THE HUMEAN M

David Hume (1711–1776) is widely acknowledged as one of the most important philosophers in the English language, with his work continuing to exert major influence on philosophy today. His empiricism, naturalism, and psychology of the mind and the passions shape many positions and approaches in the sciences and social sciences.

The Humean Mind seeks to provide a comprehensive survey of his work, not only placing it in its historical context but also exploring its contemporary significance. Comprising 38 chapters by a team of international contributors, the *Handbook* is divided into four sections:

- Intellectual context.
- Hume's thought.
- Hume's reception.
- Hume's legacy.

This handbook includes coverage of all major aspects of Hume's thought with essays spanning the full scope of Hume's philosophy. Topics explored include Hume's reception in the eighteenth and nineteenth centuries; Hume's legacy in the twentieth and twenty-first centuries; Hume's history, including an essay on Hume as historian, as well as essays on the relevance of history to Hume's philosophy and his politics, and an updated treatment of Hume's Legal Philosophy. Also included are essays on race, gender, and animal ethics.

Essential reading for students and researchers in philosophy, Hume's work is central to epistemology, metaphysics, philosophy of mind, philosophy of science, ethics, legal philosophy and philosophy of religion.

Angela M. Coventry is Associate Professor of Philosophy at Portland State University, USA. She is the author of *Hume's Theory of Causation: A Quasi-Realist Interpretation* (2006) and *Hume: A Guide for the Perplexed* (2007), co-editor (with Andrew Valls) of the volume *David Hume: Morals, Politics and Society* (2018), in addition to several articles and book reviews published in journals such as *Hume Studies*, *Locke Studies*, *Logical Analysis and History of Philosophy*, and *History of Philosophy Quarterly*. She has served as Vice President and Executive Secretary-Treasurer of The Hume Society and as co-editor of the journal *Hume Studies*.

Alex Sager is Associate Professor and Chair of the Department of Philosophy at Portland State University, USA. He has published widely in social and political philosophy on topics including migration, citizenship, and methodology, as well as on the political thought of David Hume.

THE ROUTLEDGE PHILOSOPHICAL MINDS

In philosophy past and present there are some philosophers who tower over the intellectual landscape and have shaped it in indelible ways. So significant is their impact that it is difficult to capture it in one place. The Routledge Philosophical Minds series presents a comprehensive survey of all aspects of a major philosopher's work, from analysis and criticism of their major texts and arguments to the way their ideas are taken up in contemporary philosophy and beyond. Edited by leading figures in their fields and with an outstanding international roster of contributors the series offers a magisterial and unrivalled picture of a great philosophical mind.

The Nietzschean Mind
Edited by Paul Katsafanas

The Humean Mind
Edited by Angela Coventry and Alexander Sager

The Rousseauian Mind
Edited by Eve Grace and Christopher Kelly

For more information on this series, please visit: https://www.routledge.com/Routledge-Philosophical-Minds/book-series/RPM

THE HUMEAN MIND

Edited by Angela M. Coventry and Alex Sager

Routledge
Taylor & Francis Group

LONDON AND NEW YORK

First published 2019 by Routledge

2 Park Square, Milton Park, Abingdon, Oxon, OX14 4RN
605 Third Avenue, New York, NY 10017

Routledge is an imprint of the Taylor & Francis Group, an informa business

First issued in paperback 2020

British Library Cataloguing-in-Publication Data
A catalogue record for this book is available from the British Library

Library of Congress Cataloging-in-Publication Data
Names: Coventry, Angela Michelle, editor. | Sager, Alex, edtior.
Title: The Humean mind / edited by Angela M. Coventry and Alex Sager.
Description: First edition. | Abingdon, Oxon ; New York, NY :
Routledge, 2019. | Series: The Routledge philosophical minds |
Includes bibliographical references and index.
Identifiers: LCCN 2018029330 (print) | LCCN 2018040623 (ebook) |
ISBN 9780429429996 (eBook) | ISBN 9781138909878
(hardback : alk. paper) | ISBN 9780429429996 (ebk)
Subjects: LCSH: Hume, David, 1711–1776.
Classification: LCC B1498 (ebook) | LCC B1498 .H929 2019 (print) |
DDC 192—dc23
LC record available at https://lccn.loc.gov/2018029330

ISBN: 978-1-138-90987-8 (hbk)
ISBN: 978-0-367-73292-9 (pbk)

Typeset in Bembo
by Apex CoVantage, LLC

CONTENTS

CONTRIBUTORS

James Baillie is Professor of Philosophy at the University of Portland. He has published on a variety of topics, including personal identity and philosophy of religion. He is the author of the *Routledge Philosophy Guidebook to Hume on Morality*.

Jeffrey A. Bell is Professor of Philosophy at Southeastern Louisiana University. He is the author and editor of several books, including *Philosophy at the Edge of Chaos* (2006), *Deleuze's Hume: Philosophy, Culture, and the Scottish Enlightenment* (2009), *Deleuze and History* (2009), and *Deleuze and Guattari's What Is Philosophy?: A Critical Introduction and Guide* (2016). Bell is currently working on a book on metaphysics and continental philosophy.

Christopher J. Berry is Professor (Emeritus) of Political Theory and Honorary Professorial Research Fellow at the University of Glasgow. He is the author of many books including *David Hume* (Continuum) and Essays on Hume, Smith and the Scottish Enlightenment (Edinburgh), 2018), a selection of his past work (with a new essay on Hume). Also in 2018 the Oxford University Press published his *A Very Short Introduction to Adam Smith*. He has given invited series of lectures in Japan and China on several occasions as well as in Chile, Europe, and the US. He is an elected Fellow of the Royal Society of Edinburgh (Scotland's 'National Academy').

Lorraine L. Besser is Associate Professor at Middlebury College in Middlebury, VT. Specializing in both historical and contemporary moral psychology, she is the author of *Eudaimonic Ethics: The Philosophy and Psychology of Living Well* (Routledge 2014), as well as many articles on both Hume and moral psychology.

Kristen Blair completed an undergraduate degree in philosophy at Brigham Young University in 2017, where she also acted as an undergraduate fellow at the BYU Humanities Center. She completed a minor in English, as well as significant coursework in Women's Studies. She and Dr. Paxman have been working together on topics concerning Hume and women for three years, during which time she presented research at the International Hume Conference at Brown University in 2017. She plans to pursue graduate school.

Miren Boehm is an associate professor at the University of Wisconsin, Milwaukee. Her work focuses on Hume's epistemology and philosophy of science. Her articles include "Hume's Foundational Project in the *Treatise*," *European Journal of Philosophy* (2016, 24.1: 55–77), "Hume's Definitions of 'Cause': Without Idealizations, Within the Bounds of Science," *Synthese* (2014, 191.16: 3803–3819), and "Filling the Gaps in Hume's Vacuums," *Hume Studies* (2012, 38.1: 79–99). Currently she is working on a new interpretation of moral, aesthetic, and necessary objects.

Deborah Boyle is Professor of Philosophy at the College of Charleston, where she has taught since 1999. She received a BA in Philosophy from Wellesley College and a PhD in Philosophy from the University of Pittsburgh. In addition to articles on Hume, she has published articles on Mary Astell, Margaret Cavendish, Anne Conway, Mary Shepherd, and Descartes. She is the author of *Descartes on Innate Ideas* (Continuum, 2009) and *The Well-Ordered Universe: The Philosophy of Margaret Cavendish* (Oxford, 2018).

Stephen Buckle is the author of *Hume's Enlightenment Tract* (Oxford, 2001) and editor of *An Enquiry Concerning Human Understanding* (Cambridge, 2007). He previously taught philosophy in universities in Melbourne and Sydney. Since 2016, he has been an adjunct visiting professor at the University of the Saarland in Germany and at the University of Luxembourg.

Rachel Cohon is Professor of Philosophy at the University at Albany, SUNY. She earned her PhD at UCLA and has taught at the University of California, Irvine, and Stanford University. Her book, *Hume's Morality: Feeling and Fabrication* (Oxford University Press, 2008), reinterprets Hume's meta-ethics and virtue ethics. She has published articles about Hume's philosophy as well as about reasons for action, character, and promises. She edited an anthology on Hume's ethics, *Hume: Moral and Political Philosophy* (Ashgate, 2001), and wrote the entry on Hume's moral and political philosophy in the *Stanford Encyclopedia of Philosophy*.

Mark Collier is Associate Professor of Philosophy at the University of Minnesota, Morris, and Affiliate Faculty Member at the University of Minnesota Center for Cognitive Sciences. He received an interdisciplinary PhD in Cognitive Science and Philosophy from the University of California, San Diego, and has published widely on the relationship between Hume and Cognitive Science.

Jonathan Cottrell is Assistant Professor of Philosophy at Wayne State University, USA. His work has appeared in *The Philosophical Review* and the *Journal of the History of Philosophy*.

Angela M. Coventry is Associate Professor of Philosophy at Portland State University, USA. She is the author of *Hume's Theory of Causation: A Quasi-Realist Interpretation* (Continuum, 2006) and *Hume: A Guide for the Perplexed* (Continuum 2007), co-editor (with Andrew Valls) of the volume *David Hume: Morals, Politics and Society* (Yale University Press, 2018), in addition to several articles and book reviews published in journals such as *Hume Studies*, *Locke Studies*, *Logical Analysis and History of Philosophy*, and *History of Philosophy Quarterly*. She has served as Vice President and Executive Secretary-Treasurer of The Hume Society and as the co-editor of the journal *Hume Studies*.

Tamás Demeter is Senior Research Fellow at the Institute of Philosophy, Hungarian Academy of Sciences. He has published on the relation of natural and moral philosophy in early modern philosophy. He is the author of *David Hume and the Culture of Scottish Newtonianism* (Leiden: Brill, 2016).

Don Garrett is Silver Professor of Philosophy at New York University. He is the author of *Cognition and Commitment in Hume's Philosophy* (Oxford University Press, 1997), *Hume* (Routledge, 2015), and *Nature and Necessity in Spinoza's Philosophy* (Oxford University Press, 2018). He is also the editor of *The Cambridge Companion to Spinoza* (Cambridge University Press, 1996) and has served as co-editor of *Hume Studies* and as North American editor of *Archiv für Geschichte der Philosophie*. He is an elected fellow of the American Academy of Arts and Sciences.

Gordon Graham is the series editor of Edinburgh Studies in Scottish Philosophy and editor of *Scottish Philosophy in the Nineteenth and Twentieth Centuries* (Oxford University Press, 2015). From 2007–2018 he was Director of the Center for the Study of Scottish Philosophy at Princeton Theological Seminary.

Lívia Guimarães is professor of Philosophy at Universidade Federal de Minas Gerais, Brazil. In 2000, together with graduate students and visiting scholars, she co-founded the Hume Group at University of North Carolina at Chapel Hill. In 2001, she co-founded together with undergraduate students, Grupo Hume at UFMG. She presently coordinates this Grupo which remains active since then. Her areas of study include the thought of David Hume, early modern philosophy, the philosophy of the eighteenth-century Enlightenment, philosophy of emotions, moral psychology, philosophy and literature, applied ethics, feminist philosophy, philosophy of gender, animal ethics, philosophy of education and philosophy of religion.

Thomas Holden is Professor of Philosophy at the University of California Santa Barbara. He is the author of *The Architecture of Matter: Galileo to Kant* (Oxford University Press, 2004) and *Spectres of False Divinity: Hume's Moral Atheism* (Oxford University Press, 2010).

Yumiko Inukai is Associate Professor at the University of Massachusetts, Boston, and has taught intensive courses at Kyoto University in Japan in the summer since 2013. Her recent publications include "Radical Empiricism: James and Hume on the Reality of Relations," in Alex Klein (ed.), *The Oxford Handbook of William James* (Oxford: Oxford Press, forthcoming); "The World of the Vulgar and the Ignorant: Hume and Nāgārjuna on the Substantiality and Independence of Objects," *Res Philosophica*, 92(3), 2015; and "Perceptions and Objects: Hume's Radical Empiricism," *Hume Studies* 37 (2), 2013.

P. J. E. Kail is Associate Professor in the History of Modern Philosophy and Official Fellow and Tutor in Philosophy, St. Peter's College. He is the author of *Projection and Realism in Hume's Philosophy* (Oxford, 2007) and *Berkeley's Principles of Human Knowledge* (Cambridge, 2014).

John Christian Laursen is Professor of Political Science at the University of California, Riverside. He has authored, edited, and translated many books and articles on early modern philosophy and the history of political thought, including *Skepticism in the Modern Age* (2009), *Paradoxes of Religious Toleration* (2012), *Skepticism and Political Thought in the Seventeenth and Eighteenth Centuries* (2015), and "The Moral Life of the Ancient Skeptics: Living in Accordance with Nature and Freedom from Disturbance" (*Bolletino della Società Filosofica Italiana*, 219, 2016, 5–22).

Willem Lemmens is Professor for Modern Philosophy and Ethics at the University of Antwerp, Belgium. He studied philosophy and cultural anthropology at the Catholic University of Louvain, where in 1997 he received his PhD in Philosophy with a dissertation on the moral philosophy of David Hume. He was co-editor of the translation of Hume's *Natural History of*

Religion in Dutch and of a translation of Kant's *Religion innerhalb der Grenzen der blossen Vernunft* (Boom, 2004). He edited (together with Patricia de Martelaere) an introduction in Dutch to the philosophy of David Hume: *David Hume. Filosoof van de menselijke natuur*, Pelckmans, 2001. His main research interests are: history of early modern philosophy (Spinoza and Hume), philosophy of religion, ethics, and bioethics.

Eléonore Le Jallé is Professor of Contemporary Philosophy at the University of Lille. She is the author of three books and many articles on Hume. Her last book on this author (*Hume et la philosophie contemporaine*, Paris: Vrin, 2014) deals with Hume's impact on contemporary philosophy on the following themes: induction and causality, personal identity, motivation and action, convention, and justice and social order.

Michael P. Levine is Professor of Philosophy at the University of Western Australia. His many publications include *Hume and the Problem of Miracles* (Springer, 1989); *Prospects for an Ethics of Architecture* (co-authored with Bill Taylor) (Routledge, 2011); *Thinking Through Film* (with Damian Cox) (Wiley-Blackwell, 2012); *Politics Most Unusual* (with Damian Cox and Saul Newman) (Palgrave-MacMillan, 2009); *Integrity and the Fragile Self* (with Damian Cox and Marguerite La Caze) (Ashgate, 2003); and *Engineering and War: Ethics, Institutions, Alternatives* (with Ethan Blue and Dean Nieusma) (Morgan and Claypool 2013). In 2014 he was Senior Fellow at Durham University's Institute of Advanced Study.

Emilio Mazza is Associate Professor at the Libera Università di Lingue e Comunicazione IULM in Milan. He works primarily on Hume and modern philosophy. He has published several papers on Hume, including contributions to *Impressions of Hume* (2005), *The Continuum Companion to Hume* (2012), and *Reading Hume on the Principles of Morals* (2018). He is the co-editor (with E. Ronchetti) of *New Essays on David Hume* (FrancoAngeli 2007). His last work, *Gazze, whist e verità* (Mimesis, 2016), is on Hume and the images of philosophy.

Neil McArthur is Associate Professor of Philosophy and Director of the Centre for Professional and Applied Ethics at the University of Manitoba. He is the author of *David Hume's Political Theory* (University of Toronto Press, 2007) and the co-editor of *Fragile Freedoms: The Global Struggle for Human Rights* (Oxford University Press, 2017) and *Robot Sex: Social and Ethical Implications* (MIT Press, 2017).

Katharina Paxman is Assistant Professor of Philosophy at Brigham Young University. Her work has focused on David Hume's theory of the passions and moral psychology. She has been published in *Hume Studies*, *The Journal of Scottish Philosophy*, and *Res Philosophica*, and has a forthcoming paper included in *Hume's Moral Philosophy and Contemporary Psychology* (eds. Phillip Reed and Rico Vitz, Routledge, 2018).

Stefanie Rocknak is Professor of Philosophy, Chair of the Philosophy Department, and Director of the Cognitive Science Program at Hartwick College in Oneonta, NY. She is also a professional sculptor; her work may be seen at www.steffrocknak.net.

Todd Ryan is Associate Professor of Philosophy at Trinity College, Hartford, CT. He is the author of *Pierre Bayle's Cartesian Metaphysics* (Routledge, 2009) as well as a number of articles on metaphysical and epistemological topics in Hume, Berkeley, and Bayle.

Andrew Sabl is Associate Professor of Political Science at the University of Toronto. He is the author of *Hume's Politics: Coordination and Crisis in the* History *of* England (Princeton, 2012), *Ruling Passions: Political Offices and Democratic Ethics* (Princeton, 2002), and numerous scholarly articles.

Alex Sager is Associate Professor and Chair of the Department of Philosophy at Portland State University, USA. He has published widely in social and political philosophy on topics including migration, citizenship, and methodology, as well as on the political thought of David Hume.

Frederick F. Schmitt is Oscar R. Ewing Professor of Philosophy at Indiana University. He specializes in epistemology and the history of epistemology, especially early modern empiricism. He is the author of *Knowledge and Belief* (Routledge, 1992), *Truth: A Primer* (Westview, 1995), and *Hume's Epistemology in the Treatise: A Veritistic Interpretation* (Oxford University Press, 2014), as well as editor of anthologies on epistemology and metaphysics.

Tom Seppäläinen teaches philosophy at Portland State University in Portland, Oregon, and grows Pinot Noir in Hood River, Oregon. In addition to themes in Hume's epistemology, his main research interests are in the sciences of sensory perception, including the cross-modal bases of wine-tasting classifications.

Matias Slavov defended his dissertation on Hume's natural philosophy in 2016 at the University of Jyväskylä, Finland. He currently works as a visiting scholar at UCLA's Department of Philosophy. Slavov is interested in the philosophy of Hume, the history and philosophy of science, and the philosophy of time.

Mark G. Spencer is Professor of History at Brock University. His books include *David Hume and Eighteenth-Century America* (University of Rochester Press, 2005) and, as editor, *Hume's Reception in Early America: Expanded Edition* (Bloomsbury, 2017), *The Bloomsbury Encyclopedia of the American Enlightenment* (Bloomsbury, 2015), and *David Hume: Historical Thinker, Historical Writer* (Penn State University Press, 2013). His Hume-related articles and essays have been published in collections such as *New Essays on David Hume* (2017), *The Enlightenment in Scotland: National and International Perspectives* (2015), and *David Hume* (2013), as well as in journals such as *Enlightenment and Dissent*, *The Franklin Gazette*, *Hume Studies*, and *The William and Mary Quarterly*.

Saul Traiger is Professor of Cognitive Science and Philosophy at Occidental College. His publications on Hume explore the notion of fiction, Hume's accounts of the imagination and memory, and the role of testimony in belief formation and evaluation. He is a past president of The Hume Society, the editor of *The Blackwell Guide to Hume's Treatise*, and most recently served as co-editor of *Hume Studies*.

Alessio Vaccari is Teaching Assistant in Bioethics at Sapienza University, Rome. He has done research in eighteenth-century philosophy (especially Hume and Hutcheson) and in virtue ethics. He is currently working on Hume's theory of justice and on the philosophy of emotions.

Anik Waldow is Associate Professor in the Philosophy Department at the University of Sydney. She mainly works in early modern philosophy and has published articles on the moral and cognitive function of sympathy, early modern theories of personal identity, and the role of affect in the formation of the self, skepticism, and associationist theories of thought and language. Her articles have appeared in *Philosophy and Phenomenological Research, The British Journal for the History of Philosophy, Hume Studies, History of Philosophy Quarterly* and *Philosophy*. She is the author of the book *David Hume and the Problem of Other Minds* (Continuum, 2009) and edited a special volume of the *Intellectual History Review* on *Sensibility in the Early Modern Era: From Living Machines to Affective Morality* for the *Intellectual History Review* (2014, republished with Routledge, 2016) and co-edited *Herder: Philosophy and Anthropology* (Oxford, 2017).

Carl Wennerlind is Associate Professor of History at Barnard College, Columbia University. He is the author of *Casualties of Credit* (Harvard, 2011) and, together with Margaret Schabas, the co-author of *Hume's Worldly Philosophy* (Chicago, 2019). He has also co-edited *David Hume's Political Economy* (Routledge, 2008) and *Mercantilism Reimagined* (Oxford, 2014).

Christopher Williams is Associate Professor of Philosophy at the University of Nevada, Reno. He works chiefly in aesthetics and the history of philosophy. His paper "On Mere Suffering: Hume and the Problem of Tragedy" appeared in *Suffering Art Gladly: The Paradox of Negative Emotion in Art* (Palgrave Macmillan, 2014).

Andre C. Willis is Willard Prescott and Annie McClelland Smith Assistant Professor of Religious Studies at Brown University. He is a philosopher of religion whose work focuses on Enlightenment reflections on religion, African American religious thought, critical philosophy of race, and political thought as it relates to 'religious' notions of hope, recognition, and belonging. He is the author of *Towards a Humean True Religion* (Penn State University Press, 2015) and is currently working on a manuscript about African American religion and politics called "Afro-Theism and Post-Democracy." He has published articles in the *Journal of Scottish Philosophy, Political Theology, Critical Philosophy of Race*, and *Hume Studies*.

ACKNOWLEDGMENTS

We are grateful to Nickölas Kerr and Sarah Paquette for their editorial assistance in preparing the manuscript.

ABBREVIATIONS AND CONVENTIONS FOR HUME'S WORKS

Ab.   "An Abstract of *A Treatise of Human Nature* Wherein the Chief Argument of that Book is farther Illustrated and Explained." References cite paragraph number from the Norton and Norton edition of 'T' and the page number of the Selby-Bigge edition (see below).

DP.   "A Dissertation on the Passions," in *A Dissertation on the Passions; The Natural History of Religion*, ed. Tom L. Beauchamp, Oxford: Clarendon Press, 2008. References cite section and paragraph number.

DNR.   *Dialogues Concerning Natural Religion*, in *Dialogues Concerning Natural Religion and Other Writings*, ed. Dorothy Coleman, Cambridge: Cambridge University Press, 2007. References cite part and paragraph number.

E.   *Essays: Moral, Political, and Literary*, ed. Eugene F. Miller, Indianapolis: Liberty Fund, 1985. References cite page number.

EHU.   *An Enquiry Concerning Human Understanding: A Critical Edition*, ed. T. L. Beauchamp, Oxford: Oxford University Press, 2006 and *An Enquiry Concerning Human Understanding and Enquiry Concerning the Principles of Morals*, 3rd edition, L. A. Selby-Bigge & P. H. Nidditch (eds.). Oxford: Clarendon Press, 1975. References to Hume cite the book, chapter, section, and paragraph to the most recent Oxford edition followed by page numbers from the Selby-Bigge/Nidditch editions, prefixed by 'SBN.'

EPM.   *An Enquiry Concerning the Principles of Morals: A Critical Edition*, ed. T. L. Beauchamp, Oxford: Oxford University Press, 2006 and *An Enquiry Concerning Human Understanding and Enquiry Concerning the Principles of Morals*, 3rd edition, L. A. Selby-Bigge & P. H. Nidditch (eds.). Oxford: Clarendon Press, 1975. References to Hume cite the book, chapter, section, and paragraph to the most recent Oxford edition followed by page numbers from the Selby-Bigge/Nidditch editions, prefixed by 'SBN.' The appendices to the EPM will be referred to as EPM, App. with the Appendix and paragraph number and the *Dialogue* as EPM, D with paragraph numbers and page references to Selby-Bigge/Nidditch.

H.   *History of England: from the Invasion of Julius Caesar to The Revolution in 1688*, 6 vols, Indianapolis: Liberty Fund, 1983. References cite volume and page number.

L.   *The Letters of David Hume*, ed. J.Y.T. Greig, 2 vols, Oxford: Clarendon Press, 1932. References cite volume and page number.

LG.   *Letter from a Gentleman.* References cite paragraph and page number from the Norton and Norton edition of 'T' (see below).

NHR.   "Natural History of Religion," in *A Dissertation on the Passions: The Natural History of Religion*, ed. Tom L. Beauchamp, Oxford: Clarendon Press, 2008. References cite section and paragraph number.

NL.   *The New Letters of David Hume*, ed. Raymond Kilbansky and Ernest Campbell Mossner, Oxford: Clarendon Press, 1954. References cite page number.

T.   *A Treatise of Human Nature: A Critical Edition*, ed. D. F. Norton and M. J. Norton, Oxford: Clarendon Press., 2007, and L.A. Selby-Bigge and P.H. Nidditch (eds.), Oxford: Clarendon Press, 2nd edition, 1978. References cite the book, chapter, section, and paragraph to the most recent Oxford edition followed by page numbers from the Selby-Bigge/Nidditch editions, prefixed by 'SBN.' The Appendix to T will be referred to as T App. with paragraph numbers and page references to Selby-Bigge/Nidditch.

PUBLICATION TIMELINE

1772   Ninth edition of *Essays and Treatises on Several Subjects.*
1777   *The Life of David Hume, Esq., Written by Himself*; tenth edition of *Essays and Treatises on Several Subjects.*
1779   *Dialogues Concerning Natural Religion.*
1782   "Of Suicide" and "Of the Immortality of the Soul."

INTRODUCTION

Angela M. Coventry and Alex Sager

Few today would dispute that David Hume is one of our most influential philosophers, with enduring contributions in epistemology, metaphysics, philosophy of mind, philosophy of science, ethics, economics, politics, philosophy of religion, and history. These contributions continue to exert a major influence in most areas of contemporary philosophy. Moreover, his empiricism, naturalism, and psychology of the mind and the passions shape many positions and approaches in the sciences and social sciences, at times without the awareness of researchers who continue his legacy.

The Humean Mind aims to be the most comprehensive anthology available on Hume's thought, with essays spanning the full scope of Hume's philosophy, as well as placing Hume in his own time and tracing his impact on the field from the eighteenth century until today. The goal of the anthology is to represent Hume's place in the philosophical tradition and in contemporary philosophy. For this reason, we attempt to cover all of the major topics on Hume, showcase the latest trends in Hume scholarship, and reflect how current research continues to take inspiration from his work. The essays themselves provide a critical survey of the central themes to the origins of Hume's philosophy, situate Hume in his time, and explore how Hume's ideas have been received and continue to be received in the philosophical tradition. For these purposes, we have divided the contents into four major parts: (1) Intellectual Context; (2) Hume's Thought; (3) Hume's Reception; and (4) Hume's Legacy.

Life and works

Before giving a brief outline of the major parts of the anthology, a few biographical remarks are in order. David Hume was born in Edinburgh on April 26 (old style),[1] 1711 into a family of modest wealth but decent social standing. His early childhood was spent mostly at the family estate of Ninewells near Berwick in south-east Scotland. At the age of 10 or 11, Hume accompanied his elder brother to Edinburgh University, where he matriculated in 1723. After some time studying law, he left the University in either 1725 or 1726 and went back to Ninewells to follow a self-devised academic program of study to read, ponder, and take notes on as much as possible written from ancient times to the present on literature, philosophy, and the sciences, and to learn languages. The rigorous program of study eventually hurt Hume's physical and mental health, and a change in lifestyle became necessary. He worked for a Bristol merchant briefly in

1734 and then moved to France, first to Reims, then to La Flèche in Anjou. Here Hume composed his first work, *A Treatise of Human Nature: Being an Attempt to Introduce the Experimental Method of Reasoning into Moral Subjects.*

Hume returned to England in 1737 and published the first two books, "Of the Understanding" and "Of the Passions," anonymously in 1739. The third book, "Of Morals," was published the next year with an Appendix of corrections to the first publication. The work was reviewed in many European journals to a mixed response: generally, reviewers found the work to be novel but obscure, skeptical, and paradoxical. In March 1740, Hume published anonymously an "Abstract" to the *Treatise* to clarify some of the main lines of argumentation, probably in response to some of the more negative reviews.

Hume moved back to Ninewells to write and went on to publish *Essays, Moral and Political* in 1741 and 1742, *Philosophical Essays Concerning Human Understanding* in 1748 (later known as *An Enquiry Concerning Human Understanding* in 1758), *An Enquiry Concerning the Principles of Morals* in 1751, and *The Political Discourses* in 1752. These works were successful and many editions went into print during his lifetime. Despite this success, Hume did not obtain an academic appointment on two occasions. His candidacy for a chair of ethics and pneumatical philosophy at Edinburgh University in 1744–1745 was opposed by the community, particularly by members of the clergy. Documents were produced that accused him of being a skeptical atheist intent on undermining morality, citing the *Treatise* as evidence. Hume composed a letter in response that was published anonymously as *A Letter from a Gentleman to his Friend in Edinburgh* (1745). In 1751 he again did not obtain an academic job as the chair of logic at the University of Glasgow due to controversy over his alleged skepticism and atheism.

As a result, Hume was compelled to take on a variety of jobs. He served as a tutor in 1745 and from 1746 to 1749, then served as secretary to Lieutenant-General St. Clair, whom he accompanied on military matters to Brittany, Austria, and Italy. From 1752 to 1757 he worked at the Advocates Library in Edinburgh where he used the available resources to write the bestseller *History of England from the Invasion of Julius Caesar to the Revolution of 1688.* This was published in six volumes through the period 1754–1762. Hume also published the *Four Dissertations*, comprised of the essays "The Natural History of Religion" with "Of the Passions," "Of Tragedy," and "Of the Standard of Taste" in 1757. Around the same time Hume composed his *Dialogues Concerning Natural Religion*, but he did not publish it during his lifetime on the advice of friends due to concerns of religious persecution.

His time at the library post was controversial. In 1754, his book order for the library was canceled by the trustees of the library because the books were deemed inappropriate and there was discussion to remove him from the post. In 1755 there was an attempt to formally accuse him of atheism, and in 1756, Hume prevailed over an attempt to excommunicate him by the Scottish Church's highest judicial body. Bishop William Warburton tried to stop Hume's *Four Dissertations* going into print as well in 1756. By 1761, the Roman Catholic Church had banned all of his works.

In 1763, Hume went back to France employed as the private secretary to Lord Hertford, British ambassador to France. Three years later, Hume returned to England with Jean-Jacques Rousseau, who had been ordered out of Switzerland. Hume even secured a pension for Rousseau from King George III, but Rousseau did not stay for long. He soon became convinced that Hume was plotting against him and publicly denounced him. Hume published his own version of the events in *A Concise and Genuine Account of the Dispute between Mr. Hume and Mr. Rousseau* in 1766.

Hume's final position was that of undersecretary of state at the Foreign Office for the British government from 1767 to 1769. He then retired to Scotland and spent his final years correcting editions of his works. He died on August 25, 1776 after first becoming seriously ill in the spring of 1774. His death was followed by the publication of Hume's own short autobiography, "My Own Life," accompanied by a letter by close friend Adam Smith written immediately after Hume's death. In his famous concluding sentence, Smith wrote, "Upon the whole, I have always considered him, both in his lifetime and since his death, as approaching as nearly to the idea of a perfectly wise and virtuous man, as perhaps the nature of human frailty will permit." In 1779, Hume's *Dialogues Concerning Natural Religion* were published, followed by his essays on suicide and the immortality of the soul in 1783. Though too controversial to appear while he was alive, the *Dialogues* and these essays are among the most widely read and taught texts today.

Structure of the volume

In commissioning the chapters for this volume, we faced a number of goals and challenges. First, we wanted to include chapters that highlight the range of Hume's major philosophical innovations. Topics such as Hume's empirical approach, analysis of causality and the self, his skepticism, his contributions to moral psychology, and his criticisms of religion are commonly included in anthologies of his work. These topics are indeed central and incorporated in the present anthology. But we also include chapters on his important contributions to philosophy of art, philosophy of history, and to political, economic, and legal theory that are not as commonly represented. Second, we wanted to represent Hume as a figure in the history of philosophy. This includes discussing his intellectual debts and context and his immediate reception in the eighteenth and early twentieth centuries. Finally, we take the title *The Humean Mind* to acknowledge Hume's living presence in the contemporary life of the mind. Hume is a predecessor of important work in philosophy of language, cognitive science, moral psychology, and social ontology. He also made significant contributions to questions about non-human animal minds, as well as the ethical obligations toward non-human animals. Finally, Hume left a complex and somewhat ambiguous legacy on race and on women that scholars continue to debate.

To achieve these goals, we divide the anthology into *Intellectual Context*, *Hume's Thought* (with subsections on *Mind, Knowledge, and World*; *Passions, Morals, and Taste*; and *History, Politics, and Economics*), *Hume's Reception* (focusing on the eighteenth to early twentieth centuries), and *Hume's Legacy*. The first section on Hume's intellectual context includes three chapters that allow readers to understand Hume in his time. This part of the volume aligns with recent trends in early modern scholarship that emphasize the importance of focusing on the historical and intellectual context of the period.

Hume was a careful and subtle reader of philosophy, literature, and history, and he drew upon and responded to the Ancient philosophical traditions. In his short autobiography "My Own Life," he described "devouring" the works of Cicero and Virgil at an early age. He was also familiar with the works of Seneca, Tacitus, Lucretius, and Plutarch. He devotes a section of his first work, *A Treatise of Human Nature* to Ancient philosophy (1.4.3), and his series of essays that explore different ideas of happiness, "The Platonist," "The Epicurean," "The Stoic," "The Platonist," and "The Sceptic," refer to the ancient philosophical schools. Hume also responds to his more recent predecessors in the *Treatise on Human Nature* (1.4.4). Indeed, Hume's work throughout is indebted and provides important responses to several of the major philosophers in the modern era. This includes many of the British philosophers of his time, such as Hobbes, Hutcheson, Locke, and Berkeley, as well as predecessors and cotemporaries from the continent, like the French philosophers Bayle and Malebranche.

Hume's Thought is the most substantial part of the anthology. Recent scholarship has led philosophers to reevaluate some of Hume's views and to discover aspects of his philosophy that have not received the attention they deserve. The 11 chapters in *Mind, Knowledge, and World* provide a critical survey of the major elements of Hume's epistemology, metaphysics, philosophy of mind, and philosophy of religion. Hume's empiricism and psychology – particularly his account of the origin of ideas and association – form the basis of his accounts of space and time, induction and probability, causation, the external world, and self. The first seven chapters comprise detailed treatments of these topics. The next chapter explores the role of Hume's naturalism and skepticism. The final three chapters are devoted to Hume on religion, including chapters devoted to his seminal account of miracles, his psychology of religion, and his treatment of arguments for the existence of God.

Passions, Morals, and Taste consists of seven chapters and continues to develop Hume's psychology with chapters on the passions and sympathy, Hume's philosophy of action, and his account of moral responsibility and free will. We also include chapters on sentimentalism and on convention, which form the basis of Hume's social and political philosophy. The penultimate chapter concerns beauty and how it relates to other parts of his philosophy, such as pleasure and morals. The final chapter is on the philosophy of art as presented in his classic essay, "Of the Standard of Taste."

History, Politics, and Economics consists of six chapters that acknowledge how Hume scholarship has increasingly recognized the relevance of the *History of England* and the *Essays: Moral, Political, and Literary* to Hume's philosophy. The first two chapters of this section examine Hume as a historian and lay out how Hume's history contains a sophisticated political theory. We follow these chapters with essays devoted to Hume's politics, particularly his accounts of government and the original contract, the role of custom in his political and economic thought, and his contributions to economics and philosophy of law.

Hume's Reception acknowledges how despite Hume's own protests that his *Treatise* "fell deadborn from the press," his ideas were well-received in his time. These three essays explore the reception of his works in England and the continent of Europe in the eighteenth and nineteenth centuries. This includes Hume's reception by contemporaries such as Adam Smith and Adam Ferguson, as well as Thomas Reid's reaction to Hume's work. Hume was also influential in German philosophy, not only for having wakened Immanuel Kant from his "dogmatic slumber," but also for playing a significant role in the philosophies of Johann Gottfried Herder and Johannes Nikolaus Tetens. Finally, the scientific tradition owes a debt to Hume. Charles Darwin's reading of Hume influenced his theory of evolution, including the account of ethics and psychology in *The Descent of Man*, and the biologist T.H. Huxley, known as "Darwin's Bulldog," devoted a book to Hume's philosophy in 1879. This legacy also extends to the early twentieth century in the physics of Albert Einstein. Finally, though Hume is commonly identified as an "analytic philosopher," philosophers working in the Continental tradition such as Henri Bergson, Edmund Husserl, Jean-Paul Sartre, Maurice Merleau-Ponty, and Gilles Deleuze have identified Hume as a predecessor and foil. This reveals the breadth of Hume's shadow over contemporary philosophy and invites dialogue between different contemporary traditions.

The final seven essays in *Hume's Legacy* treat Hume as a living philosopher who continues to inspire scholars in many fields. First, in metaphysics, epistemology, and the philosophy of mind, his empiricism and associationism were influential on the rise of analytic philosophy (including philosophy of language and semantics) and anticipate contemporary work in psychology and cognitive science. Hume's empiricist system also contributes to recent debates in the relatively new interdisciplinary field of social ontology. Second, Hume also continues to inform the work of ethicists, moral psychologists, and social and political philosophers. Many moral philosophers and moral psychologists work in an explicitly Humean tradition, finding parallels between Hume's account of the passions and discoveries in contemporary psychology. Applied ethicists have found unexpected resources in Hume for topics as diverse as race, gender, and animal ethics. We hope the volume as a whole reflects the wide range of approaches and interests that the span the constantly evolving Humean mind.

Note

1 Although he was born on April 26, 1711, he turned 42 years old on May 7, 1753. This is due to the calendar reform implemented by Parliament the previous September, which advanced the date by 11 days.

PART I

Intellectual context

1

HUME AND THE ANCIENTS

Lívia Guimarães

Introduction

A chapter titled *Hume and the Ancients* might well be entitled *Hume himself*, since the ancients are part of Hume's thought and life from beginning to end. Here I revisit some of Hume's references to ancient sources throughout his works. I intend to show that many of Hume's philosophical observations concerning the ancients only make sense because they come from his broad understanding of their culture. While ancient characters appear in many guises in Hume's *oeuvre*, the recurrent image of the ancient philosopher endowed with wisdom, self-sufficiency, and strength of will perplexes him. Though this figure is largely absent from Hume's philosophical theory, it reappears in the *Four Dissertations*, dedicated to the author of the play *Douglas, a Tragedy*, John Home (1722–1808). Home's tragedy dramatizes the tensions and the movement from ancient to modern ruling passions and morals, from a warrior-centered society to a gentlemanly and gentlewomanly one centered in mutual ties of love and friendship, where the issue of self-sufficiency does not arise anymore. In his life-long reading of the ancients, Hume seems to be so close to them that here he unceremoniously borrows one of their most prominent literary forms – the tragedy – as a chosen companion to his own "Of the Passions," "Of Tragedy," "Of the Standard of Taste," and "The Natural History of Religion" (among other titles) to bring into question the very foundation of their societies and his own. When human beings aspire to become a sole sage in contemplation or a sole hero in action (and there are times and places when and where they did or do), this aspiration often ends in misery by contradicting human original sociable disposition in passions and sentiments.

A survey

Hume's earliest remaining piece of writing, his very first letter – of July 4, 1727, to his friend Michael Ramsay – has references to Virgil and to Cicero, to the *Tusculan Disputations* of the latter and the former's *Aeneid* and *Georgics*. His final philosophical writing, according to the first posthumous edition of Hume's philosophical works, is the *Four Dissertations*, which overflows with references to the ancients, such as Cicero's *Against Verres*, Greek Tragedians, Virgil, Horace, and others.[1]

Hume's knowledge of ancient literature encompasses many genres and topics – history, poetry, philosophy, eloquence, and much more. Hume's erudition (i) influences the reasoning, argument, and sources of evidence in his enquiry into the principles and operations of human nature, (ii) progresses into an often sympathetic, always cultivated understanding of the morals and manners of ancient peoples, and (iii), not rarely, leads to remarkable discoveries. The essay "Of the Populousness of Ancient Nations," with its thesis that the ancient world was less populous than the modern, is an example. By careful study of a collection of primary sources, Hume reaches a conclusion that contradicts the common wisdom, according to which the world was more populous then than it is now (an example of (iii). In "The Natural History of Religion," polytheism, or ancient gods and goddesses, by their proximity to human beings and variety, favor a better morality, where humans can emulate divine counterparts, with "activity, spirit, courage, magnanimity, love of liberty" (NHR 10.2). Monotheism, or a modern god, by distancing itself from humanity, and presenting itself as "infinitely superior," favors a worse sort of morality, more prone to abasement, "and to represent the monkish virtues of mortification, penance, humility, and passive suffering" (NHR 10.2).

"The Natural History" serves a double purpose: first, it is an enquiry on the psychology of religious belief and sentiment – it discovers the origin of religion in the passions, the consequent projection of reflected passions, agency and intentionality in the personification of natural events, and the flux and reflux between monotheism and polytheism, as a result of flattery and of the mind's difficulty in sustaining a prolonged abstract idea of a single deity. It is a case study of the theory of impressions and ideas, and of the passions, direct (mainly hope and fear, in this case) and indirect (mainly flattery). Second, it is an enquiry about other civilizations: a source for the understanding of Greek and Roman conceptions of their gods and goddesses, primarily instructed by their art and epic poetry and supported by the conviction that beliefs are born from these and other practices.

Hume's opening of section 5 ("Sceptical solution of these doubts") of the *An Enquiry Concerning Human Understanding* (1748) is exemplary as well. There he writes that the passion for philosophy "aims at the correction of our manners and extirpation of our vices" (EHU 5.1; SBN 40). Yet, it sometimes happens that a philosopher is corrupted in her pursuit when her philosophy gratifies an inclination other than the proper one – and the proper one is the love of truth, a passion. Epictetus and the Stoics profess a philosophy in which the passion of selfish indolence prevails. According to Hume, they reason themselves out of all social enjoyment and out of all virtue (EHU 5.1; SBN 40).

The error of the Stoics' ways is presented in the life of a Roman citizen, to whom the meaning of a happy and well-lived life is indiscernible from her public life as a citizen, a patrician. For a Roman, no fate is more repulsive than exile or retirement, even, in some cases, voluntary retirement. Hence, the choice the Stoic argues to be admirable opposes the foundation of her society. Hume seems right in his denunciation – thinking and actual living frames or settings are not to be dissociated if they are to be properly appraised.

In the same section, Hume praises the Academics, who talk of doubt, suspension of judgment, the danger in hasty determinations, and the confinement of their inquiries within the limits of the understanding and of common life and experience. Again, in Hume's words: "Nothing, therefore, can be more contrary than such a philosophy to the supine indolence of the mind, its rash arrogance, its lofty pretensions, and its superstitious credulity" (EHU 5.1; SBN 41). The Academic or Sceptical philosophy, moved by no other passion than the love of truth, is the one true philosophical path.

In the example above Hume expresses, once again, at least two sensibilities: the sensibility to perceive and feel a thinker in her context, and the sensibility to perceive the passion and inclination of taste which lies at the bottom of any and all thought. The expression of a third sensibility consists in Hume's creative use of anyone's thoughts to freely think, write, and draw his philosophy. Hume's sensibilities color his approach to any text. In some of Hume's literary offerings we should not ask of him: is he a faithful reader of his sources or is he consistent in the judgment of the sources, but rather what role these sources have in his own philosophy.

At times, Hume explicitly mentions the *Querelle* of the ancients and moderns. He sides with the moderns, for instance, in finding their manners more polished and refined (e.g. "A Dialogue," "Of the Standard of Taste"). But does he, truly? Here, I should like to argue three points. First, Hume's experience of time is non-linear. We should only look at his "The Natural History of Religion." Religious time runs in cycles of flux and reflux between polytheism and monotheism; in the year of 1757, a Capucin walks the streets of Paris (and he is not significantly different in life and manners from a fellow monk living in the Dark Ages). Perhaps David Hume observes him from a porch in his hotel; and there they are, both, each ruled by contrary aspirations, passions, virtues, and vices (NHR 12.6). "The Natural History" demonstrates that time not only is not linear, but also that progress is a rather problematic notion for Hume in human affairs. With regard to courage or abasement, pagan polytheism is preferable to monotheism.

In the same spirit, Hume finds ancient moralists superior to modern. In his judgment, Ciceronian eloquence remains unsurpassed (e.g. "Of Eloquence"). Cicero's oratory is a delectable gift of fortune for those with a taste for it. If modern eloquence does not compare to it, what to say? Only that it is not suitable for civil matters in modern society as perceived by Hume, given the present state of arts and sciences. There is indeed a sense of history, not linear, not hierarchical, sometimes accepting of evaluations, though not *en bloc* (with the exception, maybe, of the middle ages – an epoch that he disparages thoroughly), and not out of context.

Hume soberly and wisely predicts in the "Natural History of Religion" that belief in customary doctrines of his time may appear wondrous, i.e. absurd, if not ridiculous, to future generations. He also predicts that:

> The fame of Cicero flourishes at present; but that of Aristotle is utterly decayed. La Bruyere passes the seas, and still maintains his reputation: But the glory of Malebranche is confined to his own nation, and to his own age. And Addison, perhaps, will be read with pleasure, when Locke shall be entirely forgotten.
>
> (EHU 1.4; SBN 7)

From these lines, we learn that the future is uncertain. From the examples so far, we have a glimpse at a Hume who inhabits an indefinite number of worlds, peopled by sets of persons and writings grouped within diverse, distinctive boundaries largely of his own making; a Hume who is aware of transitioning among these worlds, inviting now and then an ancient fellow writer of his choice.

Sometimes, there is no going back, either to ancient or to modern predecessors. The metaphysic of causal realism (Book 1, Part 3 of *A Treatise of Human Nature* (1739–40)), Euclidian geometry (Book 1, Part 2), moral deontology (Book 3), and political contractualism (Book 3, Part 2) have all found their tenability highly compromised by the genius of Hume's philosophy. Attending to our experience, Hume finds that:

> our ideas of bodies are nothing but collections form'd by the mind of the ideas of the several distinct sensible qualities, of which objects are compos'd, and which we find to have a constant union with each other.
>
> (1.4.3.2 SBN 219)

and that

> [t]he smooth and uninterrupted progress of the thought ... makes us ascribe an iden-
> tity to the changeable succession of connected qualities
>
> (T 1.4.3.3 SBN 220)

He is about to give the *coup de grâce* to the metaphysic of substance of the ancients – for him, "an unintelligible chimera," and begin to re-conceptualize "identity" (T 1.4.3.7 SBN 222). As a result, he will be able to achieve a non-substantial self and an ever evolving personal identity.

Although Hume is a confident reader with a keen sense of history when he wished to be, he also uses the past for his own purposes to pursue difficult problems of his philosophy. The Sceptics provide a good example: in section 12 of the first *Enquiry*, the popular or ancient Pyrrhonian is not able to attain a philosophical level in her doubting. She can triumph in the *schools* alone since the least demand of common life vanquishes her speculations and the senses and understanding themselves correct her skeptical conclusions. The philosophical Pyrrhonian, i.e. she who raises the problem of the correspondence between mind and object, the distinction between primary and secondary qualities, the very concept of extension, is invincible, for she is none other than Hume. Likewise, Hume is the Academic in which the book ends. In Hume's philosophical tale, Cicero is this Academic's ancestor, in contrast to the prevalent eighteenth-century view of Cicero as a Stoic and a strong-willed moralist. Long before the first *Enquiry*, Cicero accompanies the development of Hume's thought. He is present in the *Treatise*, in the first edition of the *Essays, Moral and Literary* (1741–1742), and in "A Letter from a Gentleman to his Friend in Edinburgh" (1745). The letter contains a confounding description of Cicero that does not fit any ready-made mold. It says:

> Were Authorities proper to be employed in any Philosophical Reasoning, I could cite
> you that of *Socrates* the wisest and most religious of the *Greek* Philosophers, as well as
> *Cicero* among the *Romans*, who both of them carried their Philosophical Doubts to the
> highest Degree of Scepticism.
>
> (LG 24)

But she who carries her doubts to the highest degree of skepticism should more properly be called Pyrrhonian, not Academic. Hence, the skepticism described in the letter is plausibly Hume's own, and the label attached to Cicero, at best, idiosyncratic.

Another good example of Hume's use of ancient eminent characters in benefit of his philosophical tale are the essays on happiness, more narrowly, on human happiness, imperiled by misfortune: "The Epicurean," "The Stoic," "The Platonist," and "The Sceptic."[2]

There is enough theatrical effect in the essays to suggest that they are not written in naïve agreement with philosophical doctrines. Hume reserves for the Sceptic the final and longest speech in the series. If someone has the last word, the Sceptic does. A dynamic story unfolds that begins with the epicurean rejection of philosophy and ends with a sort of rejection of philosophy, by the Sceptic, on higher grounds. Thus, Hume raises us, the audience, to a vantage from where the whole history of the ancient schools passes in review. We function as critical listeners, who can follow a plot in which it feels as if Hume is giving us warning: here you see philosophical paths, and they have all been followed through to the end. Uninviting, old beaten and long forgotten paths, they belong in the past, except for the skeptical, that is presently with us.

In the pursuit of happiness, the Sceptic recommends following one's inclinations, while she emphasizes the relativity of value as well. Values, she says, are relative to our particular constitution, to our nature:"objects have absolutely no worth or value in themselves. They derive their worth merely from the passion. If that be strong, and steady, and successful, the person is happy" (E 166).

Now "constitution," or the "state of passions," is under the influence of education, custom, prejudice, caprice, humor, all of these being factors that philosophy may and does affect in many different ways. But philosophy, the Sceptic adds, is not necessarily useful to bringing about the state of passions that gives support to human happiness; it may even pose an obstacle to it.

If philosophy rises too high in its abstractions, it simply does not blend with the passions; hence it does not blend with human happiness, either. This is the place where the Platonist stands – looking up to the divine, not even caring about coping with fortune. If philosophy is too narrowly principled, and opposed to the passions, it may even cause unhappiness – a cautionary word to the Stoic. The Sceptic concludes that philosophical and non-philosophical knowledge alone that "humanizes the temper and softens the passions" may agree with happiness. She takes a bow, if only a slight bow, to the Epicurean. Happiness *is* in the passions, but contrary to what the Epicurean might expect, the passions *can* mingle happily with philosophy.

The Sceptic in this essay strikingly resembles Hume. Hume trusts the explanatory power of the original principles of human nature. He is sensitive to the role of custom and culture. Hume may be making use of the effect of antiquity in the imagination for dramatic effect by sometimes clothing the complex characters of his own universe in the robes of the ancients, or making use of words already available in association with them. Book 2 of the *Treatise* notes that a distance in time elevates the mind. Both the vastness of its object and the difficulty of its conception demand constant efforts in the mind's transition through parts of time. The result is a vigorous and sublime disposition of the imagination, shown in the veneration of objects in the distant past (T 2.3.8.10; SBN 436). The veneration of objects may easily apply to veneration of persons, or actors, or thinkers. And, every once in a while, Hume does have a *penchant* for the literary (in the current sense of the word) arts, and their enchanting effects.

The third point I should like to address is the following: there is one representation of the ancients, recurrent in Hume's work, that exerts a seductive or at least unsettling influence over Hume himself. Interestingly, it is already present in the letter of 1727 to Michael Ramsey. The young, precocious Hume contemplates the ideal and raises his aspirations to the philosophical wisdom of Cicero:"This Greatness & Elevation of Soul is to be found only in Study & contemplation, this can alone teach us to look down upon humane Accident" (L 1.1). But then the young Hume, measuring himself against the ideal, modestly moderates his ambition:"My peace of Mind is not sufficiently confirm'd by Philosophy to withstand the Blows of Fortune" (L 1.1). He falls short of the high standard. At best, he may be able to live a pastoral peaceful life, the one sung in the verses of Virgil's *Georgics* he quotes:

> Untroubled calm,
> A life that knows no falsehood, rich enow
> With various treasures, yet broad-acred ease,
> Grottoes and living lakes, yet Tempes cool,
> Lowing of kine, and sylvan slumbers soft.[3]

In imitation of Cicero and Virgil, Hume is seeking to live in liberty, independence, and contempt of fame, disdain of power, in a quiet and orderly state. In this state, the philosophical mind is tranquil and peaceful, because it is self-supporting. However, "the perfectly Wise man that outbraves Fortune is surely greater than the Husbandman who slips by her" (L 1.1).

Initially, the philosophical and pastoral lives seem to be the only two possible life choices available to Hume. There is more to the letter, though. At the same time as the young Hume wavers between the two kinds of existence, the letter contains lines very true to Hume's mature philosophy, yet waiting to gain material expression over a decade ahead. He says: "for free Conversation of a friend is what I would prefer to any Entertainment" (L 1.1). In the friend's absence, his only diversion is his own company and his library's. He proceeds with a quotation of Virgil's *Aeneid*: "thus we have pleasure as our only consolation in the suffering."[4] This short sequence in the letter eschews the philosophical sage's and poetical husbandman's self-sufficiency and solitude and welcomes company and conversation, preferably live, but in the books of a library as an acceptable (if provisory) substitute. It thus hints at a philosophy that is, from its origin, social and sociable – a defining trait of Hume's thought.

Enlightened sentimentalism allied with social and sociable features define, for example, Hume's conception of the self in the *Treatise*. Book 1 overthrows the theory of a substantial self and introduces the self as a bundle of perceptions. The bundle theory of the self gains meaning and content in Book 2, when we take note that: (i) each self, susceptible of pleasure and pain, is in a continuous process of constitution, through original principles, by means of her passions and sentiments of love or hatred, relating to other selves, and pride or humility, relating to herself; and, through natural principles, conformable to the infinite variety of human lives, by relations with determinate and particular objects, places, beliefs, customs, etc. Void of relations, the self is nothing. It is from other selves that one gets a sense of one's self. If not prior, the constitution of other selves – bundles of perceptions – is concomitant with the constitution of oneself. A passage in Book 3 of the *Treatise* confirms Book 2 depiction of the human self-nesting in bundles of other selves. There, Hume notes that natural sexual appetite together with common concern with the offspring is the first and original principle of human society. Parents exert authority over children, restrained by wisdom and natural affection. By custom and habit, children are molded for society and are conscious of its advantages (T 3.2.2.4; SBN 486). While Book 2 outlines a psychology of the passions in the mind, its counterpart, Book 3, outlines a compatible sociological and historical environment.

The constitution of each and every human being is social – sociability is the most natural and agreeable of human propensities, and society is, as the essays frequently remind us, the cause of human achievements in the arts and sciences. In "Of the Rise and Progress of the Arts and Sciences," Hume affirms that the genius of the few who contribute to progress must be "antecedently diffused" in the entire society "in order to produce, form, and cultivate, from their earliest infancy, the[ir] taste and judgment" – it is not the genius of one, but the collective genius of "a whole people" that makes possible the emergence of artistic and scientific progress (E 114–115). The two first obvious causal antecedents propitious to this emergence are liberty and law, for they grant the peace and security which facilitate the cultivation of human talents. In "Of the Standard of Taste," the consensus of the critics (once again, a collective) to whose judgment a society defers (given their delicacy), and who embody its customs, manners, morals, and ways, sets the standard for that society, at that time.

In being deeply social, human, and humane, Hume's philosophy is unique among ancients and moderns. Standing apart from his modern contemporaries, he is the thinker with no debt to monotheistic religion, either constructive or destructive, who puts forward a philosophy, a politics, a system of passions, of morals and more, originating in persons joined by close ties of love, compassion, benevolence, desire, or hate, anger, revenge, of joy, sadness, hope, fear, of pleasure and pain. Sociability is a principle of human nature and its happy enjoyment is one of Hume's deepest aspirations in life. Neither an ancient sage, a superstitious monk, nor a modern romantic genius takes the lead in Hume's *repertoire*. His philosophy does not evolve from the high-souled, high-minded, wise man of the ancients, or from the *honnête homme*, *esprit-fort*, self-sufficient, autonomous subject of other moderns. It takes another path.

It does not mean, however, that the ancient myth is completely forgotten. Before being dispelled, it makes a final, ghostly, pallid apparition in the dissertation "Of the Passions," when Hume says: "What disposition of mind so desirable as the peaceful, resigned, contented; which readily submits to all the dispensations of providence, and preserves a constant serenity amidst the greatest misfortunes and disappointments?" (DP 2.41). In the sequence, wise to its inherent difficulties, he observes "this disposition is seldom the foundation of great vanity or self-applause." Moreover, Hume observes the necessity of the approbation, or the constant reassurance of the love of others, for us to feel pride in ourselves, for this passion needs fixation, confirmation, and reflection. Our very nature, our fragility, our sensitivity, susceptibility, and responsiveness call for companions and society, for our well-being and happiness. Mutual dependency is only human; it is insuperable; it is desirable.

Except for the brief apparition of the ancient philosophical sage in "Of the Passions," the *Four Dissertations* of 1757 are well adjusted to Hume's innovative philosophy of the *Treatise*. He is at ease to invite a friend, John Home, to participate in the piece; to have the friend's play appear as the specular reflection of the contents of his essay; and to extend, via the play, the reach of sociable, loving passions, opposing them, now, to a second ancient moral (not speculative anymore) myth – the courageous, heroic ideal of the warrior. Now, it is time to address the tension between the good and the great passions and virtues.

At play

The ancients reappear in the *Four Dissertations* of 1757 in a way that reveals the nature of Hume's philosophy in an unexpected and innovative way. They are prefaced by a passionate dedication[5] to John Home, the cousin and close friend of the philosopher, author of the play *Douglas, a Tragedy*,[6] and source of great national pride among fellow Scotspeople. What is first surprising about the dedication is that Hume had explicitly refused to adopt this practice throughout his career. He disdained those who did, suspicious of their interested motivations of ingratiating themselves with powerful men, and of the pernicious consequences of finding themselves subjected to benefactors.

After describing the Ancient practice of addressing a composition to friends and equals – a sign of regard and affection instead of servility and flattery, and of ancient liberty of thought – which allows authors to be friends despite differences of opinions, Hume expresses a desire to renew this practice in the Dedication of the *Dissertations*. And after celebrating Home's character (generosity of mind, cordiality of friendship, spirited honor, and integrity), Hume declares: "I own too, that I have the ambition to be the first who shall in public express his admiration of your noble tragedy of Douglas" (*Dedication*, 3–4). In pointing out the numerous qualities of Home's play, he declares: "these are incontestable proofs, that you possess the true theatric genius of *Shakespear* and *Otway*, refined from the unhappy barbarism of the one, and licentiousness of the other" (*Dedication*, 5).

The eloquence of the dedication infuses the *Dissertations* with the warmth of amiable sentiments, the feeling of good companionship, the pleasure in the contemplation of beauty. Ingeniously, it inscribes the play in the book as a fifth piece, and an extraordinary one, for it represents, on the stage, in movement, the very principles which Hume discovers in the essays, which compose the philosophical text of the volume. We may, I believe, claim that now we have a joint publication, for the play by John Home instantiates Humean principles of morals, and passions, in a work of art and taste. The playwright's theatrical genius is such that the audience, while sympathetically suffering with the play's protagonists' painful and melancholy passions, is still elated with the agreeable feeling of aesthetic pleasure in the judgment, art, and genius of the composition – an example of the conversion, overpowering, swallowing of one passion by another, stronger and opposite to it. Hume explains what happens in the mind as follows:

> By this means, the uneasiness of the melancholy passions is not only overpowered and effaced by something stronger of an opposite kind; but the whole impulse of those passions is converted into pleasure, and swells the delight which the eloquence raises in us. . . . The impulse or vehemence, arising from sorrow, compassion, indignation, receives a new direction from the sentiments of beauty. The latter, being the predominant emotion, seize the whole mind, and convert the former into themselves, at least tincture them so strongly as totally to alter their nature. And the soul, being, at the same time, rouzed by passion, and charmed by eloquence, feels on the whole a strong movement, which is altogether delightful.
>
> (E 219–220)

This confluence only touches the surface of the ties that bring together *Douglas, a Tragedy* and Hume's philosophy. The principle Hume discovers in the aesthetic essay, "Of Tragedy," operates in the economy of passions at large:

> It is a property in human nature, that any emotion, which attends a passion, is easily converted into it; though in their natures they be originally different from, and even contrary to each other. It is true, in order to cause a perfect union amongst passions, and make one produce the other, there is always required a double relation, according to the theory above delivered. But when two passions are already produced by their separate causes, and are both present in the mind, they readily mingle and unite; though they have but one relation, and sometimes without any. The predominant passion swallows up the inferior, and converts it into itself.
>
> (DP 6.2)

Aesthetic appreciation apart, Hume's dissertation on the passions and the plot and characters of John Home's tragedy form another perfect whole together. And this is a whole that exhibts some of the problems solved by Hume's philosophical stance, and which in a way singularizes it as unique in comparison with both modern and ancient predecessors. In the case of *Douglas*, the contrast between Hume and the ancients is vivid because tragedy played a political role in the Athenian *polis*, educating the citizenry, inculcating practices, customs, manners, and mores. Tragedies were live performances that revealed the possibilities of and gave direction to civic and public life.

Not unlike the ancients, eighteenth-century society flowed to the theater. We know of the cultural impact of Addison's *Cato*, of the *frisson* of a visit of a foreign opera singer to the stage in London, of the excitement succeeding any new production of Garrick at Drury Lane. Even though modern theater no longer is the cement of political instruction, it can be more than entertainment. How does John Home's tragedy fit the scene? For a theatergoer in Home's Edinburgh, the play is very much about Scottish national pride. Together with Hume's philosophy of the *Dissertations*, *Douglas* depicts the movement, the transition from a warrior society to a gentler, more sociable society, with its tensions, its conflicts, and its gains. Simultaneously, *Douglas* depicts *in vivo* the principles and operations of human nature in the passions, according to Hume's philosophical theory in "Of the Passions" – in its turn, a rewriting of Book 2 of the *Treatise*, arguably the heart and core of Hume's original thought. It is the possibility of staging the movement of passions in association with a philosophical theory grounded in the passions that turns the alliance of the play and the *Dissertations* into so rare an episode in the history of Western literature. For this chapter, in particular, it is of interest to observe effects of Hume's novelty on lingering ancient legacies.

The plot seems conventional. In her youth, Lady Randolph (of the house of Malcolm) secretly married the enemy of her family who was also a friend and savior of her brother. She had a child by her spouse (of the house of Douglas), born after his death. The long lost infant was sent away with his nanny. After giving up her child, Lady Randolph married Lord Randolph, who had saved her from the villain Glenalvon, who attempted to rape her. Her condition for the marriage was that it would be chaste, a condition Lord Randolph has honored.

The child returns now grown into a young man, endowed with gallant courage, ignorant of his true identity, in the erroneous belief that he is a humble shepherd named Norval. He defends Lord Randolph from an attack of bandits and becomes part of his army. The arrival of Old Norval, the young man's adoptive father, with the jewels with which the boy was found, discloses his true identity to Lady Randolph and her loyal maid and friend Anna: he is the Lady's lost son! Her maternal love is boundless. Norval learns that he is Douglas, awakening in him nascent sentiments of filial piety.

All the while, the villainous, treacherous Glenalvon schemes to steal Lady Randolph from his master and to ruin Douglas. A misunderstanding leads to Douglas' death by the cowardly hands of Glenalvon, soon after the reunion of mother and son. Lady Randolph, in utter despair, commits suicide by throwing herself off a precipice. Lord Randolph leaves, having decided to die in the battlefield against the Danish army about to attack.

The two main characters are Lady Randolph and Douglas. Lady Randolph stands with ease in the public and domestic domains. Daughter of a long line of prominent Scottish barons, she is kind and caring to the people living on their lands. In a telling scene of the play, she gives hope and joy to Old Norval when he realizes that young Douglas is going to reclaim the title of his forefathers, the Malcolms, reestablishing the prosperity of the old times. Within the close circle around her, she expresses a wide compass of soft, tender, caring kinds of love. Anna is a maid, a companion of almost two decades, in whom she can confide, with whom she can share happy and sad, hopeful and fearful, pleasant and painful passions and sentiments. Anna gives her comfort, advice, and loyalty, sharing experiences and a common history. Her benevolence is a relief to Lady Randolph's pains. For Lord Randolph, her spouse, she feels gratitude, esteem, and the respect due to one who stood by his promise of never forcing himself upon her after her consenting to their marriage.

For the husband of her youth, the father of Douglas, she feels amorous passion, strengthened by his abrupt loss in the height of youth, so shortly after their secret vows. For her brother, also dead, a friend of the departed husband, she feels sisterly, affectionate love. Since both brother and husband are dead, her love is melancholic, mournful, and full of woe and loneliness. For Old Norval, she feels forgiveness and understanding. Norval, having found the infant Douglas and his rich jewels in a basket floating the river, initially had avaricious inclinations, rather than fatherly ones. With the passage of time, he developed fatherly sentiments for the boy. He deserves to be forgiven. Glenalvon, she despises, hates, abhors, knowing his many vices, and his virtues, which are mostly martial: he is ungracious, subtle, predatory, irksome, shrewd, projects an artificial image of himself, and can "vary its features to the different taste of men" (*Douglas*, 12), "yet he is brave and politic in war, And stands aloft in . . . unruly times" (*Douglas*, 13). Even though Glenalvon, who is capable in the arts of war, may be admirable in warrior societies, his vices (e.g. treachery) and even warlike virtues (e.g. ferocity) turn him unacceptable in the society in which Lady Randolph conduces the play. Hume's circle of passions, their association by resemblance and conversion into others, is perfectly exemplified in Glenalvon's actions and character. Grief gives rise to anger; anger gives rise to hatred; hatred gives rise to envy; envy gives rise to malice; and malice, to grief, closing the circle.

Finally, she is so taken by Young Norval's brave, gallant, and modest deportment that she decides to protect him, and she fancies him to be what her son might have been like, had he been alive; and then, when she discovers that Young Norval is her son Douglas, her motherly love overflows with joy, pride in his excellent virtues, restless anticipation for the fulfillment of his bright destiny, and fearful anxiety for the ills that may befall him. When speculating on Douglas' uncertain future, and the revelation of Douglas' true identity to the world, Lady Randolph thinks of many possible outcomes. When she thinks of these outcomes, her passions change from hope to fear, to happiness, to sadness, as the probability appears to her to be higher of pleasant or painful outcomes.

Lady Randolph represents peaceful and amiable social aspirations. She dislikes war and the stern temper of the men – her father, her ancestors – who waged war for so long, causing so much pain and unhappiness in people's lives. She feels sympathy, initially restricted to the English, a neighboring nation, of similar customs:

> War I detest: but war with foreign foes,
> Whose manners, language, and whose looks are strange,
> Is not so horrid, nor to me so hateful.
> As that with which our neighbors oft we wage.
> A river here, there an ideal line.
> By fancy drawn, divides the sister kingdoms.
> On each side dwells a people similar.
> As twins are to each other; valiant both.
> (Douglas, 8)

Along the play, she attains the extended sympathy, from a moral point of view, able to be compassionate for the enemies, the Danes, to feel for their losses, and to disapprove of war against them. Upon the landing of the Danish invaders, she says:

> How many mothers shall bewail their sons!
> How many widows weep their husbands slain!
> Yo dames of Denmark! ev'n for you I feel,
> Who sadly sitting on the sea-beat shore.
> Long look for lords that never shall return.
> (Douglas, 30–31)

Furthermore, Lady Randolph, a woman of tender and soft passions, is also a woman of reflective nature and steady virtue. Desirous as she is to have her son's birthright asserted, and moved as she is by the opposing passions of hope and fear given the uncertainty of his present condition, still she is able to give him prudent advice, telling him to be patient and wait for corroborating testimony of his dynastic claims. Melancholy as she may feel while reminiscing about her past and youthful love, she is able to regret some choices of her young self when, confronted by the prohibitive presence of her father, the passion of fear was the motive of her actions. And, as we have just seen, her love of peace helps her attain the moral sentiment of sympathy for all who suffer from war, both friends and foes.

The other main protagonist is Douglas. Like Lady Randolph, he is a complex character. Unlike her, he has not yet made an entire transition from ancient to modern societal manners and morals. Douglas was raised as a shepherd but he is brave, valiant, and gallant. He has the temper of a warrior, of a hero. He desires to prove himself on the battlefield, to excel in the art of war, to excel in the virtue of courage, to achieve glory and greatness, and to be worthy of fame. At the same time, he is wise and sensitive. When his mother reveals herself to him, he says:

> Respect and admiration still possess me, Checking the love and fondness of a son. Yet I was filial to my humble parents. But did my fire surpass the rest of men, As thou excellent all of womankind?
>
> (*Douglas*, 38)

The words are delicate, caring, and true of the nature of the passions. Indeed, one cannot suddenly pass from reverent respect to intimate tenderness. As Hume says, differently from ideas, passions are not discrete impressions. They die slowly. And Douglas' character, his past sentiments for the adoptive parents, may be good predictors of future tender sentiments for his mother. Also, the discovery of Lady Randolph does not turn Douglas against Old Norval. Similarly to Lady Randolph, who is generous and forgiving of him, so too is Douglas.

Douglas comes to the stage with the ambition of gaining a name on the field as a warrior. In the end, because he is cowardly murdered by Glenalvon, without even a chance of self-defense, he cannot anymore prove his value and conquer a martial fame that will last to posterity. Is this his final thought? It is not. Douglas' final speech begins in a lament – he dies before his time, before achieving the greatness to which he aspired. But the speech ends not in thoughts concerning him, but concerning his mother, and in his suffering for and with her. The good, loving passions surpass the great, courageous passions in his final moments. And the tension that sustains the young hero throughout is finally resolved in the tragedy:

> DOUGLAS: Unknown I die; no tongue shall speak of me
> Some noble spirits, judging by themselves,
> May yet conjecture what I might have proved,
> And think life only wanting to my fame:
> But who shall comfort thee?
> LADY RAND: Despair! despair!
> DOUG: had it pleas'd high heav'n to let me live
> A little while! – My eyes that gaze on thee
> Grow dim apace! my mother – Oh, my mother.
>
> (*Douglas*, 51)

Douglas embodies the tension between the great heroic ancient virtues and the good, loving, and sociable modern Humean virtues. Lady Randolph embodies the latter. On this reading, John Home's tragedy is a Humean work. Embedded in the *Dissertations*, it responds well to:

(i) the solitary, contemplative, ancient sage. This figure, as we saw, appears fleetingly in "Of the Passions," soon to be dismissed. In the play, one character lives in retirement. But he is a man consumed by misery for having unknowingly killed his own brother in a fight;

(ii) the active, admirable, ancient great man of courage. In the play, he is seen through the eyes of Lady Randolph. Grouped in an army, he causes pain and destruction. Individually taken, it is not by his martial virtues that this man may add to the good of society. Indeed, such virtues may and do come in association with vices, and often with dangerous passions. Glenalvon is a villain; Lord Randolph is haughty and, because of this, unpredictable in his susceptibilities; Lady Randolph's father is a stern man who frightens his offspring, with dear and fatal consequences to both, and who can only act in secrecy; in consequence, her brother and late husband are victims of early deaths, and she of a lonely, melancholic life. Douglas alone, fortunately untainted by the horrors of the battlefield, dies in gallant greatness, easily converted into tender goodness;

(iii) the ancient active man capable of easy, free, philosophical friendship. It is true that the ancients not only emphasized war and conflict in the active life but also celebrated friendship: preferably the lasting sort, of a few trusted companions, but also that of the many fellow friends of the bottle. As we know, Hume is well-acquainted with the ancient world and literature on this subject. He alludes to it, admiringly, in the Dedication of the *Dissertations* to Home. In the same Dedication, he says he feels for Home the lasting sort: they freely express their opinions, in which they disagree without animosity and agree in inclination and manners. But this friendship is but one of many new loving possibilities present in Hume's theory of the passions, instantiated in *Douglas*. Ancient theoretical philosophies tend to be avaricious in their meager concessions to varied sorts of love and to the passions (Hume was quite right in seeking instruction from poets – not just epic ones, either – and not from philosophers alone). It is doubtful that an ancient philosopher would be so bold as to claim "reason is, and ought only to be, the slave of the passions."

Friendship is but one of several loving passions depicted in the play. The relations among characters may be seen from various different perspectives. The feelings, sentiments, affections, and emotions on display here seem richer than the scope of passions and virtues named and analyzed in the surviving literature of ancient philosophical tradition. In fact, not even modern philosophy seems comparable to Hume in the passions (hence, not to Home's tragedy, in the passions). Hume (and Home, with him) is keenly aware that pleasure and pain, good and evil, accept very many subtle variations under the same names. Lady Randolph's affects give the audience a taste of some of them. At the same time, "Of Passions" gives the reader a chance to name the different pleasures and pains felt sympathetically with characters in the play. Perceptions in the bundles are better discerned, understood, comprehended. I will not list again the loves of Lady Randolph, but recall that they exemplify, in a small scale, the range of Hume's theoretical achievement.

What is more, it is not perfect, divine, infallible beings that constitute the society, either of the play, or of Hume's theory. In both cases, good sociability is possible, although we are and will always be dealing with imperfect persons. We do get along, and lovingly so, despite our shortcomings. Also, there is a high measure of unpredictability in our behavior. Two examples: Lady Randolph's fear of Lord Randolph's haughtiness posing an obstacle to Douglas' claim to his hereditary title is key to the plot – this fear proves unfounded in the end. Lord Randolph would be fair to Douglas. Lord Randolph's susceptibility to the influence of Glenalvon, which proves his poor judgment of character, when, unaware of the villain's wile, he becomes suspicious of his wife's fidelity, is another key to the final resolution of the play. The cost of his error is enormous: Glenalvon succeeds in his murderous design against Douglas.

Finally, the play makes ingenious references to ancient and modern *motifs*, such as the infant who is sent abroad, adopted anonymously after being found in a basket floating in a river, and the villain who whispers defamatory words against the heroine's purity of character to her husband, thus leading to hers and the hero's demise. In being Humean, it does not copy and repeat the references – there is deliberate creative distortion to be seen. Sometimes it works against the theatrical tradition. We may conceivably speculate with Hume (taking Lady Randolph's point of view): the tragedy of Douglas is in his having to inhabit first the pastoral world of his upbringing, which is isolating and too confining, and second, the martial world, which is deadly. This promising youth cannot flourish in either world.

Also remarkable is the centrality of Lady Randolph in the plot – she is the heroine – a thoughtful, wise, and tender woman. With this aged woman we enter the founding, grounding, rooted, resilient world of sociable sentiments – a novelty, then and now. Through the reversals of fortune, the characters of Douglas at times mention fate, destiny, at times providence – the register oscillates between pagan and Christian references. Neither, however, appears to have intentional power or influence in the course of events. To invoke them is merely an exclamation, an expression of shock, despair, wonder – they are the play-writer's devices to signal plot twists. Any belief otherwise is, as the words of Lord Randolph indicate, idle scholastic speculation:

> Hard is his fate; for he was not to blame
> There is a destiny in this strange world.
> Which oft decrees an undeserved doom:
> Let schoolmen tell us why.
>
> (*Douglas*, 35)

Hume championed the staging of *Douglas, a Tragedy*. He attempted to influence its composition, in order to make the characters more true to life. In a letter to John Home of December, 1754, he wrote:[7]

> The more considerable objections seem to be these: *Glenalvon's* character is too abandoned. Such a man is scarce in nature; at least, it is inartificial in a poet to suppose such a one, as if he could not conduct his fable by the ordinary passions, infirmities, and vices of human nature.
>
> (L 1. 106)

And: "after *Anna* had lived 18 years with *Lady Barnet*, and yet had been kept out of the secret, there seems to be no sufficient reason why, at that very time, she should have been let into it" (*Letter*, 1.106). Hume is right: Glenalvon is too completely evil – this is not true of ordinary human beings and natural passions, nor is it necessary for the tragic beauty of the play. Lady Barnet (i.e. Lady Randolph) is not likely to keep the secret of her marriage and maternity from Anna, a trusted friend, for so long, and then, for no reason, to reveal it to her. As we know, Home did not listen to Hume, to the play's loss. And, we may see from the letter's content and advice, Hume scrutinized *Douglas* in light of the principles of human nature, in this case, principles of "Of the Passions."

The pieces are alike, first, in the broad compass of passions in display: grief, love, hate, jealousy, envy, malice, ambition, modesty, regret, courage, compassion, benevolence, pride, hope, fear, joy, sadness, despair. They are also alike in the display of the influence of the imagination on the passions, such as in: (i) the uncertainty of an object, by contrariety of views, and alternating probabilities, resulting in the alternation of hopes and fears; (ii) the possibility of passions finding strength upon the flimsiest opinions; (iii) opinions themselves being under the influence of society and sympathy. They are alike in the display of principles of the passions: (i) according to which, when passions mix, the predominant passion swallows up the other, and from it gathers added strength; (ii) finding in resemblance the principle of association of impressions. They both present the effects of sympathy: from our resemblance with them, we enter easily and familiarly into the sentiments and conceptions of others, and thus love them, desire their happiness, and are averse to their misery. They present the effects of comparison of ourselves with others, as well: comparison seems to be the source of malice and envy. They give superb analyses of love, pride, and love of fame.

The analyses, in the play and dissertation, seem superb because of the fine-tuning between the *original* principles (direct passions, and good and evil, from pain and pleasure, and indirect passions – pride and humility, love and hate – from the double association of impressions and ideas) and their natural expressions (due to custom, perspective, society, disposition, etc.). They show us that our prides and humilities, loves and hates, and the whole train of passions are not dissociable from our imaginations and are continually weaving our ever-changing selves. From 1739, with the *Treatise*, and a kind reminder in 1757, with the *Dissertations*, which include, to our delight, in *Douglas*, a fifth piece, it is time for every one of us, with a new understanding of our nature, to experience and experiment philosophical enquiry in company – un-coerced, only following our taste and sentiment – a gift from Hume to his readers.

To conclude, in Hume's theory, friendship (in a loose sense) and other loving social passions are neither complementary nor final ends to human life. They are what constitute and compose human beings themselves, always adding to, subtracting, enlivening, or fading the lines and chords of the bundle(s) of perceptions – selves in society according to original (observably steady) and natural (circumstantial) principles of human nature. This theory is at work in *Douglas*, to the delight of the reader of Hume's philosophy. In a modern seat, if we are with Hume, 'tis time, perhaps, to look into the pages of Lucian, Ovid, perhaps Horace, in acknowledgment of the timely companionship he found in congenial ancient writers, those who were, like Hume, with unclouded eyes, and open hearts and minds, keen on human nature.[8]

Notes

1 Another likely candidate for his final work are the *Dialogues Concerning Natural Religion*, since Hume was making substantial changes and corrections on them right until he died. Dialogue 8 presents us with the very plausible Epicurean cosmogony.
2 I take the analysis of the essays on happiness below from my paper *A Melancholy Skeptic*. In: Kriterion, vol. 44, no.108, Belo Horizonte – Brazil, July/December 2003.
3 Translation from the Latin: *The Spectator*, n. 414, Wednesday, June 25, 1712.
4 Translation from the Latin by Tiago Everaldo da Silva, to whom I am very thankful.
5 Hume, D. *Four Dissertations*. London: A. Millar, 1757. Hereafter: *Dedication*, paragraph.
6 Home, J. *Douglas. A Tragedy*. Glasgow, 1776. Hereafter: *Douglas*, page.
7 I very much thank Vinícius França Freitas for this reference, and also for his generous help in the composition and revision of this essay.
8 I am very grateful to Angela Coventry and Alexander Sager, and to Routledge for the kind invitation to participate in this volume, and for their kind and generous help all along – for which I feel honored, and which gives me great joy. I am also immensely grateful to the members of Grupo Hume – UFMG, Anice Lima de Araújo, Carlota Salgadinho, Stephanie Hamdan Zahredine, Vinícius França Freitas, Hugo Arruda, Andreh Sabino, Tiago Everaldo da Silva, Wendel de Holanda Campelo, Luis Felipe Lopes, Renato Fonseca, Vinícius Amaral, Weverson Lopes, and Bruno Pettersen. Without their contributions, I would not have written this chapter. This was originally given as a paper at the XVII Encontro Nacional ANPOF (Associação Nacional de Pós-Graduação em Filosofia) in Aracaju, Brazil, October, 2016, and at the seminar of Grupo Hume – UFMG, in Belo Horizonte, Brazil, January 2017. The chapter is part of a research project sponsored by Conselho Nacional para o Desenvolvimento Científico e Tecnológico (CNPq), and Fundação de Amparo à Pesquisa do Estado de Minas Gerais (FAPEMIG), Brazil.

References

Home, J. (1776) *Douglas. A Tragedy*, Glasgow.
Hume, D. (1757) *Four Dissertations*, London: A. Millar.

2

HUME'S PHILOSOPHY AND ITS MODERN BRITISH DEBTS

Stephen Buckle

Introductory textbooks typically cast Hume as the third of the British Empiricists, the heir of Locke and Berkeley. His debts to these two philosophers is undeniable, but to cast him in this frame is to distort his philosophy by artificially narrowing its scope. The main problem is that it casts Hume as a specialist epistemologist, rather than the ambitious developer of a new "science of man" which aimed at new foundations for morals, politics, and religion. In developing this new science, Hume drew on a wide array of influences, ancient as well as modern, Continental as well as British. This article will restrict itself to his modern British influences.

In his earliest published work, the *Treatise of Human Nature*, Hume is happy to identify himself as belonging to a tradition indebted to Bacon, Locke, and Newton – the three British heroes of the Enlightenment philosophers – and, in moral philosophy, to the third Earl of Shaftesbury and his inheritors. These figures give Hume's project a modern and constructive air. But other figures mentioned only in passing are no less important. One is Bishop Berkeley, but two others – the materialist Thomas Hobbes and the then-prominent Newtonian Christian Samuel Clarke – are most important for understanding the overall thrust of Hume's philosophy. In particular, Hume's dependence on key Hobbesian doctrines and his critique of Clarke's religious arguments indicate an undercurrent of materialist and irreligious themes running through his philosophy from its first formulation. The critique of religion is an obvious element in Hume's later works, but even Hume's "purely philosophical" concerns in the *Treatise* reflect its young author's intense engagement with the religious controversies of his day (Russell 2008: 25–57). This implies a wider, and rather different, set of influences than the textbook model.

The introduction to *a Treatise of Human Nature*

Perhaps the best place to begin is with Hume's own first public attempt to place himself: the opening pages of the *Treatise*. The title page announces the work to be "an attempt to introduce the experimental method of reasoning into moral subjects." The Introduction then explains the "experimental method" to be the reliance on "experience and observation" characteristic of the new natural philosophy. Hume then offers a historical parallel to illuminate the appropriateness of extending this method to "moral subjects," or "the science of man" (T Intro. §§6–10; SBN xvi–xix). He casts himself as participating in a modern version of an ancient drama: the Socratic development of moral philosophy a century after Thales had inaugurated Greek metaphysics.

23

Hume casts himself as one of the Socratics following a century after the modern Thales, Francis Bacon. This is not empty rhetoric. Bacon had himself occasionally considered the necessity of extending the methods of natural philosophy to moral philosophy, the science of man, even though, like Hume, he thought of human nature as exercising a distorting effect (Bacon 2000: 98, 41). What is more, that Hume was acquainted with those passages is shown by his very employment of the comparison of Thales with Socrates, which he has taken directly from Bacon (Bacon 2000: 65).

Hume's literary career extended to essays and history as well as philosophical works, and this also may indicate a Baconian connection. Hume first began composing essays while still working on the *Treatise*, so they cannot be attributed to his disappointment with the *Treatise*'s reception. Similarly, the *History* was in his mind long before he began work on it. So it appears that Hume had early formed an intention to write all three kinds of works – just as Bacon had done. This resemblance has not usually been recognized, because of the influence on the essays and history of more contemporary writers. Thus the *Essays* were influenced in their style, and to some extent in their choice of topics, by the example of the polished essay-writing of Joseph Addison and Richard Steele in *The Tatler* and *The Spectator*, and the *History* was influenced by the examples of Montesquieu's *Spirit of the Laws* (1748) and Voltaire's *Age of Louis XIV* (1751). These influences have occluded Bacon's example. However, the topics of Hume's essays – morals, politics, religion, and political economy, as well as matters of taste – have more in common with Bacon's choice of subject matter than with *The Tatler* or *The Spectator* (Bacon 1985); and Hume's original intention, to begin his history with the reign of Henry VII – because of its significance in undermining the old feudal order (Harris 2015: 341, 383) – was precisely to emulate Bacon's example in his *History of the Reign of King Henry VII* (Bacon 1998). There is, then, reason to believe that Hume's whole sense of a vocation was inspired by Bacon's example.

Whether or not this is so, Hume explicitly casts himself as part of a bold new current in moral philosophy traceable to the innovations provided by Bacon's natural philosophy. The other contributors are "some late philosophers in *England*, who have begun to put the science of man on a new footing." (T 1.1.1.7; SBN 17) In a footnote he tells us who they are: "Mr. *Locke*, my Lord *Shaftesbury*, Dr. *Mandeville*, Mr. *Hutcheson*, Dr. *Butler*, &c." Here we have, then, a short list of official influences. However, Locke aside, the members of this list are most relevant to the later parts of the *Treatise*; the influences on Book I are not identified explicitly.

Perhaps the most striking feature of the list is that Berkeley does not rate a mention. This is despite the fact that Berkeley's influence on some parts of the *Treatise* is very plain: Hume follows Berkeley – "a great philosopher" (T 1.1.1.7; SBN 17) – in his account of abstract ideas, in his notion of the *minimum sensibile* in his discussion of our ideas of space and time, and in his critique of the distinction between primary and secondary qualities, with all its implications for our knowledge of the external world (Berkeley 1998: 90–101, 153, 105–108). Nevertheless, Berkeley's influence on the *Treatise* is more specific than pervasive: Hume makes use of his arguments, but not to endorse his Idealist conclusions. He says, in his later estimation of "that ingenious author" that his arguments "form the best lessons of scepticism" because "*they admit of no answer and produce no conviction*" (EHU 12.15n; SBN 155). This complex attitude to Berkeley may explain his omission from Hume's list, given the positive, progressive movement it is the task of the list to endorse. But, whatever the reason, his omission suffices to show that, in the Introduction, Hume does not fully signal his debts. This needs to be kept in mind when considering the case for a pervasive Hobbesian influence.

First, though, it needs to be recognized that the pride of place accorded to Locke is no accident. The impact on the *Treatise* of Locke's *Essay Concerning Human Understanding* is considerable, in both its broad orientation, and in many of its details (Noonan 1999; Wright 2009). Hume follows Locke in insisting that the mind contains only what experience has placed in it: the fundamental role played by his "copy principle" – the principle that all our ideas are exact copies of our perceptions – is this Lockean debt in action, and it is Hume's commitment to this thesis that justifies placing him in an empiricist tradition stemming from Locke's example (Noonan 1999: 60–61). But few of the topics handled in Book I lack reference to Lockean views and arguments, whether in agreement or disagreement: Locke set the agenda for discussions of perception, language and meaning, substance and essence, power and causality, primary and secondary qualities, knowledge and probability, and so on; these topics figure prominently in Book I because Hume cut his teeth on Locke's discussion of them (Noonan 1999). In fact, in the Introduction Hume provides numerous hints of his debt. He affirms the point Locke had insisted on in the very epigraph to the *Essay*: that we know the essence of neither the mind nor the body (T Intro. §8; SBN xvii; cf. Locke 1975: 1). He also employs there some characteristically Lockean turns of phrase: he observes that we will have "lost our labour" if we do not "glean up" our experimental data from ordinary life (T Intro. §§ 3, 10; SBN xiv, xix; cf. Locke 1975: 560, 647).

The first debts Hume identifies, then, are to Bacon and Locke. This indicates a wider cultural significance that often goes unrecognized. By appealing explicitly to these two figures, Hume signals his adherence to a broad modernizing project that will come to be known as the Enlightenment. The connection becomes obvious a little later, when Bacon and Locke come to enjoy canonical status among the French *philosophes*. However, even by the time of the *Treatise*'s appearance, they had been acknowledged (alongside Descartes and Newton) as giants of the modern age in Voltaire's *Letters Concerning the English Nation*, published in London in 1733 (Voltaire 1994: 49–66). Hume shows himself fully aware of this modernizing tendency. He remarks, in typically "Enlightened" manner, that the "late philosophers in *England*" have made progress in the human sciences because "the improvements in reason and philosophy can only be owing to a land of toleration and of liberty" (T Intro. § 7; SBN xvi). Here we see scientific and moral (and political) themes being connected, as two sides of a progressive, modernizing project – in other words, as components of a new, more enlightened age.

The third, and greatest, Englishman of the Enlightenment pantheon was Sir Isaac Newton. Hume does not mention him by name in the Introduction, but he does hint broadly at a debt by including a passage which is a close paraphrase of Newton. He says:

> And tho' we must endeavour to render all our principles as universal as possible, by tracing up our experiments to the utmost, and explaining all effects from the simplest and fewest causes, 'tis still certain we cannot go beyond experience; and any hypothesis, that pretends to discover the ultimate original qualities of human nature, ought at first to be rejected as presumptuous and chimerical.
>
> (T Intro. §8; SBN xvii)

This paraphrases part of the penultimate paragraph from the last of the "Queries" that Newton had appended to his *Opticks*. Hume's purpose here is not merely to tug the forelock to the greatest Englishman, but to point the reader to his own relationship to the Newtonian outlook. In the following (closing) paragraph of that work, Newton adds that "if natural philosophy in all its parts, by pursuing this method, shall at length be perfected, the bounds of moral philosophy will also be enlarged" (Newton 2004: 140). Hume is, then, hinting, to the many readers capable of recognizing the Newtonian reference, that his own project is precisely that to which the great man had pointed.

In this and other passages, Hume conspicuously cloaks himself in Newtonian dress. The most obvious is his remark that the three principles of association of ideas can be thought of as "a kind of ATTRACTION, which in the mental world will be found to have as extraordinary effects as in the natural, and to show itself in as many and as various forms" (T 1.1.4.6; SBN 12–13). Given this explicit analogy, it seems no accident that the principles of association, like Newton's laws of motion, are only three in number. In this light, Hume's introduction of "corollaries" to his main conclusion concerning the idea of causation also appears intended to underline the Newtonian connections (T 1.3.14.32–36; SBN 171–172).

But is all this false advertising? James Noxon has pointed out that Hume's allegedly Newtonian *Treatise* is experimental only in an "attenuated" sense, and is, moreover, "as unmathematical as Ovid's *Metamorphoses*" (Noxon 1973: 112). This is true, but misses Hume's point and purpose. As the above quotation shows, it was Newton's emphasis on the limitations on our knowledge implied by experimental philosophy that was, for Hume, the central lesson to be learned (cf. H 6. 542; Buckle 2001: 70–90). This was all the more important when Newton forgot it, or failed to see how deeply such ignorance cut. Thus, he supposed that the enlargement of natural and moral philosophy could provide us with important insights into the most fundamental questions:

> For so far as we can know by natural philosophy what is the first cause, what power he has over us, and what benefits we receive from him, so far our duty towards him, as well as that towards one another, will appear to us by the light of nature.
>
> (Newton 2004: 140)

Hume shows this hope to be in vain, and does so on the very ground on which Newton had insisted. To underscore the point, he echoes this Newtonian passage in the profoundly skeptical conclusion to *Treatise* Book I:

> From what causes do I derive my existence, and to what condition shall I return? Whose favour shall I court, and whose anger must I dread? What beings surround me? and on whom have I any influence, or who have any influence on me? I am confounded with all these questions.
>
> (T 1.4.7.8; SBN 269)

Hume's point, then, is that Newtonianism does *not* deliver the positive, "enlarged" moral philosophy of which Newton – and his orthodox followers – had dreamed (Jacob 1976; cf. Demeter 2014).

In arriving at this profoundly skeptical conclusion, he is not, however, abandoning the Baconian framework. Bacon had argued that human beings are subject to illusions which block their minds, illusions he calls "idols." They are the idols of the tribe, of the cave, of the marketplace, and of the theater. These are the epistemic flaws inherent in human nature, in individuals, in talk (and in language itself), and in philosophical views. Hume's *Treatise of Human Nature* falls into place as a treatise on the idols of the tribe, of the flaws in human nature that frustrate or corrupt the pursuit of knowledge. In Bacon's words: "The human understanding is like an uneven mirror receiving rays from things and merging its own nature with the nature of things, which thus distorts and corrupts it" (Bacon 2000: 41). Hume's commitment to Newtonian strictures leads, thus – contrary to Newton's own hopes – to conclusions that give effective endorsement to the Baconian conception of the idols of the tribe. Hume's influences conspicuously include Bacon, Locke, and Newton, the heroes of the *philosophes*, but, in contrast to their optimistic outlook, the first lesson of Hume's Enlightenment is that the human being must recognize the limitations on human epistemic powers before social progress can be hoped for.

An Abstract of a Book Lately Published

It will be useful if, at this point, we step away from Hume's Introduction to the *Treatise* and consider some issues raised by his fears that the book would not sell. In *My Own Life*, he describes the *Treatise*'s reception as falling "dead-born from the press" (MoL xxxiv). This was an exaggeration, but, fearing it to be so, he composed an abstract of the book in order to encourage sales. In the *Abstract*, Hume makes two claims that are useful for identifying an unnamed influence. First, he says there that one concern of the *Treatise* that distinguishes it from other philosophical works is its focus on probabilities (Ab. §4; SBN 647). Second, he remarks, in the final paragraph, "if any thing can entitle the author to so glorious a name as that of an *inventor*, 'tis the use he makes of the principle of the association of ideas, which enters into most of his philosophy" (Ab. §35; SBN 661–662).

These remarks are significant, first, because they separate Hume's project from Locke's. Locke had devoted a chapter to probability, but Hume presents himself as following in the footsteps of "the celebrated *Monsieur Leibnitz*," who had criticized Locke's shortcomings on precisely this point (Ab. §4; SBN 646–647). Second, Locke had introduced a chapter on association of ideas only in the fourth edition of the *Essay*, and his remarks about it show him to regard it as alien to his book's central concern with rationality, the "natural Correspondence and Connexion" of the mind's ideas. Association, he admits, is not a form of rational connection, but the fruit of "Custom," which "settles habits of Thinking in the Understanding." And, because it is not a natural, rational manner of connection, it is therefore not improper to call it a kind of "Madness," a "Taint" which "infects Mankind" (Locke 1975: 394–396). Nevertheless, he concludes, this kind of connection, though not natural, is a common feature of human life, and for that reason worthy of investigation:

> This wrong Connexion in our Minds of *Ideas* in themselves, loose and independent one of another, has such an influence, and is of so great a force to set us awry in our Actions, as well Moral as Natural, Passions, Reasonings, and Notions themselves, that, perhaps, there is not any one thing that deserves more to be looked after.
>
> (Locke 1975: 397)

It is impossible to doubt that Hume read this passage, and that it helped provide him with his own project. In fact, one remark in the *Abstract* seems aimed at this passage: Hume emphasizes there the three principles of association – resemblance, contiguity, and causation – which, "notwithstanding the empire of the imagination," provide "a secret tie or union among particular ideas" (Ab. §35; SBN 662). In short, associations, although they are mere habits of thinking, are not simply "loose and independent one of another." Rather, they are subject to natural principles – even though those principles are not rational.

To give the place of associations in Hume's philosophy its due is to see that Hume's project is, in spirit, not only Lockean but also anti-Lockean – and in roughly equal measure. The empiricist copy principle he introduces at the very beginning of the *Treatise* is immediately followed by his second fundamental principle, the association of ideas (T 1.1.2–4; SBN 7–13). Moreover, Locke's "natural Correspondence and Connexion," reason, is left unmentioned – until much later, when it is firmly subordinated to passion (T 2.3.3.4; SBN 415). So, British Empiricist though he may be, Hume is, from his opening pages, not a faithful Lockean. The question is, is it possible to identify a convincing philosophical precursor of Hume's empiricist and associationist philosophy of the empire of the imagination?

Hume and Hobbes

The most plausible candidate is Thomas Hobbes. The later books of the *Treatise* are critical of Hobbesian views, but both the overall structure of the *Treatise* and the specific doctrines of Book I show striking resemblances to Hobbes' philosophical project. To take these in turn.

First, Paul Russell has shown that the structure of the *Treatise* can be fitted onto the structure of Hobbes' *The Elements of Law* (first published in 1650). *The Elements of Law* was comprised of two parts, *Human Nature* and *De Corpore Politico*: the subject matter of *Human Nature* corresponds to the subject matter of Books I and II of the *Treatise*, on the understanding and the passions; the subject matter of *De Corpore Politico* corresponds to the subject matter of *Treatise* Book III, on morals and politics. Russell also points out that, at the beginning of the second part of *De Corpore Politico*, Hobbes, in a summary of the contents of the preceding parts, refers to it as a "*Treatise of Human Nature*." So not only is there a structural correspondence between the two works, but Hume may also have found his own title in Hobbes' work (Russell 2008: 61–64).

For this to be so, Hume must have encountered *The Elements of Law*. James Harris has questioned this, since the *Elements* was not widely available in the first half of the eighteenth century, having been republished only once before 1750, in 1684. He adds: "It is at least as likely, anyway, that Hume found inspiration for the systematic study of human nature in the French Cartesian tradition. Malebranche especially seems to have had an important role in the development of Hume's ideas" (Harris 2015: 83). Hume certainly owed much to Malebranche, and it is possible that he did not encounter *The Elements of Law* first-hand – as Russell points out, much the same territory (if not the description "treatise of human nature") is covered in *Leviathan* (Russell 2008: 62). But, whatever the exact line of transmission, and whatever the precise structural parallels, it is beyond doubt that Hume's *Treatise*, Book I in particular, is organized around themes that play a prominent role in Hobbes' philosophy. The obvious difference is that Hobbes freely indulges in materialist explanations – everything reduces to matter in motion – whereas Hume largely avoids any such commitments. Nevertheless, he follows the basic Hobbesian patterns of explanation, and even a similar order of exposition. A sketch of the argument of the opening eight chapters of *Leviathan* will bring this out (Hobbes 1994: 6–50).

The mind's contents arise from sense-perceptions, in the following way. Sense-perceptions are caused by external objects pressing on the body and setting up motions within the body. These motions are, for us, feelings or ideas. Ideas are internal motions caused by external motions, and so are distinct from the external objects that cause them. The internal motions are such as to make us attribute the ideas to an external source. The repository of the images that linger in the body is the *imagination*. It is thus composed of "decaying" sensations (i.e. paler copies of original sense-perceptions). What is commonly called "the understanding" is not a distinct faculty of reason but simply those imaginings to which words have been affixed. It is, in other words, a power of the imagination (i.e. under the "empire of the imagination"). It is common to man and beast (i.e. animals also "reason").

Thought is connected imaginings. Transitions of thoughts reflect past sequences of sensations (past experience): present sensations are associated by the mind with past ones, and so a present sensation prompts the imagination to call up *the whole string* of sensations that followed the same sensation in the past. This generates expectations about the future (i.e. it is not a rational procedure but a kind of habit). "Trains of thought," when unguided, are not "wild ranging of the mind" (i.e. the imagination runs "not altogether at adventures" (EHU 3.1; SBN 23)) but are connected by associations. When guided, they are governed not by reason but by desires (a division which corresponds to the division of the *Treatise* into Books I and II).

Desire-governed trains of thought concern causes and effects.[1] When concerned with the future, they depend on the thought that like events will follow like actions – they are suppositions about the future based on experience of the past.[2] Reasoning is just a calculative power; it is not a special faculty that equips us for discovering hidden truths, but a fallible human skill improved through experience, and especially through the development of general rules (Hobbes 1994: 24; cf. T 1.3.9.6; SBN 110). Human actions begin in passions, internal motions in the body caused by internal or external motions, which therefore display predictable patterns. Reason is a "scout" for passion (its eyes and ears) and so its servant – "the slave of the passions" (Hobbes 1994: 41; cf. T 2.3.3.4; SBN 415).

These Hobbesian doctrines are all also Humean doctrines (and preoccupations). They make it plain that the basics of Hume's account of mental functioning derive from Hobbes, whatever his debts to other philosophers.[3] Hume adopts nearly all the main themes of Hobbesian psychology, even to the extent of building his account of our inductive practices and our conceptions of causal necessity and probability out of Hobbes' account of the origin of expectations (future-oriented beliefs) from the non-rational tendency to transfer past experience to the future. In fact, Hume's development of the Hobbesian doctrine shows why he should have drawn particular attention, in the *Abstract*, to Leibniz's remark about probability: it is his introduction of ideas of probability and degrees of belief that distinguishes his account from Hobbes'. Hobbes based expectations about the future on past experience; Hume sophisticated that account by explaining that varying degrees of expectation arise according to the frequency and regularity of the past experience. So Hume's emphasis, in the *Abstract*, on association and the empire of the imagination aligns him with Hobbesian psychology, while his emphasis on probability draws attention to how he has developed a distinctive Hobbesian doctrine.

To connect Hume's philosophy to Hobbes' raises some important questions, because Hobbes was notorious for his materialism and his rejection of much religious orthodoxy – so much so that he was typically attacked as an atheist. Hume, for his part, was also a sharp critic of religion – so much so that he, too, was typically attacked as an atheist – so the question is whether he can be thought of as a fellow-traveler with the materialists, and whether his religious criticisms reflect materialist sympathies.

Unlike Hobbes, Hume did not explicitly affirm the truth of materialism. Nevertheless, it is not hard to find indirect evidence of materialist sympathies in the *Treatise*. The first is the affirmation of the empire of the imagination itself. Ever since Aristotle, the imagination had, in contrast to the power of reason, been classed as a mental faculty dependent on the senses, and thus on the body (Aristotle 1986: 200; cf. Malebranche 1980: 87ff). So it is no mere accident that Hobbes' materialism denies that there is any faculty of reason independent of imagination: the understanding is merely imaginings with the use of words, "and is common to man and beast" (Hobbes 1994: 11). This connection of the empire of the imagination and materialism does not die out. Writing a century later (shortly after Hume's *Treatise*), La Mettrie and d'Holbach both insisted on the truth of materialism by arguing that there was no distinct rational faculty, that all depended on the imagination (La Mettrie 1996: 14–15; d'Holbach 1999: 84–86, 94–96). This does not prove Hume a materialist, but it does place his views in a context that strongly encourages a materialism-friendly interpretation (Buckle 2007). With this in mind, it is then possible to pick out other evidences of materialism-friendly elements in Hume's thought: the sheer passivity of the mind, as composed of mere impressions and their paler copies, and the determinism that follows from this; the reduction of reason to experience, and the willingness to treat associations, the engine of thought, as due to motions in the brain (T 1.2.5.20; SBN 60–61); and the preparedness to accept that thought might be nothing but motions (T 1.4.5.30; SBN 248). In addition, Hume employs arguments taken from the ancient

Epicureans, the aggressive materialists of the ancient world. He does so in both his discussion of materialism and his account of the origins and nature of justice. In his later works, this becomes all the more pronounced: the emphasis on utility in *An Enquiry Concerning the Principles of Morals*, and the arguments deployed in the posthumously published essay "Of the Immortality of the Soul," both reflect a marked Epicurean influence.

We can conclude that, beneath the surface, and sometimes breaking through, Hume's philosophy, from its first appearance, displayed a materialist tendency. And, since materialism was typically regarded as evidence of irreligion, this raises the question of whether, in the *Treatise*, Hume had irreligious intentions. Judging by the topics in terms of which the *Treatise* is standardly discussed – causation, induction, personal identity, etc., but not religion (e.g. Ainslie and Butler 2015) – the usual, if implicit, answer to this question is in the negative. The same assumption is betrayed by the fact that studies of Hume on religion typically refer to the *Treatise* only in passing (Gaskin 1988; O'Connor 2001). These scholarly demarcations show that, despite Hume's later frontal assaults on religious beliefs, the *Treatise* is regarded as a work apart, a work in "pure philosophy" to be contrasted with the more applied tendencies of the later, religiously critical, works. However, this perspective will not stand up. It has been comprehensively attacked by Paul Russell, in *The Riddle of Hume's Treatise* (2008); and, although Russell's arguments are not all equally compelling, he succeeds in showing that many of the topics covered in the *Treatise* have a subversive impact on religious views – particularly on then-influential philosophical arguments for religious belief.

The most significant of these is Hume's famous treatment of causation in Book 1, Part 3. Probably because this topic is commonly approached via the more streamlined account offered in the *Abstract* and *Enquiry Concerning Human Understanding*, Hume's actual target tends to be forgotten. That target is indicated in the section title, "Why a cause is always necessary." In particular, Hume's target is the belief that everything has a cause of existence. But "cause" in what sense? Since it is a *conclusion* of Hume's argument that there are only efficient causes (T 1.3.14.32; SBN 171), it must be that Hume has in mind the older, Aristotelian sense of "cause" as fundamental explanation. To put it in more familiar terms, his target is an existential version of the principle of sufficient reason – the belief in the explicability of the cosmos to the human mind, because of its divinely conferred rational powers. His much-discussed conclusion, that our belief in causal power is a product of mental habit, is thus aimed, not at determining whether there are causal powers in nature – a topic on which much ink has been spilt (e.g. Read and Richman 2007) – but at denying human beings the power of insight into nature's workings, and above all into its (and our) origins. That is, if it cannot be known that a cause is always necessary, that everything has a cause of its existence, then the central premise of the cosmological argument for God's existence cannot be affirmed. The *Treatise's* most famous section is, then, not a mere "analysis" of causation, but a long and winding road to a critique of a major plank of philosophical religion.

Hume and Clarke

This excursus into the underlying materialist and irreligious elements in the *Treatise* serves to identify a major, if negative, influence on Hume's philosophy. Samuel Clarke is not a familiar name nowadays, but he was a prominent figure in the early eighteenth-century project of reconciling Christianity with Newton's revolutionary science. His solutions were not always met with enthusiasm by other Christian philosophers, as is shown in his 1715–1716 correspondence with Leibniz over religious and scientific matters (Alexander 1956). However, his prominence was guaranteed by his very influential Boyle Lectures of 1704–1705. The first of these, published under the title *A Demonstration of the Being and Attributes of God*, is an extended argument for God's existence and nature, built precisely on the premise that everything has a cause. (It is noteworthy that Clarke does not restrict this question to efficient causation only, but also allows final causation in order to argue for God's freedom in creating the cosmos (Clarke 1998: 51)). In arguing along these lines, Clarke is following in the footsteps of Locke, who had provided a short argument of the same kind in the *Essay* (Locke 1975: 619–630). But, quite apart from Clarke's prominence (and other indirect evidence), it is known that Hume read Clarke, and indeed had him in view when composing the *Treatise*.

He is explicitly mentioned only once in the *Treatise*, but it is in the important section "Why a cause is always necessary," and it is clear that his position on the necessity of causes is one of the main targets of the whole discussion of causation in Book 1, Part 3. This is made plain in Hume's hurriedly written defense of the *Treatise*, *A Letter from a Gentleman to his Friend in Edinburgh*. The *Letter* was a reply to a hostile pamphlet circulated against the *Treatise* in 1745 in response to Hume's application for the Chair of Moral Philosophy at the University of Edinburgh. The pamphlet accuses the author of the *Treatise* with "Universal Scepticism," with "Principles leading to downright Atheism, by denying the Doctrine of Causes and Effects," "Errors concerning the very Being and Existence of a God," "Errors concerning God's being the first Cause, and prime Mover of the Universe," with "denying the Immateriality of the Soul," and with "sapping the Foundations of Morality" (LG 20; 425). In response to two of these charges – the second on causation, and the last on morality – Hume acknowledges that his arguments are opposed to Clarke's, but insists that Clarke's views do not define orthodoxy, being themselves opposed by "many Men both of Piety and Learning" (LG 27; 427). This is a fair response, even though Hume is being disingenuous in lining himself up with the pious and learned: as he had later admitted to James Boswell, "he never had entertained any belief in religion since he began to read Locke and Clarke" (Boswell 2003: 256). The relevant conclusion, then, is that Hume shows, in the *Letter*, that Clarke's Boyle Lectures are one of his targets, and that they are so because the *Treatise*'s long argument concerning causation *is* intended to have application to religious arguments; and, indeed, that Hume's exposure to Clarke's arguments played a role in his abandonment of religious belief.[4]

In this light, it is particularly striking that Clarke's work has, as its subtitle, "More particularly in answer to Mr. Hobbes, Spinoza, and their followers" (Clarke 1998: 3). It is natural to suppose, then, that, in coming to reject Clarke's views, Hume would, if he were not already aware of them, have felt curiosity aroused for the views of Clarke's targets – and also for "their followers." This places Hume's debts in a context sharply different from the usual epistemological genealogy. Hobbes and Spinoza were by-words for materialist irreligion, and "their followers" were not necessarily adherents of their specific doctrines, but fellow-travelers along the materialist and irreligious road. Most prominent among these were English Deists like John Toland, Anthony Collins, and others (many of whom claimed some measure of descent from Locke). So, although there is not much common ground between Hume's philosophy and Spinoza's doctrines, and a very mixed debt to Hobbes', Hume is known to have associated with "their followers" in London, when seeing the *Treatise* through publication (Russell 2008: 33).

All of this suggests a very different context for Hume's philosophy. Instead of situating Hume within a purely epistemological tradition, this alternative picture identifies him as someone focused on religious questions, ultimately to the cost of his initial religious beliefs. The key influences on the first book of the *Treatise* thus turn out to include not only Locke and Berkeley (and Newton) for their epistemological arguments and procedures, but also Clarke (and Locke again) as targets of its religious criticism; and, above all, Hobbes, who, despite his dogmatism, provides the bones of Hume's project. But the underlying critique of philosophical religion also draws out affinities with the heterodox or irreligious intellectual currents swirling through early eighteenth-century Britain, associated with Clarke's gang of disreputables, "Hobbes, Spinoza and their followers." The first book of Hume's *Treatise* emerges as the work of a young man growing up in a period of considerable religious disagreement, and whose interest in epistemological and metaphysical issues stems from his intense engagement with these controversies.

To cast Hume as heavily indebted to Hobbes, and even as sympathetic to his materialism, seems to run counter to the themes of Books 2 and 3. It is certainly the case that Hume resists Hobbesian doctrines in these latter books, but if we re-introduce Newton at this point, things can be fitted into a convincing frame. The key lies in the Newtonian doctrines that matter is governed by the three laws of motion and the principle of universal gravitation. We have already seen that it is significant that Hume finds *three* principles of association and underlines the Newtonian connection by describing them as kinds of *attraction*. But of equal, if not greater, importance is the sheer fact that the behavior of matter is characterized by laws of *motion*. These Newtonian doctrines allow Hume to think of the mind as if material, *without* concluding that the human being is fundamentally self-interested.

This is a break with the materialist tradition, which had followed the Stoics in holding that everything that exists seeks to preserve itself in its own being (the primary impulse, or *hormē*: in Latin, *conatus*; in English, *endeavor*). The theme is marked in both Hobbes and Spinoza (Hobbes 1994: 27–28; Spinoza 2000: 171). Hume, in contrast, breaks this link between materialist (or materialism-friendly) conceptions of the mind and self-interested behavior by drawing the Newtonian conclusion that matter does not seek its own preservation, but acts according to gravitation and the laws of its motion. Moreover, the first law is a law of inertial motion: motion, of whatever kind, once begun, will continue until overcome by some new force (Newton 2004: 70). Applied to the mind, this inertial tendency is custom or habit. Of course, many of these habits will concern self-preservation, so the older view is preserved as a special (albeit important) case. But inertial behavior is not reducible to self-interest, and Hume's accounts of the formation of probable and necessary beliefs and of practical beliefs (in the shape of the development of ideas of justice) can be seen as both developments consistent with, and perhaps inspired by, the implications of Newton's physics for understanding minds on a materialism-friendly model.

The introduction to the *Treatise* – again

This thought, that a Newtonian conception of the behavior of matter opens up the possibility of a materialism-friendly philosophy freed of the characteristic nexus between materialism and self-interest, would remain purely negative unless it could be filled out with positive content. It is at this point that the remaining members of Hume's "late philosophers in *England*" come to the fore. Hume's list – "my Lord *Shaftesbury*, Dr. *Mandeville*, Mr. *Hutcheson*, Dr. *Butler*, &c." – is chronological. In order of relevance for understanding Hume's arguments in Books 2 and 3 of the *Treatise*, however, it is Butler's moral psychology that needs to be treated first. And in this case Hume himself offers, in an early footnote to *An Enquiry Concerning Human Understanding*, a summary account of Butler's importance for Hume's psychology of the passions in Book 2. Hume there remarks that:

> It had been usual with Philosophers to divide all the Passions of the Mind into two Classes, the selfish and benevolent, which were suppos'd to stand in constant Opposition and Contrariety. . . . Philosophers may now perceive the Impropriety of this Division. It has been prov'd, beyond all Controversy, that even the Passions, commonly

esteem'd selfish, carry the Mind beyond Self, directly to the Object; that tho' the Satisfaction of these Passions gives us Enjoyment, yet the Prospect of this Enjoyment is not the Cause of the Passion, but on the contrary the Passion is antecedent to the Enjoyment, and without the former, the latter could never possibly Exist.

(EHU 232–233 (1.14n))

The fundamental distinction here, between the cause of the passion and its object, is the basis of Hume's account of the indirect passions – pride and humility, love and hatred – which makes up the bulk of Book 2. The distinction enables Hume to clarify the (necessary but only partial) role of the self in these passions, and simultaneously enables him to avoid the standard materialist analysis of them purely in terms of self-interest. Butler's analysis of the moral emotions is thus the premise on which Hume builds Book 2.

The three remaining "late philosophers" lie behind the moral theory presented in Book 3. In his *Characteristicks of Men, Manners, Opinions, Times* (1711), the third Earl of Shaftesbury developed a moral theory heavily dependent on Stoic ideas. Hume was powerfully influenced by Shaftesbury in his adolescence, even to the extent of trying to live according to a strict Stoic regimen – although he soon gave it up because of its destructive effect on his frame of mind (L i. 13–14). Nevertheless, Shaftesbury had a lasting influence on Hume's work, partly directly and partly indirectly. The direct influence included being one source of Hume's conception of the role of sympathy in the moral life – the means by which individuals "receive by communication" the "inclinations and sentiments" of others, and so move beyond a purely self-interested outlook (T 2.1.11.2; SBN 316; Shaftesbury 1999: 52, 204).

A second, related, direct influence was Shaftesbury's being the source of the idea of a *sense* of right and wrong, or moral sense (Shaftesbury 1999: 177–192). However, this influence was more profound indirectly. Shaftesbury's moral theory provoked a sharply critical response from Bernard Mandeville, whose rebukes were, in turn, met by a more philosophically sophisticated defense of Shaftesbury's basic ideas by Francis Hutcheson. Mandeville, a doctor who worked in London's slums, argued that Shaftesbury's high-minded theory showed only that he knew nothing of the self-interest, not least avarice, at the heart of human nature (Mandeville 1988: 323ff). Hutcheson replied that self-interest theories distorted the motives of "honest Hearts" – supposing them to engage in "subtle Trains of Reasoning" to which they were "often wholly Strangers" (Hutcheson 2002: 4) – and made use of Locke's account of secondary qualities to argue for the reality of a moral sense that instinctively approves of "the greatest Happiness for the greatest Numbers" (Hutcheson 2008: 125). This dispute shaped Book 3 of the *Treatise*. In Book 3, Part 1, Hume affirms the necessity of moral sensing, without which morality could not be practical. But he recasts it as the operation of a sympathetic mechanism responsive to the emotions of others, and so more local in its effects than Hutcheson's conception of an instinct for the general happiness. Then, in Book 3, Part 2, Hume offers an account of justice heavily indebted to Mandeville's very Epicurean-flavored reflections on the development of societal values in Volume 2 of *The Fable of the Bees* (Mandeville 1988). He treats justice as an "artificial" virtue – i.e. a virtue that does not reflect any natural moral approval based directly in moral sense, but as a social institution that arises gradually through a habitual acceptance of mutual self-interest, and which comes to enjoy moral approval only once its overall beneficial effects become recognized (T 3.2.2.24; SBN 498). The bulk of Book 3 thus reflects Hume's engagement with the moral theories of Shaftesbury, Mandeville, and Hutcheson – an engagement in which he navigates carefully between the providentialist cast of the moral sense theorists and Mandeville's Epicurean cynicism (Wright 2009: 286–288).[5]

Conclusion

Hume was British, and he was an empiricist. He was, therefore, a British empiricist. But to cast him as a descendent of Locke and Berkeley is to miss the extent to which he was, from his first principles, an opponent of both. He proposed a theory of human nature and of human society and its mores built on the "empire of the imagination" and its operating rules, the principles of association and the inertial mechanism (habit). These fundamental ideas, deriving from Hobbes' aggressive materialism, set him apart from his immediate empiricist predecessors. However, Hume avoided Hobbes' (and Mandeville's) self-interest theories of passion, morality, and politics by exploiting distinctions and arguments derived from Joseph Butler and Francis Hutcheson, while conceding that justice initially arises from self-interest educated by experience. He also saw, as Hobbes did not, that such an account of the mind's workings could not remove skeptical doubts about the conclusions reached; thus he rejected Hobbes' dogmatism. This meant also opposing the dogmatism of Christianity's philosophical defenders, and this brings Samuel Clarke and the other Boyle Lecturers into the frame. Hume's project was thus, from its first manifestation in the *Treatise*, a critique of the new orthodoxies being built on the new understanding of nature.

A virtue of this account is that it brings out the continuities between the *Treatise* and the more overt religious criticism of the later works. In fact, once Hume is seen to be, from the beginning, a secular critic of religious dogma, his reasons for revising the *Treatise* in the way he did becomes comprehensible. In part, he seems to have lost faith in the details of his psychological story in the *Treatise*; but he also saw, from quite early on (as the *Abstract* is enough to suggest) that the general bearing of his conception of the human being did not need all that detail in order to arrive at the conclusion that most mattered to him: that the new science, despite its inability to guarantee its own foundations, pointed firmly away from religious orthodoxy toward a skeptical standpoint.

Notes

1 Such thoughts are "nothing but *seeking*, or the faculty of invention . . . a hunting out of the causes of some effect, present or past, or the effects of some present or past cause" (Hobbes 1994: 13); cf. Hume: "The first and most considerable circumstance requisite to render truth agreeable, is the genius and capacity, which is employ'd in its *invention* and discovery . . . But beside the action of the mind . . . there is likewise requir'd a degree of success in the attainment of the end, or the discovery of that truth we examine . . . To illustrate all this by a familiar instance, I shall observe, that there cannot be two passions more nearly resembling each other, than those of *hunting* and philosophy" (T 2.3.10.3, 7, 8; SBN 449, 451–452; emphases added). Hume also goes on to compare the love of truth to the pleasures of gaming (T 2.3.10.9; SBN 452), which may perhaps be a development of Hobbes's remarks about how to become "the best guesser" (Hobbes 1994: 14).

2 "As he that foresees what will become of a criminal re-cons from what he has seen follow on the like crime before, having this order of thoughts: the crime, the officer, the prison, the judge, and the gallows" (Hobbes 1994: 13–14). Cf. Hume: "A prisoner . . . when conducted to the scaffold, foresees his death . . . His mind runs along a certain train of ideas: The refusal of the soldiers to consent to his escape, the action of the executioner; the separation of the head and body; bleeding, convulsive motions, and death" (T 2.3.1.17; SBN 406).

3 Hobbes is an advocate of compatibilism before Hume (Hobbes 1994: 137), but he is not unique in this respect: Spinoza, Locke, and others also argued for compatibilist views. Hume's account of personal identity may also have Hobbesian debts (Hobbes 1994: 516). (My thanks to Deborah Brown for drawing my attention to this point.)

4 Hume also seems to have Clarke in view in his discussions of free will, personal identity, and ethical rationalism (including the famous "is–ought" paragraph).

5 The third and final Part of Book 3, in which Hume offers his account of the natural virtues, is indebted more to ancient moralists – Cicero in particular – than to this contemporary British debate.

References

Ainslie, D. and A. Butler (2015) *The Cambridge Companion to Hume's Treatise*, Cambridge: Cambridge University Press.

Alexander, H., ed. (1956) *The Leibniz-Clarke Correspondence (1717)*, Manchester: Manchester University Press.

Aristotle (1986) *De Anima (On the Soul)*, trans. H. Lawson-Tancred, London: Penguin Books.

Bacon, F. (1985) *The Essays (1597–1625)*, edited by J. Pitcher, London: Penguin Books.

———. (1998) *The History of the Reign of King Henry VII (1622)*, edited by B. Vickers, Cambridge: Cambridge University Press.

———. (2000) *The New Organon (1620)*, edited by L. Jardine and M. Silverthrone, Cambridge: Cambridge University Press.

Berkeley, G. (1998) *A Treatise Concerning the Principles of Human Knowledge (1710)*, edited by J. Dancy, Oxford: Oxford University Press.

Boswell, J. (2003) *Boswell's Edinburgh Journals 1767–1786*, edited by H. Milne, rev. edn, Edinburgh: Mercat Press.

Buckle, S. (2001) *Hume's Enlightenment Tract: The Unity and Purpose of an Enquiry Concerning Human Understanding*, Oxford: Clarendon Press.

———. (2007) "Hume's Sceptical Materialism," *Philosophy* 82: 553–578.

Clarke, S. (1998) *A Demonstration of the Being and Attributes of God and Other Writings*, edited by E. Vailati, Cambridge: Cambridge University Press.

D'Holbach, P. (1999) *The System of Nature (1770)*, edited by M. Bush, Manchester: Clinamen Press.

Demeter, Tamás (2014) "Enlarging the Bounds of Moral Philosophy: Newton's Method and Hume's Science of Man," in Z. Biener and E. Schliesser (eds.), *Newton and Empiricism*, New York: Oxford University Press.

Gaskin, J. (1988) *Hume's Philosophy of Religion*, 2nd edn, London: Palgrave Macmillan.

Harris, J. (2015) *Hume: An Intellectual Biography*, Cambridge: Cambridge University Press.

Hobbes, T. (1994) *Leviathan (1651)*, edited by E. Curley, Indianapolis, IN: Hackett Publishing.

Hutcheson, F. (2002) *An Essay on the Nature and Conduct of the Passions and Affections (1728)*, edited by A. Garrett, Indianapolis, IN: Liberty Fund.

———. (2008) *An Inquiry into the Original of Our Ideas of Beauty and Virtue (1725)*, edited by W. Leidhold, rev. edn, Indianapolis, IN: Liberty Fund.

Jacob, M. (1976) *The Newtonians and the English Revolution 1689–1720*, Ithaca, NY: Cornell University Press.

La Mettrie, J. (1996) *Machine Man and Other Writings*, edited by A. Thomson, Cambridge: Cambridge University Press.

Locke, J. (1975) *An Essay Concerning Human Understanding (1704)*, edited by P. Nidditch, Oxford: Clarendon Press.

Malebranche, N. (1980) *The Search After Truth*, trans. T. Lennon and P. Olscamp, Columbus: Ohio State University Press.

Mandeville, B. (1988) *The Fable of the Bees (1723–1728)*, 2 vols, edited by F. Kaye, Indianapolis, IN: Liberty Fund.

Newton, I. (2004) *Philosophical Writings*, edited by A. Janiak, Cambridge: Cambridge University Press.

Noonan, H. (1999) *Hume on Knowledge*, London: Routledge.

Noxon, J. (1973) *Hume's Philosophical Development*, Oxford: Clarendon Press.

O'Connor, D. (2001) *Hume on Religion*, London: Routledge.

Read, R. and K. Richman (2007) *The New Hume Debate*, rev. edn, Abingdon: Routledge.

Russell, P. (2008) *The Riddle of Hume's Treatise: Skepticism, Naturalism, and Irreligion*, New York: Oxford University Press.

Shaftesbury, Third Earl (1999) *Characteristics of Men, Manners, Opinions, Times*, edited by L. Klein, Cambridge: Cambridge University Press.

Spinoza, B. (2000) *Ethics (1677)*, edited by G. Parkinson, Oxford: Oxford University Press.

————. (2007) *Theological-Political Treatise (1669–1670)*, edited by J. Israel, Cambridge: Cambridge University Press.

Voltaire (1994) *Letters Concerning the English Nation (1733)*, edited by N. Cronk, Oxford: Oxford University Press.

Wright, J. (2009) *Hume's A Treatise of Human Nature: An Introduction*, Cambridge: Cambridge University Press.

3

THE FRENCH CONTEXT OF HUME'S PHILOSOPHY

Todd Ryan

In presenting his philosophical project in the Introduction to the *Treatise of Human Nature*, Hume acknowledges the important contributions that "some late philosophers in *England*" have made toward the new experimental "science of man." In addition to Bacon, Hume singles out for special mention "Mr. Locke, my Lord Shaftesbury, Dr. Mandeville, Mr. Hutcheson [and] Dr. Butler" (T Intro.7; SBN xvii; Ab. 2; SBN 646). However, if Hume's publicly acknowledged debts are to his great British predecessors, his private correspondence tells a somewhat different story. Writing to his friend Michael Ramsay in 1737, Hume proposed a list of suggested reading as an aid to understanding the recently completed *Treatise*. Hume writes,

> I desire of you, if you have Leizure, to read over once le Recherche de la Verité of Pere Malebranche, the Principles of Human Knowledge by Dr Berkeley, some of the more metaphysical Articles of Bailes Dictionary; such as those [of] Zeno, & Spinoza. Des-Cartes Meditations would also be useful but don't know if you will find it easily among your Acquiantances. These Books will make you easily comprehend the meta-physical Parts of my Reasoning and as to the rest, they have so little Dependence on all former systems of Philosophy, that your natural Good Sense will afford you Light enough to judge of their Force and Solidity.
>
> (Mossner 1980: 627)

Perhaps the most striking feature of Hume's list is that apart from Berkeley, all of the recom-mended authors are French. Nor will this seem particularly surprising, when we recall that the first two books of the *Treatise* were almost entirely composed during Hume's three-year sojourn in France. Of course, this is not to say that in the Introduction to the *Treatise* Hume was merely flattering the national pride of his British audience or that the authors he names there were not of decisive importance in the development of his thought. Nevertheless, Hume's private recom-mendation highlights the importance of the French context – and in particular the Cartesian tradition, broadly understood – as part of the philosophical background to which Hume was reacting. This is particularly true of Book 1 of the *Treatise*, which includes many of the most "metaphysical Parts" of the work. Naturally, a comprehensive account of this context would include a wide range of authors and touch on almost every major area of Hume's thought. In this chapter, I shall follow Hume's lead by examining the influence of Descartes, Malebranche, and Bayle on those aspects of Hume's philosophy where it weighed most heavily, namely his metaphysics and epistemology.

Space and time

In Book 1, Part 2 of the *Treatise*, Hume advances a highly original account of space and time as they appear to the senses. In undertaking to explain the nature of space in particular, Hume was entering into a longstanding debate concerning the composition of physical extension. The framework of this debate had been clearly articulated by Pierre Bayle, most famously in the *Dictionary* articles "Zeno of Elea" and "Zeno, the Epicurean" as well as in his lectures on physics. According to Bayle, there are only three possible views with regard to the composition of physical extension. Either it is composed of mathematical points or it is composed of physical atoms or it is composed of parts, each of which is infinitely divisible. According to Bayle, each of the three possibilities is subject to unanswerable objections. From this, Bayle concludes that physical extension cannot exist, a claim to which I shall return below. For the moment, we must briefly consider Bayle's arguments against each of the three alternatives.

Against the possibility that physical extension is ultimately composed of mathematical points, Bayle argues that no collection of such points can constitute a real extension. The objection takes two forms. The first is what has been called the Summation Problem (Falkenstein 2013). By definition, mathematical points are dimensionless and so have zero magnitude. Now, no collection or aggregation of dimensionless points can produce a spatially extended entity. The second argument, which we might call the Mereological Problem, takes as its crucial premise the observation that mathematical points are conceived not as material objects but as "a pure nothing" (Bayle 1737 4: 300). However, no physical entity can be wholly composed of parts that are literally nothing. Therefore, no extended entity can be wholly composed of mathematical points. Additionally, in his lectures on physics Bayle offers a third objection, which we might call the Penetration Problem. According to this argument, a multiplicity of mathematical points cannot form a real extension, because any two such points when placed in contact with one another would interpenetrate. The points would interpenetrate because, being simple and indivisible, they cannot be arranged such that only a part of one is contiguous with a part of the other. Rather, the whole of the one must touch the whole of the other (*segundum se tota*). Consequently, the resulting compound would have no greater magnitude than either of the points considered individually (Bayle 1737 4: 293).

Against the claim that physical extension is ultimately composed of atoms or physical points, Bayle observes that by definition such atoms are supposed to be extended, yet indivisible entities. However, according to Bayle, whatever is extended consists of distinguishable parts (it has, for example, a left side and a right side) and whatever consists of distinct parts may be divided, if not physically, then at least conceptually. It follows that the very notion of an indivisible, extended atom is contradictory, and consequently the existence of such atoms is impossible. The final view, which Bayle associates with the Scholastics, is that physical extension is composed of parts, each of which is infinitely divisible. Bayle's principal objection to this alternative is that of necessity, a thing that is infinitely divisible is composed of an infinite number of actually distinct parts. However, according to Bayle, an infinite collection of actual parts would combine to form an infinite extension. Therefore, no finite extension can be composed of infinitely divisible parts.

It is within this framework that Hume offers his own account of space. Like Bayle, Hume quickly dismisses the notion of physical points or extended, indivisible atoms on the grounds that every extended object consists of really distinct parts. Consequently, such atoms must be divisible, which is contrary to the supposition (T 1.2.4.3; SBN 40). For Hume, then, infinite divisibility and mathematical points are the only serious contenders. Hume argues in favor of the latter. This requires him to do two things: first he must establish that we have an idea of a mathematical point, that is of an unextended, indivisible entity, such that a collection of these points is capable of forming a real extension. Second, he must argue against the possibility of infinite divisibility.

Hume begins with the latter. Like Bayle, Hume understands "the doctrine of infinite divisibility" to imply not only that every extended entity is infinitely divisible, but also that it consists of parts, each of which is infinitely divisible (Baxter 2008: 22). Hume first argues that, owing to the limited capacity of the human mind, any idea of finite extension we can form can contain only a finite number of parts or component ideas. Now, because infinite divisibility implies the existence of an infinite number of really distinct parts, it follows that we can form no idea of an extension that is infinitely divisible. Furthermore, in dividing any one of our ideas of extension into its component parts, we must arrive at the idea of a part that is absolutely simple and indivisible. Hume calls such parts 'minima.' Because they contain no component parts into which they can be divided, such ideas represent the smallest conceivable quantity.

Hume next argues that no finite extension can be infinitely divisible. His argument turns on the claim that because our idea of a minimum represents the smallest conceivable quantity, it follows that if no finite extension can contain an infinite number of these minimal parts, then no finite extension can contain an infinite number of parts of any magnitude whatsoever. Hume then imagines the result of conjoining several such minima together:

> I then repeat this idea once, twice, thrice, &c. and find the compound idea of extension, arising from its repetition, always to augment, and become double, triple, quadruple, &c. till at last it swells up to a considerable bulk, greater or smaller, in proportion as I repeat more or less the same idea.
>
> (T 1.2.2.2; SBN 29)

According to Hume, we clearly conceive that were we to continue this process of concatenation to infinity, the result would be an extension of infinite length. From this he concludes that no finite spatial extent can comprise an infinite number of parts and consequently no such extent is infinitely divisible.

Having rejected the doctrine of infinite divisibility in favor of mathematical points, Hume turns to defend this latter theory against several of the key objections raised by Bayle. Against the claim that the idea of a mathematical point is the idea of "a mere nothing," Hume concedes that were our idea of a minimum merely that of a simple, indivisible entity, the objection would hold. However, he insists that these points are not merely nothing since they are endowed with color or tactile qualities. As such, they are real entities capable of composing a real extension (T 1.2.4.3; SBN 40). In response to the Summation Problem, Hume argues that although minimum visible and tangible points are perfectly simple, and so lacking in length, breadth, and depth, nevertheless, as the above thought experiment shows, a finite number of such points juxtaposed to one another constitutes an entity with real finite magnitude. Finally, in response to the Penetration Problem, Hume once again appeals to experience. If we place two minimum visible points side by side, we find that they do not interpenetrate, but form "an object, which is compounded and divisible, and may be distinguish'd into two parts, of which each preserves its existence distinct and separate, notwithstanding its contiguity to the other" (T 1.2.4.6; SBN 41).

Hume maintains that all of the arguments that establish the impossibility of infinite divisibility in the case of extension are equally applicable to time. However, Hume adduces an additional argument against the infinite divisibility of time that once again has a direct antecedent in

Bayle (Bayle 1991: 353–354). The argument turns on the traditional (Aristotelean) distinction between two kinds of quantity: spatial and temporal. What distinguishes these two kinds of quantity is how their parts stand in relation to one another. Spatial quantity, or extension, consists of parts that are coexistent. Duration consists of parts that are successive – that is, existing one after the other. As Hume puts the point with regard to the parts of time, "'tis also evident, that these parts are not co-existent: For that quality of the co-existence of parts belongs to extension, and is what distinguishes it from duration" (T 1.2.3.8; SBN 36). For both Hume and Bayle, this means that each successive part of time must exist alone (Baxter 2008: 28–29). Now, because no two successive parts of time can coexist, it follows that time must be composed of indivisible moments. For if the present moment were infinitely divisible, its parts would exist not one after another, but simultaneously, contrary to the essence of temporal quantity (for more on Hume's theory of space and time, see Chapter 6 of this volume).

Causation

Commentators have long recognized the influence of Malebranche on many aspects of Hume's philosophy (McCracken 1983; Wright 1983). Here I shall focus on the most important of those influences, Malebranche's occasionalist theory of causation. On this theory, God alone is a true cause. Finite created objects are devoid of real causal power. Thus, for example, when one billiard ball strikes another, setting it in motion, it is God alone who produces motion in the second ball. The impact of the moving ball provides nothing more than the "occasion" for God to exercise his unlimited causal power. While Malebranche offers a variety of arguments for this view over the course of his long career, the one that figures most prominently in his earliest work, the *Search After Truth*, turns on the claim that one object or event is the cause of another only if there is a necessary connection between the occurrence of the cause and the occurrence of the effect. This argument, which has come to be known as the No Necessary Connection Argument, is formulated by Malebranche as follows:

> a true cause as I understand it is one such that the mind perceives a necessary connection between it and its effect. Now the mind perceives a necessary connection only between the will of an infinitely perfect being and its effects. Therefore, it is only God who is the true cause and who truly has the power to move bodies.
>
> (OCM 2: 316; LO 450)[1]

What exactly is meant by a necessary connection is a matter of some debate. However, the most natural reading suggests that, for Malebranche, there is a necessary connection between the occurrence of the cause and the occurrence of the effect just in case it would be a contradiction for the effect to fail to occur upon occurrence of the cause (Nadler 1996). From the claim that genuine causation requires a necessary connection between cause and effect, Malebranche draws two conclusions. First, because we never perceive a necessary connection between any two natural events, no natural event is the real cause of any other. Second, because it is a contradiction that an omnipotent being wills a certain state of affairs and yet that state of affairs fails to obtain, the mind clearly perceives that there is a necessary connection between God's willing some event and the occurrence of that event. Therefore, God is a real cause (OCM 10: 64). Taken together, these two theses imply that God alone is the true cause of every effect.

In addition to this general argument for the occasionalist thesis, Malebranche deploys a host of particular arguments intended to show that neither finite bodies nor finite minds possess the requisite power or force to produce any effect. Against the real causal efficacy of body, or material substance, Malebranche argues (following Descartes) that we have a clear and distinct idea of the essence of body as extension. This idea informs us that all of the various modes of which body is capable are nothing more than relations of distance between its parts. Now, because power or force cannot be conceived as a mere relation of distance, it follows that by its very nature body lacks real causal power and so cannot be a true cause of change (OCM 12: 150).

The case of finite minds is importantly different from that of bodies, since for Malebranche we lack a clear and distinct idea of the nature or essence of mind.[2] Consequently, any particular argument to show that finite minds lack real causal power must appeal to our conscious awareness (*sentiment intérieur*) of our internal mental operations and, in particular, our volitions. Malebranche denies that this inner consciousness makes us aware of any real causal power in our will. On the contrary, motion in my arm is the result of a complex sequence of physiological changes of which I am largely or wholly ignorant and which are in no way the object of my volition when I choose to move my arm. Nor is my will the true cause of the ideas that appear before my mind when I choose to contemplate them. For I am wholly ignorant of the nature of these ideas and of the means by which they are produced. Indeed, "I do not know whether they are produced from nothing and whether they return to nothingness as soon as we cease to perceive them" (OCM 3: 226; LO 669).

According to Malebranche, although we never perceive a necessary connection between any two finite events, we are prone to believe that such events are real causes because we observe them to occur in regular patterns or sequences. Thus, we observe one billiard ball approaching another and upon collision we see that the latter is set into motion at a determinate speed and direction. The regular and uniform occurrence of these events deceives us into thinking that the former is the true cause of the latter. Against this tendency, Malebranche warns that we ought

> never judge in the case of natural events that one thing is the cause of another, because experience shows you that the one never fails to follow the other. For, of all false principles this one is the most dangerous and the greatest source of errors.
>
> (OCM 10: 59)

In reality, these regular patterns among events – what Hume would call their "constant conjunction" – are the result of God's lawful causal activity. God's infinite wisdom requires that he act in the simplest and most uniform manner. As a result, God's (non-miraculous) causal activity takes the form of freely established general laws which dictate that whenever an event of type A occurs it will be followed by an event of type B.

Although Hume has little sympathy for the positive claim that God is the immediate cause of every natural event, much of what Malebranche has to say about causation is reflected in Hume's own account. Hume follows Malebranche in maintaining that an essential component of our idea of causation is necessary connection (T 1.3.2.11; SBN 77). Furthermore, Hume agrees with Malebranche that the mind never perceives a necessary connection between any two natural objects or events. Hume defends this claim by arguing that such a connection is discoverable by neither reason nor experience. In both cases, his arguments draw heavily on his French predecessor.

Hume's assertion that causal relations are not knowable by reason rests on a version of Malebranche's No Necessary Connection Argument (Nadler 1996), although Hume arguably gives a much clearer and more incisive formulation of the argument. For Hume, all objects of human knowledge are either relations of ideas or matters of fact.[3] Relations of ideas are knowable independently of experience; they are *a priori* truths. The certainty of such truths is owing to the fact that their denial implies a contradiction and so is strictly inconceivable. Now, according to Hume,

> there is no object, which implies the existence of any other if we consider these objects in themselves, and never look beyond the ideas which we form of them. Such an inference wou'd amount to knowledge, and wou'd imply the absolute contradiction and impossibility of conceiving any thing different. But as all distinct ideas are separable, 'tis evident there can be no impossibility of that kind.
>
> (T 1.3.6.1; SBN 86–87; cf. EHU 4.6–11)

Every cause is distinct from its effect. Therefore, it is always possible to conceive of the one as existing in the absence of the other. Now, because whatever is clearly conceivable is possible, there can be no impossibility in the occurrence of the cause without the corresponding effect.

Likewise, Hume argues that when we consult experience we are equally incapable of perceiving any necessary connection between the occurrence of any two finite events or objects. Here again in establishing this conclusion Hume draws heavily on particular arguments advanced by Malebranche. Thus, Hume appeals to our ignorance of the chain of physiological events that terminates in the raising of our arm to argue that we are not aware of any power to move our arm (EHU 7.14; SBN 66). Similarly, in the case of our voluntary control of our ideas, Hume observes that far from perceiving the power by which the will is able to summon forth ideas, we do not even know what an idea is or whether its occurrence amounts to an instance of creation ex nihilo (EHU 7.17; SBN 68). However, whereas Malebranche had used such considerations to maintain that there was no necessary connection between finite objects and that therefore such objects were not true causes, Hume deploys similar arguments to show that we are never aware of a necessary connection among natural objects or events. From this he concludes not that such objects and events are not genuine causes, but that they are not the immediate source of our idea of necessary connection.

Despite the obvious importance of Malebranche for understanding Hume's account of causation, Hume offers a powerful criticism of both the conclusion that no finite objects or events are true causes and the attempt to establish God as the one true cause. In summarizing the occasionalist argument in the *Treatise*, Hume emphasizes Malebranche's denial of real causal power in material objects based on the assertion that we have an adequate – that is, clear and distinct – idea of the essence of matter, on the basis of which we clearly perceive that material objects possess no true power or force. Hume portrays Malebranche as drawing the conclusion that the power to move bodies must reside in God, whose omnipotence we conceive by means of an innate idea. Hume's principal objection to this line of reasoning is based on the Copy Principle – that is, his claim that all simple ideas are copies of antecedent impressions. From this, it follows that if we have no impression of power from either the senses or reflection, then we can form no idea of power at all, much less an idea of supreme power or omnipotence. Hume writes:

> if every idea be deriv'd from an impression, the idea of a deity proceeds from the same origin; and if no impression, either of sensation or reflection, implies any force or efficacy, 'tis equally impossible to discover or even imagine any such active principle in the deity. Since these philosophers, therefore, have concluded, that matter cannot be endow'd with any efficacious principle, because 'tis impossible to discover in it such a principle; the same course of reasoning shou'd determine them to exclude it from the supreme being.
>
> (T 1.3.14.10; SBN 160)

Consequently, if we continue to insist with Malebranche that an object is a real cause only if the mind perceives a necessary connection between it and its effect, we are left with the following dilemma:

> either to assert, that nothing can be the cause of another, but where the mind can perceive the connexion in its idea of the objects: Or to maintain, that all objects, which we find constantly conjoin'd, are upon that account to be regarded as causes and effects.
>
> (T 1.4.5.31; SBN 248; Cf. EHU 7.25; SBN 72–73)

While this criticism has often been portrayed as constituting Hume's decisive objection to occasionalism, I think we can see that Malebranche was much closer to Hume on this point than is commonly imagined. To be sure, Malebranche had asserted in the *Search* that "whatever effort of mind I make, I can find force, efficacy, or power only in the will of the infinitely perfect Being" (OCM 3: 205; LO 658). This might be taken to suggest that what distinguishes divine volition from ordinary finite objects is that in the case of God we have a clear idea of the power by which he is able to bring about any possible effect. However, as Malebranche makes clear in subsequent works, not only do we have no clear idea of omnipotence or supreme power, but we have no clear and distinct idea of power at all. This point is brought out most clearly in the *Méditations Chrétiennes*, where Malebranche considers the objection that the Christian doctrine of creation ex nihilo should be rejected, since we cannot comprehend by what power God could create matter out of nothing. Malebranche replies that God reveals to us no idea of power whatsoever. Thus, the Word says:

> you ask me for a clear and distinct idea of this infinite efficacy which gives and preserves being in all things. . . . I give men no distinct idea corresponding to the word 'power' or 'efficaciousness'. . . . For even if you believe that God does whatever he wills, this is not because you clearly perceive that there is a necessary connection between God's will and its effects, since you do not so much as know what God's will is.
>
> (OCM 10: 96)[4]

Malebranche goes on to formulate the following dilemma. If we deny that God has the power to create ex nihilo on the grounds that we have no clear idea of a power that can bring about such an effect, then we must likewise deny that God has the power to do anything, since we have "no clear idea of efficaciousness or power" whatsoever. As a result, we would be forced to acknowledge that there is no such thing as causation nor any real causes in the world. Thus, Malebranche had already conceded that we have no more an idea of power in the case of God than in the case of finite objects. Nevertheless, he believed that he could escape the dilemma and preserve God's real causal power on the grounds that it would be a contradiction for an omnipotent being to will some possible event and for that event to fail to occur. As Malebranche puts the point, "it is evident that God would not be all-powerful if his absolute volitions remained inefficacious" (OCM 10: 96). In effect, Malebranche claims that while it is true that the mind perceives no necessary connection between God's will and its effects, nevertheless because God is an omnipotent being, we perceive *that there must be* such a connection.

It is here that we find Hume's crucial insight in response to Malebranche's occasionalism. As Hume points out, if it is true that we have no idea of divine power, then Malebranche's claim to know that there must be a necessary connection between the will of an omnipotent being and the occurrence of what he wills proves to be nothing more than an empty tautology:

> As to what may be said, that the connexion betwixt the idea of an infinitely powerful being, and that of any effect, which he wills, is necessary and unavoidable; I answer,

that we have no idea of a being endow'd with any power, much less of one endow'd with infinite power. But if we will change expressions, we can only define power by connexion; and then in saying, that the idea of an infinitely powerful being is connected with that of every effect, which he wills, we really do no more than assert, that a being, whose volition is connected with every effect, is connected with every effect; which is an identical proposition, and gives us no insight into the nature of this power or connexion.

(T 1.4.5.31; SBN 248–249)

From this, Hume concludes that we must choose "the other side of the dilemma" and agree that constant conjunction constitutes the essence of real causation (T 1.4.5.32; SBN 249).

Skepticism

Throughout the seventeenth and early eighteenth centuries, skepticism was largely, if not exclusively, a French phenomenon. Montaigne, Descartes, Pascal, and Bayle as well a myriad of lesser known figures such as Simon Foucher and Pierre-Daniel Huet each placed skepticism at the center of their philosophical reflections. However, although Hume was well-acquainted with the arguments of the major figures of French skepticism, their influence on him appears to have been mostly negative. For not only are Hume's most powerful skeptical arguments largely of his own devising, but he also goes out of his way to challenge the nature and role of skepticism in two of his most famous French predecessors: Descartes and Bayle.

In Section 12 of the first *Enquiry*, Hume offers his most extensive discussion of the various kinds of skepticism and their relation to his own. Hume first draws a distinction between antecedent skepticism and consequent skepticism. Antecedent skepticism is a kind of skeptical methodology for acquiring certain knowledge. It seeks to insulate the investigator from prejudice and error by calling all of one's previously held beliefs into doubt as a preliminary to philosophical investigation. According to Hume, antecedent skepticism comes in both a strong and a moderate form, the former of which he explicitly associates with the skeptical procedure employed by Descartes in the First Meditation. On the strong version of this methodology, the investigator is to find reasons for doubting "not only of all our former opinions and principles, but also of our very faculties" (EHU 12.3; SBN 149). Hume offers three criticisms of the Cartesian method of doubt so conceived. First, Hume denies that among the various self-evident principles, there is some one that is uniquely suited to serve as the starting point for a demonstration of the reliability of our cognitive faculties. Second, the method imposes on the investigator the impossible demand of justifying reason by means of rational argument. This is because, as Hume understands the Cartesian method, we are required to call into doubt not only all previously held beliefs, but also the reliability of our cognitive faculties themselves. However, having once placed ourselves in such a skeptical posture, it would be impossible to escape, since any argument subsequently adduced in support of the reliability of reason must presuppose the very thing in question – namely, the reliability of our faculty of reasoning. Finally, the universal doubt prescribed by the method is, as a matter of psychological fact, impossible to achieve. For Hume, the human mind is literally incapable of the universal suspension of judgment that the method demands.

Some recent commentators have questioned whether in fact Descartes' method of doubt involves calling into doubt not only our opinions, but even self-evident truths or "common notions" (what Hume refers to as "principles"). Others have wondered whether Descartes conceives of the *cogito* as foundational in the sense suggested by Hume – that is, as a first principle from which all further metaphysical truths can be logically deduced. Nevertheless, Hume is surely right that if the scope of Cartesian doubt is meant to extend to both self-evident truths and our very cognitive faculties, the prospect of escaping such radical, universal doubt seems very dim indeed. With regard to Hume's final criticism, David Fate Norton (1994) has shown that the objection reveals a fundamental disagreement concerning the degree to which ordinary belief is subject to our voluntary control. For Descartes, whenever the mind entertains a proposition the truth or falsity of which it does not clearly and distinctly perceive, it remains free to affirm or deny the proposition, or to withhold judgment altogether. For Hume, by contrast, belief concerning matters of fact is not subject to direct voluntary control (EHU 5.10–11; SBN 47–48). It is for this reason that Hume considers the methodological directive to voluntarily suspend judgment with regard to all of our previously held beliefs to be psychologically impossible.

However, while Hume rejects the Cartesian method of doubt, he acknowledges that a more moderate version of antecedent skepticism is not only salutary but even "necessary" for philosophical investigation. On this more moderate view, the investigator aims to avoid error arising from prejudice and hasty judgment by conducting his investigation with extreme caution, beginning with self-evident truths and slowly and carefully drawing conclusions from them. Several commentators have seen in these recommendations an echo of the methodological rules set out by Descartes in Part 2 of the *Discourse on Method* (Maia Neto 2015: 383–384).

Surprisingly, there exists no comprehensive study of the influence of Bayle's skeptical philosophy on Hume. Nevertheless, given Hume's well documented interest in Bayle's works, many commentators have assumed that there is some important commonality between Bayle's skepticism and Hume's. According to Richard Popkin, Hume took the skeptical arguments of Bayle to be both "unavoidable and unanswerable" (Popkin 1980: 155). However, with regard to Bayle's most original and far-reaching skeptical arguments, the case seems to be quite the reverse. In both the *Historical and Critical Dictionary* and subsequent works, Bayle claimed repeatedly to have uncovered contradictions among several of the clearest and most evident notions of human reason. Not only did Hume reject the specific instances of conflict put forward by Bayle, but Hume was unwilling to countenance even the possibility of such radical skepticism (Ryan 2013).

Earlier in our discussion of Hume's theory of space and time, we saw how Bayle had argued that there are only three possibilities concerning the composition of extension and that each can be shown to be impossible, insofar as it is contradicted by one or more evident principles of reason. The conclusion Bayle draws from this conflict is variously stated. Sometimes he maintains that what the argument shows is that extension cannot exist in reality, but only "mentally." Understood in this way, the problem of the continuum is similar in form to Zeno's paradoxes of motion in that it pits evident principles of reason against the clear testimony of the senses: we know by sense experience that extended matter exists, and yet our clear and distinct ideas of extension suggest that its existence is impossible. In a similar vein, Bayle maintains that although the sciences of mathematics and geometry are absolutely certain, the objects of these sciences are impossible objects that cannot exist in reality. As Bayle puts the point in "Zeno, the Epicurean," there is

> an irreparable and most enormous difficulty with mathematical objects – they are chimeras that cannot exist. Mathematical points, and therefore lines and geometrical surfaces, globes, and axes are fictions that can never have any existence.
>
> (Bayle 1991: 390)

That is, we have a perfectly adequate concept of extension *qua* object of geometry. Nevertheless, the nature of the concept is such that it cannot be instantiated in the physical world.

On other occasions, however, Bayle goes further and suggests that what the impasse concerning the composition of the continuum reveals is that there are contradictions among our clear and distinct ideas – that is, among the most evident principles of reason. According to Bayle, "the mind of man has no ideas more clear and distinct than those of the nature and attributes of extension," and these ideas inform us that it is of the very essence of extension to be actually divisible into parts, each of which is itself extended and so divisible into parts, and so on to infinity (Bayle 1991: 138). Nevertheless, reason shows this to be impossible, since, to take just one consideration, no finite extended object can contain within it an infinite number of extended parts. Similarly, Bayle cites with approval a discussion of Malezieu in which he offers a mathematical demonstration of the infinite divisibility of extension, while at the same time developing a metaphysical proof that extension must be composed of indivisible units and so only finitely divisible.

With regard to the particular case of the composition of the continuum, we have seen how Hume attempts to answer Bayle's skeptical challenge by developing an account of simple and indivisible mathematical points, which are able to serve as the ultimate constituents of extension. In this way, Hume claims to have resolved Bayle's trilemma concerning the composition of the continuum. However, of greater importance for understanding the nature and limits of Hume's skepticism is that, even independent of his own preferred solution, Hume categorically refuses to accept the very possibility of the kind of radical conflict among our clear and distinct ideas that Bayle claims to uncover. Thus, having rehearsed Bayle's position that although the sciences of mathematics and geometry are absolutely certain, their objects cannot exist in reality, Hume asks

> but can any thing be imagin'd more absurd and contradictory than this reasoning? Whatever can be conceiv'd by a clear and distinct idea necessarily implies the possibility of existence; and he who pretends to prove the impossibility of its existence by any argument deriv'd from the clear idea, in reality asserts, that we have no clear idea of it, because we have a clear idea.'Tis in vain to search for a contradiction in any thing that is distinctly conceiv'd by the mind. Did it imply any contradiction, 'tis impossible it cou'd ever be conceiv'd.
>
> (T 1.2.4.11; SBN 43)

Thus, on the strength of his Conceivability Principle, Hume rejects the very possibility of a clear and distinct idea whose object cannot exist. The case is much the same with regard to the stronger version of Bayle's skepticism, according to which there are contradictions among the most evident principles of human reason. In the *Treatise*, Hume does not so much argue against such logical incompatibilities as presuppose their impossibility. Thus, having proved to his own satisfaction the possibility of a finite extension composed of visible or tangible mathematical points, Hume immediately concludes that no purported demonstration of the necessity of infinite divisibility can be sound, on the grounds that this would entail the impossibility of mathematical points (T 1.2.2.7–10; SBN 32–33). However, the conclusion follows only if it is not possible for there to be sound demonstrations of logically incompatible propositions. Moreover, in the corresponding discussion of skepticism with regard to abstract reason in the first *Enquiry*, Hume makes his disagreement with Bayle more explicit. Hume writes:

> how any clear, distinct idea can contain circumstances, contradictory to itself, or to any other clear, distinct idea, is absolutely incomprehensible; and is, perhaps, as absurd as any proposition, which can be formed.
>
> (EHU 12.20; SBN 157–158)

Thus, even independent of the details of his preferred resolution of Bayle's various skeptical paradoxes, Hume clearly rejects the very possibility of the kind of logical contradictions among our clear and distinct ideas of the kind propounded by Bayle.

In his discussion of the principal skeptical arguments against abstract reason in the *Enquiry*, Hume hints at a further reason for opposing the sort of radical skepticism propounded by Bayle. There Hume exclaims, "no priestly *dogmas*, invented on purpose to tame and subdue the rebellious reason of mankind, ever shocked common sense more than the doctrine of the infinite divisibility of extension" (EHU 12.18; SBN 156). In Hume's time, it was a commonplace of Christian apologetics to rehearse the supposed paradoxes surrounding the nature of infinity, and in particular of the infinite divisibility of extension, as a caution to those who would presumptuously reject the Christian mysteries on the grounds of their incomprehensibility. However, Bayle had gone much further than such conventional appeals to intellectual humility by insisting that several of the fundamental dogmas of the Christian religion, such as the Trinity and the Incarnation, were not only above reason, but contrary to reason. In other words, for Bayle, these Christian doctrines contradict certain evident principles of logic, metaphysics, and ethics. Bayle argued that when faced with such conflicts, the true Christian believer ought to accept the religious doctrines and reject the evident principles of reason which oppose them. Bayle defended the sincerity of this conception of faith on the grounds that the principle that God can neither deceive nor be deceived is more evident than any of the opposing demonstrations of the falsity of the Christian mysteries. Therefore, it is reasonable to accept revelation and to reject the philosophical principles that seem to oppose it.

Hume's response to such a maneuver is clear. Not only does he reject the suggestion that clear and distinct propositions might be mutually contradictory, but he also further argues that the sort of weighing of one allegedly demonstrative argument against another has no place in philosophy. Hume writes:

> 'Tis not in demonstrations as in probabilities, that difficulties can take place, and one argument counter-ballance another, and diminish its authority. A demonstration, if just, admits of no opposite difficulty; and if not just, 'tis a mere sophism, and consequently can never be a difficulty. 'Tis either irresistible, or has no manner of force. To talk therefore of objections and replies, and ballancing of arguments in such a question as this, is to confess, either that human reason is nothing but a play of words, or that the person himself, who talks so, has not a capacity equal to such subjects.
>
> (T 1.2.2.6; SBN 31–32)

Once again, for Hume, there can be no question of logical conflicts between the evident principles of reason, and so no rational justification for abandoning some ones of these principles in favor of others.

This reference to the irrational nature of Christian faith brings us to one final, though somewhat more elusive, influence on Hume's skepticism: Pascal. Although we have no direct evidence of Hume's first-hand knowledge of Pascal's works, several commentators have drawn attention to a number of striking parallels between the two thinkers, particularly with regard to their respective accounts of the inescapable force of radical skeptical arguments. Like Hume, Pascal maintains that the most destructive skeptical arguments (which Pascal generally refers to as "Pyrrhonian") cannot be adequately resolved by human reason. Also like Hume, Pascal maintains that nevertheless human nature prevents us from falling into the universal suspension of judgment that would seem to be the logical outcome of the Pyrrhonian arguments. Underlying their shared belief in the ultimate futility of skeptical arguments is the conviction that much of what humans believe is owing not to reason but to custom and the imagination (Penelhum 1993). Indeed, in a striking anticipation of Hume, Pascal affirms that "nature confounds the Pyrrhonians; and reason the dogmatist" (Pascal 1670: 161).

In the wake of this confrontation with radical skepticism, Pascal offers an anxious account of the human condition as presenting a choice between a philosophical reason, which inevitably leads to skepticism, and an irrational faith in the God of Christianity. While Hume's account of the "dangerous dilemma" to which the philosopher is reduced by skeptical argument is somewhat less anguished than the corresponding passages in Pascal, nevertheless Hume famously portrays his state as one of "philosophical melancholy" full of anxiety and "dread."[5] Furthermore, in both the *Treatise* and first *Enquiry*, Hume frames the choice we confront as one between philosophy and "superstition" (T 1.4.7.13; SBN 271; EHU 1.11–12; SBN 11–12; cf. Maia Neto 1991). The difference, of course, is that whereas Pascal counseled a turn to God, Hume proposes a purely secular resolution to the dilemma by embracing the philosophical pursuits of "moderate" skepticism.

Naturally, the influence of French philosophy on Hume was of far greater extent than what I have been able to discuss here. Within the *Treatise* itself, the influence of Malebranche in particular can be readily discerned in a whole host of issues, including knowledge of the self, the explanation of error by appeal to the "fictions" of the imagination, projection, and the theory of the passions (Kail 2007). Hume's subsequent work in history, politics, and natural religion shows his continuing engagement with post-Cartesian French thought. Thus, Voltaire's *Siècle de Louis XIV* may well have provided Hume with a model for his own approach to writing "philosophical" history. In addition, as James Harris (2015) has recently shown, Montesquieu's *L'Esprit des Lois* exercised an important influence on Hume's moral and political thought, prompting him to consider how the great diversity of political and moral systems can be explained on the basis of a shared human nature. Moreover, Hume's later travel to Paris as secretary to the embassy brought him into contact with many of the leading figures of the French Enlightenment, including d'Alembert and Diderot. Thus, throughout his literary career we can see in Hume's writings a constant dialogue with French philosophy and learning.

Notes

1 OCM refers to the French edition of Malebranche's collected works; LO refers to the standard English translation of *The Search After Truth*. See the bibliography for full references.
2 Several commentators have drawn a connection between Malebranche's denial that we have a clear and distinct idea of the mind and Hume's discussion of personal identity. See McCracken (1983) and Kail (2007).
3 McCracken (1983) draws a parallel between Hume's distinction between relations of ideas and matters of fact and Malebranche's similar account of the objects of knowledge.
4 It is difficult to say with confidence precisely which works of Malebranche Hume was familiar with beyond the *Search After Truth*. However, even if he had no direct acquaintance with the *Méditations Chrétiennes*, Hume would almost certainly have been aware of this passage on the basis of Bayle's rather ostentatious appeal to it in remark T of the *Dictionary* article "Epicurus."
5 On this score, the conclusion of Book 1 of the *Treatise* is much closer in spirit to Pascal than the corresponding passage in Section 12 of the first *Enquiry*. In this latter work, the sense of crisis in the face of irresolvable skeptical arguments is completely absent. Indeed, so free of anxiety is Hume that he is able to characterize the human predicament as the "whimsical condition of mankind" (EHU 12.23; SBN 160). For a detailed comparison of Hume's skeptical crisis with Pascal, see Maia Neto (1991).

References

Baxter, D. (2008) *Hume's Difficulty*, New York: Routledge.
Bayle, P. (1737) *Oeuvres Diverses de Mr. Pierre Bayle*, 4 vols. The Hague: Compagnie des Librairies.

————. (1991) *Historical and Critical Dictionary: Selections*, edited by Richard Popkin, Indianapolis, IN: Hackett Publishing.

Falkenstein, L. (2013) "Hume on the Idea of a Vacuum," *Hume Studies* 39: 131–168.

Harris, J. (2015) *Hume: An Intellectual Biography*, Cambridge: Cambridge University Press.

Kail, P. (2007) "On Hume's Appropriation of Malebranche: Causation and Self," *European Journal of Philosophy* 1–26.

Maia Neto, J. (1991) "Hume and Pascal: Pyrrhonism vs. Nature," *Hume Studies* 17: 41–50.

————. (2015) "The Sceptical Cartesian Background of Hume's 'Of the Academical or Skeptical Philosophy' (First Inquiry, Section 12)," *Kriterion* 371–392.

Malebranche, N. (1958–1978) *Oeuvres Complètes*, 20 vols, edited by André Robinet, Paris: Vrin.

————. (1980) *The Search After Truth*, edited by Thomas Lennon and Paul Oscamp, Columbus: Ohio State University Press.

McCracken, C. (1983) *Malebranche and British Philosophy*, Oxford: Clarendon Press.

Mossner, E. (1980) *The Life of David Hume*, 2nd edn, New York: Oxford University Press.

Nadler, S. (1996) "'No Necessary Connection': The Medieval Roots of the Occasionalist Roots of Hume," *The Monist* 79: 448–466.

Norton, D. F. (1994) "How a Sceptic May Live Scepticism," in J. J. McIntosh and H. A. Meynell (eds.), *Faith, Skepticism and Personal Identity*, Calgary: University of Calgary Press.

Pascal, B. (1670) *Pensées* (Port Royal).

Penelhum, T. (1993) "Human Nature and Truth: Hume and Pascal," *Lumen: Selected Proceedings from the Canadian Society for Eighteenth-Century Studies* 12: 45–64.

Popkin, R. (1980) "Hume and Bayle," in R. Watson and J. Force (eds.), *The High Road to Pyrrhonism*, Indianapolis, IN: Hackett Publishing.

Ryan, T. (2013) "Hume's Reply to Baylean Scepticism," in P. J. Smith and S. Charles (eds.), *Skepticism and the Eighteenth Century: Enlightenment, Lumières, Aufklärung*, Dordrecht: Springer.

Wright, J. (1983) *The Skeptical Realism of David Hume*, Minneapolis: University of Minnesota Press.

PART II

Hume's thought

PART IIA

Mind, knowledge, and world

PART IIA

Mind, knowledge and world

4

HUME'S SYSTEM OF THE SCIENCES

Don Garrett

David Hume has frequently been assigned a negative or destructive role in the narratives of the history of philosophy and science constructed by his successors. Thomas Reid, for example, declared that Hume "has reared a system of absolute skepticism, which leaves no rational ground to believe any one proposition, rather than its contrary" (Reid 2010: 2.12). Immanuel Kant remarked that Hume "ran his ship ashore, for safety's sake, landing on skepticism, there to let it lie and rot" (Kant 1902: Preface). John Stuart Mill concluded, "England (or rather Scotland) had the profoundest negative thinker on record, David Hume" (Mill 1867: 79).

These judgments stand in very stark contrast with Hume's own stated ambitions in *A Treatise of Human Nature: Being an Attempt to Introduce the Experimental Method of Reasoning into Moral Subjects*. In his Introduction to that work, he promises not only to "explain the principles of human nature" but also, in doing so, to "propose a compleat system of the sciences, built on a foundation almost entirely new, and the only one upon which they can stand with any security" (T Intro: 6; SBN xvi). Books 1 and 2 of the *Treatise* were published together, anonymously, in two volumes, in 1739. In the following year (and before publishing Book 3), he published an anonymous pamphlet review of them, *An Abstract of a Book lately Published; Entitled, A Treatise of Human Nature, &c. Wherein The Chief Argument of that Book is farther Illustrated and Explained*. In it he reports, "This treatise therefore of human nature seems intended for a system of the sciences" (T Abstract 3; SBN 646), and he remarks that "the Author seems to insinuate, that were his philosophy receiv'd, we must alter from the foundation the greatest part of the sciences" (T Abstract Preface 2; SBN 643). Hume's famous and self-professed "scepticism" in the final section of *Treatise* Book 1 notwithstanding, he evidently intends these grand pronouncements to be taken seriously – but how?

In order to answer this question fully, I will first explain the significance, rationale, and method of Hume's project of "founding" all of the sciences in the science of human nature – what Miren Boehm, in an important paper to which this chapter is much indebted, has rightly dubbed "Hume's foundational project" (Boehm 2013). Second, I will survey the main foundations in the science of human nature that he provides in *Treatise* Book 1 for what he calls the science of "logic," foundations that notably include his accounts of causal (i.e. "probable") reasoning and the concept of causation. Third, I will describe the applications he makes of these accounts to provide foundations for sciences other than mathematics – what I will call the "causal sciences" – generally. Fourth, I will explore the additional foundations he provides for three sciences that he describes as being closely connected to human life: aesthetic criticism, morals, and politics. Fifth, I will examine the additional foundation he provides, or fails to provide, for three sciences that he describes as being less closely connected to human life: mathematics, natural philosophy, and natural religion (i.e. religion not derived from special revelation). Finally, I will briefly outline an understanding of how Hume intends these foundations to survive the skepticism that results from a set of disturbing discoveries about our cognitive faculties that occur in the course of investigating human nature. Many facets of both Hume's foundational aspirations and his skepticism survive and flourish in his later writings, but the present discussion will largely be limited to the *Treatise*, where the foundational project is most fully elaborated. One effect, I hope, will be to counteract the still-common representation of Hume as a thinker who rejects all serious pursuit even of probable truth, and who therefore has little serious interest in contributing to the achievement of scientific knowledge.

1. Hume's project

Throughout his writings, Hume employs the terms "founded" and "foundation" very broadly, sometimes signifying a causal relation in which one thing makes possible the existence of another, sometimes signifying a normative relation in which one thing makes another legitimate, and sometimes both at once. In proposing to provide a foundation in the science of human nature that will "improve" all of the other sciences with an eye to "truth" and render them more "secure," he evidently means to provide what these other sciences need for their development as sciences and for their capacity to achieve a legitimate claim to knowledge. Elements of such a "foundation" may include concepts, methodological principles, and theoretical principles.

Significance

Hume is by no means alone among early modern philosophers in proposing that a better understanding of the operations of the human mind can bring "improvements" in the sciences, but the scope of his ambitions in this respect is nevertheless distinctive. Whereas John Locke declares of himself, "'tis Ambition enough to be employed as an Under-Labourer in clearing Ground a little, and removing some of the Rubbish, that lies in the way to Knowledge" (Locke 1975: 10), Hume proposes to develop the understanding of the human mind into a science in its own right. Locke modestly offers assistance to "the incomparable Mr. Newton" and other "Master-Builders, whose mighty Designs, in advancing the Sciences, will leave lasting Monuments to the Admiration of Posterity" (Locke 1975: 9). Hume, in contrast, implicitly positions himself not only as the Isaac Newton of "moral philosophy" (meaning by this all of the human sciences, not just morality or "morals"), but also as a provider of foundations for Newtonian "natural philosophy" (that is, the natural sciences) and even as an authoritative interpreter of how Newton's natural philosophy is to be "rightly understood" (T 1.2.5.26n; SBN 639). Improvements in the science of human nature should carry not just equal but "greater glory" than do recent improvements in natural philosophy, he asserts, "upon account of the greater importance of that science" to human life.

Rationale

In the "Introduction" to the *Treatise*, Hume distinguishes the sciences into two classes, as they "have a relation, greater or less, to human nature." Those with less relation include "*Mathematics, Natural Philosophy*, and *Natural Religion*." However, even those, he asserts, "are in some measure dependent on the science of MAN; since they lie under the cognizance of men, and are judg'd of by their powers and faculties." Hence, he remarks,

'Tis impossible to tell what changes and improvements we might make in these sciences were we thoroughly acquainted with the extent of human understanding, and cou'd explain the nature of the ideas we employ, and of the operations we perform in our reasonings.

(T Intro: 4; SBN xv)

Yet more improvements, of course, may be expected in those sciences "whose connexion with human nature is more close and intimate," namely, "*Logic, Morals, Criticism,* and *Politics.*" Thus, he generalizes,

There is no question of importance, whose decision is not compriz'd in the science of man; and there is none, which can be decided with any certainty, before we become acquainted with that science.

(T Intro: 6; SBN xvi)

Method

The foundational science of human nature finds its own foundation, for Hume, in the "experimental method" invoked by the subtitle of the *Treatise*:

And as the science of man is the only solid foundation for the other sciences, so the only solid foundation we can give to this science itself must be laid on experience and observation.

(T Intro: 7; SBN xvi)

He continues immediately by sketching a history of natural and moral philosophy that leaves the reader to infer that, just as Newton has perfected natural philosophy after Francis Bacon's original introduction of the experimental method into it, so Hume will perfect moral philosophy after the introduction of the experimental method into it by "some late philosophers in England" (identified in a footnote as "Mr. *Locke*, my Lord *Shaftesbury*, Dr. *Mandeville*, Mr. *Hutcheson*, Dr. *Butler*, &c.")." The passage might well be taken as arguing, at least implicitly, for an expanded use of the experimental method in moral philosophy on the *grounds* of its recent successes in natural philosophy. However, Hume's only explicit argument for its use is that the contrasting method of proceeding instead from "essences" is simply unavailable to us:

The essence of the mind being equally unknown to us with that of external bodies, it must be equally impossible to form any notion of its powers and qualities otherwise than from careful and exact experiments, and the observation of those particular effects, which result from its different circumstances and situations.

(T Intro: 8; SBN xvii)

An "essence," for Hume – as for such predecessors as Spinoza and Locke – is something from which all the permanent and inseparable qualities (i.e. "properties" in the technical sense that translates the Latin "*propria*") of a thing follow.[1]

As his phrase "careful and exact experiments" suggests, Hume means much more by "the experimental method" than simply the observation and cataloguing of patterns or regularities (Demeter 2012). Rather, he means especially the use of "crucial experiments," understood as the process of repeating with a single difference what are otherwise the same circumstances, so that any difference in outcome can be attributed to the changed circumstance. The concept of such crucial experiments can be traced to Bacon, a fact that helps to explain Hume's care to credit him with introducing the experimental method into natural philosophy. Hume emphasizes, however, that we cannot perform experiments of the kind he has in mind directly on ourselves because the "reflection and premeditation" required would introduce a further and potentially disturbing (second) alteration into the circumstances. For this reason, he declares, we must instead "glean up our experiments" in the science of human nature from "a cautious observation of human life." The *Treatise* explicitly invokes dozens of just such crucial experiments at various points.[2] When they are properly deployed and compared, Hume proposes, "we may hope to establish on them a science, which will not be inferior in certainty, and will be much superior in utility to any other of human comprehension" (T Intro: 10; SBN xix).

2. Logic

"The sole end of logic," Hume writes in the "Introduction" to the *Treatise*, "is to explain the principles and operations of our reasoning faculty, and the nature of our ideas" (T Intro: 5; SBN xv). He repeats this psychological characterization of logic verbatim in his *Abstract* of the *Treatise* and adds that "the author has finished what regards logic" (Ab. 3; SBN 646). In fact, as one might expect, logic is treated primarily in Book 1, "Of the Understanding."

The nature of our ideas

In Book 1, Hume makes and defends five especially important claims about "the nature of our ideas," which are the mental entities employed in thinking. First, the different parts of complex ideas are always separable from one another by "the imagination" – that is, the faculty of having ideas that are not simply memories.[3] Second, ideas differ from "impressions" – that is, sensations, passions, and other strong feelings – not by their qualitative character but by their degree of felt "liveliness" (which he also calls "force" and "vivacity"). Third, ideas are copied, or composed of simpler parts that are copied, from impressions. Fourth, the "reference of the idea to an object [is] an extrinsic denomination, of which in itself it bears no mark or character" (T 1.1.7.6; SBN 20). In other words, what an idea represents (is of, or is about) is not an intrinsic feature of the idea itself. For this reason, ideas that are qualitatively indistinguishable from one another can nevertheless represent various different things – including impressions, external objects, and other ideas, singly or in groups – in virtue of the different causal roles they are playing in the mind's operations (Garrett 2015). Fifth, when the objects of ideas are taken by the mind to be related by any of the three relations of "resemblance," "contiguity in time or place," or "cause and effect" (also called "causation"), the ideas become naturally associated in the mind in such a way as to introduce one another and to generate synchronic and diachronic complexes.

Hume also distinguishes a number of important *kinds* of ideas. One of these consists of ideas of memory, which have less liveliness than impressions but more liveliness than ideas of imagination, and which retain the order of the previous impressions from which they are copied. He also distinguishes three distinctive kinds of complex ideas – of "relations," "substances" (things), and "modes" (complex qualities) respectively. Finally, he discusses "abstract ideas" – what we would call *concepts* – which allow the mind to think with generality and to form judgments involving "a subject and predicate." They require a particular determinate idea (the *exemplar*, we may call it) associated with a "general term" of language disposing the mind to "revive" ideas of other objects that resemble the object of the exemplar (ideas constituting the remainder of a *revival set*, we may say) in some relevant way (T 1.1.7.7–10; SBN 20–22).

The principles and operations of our reasoning faculty

Concerning "our reasoning faculty" – which he also calls simply "reason" – Hume asserts, "All kinds of reasoning consist in nothing but a comparison, and a discovery of those relations, either constant or inconstant, which two or more objects bear to each other" (T 1.3.2.2; SBN 73). He recognizes two kinds of reasoning, "demonstrative" and "probable," derived from constant and inconstant relations respectively. Demonstrative reasoning produces "knowledge" (in a strict sense derived from Locke), while probable reasoning produces "belief."

The constant relations are those that could not be altered without altering the intrinsic character of the related things themselves. For example, if one thing is darker in color than another, it cannot become lighter than the other without at least one of them changing its intrinsic color; this is because "degrees of any quality" is a species of constant relation. "Inconstant" relations, in contrast, are those that can be altered without altering the intrinsic character of the related things themselves. For example, two objects that are adjacent at one time can become distant at another simply through motion, without either of the moving objects changing its intrinsic character; this is because "relations of space and time" is a species of inconstant relation. Some propositions, Hume holds, owe their truth entirely to constant relations: because the ideas involved in the proposition stand in certain constant relations, we can be sure that any objects adequately represented by them as having the same intrinsic qualities – if any such objects should actually exist – would necessarily stand in the same relations. Propositions of this kind he calls "relations of ideas." The denial of a relation of ideas is inconceivable and (at least in an informal sense) contradictory, he holds, because an attempted denial will be incompatible with the nature of the ideas involved. Other propositions, he maintains, owe their truth to inconstant relations; he calls propositions of this kind "matters of fact." A matter of fact and its denial are equally conceivable, and the truth of a matter of fact can therefore be ascertained only by means of experience.

Relations of ideas are known either by immediate intuition (that is, self-evidence) or by demonstrative reasoning. The constant relations of "resemblance," "contrariety," and "degrees of any quality" are generally subjects of immediate intuition, with little or no need for any reasoning. Accordingly, he declares, the important and useful operations of demonstrative reasoning[4] are typically those that serve to "discover" the constant relations of "proportion in quantity or number." It is these reasonings that provide the basis for the science of mathematics. Matters of fact are ascertained by present perception (including sense perception), memory, or probable reasoning. Reasoning that is not demonstrative is always "probable" for Hume (in a technical sense that is also derived from Locke) even when the degree of assurance is very high. Of the inconstant relations – those of causation (that is, cause and effect), identity, and relations of time and place – only causation, Hume argues, can provide the basis for beliefs that go beyond the deliverances of present perception and memory. Accordingly, all probable reasoning is in some way or other a "discovery" of causal relations.

Such probable reasoning, as Hume famously explains it, requires and depends on experience of the "constant conjunction" of objects: that is, things or events of one kind consistently followed by things or events of a second kind. Once the mind has experienced such a constant conjunction, then an impression or memory of something of one of the two kinds will elicit from the mind a belief in an object of the second kind. In all probable reasoning, the mind thus "supposes" or "makes the presumption" – that is, *operates as if it believed* – that the future will resemble the past or, more generally, that nature is uniform. Hume argues, however, that this transition is not itself produced by a mediating piece of reasoning to a belief with the content "nature is uniform." For if it were, the reasoning would have to be either demonstrative or probable. But it could not be demonstrative, because the non-uniformity of nature is conceivable and does not involve a contradiction; and it cannot be probable, because all probable reasoning *already* presupposes the uniformity of nature and hence cannot be the source of that supposition. Instead, Hume concludes, the transition is a product of the mental operation of "custom" (or "habit"), defined as "every thing which proceeds from a past repetition, without any new reasoning or conclusion" (T 1.3.8.10; SBN 102). In this way, custom produces the supposition of the uniformity of nature – not, as reason would have to do, by producing a *belief* in the uniformity, but rather by creating an habitual *association* between kinds of things that have been constantly conjoined in experience. Crucially, this habitual association also allows the originating impression or memory to convey some of its liveliness to the new idea produced. The resulting degree of liveliness, he argues, constitutes belief itself, and this explains why conclusions of probable reasoning are not merely entertained but affirmed.

Hume considers this account of belief, as the felt liveliness of ideas, to be one of his most original contributions to logic, and he seeks to employ it to explain many doxastic phenomena. One of its most important consequences is that the belief produced by probable reasoning is analogous to other feelings, such as the sentiment of beauty that underlies aesthetics:

> Thus all probable reasoning is nothing but a species of sensation. 'Tis not solely in poetry and music, we must follow our taste and sentiment, but likewise in philosophy. When I am convinc'd of any principle, 'tis only an idea, which strikes more strongly upon me. When I give the preference to one set of arguments above another, I do nothing but decide from my feeling concerning the superiority of their influence. Objects have no discoverable connexion together; nor is it from any other principle but custom operating upon the imagination, that we can draw any inference from the appearance of one to the existence of another.
>
> (T 1.3.8.12; SBN 103)

Furthermore, just as sentiments of beauty come in varying degrees, so does the feeling or "sentiment" of belief. Hume distinguishes several psychological operations – the "probability of chances," "the probability of causes," and "analogy" (T 1.3.11–12) – through which defects in the complete constancy of conjunction or in the complete resemblance of conjoined objects yield lower degrees of belief than the certainty of "proof" that results from the experience of pervasive and exceptionless constant conjunctions. These psychological operations are "philosophical," in the sense that they are approved upon epistemic reflection. He distinguishes them from a variety of other psychological operations collected under the heading "unphilosophical probability" that "have not had the good fortune to obtain the same sanction" (T 1.3.13.1; SBN 143). In these latter cases, as in others, we "correct" the felt degree of probability by appeal to what he calls "general rules" (T 1.3.9.6; SBN 109; T 1.3.10.12; SBN 632; T 1.3.13.9–12; SBN 147–150).

The idea of causation

Because probable reasoning is the discovery of causal relations for Hume, his account of its operation allows him to make one more contribution to logic's explanation of "the nature of our ideas," by defining the term "cause" for which the abstract idea of causation stands. In fact, he provides two definitions, because there are two ways to specify the ideas of cause-and-effect pairs that together constitute what we have just called the *revival set* of the abstract idea of causation (see Garrett 1997: 96–117 for more detail). The first definition appeals to the constant conjunction in which the pairs participate:

> An object precedent and contiguous to another, and where all the objects resembling the former are plac'd in a like relation of priority and contiguity to those objects, that resemble the latter.
>
> (T 1.3.14.35; SBN 172)

The second definition appeals to the effect on the mind of that conjunction:

> An object precedent and contiguous to another, and so united with it in the imagination, that the idea of the one determines the mind to form the idea of the other, and the impression of the one to form a more lively idea of the other.
>
> (T 1.3.14.35; SBN 172)

3. Foundations of causal sciences

Whereas mathematics concerns constant and unalterable relations of ideas, the other sciences that Hume mentions by name in the Introduction all chiefly concern matters of fact. Most of the inferences that occur within these non-mathematical sciences are therefore of the kind that discover the relation of causation; and because these sciences at least partly concern "general facts," prominent among their elements as sciences are general truths about causal laws.[5] Within the branch of the science of human nature pertaining to the foundations of logic, Hume has examined the causal ways in which the mind makes causal/probable inferences and through which it recognizes and classifies pairs of event as causes and effects. On this basis, he provides foundations for the causal sciences in at least three different ways: (i) through the four corollaries he immediately draws from his two definitions of "cause"; (ii) through his eight methodological "rules by which to judge of causes and effects"; and (iii) through his clarifying account of causal explanation.

Corollaries of the definitions

Hume's first corollary is that "all causes are of the same kind." Specifically, all causes are "efficient" causes – that is, causes through which an effect is made actual. His argument is simple: if there is constant conjunction of the sort leading to inference and association, then there is causation that qualifies as efficient; if there is not, then there is no kind of cause at all. He thus rejects in principle the distinction between efficient causes and necessary background causes ("causes *sine qua non*"), on the grounds that any element that is essential to the constant conjunction is as much a part of the total efficient cause as any other. Similarly, of the four kinds of explanatory factors that Aristotle distinguishes as "causes" – "formal," "material," "final," and "efficient"[6] – he recognizes only the efficient as genuinely causal. Finally, he disallows the distinction drawn by Malebranche and "other Cartesians" between real causes and occasional causes (or "occasions") – the latter being merely "occasioning" circumstances in which God exerts the sole causal power that produces some effect. Because such conditions are, by hypothesis, constantly conjoined with the specified outcome, they must qualify for Hume as real and hence "powerful" efficient causes in their own right.

Hume's second corollary is that we must reject as "without any foundation in nature" the (then-common) distinction between "moral" and "physical" necessity. Whereas physical necessity was understood to reflect an irresistible force that absolutely necessitated the motions of bodies, merely moral necessity was understood to reflect only a metaphysically weaker influence that "determined" rather than necessitated intentional human action through the judged or felt weight of reasons. Once again, however, given the two definitions, if there is enough constant conjunction to determine the mind to association and inference, then there is causal necessity simpliciter; if not, there is mere chance and so no kind of necessity at all. In this respect, it matters not whether the events in question are the blind motions of bodies or voluntary human actions, nor whether they are preceded by other bodily motions or by passions and beliefs.

Hume's third corollary is that "we may now be able to fully overcome all that repugnance, which 'tis so natural for us to entertain" against his own earlier argument (of T 1.3.3) that the "necessity of a cause to every beginning of existence" is not founded on either demonstration or intuition. For the sense that such a claim should be either demonstrative or intuitive results from a now-diagnosed conflation of "metaphysical" necessity (i.e. that pertaining to relations of ideas) with merely causal necessity. Once it is recognized that causes are discerned only by constant conjunction – with its associative and inferential effects on the mind – we can concede more readily that there is no contradiction in the thought that a distinct thing might come into existence without being the second element of such a pair. This is not, however, to deny that – as a matter of fact – every beginning of existence *does* have a cause in accordance with causally necessary laws.

Hume's fourth and final corollary is that "we can never have reason to believe that any object exists of which we cannot form an idea." This follows because sound beliefs about the existence of unperceived objects must result from probable, and hence causal, inferences, and these inferences require experience of constant conjunctions – experience that will thereby provide some idea of both the cause and the effect. Of course, Hume's view that belief is a lively idea also entails that, with or without reasons, we cannot believe in the existence of objects of which we cannot form any idea at all, nor can we believe clearly and definitely in the existence of objects of which we cannot form a clear and definite idea. Boehm (2013) argues that Hume's fourth corollary is the primary methodological principle that he draws from the science of human nature for the other sciences, a principle that allows him to deny explanatory roles to such theoretical entities as empty space and temporal duration without change. Hume himself mentions only one application, however, writing of the corollary, "This is so evident, that 'twou'd scarce have merited our attention, were it not to obviate certain objections of this kind, which might arise against the following reasonings concerning *matter* and *substance*" as hypothesized substrata that support and unify qualities. In any case, he immediately adds a qualification: "I need not observe, that a full knowledge of the object is not requisite, but only of those qualities of it, which we believe to exist" (T 1.3.14.36; SBN 172). Presumably, such ideas may sometimes be what he calls "relative" ideas – that is, ideas by which we conceive of something potentially unknown in some of its qualities simply as *whatever it is* that stands in a known relation to a known object (for example, *Sam's sister*). In the limiting case in which experience has led us to infer that an event has some cause or other, he thinks, we may believe in the existence of a cause of that event simply via a relative idea such as that expressed by a phrase like "the cause of that event" (T 1.2.6.9; SBN 69).

Rules by which to judge

Just as Hume recognizes "general rules" by which to make or correct judgments of degrees of probability, he devotes a section of the *Treatise* (T 1.3.15) to eight "rules by which to judge of causes and effects." These rules are "form'd on the nature of our understanding, and on our experience of its operations in the judgments we form concerning objects" (T 1.3.13.11; SBN 149) – that is, they are derived from past experience of satisfactory and unsatisfactory inferential predictions and judgments of causal relations. As such, they assist us in anticipating what judgments would be made from a perspective of greater experience and relevant cognitive endowments.

The first three rules express the requirements of the first definition of "cause" – namely, that causes be spatially and temporally contiguous with, prior to, and constantly conjoined with their effects. (Elsewhere in the *Treatise*, Hume effectively withdraws the requirement of spatial conti-guity for entities – including many impressions and ideas – that lack spatial locations altogether [T 1.3.2.6,n; SBN 75; T 1.3.14.25,n; SBN 167]). The fourth rule is particularly important: "The same cause always produces the same effect, and the same effect never arises but from the same cause." "This principle," Hume emphasizes, "we derive from experience, and is the source of most of our philosophical reasonings." As he employs it, the rule implies a universal causal determinism that supports and justifies the use of crucial experiments, and even the drawing of a causal conclusion from a single crucial experiment once we have extensive experience sup-porting the general principle (T 1.3.12.3; SBN 131). It also implies, as a fifth rule, that any given kind of effect must be attributed to some commonality among its causes and, as a sixth, that any difference in effects must be attributed to a difference in causes. The seventh rule requires that, where causes and effects co-vary in degree, the effect should be considered a compound one resulting from a compound cause. The eighth rule requires that any cause that does not produce its effect immediately must be only a partial cause.

Using the term 'logic' in the narrower sense of a set of rules by which to conduct reasoning – and disparaging the value of rules of demonstrative reasoning – Hume writes, of these eight rules: "Here is all the LOGIC I think proper to employ in my reasoning" (T 1.3.15.11; SBN 175). Later in the *Treatise*, when discussing the possibility of mind–body interaction, he explicitly cites these rules to support what is in effect a further, cautionary rule. Because any two kinds of objects can be conceived to be constantly conjoined, he writes:

> I have inferr'd from these principles [footnote reference to T 1.3.15], that to consider the matter *a priori*, any thing may produce any thing, and that we shall never discover a reason, why any object may or may not be the cause of any other, however great, or however little the resemblance may be betwixt them.
>
> (T 1.4.5.30; SBN 247)

Causal explanation

Nearly every occurrence of the term "explain" in the *Treatise*, outside the context of mathemati-cal demonstration, exemplifies one of two uses: (i) explaining *what something is*, by describing its parts, qualities, and/or history; or (ii) explaining *why something occurs*, by appeal to a causal generalization of which it is an instance. Much as the topics of Humean logic are "the nature of our ideas" and "the principles and operations of our reasoning faculty," we may infer that a part of any causal science, for Hume, consists in explaining what its objects of study are, while at least much of the rest consists in discovering appropriate causal generalizations that apply to the phenomena under study. In the case of the entire science of human nature more broadly, he later calls the first explanatory element "mental geography" and the second "discover[ing] at least in some degree, the secret springs and principles, by which the human mind is actuated in its operations" (EHU 1.13–15; SBN 13–14).

Crucially, Hume distinguishes two kinds of explanation by appeal to causal generalizations.[7] The first is explaining an event by establishing a causal generalization of which it is an immediate instance. The second is explaining a lower-level causal generalization, along with its instances, as an instance of a higher-level and more inclusive causal generalization. Thus he summarizes in the *Abstract*:

> If, in examining several phænomena, we find that they resolve themselves into one common principle, and can trace this principle into another, we shall at last arrive at those few simple principles, on which all the rest depend. And tho' we can never arrive at the ultimate principles, 'tis a satisfaction to go as far as our faculties will allow us. (Ab. 1; SBN 646; see also T Intro. 8; SBN xvii)

4. Morals, criticism, and politics

After describing the science of logic in the Introduction as explaining "the principles and operations of our reasoning faculty, and the nature of our ideas," Hume immediately goes on to describe "morals and criticism" as the sciences that "regard our tastes and sentiments" and politics as the science that "considers men as united in society, and dependent on each other." In the 1739 Advertisement attached to the first two books of the *Treatise* ("Of the Understanding" and "Of the Passions," respectively), he writes:

> The subjects of the *Understanding* and *Passions* make a compleat chain of reasoning by themselves; and I was willing to take advantage of this natural division, in order to try the taste of the public. If I have the good fortune to meet with success, I shall proceed to the examination of *Morals*, *Politics*, and *Criticism*; which will compleat this Treatise of Human Nature.

In the *Abstract* of the *Treatise*, he repeats verbatim his Introduction descriptions of the scope of morals, criticism, and politics, and he adds that "the author . . . has laid the foundation" for these "other parts in his account of the passions." In fact, while the science of morals receives its own dedicated book (Book 3, "Of Morals"), which also includes some related treatment of politics, the completed *Treatise* contains little or no further examination of aesthetic criticism. Nevertheless, we can see how the science of human nature was intended to provide foundations for each of these sciences.

Morals

It may initially seem surprising that Hume regards his Book 2 account of the passions as laying the foundations for morals, but there are at least four ways in which it does so. First, it introduces the distinction, within "mental geography," between the faculties of "the passions" and "taste": both provide "impressions of reflection" (that is, impressions that are not produced immediately by the senses), but the impressions of taste are typically calmer and less violent than the passions. His technical term for an impression of taste is "sentiment"; although this is a narrower usage of the term than the one in which he calls the feeling of liveliness in ideas "the sentiment of belief," his willingness to use the same term in both contexts is revealing of the analogy he sees. Moreover, Book 2 already suggests that moral sentiments are the ultimate source of moral distinctions (T 2.1.7.1–5; SBN 294–297). Book 3 develops this suggestion, arguing that the capacity to feel the sentiments of "moral approbation" and "moral disapprobation" when considering traits of character in a general, non-self-interested way constitutes the "moral sense" from which our fundamental moral concepts of virtue and vice develop (T 3.1.2.4–5; SBN 471–472).

Second, Book 2 contains Hume's causal account of the mental operation of sympathy. In this operation, a belief about another person's state of mind becomes further enlivened through the resemblance between one's idea of that person and the "idea, or rather impression of oneself," to the point at which one feels a similar state of mind oneself (T 2.1.11.1–6; SBN 316–319). Sympathy with those who are affected by a character trait (including the trait's possessor) proves in Book 3 to be, in almost every case, the immediate causal stimulus to the moral sentiments of approbation and disapprobation.

Third, Book 2 contains Hume's discussion of "liberty and necessity," or freedom of the will (T 2.3.1–2). Drawing on the second corollary of his definitions of "cause" and his fourth rule for judging causes and effects, he argues that voluntary actions are causally necessitated in just the same sense and to the same extent that physical events are. Most generally, this conclusion helps to confirm the possibility of a science of human nature bearing on morals; more specifically, Hume uses it to explain how voluntary actions can serve as reliable signs of the enduring character traits that are the primary causes of moral sentiments.

Finally, Book 2 provides Hume's account of how virtue causes the passions of pride and love, while vice causes the passions of humility and hatred. Indeed, as he later remarks in Book 3, the inciting of pride and humility, love and hatred "is, perhaps, the most considerable effect that virtue and vice have upon the human mind" (T 3.1.2.5; SBN 473). Furthermore, Book 2 examines the way in which love causes benevolence or the desire to benefit another, while hatred causes anger, or the desire to harm another. In this way, Book 2 provides the basis for a naturalistic account of how virtue and vice come to be to the subjects of socially shared appreciation and deprecation, respectively, and how their possession has important interpersonal consequences that can explain why the terms expressing concepts of virtues are, as he later puts it, "taken in a good sense" (EPM 1.10; SBN 174) – that is, as expressing normative approval.

Hume's science of morals includes psychological explanations *of* moral evaluations, but it also includes such evaluations themselves. He concludes Book 3 by reminding his readers that the promise of the Introduction to build a science of morals on the science of human nature has been met, and he notes that this science is practical and contains moral precepts:

> And thus the most abstract speculations concerning human nature, however cold and unentertaining, become subservient to *practical morality*; and may render this latter science more correct in its precepts, and more persuasive in its exhortations.
>
> (T 3.3.6.6; SBN 621)

These precepts presumably include truths concerning which character traits are virtues and vices, as well as about the kinds of actions that manifest them. That there can be such truths for Hume may itself be surprising, especially given that his later *Enquiries* distinguish sharply between a domain of "reason" or "understanding" on one hand and "taste" or "sentiment" on the other, with both morals and criticism in the latter domain (EHU 12.33; SBN 165; EPM, App. 1.21; SBN 294). In both *Enquiries*, however, he immediately goes on to cite the existence of a "standard" of judgment for taste, which provides a basis for judgment and reasoning.

A standard of judgment is the consequence of "correcting [of our] sentiments . . . to regulate our abstract notions" (T 3.3.1.21; SBN 585) – that is, our abstract ideas – in cases in which the abstract idea arises from a distinctive felt sentimental or sensory response to stimuli. As Hume explains, while the similarities of distinctive felt responses tend naturally toward the development of an abstract idea, differences in either the conditions of observation or the state of the respondents will often result in different responses to the same stimulus, both within a single person at different times and among different persons even at the same time. In the case of moral responses, the degree of sympathy varies with each individual's psychological distance from the object of sympathy, and this leads, in turn, to differences in degree of moral approbation or disapprobation. These differences of response are often naturally disturbing to the individuals who experience or observe them, leading them to incline naturally toward some way of achieving and maintaining greater intrapersonal and interpersonal uniformity and agreement in their reactions. This is achieved primarily by the gradual adoption and refinement, through a tacit convention, of what Hume calls a "standard" by which to judge. In its general form, a standard of judgment for a concept derived from a "sense" consists of a standard (idealized) perspective or "point of view" *from which* to be responsive plus standard (idealized) endowments or "qualities" *with which* to be responsive. In the case of morals, this standard lies in what Hume calls the "steady and general points of view" of all those who constitute the "narrow circle" of the individual judged, together with qualities of sympathy, delicate moral sentiments, and comprehensive understanding of causes and effects in human life (T 3.3.1, "Of the origin of the natural virtues and vices"). The acceptance of this standard as authoritative makes possible the development of moral concepts, the correct or incorrect applications of which can be matters of truth, reasoning, and science (for details, see Garrett 2015: 117–129).[8]

Criticism

Although Hume returns to examine criticism only in his much later essay "Of the Standard of Taste," that essay is organized specifically as an investigation of the standard of judgment for aesthetic criticism, parallel to the standard of judgment for morals. In this case, the idealized point of view is one "cleared of all prejudice" by sympathetically occupying the position of the intended audience of a work, while the idealized endowments are "strong sense, delicacy of sentiment, improved by practice, and perfected by comparison." With this standard understood, criticism can be a subject of truth, reasoning, and science, just as morals can.

Moreover, the foundations laid for the examination of criticism in *Treatise* Book 2 resemble those laid for morals. First, Hume's distinction between the passions and taste is again relevant, for criticism derives from sentiments of "beauty" and "deformity," much as morals derive from moral sentiments (T 2.1.8, "Of beauty and deformity"). Second, his account of the operation of sympathy is relevant as well, for in many cases sentiments of beauty or deformity are felt in response to sympathy with those who will use an object (T 2.2.5.16; SBN 363–364). Third, his accounts of pride, humility, love, and hatred, with their passionate and practical consequences, again help to provide a naturalistic explanation of why there is shared appreciation and deprecation of beauty and deformity, respectively, and hence also of why aesthetic judgments have a normative character.

Politics

It is uncertain whether Book 3 of the *Treatise* contains as extensive an examination of politics as was originally intended in the Advertisement to the first two volumes. Indeed, it is very possible that he originally intended to devote a further Book to it, including some of the material that appeared in his later political essays, such as the causal generalizations about different forms of government in "That Politics May be Reduced to a Science." However, Book 3 does contain four sections specifically devoted to government and "allegiance" – that is, the trait of obeying and upholding a government, which is generally a moral virtue. It also considers the role of government in enforcing the rules of property (respect for which he calls "justice") and the rules of promising-keeping and contract (respect for which he calls "fidelity"). Under the broad definition of 'politics' that he provides in the Introduction and *Abstract*, his extensive discussions of property and promises themselves qualify as politics, as does his section "Of the laws of nations" (T 3.2.11) and even perhaps "Of modesty and chastity" (T 3.2.12).

Foundations for these discussions are laid in Book 2's account of the passions in at least two respects. First, that account describes many of the specific passions – including self-love, love of relations, desire for property and riches, and "the amorous passion" – that lead human beings into society and govern their conduct within it. (See especially T 2.3.1.8; SBN 401–402.) Second, in providing a basis for understanding moral normativity, it also provides the psychological basis for understanding the specific moral obligations to justice, fidelity, and allegiance. Book 3 then goes on (i) to distinguish between self-interested and moral obligation; (ii) to explain the nature of "convention" as a coordinated course of action in which each party sees and acknowledges the advantage of performing one's part on condition that the others perform their parts (T 3.2.2.10; SBN 490); (iii) to explain the origins of justice, fidelity, and allegiance in distinctive conventions; and (iv) to explain the moral obligation to them on the basis of moral approval of the desires to respect the conventions, approval that results from sympathy with the public interest of all those who benefit from them. Especially notable is the way in which Hume often appeals to the principles of association among ideas, and to other features of the imagination discussed in Book 1, to help explain many of the common rules and principles of property and political legitimacy.

5. Mathematics, natural philosophy, and natural religion

Part 2 of *Treatise* Book 1 is entitled, "Of the ideas of space and time," and Hume describes his "system concerning space and time" as consisting of two doctrines (T 1.2.4.1–2; SBN 39–40). The first is that the infinite divisibility of space and time is "utterly impossible and contradictory." The second is that "'tis impossible to conceive either a vacuum and extension without matter, or a time, when there was no succession or change in any real existence." As he later indicates, his discussion of the first doctrine involves "examining the foundation of mathematics" (T 1.4.2.22,n; SBN 199,n); the second involves the foundation of natural philosophy.

Mathematics

The science of human nature shows, according to Hume, that the mind's ideas of space and time are literally composed of finite numbers of spatial and temporal minima individually lacking extension and duration, respectively, but capable of constituting extension and duration by their finite combination. Since nothing at all can be smaller than an unextended minimum, or shorter than a durationless moment, he argues, it follows that space and time themselves cannot be composed of any parts that are smaller. Because their division always reaches such indivisible minima, finite extensions and durations cannot be infinitely divisible.

After providing further arguments to reinforce this conclusion, Hume sets out to "defend the definitions" of geometers and to "refute the[ir] demonstrations" of the infinite divisibility of finite extensions. The definitions he has in mind are those of a plane or surface as "what has length and breadth without depth"; of a line as "what has length without breadth or depth"; and of a point as "what has neither length, breadth, nor depth" (T 1.2.4.8–9; SBN 42). Only on his doctrine of minima individually lacking extension but capable of constituting it by their contiguous combination, he argues, can these definitions be understood to apply to anything. In order to refute geometers' proposed demonstrations of the infinite divisibility of finite extensions, he denies the precise truth of the Euclidean axioms of geometry on which they are based. The concept of "straightness," he urges, is simply that of an indefinable appearance, which may conform only approximately to the axioms. A similar point applies to the only usable concept of "equality of size," since the obvious standard of an equal number of minima is not practically applicable. Thus Hume draws a sharp distinction between other branches of mathematics, where a precise standard of equality (one-to-one correspondence of elements, now called "Hume's Principle") is available, and geometry, where our judgments can only be known to be approximately accurate (T 1.3.1.4–5; SBN 70–71).

Natural philosophy

Hume also derives the second doctrine of his system of space and time – that "'tis impossible to conceive either a vacuum and extension without matter, or a time, when there was no succession or change in any real existence" – from the science of human nature. The mind's only ideas of extension represent qualities in spatial arrangement, and its only ideas of duration represent qualities in successive arrangement, leaving "empty space" and "changeless duration" literally inconceivable. In maintaining that the extended world is necessarily a plenum (i.e. completely full of matter), Descartes denies the possibility of a vacuum, whereas Newton accepts that possibility. It may appear, therefore, that in declaring a vacuum to be "inconceivable," Hume is declaring the Cartesian view to be demonstrable.

In fact, however, that appearance is misleading. For Hume denies neither that there can be, nor that we can conceive, bodies that are not contiguous while having no bodies between them, and which might "receive" other bodies between them without themselves moving. This arrangement of bodies is perfectly conceivable, involves no contradiction, and hence is metaphysically possible. What he denies is only that we can conceive of *some thing which is the vacuum* – that empty space as a *thing* existing between bodies and capable of remaining when they are gone. Similarly, he denies that we can conceive of *some thing* which has duration in the absence of any change in the universe – that is, a thing that is duration empty of succession or change. Yet it is in just these ways that Newton treats what he calls "absolute space" and "absolute time" as beings in their own right that can be co-located with objects and relative to which objects can be said to move or change. As Boehm (2013) rightly emphasizes, Hume in effect proposes that Newtonian natural philosophy be reformulated to remove reference to these reified entities, most explicitly in a footnote added in his Appendix to the *Treatise*:

> If the Newtonian philosophy be rightly understood, it will be found to mean no more. A vacuum is asserted: That is, bodies are said to be plac'd after such a manner, as to receive bodies betwixt them, without impulsion or penetration. The real nature of this position of bodies is unknown.
>
> (T 1.2.5.26n; SBN 639)

Hume does not go on to explain *how* Newtonians should reformulate the laws of motion without reference to absolute motion and rest defined in relation to absolute space and time; it is notable, however, that Albert Einstein (1949) credits his reading of Hume on space and time with helping to stimulate his discovery of the theory of special relativity.[9]

Hume's general foundations for causal sciences, examined previously, also bear on Newtonian natural philosophy, in two ways. First, his rule that causes be spatially contiguous to their effects (at least when they are spatially located at all) is incompatible with the attempt to understand gravitation simply as causal "action at a distance," and it therefore supports Newton's own hope that gravitation might be explained instead through the local propagation of effects through some intervening medium between the attracting bodies. Second, his cautionary rule that "to consider the matter *a priori*, any thing may produce any thing" allows that such action need not be understood as the communication of motion from one body to another, which the earlier "mechanical" natural philosophy had considered to be the only intelligible kind of physical causation.

In the section of Book 1 entitled "Of the modern philosophy" (T 1.4.4), Hume examines a more general problem for modern natural philosophy that concerns the qualitative representation of extended bodies. He provides an argument drawn from the relativity of sense perception, and appealing to the fourth of the "rules by which to judge of causes and effects," for the conclusion that bodies do not have qualities resembling any of the ideas we have of color, sound, taste, or smell, nor of heat, cold, or other tactile qualities. As a result, natural philosophers cannot conceive the specific qualitative character of the qualities that must fill the spatial extension of bodies, and their attempts to do so can therefore at best appeal to mere relative ideas. In the immediately preceding section, Hume appeals to principles of the science of human nature to explain the origins in features of the imagination of such scholastic notions as "substantial forms," "accidents," and "occult powers and faculties," and to rule them out as useless for natural philosophy, presumably in accordance with the fourth corollary from his definitions of "cause."

Natural religion

In the Introduction, Hume lists "Natural Religion" as the third of the three sciences that are less closely connected with human nature. In doing so, he remarks that it is nevertheless more closely connected to human nature than are mathematics and natural philosophy because "it is not content with instructing us in the nature of superior powers, but carries its views farther, to their disposition towards us, and our duties towards them" (T Intro. 4; SBN xv). In fact, however, the *Treatise* says very little to found any doctrines of natural religion, and this is no doubt intentional. He observes in a subsequent defense of the *Treatise* (*A Letter from a Gentleman to his Friend in Edinburgh*) that his third corollary of the two definitions, which affirms the metaphysical possibility of a beginning of existence without a cause, undermines Samuel Clarke's argument for the existence of God as a necessarily existent being, although he also emphasizes (against the charge of atheism) that it leaves many other arguments for God's existence unaffected. The *Treatise* does mention in passing but without endorsement the doctrine of a deity who "is the prime mover of the universe, and who . . . first created matter, and gave it its original impulse" (T 1.3.14.9; SBN 159). Its only remark specifically about "the nature of superior powers," however, is added in the Appendix as a footnote to a passage commenting that we cannot obtain an impression of causal necessary connection or power from experience of God. The footnote reads:

> The order of the universe proves an omnipotent mind; that is, a mind whose will is *constantly attended* with the obedience of every creature and being. Nothing more is requisite to give a foundation to all the articles of religion.
>
> (T 1.3.14.12n; SBN 633)

How the order of the universe could prove an unobserved omnipotent mind in accordance with the rules by which to judge of causes and effects, Hume notably does not say. Presumably any such argument would be one from "analogy," of the kind discussed – and mostly criticized – in his later *Dialogues Concerning Natural Religion*.[10]

Concerning "the dispositions of superior powers towards us" – a matter that was for many other philosophers a key element in the foundation of morals – Hume remarks only that a doctrine of divine rewards and punishments, whether understood instrumentally or retributively, presupposes the causal necessity of human voluntary actions (T 2.3.26; SBN 410–411).[11] He does nothing in the *Treatise* to endorse or support the doctrine that there *are* divine rewards and punishments in an afterlife. Furthermore, his investigation of the nature of personal identity leads him to the conclusion that the very distinction between continuing to exist as the same person and not continuing to exist as the same person depends on a kind of association-inducing causal interrelatedness among impressions and ideas that is a matter of degree, with the consequence that "all the nice and subtle questions concerning personal identity can never possibly be decided, and are to be regarded rather as grammatical than as philosophical difficulties" (T 1.4.6.21; SBN 272). He does remark that, *if* moral requirements were entirely determined by relations of ideas grasped by reason alone, *then* any deity would have to be determined by reason in its moral dealing with human beings; but he positively rejects that view of morality (T 3.1.1.4; SBN 456–457; and T 3.1.1.22; SBN 465).

Finally, Hume provides no account at all of any "duties" of human beings "towards" superior powers. On the contrary, his account of moral distinctions as derived from sympathy-inspired moral sentiments implies that we could have duties towards superior beings only if we could harm or benefit them and they were sufficiently like us for us to sympathize with them.

6. Science and skepticism

As Hume concludes his examination of the foundations of logic in Book 1, and before he goes on to provide foundations for morals, criticism, and politics in Book 2, he surveys a set of troubling findings about human cognitive faculties that have resulted from his investigations. This survey produces a skeptical crisis, which he narrates in the final section of Book 1. He is often interpreted as concluding from this survey that no beliefs are more probable or justified than others, although at the same time allowing that it might be both more enjoyable and psychologically inevitable to proceed as if this were not true. If this were indeed Hume's conclusion, then Reid, Kant, and Mill would be correct, and Hume would have abandoned his promise in the Introduction to "propose a compleat system of the sciences, built on a foundation almost entirely new, and the only one upon which they can stand with any security." Strong evidence against this interpretation, however, is provided by the facts that Hume did not change his Introduction prior to publication; that he took such elaborate care in Book 1 to provide foundations for logic, mathematics, and the causal sciences; and that in the *Abstract* he repeated his ambitions and reported himself already to have completed a treatment of logic and laid the foundation for morals, criticism, and politics as sciences.

In fact, although Hume reports briefly *feeling*, at the height of the crisis, that no belief is more probable than another (T 1.4.7.8; SBN 268), he does not adopt or endorse this radically negative conclusion. The troubling findings about human cognition do serve as the basis for probable arguments – employing the "probability of chances" and "the probability of causes" – for the conclusion that our reasoning faculty produces beliefs that are not probably true; but these second-order probable arguments are opposed by first-order information, in the form of sentiments of belief, supporting the (second-order) conclusion that those beliefs *are* at least probably true (Garrett 2015: 213–237). As in the case of conflicting moral sentiments, conflicting sentiments of probability must be corrected and adjudicated from a standard of judgment. Hume reports that the outcome of that adjudication is an overall lowering of credence and probability – which he calls "moderate scepticism" – but not its annihilation. Just as he affirms the reality of *moral* distinctions in the science of morals (see also EPM 1.1–2; SBN 169–170), so he affirms the reality of *probability* distinctions in the science of logic. Such probable truth is, in his view, sufficient to provide a foundation for all of the sciences.[12]

Notes

1 In other contexts, Hume uses the term "essence" more permissively, although with the same general meaning. Thus, the sentiment of beauty is "the essence of beauty" (T 2.1.8.2; SBN 299), and "the constant conjunction of objects is the very essence of cause and effect" (T 1.4.5.33; SBN 250), because these are what account for (what are in context) the most important features of the phenomenon under consideration.

2 Notable examples include: (i) T 1.3.8.3–15; SBN 99–106; (ii) T 1.4.2.44–45; SBN 210–211; (iii) T 1.4.6.8–10; SBN 255–256; (iv) T 2.1.8.7; SBN 301–302; (v) T 2.1.12.2; SBN 325; and (vi) T 2.2.2.1–28; SBN 332–347. The use of experiments is also discussed in T 1.3.12–13 ("Of the probability of causes" and "Of unphilosophical probability") and T 1.3.15 ("Rules by which to judge of causes and effects"). In the latter section, Hume declares, "There is no phænomenon in nature, but what is compounded and modify'd by so many different circumstances, that in order to arrive at the decisive point, we must carefully separate whatever is superfluous, and enquire by new experiments, if every particular circumstance of the first experiment was essential to it" (T 1.3.15.11; SBN 131), and he emphasizes that this is even more true in moral philosophy than in natural philosophy.

3 Hume also uses the term "imagination" in a narrower sense that excludes "our demonstrative and probable reasonings," but that sense need not concern us here.

4 Because he also calls this "abstract reasoning," it seems plausible that it will typically involve combinatorial operations involving the revival sets of abstract ideas.

5 Hume distinguishes sciences concerning "general facts" from those concerning "particular facts," citing "history, chronology, geography, and astronomy" as examples of the latter (EHU 12.30–21; SBN 165).

6 For Aristotle, a formal cause provides the form of an effect, a material cause provides its matter, and a final cause is the end toward which it is directed. Hume gives no important technical role to the form/matter distinction, but in particular cases a source of form or matter might be part of an efficient cause. He recognizes that many things have parts that consistently interact in producing an outcome that is beneficial in some way to the whole; but this outcome is itself only a further (expected) effect, not itself the causal source of the earlier activity. In the case of end-directed human activity, it is the desire and volition that are the causes, not the end desired.

7 Causal explanations are psychologically satisfying, Hume would likely speculate, in part because they determine the mind to think in a particular way without painful vacillation or doubt about what has occurred or will occur.

8 As this naturalistic account of their development implies, standards of judgment for concepts are not fixed immutability; their constituents, and the shared understanding of their constituents, can change over time.

9 For more about Hume's treatment of space and time, see the chapter by Jonathan Cottrell in this volume.

10 For an explanation of this argument and Hume's assessment of it in accordance with the rules of probability, see Garrett 2012.

11 More specifically, he argues that rewards and punishments can be effective in producing obedience only if voluntary actions are caused partly by motives and circumstances; and they can be appropriate responses to the moral quality of voluntary actions only if they are caused partly by motives and character. He also questions whether people really believe in an afterlife as much as they profess to do (T 1.3.9.13–15; SBN 113–115).

12 I thank participants in the 2015 Kline Workshop on Philosophy and Science in the British Empiricist Tradition at the University of Missouri, and participants in the 2014 Center for the Study of Scottish Philosophy Conference at Princeton Theological Seminary for helpful discussion of the topics of this chapter. I especially thank Jonathan Cottrell and Miren Boehm for comments and suggestions on earlier drafts.

References

Boehm, M. (2016) "Hume's Foundational Project in the *Treatise*," *European Journal of Philosophy* 24(1): 55–77 (online publication 2013 with doi:10.1111/ejop.12056).

Demeter, T. (2012) "Hume's Experimental Method," *British Journal for the History of Philosophy* 20(3): 577–599.

Einstein, A. (1949) *Autobiographical Notes*, trans. P. A. Schilpp, LaSalle and Chicago, IL: Open Court.

Garrett, D. (1997) *Cognition and Commitment in Hume's Philosophy*, New York: Oxford University Press.

———. (2006) "Hume's Naturalistic Theory of Representation," *Synthese* 152(3): 301–319.

———. (2012) "What's True About Hume's 'True Religion'?" *Journal of Scottish Philosophy* 10(2): 199–220.

———. (2015) *Hume*, London and New York: Routledge.

Kant, I. (1902) *Prolegomena to Any Future Metaphysics*, trans. P. Carus, Chicago, IL: Open Court.

Locke, J. (1975) *An Essay Concerning Human Understanding*, edited by P. H. Nidditch, Oxford: Clarendon Press.

Mill, J. S. (1867) *Dissertations and Discussions*, Toronto: University of Toronto Press.

Reid, T. (2010) *Essays on the Intellectual Powers of Man*, edited by D. Brookes, University Park, PA: Pennsylvania State University Press.

5

IDEAS AND ASSOCIATION IN HUME'S PHILOSOPHY

Saul Traiger

In *A Treatise of Human Nature*, Hume notes that while the imagination can separate and reunite our simple ideas "in what form it pleases," without some "universal principles" uniting our ideas together, "nothing wou'd be more unaccountable than the operations of that faculty" (T 1.1.4.1; SBN 10). The possibility of success for Hume's science of human nature, then, depends on the discovery of principles of association, since without them the imagination would be an unordered jumble of simple perceptions. It is interesting that Hume first raises the possibility of the randomness of the mind four sections into the *Treatise* when he has already discovered and reported some of the imagination's law-like behavior. Pausing here to note the significance of his nascent discovery of the association of ideas, he begins to explore "the full extent of these relations" (T 1.1.4.3; SBN 11). In the *Abstract*, Hume concludes his overview of the *Treatise* by pointing to the principles of association as his most significant discoveries; he refers to the use to which he puts them as his inventions. The principles of association, resemblance, contiguity, and cause and effect

> are the only links that bind the parts of the universe together, or connect us with any person or object exterior to ourselves. For as it is by means of thought only that any thing operates upon our passions, and as these are the only ties of our thoughts, they are really *to us* the cement of the universe, and all the operations of the mind must, in a great measure, depend on them.
>
> (Ab. 35; SBN 661–662)

In what follows, we will explore Hume's remarkable claim to have discovered both the "cement of the universe" and the objects bound together by that cement.

The objects which are joined together by the principles of association are ideas, and Hume begins both the *Treatise* and *An Enquiry Concerning Human Understanding* (hereafter, "first *Enquiry*") with sections entitled "Of the origin of our ideas" and "Of the origin of ideas," respectively. Ideas are one of two kinds of "perceptions of the human mind." The other kind are impressions, perceptions "which enter with most force and violence . . . and under this name I comprehend all our sensations, passions and emotions, as they make their first appearance in the soul" (T 1.1.1.1; SBN 2). Impressions of sensation arise "in the soul originally, from unknown causes" (T 1.1.2.1; SBN 8).[1] Hume emphasizes this point in section 5:

As to those impressions, which arise from the senses, their ultimate cause is, in my opinion, perfectly inexplicable by human reason, and 'twill always be impossible to decide with certainty, whether they arise immediately from the object, or are produc'd by the creative power of the mind, or are deriv'd from the author of our being.

(T 1.1.5.2; SBN 14)

In contrast, impressions of reflection are "deriv'd in great measure from our ideas" (T 1.1.2.1; SBN 8). This distinction has important consequences in the structuring of Hume's science of human nature. Hume will not attempt a science of sensation, but he will offer a science of the understanding, which concerns the ideas derived from impressions of sensation, and later a science of the passions and of morals, which concern the impressions of reflection, derived in part from our ideas.

Ideas, in contrast to impressions, are "faint images" of impressions, occurring in "thinking and reasoning"[2] (T 1.1.1.1; SBN 2). Impressions are felt; ideas are thought. This is connected to the fact that ideas are effects of their causes, sensory impressions, while we are ignorant of the causes of those impressions. Although impressions differ from ideas in liveliness or vivacity, our simple ideas, those that "admit of no distinction or separation" (T 1.1.1.2; SBN 2), are "exact representations of the impressions" (T 1.1.1.3; SBN 3). Hume maintains that a careful examination of the mind reveals that the simple perceptions of the mind are "double," and "that every simple idea has a simple impression, which resembles it; and every simple impression a correspondent idea" (T 1.1.1.5; SBN 3). Although his examination is not exhaustive, Hume is confident that anyone who attempts such an examination will concur with him, "*that all our simple ideas in their first appearance are deriv'd from simple impressions, which are correspondent to them, and which they exactly represent*" (T 1.1.1.6; SBN 4). Hume's general proposition, which he refers to as his "first principle" (T 1.1.1.12; SBN 7), customarily referred to in the literature as the *Copy Principle*, is couched in terms of the relation of exact correspondence, which includes both resemblance and causation.[3] Perhaps emboldened by this discovery, Hume finds that, "having discovered this relation," he is "curious to find some other of their qualities." What perceptions exist, and which are causes and which are effects? Hume succinctly characterizes the work ahead of him: "The *full* examination of this question is the subject of the present treatise" (T 1.1.1.6; SBN 4). If the contents of the mind are not random, then there is something to be discovered about human nature, and such discoveries will determine what perceptions exist, and how perceptions are related.

In both the *Treatise* and the first *Enquiry*, Hume calls attention to his choice of the terms "impression," "idea," and "perception," and complains that the sense of "idea" employed by Locke and others is "loose" (E 2.n1; SBN 22; T 1.1.1.n2; SBN 2). Locke's usage doesn't distinguish the perceptions which are original, our sensory impressions, from those which are derived, our ideas and our impressions of reflection. Making the distinction also allows Hume to weigh into the debate concerning innate ideas. If by "innate" one means "what is original or copied from no precedent perception, then may we assert, that all our impressions are innate, and our ideas not innate" (E 2.n1; SBN 22).[4] This deflated or naturalized sense of innateness, which does not apply to ideas, is the only sense Hume will grant.

By characterizing impressions as original or innate in this limited sense, Hume also distinguishes his view from that of Locke, who held that our sensations, *qua* ideas, derive from the primary qualities in objects which bring about the secondary qualities we sense. Hume rejects Locke's view as an abstruse hypothesis that has no evidence to support it.[5]

Hume adduces further evidence for the exact correspondence of simple ideas with simple impressions. As we noted, the claim is that simple impressions resemble simple ideas, and are caused by them. Although Hume does not yet have an account of causation on board, he anticipates that account by inferring that impressions are the cause of resembling simple ideas from their constant conjunction. "From this constant conjunction of resembling perceptions I immediately conclude, that there is a great connexion betwixt our correspondent impressions and ideas" (T 1.1.1.8; SBN 4). That our ideas are caused by the corresponding impressions is supported by the observation of the temporal priority of impressions to their ideas. Further, Hume observes that one who fails to have certain impressions, due to the lack of the requisite sensory modalities, or their limited employment, will fail to have the corresponding ideas.

In the Introduction to the *Treatise*, Hume recommended that we "glean up our experiments in this science from a cautious observation of human life, and take them as they appear in the common course of the world, by men's behavior in company, in affairs, and in their pleasures" (T Introduction 10; SBN xix). So it is surprising when Hume introduces a "contrary phenomenon" to the Copy Principle, the case of the missing shade of blue, which seems not to be drawn from common life. Hume imagines an individual who has seen every shade of blue except for one, who then observes all the shades of blue, in order from lightest to darkest, with the one shade that hasn't been experienced missing. Hume asserts that such an individual would both notice that the one shade is missing, and form the idea of the missing shade. This, however, would be a case of someone having a simple idea without having an antecedent exactly resembling impression.

Hume accepts that the missing shade of blue is a counterexample to the Copy Principle, but does not think that the existence of this counterexample merits rejecting "our general maxim" because "the instance is so particular and singular, that 'tis scarce worth our observing" (T 1.1.1.10; SBN 6). Interpreters have struggled to make sense both of Hume's introduction of this example and his quick dismissal of it. Some commentators argue that in the circumstances Hume describes, one would not have the idea of the missing shade; at best one might notice that a shade was missing, but noticing the absence of a shade is different from having an impression of the missing shade.[6] Durland offers a novel account of how Hume could account for the formation of the idea of the missing shade by means of distinguishing the hue, brightness, and saturation of the surrounding patches of blue. One could construct the missing shade by combining these into an idea of the missing shade. Durland (1996) argues that Hume thinks that such an imaginative feat is possible without the resulting idea being a complex idea. She cites Hume's use of the idea of a "distinction of reason" (T 1.1.7.17; SBN 24) as the mechanism for attaining simple ideas not derived from simple impressions.

Fogelin (1984) suggests that Hume's dismissal of the missing shade of blue makes sense in light of Hume's particular philosophical concerns. While one could imagine a whole host of cases of missing impressions based on graded presentations across different sensory modalities, such as temperature or pitch, these are far from the main topics of the *Treatise* and first *Enquiry*. Hume is simply acknowledging this in his dismissal of the importance of the thought experiment.[7]

Fogelin is certainly correct that Hume does not concern himself with alternative sensory analogues of the missing shade of blue, but he does take up other phenomena that may be related to that case. For example, Hume considers the "loose idea of a perfect standard" of length (T 1.2.4.25; SBN 49). Hume offers an explanation of how we form such ideas, by extrapolation from a series of increasingly precise standards. He mentions other perfect standards and suggests that his explanation applies to them as well. Further, the *Treatise* is peppered with discussions of ideas or purported ideas that cannot be derived from simple impressions, including, most notably, the idea of power or the efficacy of causes, the idea of continued and distinct existence, and the idea of the self. The nature and status of such purported ideas presents a significant challenge to Hume interpreters.

If the Copy Principle is understood as a criterion of empirical adequacy, and if Hume's position requires empirical adequacy for legitimate or meaningful ideas to be admitted into philosophical theorizing, then Hume must be understood as rejecting those purported simple ideas which fail to have corresponding antecedent simple impressions. Indeed, Hume seems to employ the Copy Principle to question the adequacy of a number of venerable philosophical concepts, based on their use of ideas which cannot be traced to impressions. Hume begins with the purported idea of substance. Failing to find an impression of substance, Hume concludes that we have no such idea (T 1.1.6.1; SBN 16). There are also no abstract ideas, since "all ideas are deriv'd from impressions, and are nothing but copies and representations of them," and the purported abstract ideas are wholly different from impressions, in lacking determinate degrees of quantity and quality (T 1.1.7.5–6; SBN 19). The failure to locate antecedent resembling impressions leads to the denial of the corresponding idea of substance (T 1.1.6.2; SBN 16), duration without change (T 1.2.3.11; SBN 37; T 1.2.5.29; SBN 63), the idea of a vacuum (T 1.2.5.1; SBN 54), perfect equality (T 1.2.4.24; SBN 48), power or agency (T 1.4.3.9; SBN 223), the substance of the soul (T 1.4.5.27; SBN 245), and the self (T 1.4.6.2; SBN 251).

The Copy Principle has often been interpreted as Hume's vehicle for dismissing traditional philosophical concepts and their associated views outright. Jonathan Bennett calls it Hume's "weapon of destructive criticism."[8] Oliver Johnson shares this interpretation, attributing to Hume the view that knowledge of the self is impossible. "Since we have no impression, hence no idea of it, our self or mind must be inconceivable."[9] If self, mind, duration without change, and the vacuum, to name a few, are truly inconceivable, then there is nothing more to be said. Hume must move on to genuine ideas, those derivable from antecedent impressions. This interpretation of Hume was implicit in the constructive or concept empiricism of early twentieth-century philosophy.[10]

When we attend to what Hume says immediately after invoking the Copy Principle in all these cases, we find, perhaps surprisingly, that Hume does not simply dismiss the purported ideas as inconceivable and move on. We do not have an idea of substance derived from a simple impression, but we can make sense of it as "a collection of particular qualities" (T 1.1.6.1; SBN 16). There is no idea of duration without change, yet we "fancy we have that idea" (T 1.2.5.29; SBN 63). A musician lacks the antecedent impression, yet she still "entertains a notion of a compleat *tierce* or *octave*" (T 1.2.4.24; SBN 48). After rejecting idea of efficacy because there is no impression, Hume writes: "Our present business, then, must be to find some natural production, where the operation and efficacy of a cause can be clearly conceiv'd and comprehended by the mind, without any danger of obscurity or mistake" (T 1.3.14.6; SBN 158). In each of these cases, and in others, Hume's announcement that there is no idea of x is followed by an account of how it is that we think that there is an idea of x. Sometimes this is described as mistake or conflation, where we use one idea, thinking that it is another. In other cases Hume accounts for our thinking that we have an idea in terms of a conflation of mental operations (T 1.2.5.21; SBN 61).

Toward discovering the "natural productions" that issue in such conceptions of substance, efficacy, and the self, Hume follows his account of the origin of ideas with an explanation of the ways "one idea naturally introduces another" (T 1.1.4.1; SBN 10). As already noted, Hume cites the existence of "universal principles" of the union or connection of our ideas underpinning the regularities we discover in carrying out a science of human nature. Hume finds three kinds of natural unions or relations, which are characterized in terms of the "qualities" which give rise to them. They are "RESEMBLANCE, CONTIGUITY in time or place, and CAUSE and EFFECT" (T 1.1.4.1; SBN 10).

In the *Treatise* and more forcefully in the first *Enquiry*, Hume makes the general case for the principles of association before introducing the three principles of resemblance, contiguity, and cause and effect. In the *Treatise*, Hume cites the "gentle force" of the associative principles as the cause of what he describes as the correspondence of different languages, in particular a correspondence of terms for complex ideas (T 1.1.4.1; SBN 10). Regardless of what language we speak, we associate ideas in the same way, and so form the same complex ideas. Thus, where we have terms for particular complex ideas in one language, we will discover corresponding terms for those same complex ideas, terms with the same meaning, in other languages.[11]

In the first *Enquiry*, a broad survey of the mind in its various cognitive postures requires reference to the association of ideas. Hume begins with our "serious thinking or discourse." If we are engaged in a proof in geometry, then the introduction of the idea of ice cream into the proof would be immediately rejected as irrelevant because it is not part of "the regular tract or train of ideas" (EHU 3.1; SBN 23). Hume then turns to harder cases, our imaginings and dreams. Though Hume earlier described the imagination as "free" (T 1.1.4.1; SBN 10), here he insists, perhaps anticipating the psychoanalytical theory of Freud and others, that were we to examine the content of someone's dream, we would easily discover the connections between seemingly unrelated thoughts. If the connections of "the loosest and freest conversation" are not immediately discoverable, Hume claims, one need only query the subject, who "might still inform you, that there had secretly revolved in his mind a succession of thought, which had gradually led him from the subject of conversation" (EHU 3.1; SBN 23). Hume has pushed into difficult territory here, and the case for the application of principles of association to all cognitive acts is clearly speculative, though also fertile material for future theorists.[12]

The influence of Locke's *Essay*, Book II, Chapter XXXIII, "Of the Association of Ideas," is worth noting, particularly for the ways Hume's associationism differs from Locke's. Locke distinguishes two kinds of association of ideas, a "natural Correspondence and Connexion" and one "wholly owing to Chance or Custom."[13] Natural connections are discovered by reason. Most connections, however, are the result of the contingent pairing of ideas, and their repetition through custom, which for Locke includes the influence of our inclinations, education, and interests. Locke speculates that there are natural causes of these connections in the motions of the body, though as "Intellectual Habits" they are natural only in the sense of being expected, once we are aware of them. Unlike Hume, Locke does not distinguish types of connections, and many of his examples are what he calls "wrong Connexions": being surfeited with honey, and the formation of hatred by associating pain or injury with the individual who caused the injury, or the school at which the injury occurred.

By distinguishing three kinds of association – resemblance, contiguity, and cause and effect – Hume can say more about the examples of association that Locke only characterizes as being due to chance or custom. For example, Hume would explain Locke's case of hatred or ill feeling when thinking about the school at which one suffered an injury as a due to the association of ideas by spatial contiguity. Hume's own example of contiguity is more mundane: when someone mentions an apartment in a building, she tends to think of the other apartments in that same building. But like Locke, Hume provides an example of the association of ideas of pain, naturally following the idea of its cause, a wound (EHU 3.3; SBN 24).

Both Locke and Hume use similarly titled sections to introduce the association of ideas, but the difference in the examples cited as well as the relative placement of the sections in the texts is telling. In the *Essay*, the section closes out Book II, an account of aberrations or mistakes in thinking, which Locke describes as the unnatural fusing of ideas, not the fundamental, natural principles of the operation of the mind. For Hume, in contrast, the sections on the association of ideas in both the *Treatise* and the first *Enquiry* are among the earliest sections and play a central role in all that follows.[14]

In accounting for the origin of ideas and in distinguishing memory and imagination, the three qualities of the association of ideas were already referenced by Hume as relations among impressions and ideas before they are introduced in the Section 4 of the *Treatise*, "Of the connexion or association of ideas." Simple ideas resemble the impressions from which they are derived, and impressions are also the causes of their corresponding ideas.[15] Ideas of memory present ideas "in the original form in which its objects were presented" (T 1.1.3.3; SBN 9). Hume characterizes the original form as retaining the "order and position" of the experienced impressions. His example from history suggests that this is at least a preservation of temporal contiguity. This more general sense of "relation" is clarified in the *Treatise* in the section, "Of relations," which follows shortly after "Of the connexion or association of ideas." In addition to resemblance, contiguity, and cause and effect, which are "natural relations," Hume counts the relations of identity, quantity or number, degrees of quality, and contrariety as joining the three natural relations to form the complete set of relations. Hume describes these as "philosophical relations," the possible relations any object can compared to another, whether or not such objects naturally stand in such a relation in our experience. Resemblance, contiguity, and cause and effect are both natural and philosophical relations. Identity, quantity, quality, and contrariety are philosophical relations.

Hume has, then, described two distinct causes for ideas to become present to the mind. The first causes are impressions. Impressions produce their corresponding ideas. The second causes are ideas and a quality, of resemblance, contiguity, or cause and effect, which produces an association of ideas, whereby "one idea naturally introduces another" (T 1.1.4.1; SBN 10). We noted that Hume has described the first of these two causes, impressions, as *original*, that is, as causally inexplicable (T 1.1.2.1; SBN 9). Similarly, Hume can account for the effects of the association of ideas, but the causes of the association of ideas "are mostly unknown, and must be resolv'd into *original* qualities of human nature, which I pretend not to explain" (T 1.1.4.6; SBN 13). We can account for the origin of ideas from original causes, the impressions of which they are copies, and we can account for complex ideas, including relations, modes, and substances, from those ideas together with one or more of the original qualities of the three natural relations.

How does the association of ideas work? How does the presence of one idea bring about a resembling, contiguous, or causally related idea? It is not clear that Hume thinks it makes sense to attempt to answer this question, since association is original, and thus not subject to causal investigation. However, we can ask about the conditions under which ideas naturally introduce other ideas, beyond saying simply that they do so when a relation of resemblance, contiguity, or causation holds. And in fact, Hume does have something to say about each of the three kinds of association.

Resemblance, Hume says, can be understood as the basis for any comparison. Thus, resemblance is "necessary to all philosophical relations" (T 1.1.5.3; SBN 14). Yet, not all resemblances produce an association of ideas. The idea of a tomato resembles the idea of an automobile, in that both are ideas of physical objects. But resemblances at this degree of abstraction or generality do not bring about associations. The thought of a tomato does not naturally lead to the thought of an automobile. Hume explains:

> When a quality becomes very general, and is common to a great many individuals, it leads not the mind directly to any one of them; but by presenting at once too great a choice, does thereby prevent the imagination from fixing on any single object.
>
> (T 1.1.5.3; SBN 14)

For the relation of resemblance to serve as a principle of association, the idea which leads to a resembling idea must be specific enough to limit the imagination's "choice" of resembling ideas, and it does that by having particular qualities that can be matched by a selection of ideas via resemblance.[16] Hume does not say how the imagination selects a target idea from the ideas that match the associating idea.

Hume also has something to say about the conditions under which we form associations via contiguity. As we customarily sense objects that are contiguous in space and time, Hume says that the imagination has no choice but to order its objects in the same manner. That is, we associate contiguous ideas in thought, matching the experienced contiguity of our sense impressions.[17]

Associative connections are enhanced by the imagination's capacity to form long chains of associated ideas. Hume's example is that of "cousins in the fourth degree" who, though related by blood, are not related "so closely as brothers, much less as child and parent" (T 1.1.4.3; SBN 12). Hume also notes that causal associations can be dispositional as well as occurrent. He illustrates this through examples of social relationships such as duty, interest, government and judicial relationships, and obedience to authority generally.

Hume's commentary on the natural relations raises several questions. Kemp Smith questions whether resemblance should be counted as a natural relation, particularly when we compare it to contiguity.[18] While association by contiguity plausibly trades on the contiguity of impressions in our sensory experience, we cannot describe our sensory experience as customarily group-ing resembling impressions. If we have to notice that our perceptions resemble one another, then that would make the association one based on reflection, and so not the result of natural association.

A related problem is raised by Hume's appeal to sensory experience as underlying the asso-ciation by contiguity and his explication of causation by appeal to biological and social rela-tionships. Hume's description of our sensation of objects that are in proximity to one another appears to be a claim about the nature of physical objects, and their spatial and temporal dis-position. Hume is not in a position to make claims about physical objects and their spatial and temporal relations, at this stage of his science of human nature, at any rate. The same worry applies to Hume's use of biological and social relations to account for the association of causally related ideas.

In Part 2 of Book 1, in accounting for our purported idea of a vacuum, Hume notes that he has resisted the temptation to explain the relations of ideas in physiological terms, but he now finds it necessary to do so, in order to explain more nuanced aspects of the imagination. Here Hume describes resemblance, not among ideas, but among actions of the mind. We tend to conflate similar actions of mind, and thereby conflate the ideas each action of the mind produces. The related acts of mind occur in "animal spirits" occupying contiguous "traces" in a "region of the brain." The mingling of these traces is responsible for the conflation (T 1.2.5.20; SBN 60–61).

Kemp Smith raises several questions about these elaborations of Hume's associationism, but his fundamental concern is that these extended descriptions of the three natural relations are incompatible with their status as *natural* relations. By appealing to the structure and organization of the brain, the relationships between family members and among social structures and institu-tions, Hume is not describing relations that are basic or original, but relations that are formed by reflection on these structures and institutions.[19] Kemp Smith argues that the only way to resolve these difficulties is to see the material in Book 1 of the *Treatise* as following the account of the association in Book 2, where Hume is concerned with the relations among persons, the passions, and their role in morals. This interpretation requires jettisoning Hume's Book 1 claims about the fundamental status of the natural relations, as relations that hold among ideas before reflection.

Baier (1991) does not second Kemp Smith's reconstruction of the order of Hume's writing of the *Treatise*, but she does urge us to see Hume's introduction of the association of ideas in the broader context of his interest in the full variety of kinds of association discussed throughout the *Treatise*, including those of Books 2 and 3. Baier points out that in addition to the association of ideas, that Hume is interested in the association of passions, or impressions of reflection, in Book 2, and in the association of persons, in Book 3. Given those interests in the full extent of human nature, she suggests, it is no surprise that Hume's elaborations of the association of ideas are couched in terms that refer to associated spatio-temporal objects and persons.

Instead of seeing Hume's appeal to the associations of physical objects and persons to explain the association of ideas as a lapse or mistake, Baier argues that it is a strength of Hume's approach. If our access to association by resemblance, contiguity, and cause and effect were really based on our fleeting mental images, we would be unable to assess them. What we do have access to are durable representations, such as paintings, images in mirrors, and texts whose accurate reproduction is due to the fidelity of "printers and copists" (T 1.3.13.6; SBN 146). Although Hume presents the association of ideas as "original," it is the other way around. Baier writes: "Persons and their works are primary; one is tempted to say that for Hume *they* are the 'original existences.'"[20] On her view, the association of ideas is modeled on the thicker associations of objects and persons.[21]

What of Kemp Smith's objection that such a shift renders associations reflection-based and so not natural? How can the three natural relations among ideas be the cement of the universe if our understanding of them depends on other relations between other kinds of objects? The purported difficulty results from the failure to distinguish between our philosophical reflection on the natural relations, and the natural relations as they occur in both vulgar and philosophical minds. It is not necessary for us to be consciously aware of the resemblance, much less that we have a philosophical view about the nature of the relation of resemblance itself, for the associative principle of resemblance to do its work. Hume notes, for example, that when we come to a river we infer the effect of water on animal bodies without engaging in any reflection (T 1.3.13; SBN 104). The achievement of the association of ideas in the mind does not depend on the recognition of the association, though such recognition can be achieved and can be made use of to understand the imagination, and to critique and improve our cognitive efforts. Hume shows this in his treatment of our ideas space and time and in his account of belief and his account of the norms of causal reasoning.[22]

In the *Treatise*, Hume characterizes complex ideas as combinations of simple ideas brought together by the natural relations.[23] Hume divides complex ideas into three types: relations, modes, and substances. In doing so, Hume is clearly acknowledging these kinds of complex ideas as philosophical terms of art. His point is to show how traditional distinctions other philosophers have drawn can be accommodated in terms of the natural relations. However, this does not mean that Hume accepts the distinction. As we've already noted, Hume begins his explanation of how the natural relations give rise to our ideas of substances by first challenging the very distinction. There is no impression from which the idea of substance is derived. So there is no idea of substance, and so no distinction between substances and modes. The best we can do is distinguish the complex ideas we *call* substances from those we *call* modes, and to do this we need only investigate the "principle[s] of union," contiguity and causation, responsible for our grouping simple ideas together (T 1.1.6.2; SBN 16). In substances, the simple ideas or "qualities" united in the complex idea are taken to be inseparable from each other. In modes or accidents, the ideas can be separated.

When Hume introduced the principles of association, he introduced them as relations among simple ideas. The account of complex ideas conforms to that characterization. However, he clearly does not intend to restrict the associative relations to simple ideas. We have seen that he also thinks that impressions of reflection are associated, and that we find associative connections among physical objects, persons, and institutions. Nor does Hume limit the kinds of complex ideas formed by association to substances, modes, and relations. Hume says only that these three are the most "remarkable." He is open to other ways perceptions can be united in the imagination.

The last significant addition to Hume's introduction of ideas and their association in Book 1 of the *Treatise* to be canvassed here is his treatment of abstraction. Hume explicitly endorses Berkeley's view that any idea "has in its appearance in the mind a precise degree of quantity and quality; however it may be made to represent others, which have different degrees of both" (T 1.1.7.3; SBN 19). There are no ideas that lack precise degrees of quantity and quality, a conclusion Hume supports with three arguments. One argument employs the Copy Principle. All ideas are derived from impressions, which differ from ideas only in vivacity, and so have the same "determinate quantity and quality" as their impressions (T 1.1.7.5; SBN 19).

Although completely determinate, ideas can operate "beyond their nature" and apply to objects that vary in their quantity and quality, abstract ideas by function, if not by nature. This is achieved by the custom of joining an idea to resembling ideas and applying the same name to each member of this group. When we hear the name applied to each member of the group of resembling ideas, we have the idea of one of them, and it also "revives the custom, which we have acquir'd by surveying them" (T 1.1.7.7; SBN 20). The revival of the custom is a readiness to recall any of the resembling ideas, as needed. This is clearly a case of association by resemblance, where ideas introduce one another in the imagination. Recall Hume's description of the relation of resemblance itself, which, we noted earlier, makes reference to sets of resembling ideas based on the specific properties of the ideas selected for resemblance.[24]

Hume's theory of ideas and their associative relations figure centrally in the *Treatise*, and in his other philosophical works. Most notably in Book 1 of the *Treatise*, Hume attempts to follow his curiosity to fully examine and attempt to discover the "other qualities" beyond the origin of simple ideas in simple impressions. As we have already noted, he describes this as the subject of the *Treatise*. The application of the theory to our understanding of space and time, causation, belief, our conception of the external world, and the self, is extensive.

There is a subtle but important application of the association of ideas which highlights the reach of the natural relations in Hume's philosophy. In T 1.3.9, "Of the effects of other relations and other habits," Hume claims that we often mistake inferences for matters of direct perception. For example, whether we observe the "vast extent of the ocean" from "a high promontory" or we look at an object in our study, "the eye at all times sees an equal number of physical points" (T 1.3.9.11; SBN 112). So the conclusion that the ocean is larger and more distant than the object in our study is a matter of causal inference, enhanced by the resemblance between the image present to our senses, the impression, and the lively idea. Here, like Locke, Hume credits a mistake, in this case a conflation of perception and judgment, to association. Unlike Locke, Hume does not take the mistake to indicate a defect in human nature.

Notes

1 See T 1.3.5.2; SBN 84.
2 It is a matter of debate how much emphasis to put on Hume's description of ideas as "images." Pears (1990: 6), for example, describes an idea as "a replica of a sense-impression and is therefore an image."
3 Williams (1985). Garrett (1997) is often credited for naming this principle, but Garrett does not himself claim to have named it.

4 Hume does not restrict the "innate" ideas to impressions of sensation, though he should, since impressions of reflection are not original. They are derived in the sense of being the effects of causes.

5 See Brown and Morris (2012: 39–41).

6 See Fogelin (1984) and Durland (1996) for a review of some of the main interpretive moves.

7 Recent commentary attempts to resolve the counterexample in a way that explains Hume's casual dismissal of it include Brown and Morris (2012); Garrett (2015); and Landy (2006). See also Morreal (1982) and Nelson (1989). Among those who see the counterexample as a serious problem are Johnson (1984); Losee (1992); Rollin (1971); and Russow (1980).

8 Bennett (1971: 223).

9 Johnson (1995: 287).

10 See Palaluk (1989).

11 Hume does not indicate which languages fall within his survey here.

12 Weintraub (2002) suggests that Hume is not claiming that there are exceptionless laws here. Cf. p. 234.

13 Locke (1975: 395).

14 Millican (2002) takes Hume to have largely abandoned his commitment to associationism, the attempt to explain the operations of the mind in terms of the natural association of ideas by resemblance, contiguity, and cause and effect, in his later writings. Millican notes that Hume reduced the size of section 3 of the first *Enquiry* for the 1777 edition from the 1772 edition. However, the 2000 Critical Edition of the *Enquiry* restored the reduced passages, which appear in all editions, and which apply the principles of association to the analysis of human action, as represented in literature, history, and criticism. Hume ends the section with the conclusion: "It is sufficient, at present, to have established this conclusion, that the three connecting principles of all ideas are the relations of *Resemblance, Contiguity, and Causation*" (EHU 3.18).

15 Note, however, that Hume always describes resemblance, contiguity, and causation as relations of *ideas*, not more generally as relations among *perceptions*, However, Hume is clearly committed to the resemblance of simple impressions with their corresponding ideas. He describes ideas as "images" and "exact representations" of impressions, in virtue of their "same resemblance and representation" (T 1.1.1.3; SBN 3). Hume also appeals to the temporal and spatial contiguity of our impressions to explain spatial and temporal association in the imagination (T 1.1.4.2; SBN 11). In Book II, Hume introduces a principle of the association of *impressions* as separate from the association of ideas. Resembling impressions naturally introduce one another (T 2.1.4.3; SBN 283). Hume's examples of the association by resemblance of impressions are all impressions of reflection, as they must be, given his claim that we cannot fathom the causes of impressions of sensation.

16 Hume develops this idea of the generality and specificity of comparisons in T 1.1.7, "Of abstract ideas."

17 That leaves cause and effect, which Hume notes he will have much more to say about later in the *Treatise*. For now he emphasizes only that it brings about the strongest connections of the three.

18 Kemp Smith (1941: 240 ff).

19 This line of objection is also developed by Weintraub (2002).

20 Baier (1991: 33).

21 The view that our account of perceptions is modeled on our concepts of ordinary objects and persons has some similarity to the view of Wilfrid Sellars (Sellars, Rorty, and Brandom, 1997), who argues that appearance talk is parasitic on physical object talk, that the claim that an object appears green depends on our already having the concept of a physical object being green.

22 See T 1.2.5.20; SBN 61, T 1.3.6; SBN 87, and T 1.3.13, SBN 143.

23 That Hume does not include this or a revised account of complex ideas as ideas united by the three natural relations is among the grounds Millican has for his claim that Hume largely jettisoned the associationism of the *Treatise* in the first *Enquiry*.

24 Hume's account of the custom seems clear for complex ideas, which can form resemblances by having qualities, component simple ideas, in common. The worry that simple ideas, e.g. ideas of individual colors, cannot be associated by resemblance, is raised and answered. There can be a "point of resemblance" even where separation is not in question (T App. 5; SBN 626).

References

Baier, Annette C. (1991) *A Progress of Sentiments: Reflections on Hume's Treatise*, Cambridge, MA: Harvard University Press.

Bennett, Jonathan (1971) *Locke, Berkeley, Hume: Central Themes*, Oxford: Oxford University Press.

Brown, C. R. and W. E. Morris (2012) *Starting with Hume*, London: Continuum.

Durland, Karann (1996) "Hume's First Principle, His Missing Shade, and His Distinctions of Reason," *Hume Studies* 22(1): 105–122.

Fogelin, R. (1984) "Hume and the Missing Shade of Blue," *Philosophy and Phenomenological Research* 45(2): 263–271.

Garrett, Don (1997) *Cognition and Commitment in Hume's Philosophy*, Oxford: Oxford University Press.

———— (2015) *Hume*, London: Routledge.

Johnson, D. M. (1984) "Hume's Missing Shade of Blue, Interpreted as Involving Habitual Spectra," *Hume Studies* 10(2): 109–124.

Johnson, Oliver A. (1995) *The Mind of David Hume: A Companion to Book I of "A Treatise of Human Nature,"* Urbana: University of Illinois Press.

Kemp Smith, Norman (1941) *The Philosophy of David Hume: A Critical Study of Its Origins and Central Doctrines*, London: Palgrave Macmillan.

Landy, David (2006) "Hume's Impression/Idea Distinction," *Hume Studies* 32(1): 119–140.

Locke, John and Peter H. Nidditch, eds. (1975) *An Essay Concerning Human Understanding*, Oxford: Oxford University Press.

Losee, John (1992) "Hume's Demarcation Project," *Hume Studies* 18(1): 51–62.

Millican, Peter (2002) "The Context, Aims, and Structure of Hume's first *Enquiry*," in *Reading Hume on Human Understanding: Essays on the First "Enquiry,"* Oxford: Oxford University Press.

Morreall, John (1982) "Hume's Missing Shade of Blue," *Philosophy and Phenomenological Research* 42(3): 407–415.

Nelson, John O. (1989) "Hume's Missing Shade of Blue Re-Viewed," *Hume Studies* 15(2): 353–364.

Palaluk, Michael (1989) "Quine's 1946 Lectures on Hume," *Journal of the History of Philosophy* 27(3): 445–459.

Pears, David (1990) *Hume's System: An Examination of the First Book of His Treatise*, Oxford: Oxford University Press.

Rollin, Bernard E. (1971) "Hume's Blue Patch and the Mind's Creativity," *Journal of the History of Ideas* 32(1): 119–128.

Russow, Lilly-Marlene (1980) "Simple Ideas and Resemblance," *The Philosophical Quarterly* 30(121): 342–350.

Sellars, Wilfrid, Richard Rorty and Robert Brandom (1997) *Empiricism and the Philosophy of Mind*, Cambridge, MA: Harvard University Press.

Weintraub, Ruth (2002) "Hume's Associations," *Hume Studies* 28(2): 231–246.

Williams, Michael (1985) "Hume's Criterion of Significance," *Canadian Journal of Philosophy* 15(2): 273–304.

6

HUME ON SPACE AND TIME

A limited defense

Jonathan Cottrell

Treatise Book 1, Part 2, addresses two major early modern debates about space and time. First, are spatially extended and temporally enduring things "infinitely divisible" – that is, divisible into infinitely many parts? Second, could there be empty regions of space (vacua) and things that endure without changing? (Hume regards something that endures without changing as the temporal analog of a vacuum.)

For much of the twentieth century, Hume's contributions to these debates were poorly received. The few scholars who addressed them claimed to find them riddled with inconsistencies, conflations, and fallacies.[1] Perhaps for this reason, other scholars simply ignored them. While recent scholarship has been more favorable, some of Hume's most sympathetic and judicious critics still reject important parts of what Hume calls his "system concerning space and time" (T 1.2.4.1; SBN 39).[2] Here, I aim to defend this system as far as possible.

As indicated by the title of Hume's discussion – "Of *the ideas of* space and time" (emphasis added) – he does not address the topics of space and time directly. Instead, he approaches them via his theory of the ideas by which we conceive of space and time. I will therefore examine this theory (§§2–3) before turning to his arguments about space and time themselves (§§4–5). First, however, I will explain why the debates Hume addresses were theologically significant for him and his contemporaries (§1).

§1 Two debates about space and time

The two debates that Hume addresses concern the divisibility of extended and enduring things, and the existence of empty space or vacuum. For him and his contemporaries, both were theologically significant.

In the *Historical and Critical Dictionary* (first published in 1697), Pierre Bayle uses considerations about divisibility and vacua to argue that there is no motion. First, he argues that there is no motion because only extended things can move, but such things cannot exist because there is no coherent account of an extended thing's parts: there are only three possible accounts – its parts each have further parts, it has extended simple parts, or it has extensionless simple parts – and each is incoherent (1991: 359–362). Second, he argues that there is no motion because motion requires a vacuum, but there is no vacuum (1991: 377–383; for a fuller statement of this argument, see §5 below).

Bayle's use of these arguments is subtle. He does not think they should convince us that there is no motion. Instead, from our inability to answer them, he concludes that we do not understand motion (1991: 372). He quotes and endorses a passage by Arnauld and Nicole claiming that such unanswerable arguments serve religion in two ways. They "check [our mind's] presumption and . . . keep it from ever being foolhardy enough to oppose its feeble light to the truths that the Church proposes" (*Logic*, Part IV, Chapter i; quoted in Bayle 1991: 372). And they undermine the view that we should not believe in God because we cannot understand Him: we cannot consistently take this view, because we believe in motion even though we cannot understand it (Bayle 1991: 372). So, as Bayle presents them, his arguments against motion support *fideism*: the view that belief in God may be accepted on faith, independently of reason. We all accept the existence of motion as an article of faith, even though reason speaks against it. What obstacle, then, to accepting the existence of God as an article of faith, even though reason speaks against it, too?

Samuel Clarke, an ally of Isaac Newton, also used considerations about space and vacua to support belief in God.[3] In his *Demonstration of the Being and Attributes of God* (first published in 1705), Clarke argues that there is a necessarily existing substance – one that cannot fail to exist. One of his arguments is as follows (1998: 13): space or "immensity" exists necessarily; space is a "mode" or "attribute"; as such, it requires a substance; so, there is a necessarily existing substance, of which space or immensity is a mode or attribute. As we will see, Clarke holds that the material world does not exist necessarily (1998: 19–20). So, in the context of this argument, 'space' must be understood to mean *absolute space* – something that could exist even if there were no material objects to occupy it. The concepts of absolute space and vacuum are related: if we cannot conceive a vacuum, then we cannot understand the claim that space could exist even if there were no material objects to occupy it.

Clarke also wishes to show that the necessarily existing substance is God. In order to do so, he needs to rule out the possibility that the material world is the necessarily existing substance. To this end, he offers the following argument (1998: 19–20): there is a vacuum; if there is a vacuum, then matter is "absent from one place"; if matter is absent from one place, then matter can be absent from every place, i.e. can fail to exist altogether; so, the material world does not exist necessarily.

One of Hume's goals in discussing space and time is to answer these theistic arguments.[4] To a first approximation, he does so as follows. To Bayle's divisibility-based argument, he replies that there is a coherent account of an extended thing's parts: extended things are ultimately composed of extensionless simple parts. (This view seems paradoxical to Bayle; §4 aims to explain why it is not.) To Bayle's vacuum-based argument, he replies that motion does not require a vacuum; it requires only "invisible and intangible distance," which he distinguishes from vacuum. And to Clarke's vacuum-based arguments, he replies that we cannot conceive or form an idea of a vacuum, so Clarke's arguments are unintelligible – they lack a conceivable subject matter.

Hume's reply to Bayle's divisibility-based argument seems to involve a metaphysical claim about the nature of extended things. Elsewhere in his writings, however, Hume argues only for *qualified* metaphysical claims. For example, when discussing the nature of a mind or self, his conclusions concern what a mind is "as far as we can conceive it" (Ab. 28; SBN 657) or as far as we have any "notion of it" (T App. 19; SBN 635), not what a mind is, unqualifiedly. Similarly, in the *Treatise* section "Of the idea of necessary connexion," Hume aims to explain what we can conceive causal necessity to be, rather than what it is, unqualifiedly: he argues that we cannot form "the most distant idea" of causal necessity "when it is not taken for the determination of the mind, to pass from the idea of an object to that of its usual attendant" (T 1.3.14.25; SBN 167). And when he considers spatial vacua, he argues for a claim about what we can conceive there to be, not about what there is: he argues that we cannot conceive of a vacuum, not that there is no such thing (T 1.2.5.1; SBN 53). In light of this, it seems likely that Hume means to make only a qualified claim about divisibility: that, "as far as we can conceive" them, extended things are ultimately composed of extensionless simple parts.[5]

Because Hume's views on divisibility and the vacuum concern what we can conceive, let us approach them via his theory of thought or conception.

§2 Conception and its limits

According to Hume, the ingredients of our mental lives are *perceptions*. He distinguishes these into *impressions*, which are the ingredients of our sensory and passionate experiences, and *ideas*, which are the ingredients of thinking (T 1.1.1.1; SBN 1). Conceiving or thinking of something, then, involves forming an *idea* (T 1.2.2.8, 1.2.6.8; SBN 32, 67). In Hume's view, the nature of our perceptions and the origins of our ideas place limits on what we can conceive. This section aims to explain what these limits are and why Hume thinks they apply to us.

Perceptions, be they impressions or ideas, are either simple or complex. A simple perception has no parts; it is a true atom. Perceptions of a single colored point and of a single musical note may be examples. In contrast, a complex perception has parts: it is composed of other perceptions – ultimately, of simple ones. For example, an auditory perception of a C major triad is complex: it is composed of perceptions of the notes C, E, and G.

Hume argues that each of one's *simple* ideas is copied from – that is, causally derives from and resembles – a simple impression one has previously had (T 1.1.1.7; SBN 4). Scholars call this the Copy Principle. Assuming that an idea of middle C is simple, the Copy Principle implies that anyone who auditorily imagines (and so forms an auditory idea of) this note has previously heard it (had an auditory impression of it).

A *complex* idea may also be copied from a single past impression, but need not be. In visualizing Oxford's Balliol College, I form a complex idea that is copied from a previous complex visual impression of this college. But in visualizing Hogwarts School of Witchcraft and Wizardry, I form a complex idea that is not copied from any one previous impression, for I have never seen Hogwarts, nor anything that exactly resembles it. Instead, I visualize Hogwarts by assembling many ideas – ultimately, many simple ideas of colored points – into a complex one. Of course, per the Copy Principle, each of these simple ideas must be copied from a previous simple impression.

When we conceive of objects, we do not merely pick them out in thought, or mentally point to them. We also conceive them *as* having certain features and *as* being related in certain ways. For example, when I visualize Balliol College, I conceive it *as* having a certain shape and color, *as* being adjacent to Trinity College, and so forth. In Hume's view, the origins of our ideas constrain the range of features that we can conceive objects as having:

> As every idea is deriv'd from a preceding perception, 'tis impossible our idea of a perception, and that of an object or external existence can ever represent what are specifically different from each other. Whatever difference we may suppose betwixt them, 'tis still incomprehensible to us; and we are oblig'd either to conceive an external object merely as a relation without a relative, or to make it the very same with a perception or impression.
>
> (T 1.4.5.19; SBN 241; see also T 1.2.6.8; SBN 67)

When conceiving of an object, Hume claims, we have only two options. First, we can "conceive . . . [it] merely as a relation without a relative." That is, we can conceive the object as having a certain relation to another thing, without conceiving it as having any specific intrinsic properties. For example, I might conceive an object simply as *the cause of my perceptions*. (I thereby conceive the object as "a relation without a relative" because I conceive it merely by conceiving a relation in which it stands, without conceiving the intrinsic character of the "relative" – that is, the object itself that stands in this relation.) Second, we can conceive the object as being "the very same with a perception or impression" – in other words, conceive it as having the same intrinsic features as a perception. There is no third option. So, if we are to conceive an object as having any specific intrinsic features at all, we must conceive it as having the intrinsic features of a perception. This explains why Hume says that we cannot "conceive or form an idea of any thing specifically different from ideas and impressions" (T 1.2.6.8; SBN 67). In his sense, conceiving of something "specifically different" from a perception would involve conceiving it as having intrinsic features that no perception has – and, as we have seen, he thinks we cannot do this.

In Hume's view, we are subject to this constraint because our ideas are "deriv'd from" (or caused by) previous perceptions (T 1.2.6.8, 1.4.5.19; SBN 67, 241). We might interpret him as saying that each idea is limited to representing the intrinsic features of the perception from which it is derived – hence, that one can conceive an object as having a certain intrinsic feature only if one has previously had a perception with that very feature. But this constraint seems too strong, even by Hume's own lights. He allows that, by assembling simple ideas into a novel complex idea, one can conceive an object as having certain intrinsic features that none of one's previous perceptions have had: for example, one can conceive something as having the distinctive shape of a winged horse (T 1.1.3.4; SBN 10), without previously having had a perception with that shape. Therefore, it is more plausible to interpret him as accepting the following, weaker Constraint Principle:

> *Constraint Principle:* Someone can conceive an object as having a certain intrinsic feature, F, only if *either* a) she has had a perception that is F *or* b) she can now form a perception that is F, given her stock of simple ideas and the ways in which she can combine them.

If this principle is true, then someone can conceive an object as having intrinsic spatial features, such as extension or shape, only if she has had, or can now form, *spatial perceptions* – perceptions that are, themselves, extended or shaped. And she can conceive an object as having intrinsic temporal features, such as duration, only if she has had, or can now form, *temporal perceptions* – perceptions that are, themselves, enduring. The next section examines Hume's views about these spatial and temporal perceptions.[6]

§3 Spatial and temporal perceptions

In Hume's view, then, some of our perceptions are spatial: they are literally extended and, in some cases, shaped. And some perceptions are temporal: they are literally enduring – it takes time to have them. Some scholars think it incoherent to say that *perceptions* are extended.[7] Incoherent or not, there is clear evidence Hume accepts this: "there are impressions and ideas really extended" (T 1.4.5.16; SBN 240; see also T 1.4.5.9, 1.4.5.15; SBN 235, 239–240).

The Constraint Principle implies that the intrinsic features of our spatial and temporal perceptions constrain the range of features that we can conceive extended and enduring things as having. The rest of this section examines three claims about the intrinsic features of these perceptions, for which Hume argues or to which he is committed. First, these perceptions are complex: they are composed of parts arranged in certain distinctive ways. Second, they are only finitely, not infinitely, divisible. Third, every part of a spatial perception is either colored or tangible.

Let us start with Hume's claim that these perceptions are complex. The complexity of spatial perceptions follows from his view that they are extended, together with his view that everything extended is composed of spatial parts (T 1.2.4.3; SBN 40). Accordingly, he writes that the spatially extended impression of a table "consists of parts" and that "these parts are so situated, as to afford us the notion of distance and contiguity; of length, breadth, and thickness" (T 1.4.5.15; SBN 239). A spatial perception, then, is ultimately composed of simple perceptions that are spatially arranged: that are above, below, to the left of, and to the right of each other – and, if it is a tactile perception, in front of and behind each other. (Hume thinks visual perceptions have only two spatial dimensions, while tactile ones have three: see T 1.2.5.8 (SBN 56) and Hume's letter to Hugh Blair of 4 July, 1762, in Reid 2002: 256–257.) Similarly, Hume holds that a temporal perception is a complex composed of "successive perceptions" (T 1.2.3.7; SBN 35), i.e. perceptions that occur before and after each other. He calls the spatial and temporal arrangements of simple perceptions their "manner[s] of appearance" or "disposition[s]" (T 1.2.3.5, 1.2.3.10; SBN 34, 36–37).[8]

Let us next consider Hume's claim that our spatial and temporal perceptions are only finitely divisible – that is, divisible only into a finite number of parts, not into infinitely many parts. This has two implications. First, each spatial or temporal perception is ultimately composed of simple, indivisible parts. (If it were not – if each of its parts were divisible into further parts – then it would be divisible into infinitely many parts.) Second, the simple parts that compose a spatial or temporal perception are not densely ordered: in other words, it is not the case that, between any two such parts, there is a further part. (If a perception's simple parts were densely ordered, then it would have infinitely many parts: between any two parts, *a* and *b*, there would be a further part, *c*; between *a* and *c*, a further part, *d*; and so on, to infinity.)

Why should we accept that our spatial and temporal perceptions are only finitely divisible? Hume argues the case for spatial and temporal *ideas* as follows:

> 'Tis universally allow'd, that the capacity of the mind is limited, and can never attain a full and adequate conception of infinity: And tho' it were not allow'd, 'twou'd be sufficiently evident from the plainest observation and experience. 'Tis also obvious, that whatever is capable of being divided *in infinitum*, must consist of an infinite number of parts . . . It requires scarce any induction to conclude from hence, that the *idea*, which we form of any finite quality, is not infinitely divisible, but that by proper distinctions and separations we may run this idea up to inferior ones, which will be perfectly simple and indivisible.
>
> (T 1.2.1.2; SBN 26–27)

Let us call this the Argument from Limited Capacity:

[1]   A human mind can contain only finitely many ideas.
[2]   If a human mind contains an idea that is infinitely divisible, then that mind contains infinitely many ideas.

Therefore,

[3]   No human mind contains an idea that is infinitely divisible. (From 1, 2)
[4]   Our spatial and temporal ideas are divisible. (Suppressed premise)

Therefore,

[5] Our spatial and temporal ideas are only finitely divisible. (From 3, 4)

This argument is valid. Premise [4] follows from Hume's claim that our spatial and temporal ideas are complex. But why should we accept premises [1] and [2]?

Hume claims that [1] is "evident from the plainest observation and experience." This is dialectically problematic. The only ordinary (or "plain") form of "observation and experience" that bears upon this issue is introspection. But, for all I can tell introspectively, my spatially extended ideas may be infinitely divisible – and hence, by premise [2] of Hume's own argument, may involve my having infinitely many ideas. (For example, for all I can tell introspectively, the extended idea that I form, when visualizing a table, may be divisible into parts that each have further parts: two ideas half its size, which are each divisible into two ideas quarter of its size . . . and so on, to infinity.) Of course, Hume wants to say that my spatial ideas are *not* counterexamples to premise [1], because they are only finitely divisible. But this is his *conclusion*. If he relies on it to defend a *premise* against putative counterexamples, then he begs the question.

What of premise [2]? It seems to rest on three assumptions. First, Hume assumes that if something is now divisible, then all of the parts into which it is divisible actually now exist. Thomas Holden calls this the "actual parts doctrine"; it opposes the "potential parts doctrine," which says that an object's parts do not actually exist until it is divided into them (Holden 2004: Ch. 2). The actual parts doctrine implies that, if an idea is infinitely divisible, then all of the infinitely many parts into which it is divisible actually now exist. Hume also assumes that every part of an idea is an idea, and that if a human mind contains an idea, it contains every part of that idea. Taken together, these assumptions imply premise [2].

So, Hume cannot claim to have established the Argument from Limited Capacity's premises beyond reasonable doubt: [1] is not defended satisfactorily, and [2] rests on several undefended assumptions. Nonetheless, these premises seem plausible and may well be true – nothing we have seen suggests otherwise. Moreover, both premises may draw support from views still held by philosophers today. Certain computational theories of the mind developed in the twentieth century imply that a human being can have only finitely many representational mental states – the analogues of Humean ideas in current philosophy of mind – as premise [1] claims. And the "actual parts doctrine," on which premise [2] rests, survives in the form of the "doctrine of arbitrary undetached parts," which is widely accepted in current metaphysics (Holden 2004: 82–83). Those of us who are sympathetic to these present-day theories may be committed to the premises of Hume's argument, and thereby committed to its conclusion. So, despite Hume's own failure to establish that its premises are true, the Argument from Limited Capacity deserves our serious consideration.

As Hume presents it, this argument concerns only *ideas*. He offers a further argument that our spatial *impressions* are only finitely divisible:

> Put a spot of ink upon paper, fix your eye upon that spot, and retire to such a distance, that at last you lose sight of it; 'tis plain, that the moment before it vanish'd the image or impression was perfectly indivisible.
>
> (T 1.2.1.4; SBN 27)

Let us call this the Inkspot Argument. It has several problems. First, it establishes at most that our spatial impressions are ultimately composed of simple or indivisible parts. This does not imply that they are only finitely divisible. Perhaps the simple parts of our spatial impressions are densely ordered. If so, then our spatial impressions are infinitely divisible, despite being composed of indivisible parts. So, even if it is sound, the Inkspot Argument does not establish Hume's desired conclusion.

Second, the Inkspot Argument assumes that it cannot be a vague matter whether you see the inkspot or not: as you walk back from the spot, Hume supposes, there must be a definite moment when you cease to see it. This is not obviously true. If we remove grains of sand from a heap one by one, there will eventually cease to be a heap before us. But there need be no particular grain of sand such that, when we remove it, there ceases to be a heap. More plausibly, for a while, it will be vague – there will be no fact of the matter – whether the grains of sand before us form a heap or not. Perhaps stepping back from the inkspot is like removing grains from a heap: eventually, you cease to see the spot, but there is no definite moment when you cease to see it; instead, for a while, it is vague whether you see the spot or not.

Third, the Inkspot Argument assumes that time is *not* composed of densely ordered moments. If it were, then there would be no such thing as "the moment before [the inkspot] vanish'd": between any moment when you did not see the inkspot, and any moment when you did, there would be a further moment. But Hume uses his views about our spatial and temporal perceptions to support his views about space and time (§§4–5). On pain of circularity, he cannot rely on the latter to support the former.

However, insofar as it is plausible that we can have only finitely many *ideas*, it is also plausible that we can have only finitely many *impressions*.[9] Instead of using the Inkspot Argument, Hume could use this claim to argue that our spatial and temporal impressions are only finitely divisible, along the lines of the Argument from Limited Capacity.

Lastly, let us consider Hume's third claim about the intrinsic features of our perceptions: every part of a spatial perception is colored or tangible. He does not state this outright, but he is committed to it, for at least two reasons. First, he claims that everything extended – hence, every spatial perception – is wholly composed of colored or tangible parts (T 1.2.3.15–16; SBN 38–39). Second, he holds that our visual impressions are colored or, perhaps better, are instances of color (T 1.1.6.1; SBN 15–16). Therefore, the simple parts of an extended idea copied from any visual impression must also be colored. Presumably, Hume would accept similar claims about tactile impressions and ideas – that each of them must have (or be an instance of) some tactile quality, such as a degree of heat or cold.

This section has focused on three of Hume's claims about our spatial and temporal perceptions: they are complex perceptions composed of simple perceptions in spatial or temporal arrangements; they are only finitely divisible; and spatial perceptions' simple parts are colored or tangible. The remaining sections aim to show how these claims about our perceptions allow him to defend his views about space and time, and how these views, in turn, allow him to answer Bayle's and Clarke's theistic arguments.

§4 Finite divisibility

Let us now consider Hume's view of divisibility, and how it allows him to answer Bayle's divisibility-based argument for fideism. Hume claims that, as far as we can conceive them, extended and enduring things of finite size are composed of finitely many simple or indivisible parts (T 1.2.2.1–2; SBN 29–30). If he can show that this claim is coherent, then he can answer Bayle's argument, which has the premise that there is no coherent account of an extended thing's parts (see §1, above).

Hume's main argument for his view of divisibility uses the premise that our simple visual and tactile ideas "are adequate representations of the most minute parts of extension" (T 1.2.2.1;

SBN 29). This premise may seem to beg the question, by assuming that extended things have indivisible (or "most minute") parts. But all Hume means here is that "there is nothing more minute than" our simple visual and tactile ideas (T 1.2.2.2; SBN 29) – in other words, that every part of an extended thing is at least as large as one of these simple ideas (Baxter 2009: 110). This is not to assume that extended things have indivisible parts: it allows that each of their parts has further parts, and so is larger than a simple visual or tactile idea.

Using this premise, Hume argues as follows (T 1.2.2.1–2; SBN 29–30):

[1]   Every part of an extended thing is at least as large as a simple visual or tactile idea.
[2]   If [1], then every extended thing with a certain number of parts is at least as large as a spatial idea composed of the same number of simple ideas.
[3]   A spatial idea composed of infinitely many simple ideas is infinitely large.

Therefore,

[4]   Every extended thing with infinitely many parts is infinitely large. (From 1, 2, 3)

Therefore,

[5]   Every extended thing of finite size has only finitely many parts. (From 4)

(At T 1.2.2.4 (SBN 31), Hume claims that a parallel argument would show that nothing of finite duration is composed of infinitely many successive, temporal parts.)

Let us call this the Argument from Adequate Ideas. It has a serious shortcoming. In asserting premise [2], Hume assumes that an extended thing's size depends only on the sizes and number of its parts. But this is false. An extended thing's size also depends on *how its parts are related*. If infinitely many extensionless points are densely ordered, then they may compose something of finite length. (For example, in mathematics, a line segment is regarded as containing infinitely many, densely ordered points.) But if infinitely many extensionless points are *not* densely ordered – if they are related so that, between two adjacent points, there can be no further point – then they will compose something of infinite length. So, extended things of different lengths – one finite, the other infinite – can have the same number of same-sized parts, contrary to Hume's assumption.[10]

Hume may reply that our simple visual and tactile ideas cannot be densely ordered; therefore, the parts of extension they adequately represent cannot be densely ordered, either (T 1.2.2.1–2; SBN 29–30). But he has not shown that our simple ideas cannot be densely ordered. At most, he has shown that they cannot be densely ordered *in a mind of limited capacity*. This does not imply that they cannot be densely ordered, period. Perhaps they can be, if located in an unlimited mind. (In Hume's view, ideas do not essentially belong to the mind that has them: numerically the same ideas could belong first to one mind, then to another – hence, could belong first to a limited mind, then to an unlimited one. See T 1.4.2.39–40; SBN 207–208.)

So, the Argument from Adequate Ideas is unpersuasive. But Hume's views about our spatial and temporal perceptions afford him an alternative argument for his desired conclusion. Assuming it is successful, the Argument from Limited Capacity shows that we cannot form an extended idea that is infinitely divisible; a parallel argument would show that none of our extended impressions is infinitely divisible (§3). So, we have not had, and cannot form, an infinitely divisible perception. *Being infinitely divisible* is an intrinsic feature. So, by the Constraint Principle, we cannot conceive of anything as being infinitely divisible. So, we cannot conceive an extended thing of finite size as being infinitely divisible. And so, as far as we can conceive them, extended things of finite size are only finitely divisible. (A parallel argument would support Hume's view that, as far as we can conceive it, nothing of finite duration is divisible into infinitely many temporal parts.)

This argument supports Hume's desired conclusion, while avoiding the shortcoming of the Argument from Adequate Ideas. Of course, it is only as persuasive as the Argument from Limited Capacity and the Constraint Principle, whose correctness it assumes.

If Hume's account of divisibility is coherent, then Bayle is incorrect to say that there is no coherent account of an extended thing's parts, and so Bayle's divisibility-based argument for fideism is unsound. But Hume's account may seem vulnerable to one of Bayle's objections: simple parts are extensionless – a claim Hume also accepts (T 1.2.4.3; SBN 40) – but extensionless parts cannot compose something extended. As Bayle puts it, "several nonentities of extension joined together will never make up an extension" (1991: 359–360).

We can interpret Bayle's objection in two ways. When he calls extensionless simples "nonentities of extension," he might mean that they do not really exist in nature – that they are merely mathematical abstractions from, not real constituents of, extended things. Hume can readily answer this. Although they are extensionless, the simple things his theory posits are not "nonentities," in this sense: they have sensible qualities, like color and solidity; hence, they must really exist in nature (T 1.2.4.3; SBN 40).

However, we might interpret Bayle as arguing that, even if extensionless simples really exist in nature, they cannot compose something extended because they lack extension themselves. How could we create something extended by combining parts that are each extensionless? Again, though, Hume has an answer. He indicates that, as far as we can conceive them, two simple, colored points can be placed next to each other, in such a way that no further point can be placed between them (T 1.2.4.6; SBN 41). Two such points are at the smallest possible distance from each other; they are the endpoints of the shortest possible line. And, where there is a line, there is extension – in this case, the shortest possible extension, but extension nonetheless. So, as far as we can conceive them, extensionless simples can compose something extended, given that they can be placed at smallest possible distances from each other.[11]

I conclude that, given his views about our spatial and temporal ideas – in particular, the Argument from Limited Capacity and the Constraint Principle – Hume can defend his view about the finite divisibility of extended and enduring things. This view allows him to answer Bayle's divisibility-based argument for fideism.

§5 Empty space and duration without change

Lastly, let us consider Hume's view of vacua and things that endure without changing, and how this view allows him to answer the vacuum-based arguments for theism given by Bayle and Clarke. Bayle's article on Zeno of Elea provides helpful background here. Bayle distinguishes two conceptions of a vacuum (1991: 380). First, a vacuum may be conceived as "a positive being": a real, existing thing that is extended but (unlike a body) is immobile, indivisible, penetrable, and lacking sensible qualities such as color, heat and cold, and so forth. Let us call a vacuum, conceived in this first way, a *positive vacuum*. Second, a vacuum may be conceived as a mere absence or "privation" of bodies; for Bayle, this is to say that a vacuum "has no reality" and "properly speaking . . . is nothing." So conceived, a vacuum is akin to a hole (an absence of matter) or a shadow (an absence of light). Let us call a vacuum, conceived in this second way, a *privative vacuum*.

Newton and Clarke purport to be able to conceive of a positive vacuum. In their view, a vacuum is an empty region of "absolute space," which they take to be a real, existing thing that is independent of bodies and their arrangement.[12] In the *Demonstration*, Clarke relies on the supposed conception of a positive vacuum. For example, his argument that there is a necessary, immaterial being assumes that we can conceive of space or "immensity" as a positive vacuum – as something that can exist, even if there are no bodies to occupy it (Clarke 1998: 13).

Hume argues that we cannot conceive of a positive vacuum: "the idea of space or extension is nothing but the idea of visible or tangible points distributed in a certain order"; therefore, "we can form no idea of a vacuum, or space, where there is nothing visible or tangible" (T 1.2.5.1; SBN 53). We have seen that, in his view, every extended perception is composed of simple perceptions that are colored or tangible (§3). Taken together with the Constraint Principle, this implies that we cannot conceive of something as extended but not composed of colored or tangible points. But a positive vacuum is, precisely, something extended yet lacking sensible qualities. So, we cannot conceive of a positive vacuum.

If this argument is correct, then Hume has grounds for rejecting Clarke's vacuum-based arguments for theism: he can say that Clarke's arguments are unintelligible because their supposed subject matter – a positive vacuum – is, in fact, inconceivable.

Hume realizes that his conclusion may seem incredible. Whether or not there are any positive vacua, the fact that we debate this question seems to show that it is intelligible – and if it is intelligible, then we must be able to conceive of a positive vacuum (T 1.2.5.2; SBN 54). Further, it may be objected that Hume's own views about the separability of ideas imply that we can conceive of a positive vacuum: our ideas of a room's contents are separable from those of its walls, floor, and ceiling; so, we can conceive of its contents' being annihilated, while its walls, floor, and ceiling remain in place; and this involves conceiving of a positive vacuum in the room, where its contents used to be (T 1.2.5.3; SBN 54–55). Hume answers that we do not really debate the existence of a positive vacuum, and do not form an idea of a positive vacuum when thinking about the empty room – we have only an illusion as of doing these things.

The illusion arises, Hume argues, because we tend to confuse two kinds of idea. Neither represents a positive vacuum. But confusing the two leads us to talk as if we can conceive such a vacuum. The first kind of idea represents what Hume calls a "real extension" (T 1.2.5.14; SBN 58): numerous points placed adjacently (that is, at smallest possible distances from each other), like the letters A through E in this diagram:

ABCDE

The second kind of idea represents what Hume calls an "invisible and intangible distance" (T 1.2.5.16, 1.2.5.24; SBN 59, 63): points arranged in such a way that further points could be placed between them, without having to move any of the original points, like the letters F and G in this diagram:

F   G

These two kinds of ideas are crucially different. An idea of a real extension represents something extended between the two endpoints: namely, the line composed of the intervening points. In contrast, an idea of an invisible and intangible distance does not represent anything extended between the distant points. Hume says that it represents only "darkness" – the "negation" or absence of visible (and tangible) things – between the two distant points (T 1.2.5.11; SBN 57). In other words, it represents privative vacuum.

Despite their differences, Hume claims that these two kinds of ideas resemble each other in several ways. For example, an idea of an invisible, intangible distance can become an idea of a real extension, if further ideas are added to it (T 1.2.5.16; SBN 59). According to Hume, these resemblances lead us to confuse the two kinds of idea (T 1.2.5.19; SBN 60). In turn, this leads us to combine forms of speech that are appropriate only to one kind of idea with forms appropriate only to the other (Baxter 2009: 137–138). For example, we may speak of 'points separated by something extended but not colored or tangible.' Here, we combine language appropriate only to the idea of a real extension – 'points separated by something extended' – with language appropriate only to that of an invisible, intangible distance – 'points separated by nothing colored or tangible.' This combination would be appropriate only if we could conceive of a positive vacuum – that is, of something extended but neither colored nor tangible.

This confusion explains why we seem to debate whether there are positive vacua: we use words as if we were conducting a meaningful debate, but in fact we are not, because we cannot form suitable ideas corresponding to those words. (In Hume's view, a form of words is meaningful only if suitable ideas correspond to it: see Ab. 7; SBN 648–649.) It also explains why we mistakenly suppose that thinking about the emptied room involves conceiving of a positive vacuum. Imagining the room's contents annihilated leaves us with an idea of invisible, intangible distances (or "fictitious" distances) between its walls, floor, and ceiling (T 1.2.5.23; SBN 62–63) – not an idea of a positive vacuum. But we talk as if this is an idea of a positive vacuum, thanks to our confusion of ideas and words.

Some scholars protest that an idea of an invisible, intangible distance represents the kind of vacuum that Hume says we cannot conceive – and so, by allowing that we have this idea, Hume inadvertently contradicts himself.[13] But this is incorrect. Hume aims to show that we cannot conceive of a *positive* vacuum. To represent two colored or tangible things as separated by a positive vacuum, an idea must represent *a third positive being* – the vacuum – in addition to the two colored or tangible things. An idea of an invisible, intangible distance does not do this. It represents two colored or tangible things as distant from each other, but does not represent any positive being located between them; it represents only a "negation" or absence of colored or tangible things between them. So, an idea of invisible, intangible distance does not represent the kind of vacuum that Hume says we cannot conceive: a positive vacuum. (The objection may arise from conflating the two conceptions of vacuum that Bayle distinguishes.)

Hume's account of "invisible and intangible distance" allows him to answer Bayle's vacuum-based argument for fideism. Recall that Bayle's article on Zeno of Elea aims to support fideism by arguing that there is no motion (§1). Bayle's vacuum-based argument for fideism is that motion requires a vacuum; but there is no positive vacuum; and privative vacuum is "absurd" or inconceivable; so, there is no motion (1991: 377–380). Hume can reply that privative vacuum is not "absurd" or inconceivable. We can have impressions of objects that are at an "invisible and intangible distance" from each other: for example, we can have a complex impression of two luminous bodies that appear "separate[ly]" in an otherwise completely dark environment (T 1.2.5.10; SBN 57). An idea copied from such an impression represents an instance of "invisible and intangible distance" or privative vacuum. So, privative vacuum is conceivable. Hume argues that motion requires only "invisible and intangible distance" or privative vacuum, not a positive vacuum: if two bodies are arranged like the letters F and G, in the diagram above, then a third body can move in between them without either of these two bodies having to move out of its way (T 1.2.5.24; SBN 63). So, Bayle's vacuum-based argument fails to show that there is no motion.

I conclude that, given his views about our spatial perceptions – in particular, his view that they are composed of colored or tangible parts – Hume can support his view that positive vacuum is inconceivable; and this view does not conflict with his further claim that we can conceive of "invisible and intangible distance," as some scholars allege. Hume's views about positive vacuum and "invisible and intangible distance" allow him to answer theistic arguments given by Clarke and Bayle.

Hume claims that we are subject to an illusion about time analogous to the one about spatial vacua (T 1.2.5.28–29; SBN 64–65). This results from confusing an idea of a succession of things, which represents both duration and change, with an idea of an unchanging or "stedfast" object, which represents neither duration nor change. Consequently, we talk as if we can conceive of something enduring (like the succession) yet unchanging (like the steadfast object). Hume's account of this illusion about time plays an important role in his philosophy. He argues that we must succumb to it, in order to form an idea of identity (T 1.4.2.29; SBN 200–201). This account of identity shapes his accounts of our beliefs about the external world (T 1.4.2.31–43; SBN 201–210), substances (T 1.4.3.3–4; SBN 220), and personal identity (T 1.4.6.5–21; SBN 253–262).

Conclusion

Hume does not establish his views about our spatial and temporal perceptions beyond reasonable doubt. Nonetheless, the arguments by which he supports them – especially the Argument from Limited Capacity – deserve our serious consideration. Given these views, he can defend his two main claims about space and time: that things of finite extent and duration, as far as we can conceive them, are only finitely divisible; and that we cannot conceive of a positive vacuum (though we can conceive of "invisible and intangible distance"). Based on these claims, he can answer Bayle's and Clarke's theistic arguments.[14][15]

Notes

1　For example, see Flew (1976).
2　For example, see Falkenstein (2015).
3　For helpful discussion of these arguments, see Russell (2008: 99–103).
4　Hume's letter to Ramsay of August 31, 1737, in Popkin (1964), provides evidence that he means to engage with Bayle on these issues: he recommends Bayle's article on Zeno of Elea, which contains the divisibility- and vacuum-based arguments sketched here, as helpful background to the *Treatise*. See also T 1.2.4.3 (SBN 40), where Hume engages with Bayle, and T 1.2.4.15 (SBN 44), where he borrows from him; cf. Bayle (1991: 359–362, 370). For evidence that Hume means to engage with Clarke on the vacuum, see Russell (2008: 103–105).
5　Here, I am indebted to Baxter (2009) and Ainslie (2010).
6　For the claim that, in Hume's view, we conceive objects as having intrinsic spatial and temporal features by forming perceptions that themselves have these features, see Falkenstein (2015) (especially pages 36–37 and 48–50), to whom I owe the terms 'spatial perception' and 'temporal perception'.
7　For a discussion and reply, see Falkenstein (1997: 196–198).
8　Norman Kemp Smith (1941: Chapter XIV) objects that if a spatial or temporal idea involves a "disposition" of simple ideas, then it has an ultimate part – the "disposition" – that is not copied from any simple impression, contrary to Hume's own views. Falkenstein (1997) and Garrett (1997: 52–54) reply to this objection on Hume's behalf; Coventry (2010) critically discusses their replies and proposes an alternative.
9　For this point, see Garrett (2015: 62).
10　For this point, see Falkenstein (2015: 60).
11　For this line of response to Bayle, see Allison (2008: 39–44) and Falkenstein (2015: 37–39).
12　For Newton's view of absolute space, see his Scholium to the *Principia* (Newton 1999: 408–415). For Clarke's, see his correspondence with Leibniz, especially his Fourth Reply and the footnote to §§36–48 of his Fifth Reply (Leibniz and Clarke 1956: 45–54, 120–121).
13　For example, Allison (2008: 57) and Falkenstein (2015: 62–63).

14 For further reading, see Baxter (2009) for a clear, comprehensive and illuminating defense of Hume's views on space and time, and Bayle's (1991) article on Zeno of Elea, which provides crucial background to Hume on space and time. For an historically rich discussion of Hume's arguments about space and time, focusing on their theological significance, see Russell (2008).

15 Thanks to Eric Ash, Simone Chess, Thomas Cottrell, Hilary Fox, Don Garrett, Eric Hiddleston, Bosik Kim, Sean Levenson, and the editors of this volume.

References

Ainslie, D. C. (2010) "Adequate Ideas and Modest Scepticism in Hume's Metaphysics of Space," *Archiv für Geschichte der Philosophie* 92: 39–67.

Allison, H. E. (2008) *Custom and Reason: A Kantian Reading of the First Book of the Treatise*, New York: Oxford University Press.

Baxter, D. L. M. (2009) "Hume's Theory of Space and Time in Its Skeptical Context," in D. F. Norton and J. Taylor (eds.), *The Cambridge Companion to Hume*, 2nd edn, New York: Cambridge University Press, pp. 105–146.

Bayle, P. (1991) *Historical and Critical Dictionary*, trans. R. H. Popkin, Indianapolis, IN: Hackett Publishing.

Clarke, S. (1998) *A Demonstration of the Being and Attributes of God and Other Writings*, edited by E. Vailati, New York: Cambridge University Press.

Coventry, A. (2010) "Hume's System of Space and Time," *Logical Analysis and History of Philosophy* 13: 76–89.

Falkenstein, L. (1997) "Hume on Manners of Disposition and the Ideas of Space and Time," *Archiv für Geschichte der Philosophie* 79: 179–201.

———. (2015) "The Ideas of Space and Time and Spatial and Temporal Ideas in *Treatise* 1.2," in D. C. Ainslie and A. Butler (eds.), *The Cambridge Companion to Hume's Treatise*, New York: Cambridge University Press, pp. 31–68.

Flew, A. (1976) "Infinite Divisibility in Hume's *Treatise*," in D. W. Livingston and J. T. King (eds.), *Hume: A Re-evaluation*, New York: Fordham University Press, pp. 257–269.

Garrett, D. (1997) *Cognition and Commitment in Hume's Philosophy*, New York: Oxford University Press.

———. (2015) *Hume*, New York: Routledge.

Holden, T. (2004) *The Architecture of Matter: Galileo to Kant*, New York: Oxford University Press.

Kemp Smith, N. (1941) *The Philosophy of David Hume*, New York: Palgrave Macmillan.

Leibniz, G. and S. Clarke. (1956) *The Leibniz – Clarke Correspondence*, edited by H. G. Alexander, Manchester: Manchester University Press.

Newton, I. (1999) *The Principia: Mathematical Principles of Natural Philosophy*, trans. and edited by I. B. Cohen and A. Whitman, Berkeley and Los Angeles: University of California Press.

Popkin, R. H. (1964) "So Hume Did Read Berkeley," *Journal of Philosophy* 61: 773–778.

Reid, T. (2002) *An Inquiry into the Human Mind on the Principles of Common Sense*, edited by D. R. Brookes, Edinburgh: Edinburgh University Press.

Russell, P. (2008) *The Riddle of Hume's Treatise: Skepticism, Naturalism, and Irreligion*, New York: Oxford University Press.

7

HUME ON INDUCTION AND PROBABILITY

Frederick F. Schmitt

I begin this review of Hume's treatment of induction and probability by explaining the significance of the category of probability in his psychology. In his most ample presentation of his account of probability (*A Treatise of Human Nature*, Book 1, "Of the Understanding," Part 3, "Of knowledge and probability"), Hume follows tradition by contrasting probability with knowledge as one of two broad, disjoint classes of cognition. However, he departs from tradition in decisively assigning causal inference (i.e. "the inference we draw from cause to effect," T 1.3.6.1; SBN 86) entirely to the class of operations that produce probability rather than to the class of those that produce knowledge. Moreover, he rejects the traditional view that operations that produce probability are cogitative in nature. He argues, to the contrary, that causal inference has a habitual and sensitive character, arising from custom and the association of perceptions: "reason [i.e. causal inference] is nothing but a wonderful and unintelligible instinct in our souls," like the instincts of animals (T 1.3.16.9; SBN 179). Hume generalizes this associationist account of causal inference to many other probable inferences. After sketching this generalization, I will turn to the focus of the literature on Hume on probability – the question whether he is a skeptic about causal inference. Both his argument for classifying causal inference under probability and his associationist account of it have customarily been interpreted as intended to support such skepticism. But we will see some advantages in nonskeptical interpretations.

Knowledge and probability

Hume's position in the history of theories of knowledge and probability is most readily appreciated by comparing his views with those of Locke. Like Locke, Hume takes knowledge to be certain and probability to be uncertain. He follows Locke in treating both knowledge and probability as cognitions of relations that derive from comparisons – comparisons of ideas in the case of knowledge, and of objects in the case of probability. For Locke, the certainty of knowledge is afforded by its being a perception of the agreement or disagreement of the ideas compared. By contrast, the uncertainty of a probable conclusion derives from its reliance on a "presumption" of relations "extraneous" to the relation of the objects compared (Locke, *An Essay Concerning Human Understanding*, E IV.xv.3; Nidditch 655). In explaining the difference between knowledge and probability, Hume preserves something closely analogous to Locke's contrast between a perception of ideas and a presumption of extraneous relations:

knowledge is of a relation that depends "entirely on the ideas" compared, such as resemblance or proportion in number; whereas probability is of a relation that "may be chang'd without any change in the ideas" (T 1.3.1.1; SBN 69), such as spatio-temporal contiguity or identity. For Hume, knowledge is a product of intuition and demonstration (though he forgoes Locke's additional category of sensitive knowledge, and he allows knowledge of perceptions by consciousness where Locke treats this as intuitive knowledge); and induction (in the sense of an inference that depends on repeated experience of objects with certain qualities) belongs to probability. So far, Hume's account of knowledge and probability is traditional and not far from Locke's.

But Hume departs from Locke in important respects. For one thing, he holds that both knowledge and probability involve belief, whereas for Locke knowledge involves perception of the relation of ideas rather than belief, and judgment (the attitude in Locke closest to belief in Hume) contrasts with knowledge. Hume conceives of belief, even that involved in knowledge, as "*more properly an act of the sensitive, than of the cogitative part of our natures*" (T1.4.1.8; SBN 183), whereas Locke conceives of judgment as cogitation. And Hume departs radically from Locke in excluding the relation of causation from the objects of knowledge, admitting it as an object of probability only. Hume is driven to assign causation to probability by his argument that we cannot know causal conclusions by demonstration. For a demonstration of an effect from a cause would require that the cause implies the effect; yet "there is no object, which implies the existence of any other" (T 1.3.6.1; SBN 86). Hume subsequently argues that causal inference must be assimilated to induction. We will consider this argument at length below.[1]

Hume's argument for assigning causal inference to probability comes at a price. His premise that a cause does not imply its effect requires him to reject the traditional metaphysical view that a cause necessitates its effect in the sense of implying it and that causal inference proceeds by a perception of this relation of necessitation (thereby producing an idea of necessity). Hume wishes, however, to preserve something of the view that a cause necessitates its effect and that we have an idea of such necessity. He does so by maintaining that something that passes for an idea of necessity results from, rather than affords, the causal inference: "Perhaps 'twill appear in the end, that the necessary connexion depends on the inference, instead of the inference's depending on the necessary connexion" (T 1.3.6.3; SBN 88; cf. T 1.3.3.9; SBN 82; T 1.3.2.13; SBN 78; EHU 7.2.27–29; SBN 74–77). We form the idea of necessity as part of "an illusion of the imagination" (T 1.4.7.5–6; SBN 266–267) in which an idea of mental determination is "*wrong apply'd*" to the cause (T 1.3.14.14; SBN 162).

This explanation of our ascription of necessity to the cause rests on Hume's associationist account of causal inference. According to this account, a causal inference arises in this way. We experience a conjunction of objects of two species; this leads to the formation of a "habit" of "association" of a present impression of an object of the one species with an idea of an object of the other species (T 1.3.12.2; SBN 130–131). When the habit is strong enough, the association produces a belief in or "full assurance" of the latter object. The causal inference itself is a "transition" from the impression to this belief, and our belief in the object is or is accompanied by a belief that the object is a cause or effect, presumably in virtue of the belief's having been produced by this transition. Something that passes for an idea of necessity is produced in this way: whenever we manifest the habit of association, we feel a determination to infer from the impression of the one object the belief in the other. From this feeling we form an idea of this mental determination, which we then wrongly apply to the cause itself, giving us a sense that the cause necessitates. Hume leaves it ambiguous whether we have a genuine idea of causal necessity: "Either we have no idea of necessity, or necessity is nothing but that determination of the thought to pass from causes to effects and from effects to causes, according to their experienc'd union" (T 1.3.14.22; SBN 166). This is as far as Hume goes in making room for an idea of necessity in our ordinary idea of cause.[2]

Associationist accounts of probable inferences

Hume generalizes his associationist psychology of causal inference to diverse probable inferences. The psychological differences among these inferences are explained by differences in the associations they make, as are differences in their epistemic value and practical significance:

(1) A *proof* is a transition that manifests a habit formed by experience of sufficiently many and "constant" (i.e. exceptionless) conjunctions of objects, where objects of each species sufficiently resemble others of the species, producing a "full assurance" in an unobserved object and cause (T 1.3.11.2; SBN 124; T 1.3.13.19; SBN 153–154). A proof that "the sun will rise to-morrow" yields a certain and not a merely probable belief, despite falling short of making the contrary inconceivable, as in cases of knowledge.

(2) An *inference to* a mere *probability of causes* is an "imperfect" transition, from a habit formed by experience either of few conjunctions or of a less-than-constant conjunction (T 1.3.12.2–4; SBN 131). A merely probable inference produces "a kind of hesitating belief" in a causal conclusion, where the degree of hesitation is inversely proportioned to the number and frequency of observed conjunctions of objects of the two species (T 1.3.12.2–6; SBN 130–132). Hume speaks as if we should proportion our belief to the evidence (e.g. inversely proportion our hesitation to the frequency of the conjunction, as the "full assurance" of a proof is proportioned to the constancy of the conjunction), but he does not make clear that this provides a degree of justification for our hesitating beliefs equal to that provided by the certainty of proofs. Hume applies his account of inference to the probability of causes to the case of inference from testimony, which is "derived from no other principle than our observation of the veracity of human testimony, and of the usual conformity of facts to the reports of witnesses" (EHU 10.1.5; SBN 111). Like other inferences to the probability of causes, inferences from testimony are often made uncertain by a "contrariety of evidence . . . derived from several different causes; from the opposition of contrary testimony; from the character or number of the witnesses; from the manner of their delivering their testimony; or from the union of all these circumstances" (EHU 10.1.7; SBN 112): "We balance the opposite circumstances, which cause any doubt or uncertainty; and when we discover a superiority on any side, we incline to it; but still with a diminution of assurance, in proportion to the force of its antagonist" (EHU 10.1.6; SBN 112). Hume relies on this calculus to argue that testimony to miracles gives us no probability at all: "A miracle is a violation of the laws of nature . . . a direct and full *proof*, from the nature of the fact, against the existence of any miracle" (EHU 10.1.12; SBN 114–115).

(3) Chance "is merely the negation of a cause" and requires us "to leave the imagination perfectly indifferent" between the existence and the non-existence of the object (T 1.3.11.4; SBN 125). Accordingly, in an *inference to* a *probability of chances*, we divide the possible outcomes of the roll of a die into equal chances, and a superior number of chances causes the mind to affirm a belief in one of these outcomes. Hume argues, in a manner parallel to his famous argument regarding proofs at T 1.3.6 (discussed below), that an inference to a probability of chances does not produce belief by "demonstration nor probability" (T 1.3.11.7; SBN 126). Rather, the circumstances of the inference "direct us to the whole six sides [of the die] after such a manner as to divide its force equally among them," and "as the same figure is presented by more than one side . . . the impulses belonging to all these sides must

re-unite in that one figure," producing a hesitating belief that the die will land on one of these sides, which belief is proportioned to their number (T 1.3.11.12; SBN 129; see Loeb 2008: 121).

(4) An *analogical* inference is a transition from a habit formed by an observed conjunction and yielding a causal conclusion, in which the objects of one or the other species do not closely resemble one another (T 1.3.12.25; SBN 142). The conclusion of an analogical inference approximates the certainty of the conclusion of a proof in proportion to how closely the two objects (one observed on the occasion of inference and the other inferred from it) resemble the previously observed conjoined objects. Hume applies the requirement of resemblance for an analogical inference to raise doubts about the argument from design for the existence of God. The dissimilarity of God to the observed causes of order, and of the universe to machines, prevents the argument from design from conferring high probability on its conclusion (EHU 11.12–27; SBN 136–147; DNR 2; see Loeb 2008: 118–120).

(5) We sometimes infer by the application of a *general rule*. We form a general rule by an analogical inference. General rules are sometimes "rashly formed" by associating objects that little resemble one another: "In proportion as the resemblance [between the objects observed to be conjoined] decays, the probability [of the general rule] diminishes; but still has some force as long as there remain any traces of the resemblance" (T 1.3.13.8; SBN 147). Such rashly formed general rules may then explain "prejudice": "An *Irishman* cannot have wit, and a *Frenchman* cannot have solidity; for which reason, tho' the conversation of the former in any instance be visibly very agreeable, and of the latter very judicious, we have entertain'd such a prejudice against them, that they must be dunces or fops in spite of sense and reason" (T 1.3.13.7; SBN 146). Hume does not, however, make it clear how the application of a less probable, hence less vivacious, general rule can impart high vivacity to our attribution of a quality visibly lacking in the person to whom we apply it. By using the epithets "prejudice" and "rashly," Hume condemns rashly formed rules and their applications as lacking justification. But he maintains that the use of general rules is essential for correcting rash inferences. We form second-order general rules governing first-order general rules regarding specific instances (such as those of the Irishman and the Frenchman) by a second-order causal inference from our observation of which first-order general rules lead to true conclusions and which do not (see Falkenstein 1997; Loeb 2002: 105–111). And even though we apply a second-order general rule to a rashly formed first-order general rule that is itself applied in a manner contrary to that required by the second-order general rule, so that the two general rules are "set in opposition" to one another, we prefer the second-order general rule "as being more extensive and constant" than the first-order general rule, which is "more capricious and uncertain" (T 1.3.13.11–12; SBN 149–150).

(6) The "Rules by which to judge of cause and effect" listed by Hume in T 1.3.15 are formed by *second-order causal inferences* from our observation of our success and failure in first-order causal inferences. For example, we infer from our winding of the watch that its hands will move, but we are disappointed to discover that they remain still. How are we to correct our error in this case or make future predictions on the basis of our disappointment? Hume notes that an artisan "easily perceives" that the winding "fails of its usual effect, perhaps by reason of a grain of dust, which puts a stop to the whole movement. From the observation of several parallel instances, philosophers form a maxim, that the connexion betwixt all causes and effects is equally necessary, and that its seeming uncertainty in some instances proceeds from the secret opposition of contrary causes" (T 1.3.12.5; SBN 132). By this second-order causal inference, Hume establishes Rule 6 of T 1.3.15, that such

disappointments stem from secret causes. This rule suggests a norm for correcting our error in such a case, by finding the secret cause responsible for disappointing our expectation.

(7) Finally, an *enumerative induction* (in our contemporary sense of the term) is the portion of a causal inference (whether that inference is a proof or a probable inference to a cause) that produces the qualitative conclusion of the inference, i.e. the belief (whether full or hesitating) in the existence of the object, rather than the portion that produces the causal conclusion of the inference, i.e. the belief that the object is a cause (T 1.3.6.15; SBN 93).

Hume's explanation of this variety of inferences by appeal to differences in the associations they make provides a systematic associationist account of a family of probable inferences: "What gives authority to this system is, beside the undoubted arguments, upon which each part is founded, the agreement of these parts, and the necessity of one to explain another" (T 1.3.13.20; SBN 154).

Hume also explains many *non-associative* inferences that belong to the domain of probability in the sense that beliefs they produce fall short of the certainty of knowledge. These include:

"education," i.e., inculcation, or the production of belief by "The frequent repetition of any idea" (T 1.3.9.17; SBN 116);

the propensity to complete a uniformity, of which the inference from coherence to the belief in continued and distinct body is a species (T 1.4.2.22; SBN 198);

the propensity "to compleat the union," of which our tendency to locate taste in a body is a species (T 1.4.5.12; SBN 237–238); and

the propensity to ascribe identity to resembling objects, of which the inference from constancy to the belief in continued and distinct body is a species (T 1.4.2.31–37; SBN 201–206).

Hume highlights the psychological differences between these non-associative operations and causal inference, and he argues that the former are inferior to the latter in justificatory power.

Is causal inference justifying? The skeptical interpretation

We have so far discussed Hume's classification of causal inference under probability and his unified associationist psychology of proofs, merely probable inferences, and induction. I want to turn now to the question that has long occupied the most attention in the Hume literature on causal inference and probable inference more generally: does Hume take causal inference to produce justified (or "just") beliefs?[3]

The traditional answer is negative: Hume is a skeptic about causal inference. I begin by considering the traditional skeptical interpretation of Hume's famous argument of T 1.3.6, which dominated the literature on Hume on causal inference from the 1940s to the 1970s and continues to be influential.[4] I will then turn to the case for reading that argument as committing Hume to the opposite view. After that, we will consider whether Hume argues for skepticism about causal inference in a different place, "Conclusion of this book," T 1.4.7.

According to the skeptical interpretation, Hume's argument of T 1.3.6 poses what we now call the problem of induction: there is an epistemic gap between the premises of a causal inference and its conclusion, making the conclusion arbitrary given the premises and depriving the inference of justification. I set out here the steps in Hume's argument of T 1.3.6.1–7 that would be attributed by an optimal version of the skeptical interpretation.[5]

Hume first rules out that we infer from the cause to the effect by demonstration:

> There is no object that implies the existence of any other if we consider these objects in themselves, and never look beyond the ideas which we form of them. Such an inference wou'd amount to knowledge, and wou'd imply the absolute contradiction and impossibility of conceiving any thing different.
>
> (T 1.3.6.1; SBN 86–87)

From the result that causal inference is not demonstrative inference, Hume infers that it justifies its conclusion only if it is what I will call *an inference from experience via reason*: "the transition from an impression present to the memory or senses to the idea of an object, which we call cause or effect, is founded on past *experience*, and on our remembrance of their *constant conjunction*," and "experience produces the idea by means of the understanding . . . we are determin'd by reason to make the transition" (T 1.3.6.4; SBN 88–89). Thus, Hume's argument assumes that causal inference can justify its conclusion only if the inference is either demonstration or inference from experience via reason. Hume's "determin'd by reason" evidently means that the transition must proceed by a recognition of a connection between the impression and an idea of the cause or effect. For he proposes that inference from experience via reason "wou'd proceed upon that principle, *that instances, of which we have had no experience, must resemble those, of which we have had experience, and that the course of nature continues always uniformly the same*" (T 1.3.6.4; SBN 89).

Hume then asks whether we can be justified in believing the Uniformity Principle:

> let us consider all the arguments, upon which such a proposition may be suppos'd to be founded; and as these must be deriv'd either from *knowledge* or *probability*, let us cast our eye on each of these degrees of evidence, and see whether they afford any just conclusion of this nature.
>
> (T 1.3.6.4; SBN 89)

Hume's asking this question is best explained by attributing the plausible presupposition that an inference from experience via reason relying on the Uniformity Principle justifies its conclusion only if the belief in the Uniformity Principle on which it relies is itself justified.

At this point, according to the skeptical interpretation, Hume argues that no belief in the Uniformity Principle is justified. He notes that a belief in the Uniformity Principle cannot be demonstratively justified, for the same reason that causal inference cannot be a demonstration: "We can at least conceive a change in the course of nature; which sufficiently proves, that such a change is not absolutely impossible" (T 1.3.6.5; SBN 89). Nor can a belief in the Uniformity Principle be justified by an inference from experience via reason. For, as already stated, any such inference is justifying only if it relies on the Uniformity Principle. Such an inference would therefore require a prior belief in the Uniformity Principle, in which case the belief in the Uniformity Principle would produce itself – an impossible causal circularity: "The same principle cannot be both the cause and effect of another" (T 1.3.6.7; SBN 90). Demonstration and inference from experience via reason are, however, the only options for justifying a belief in the Uniformity Principle, for the same reason that, as Hume assumes, demonstration and inference from experience via reason are the only options for operations with which to identify a justifying causal inference. So causal inference cannot justify its conclusion.[6]

Objections to the skeptical interpretation of T 1.3.6

This skeptical interpretation faces two objections.

First, according to the interpretation, in arguing that causal inference is not inference from experience via reason, Hume assumes that the Uniformity Principle can be justified only by demonstration or an inference from experience via reason. But in fact Hume makes no such assumption. He makes only the weaker assumption (in T 1.3.6.4) that the Uniformity Principle is justified only if it is derived either from "*knowledge*" (i.e. from demonstration) or from "*probability*." The crucial point is that Hume does not *assume* that a justifying derivation from probability is restricted to a justifying inference from experience via reason (so e.g. excludes an associative inference). Rather, he *argues* for this claim. More exactly, he argues at T 1.3.6.6–7 for the lemma that, given the hypothesis operative at T 1.3.6.4–7 (as I take it, a hypothesis for the reductio, that causal inference is an inference from experience via reason), a belief in the Uniformity Principle is justified only if it is produced by an inference from experience via reason.

Hume's argument for this lemma is the following:

(a) By an earlier argument (presented at T 1.3.2.2; SBN 73–74), only causal inference can justify a belief in an unobserved object, given an observed object: "'tis the only [inference], on which we can found a just inference from one object to another" (T 1.3.6.7; SBN 89).

(b) Belief in the Uniformity Principle is a belief in unobserved objects, given observed objects.

(c) So only causal inference can justify the Uniformity Principle: "The only connexion or relation of objects, which can lead us beyond the immediate impressions of our memory and senses, is that of cause and effect" (T 1.3.6.7; SBN 89).

(d) So if the Uniformity Principle is justified by probable inference (the option under consideration at T 1.3.6.6–7), it must be justified by causal inference.

(e) Then by the hypothesis operative at T 1.3.6.4–7 (a hypothesis for the reductio, that causal inference is an inference from experience via reason), it follows that the Uniformity Principle is justified by probable inference only if it is produced by an inference from experience via reason. This is the lemma that was to be proved.

In the remainder of his argument of T 1.3.6.6–7, Hume draws a contradiction from this lemma given the option under consideration at T 1.3.6.6–7, that the Uniformity Principle is justified by probable inference. For the lemma entails that given this option, the Uniformity Principle must be justified by an inference from experience via reason. Yet as Hume has already claimed, any justifying inference from experience via reason must rely on the Uniformity Principle. From this it follows that a belief in the Uniformity Principle must be produced by a belief in the Uniformity Principle – an impossible causal circularity. The argument of T 1.3.6.4–7, then, so far shows that, under the operative hypothesis that causal inference is an inference from experience via reason, the Uniformity Principle is not justified, and so on that hypothesis causal inference cannot be justifying. This result of course does not entail that the Uniformity Principle is not justified, or that causal inference is not justifying, if causal inference is any operation other than an inference from experience via reason – if it is an associative inference, for example. Since Hume holds that causal inference is an associative inference, it follows that his argument at T 1.3.6.4–7 cannot be designed to establish skepticism about causal inference.

The present objection to the skeptical interpretation, then, is that it omits Hume's actual argument at T 1.3.6.6–7 (to show that under the hypothesis for the reductio that causal inference is an inference from experience via reason, the Uniformity Principle cannot be justified by probability); and in its place attributes an argument from an assumption not expressed in the text: that the Uniformity Principle is justified only if it is produced either by demonstration or inference from experience via reason. The text in fact supports reading Hume as not accepting this assumption. For if he did accept it, he could argue from it directly to the result (one he desires, on the skeptical interpretation) that the Uniformity Principle cannot be justified by probability (since he has already claimed that inference from experience via reason must proceed by the Uniformity Principle, and so he can infer that it cannot produce the Uniformity Principle without causal circularity). This is a key point. For if Hume does not accept the assumption in question, he can hold, consistently with the argument of T 1.3.6.1–7, that the Uniformity Principle can be justified by causal inference even if causal inference is not demonstration or inference from experience via reason – even if it is an *associative* inference. In this case, Hume's argument of T 1.3.6.4–7 cannot be designed to show that the Uniformity Principle is not justified by any operation, nor that causal inference is not justifying.

This brings us to the second objection to the skeptical interpretation. If, as I have suggested, the argument of T 1.3.6.4–7 purports to show that, under the operative hypothesis that causal inference is an inference from experience via reason, causal inference cannot be justifying, then it establishes a dilemma: either causal inference is not an inference from experience via reason, or it is not justifying. The ultimate conclusion of this argument must then be one or the other horn of this dilemma. The argument cannot establish both horns of the dilemma (as Beebee 2006: 55–56 observes). On the skeptical interpretation, the ultimate conclusion is that causal inference is not justifying. But this cannot be right if the argument is supposed to eliminate inference from experience via reason as an account of causal inference, to clear the way for Hume's associationist view of causal inference. This is why I suggested above that at T 1.3.6.4–7 Hume takes as hypothesis for the reductio that causal inference is an inference from experience via reason.

That Hume aims to eliminate inference from experience via reason as an account of causal inference is explicit as early as T 1.3.6.4, where he sets out the alternatives to identifying causal inference with demonstration: "Whether experience produces the idea by means of the understanding or of the imagination; whether we are determin'd by reason to make the transition, or by a certain association and relation of perceptions" (SBN 88–89). Having eliminated the option that causal inference is inference from experience via reason by the end of T 1.3.6.11; SBN 91–92, Hume decisively affirms associationism about causal inference at T 1.3.6.12:

> When the mind, therefore, passes from the idea or impression of one object to the idea or belief of another, it is not determin'd by reason, but by certain principles, which associate together the ideas of these objects, and unite them in the imagination.
>
> (SBN 92)

The key point here for interpreting the argument of T 1.3.6.1–7 is that Hume uses that argument to show that causal inference is neither demonstrative inference nor inference from experience via reason. Of course, to argue for that conclusion, he must assume that causal inference is justifying.

These are serious objections to the skeptical interpretation of T 1.3.6. I will return below to the question whether Hume commits himself to skepticism about causal inference in T 1.4.7.

The positive epistemological interpretation of the argument of T 1.3.6

Noting that Hume does not aim in T 1.3.6 to establish the epistemological conclusion that causal inference is not justifying, but only the psychological conclusion that it is an associative belief-forming operation, some interpreters go on to deny that he makes any epistemologi-cal claims at all in the course of his argument (Garrett 1997: 91–95; Owen 1999: 113–146). It is undeniable that Hume's primary concern in T 1.3.6, and in *Treatise* 1.3 more broadly, is to develop an associationist psychological account of causal inference. But the second objection to the skeptical interpretation above also tells against a purely psychological interpretation of T 1.3.6, since the objection entails that Hume assumes that causal inference is justifying in the course of his argument. This is the core of what I will call the *positive epistemological interpretation* of T 1.3.6.1–7 (Millican 2002: 132; Loeb 2006; Beebee 2006: 55–56; Schmitt 2014: 145–171; cf. Qu 2014).

On this interpretation, Hume's argument of T 1.3.6.1–7 proceeds as follows. Having shown that causal inference is not demonstrative inference, Hume undertakes at T 1.3.6.4–7 to show that causal inference is not inference from experience via reason, from which he will infer that causal inference is associative inference. To show that causal inference is not inference from experience via reason, he assumes that if causal inference is such an inference, it relies on a belief in the Uniformity Principle. He then asks how we could reach "any just conclusion" of the Uniformity Principle. His insistence on a "just" (i.e. justified) conclusion of the Uniformity Principle assumes that if causal inference is an inference from experience via reason, it relies on a justified belief in the Uniformity Principle. His choice of the belief in the Uniformity Principle as that on which the causal inference must rely is explained if he assumes: that a causal inference is justifying; that a justifying inference must rely on a justified belief; and finally that the belief in the Uniformity Principle is the only justified belief on which a justifying causal inference could rely if it is an inference from experience via reason. Thus, Hume assumes that causal inference is a justifying inference. He proceeds to show that the Uniformity Principle could not be justified by demonstration, because "a change in the course of nature . . . is not absolutely impossible" (T 1.3.6.5; SBN 89). And the Uniformity Principle could not be justified by any probable infer-ence. For the only probable inference (indeed, the only inference) that justifies a belief in the existence of an unobserved object given an observed one is a causal inference, and thus (by the hypothesis for the reductio, that a causal inference is an inference from experience via reason) the justification of the Uniformity Principle would require that the belief in the Uniformity Principle produces itself – an impossible causal circularity.

Why does Hume argue for this conclusion from the stronger assumption that causal infer-ence is justifying regardless of whether it is an inference from experience via reason? Why does he not argue instead from the weaker assumption that if causal inference is an inference from experience via reason, then it is justifying? This weaker assumption would indeed suffice to generate the causal circularity. But no argument from it would be sound. For this assump-tion is not true, unless causal inference is also justifying whether or not it is an inference from experience via reason. The difficulty is that an inference from experience via reason need not be justifying: it may rely on an unjustified Uniformity Principle. Hume must therefore make the stronger assumption that causal inference is justifying whether or not it is an inference from experience via reason.

The assumption that causal inference is justifying is one that Hume must endorse as long as he supports his associationism by the argument of T 1.3.6. He clearly cannot intend it merely as his report of our actual evaluative attitude toward causal inference, whether that of the vulgar or of philosophers, since a mere report of our attitude would not provide a premise from which Hume could argue for his associationism. The assumption is a core theoretical commitment of his philosophy.

Is it merely an assumption, or does Hume have some justification for it? Plausibly he does on the reliability interpretation of justification, according to which causal inference is justifying just in case it tends to produce true beliefs. On this interpretation, the claim that causal inference is justifying is equivalent to the truth of the Uniformity Principle. By Hume's claim of T 1.3.6.7 that only causal inference can justify a belief in the unobserved, the Uniformity Principle can be justified only by a causal inference. And there is in fact evidence that Hume takes our belief in the Uniformity Principle to be justified by a causal inference (T 1.3.8.13–14; SBN 104–105; see Schmitt 2014: 175–194). On the stability interpretation of justification as well (Loeb 2002: 87–98), Hume plausibly takes justification to be available for the assumption that causal inference is justifying, since we have justification for believing that causal inference yields stable beliefs, as required for it to be justifying on that interpretation.

Further evidence for a positive epistemology of causal inference

If Hume's argument for associationism commits him to the view that causal inference is justifying, then we would expect to find evidence outside of T 1.3.6 that he evaluates causal inference positively. We do indeed find extensive evidence of this sort (Garrett 1997: 78; Loeb 2008: 112–114):

(i) Hume applies "just" and its cognates to causal inferences – those of common life (T 1.3.13.3; SBN 144), those of "true" philosophy (T 1.4.3.9; SBN 223), and his own philosophical inferences (T 3.3.5.5; SBN 616). He calls the conclusions of proofs "free from doubt and uncertainty" (T 1.3.11.2; SBN 124) and instances of "knowledge" (T 1.3.8.13; SBN 103; T 1.3.15.2; SBN 173). Indeed, he speaks of "just" philosophy (T 1.4.7.13; SBN 272) only five paragraphs after his deepest expression of skepticism. These are or obviously imply affirmations that causal inference is justifying.

(ii) Hume repeatedly uses causal inference to establish the laws of human nature, some of which he regards as certain. He is explicit that his most important psychological principle, the Copy Principle, rests on an observed constant conjunction (T 1.1.1.8; SBN 4–5) and that he employs analogical inference to establish laws (T 2.1.12.2; SBN 325–326). How rational would it be to construct an entire philosophy by employing causal inference to derive laws of human nature if one at the same time denied, or for that matter, merely hoped but did not accept, that causal inference justifies these laws?

(iii) Hume officially restricts his laws of psychology to generalizations over perceptions ("inferences from the coherence [i.e. constant conjunction] of our perceptions"), rather than speculations about the original causes of perceptions, because the former are certain and the latter uncertain (T 1.3.5.2; SBN 84). This reason for the restriction entails that we can achieve certainty, hence justified belief, by using causal inferences.

(iv) Hume distinguishes better and worse causal inferences (e.g. T 1.3.11–13). How plausible is it that in making such distinctions he is claiming only that the worse causal inferences are not justifying, and the better ones might be justifying? That commitment falls short of distinguishing the better and worse inferences with respect to their justifying power, since it entails only a distinction with respect to our *belief* as to their justifying power.

(v) As I have already noted, Hume argues that the justificatory power of causal inference is greater than that of non-associative non-demonstrative operations – e.g. education, the propensity to complete a uniformity, and the like. How plausible is it that he is merely saying that these other inferences are not justifying, though for all we know causal inference might be justifying?

Here we have substantial confirmation that Hume evaluates causal inference as justifying.

Reconciling positive and negative evaluations of causal inference

I have displayed reasons to doubt that Hume argues for skepticism about causal inference in T 1.3.6 and even to think that his argument rests on a positive evaluation of causal inference. But we must wrestle with the evidence of Hume's skepticism about causal inference from a later section of Book 1, "Conclusion of this book," T 1.4.7.[7] At T 1.4.7.2–7, Hume lists doubts about causal inference that he clearly takes to count to some extent against the justifying power of causal inference. On the basis of these doubts, he delivers his most forthright expression of skepticism in the *Treatise*: "I am ready to reject all belief and reasoning, and can look upon no opinion even as more probable or likely than another" (1.4.7.8; SBN 268–269). It is common to read this sentence as denying that any beliefs, including those produced by causal inference, are justified. But a close look reveals that it expresses only the more modest *skepticism about evaluation*: that we are not justified in evaluating any belief ("can look upon no opinion") as more justified ("probable") than another or indeed as having any justification at all ("reject all belief"). Skepticism about evaluation does not entail that no causal inferences are justifying. This skeptical interpretation of T 1.4.7.8, then, is compatible with the positive epistemological interpretation of T 1.3.6.1–7 attributing the assumption that causal inference is justifying.[8] However, the skeptical interpretation of T 1.4.7.8 does entail that our positive evaluations of causal inferences as justifying are not justified, and this seems to be inconsistent with what is suggested by points (i)–(v) above, that Hume takes a positive evaluation of causal inference to be justified. Writers on Hume's skepticism have attempted to mitigate this apparent inconsistency by maintaining either that it is merely apparent, that it is genuine but harmless, or that it is instrumental to Hume's greater philosophical and practical purposes in the *Treatise*.[9] Here are three such attempts:

(1) According to a *perspectival* interpretation, the justifiedness of Hume's positive evaluations of causal inference as justifying in *Treatise* 1.3 is compatible with his skepticism about evaluation at T 1.4.7.8.[10] For the positive evaluations are justified in virtue of the applicability of standards appropriate to the perspective represented in *Treatise* 1.3, that of common life and science (as codified in the rules of causal inference of T 1.3.15.3–10; SBN 173–175); whereas skepticism about evaluation holds (i.e. the positive evaluations are not justified) in virtue of the applicability of standards appropriate to the perspective represented in T 1.4.7, that of intense philosophical reflection, which requires giving free reign to doubts in a way that we are not required to do in common life and science.

(2) The justifiedness of the positive evaluations of causal inferences as justifying varies with the accumulation of considerations about the justifying power of causal inference (Schmitt 2014: 362–375; cf. Loeb 2002: 88–100). The justifiedness of these evaluations is defeated at T 1.4.7.7 by the "very dangerous dilemma"; this explains Hume's evaluational skepticism at T 1.4.7.8. But afterward this defeater is itself defeated, restoring the justifiedness of the positive evaluations of causal inference as justifying. This defeat of a defeater may be regarded as the result of the development of cognitive resources, in particular the formulation of a principle (the Title Principle, Garrett 1997: 233–237, 2016) that can defeat the defeater. It may also be regarded as the result of a progress of passions that afford recognition of the defeater (cf. Baier 1991: 20).

(3) Hume's positive evaluations of causal inferences as justifying in *Treatise* 1.3, and his suspension of such positive evaluations at T 1.4.7.8 because these are defeated, are two successive attitudes, each justified in turn, in a dialectic that subsequently replaces them with a median attitude that avoids overconfidence and underconfidence (Cummins 1999). The suggestion is that the experience of the doubts of T 1.4.7.2–7 at first justifiedly reduces evaluations

to suspension of judgment; but "nature . . . cures me of this philosophical melancholy and delirium" (T 1.4.7.9; SBN 269); upon this cure, "my animal spirits and passions reduce me to this indolent belief in the general maxims of the world" (T 1.4.7.10; SBN 269); but curiosity about the world returns, until at last "a true skeptic" "studies philosophy in this careless manner," inquiring with "modesty" (T 1.4.7.15; SBN 274), "diffident of his philosophical doubts, as well as of his philosophical conviction" (T 1.4.7.14; SBN 273).

While it is beyond our scope here to choose among these attempts to mitigate the apparent inconsistency between points (i)–(v) and Hume's skepticism about evaluation, I remark that attempts (2) and (3) are mutually compatible.[11]

Notes

1 Hume treats causal inference primarily in *A Treatise of Human Nature* T 1.3.2–16 and T 1.4.7 and in *An Enquiry Concerning Human Understanding* 4–7 and 12. It is a matter of controversy whether Hume's view of causal inference in the latter work departs substantially from his view in the former (Millican 1998: 154–156; 2002: 109; Broughton 2008b: 436–439). However, this controversy is beyond the scope of the present article, which focuses on his view in the *Treatise*. See Garrett 2015 for an overview of Hume on causal inference.

2 We lack space here to discuss the "new Hume" controversy as to whether Hume allows that there is some causal necessity not recognized by our ordinary idea of cause (Read and Richman 2000; Beebee 2006: 75–225; Kail 2007: 77–124).

3 See Morris (2006); Loeb (2008); and Winkler (2016) for surveys of Hume on the epistemology of causal inference. For a case that Hume's "just" belief means justified belief in our contemporary sense of proper belief of the sort required for knowledge in its colloquial sense, see Schmitt (2014: 81–88, 115–128).

4 For skeptical interpretations of T 1.3.6, see Price (1940); Stove (1973); Bennett (1971: 299–304); Penelhum (1975); Stroud (1977, 1991); Kemp Smith (1983: 46, 121, 374–375); Meeker (1998); Winkler (1999; cf. 2016: 214–221); and De Pierris (2015: 197–258).

5 Hume's argument of T 1.3.6 is explicitly about proofs, but he offers a parallel argument for lesser probable inferences to a cause (T 1.3.12.20; SBN 139).

6 I note that some interpreters of the argument of T 1.3.6.1–7 have offered a limited version of the skeptical interpretation, on which the conclusion of the argument is not a fully general skepticism about causal inference but rather the conclusion that causal inference does not produce the certainty of demonstrative or deductive conclusions (e.g. Beauchamp and Rosenberg 1981; Arnold 1983; Broughton 1983, 2008a; Baier 1991: 54–77). But as Garrett observes, taking Hume merely to target such rationalism "cannot account for the structure of Hume's argument, which gives a prominent role to establishing that the Uniformity Thesis cannot be supported by a probable argument" (1997: 91).

7 For interpretations of Hume's skepticism in T 1.4.7, see Popkin (1980); Fogelin (1985: 20–24); Baier (1991: 1–27); Waxman (1994); Singer (1995); Garrett (1997: 205–241; 2006); Cummins (1999); Morris (2000); Loeb (2002); Broughton (2004, 2008b: 429–432); Schmitt (2014: 341–379); De Pierris (2015); and Ainslie (2015: 226–246).

8 See Schmitt (2014: 161, 355–358) for further discussion of the compatibility.

9 For reviews of these attempts, see Broughton (2008b); Durland (2011); and Ainslie (2015: 226–246).

10 For perspectival interpretations, see Williams (1995: 355–359); Fogelin (1998: 163; 2009: 6–7); Broughton (2004, 2008b); and De Pierris (2015: 19–24, 283–306).

11 I wish to thank Angela Coventry, Louis Loeb, and Alex Sager for valuable comments.

References

Ainslie, Donald (2015) *Hume's True Scepticism*, Oxford: Oxford University Press.

Arnold, N. Scott (1983) "Hume's Skepticism about Inductive Inference," *Journal of the History of Philosophy* 21: 31–55.

Baier, Annette C. (1991) *A Progress of Sentiments: Reflections on Hume's "Treatise,"* Cambridge, MA: Harvard University Press.

Beauchamp, Tom L. and Alexander Rosenberg (1981) *Hume and the Problem of Causation*, Oxford: Oxford University Press.

Beebee, Helen (2006) *Hume on Causation*, London: Routledge.

Bennett, Jonathan (1971) *Locke, Berkeley, Hume: Central Themes*. Oxford: Oxford University Press.

Broughton, Janet (1983) "Hume's Skepticism about Causal Inference," *Pacific Philosophical Quarterly* 64: 3–18.

———— (2004) "The Inquiry in Hume's *Treatise*," *The Philosophical Review* 113: 537–556.

————. (2008a) "Hume's Explanation of Causal Inference," in Paul Hoffman, David Owen and Gideon Yaffe (eds.), *Contemporary Perspectives on Early Modern Philosophy: Essays in Honor of Vere Chappell*, Peterborough, ON: Broadview Press, pp. 289–305.

————. (2008b) "Hume's Naturalism and His Skepticism," in Elizabeth Radcliffe (ed.), *A Companion to Hume*, Oxford: Wiley-Blackwell, pp. 477–492.

Cummins, Phillip D. (1999) "Hume's Diffident Scepticism," *Hume Studies* 25: 43–65.

De Pierris, Graciela (2015) *Ideas, Evidence, and Method: Hume's Skepticism and Naturalism Concerning Knowledge and Causation*, Oxford: Oxford University Press.

Durland, Karánn (2011) "Extreme Skepticism and Commitment in the *Treatise*," *Hume Studies* 37: 65–98.

Falkenstein, Lorne (1997) "Naturalism, Normativity, and Scepticism in Hume's Account of Belief," *Hume Studies* 23: 29–72.

Fogelin, Robert (1985) *Hume's Skepticism in the Treatise of Human Nature*, London: Routledge & Kegan Paul.

————. (1998) "Garrett on the Consistency of Hume's Philosophy," *Hume Studies* 15: 161–169.

————. (2009) *Hume's Skeptical Crisis: A Textual Study*, New York: Oxford University Press.

Garrett, Don (1997) *Cognition and Commitment in Hume's Philosophy*, Oxford: Oxford University Press.

————. (2006) "Hume's Conclusions in 'Conclusion of This Book'," in Saul Traiger (ed.), *The Blackwell Guide to Hume's Treatise*, Oxford: Wiley-Blackwell, pp. 151–175.

————. (2015) "Hume's Theory of Causation: Inference, Judgment, and the Causal Sense," in Donald C. Ainslie and Annemarie Butler (eds.), *The Cambridge Companion to Hume's Treatise*, Cambridge: Cambridge University Press, pp. 69–100.

————. (2016) "Reason, Normativity, and Hume's 'Title Principle'," in Paul Russell (ed.), *The Oxford Handbook of Hume*, Oxford: Oxford University Press, pp. 32–53.

Kail, P. J. E. (2007) *Projection and Realism in Hume's Philosophy*, Oxford: Oxford University Press.

Kemp Smith, Norman (1983) *The Philosophy of David Hume: A Critical Study of Its Origins and Central Doctrines*, New York: Garland.

Loeb, Louis E. (2002) *Stability and Justification in Hume's Treatise*, Oxford: Oxford University Press.

————. (2006) "Psychology, Epistemology, and Skepticism in Hume's Argument About Induction," *Synthese* 152: 321–338.

————. (2008) "Inductive Inference in Hume's Philosophy," in Elizabeth Radcliffe (ed.), *Blackwell Companion to Hume*, Oxford: Wiley-Blackwell, pp. 106–125.

Meeker, Kevin (1998) "Hume: Radical Sceptic or Naturalized Epistemologist?" *Hume Studies* 24: 31–52.

Millican, Peter J. R. (1998) "Hume on Reason and Induction: Epistemology or Cognitive Science?" *Hume Studies* 24: 141–159.

————. (2002) "Hume's Sceptical Doubts Concerning Induction," in Peter Millican (ed.), *Reading Hume on Human Understanding: Essays on the First Enquiry*, Oxford: Clarendon Press, pp. 107–173.

Morris, William Edward (2000) "Hume's Conclusion," *Philosophical Studies* 99: 89–110.

————. (2006) "Belief, Probability, and Normativity," in Saul Traiger (ed.), *The Blackwell Guide to Hume's Treatise*, Oxford: Wiley-Blackwell, pp. 77–94.

Owen, David (1999) *Hume's Reason*, Oxford: Oxford University Press.

Penelhum, Terence (1975) *Hume*, London: Palgrave Macmillan.

Popkin, Richard H. (1980) "David Hume: His Pyrrhonism and His Critique of Pyrrhonism," in Richard H. Popkin, Richard A. Watson and James E. Force (eds.), *The High Road to Pyrrhonism*, San Diego: Austin Hill Press, pp. 103–132.

Price, H. H. (1940) "The Permanent Significance of Hume's Philosophy," *Philosophy* 15: 7–37.

Qu, Hsueh (2014) "Hume's Positive Argument on Induction," *Nous* 48: 595–625.

Read, Rupert and Kenneth A. Richman, eds. (2000) *The New Hume Debate*, London: Routledge.

Schmitt, Frederick F. (2014) *Hume's Epistemology in the Treatise: A Veritistic Interpretation*, Oxford: Oxford University Press.

Singer, Ira (1995) "Hume's Extreme Scepticism in I.iv.7," *Canadian Journal of Philosophy* 25: 595–622.

Stove, D. C. (1973) *Probability and Hume's Inductive Scepticism*, Oxford: Clarendon Press.

Stroud, Barry (1977) *Hume*, London: Routledge & Kegan Paul.

———. (1991) "Hume's Scepticism: Natural Instincts and Philosophical Reflection," *Philosophical Topics* 19: 271–291.

Waxman, Wayne (1994) *Hume's Theory of Consciousness*, Cambridge: Cambridge University Press.

Williams, Michael (1995) *Unnatural Doubts: Epistemological Realism and the Basis of Scepticism*, Princeton: Princeton University Press.

Winkler, Kenneth (1999) "Hume's Inductive Scepticism," in Margaret Atherton (ed.), *The Empiricists: Critical Essays on Locke, Berkeley, and Hume*, Lanham, MD: Rowman & Littlefield, pp. 183–222.

———. (2016) "Hume's Skeptical Logic of Induction," in Paul Russell (ed.), *The Oxford Handbook of Hume*, Oxford: Oxford University Press, pp. 191–227.

8

CAUSALITY AND HUME'S FOUNDATIONAL PROJECT

Miren Boehm

The concept of causation is fundamental to all science and philosophy. Both our explanations of changing events and our conceptions of the nature of change itself are formulated in causal language. However, throughout history philosophers have found it rather difficult to agree on the nature of this concept. And this is why Hume writes:

> There is no question, which on account of its importance, as well as difficulty, has caus'd more disputes both among ancients and modern philosophers, than this concerning the efficacy of causes, or that quality which makes them be follow'd by their effects.
>
> (T 1.3.14.3; SBN 156–157)

This passage appears in a section of his masterpiece, *A Treatise of Human Nature*, where Hume anticipates the revolutionary nature of his account of the idea of causation.

Some elements of Hume's theory of causation have been controversial ever since Hume put ink to paper. Hume proposes *two* definitions of the concept of 'cause,' insisting that they are essentially the same, although they appear to be fundamentally different. Hume also famously compares necessity to sounds and other sensible qualities, which we believe are mind-independent properties of objects but turn out to be instead projections of the mind onto the world. Unsurprisingly, there are disputes about the right interpretation of these issues. But for the last 30 years or so interpreters have engaged in contentious and exciting debates over fundamental, core elements of Hume's theory of causation. Indeed, what has been challenged is what seemed most unassailable, what is almost synonymous with the name "Hume," *the regularity theory*, the view that all that causation amounts to in mind-independent world is mere regularity, or what Hume refers to as "constant conjunction." Causation, on this view, reduces to the observable fact that some objects or events are constantly conjoined with other objects or events, without necessity or reason in nature for these constant conjunctions.[1]

The regularity theory can only be challenged, of course, by attacking fundamental structures of Hume's philosophy. Indeed, "New Hume" (Winkler 1991) defenders have questioned the primacy of Hume's theory of ideas, his semantic theory, and his metaphysics.[2] Hume approaches the subject of causation by examining the *idea* of cause, but is Hume's account of this idea an answer to the question of the *nature* of causation? Or is the idea of cause only an account of what causation is *for us*, or what we can *know* of causation? If the latter, does Hume then leave open the metaphysical possibility that there is "real" or mind-independent causation? Hume claims that the meaning of the term 'necessity' is given by the idea associated with it, but what does Hume mean by 'meaning' anyway? And what meaning, if any, bridges over to metaphysics?

The "old–new Hume debate" has generated scores of answers to these and related questions concerning Hume's views on the external world. I believe that the controversy can benefit from a widening of the perspective in which we reflect, more systematically, on the role of ideas in Hume's philosophy, his position on meaning, and his metaphysical (or anti-metaphysical) views. In this chapter, I consider these fundamental questions against the background of what I take to be Hume's overarching philosophical intention, namely to establish his "science of man" as the foundation of the other sciences. This project has a method, with identifiable patterns of argumentation that I think are important to the old–new Hume debate.

Hume introduces his "foundational project" in his first philosophical work, the *Treatise*, and it is in this text that he articulates the project most fully and carries it out most deliberately. Thus, given my aim in this chapter to place Hume's account of our idea of causation against the background of his foundational project, I will appeal mostly to this text for my presentation of Hume's treatment of causation. I start by providing an outline of Hume's approach to the subject of causation, which begins with an examination of our idea of 'cause' and culminates in an account of the idea of necessary connection. I then sketch some of the central moves at the heart of the old–new Hume controversy. This is followed by a discussion of other cases in which Hume appeals to *ideas* to settle central debates within the sciences, which I relate to Hume's foundational project in the *Treatise*. At the end, I return to the old–new Hume debate and assess some of the contested claims against the background of Hume's project.

The idea of 'cause'

Hume's discussion of causation extends over a large part of Book I of the *Treatise*. In *Treatise* 1.3 (SBN 69), entitled "Of Knowledge and Probability," Hume begins by identifying the seven philosophical relations we employ when we reason in general.[3] The relation of causation is one of these relations, and although it does not generate knowledge, Hume recognizes it as exceptional and of utmost importance. The relation of causation, Hume explains, is the only relation "which produces such a connexion, as to give us assurance from the existence or action of one object, that 'twas follow'd or preceded by any other existence or action." Causation, he continues, is the only relation that "informs us of existences and objects, which we do not see or feel" (T 1.3.2.2; SBN 73). Hume's goal then is to "endeavour to explain fully" this relation.

Hume claims to "begin regularly" by considering "the idea of *causation*, and see from what origin it is deriv'd" (T 1.3.2.4; SBN 74–75). So, to understand the relation of causation, Hume begins by examining the *idea* of causation, and to do this, Hume turns to the objects in experience that we are confident are causally connected, in order to discover the relations or circumstances that unite the two causally related objects.[4] He learns that these objects are contiguous to each other and that the cause is prior to the effect. When he enlarges his observations across time, he determines that cause and effect are *constantly conjoined*.

As long as we consider only the *objects* that are causally related, we cannot discern any other relations beyond constant conjunction. But Hume maintains that there is another component of our idea of causation, which is "of much greater importance" than contiguity and priority, namely "NECESSARY CONNEXION" (T 1.3.2.11; SBN 77). Because the source of this idea is not found in objects, it is not something we detect out there, Hume proceeds "to beat about all the neighbouring fields" (T 1.3.2.13; SBN 77–78) in search of the source of the idea of necessary connection. Many pages later, in *Treatise* 1.3.14, entitled "Of the idea of necessary connexion," Hume recaptures his main question, his commitments and his findings:

> *What is our idea of necessity, when we say that two objects are necessarily connected together?* Upon this head I repeat what I have often had occasion to observe, that as we have no idea, that is not deriv'd from an impression, we must find some impression, that gives rise to this idea of necessity, if we assert that we have really such an idea.... For after a frequent repetition, [or constant conjunction] I find, that upon the appearance of one of the objects, the mind is *determin'd* by custom to consider its usual attendant, and to consider it in a stronger light upon account of its relation to the first object.'Tis this impression, then, or *determination*, which affords me the idea of necessity.
>
> (T 1.3.14.1; SBN 155)

The idea of *necessary connection* has its origin in the mind, in the process of causal reasoning, and not in the world we experience. The idea traces back to an impression or determination that is the mind's response to the contribution of sense experience to the idea of causation: constant conjunctions or regularities.[5]

Toward the end of this crucial section, *Treatise* 1.3.14, Hume puts forward two definitions of 'cause.' The first defines 'cause' as:

> an object precedent and contiguous to another, and where all the objects resembling the former are plac'd in like relations of precedency and contiguity to those objects, that resemble the latter.
>
> (T 1.3.14.31; SBN 169–170)

The second defines 'cause' as:

> an object precedent and contiguous to another, and so united with it, that the idea of the one determines the mind to form the idea of the other, and the impression of the one to form a more lively idea of the other.
>
> (T 1.3.14.31; SBN 169–170)

Traditionally, these definitions have been interpreted as answering the question of the meaning of 'cause' by stating the necessary and sufficient conditions for causation. But there are substantial problems with this traditional reading of Hume's definitions. The core problem is this: how can both definitions be taken to specify the necessary and sufficient conditions for causation given that they are, or at least appear to be, very different? The first definition captures regularities in the world, the objects that are constantly conjoined. The second definition appeals to the determination or impression in the mind produced by observed regularities. Obviously, the definitions differ in their meaning or intension, but even more problematically, they also seem to differ in their extension: different objects seem to fall under the scope of each definition.[6] Any pair of objects that are constantly conjoined satisfy the first definition of 'cause.' But, someone can respond with a determination or impression of the mind to observed constant conjunctions that are not, in fact, universal. And there likely are many constantly conjoined objects that are never observed and thus satisfy the first but not the second definition. Did Hume really think that his two definitions were the same, that is, definitions of the same concept? It appears that he did, for in the (first) *Enquiry* Hume once again puts forward two definitions of 'cause,' and again insists that the two definitions are "at bottom the same" (EHU 8.27; SBN 97). But that is not how most interpreters have seen it. Some have argued that only the *first* definition is the true definition of 'cause' for Hume. It alone captures the metaphysics of causation: what causation is independently of the mind. On this view, the second "definition" merely describes what happens when observers witness regularities. Thus, causation just is regularity. Other interpreters, however, insist on the role of necessary connection in the concept of 'cause,' and thus in the definition of 'cause.' Indeed, recall that Hume explicitly states that the element of necessary connection is "of greater importance" than contiguity and priority (T 1.3.2.11; SBN 77). Because in Hume's account of our idea of cause the element of necessary connection is identified with an impression or determination of the mind, the second definition seems to be the true definition of causation. Yet other commentators have maintained that neither definition is a true definition in the sense that neither states the necessary and sufficient conditions for causation.[7] Don Garrett, however, has offered an influential interpretation, which aims to render the two definitions extensionally equivalent by interpreting both as relative to an ideal observer. However, Garrett's reliance on an ideal observer has been challenged recently (Boehm 2014).[8]

Old Hume vs. New Hume

The traditional reading takes Hume's account of our idea of cause to yield the *metaphysical* conclusion that all that causation amounts to in a mind-independent world is constant conjunction or mere regularity. There are no necessary connections in mind-independent nature because Hume's account of our idea of necessary connection identifies a feeling in the mind as source of this idea. Although Hume suggests that the mind somehow projects or "spreads" this feeling onto the world, the fact remains that in mind-independent world all there is to causation is mere regularity.[9]

The step or inference from Hume's account of the idea of 'cause' to the metaphysical, regularity theory is supported by a certain theory of *meaning*. As we have seen, Hume's first definition of 'cause' identifies the "external" conditions for causation: constant conjunction. But there are additional remarks Hume makes about the meaning of "necessity" or its Humean cognates: "force," "energy," "power," and others, which are pivotal to old–new Hume debate. In the *Treatise*, Hume writes: "Necessity, then, is nothing but an internal impression of the mind. . . . Without considering it in this view, we can never arrive at the most distant notion of it, or be able to attribute it either to external or internal objects" (T 1.3.14.20; SBN 164–165). In the *Abstract*:

> The question is, what idea is annex'd to these terms [power or force or energy]. . . . Upon the whole . . . either we have no idea at all of force and energy, and these words are altogether insignificant, or they can mean nothing but that determination of the thought, acquir's by habit, to pass from the cause to its usual effect.
>
> (Ab.26; SBN 656–657)

In the *Enquiry*, Hume comments that

> no ideas, which occur in metaphysics, [are] more obscure and uncertain, than those of power, force, energy, or necessary connexion. . . . it is impossible for us to think of any thing, which we have not antecedently felt, either by our external or internal sense . . . this customary transition of the imagination from one object to its usual attendant, is the sentiment or impression, from which we form the idea of power or necessary connexion.
>
> (EHU 3, 7.4, 7.28; SBN 62, 75–76)

Responding to these and other passages, which I shall refer to as *meaning passages*, Peter Millican, a strong defender of the Old Hume reading, notes that "the ultimate aim of Hume's quest for the impression of necessary connexion is the clarification of meanings." And, Millican continues: "If this is the case, then the result of that quest would seem to imply a constraint on what we can mean by 'necessary connexion,' thus giving rise to the Old Hume interpretation" (Millican 2011: 128).

But *meaning passages* do more than support the regularity theory; they seem to block the very possibility of *having the thought* of mind-independent necessary connections. If the meaning of "necessity" is a feeling in the mind, then when we ask whether there are necessary connections in nature, we are asking something that is not really intelligible. Of course, there is a sense in which we *can* seriously ask the question of whether the mind-independent world contains necessary connections, just as we *can* earnestly ask whether bachelors are married. Such questions, however, merely reveal a fundamental lack of understanding of the meaning of our words; they display only conceptual confusion.

But now consider the following striking, polemical passages. In the *Treatise*, Hume maintains that "we can never penetrate so far into the essence and construction of bodies, as to perceive the principle, on which their mutual influence depends" (T 2.3.1.4; SBN 400–401). In the *Enquiry*, Hume asserts that we are "ignorant . . . of the manner in which bodies operate on each other. Their force or energy is entirely incomprehensible" (EHU 7.1.25; SBN 72). Hume claims that the "ultimate springs and principles are totally shut up from human curiosity and enquiry. . . . The most perfect philosophy of the natural kind only staves off our ignorance a little longer" (EHU 4.1.12; SBN 30–31). Hume insists that "we are ignorant of those powers and forces, on which this regular course and succession of objects totally depends" (EHU 5.2.22; SBN 55). I shall refer to these as *ignorance passages*. In these texts, Hume appears to allow, at least, for the possibility of mind-independent necessary connections. Is Hume deeply confused about the meaning of the term "necessity"? Or did we misinterpret the significance of *meaning passages*?

So here is the crucial puzzle at the heart of the old–new Hume debate: if "necessity" can mean nothing other than a determination or impression of the mind, because that is what the idea of necessity represents, then how *could* we be ignorant of the force or energy or ultimate springs between bodies? How could the force or energy or necessity of objects be hidden from us? This puzzle has prompted a thorough investigation into the status of Hume's theory of ideas, and in particular, Hume's position on meaning.[10]

Old Humeans privilege *meaning passages* and interpret *ignorance passages* as texts in which Hume is not strict in the use of his words. Hume himself, in an important *Enquiry* passage, claims to have used "the word, Power . . . in a loose and popular sense." He then adds that he will proceed to offer a "more accurate explanation of it," and this explanation makes reference to the impression or determination of the mind (EHU 4.2.16n; SBN 33n). This passage gives strong ammunition to Old Humeans who distinguish between genuine meaning, which only terms associated with *ideas* traceable to impressions have, and "loose and popular" meaning. Unlike genuine, empirical meaning, loose meaning is not metaphysically significant. Ken Winkler appeals to this *Enquiry* footnote (EHU 4.2.16n; SBN 33n) to argue for a "retrospective reinterpretation" of Hume's employment of 'necessity' and its cognates (Winkler 2000: 54–55). Anne Jaap Jacobson, in contrast, defends the Old Hume reading by arguing that claims of ignorance of x do not commit one to the belief that x exists. According to Jacobson, in *ignorance passages*, Hume is appealing only to the meaning that *others* give to their words, for dialectical purposes, without endorsing this meaning himself (Jacobson 2000: 163).[11]

New Humeans, in contrast, prioritize *ignorance passages*; they take Hume's language in these texts to be significant, and thus their strategy is to reinterpret the scope of *meaning passages*. Peter Kail points out that despite Hume's account of our *idea* of cause, Hume never argues *directly* against the view that there is more to mind-independent causation than regularity. Kail singles out this *minimal fact*, that Hume never explicitly makes what Kail calls the "anti-realist" argument, as the common thesis that unites all New Humeans (Kail 2000: 254–255). Kail maintains that Hume's account of the idea of cause is an account of *what we can understand or know* about causation, not an account of what causation *is*. Commenting on Hume's two definitions of 'cause,' Kail writes: "the two definitions circumscribe very severely what we can understand by causation, and capture what causation is *for us*. Hume then (at least) allows that what causation *consists* in metaphysically speaking may outrun what we can understand of it" (Kail 2014: 246–247; Kail 2007). Of course, to leave this metaphysical possibility open, we must be able to *think* the possibility; we must be able to form some meaningful thought about this possibility. New Humeans identify a number of alternative cognitive tools, different from *ideas*, which they argue are also genuinely meaningful and metaphysically significant. Some of these "idea-alternates," as I shall refer to them, are *suppositions, assumptions, relative ideas*, and *bare thoughts* (Wright 1983; Wright 2000; Strawson 2000; Kail 2007; Beebee 2006).[12] Kail, in particular, argues that Hume has the resources for constructing a "bare thought" that allows us to think beyond the regularities. I shall discuss this bare thought later (Kail 2007: 83–90).

Despite the differences, Old Humeans and New Humeans share fundamental assumptions. Both conceive of metaphysics as the ultimate prize. Their fight is ultimately over the metaphysics of causation: either causation is mere regularity, or it accommodates mind-independent necessary connections. And both identify meaning as the bridge to Hume's metaphysical views. Old Humeans insist that only *ideas* are genuine bearers of meaning and thus metaphysically significant. New Humeans maintain that ideas only tell us what we can *know* about causation, and idea-alternates are genuinely meaningful and reach beyond the content of ideas to metaphysical possibilities.

In what follows, I do some beating about "the neighbouring fields" myself and consider the role *ideas* play in Hume's discussion of other topics; my aim is to see whether there is a general pattern that we can identify and apply to the particular case of the idea of cause and thus shed light on its implications. As we shall see, Hume appeals to ideas strategically, to adjudicate on discussions concerning the nature of a number of subjects. I connect Hume's discussion and his strategy to the project to establish a foundation for the sciences, which he announces in the introduction to the *Treatise*. Because we are interested in the consequences of Hume's denial of the idea of mind-independent necessary connections, I focus on the implications of Hume's denial of other ideas. I argue that meaning does not appear to be central to Hume's concern, and I raise another possibility for understanding the implications of Hume's denial of ideas.

The nature of ideas before the nature of things; the foundational project

When Hume first approaches the question of the nature of the relation of causation he proceeds, as we saw earlier, to "begin regularly . . . [and] consider the idea of *causation*, and see from what origin it is deriv'd" (T 1.3.2.4; SBN 74). To understand the nature of the relation of causation, we must first understand the nature of the *idea* of causation. This has been indeed Hume's "regular beginning," as he makes explicit in a number of texts before *Treatise* 1.3. Consider the following passage concerning the nature of mathematical points:

> Here, therefore, I must ask, *What is our idea of a simple and indivisible point?* No wonder if my answer appear somewhat new, since the question itself has scarce ever yet been thought of. We are wont to dispute concerning the nature of mathematical points, but seldom concerning the nature of their ideas.
>
> (T 1.2.3.14; SBN 38)

Here Hume argues that prior to the question of the nature of mathematical points is the question of the nature of our *idea* of the mathematical point. Hume also enters the dispute in natural philosophy concerning the Newtonian posit of a vacuum by examining whether we have an idea of a vacuum. Thus he begins *Treatise* 1.2.5:

> If the second part of my system be true, *that the idea of space or extension is nothing but the idea of visible or tangible points distributed in a certain order*, it follows, that we can form no idea of a vacuum, or space, where there is nothing visible or tangible.
>
> (T 1.2.5.1; SBN 53)

Toward the end of *Treatise* 1.2.5, Hume explicitly extends his results about *ideas* to the domain of metaphysics and mechanics: "After this chain of reasoning and explication of my principles, I am now prepar'd to answer all the objections that have been offer'd, whether deriv'd from *metaphysics* or *mechanics*" (T 1.2.5.22; SBN 62). And a few lines later, he explicitly draws an important implication. Hume writes:

> If the *Newtonian* philosophy be rightly understood, it will be found to mean no more. A vacuum is asserted: That is, bodies are said to be plac'd after such a manner, as to receive bodies betwixt them, without impulsion or penetration.
>
> (T 1.2.5n12; SBN 639)

Hume's denial of the idea of a vacuum has implications for the Newtonian philosophy; in particular, it restricts what we can justifiably say about bodies and vacuums in nature (Boehm 2012).

Now consider the beginning of Hume's discussion "Of the idea of necessary connexion" in *Treatise* 1.3.14. Hume starts this section by identifying the debate to which he aims to contribute. He writes:

> There are some, who maintain, that bodies operate by their substantial form; others, by their accidents or qualities; several, by their matter and form . . . the supposition of an efficacy in any of the known qualities of matter is entirely without foundation.
>
> (T 1.3.14.7; SBN 158)

He continues:

> at last [. . .] philosophers [have been obliged] to conclude, that the ultimate force and efficacy of nature is perfectly unknown to us, and that 'tis in vain we search for it in all the known qualities of matter. . . . For some of them, as the *Cartesians* in particular, having establish'd it as a principle, that we are perfectly acquainted with the nature of matter, have very naturally inferr'd, that it is endow'd with no efficacy, and that it is impossible for it of itself to communicate motion, or produce any of those effects, which we ascribe to it.
>
> (T 1.3.14.8; SBN 159)

Hume is here rehearsing a debate about matter, about the efficacy of causes in nature. These are *not* claims about *ideas*. They are claims made within natural philosophy. But now, here is how Hume aims to contribute to these debates within natural philosophy:

> But before they enter'd upon these disputes, methinks it wou'd not have been improper to have examin'd what idea we have of the efficacy, which is the subject of

the controversy. This is what I find principally wanting in their reasonings, and what I shall here endeavour to supply.

(T 1.3.14.3; SBN 156)

Hume makes the same argument about necessity and the idea of necessity in Book 2 of the *Treatise* in "Of liberty and necessity":

> 'Tis universally acknowledg'd, that the operations of external bodies are necessary, and that in the communication of their motion, in their attraction, and mutual cohesion, there are not the least traces of indifference or liberty [. . .] The actions, therefore, of matter are to be regarded as instances of necessary actions; and whatever is in this respect on the same footing with matter, must be acknowledg'd to be necessary. That we may know whether this be the case with the actions of the mind, we shall begin with examining matter, and considering on what the idea of a necessity in its operations is founded, and why we conclude one body or action to be the infallible cause of another.

(T 2.3.1.3; SBN 399–400; see also EHU 8.4; SBN 82)

The question of the *idea* of efficacy is prior to the question of the efficacy of matter and mind.

These passages reveal a common aim and method.[13] The *examination of ideas* is supposed to adjudicate on contested questions within other domains, such as mathematics and natural philosophy. Hume is arguing that the question of the nature of our ideas is *prior* to the question of the nature of mathematical points, the existence of vacuum, and the efficacy of matter. But what is Hume's argument for this *priority*? Hume presents this argument in the introduction to the *Treatise* where he announces his intentions or project for the *Treatise*.

Hume opens the *Treatise* by vividly describing the appalling condition of philosophical systems, identifying the core problem with their "weak foundation" (T Intro. 2; SBN xiii–xiv). Hume quickly announces his intention for the *Treatise*; he aims "to establish a compleat system of the sciences, built on a foundation almost entirely new, and the only one upon which they can stand with any security" (T Intro. 6; SBN xvi). His "science of man" will be foundational to *all* sciences: "there is no question of importance whose decision is not compriz'd in the science of man; and there is none which can be decided with any certainty, before we become acquainted with that science" (T Intro. 6; SBN xvi). The science of man, Hume declares, is "the only solid foundation for the other sciences" (T Intro. 7; SBN xvi). This project is confirmed after the writing of the *Treatise*. In the preface to the *Abstract*, Hume claims that if we take the philosophy of the *Treatise* seriously then "*we must alter from the foundation the greatest part of the sciences*" (Pref. 2; SBN 643). In the *Abstract* itself, he concludes: "This Treatise therefore of human nature seems intended for a system of the sciences" (Ab. 3; SBN 646).

In the introduction to the *Treatise*, Hume puts forward the chief argument that establishes the relation between his science of man and some of the other sciences.

> Even *Mathematics, Natural Philosophy, and Natural Religion*, are in some measure dependent on the science of Man; since they lie under the cognizance of men, and are judged of by their powers and faculties.'Tis impossible to tell what changes and improvements we might make in these sciences were we thoroughly acquainted with the extent and force of human understanding, and cou'd explain the nature of the ideas we employ, and of the operations we perform in our reasoning.

(T Intro. 4; SBN xv)[14]

The key premise in Hume's *dependence argument* is the phrase: "since they lie under the cognizance of men, and are judged of by their powers and faculties." Natural philosophers (and mathematicians, etc.) employ their cognitive faculties when they engage in natural philosophy: to do natural philosophy, natural philosophers must *think* and *reason*. Natural philosophy is dependent on Hume's science of man because it "explain[s] the nature of the ideas we employ, and of the operations we perform in our reasoning" (T Intro. 4; SBN xv).

In the *Abstract* to the first two books of the *Treatise*, Hume indicates that the project of founding the sciences has already "finished what regards to logic" and has already "laid the foundation of the other parts in [the] account of the passions" (Ab. 3; SBN 646). Logic and the passions are the two most general branches of the science of man; of logic Hume writes: "The sole end of logic is to explain the principles and operations of our reasoning faculty, and the nature of our ideas" (T Intro. 5, Ab. 3; SBN xv, 646). We can now see most clearly that Hume's dependence argument establishes the dependence of natural philosophy on logic, the logic that Hume claims to have "finished" in Book 1 of the *Treatise*.[15] Logic is *prior* to the other sciences because to do science one must employ ideas and reasoning. Thus the examination of our ideas and the explanation of the operations of our reasoning faculty is prior, or more fundamental, than any other question in the sciences concerning the nature of things.

Here we are concerned with Hume's examination of the nature of ideas and, in particular, with the idea of necessary connection. Hume clarifies the nature or content of ideas by tracing them back to their original impressions. In the case of the idea of necessary connection, we have seen that its original impression is a feeling in the mind. We do not have an idea of necessary connection that traces back or represents a sense impression or anything detected in sense experience. And now the question we must ask, from the standpoint of Hume's project, is this: what follows *in general*, when Hume's logic reveals that some putative idea does not trace back to impressions of sensation?

Old, new, and foundational Hume

We know that Hume answers the *particular* question of the implications of our lack of the idea of mind-independent necessary connection explicitly in a number of places. For instance, terms like 'necessity' and 'power' and 'energy' are "altogether insignificant" (Ab. 7; SBN 649). But, as we have seen, these *meaning passages* appear to be in tension with *ignorance passages*. The conflict arises because Hume seems to mean what he says in both sets of passages, and yet his claims are at odds with each other. Old Humeans privilege *meaning passages* and relieve the tension by interpreting the Hume of *ignorance passages* as giving his words meaning that he ultimately does not endorse. But we have seen now that Hume's argumentative strategy in his discussion of necessity mimics his argumentative strategy in his discussion of other topics; the general argument is that the nature of ideas is prior to the nature of objects. From this larger context, part of the justification, at least, for privileging *meaning passages* would have to be that they instantiate, i.e. that they are an instance of a general theory of meaning, a theory according to which only terms associated with ideas traceable to impressions have meaning. The problem is that there appears to be no such general theory. Hume's claims about the meaninglessness of "necessity" simply do not generalize to other cases in which we fail to have an idea. For instance, Hume considers the claims that space and time are both infinitely divisible simply to be false, not meaningless. Hume denies that we have an idea of a vacuum, as the idea of space without something visible or tangible, but he never says that "vacuum" is insignificant. Hume argues that we fail to have an idea of changeless duration, but he does not maintain that claims about enduring unchanging objects are meaningless or incomprehensible. Hume denies that we have an idea of a mathematical point as defined within classical geometry, but he never claims that the expression 'mathematical point' is meaningless. When Hume assesses the ideas of geometry, including the idea of a straight line and the standard of equality, his position is not that the terms central to geometry are meaningless; instead he says: "the ideas which are most essential to geometry ... are far from being exact and determinate" (T 1.2.4.29; SBN 50–51).[16] And Hume denies that we have an idea of gravity as a distinct thing, but he does not conclude that 'gravity' is meaningless. If there is a "criterion of meaninglessness," or if there is a criterion according to which only terms associated with ideas have (genuine) meaning, then Hume does not apply it consistently. This is a serious methodological problem because if the empirical meaning of terms was even part of Hume's project of reforming the sciences, then we would expect him to condemn terms like "gravity," "mathematical point," "vacuum," and "equality" as meaningless. These terms are at the heart of scientific/mathematic theory, but Hume fails to stigmatize them as meaningless or as insignificant.[17]

Hume's "inconsistency" above is also a problem for New Humeans, not just Old Humeans. For the passages above suggest that meaning does not occupy a central place in Hume's project as a whole, and this suggests that, at least from the wider perspective of Hume's foundational project, the old–new Hume fight over meaning might be misguided. However, meaning in this debate is, as I remarked earlier, a means to an end; the end is the metaphysics of causation. Old Humeans insists that only terms associated with ideas are meaningful and thus, given Hume's account of the idea of necessary connection, there *couldn't possibly* be mind-independent necessary connections. New Humeans insist that we can think of mind-independent necessary connections via idea-alternates, which are also meaningful, and thus that the *metaphysical possibility* of mind-independent necessary connections is left open.

There is a direct answer to the question I asked regarding the general implications of our lack of ideas in Hume's system, and it has nothing to do with metaphysics. Hume answers this general question, interestingly, at the end of his discussion of the idea of "necessary connexion," where he draws a number of corollaries. The one that concerns us here is one that Hume considers "so evident," so basic or fundamental to his whole philosophy, that he wonders whether he needs to state it explicitly: "we can never have reason to believe that any object exists, of which we cannot form an idea" (T 1.3.14.36; SBN 172).[18] If we cannot form an idea of x, then *we can have no reason* to believe that x exists. Our inability to form ideas does not affect the nature of things or the possible existence of things, but our *attitude* toward such questions; it restricts which beliefs we can justifiably maintain.

Hume's "no reason to believe" principle answers the question of how Hume's logic is *prior* to the other sciences. Prior to the question of the nature of vacuum, or the efficacy of causes, we must ask what idea we have of these things. The consequence of our inability to form an idea of mind-independent necessary connection is *not* that there are no such necessary connections in nature. The consequence Hume draws from our inability to form an idea of mind-independent necessary connection is that we cannot justify the belief in such necessary connections. The "no reason to believe" principle is not metaphysical, but I think Hume intends it as a non-metaphysical answer to a metaphysical question. Once we understand that we have no reason to believe in the existence or possible existence of mind-independent necessary connections, the metaphysical question is closed. We can only *judge* mind-independent necessary connections to be possible when we can form an idea of them. And, throughout his writings, Hume is absolutely clear about this: we cannot form an *idea* of mind-independent necessary connection.

New Humeans insist that idea-alternates allow us to think that which cannot be thought with ideas. Galen Strawson argues that we can think of real, metaphysical connections via a *relative idea*.[19] Kail maintains that we can form the *bare thought* of mind-independent necessary connections. Against the old, traditional reading of Hume, Kail argues that Hume's account of the *idea* of cause does not provide an answer to the metaphysical nature of causation, and Hume never, as Kail insists, makes the anti-realist argument that there are no mind-independent necessary connections. Hume's account of the nature of our idea of causation is meant to answer the question of what we can know of causation. The bare thought, in contrast, represents the possibility of mind-independent necessary connections.

I shall focus on a few general problems with these claims. If ideas cannot deliver metaphysical theses, why would idea-alternates be able or qualified to do so? One answer is that ideas are empirically constrained; they are limited by the straightjacket of experience. But what liberates idea-alternates? Why would idea-alternates enjoy this lack of restraint? Additionally, one danger with liberating idea-alternates in this way is the possible proliferation of thoughts, the possibility of which Hume seems bent on denying. In his characterization of the bare thought of causal power, Kail claims that

> we can specify uniquely that which we cannot understand (causal power) by saying that it is that feature that, were we acquainted with it, would yield *a priori* inference and render it inconceivable that the cause not be followed by its effect.
>
> (Kail 2007: 84)

But might we not similarly form, for instance, the *bare thought* of infinity? We could form the bare thought of the infinite via the thought of the finite and then add a denial. Or, we could form the bare thought of infinity by stating what it would be like to count to infinity: we would count forever, never reaching an end. Could this bare thought of the infinite be then used to counter Hume's own argument against the infinite divisibility of extension?

There is also, as we discussed above, Hume's "no reason to believe" principle, which is a principle about *ideas*, not idea-alternates. If we do not have an *idea* of mind-independent necessary connection, as it is the case, we *can have no reason* to believe in the existence or possible existence of these necessary connections. This principle privileges ideas and identifies the ability to form an *idea* as the *necessary* (but not sufficient) condition for having reason to believe in the existence of something.[20]

Kail finds significance in the fact that Hume's denial of the idea is not accompanied by the anti-realist claim that there are no mind-independent necessary connections. This minimal fact, Kail suggests, unites all New Humeans. But Hume also denies the existence of the idea of vacuum, the idea of time without change, and others, and these denials are also not accompanied by anti-realist claims. One can construe this as evidence that Hume allows for the existence of vacuum and time without change. But we could also, and much more plausibly, interpret the absence of these explicit denials to follow from the fact that Hume considers the "no reason to believe" principle to be, indeed, absolutely *evident*. We simply have no reason to believe in the existence of vacuum or time without change or mind-independent necessary connections. And once we understand that, there remain no metaphysical questions about these objects to be answered.

Against the background of Hume's foundational project, New Humeans are right that Hume's examination of ideas is not meant to provide metaphysical accounts of the nature of reality. And if the regularity theory is a metaphysical theory, Hume is not a regularity theorist. But New Humeans are wrong and misguided in their attempt to reinsert metaphysics (or metaphysical possibilities) into Hume's system with idea-alternates. Old Humeans are right that ideas are king, but they are wrong about the nature of their power.

The idea of causation is not just fundamental to all science and philosophy; it also plays an essential role within Hume's own system. Hume's examination of this idea leads him to articulate what is perhaps the most famous argument in philosophy: the problem of induction. Hume shows that our beliefs in unobserved events, such as those that take place in the future, cannot be justified either by demonstrative or probabilistic reasoning. Hume's groundbreaking account of the self crucially relies on his treatment of causation. Hume's influential discussion of freedom of the will, of "liberty and necessity," is founded on his account of causation. Hume's account of causation is fundamental to his whole philosophy, and it is for his treatment of causation that he is most famous. Although Hume anticipates the revolutionary character of his account of the idea of causation, he might still have been surprised by the enormous impact his views have had on the entire field of philosophy.[21]

Notes

1 For a good general discussion of Hume's account of causation, see Garrett, D. (2009) "Hume," in Beebee, H., Hitchcock, C., Menzies, P., *The Oxford Handbook of Causation*, Oxford: Oxford University Press, pp. 73–91.

2 The phrase "New Hume" was coined by Kenneth Winkler in his 1991 landmark paper. For another paper that is critical of what was then referred to as the "skeptical realist" position, see Blackburn (1990).

3 Hume introduces these philosophical relations earlier in the text in *Treatise* 1.1.5.

4 This might be the beginning, at least, of a response to Thomas Reid's famous objection involving the constant conjunction of day and night (Reid 2002). We are not confident, indeed we do not at all believe, that day and night are causally related. Instead of using this example to criticize Hume's account of causation, Reid might have investigated the *reasons* we do not consider day and night to be causally connected. There might be many. It is hard to determine which one is the cause and which is the effect. Would each be both the effect *and* the cause of the other? Are day and night two different *things*, or two presentations of the same thing? If they are not two distinct things, can they be constantly conjoined? Why don't we consider the red tomato to be the effect of the same but previously green tomato? These and other related questions might reveal our reasons for not considering day and night to be causally connected.

5 I ignore the difficult question of Hume's apparent identification of a *determination* of the mind with an *impression* of reflexion.

6 J.A. Robinson seems to be the first interpreter to point to this problem of extension of Hume's definitions of 'cause' (Robinson 1966).

7 For a helpful discussion of all of these different positions, and their problems, see Garrett (1997), pp. 96–117. For a discussion that places the question of Hume's view of causation against the larger background of philosophical realism and anti-realism, see Coventry, A. (2006).

8 Garrett distinguishes between a subjective and an absolute reading of the definitions but ascribes to Hume the absolute reading (Garrett 1997). I have argued against the absolute reading on both textual and philosophical grounds and have proposed instead an expert-relative reading (Boehm 2014).

9 Hume writes that "the mind has a great propensity to spread itself on external objects. . . . Thus as certain sounds and smells are always found to attend certain visible objects, we naturally imagine a conjunction, even in place, betwixt the objects and qualities, tho' the qualities be of such a nature as to admit of not such conjunction, and really exist no where . . . the same propensity is the reason, why we suppose necessity and power to lie in the objects we consider, no in our mind, that considers them" (T 1.3.14.25; SBN 167).

10 Galen Strawon aptly refers to this tension as "the meaning tension" (Strawson 1989).

11 For a good discussion of these interpretative strategies, see Beebee (2006: 180–192).

12 Beebee and Kail offer extensive discussion of these strategies and some of their problems (Beebee 2006: 173–225; Kail 2007: 56–102).

13 I discuss more contexts in which Hume is employing this argumentative method in Boehm 2016: 55–77.

14 Although the dependence here is qualified with "in some measure," in the paragraph that follows Hume writes: "If therefore the sciences of Mathematics, Natural philosophy and Natural religion, have

such a dependence on the knowledge of man" (my emphasis) (T Intro. 5). This suggests that Hume does not regard the dependence in question of little significance.

15 The passions, the subject of Book 2, provide the foundations for morality.
16 Hume does claim that the *fiction*, not the term 'equality,' by which we arrive at the notion of equality is "useless as well as incomprehensible" (T 1.2.4.24; SBN 48).
17 Alexander Rosenberg notes that Hume employs the criterion of meaning "mainly to condemn a wide variety of concepts of traditional philosophical thought,", concepts such as "*substance, substantial form, mode, essence*." But Hume could hardly be said to reform the sciences simply by pointing out that *such* terms were meaningless. As Rosenberg acknowledges, Hume stigmatizes "many of the terms of Aristotelian metaphysics, terms that few empiricists would identify as practically or scientifically useful" (Rosenberg 1993: 70).
18 I discuss this principle and how it applies to cases in which Hume denies ideas in Boehm (2016).
19 Flage mounts a convincing argument against the relative idea of cause in Flage (2000: 153).
20 I can obviously think about the golden mountain, but my ability to form this idea does not give me reason to believe in its existence. The ability to form a given idea then gives me necessary but not sufficient reason for believing in the existence of something.
21 I want to thank audiences for their valuable questions and comments at a number of places where I have presented the material included in this chapter in 2016: the Central APA Hume Meeting in Chicago, the workshop in Early Modern Philosophy at the University of Helsinki, the University of Jyväskylä in Finland, and the Research Institute in Budapest, Hungary. I also want to thank the editors of this volume for very helpful and friendly comments. Finally, I am grateful to Peter Millican and Don Garrett for discussion that improved this chapter.

References

Beebee, H. (2006) *Hume on Causation*, London: Routledge.
Blackburn, S. (1990) "Hume and Thick Connexions," *Philosophy and Phenomenological Research* L: 237–250.
Boehm, M. (2012) "Filling the Gaps in Hume's Vacuums," *Hume Studies* 38(1): 79–99.
———. (2014) "Hume's Definitions of 'Cause': Without Idealizations, Within the Bounds of Science," *Synthese* 191(16): 3803–3819.
———. (2016) "Hume's Foundational Project in the *Treatise*," *European Journal of Philosophy* 24(1): 55–77.
Coventry, A. (2006) *Hume's Theory of Causation: A Quasi-Realist Interpretation, Continuum Studies in British Philosophy*, London: Continuum.
Flage, D. (2000) "Relative Ideas Re-Viewed," in R. Read and K. Richman (eds.), *The New Hume Debate*, London: Routledge, pp. 138–155.
Garrett, D. (1997) *Cognition and Commitment in Hume's Philosophy*, Oxford: Oxford University Press.
———. (2009) "Hume," in H. Beebee, C. Hitchcock and P. Menzies (eds.), *The Oxford Handbook of Causation*, Oxford: Oxford University Press, pp. 73–91.
Jacobson, A. (2000) "From Cognitive Science to a Post-Cartesian Text: What Did Hume Really Say?" in R. Read and K. Richman (eds.), *The New Hume Debate*, London: Routledge, pp. 156–166.
Kail, P. (2000) "How to Understand Hume's Realism," in R. Read and K. Richman (eds.), *The New Hume Debate*, London: Routledge, pp. 253–269.
———. (2007) *Projection and Realism in Hume's Philosophy*, Oxford: Oxford University Press.
———. (2014) "Efficient Causation in Hume," in Tad Schmaltz (ed.), *Efficient Causation, a History*, Oxford University Press, pp. 231–257.
Millican, P. (2011) "Hume, Causal Realism, and Free Will," in Keith Allen and Tom Stoneham (eds.), *Causation and Modern Philosophy*, London: Routledge, pp. 123–165.
Reid, T. (2002) *Essays on the Intellectual Powers of Man*, edited by D. R. Brookes and K. Haakonssen, University Park, PA: Pennsylvania State University Press.
Robinson, J. A. (1966) "Hume's Two Definitions of 'Cause'," in V. C. Chappell (ed.), *Hume, a Collection of Critical Essays*, New York: Anchor Books and Doubleday & Company.
Rosenberg, A. (1993) "Hume and the Philosophy of Science," in David Fate Norton (ed.), *The Cambridge Companion to Hume*, Cambridge: Cambridge University Press, pp. 64–89.
Strawson, G. (1989) *The Secret Connexion: Causation, Realism and David Hume*, Oxford: Clarendon Press.
———. (2000) "David Hume: Objects and Power," in R. Read and K. Richman (eds.), *The New Hume Debate*, London: Routledge, pp. 31–51.

Winkler, K. (1991) "The New Hume," *The Philosophical Review* 100(4): 541–579.

———— (2000) "'All Is Revolution in Us': Personal Identity in Shaftesbury and Hume." *Hume Studies* (26.1): 3–40.

Wright, J. (1983) *The Sceptical Realism of David Hume*, Manchester: Manchester University Press.

————. (2000) "Hume on Causal Realism," in R. Read and K. Richman (eds.), *The New Hume Debate*, London: Routledge, pp. 88–99.

9

HUME AND
THE EXTERNAL WORLD

Stefanie Rocknak

§1 Introduction

Hume's understanding of the external world, particularly his conception of objects, or what he occasionally refers to as "bodies," is the subject of much dispute. Are objects mind-independent? Or are they just what we see, feel, smell, taste, or touch? In other words, are objects just sense data? Or are they ideas *about* sense data? Or are objects, somehow, mind-independent, but we have ideas *of* them, and we receive sense data *from* them?

Contrary to the "rationalist" tradition from which Hume was emerging, Hume thought that our only access to the world was by way of the data that we receive from our five senses, i.e. what he called sense "impressions." Unlike Descartes and Leibniz, Hume thought that we cannot use anything like "pure rational thought" – i.e. thought devoid of sense data – to grasp or understand the world. This methodology constitutes Hume's "naturalistic" or scientific approach: because we do not have access to anything *beyond* our sense impressions (and any ideas that are caused by them), "reality" can *only* be defined in terms of impressions and ideas. According to Hume, ideas and impressions constitute the only fabric of "reality" that we have access to and that we know. Though a reality or "external world" might or *could* exist beyond our impressions and ideas, Hume believed we have no way of telling, one way or the other.

To some degree, this reading of Hume aligns with what some scholars have characterized as Hume's "phenomenonalist" reading of the external world. According to this interpretation, objects are *just* sense impressions, i.e. they are literally what we feel, see, touch, taste, or hear.[1] In this case, an object such as an "apple" would literally be how the apple tastes, feels, smells, etc.

The phenomenonalist position competes with three other major interpretations of Humean objects. Some scholars have argued that, according to Hume, objects are "intentional," i.e. they are the objects of thought (Salmon 1983). In this case, an object, e.g. an "apple," would be an idea that we necessarily think *about*. Still others interpret Hume as a realist, i.e. objects are mind-independent.[2] In this case, an "apple" would be a thing that exists independently of how we sense or think about it. And finally, some think that Hume maintained that objects are imagined ideas, but they are not imagined to be the causes of our perceptions.[3] In this case, the object "apple" would be an imagined idea, but we do not also imagine that it causes our sense impressions of it.

Clearly, then, much is at stake in regard to how one interprets Hume's conception of an "object." Doing so directly affects how one understands Hume's notion of a "world" that may or may not exist "externally" to the human mind. For, as just noted, some scholars claim that Hume thought that objects, and so the external world, consist of just sense impressions (i.e. the phenomenonalist position), while in other cases, it seems that Hume thought that objects and the external world are just the objects of our thought (i.e. the intentional position). Meanwhile, the realists interpret Hume as believing in a mind-independent world, i.e. a truly *external* world, while others think that external world is, to some degree, *imagined* (i.e. the imagined but non-causal interpretation).

However, although Hume occasionally uses the word 'object' in a phenomenonalist, intentional, realist, and/or imagined but not causal sense, his position on objects, his position on the "external world," is not effectively captured by any of these scholarly interpretations. Thus, in this chapter, focusing primarily on Book I of the *Treatise*,[4] I present an overview of a fifth, more complicated, and, I think, more accurate interpretation of Hume's notion of objects.

In particular, I suggest that we must distinguish between: (a) Hume's conception of the "vulgar" notion of objects (which may be equated with the "phenomenonalist" reading of Hume, noted above), (b) Hume's conception of the "philosophical" position on objects, and (c) Hume's *own* position on objects. In all three cases, we do, indeed, *imagine* ideas of objects. Thus, we will see that regardless of if we are in a vulgar, philosophical, or Humean state of mind, *Hume thought that we imagine the external world*.[5] As a result, as already suggested above, Hume was by no means a realist, and so, we can immediately rule out the realist interpretation. How the other three scholarly interpretations sketched above relate to my reading will be explained as we proceed.

In the meantime, we must immediately call our attention to three fundamental differences between the vulgar position, the philosopher's position, and Hume's position: (1) the vulgar imagine that objects are identical to impressions; (2) the philosophers, in virtue of making a reasoned rejection of the vulgar position, imagine that objects are mind-independent and are the causes of our perceptions. However, they are *unaware* that they are imagining objects. Instead, they think that reason, and reason alone, shows that objects exist as mind-independent entities; and (3) Hume thinks that we always imagine that objects are the "invariable and uninterrupted"[6] causes of our perceptions; this is a condition of possibility for almost all thought, including our ability to reason.

In this very general respect, we may refer to this third position that I am identifying as *Hume's* position, as a *transcendental* conception of objects. Accordingly, all humans must, in order to function properly, almost immediately imagine invariable and uninterrupted objects – i.e. objects that admit of what he calls a "perfect identity." Thus, this process must occur before we employ any kind of reasoning regarding what we believe are uninterrupted and invariable objects. And so, this transcendental process must take place well before the philosopher can use reason to reject the vulgar position and subsequently imagine that objects are mind-independent objects; the transcendental process is a condition of possibility for the philosophical process – it is what some might refer to as "pre-theoretical" (cf. (Mounce 1999), (Pears 1990)).[7]

To illustrate the general distinctions between (1) the vulgar position, (2) the philosophical position, and (3) Hume's position, I have divided this chapter as follows. In §2, I give a general overview of "perfect identity," since it frames all of Hume's discussions of objects in the *Treatise*, regardless of if he is discussing his own position, the vulgar view, or the philosophical position. In §3, I provide a general explanation of the relationship between the following two pairs of properties: uninterruptedness and invariability vs. continuity and distinctness. In §4, I summarize the vulgar position on objects. In §5, I summarize the philosophical conception of objects. In §6, I summarize the transcendental conception of objects which is what I take to be Hume's own position on objects. In §7, I summarize the distinction between natural and philosophical causation, and in §8, I summarize transcendental causation. Finally, in §9, I present my conclusion.

§2 Perfect identity: a summary

Hume introduces what he calls "perfect identity" in the *Treatise* section "Of skepticism with regard to the senses," which culminates in the statement that the two essential properties of identity are invariability and uninterruptedness (T 1.4.2.30; SBN 199–201). Hume repeats this claim in "Of personal identity" (T 1.4.6.6; SBN 253–255). According to Hume, "perfect identity" is the paradigmatic definition of how he thinks we conceive of identity – it allows us to determine how and when an "object" may be characterized as such, e.g. how and when a "chair" is actually a "chair."

Moreover, it is *ideas* that admit of perfect identity, not impressions and not mind-independent objects ("Of skepticism with regard to the senses," i.e. T 1.4.2.29; SBN 200–201, and "Of personal identity," i.e. T 1.4.6.6; SBN 253). Also, Hume tells us in "Of skepticism with regard to the senses" and "Of personal identity" that the properties of invariability and uninterruptedness are *imagined*.[8] This is the case because, according to Hume, our perceptions, by their very nature, are never invariable and/or uninterrupted. And thus, neither impressions nor any idea that exactly represents[9] an impression could be invariable and uninterrupted. However, impressions and ideas may surely *resemble* each other to a very high degree, and thus, they do admit of a certain kind of "constancy" (T 1.4.2.18; SBN 194–195). However, *this* kind of constancy (resemblance) is not invariability, although, confusingly enough, Hume also uses the word 'constant' to mean "invariable," especially when claiming that we never experience invariable and uninterrupted impressions.[10]

Regardless of this confusion regarding the word 'constant' – i.e. in some cases it means "resembling" and in other cases it means "invariable" – Hume makes it abundantly clear that although we can perceive a high degree of resemblance among our impressions and any idea or ideas that exactly represent them, we never perceive them to be uninterrupted and/or invariable, unless we *imagine* them to be so.[11]

According to Hume, when we imagine that something has a perfect identity, we are imagining an idea of a thing, say a chair, that we *think* is uninterrupted. This means, in brief, that even if we stop having chair perceptions (e.g. by looking away), we *imagine* that the object "chair" does not become interrupted. Similarly, although our chair perceptions might vary, e.g. they shift with the changing light, we *imagine* that the object "chair" does not vary.

§3 Invariability and uninterruptedness vs. continuity and distinctness

Throughout Book I, Hume seems to use the property of continuity interchangeably with the property of uninterruptedness. In some places, he speaks of imagining a continuous object (T 1.4.2; 15–24; SBN 194–199), and in other places, he speaks of an uninterrupted object (T 1.3.2.2; SBN 74). However, in both cases, he seems to mean the same thing: we are imagining an object that is not affected by the way in which we intermittently perceive it. In other words, if an object is conceived of as uninterrupted, then it is, simply by definition, also conceived of as continuous, and *vice versa*; an uninterrupted "object" continues in the respect that its existence is not interrupted when we are not perceiving it. Likewise, an "object" that is not interrupted by our gaps in perceiving it, continues. Moreover, according to Hume, if an object is conceived of as continuous, it must also be conceived of as distinct. This also makes sense; for instance, if I believe that an "object," say, a melon, continues to exist when I am not having impressions of it, then I must also believe that the melon exists *distinctly* from my perceptions – such that it is not affected when I stop perceiving it (T 1.4.2.2; SBN 187–188).

However, although uninterruptedness and continuity are interchangeable, distinctness and invariability are not: I could easily imagine an object existing distinctly from my perception of it, while simultaneously imagining that it varies, or changes, e.g. with time. Thus, we must conclude that the two pairs of properties, i.e. continuity and distinctness vs. uninterruptedness and invariability are not strictly interchangeable.

Throughout Book I of the *Treatise*, Hume alternates between talking about imagining continuous and distinct objects vs. imagining uninterrupted and invariable objects. It is entirely plausible that Hume switches from discussing objects that we imagine to be continuous and distinct to objects that we think are uninterrupted and invariable in order to introduce the notion of "time." In particular, in "The same subject continu'd" and in "Of skepticism with regard to the senses," he explains how "time" – which in one respect is an imagined object[12] – can change or vary the perceptions of those things that we imagine to be otherwise uninterrupted and invariable (T 1.2.5.29; SBN 65; T 1.4.2.29; SBN 200–201). With this caveat in mind, we will use the two pairs of imagined properties interchangeably.

§4 The vulgar conception of objects

Hume explains in "Of skepticism with regard to the senses" that the "vulgar," or everyday person – which includes all of us at least some of the time – is consistently fooled into thinking that certain resembling sense impressions may be identified with each other (T 1.4.2.36, 38; SBN 205, 207). As a result of doing so, we tend to think that sets of resembling perceptions constitute the objects of the world. For example, if I look at, say, a bicycle, at time T_1, and then again at time T_2, and still again at time T_3–T_n, my current sense-perceptions and my past impressions of the bicycle would all seem to significantly *resemble* each other. In this respect, they are "constant" but not invariable. However, the vulgar mistake this constancy for invariability, and so, they are led to imagine an idea of an "invariable" object ("Of skepticism with regard to the senses," i.e. T 1.4.2.31; SBN 201–202).

Through a very complex process involving dispositions (states of mind) and the imagination, the vulgar proceed to imagine an idea of a sense impression that they think is not only invariable, but also uninterrupted (T 1.4.2.31–35; SBN 201–204). However, the vulgar ultimately reject this position because it becomes clear to them that they cannot simultaneously believe that a perception is both interrupted and not interrupted (T 1.4.2.36; SBN 205). In turn, they posit the existence of an uninterrupted and invariable unperceived perception (i.e. an unperceived impression (T 1.4.2.37–40; SBN 205–208).[13] However, the "philosophers" proceed to make short work of the idea of an unperceived perception, i.e. they summarily reject it by using simple logic (modus tollens) and a thought experiment (T 1.4.2.45; SBN 210–211).[14]

In sum, the vulgar a.) think that objects are impressions; b.) are initially inclined to imagine that impressions are uninterrupted and invariable thanks to resembling dispositions (states of mind); c.) upon rejecting this conception of objects, posit the existence of an unperceived perception; and d.) themselves reject the first phase of the vulgar position (i.e. b.) above), while the second phase (i.e. c.) above is rejected by the philosophers.

In all cases, the vulgar *imagine* that they are thinking of an object with a perfect identity, but they are not because, as noted above, they cannot effectively imagine the property of uninterruptedness.[15] Not surprisingly, in "Of personal identity," Hume explicitly refers to the vulgar position on objects as "improper" (T 1.4.6.7; SBN 255). As such, it is an instance of "*im*perfect identity" (T 1.4.6.9; SBN 256; emphasis added).

At this point, it should be clear that the vulgar position clearly captures the "phenomenalist" position sketched in the Introduction to this chapter, where, it is alleged, Hume identified objects with impressions. However, as we will see, Hume's conception of objects, and so his conception of the external world, is surely not to be confused with the vulgar position. For one thing, as noted above, he clearly must reject the vulgar position; it does not allow for an effective conception of perfect identity as it is "improper" and "imperfect." Second, and most importantly, he presents an entirely different psychological process of imagining ideas of objects that, as such, (a) cannot be conflated with either the vulgar or the philosophical process and (b) is never explicitly rejected by Hume.[16] Thus, Hume was not a "phenomenalist" when it came to the external world. He did *not* simply identify objects with sense impressions.

§5 The philosophical conception of objects

As already noted above, the philosophical position emerges as a result of rejecting the vulgar position, particularly the second phase of vulgar thought, i.e. the idea of an "unperceived perception." More specifically, according to Hume, the philosophers conclude that reason (and reason alone) shows that the vulgar perspective of objects is false. Concomitantly, it seems that reason (and reason alone) shows that there must be mind-independent objects, particularly objects that are the continued and distinct causes of our perceptions (T 1.4.2.46; SBN 211).[17]

However, Hume explains, although the philosophers think that reason is solely responsible for proving that mind-independent objects exist, this is not entirely accurate. Rather, Hume argues, in conjunction with their reasoned rejection of the vulgar conception of objects, the philosophers must inevitably employ the imagination; philosophers are actually *imagining* ideas of continued and distinct objects that, as such, allegedly cause our interrupted and varied perceptions of them (T 1.4.2.49–50; SBN 213). In this respect, he explains in "Of skepticism with regard to the senses" that the philosophical conception of objects is the "monstrous offspring" of reason *and* the imagination (T 1.4.2.52; SBN 215).

Hume's first extended account of the philosophical position on objects occurs at the end of the section "Of skepticism with regard to the senses," where he discusses the philosopher's rejection of the vulgar perspective (T 1.4.2.43–53; SBN 209–216). Hume's second extended account occurs in the course of discussing three variants of the philosophical conception of objects, namely, the ancient conception of objects ("Of the antient philosophy," i.e. T 1.4.3.1–11; SBN 219–225), the modern conception of objects ("Of the modern philosophy," i.e. T 1.4.4.1–15; SBN 225–231), and the notion of an immaterial soul ("Of the immateriality of the soul," i.e. T 1.4.5.1–35; SBN 232–251). Hume's final extended account of the philosophical position on objects occurs in the course of discussing personal identity in 1.4.6, i.e. "Of personal identity."

§6 The transcendental conception of objects

There are three moments in Book I of the *Treatise* where Hume discusses a process of imagining ideas of objects that is clearly distinct from the way in which the vulgar and the philosophers respectively imagine ideas of objects. These occur in: (1) "Of probability; and of the idea of cause and effect" (T 1.3.2.1–2; SBN 73–74), where Hume discusses "secret causes"; (2) "Of skepticism with regard to the senses" (T 1.4.2.15–24; SBN 194–199), which occurs in the course of a discussion of the role that the two levels of constancy and coherence of our impressions play in regard to our conception of objects; and (3) "Of skepticism with regard to the senses" (T 1.4.2.25–30; SBN 199–201), which constitutes part 1 of 1.4.2's four-part system, where Hume presents his "*principium individuationis*," i.e. the principle of identity.[18] These three moments provide the textual evidence for my transcendental interpretation of objects.

In particular, in the second moment (T 1.4.2.15–24; SBN 194–199), we must imagine an idea of an object that we think represents the properties of continuity and distinctness, while in the two other cases (T 1.3.2.2; SBN 73–74; T 1.4.2.25–30; SBN 199–201), we must imagine an idea of an object that we think represents the properties of invariability and uninterruptedness (where, as noted above, for our purposes, we may assume that invariability and uninterruptedness are roughly interchangeable with the properties of continuity and distinctness). This means that, according to Hume, particular objects that seem to admit of what he calls a "perfect identity" are imagined, complex ideas.

Moreover, ideas of objects that we think admit of a perfect identity appear to be very similar to abstract ideas. However, these ideas represent *particular* objects, not general objects. To understand why this is the case – at least in broad terms – recall that Hume, similar to Berkeley, defines an abstract object as follows: "all general ideas are nothing but particular ones, annexed to a certain term, which gives them a more extensive signification, and makes them recall upon occasion other individuals, which are similar to them" (T 1.1.7.1; SBN 17). According to Hume, a general idea is actually a particular idea with a "certain term" attached to it. For instance, upon experiencing a set of resembling ideas of "objects" (say, of dogs), we generally call them by the same name, regardless of any small variations (T 1.1.7.7; SBN 20). Afterwards, whenever we hear the name "dog," we call to mind one of the particular ideas of the set which "revives the idea of one of these objects, and makes the imagination conceive it with all its particular circumstances and properties" (T 1.1.7.7; SBN 20). This means that a particular idea represents not only a particular impression, but also the entire "revival set" (Garrett 1997: 53). However, it does not exactly represent the entire revival set since "the word not being able to revive the idea of all these individuals, only touches the soul, if I may be allow'd so to speak, and revives that custom, which we have acquir'd by surveying them" (T 1.1.7.7; SBN 20). Thus, our idea of a dog (in general) brings to mind a great deal of what we have experienced upon perceiving dogs, but not everything. When we think of a dog, in general, we bring to mind the idea of a particular dog that we have had an impression of, but now augmented with an imagined compilation of other dog perceptions.

Hume has a very similar process in mind in the three sets of passages noted above regarding particular objects. More specifically, we must first experience respectively, a "species" (T 1.3.2.2; SBN 74) or a number of "constant and coherent" perceptions (T 1.4.2.15–24; SBN 194–199) or a "number" of "resembling" perceptions (T 1.4.2.27; SBN 200). Following, we imagine a "secret cause" (T 1.3.2.2; SBN 74) of this set of resembling perceptions, which is explained below.

In particular, we imagine an object that we think is invariable and uninterrupted (or continuous and distinct). To do so, we imagine that one of the perceptions from the set of resembling perceptions is (a) the cause of that set and (b) invariable and uninterrupted (or continuous and distinct). In other words, we imagine that it has a *perfect identity*. As such, as in the case with a general, abstract idea, we use a particular perception from a revival set, i.e. the "species" or "number" to represent the whole set. However, this particular perception does not *exactly* represent any impression because it has certain imagined qualities, particularly: (a) we imagine that it is invariable and uninterrupted (or continuous and distinct), where, recall, we never perceive any of these qualities. In precisely this respect, it is a "secret cause"; we do not "see or feel" it (T 1.3.2.3; SBN 74); and (b) we imagine it to be a cause, where we never perceive it to be what Hume refers to as "constantly conjoined" with the perceptions that we imagine that it causes (T 1.3.6.12; SBN 92). This is the case because, as just noted, we never "see or feel" it, so we cannot *perceive* it, much less perceive it as being constantly conjoined with another perception.

For instance, although our idea of a particular chair object would be based on a particular chair impression that we have actually had, we must *imagine* that this idea is not only invariable and uninterrupted (or continuous and distinct), but that it is the *cause* of any perception that resembles it, i.e. the set of our resembling (but invariable and interrupted) chair perceptions. And thus, Hume explains, our imagined idea of an object that admits of perfect identity is "oblique[ly]" and "indirect[ly]" related to our experience (T 1.4.2.21; SBN 197), precisely because it does not exactly represent an impression. However, it is *based* on an impression; in particular, it belongs to the "species" noted above, but with imagined qualities.[19]

Moreover, our ability to imagine such causes seems to be *presupposed* by, at least, our ability to employ what Hume calls philosophical causation. And thus, this process is fundamentally distinct from the philosophical process of imagining causes, which, recall, only occurs by way of rejecting the vulgar position, a rejection that necessarily incurs the use of, at least, philosophical probable reasoning. To understand why this is the case – at least in general terms – we need to briefly examine i.) the distinction between "natural" and "philosophical" causation and ii.) the way in which we imagine a "secret cause."

§7 Natural causation vs. philosophical causation: a brief overview

For our purposes, we can distinguish between what Hume refers to as the "natural" and "philosophical" relations of causality as follows: the natural relation of causality is the product of a conditioning process (specifically, the repetitive association of impressions [T 1.3.14; SBN 155–172]). In this respect, the natural relation of causality is reflexive, not reflective. Indeed, this is what the negative argument concerning induction is meant to show: the natural relation of causality is not a reasoning (comparing) process,[20] nor is it justified by any reasoning process or reasons. Philosophical relations of causality, however, are not mere reflexes. Rather, after we have become conditioned to think in terms of natural relations of causality, we use "reason" – i.e. a comparing process – to determine if two objects are causally related (T 1.1.5.1–2; SBN 13–14; T 1.3.6.12–16; SBN 92–93; T 1.3.14.31; SBN 169–170).[21]

Consider the following example. One may become conditioned through "constant conjunction" (T 1.1.1.8; SBN 4) to think that fire causes paper to burn. And so, every time she sees fire engulfing paper (or remembers fire engulfing paper), the enlivened idea of paper burning reflexively comes to mind. Thus, according to one of Hume's many senses of belief,[22] she believes that the paper will burn; indeed, the enlivened idea *is* the belief (T 1.3.7.5–6; SBN 96). This is what we may think of as a causally produced belief; it occurs as the result of a conditioning process, which comprises the natural relation of causality. However, as a result of reflection, i.e. "reason," she may also come to believe the causal *relation* that "every time fire engulfs paper, it will burn." In this respect, a causal relation is, in effect, a "principle"; it is a causal relation that we believe to obtain between "fire," i.e. the cause, and "paper burning," i.e. the effect. Thus, we may refer to this kind of belief, and, in fact, any kind of belief that is based on the comparison of a cause and an effect as a *philosophical* probable belief. As such, philosophical probable belief is a result of reason, not a conditioning process. We can call this reasoning process "philosophical probable reason."

In order to engage in philosophical probable reason, we must, it seems, be able to explicitly distinguish between the cause and the effect, e.g. we must be able to distinguish "fire" from "paper burning." We must also be able to distinguish these causes and effects from *ourselves*, or at least, be capable of thinking of these things as existing independently from our perceptions of them. Otherwise, it seems, our situation would be hopelessly complicated; e.g. if we thought that both "fire" and "paper burning" were actually parts of ourselves, then the fire would not actually cause the "paper" to burn. Rather, somehow, we would be "causing" a part of ourselves to "burn." In other words, we would lack what Bennett calls "objectivity concepts" (1971: 324), concepts that Bennett disparages Hume for not employing in the *Treatise*.[23]

However, it seems that such "objectivity concepts" need not be in place when it comes to thinking in terms of *natural* causation, e.g. whenever we have an impression of fire engulfing paper, we automatically and reflexively think of paper burning, without necessarily thinking of these perceptions as being distinct from ourselves. Moreover, we do not even reflectively distinguish these ideas from each other; we are just compelled to think of one whenever we have the impression of the other one. Thus, although Hume does not explicitly say as much, this seems to be another aspect of the distinction between natural and philosophical causation: the former does not, it seems, necessarily invoke objectivity concepts, while the latter does.[24]

§8 Transcendental causation

At this point, we may consider, in bit more detail, the process behind imagining "secret causes." Doing so will show us how this process is fundamentally different from the process where, by way of a reasoned reaction to the vulgar, the philosophers imagine that objects are the causes of our perceptions.

Recall that Hume explains in the first passage pertaining to what I call transcendental causation that we must move "beyond the impressions of the senses" to imagine a "secret cause" such that in turn, we are better able to make comparisons (i.e. reason about) of objects that admit of a perfect identity (T 1.3.2.2; SBN 73–74). In particular, as explained earlier, we experience a set of resembling impressions that we imagine are caused by an object with a perfect identity. Thus, we are thinking in terms of *some* kind of causal inference, particularly, one that associates a set of resembling impressions with an idea (i.e. an imagined cause).

Indeed, Hume tells us in the second portion of text pertaining to transcendental causation – found in "Of skepticism with regard to the senses" – that this is a very *special* "kind of . . . causation" (T 1.4.2.19; SBN 195)) which, by virtue of being "considerably different" (T 1.4.2.21; SBN 197) from other kinds of causation, enables us to imagine an "insensible" (T 1.4.2.21; SBN 198) idea of an object that admits of a perfect identity. In particular, Hume explains, before we imagine their respective and "insensible" causes, our perceptions appear to us as "loose[ly]" (T 1.4.2.22; SBN 198) and "irregular[ly]" (T 1.4.2.21; SBN 197) "constant and coherent" (T 1.4.2.20; SBN 195). However, once we imagine that an object with perfect identity is causing such perceptions, the constancy and coherence of our perceptions appears more "regular," "compleat," and "uniform" (T 1.4.2.22; SBN 198). Hume explains that this phenomenon is somewhat analogous to the way in which we might imagine a "correct and exact" standard of equality when doing mathematics. This standard is based on the "loose" notions of equality that we actually perceive. In virtue of imagining an exact standard, it makes what we actually perceive, i.e. our "loose standards" (T 1.4.2.22; SBN 198), seem more precise. Moreover, imagining such causes enables us to coherently think in terms of ordinary (i.e. non-transcendental) causal relationships which obtain between objects that *do* admit of a perfect identity (T 1.4.2.20; SBN 196).[25]

In the third portion of text pertaining to transcendental causation – also found in "Of skepticism with regard to the senses" – Hume explains how we imagine the object "time" as a cause of change, similar to how we imagine objects that admit of perfect identity to cause sets of resembling perceptions. Doing so, very generally speaking, allows Hume to explain how we might imagine ideas of objects with perfect identities that persist in "time," although our *perceptions* of such objects change, i.e. vary with "time." Thus, in order to even think of anything as occurring in "time," we must first imagine time as a cause and, more complicated still, imagine objects that admit of a perfect identity as persisting "in time." Again, this is a very special "kind" of causation because the cause that we imagine is never perceived, regardless of if it is the object "time" or the typical objects that we imagine to admit of a perfect identity, i.e. objects that we believe we have impressions of, e.g. tables, chairs, etc.

However, in all three cases, although it is abundantly clear that Hume thinks that this process involves some kind of inference, i.e. a *special* kind of causation, it does *not*, at least initially, seem to involve any kind of a comparison or reasoning process. For, like natural causation, this process seems to be almost reflexive, in the respect that upon experiencing a set of resembling perceptions, we are naturally and "always" and "almost universally" (T 1.4.2.29; SBN 201) led to imagine an invariable and uninterrupted (or continuous and distinct) cause of those perceptions. Indeed, Hume writes just before discussing "secret causes" that: "we ought not to receive as reasoning any of the observations we may make concerning *identity*" (T 1.3.2.2; SBN 73) He also claims – in no uncertain terms – that we do *not* use "reason" to establish "the belief of objects independent of the mind," as the philosophers mistakenly do. Rather, this belief is "*entirely* [owed] to the imagination" (T 1.4.2.14; SBN 193).

It is entirely plausible, then, that, like natural causation, transcendental causation is a kind of inference, but it is reflexive – we do not think about it, we just "universally" and "always" do it. However, like natural causation, it may eventually *yield* a comparison, i.e. what we might characterize as a kind of "philosophical" transcendental causation. For example, we may eventually compare what we take to be a mind-independent thing that causes our perceptions with the perceptions themselves; at this point we would be explicitly aware of our "objectivity concepts," although we would not, it seems, be aware that we imagined them. Indeed, when such "objectivity concepts" are in place – i.e. when we are made aware of them *via* what we may characterize as transcendental philosophical reasoning – we may then, and only then, proceed to engage in philosophical probable reasoning, where we compare ideas of objects that we think are not only independent of each other, but also independent of ourselves. Indeed, in order to use basic logic, e.g. the modus tollens that the philosophers use to refute the vulgar, we must be able to think in terms of objectivity concepts and, at least, philosophical probable reasoning, where the latter presupposes the former, as explained above. For how else could we think in terms of "if p then q" where we distinguish p and q not only from each other, but from ourselves, and in turn, think of "if p then q" as a principle, which, it seems, is derivative of the philosophical probable relation of "p causes q?"

Thus, the philosophers simply could not reject the vulgar without having objectivity concepts in place, i.e. without first imagining causes. And thus, the philosophical position on the external world is fundamentally distinct from Hume's transcendental account of the external world; the former presupposes the latter.

§9 Conclusion

We have seen that Hume thinks that we *imagine* objects, and so, *we imagine the external world*. Moreover, we have seen that the process described in what I call the three transcendental moments of Book I of the *Treatise* is fundamentally different from both the vulgar process of imagining objects and the philosophical process of imagining objects. In particular, the transcendental process differs from the vulgar process in the respect that (1) the transcendental process does not assume that objects *are* impressions, while the vulgar process does; (2) rather, in the transcendental process, objects are imagined to be the *causes* of our interrupted and variable impressions; and (3) moreover, in the transcendental process, objects are *effectively* imagined to have a perfect identity, i.e. they are effectively imagined to be uninterrupted and invariable, or (roughly) equivalently, that they are continuous and distinct. However, Hume characterizes the vulgar conception of identity as "improper" and "imperfect" because the vulgar *cannot* effectively imagine the property of uninterruptedness (T 1.4.6.9; SBN 255–256).

Meanwhile, the transcendental process differs from the philosophical process of imagining objects in the respect that: (1) in all three cases of the transcendental process, objects are *not* imagined as a result of a calculated, conscious rejection of the vulgar position, which, in turn, inspires a rather troublesome union between reason and the imagination. Rather, in all three cases, it seems clear that Hume was committed to a process that is a necessary condition of possibility for ordinary experience; this is something that, Hume claims, we must "always" "almost universally" and, it seems, *reflexively* do (T 1.3.2.2; SBN 74; T 1.4.2.29; SBN 201). In particular, we must be able to effectively imagine ideas of invariable and uninterrupted objects such that we may, in turn, reason *about* objects; generally speaking, such ideas constitute what Bennett calls the missing "objectivity-concepts" (1971: 324) in Book I of the *Treatise*. Similarly, they constitute what Pears (1990) and Mounce (1999) would refer to as "pre-theoretical" aspects of the *Treatise*; (2) moreover, in the case of the ancient and modern philosophical position on objects, as well as cases where philosophers imagine immaterial soul-objects, ideas of objects are not based on impressions (T 1.4.3–5; SBN 219–251). For instance, the Ancients' idea of a "substance" is not based on any substance impression. In principle, it could not be; by definition, "substances" cannot be apprehended with our senses – they are, as Hume puts it, "invisible" (T 1.4.3.4; SBN 220). Similarly, Modern philosophers who believe in primary qualities and immaterial souls maintain that we never have an impression of either. As a result, Hume thinks that all of these philosophical conceptions of objects are utterly "incomprehensible" and smack of the "occult" (T 1.4.3.8; SBN 222). However, in the three instances where Hume discusses the transcendental account of objects, the ideas that we imagine are *not* incomprehensible. Rather, they are based on impressions, specifically sets, or what Hume refers to as "species" of "perfectly resembling" but interrupted perceptions (T 1.3.2.2; SBN 74).

Finally, we might conclude that in a very general respect, Hume anticipated Immanuel Kant's later work in the *Critique of Pure Reason*, written approximately 40 years after Hume's *Treatise*. There, Kant presented a complicated and lengthy account of transcendental conditions, including "objectivity concepts." Thus, in many respects, both Hume and Kant influenced the field of what we currently call "psychology"; both philosophers were deeply concerned with understanding how the human mind works, especially with regard to how it allows us to articulate what we think is the "external world."

Notes

1 Grene (1994); Bennett (1971); Steinberg (1981); and Dicker (2007).
2 Wilson (1989); Flage (1990); Costa (1989); G. Strawson (2007); and Wright (2007).
3 Price (1940); Kemp Smith (1941); Wilbanks (1968); and Waxman (1994).
4 Because the *Treatise* is so unique and complicated, I cannot properly contextualize it with Hume's broader corpus without a great deal of explanation. For this reason, we will not take Hume's other work (e.g. *The Enquiry*) into consideration here.
5 Hume also thought that the "self" is imagined. However, most would argue that the "self" is not a part of the "external world," and thus, the "self" falls outside the purview of this chapter.
6 Or, alternatively, the "continuous and distinct" causes; see §3 of this chapter.
7 However, it is not my intention to carefully explicate the textual evidence needed to show that Hume did, indeed, present a transcendental position in the *Treatise*. For such evidence, I point the reader to my

book, *Imagined Causes: Hume's Conception of Objects* (Springer, 2013). In this chapter, by summarizing the evidence, I hope to show the reader why it is, at least on a very general level, *plausible* to conclude that Hume employed a transcendental conception of objects.

8 T 1.4.2.29–30; SBN 200–201; T 1.4.6.6; SBN 200–201; T 1.4.6.15; SBN 259.

9 A careful discussion of Hume's notion of representation would take us too far afield. Thus, for our purposes, we can think of it as a kind of copying. For more detail, see Rocknak (2013: 15–27).

10 Note: "'Tis impossible for the mind to fix itself steadily upon one idea for any considerable time; nor can it by its utmost efforts ever arrive at such a constancy" (T 2.1.4.2; SBN 283; emphasis added). That is, we cannot fix our minds upon one object such that it appears "steady" or "constant" to us, i.e. *invariable*. Also consider 1.4.6.2; SBN 251: "*there is no impression constant and invariable.* Pain and pleasure, grief and joy, passions and sensations succeed each other, and never all exist at the same time" (emphasis added). Here again, in the course of explaining that we never experience an invariable impression, Hume uses 'constant' interchangeably with 'invariable.'

11 To see that is the case, in no uncertain terms, consider: 1.3.2.1–2; SBN 73–74; 1.4.2.11; SBN 192; 1.4.2.15–22; SBN 194–198; 1.4.2.3–10; SBN 188–191; 1.4.6.2; SBN 251–252; 1.4.6.4; SBN 252–253; 1.4.6.5; SBN 253; 1.4.6.6; SBN 253–255. Cf. Rocknak (2013: 125–138).

12 See Rocknak (2013: 138–151).

13 See Rocknak (2013: 159–178) and Rocknak (2007).

14 Hume presents us with the following biconditional, where 'C' denotes "continued existence," and 'I' denotes an "independent existence": (I → C) & (C → I). The philosophers conclude that, by definition, perceptions cannot exist unperceived, i.e. they do not exist *independently* of our perception. Thus, using the second half of the biconditional and modus tollens, they conclude that sense impressions cannot be continuous i.e. ~C. However, it must also be *shown* why perceptions do not have an independent existence, i.e. ~I must be derived rather than merely stipulated, as it was above. So, press an eye with a finger, which will effectively double all your current visual sense impressions. As a result of doing so, you will conclude that our perceptions do not continue when we are not perceiving them because their existence clearly depends on the way in which our eyes perceive them. Thus, you will conclude ~C. Following, using the first half of the biconditional and modus tollens, you will conclude ~I. This leads to a logical contradiction (or, as Hume puts it, a "fallacy" (T 1.4.2.44; SBN 210)): the vulgar assume I, but given what we have seen above, we must conclude ~I. Thus, we have both I and ~I, and so, a formal *reductio*, where the conclusion is ~I. Following, Hume explains that our impressions obviously vary according to which physical position we might view them from, and according to what state of health we are in, etc. (T 1.4.2.45; SBN 211). As a result, Hume concludes that we have still more evidence to show that impressions are not independent of our bodies – given that they obviously depend on the current physical condition of our bodies. That is, we may conclude, again, ~I, and thus, again using the second half of the biconditional and modus tollens, we may conclude ~C. Thus, mirroring what we saw above, the logical contradiction (or again, as Hume puts it, the "fallacy") is: the vulgar assume C, but must conclude ~C, so, we have both C and ~C, and thus, a formal *reductio*, where the conclusion is ~C. Thus, the ultimate conclusion is that impressions are neither independent of our perception, nor do they continue when we are not perceiving them. See Rocknak (2013: 181–183).

15 The bulk of Hume's discussion of the vulgar position is discussed in T 1.4.2.31–40; SBN 201–208, and intermittently in 1.4.3–1.4.6.

16 See Rocknak (2013: 228–230) to see how Hume's rejection of the vulgar position relates to what he refers to as "true philosophy" on T 1.4.3.9; SBN 223.

17 See Rocknak (2013: 181–188). Also, recall that for the purposes of this chapter, we are using continuity and distinctness interchangeably with uninterruptedness and invariability.

18 Although Hume discusses variants of 1.4.2's principle of identity in 1.4.6, the bulk of 1.4.6 consists of giving three separate accounts of the transition from the vulgar perspective to the philosophical perspective. See Rocknak (2013: 189–217) for more detail.

19 And so, we must rule out those scholars who maintained that Hume thought that we imagine objects, but we do not imagine them to be causes, e.g. Price (1940), Kemp Smith (1941), Wilbanks (1968), and Waxman (1994). Moreover, we can also rule out the theory that Hume primarily used the word 'object' in an intentional sense (cf. Salmon 1983). For although Hume did have occasion to use the word 'object' in this sense (e.g. T 1.2.6.2; SBN 66), such usage does not reflect his more comprehensive position on objects.

20 See T 1.3.2.2; SBN 73 and Rocknak (2013: 29–50). Moreover, it needs to be noted that Hume does, confusingly enough, periodically refer to the natural relation of causality as an "inference" (e.g. T 1.3.6.2;

SBN 87, T 1.3.6.12; SBN 92, 1.3.12.20; SBN 139) or as "reason" (T 1.3.8.12; SBN 103). In fact, he even titles 1.3.16 "Of the reason of animals," where he discusses non-human animal thought, which is equivalent to the way in which humans naturally associate perceptions. Regardless, this process does not consist of any kind of "comparing."

21 Cf. De Pierris (2002: n. 20), Schliesser (2007), and Owen (1999: 151–153). See also Rocknak (2013: 29–51).

22 Hume employs a number of different kinds of belief in Book I of the *Treatise*. See Rocknak (2013: 241–243).

23 Bennett writes: "The notion of 'contradiction' has no place here unless I already accept a large body of theory: the proposition that I inhabit a world of objects, many hypotheses about their general behavior, and some hypotheses of the form 'I have perceptions of kind K only when in the presence of objects of kind K'" (p. 324). Bennett concludes, "This is the greatest case yet of Hume's failure [to properly] set the scene for an analysis of objectivity-concepts" (p. 324). However, as shown above, Hume does, indeed, take great pains to present "objectivity concepts" on T 1.3.2.1–2; SBN 73–74; T 1.4.2.15–24; SBN 194–199; and T 1.4.2.25–30; SBN 199–201. See Rocknak (2013: 105–122), where I address Bennett's concerns in the context of the passages that concern him.

24 See Rocknak (2013), Chapter 2 and pp. 254–259.

25 See Rocknak (2013: 112–118).

References

Bennett, J. (1971) *Locke, Berkeley and Hume: Central Themes*, Oxford: Oxford University Press.

Costa, M. J. (1989) "Hume and Causal Realism," *Australasian Journal of Philosophy* 67(2): 172–190.

DePierris, G. (2002) "Causation as a Philosophical Relation in Hume," *Philosophy and Phenomenological Research* 64(3): 499–545.

Dicker, G. (2007) "*Hume on the Intermittent Existence of the Objects of the Senses*," Paper presented at the 153rd Creighton Club Conference, Hobart and William Smith Colleges, Geneva, NY.

Flage, D. (1990) *David Hume's Theory of Mind*, London: Routledge.

Garrett, D. (1997) *Cognition and Commitment in Hume's Philosophy*, Oxford: Oxford University Press.

Grene, M. (1994) "The Objects of Hume's Treatise," *Hume Studies* 20(2): 163–177.

Mounce, H. O. (1999) *Hume's Naturalism*, New York: Routledge.

Owen, D. (1999) *Hume's Reason*, Oxford: Oxford University Press.

Pears, D. (1990) *Hume's System*, Oxford: Oxford University Press.

Price, H. H. (1940) *Hume's Theory of the External World*, Oxford: Oxford University Press.

Rocknak, S. (2013) *Imagined Causes: Hume's Conception of Objects*, Dordrecht: Springer.

———. (2007) "The Vulgar Conception of Objects in 'Of Skepticism with Regard to the Senses," *Hume Studies* 33(1): 67–90.

Salmon, C. V. (1983) *The Central Problem of Hume's Philosophy*, New York: Garland.

Schliesser, E. (2007) "Two Definitions of 'Cause', Newton and the Significance of the Humean Distinction Between Natural and Philosophical Relations," *The Journal of Scottish Philosophy* 5(1): 83–101.

Smith, N. K. (1941) *The Philosophy of David Hume: A Critical Study of its Origins and Central Doctrines*, New York: Palgrave Macmillan.

Steinberg, E. (1981) "Hume on the Continued Existence and the Identity of Changing Things," *Hume Studies* 7(2): 105–120.

Strawson, G. (2007) "David Hume: Objects and Power," in R. Read and K. Richman (eds.), *The New Hume Debate*, rev. edn, New York: Routledge, pp. 31–51.

Waxman, W. (1994) *Hume's Theory of Consciousness*, Cambridge: Cambridge University Press.

Wilbanks, J. (1968) *Hume's Theory of Imagination*, The Hague: Martinus Nijhoff.

Wilson, F. (1989) "Is Hume a Skeptic with Regard to the Senses?" *Journal of the History of Philosophy* 27(1): 49–73.

Wright, J. P. (2007) "Hume's Causal Realism: Recovering a Traditional Interpretation," in R. Read and K. Richman (eds.), *The New Hume Debate*, rev. edn, New York: Routledge, pp. 88–99.

10

HUME'S SELF

Yumiko Inukai

Hume put forward a radical view of the self[1] and personal identity in which he rejects the self as substantial and identical over time. A popular conception of Hume's account of the self suggests that he essentially denies the reality of the self altogether. This popular conception is not entirely wrong: Hume maintains that the idea of an identical, simple self is a fiction. Nonetheless, Hume does not reject the existence of the self altogether. He tackles the issues of the self as an empirical matter and addresses them solely on an empirical basis. This allows him to affirm the existence of the self and personal identity by explaining the psychological mechanisms that give rise to them.[2] Hume's *radical* attitude as a philosopher does not stop at providing an ingenious account of the self and personal identity.

He, interestingly and peculiarly, expresses his dissatisfaction with some aspects of his account later in the Appendix to the *Treatise*. He confesses that he is unable to resolve a contradiction that he finds between two principles that are intimately implicated in his account, which are (1) "all our distinct perceptions are distinct existences" and (2) "the mind never perceives any real connexion among distinct existences" (T App. 20; SBN636). The passages in the Appendix are both illuminating and puzzling: *illuminating*, because Hume reiterates "a promising aspect" of his earlier account; puzzling, because the two principles above are not inconsistent with each other and it is not clear what problem they pose to his account of personal identity (T App. 21; SBN 635–636). These puzzles have generated a number of different interpretations of Hume's dissatisfaction, and no agreement has been reached among interpreters so far.

Hume's legacy is not just the continuing interpretive dispute among commentators. His ingenuity in creating a rigorously empirical account of the self has remained highly influential. William James, even more than 100 years later, openly praised Hume for his empirical approach: he writes, "it is to the imperishable glory of Hume . . . to have taken so much of the meaning of personal identity out of the clouds and made of the Self an empirical and verifiable thing" (James 1890: 319). In the contemporary discussions of the self, Hume's analysis of the self is often a touchstone that is passionately defended or dismissed. Dennett, for example, ends his argument for the narrative conception of the self with the passage from T 1.4.6. in which Hume reports that he cannot find a self but only various perceptions (1992: 115). Zahavi, on the other hand, uses the same passage to criticize Hume's mistake, arguing for his minimal conception of the self (2005: 126).[3] Given their continued influence, Hume's views about the self clearly warrant careful scrutiny.

This chapter aims to clarify Hume's account of the self through careful analysis of his writings. I first examine the ideas of the self that Hume rejects and then investigate his positive stance and view of the self by drawing a parallel between his accounts of external objects and the self. Finally, I discuss his psychological account of our belief in the identical self in detail.

Of rejected ideas of the self

Before delving into "Of personal identity," it is worth noting two points that Hume makes in "Of the immateriality of the soul," which amount to the rejection of an idea of the self as a substance. He argues that (1) the idea of an immaterial substance is unintelligible, and (2) perceptions can exist independently, that is, without the need for a substance to support for their existence. Hume understands a substance to be something that the philosophers posit as a subject to which our perceptions belong (T1.4.5.2; SBN232). Applying his familiar Copy Principle[4] to probe this idea, Hume asks: from what impressions are the ideas of substance and of inhesion derived? Given that a substance is supposed to be something in which perceptions inhere, Hume argues that it must be different in *kind* from perceptions. If so, any impression, being a mere accident of a substance, would not be able to represent adequately, or "resemble," a substance itself. Therefore, there cannot be an impression of a substance. The idea of an immaterial substance is therefore empty and unintelligible (1).

The philosophers can respond by defining a substance as "*something which may exist by itself*" and claim that perceptions are merely "accidents," which need a support for their existence (T 1.4.5.5; SBN 233). Interestingly, Hume's response illuminates his view on the nature of perceptions:

> Whatever is clearly conceiv'd may exist; and whatever is clearly conceiv'd, after any manner, may exist after the same manner. This is one principle. . . . Again, every thing, which is different, is distinguishable, and every thing, which is distinguishable, is separable by the imagination. This is another principle. My conclusion from both is, that since all our perceptions are different from each other, and from every thing else in the universe, they are also distinct and separable, and may be consider'd as separately existent, and may exist separately, and have no need of any thing else to support their existence. They are, therefore, substances, as far as this definition explains a substance.
>
> (T 1.4.5.5; SBN 233)

According to the so-called Conceivability Principle, there is no metaphysical absurdity or impossibility for something to actually exist in the way that it can be conceived. Since it is conceivable that perceptions separable by the imagination exist separately from other things, it is possible that they exist by themselves. This possibility suggests that perceptions could exist on their own (2), which satisfies the definition of substance.[5] Therefore, the philosophers' definition also fails to provide a sufficient notion to differentiate a substance from perceptions. Moreover, this also shows that the idea of inhesion, supposed in the relationship between a substance and perceptions, is unintelligible because "nothing appears requisite to support the existence of a perception" (T 1.4.5.6; SBN 234).

Having argued that both views of substance are unintelligible, Hume considers the idea of the self that "some philosophers" supposedly have in the following section, "Of personal identity." On their view, the self is something with "perfect identity and simplicity . . . to which our several impressions and ideas are suppos'd to have a reference" (T 1.4.6.1–2; SBN 252).[6] Hume also reports that they "imagine we are every moment *intimately conscious of*" such a self, and its existence is so certain that it is "beyond the evidence of a demonstration" (T 1.4.6.1; SBN 252).

Before considering Hume's objections, it is worth considering whose view of the self he is engaged with. Descartes' view of the mind seems to fit the bill.[7] For Descartes, the mind *is* a "created thinking substance" that "exists in such a way as to depend on no other thing for its existence" (except God's concurrence) (Descartes 1985: vol. 1, 210). It is capable of having different thoughts, which are modes of the mind and whose existence depends on the mind by inhering in it (Descartes 1985: vol. 1, 215–216). Furthermore, the mind as immaterial substance is distinguished from material substance as indivisible and uncompounded (Descartes 1985: vol.2, 59); thus, it is simple and unchanging. Such a thinking substance is clearly identified as him*self* as his *Cogito* reasoning shows: his own existence as a thing that thinks is affirmed by the awareness of thoughts. Descartes is also certain that the "I" whose existence is grasped here is also one and the same "I" responsible for various mental activities like doubting, understanding, and willing. Finally, Descartes declares that the existence of the "I" is grasped through an intuitive, immediate awareness of thoughts, and not established by any inferential argument (Descartes 1985: vol. 2, 100; Descartes 1991: vol.3, 333), although he also makes it clear that we cannot be directly aware of a substance but can come to know it indirectly by the awareness of its attribute (Descartes 1985: vol. 1, 210; Descartes: 1985: vol. 2, 124). Therefore, for Descartes, the mind, or the self, is something that is simple, exists identically and continuously over time, has various thoughts, and most importantly reveals itself in our immediate awareness of particular thinking activities.[8]

Locke clearly maintains that the self or a person is a thinking thing who is always aware of itself as a subject of thinking or perceiving; thus he says, "it being impossible for anyone to perceive, without perceiving, that he does perceive" (Locke 1975: 138).[9] According to Locke, when I am drinking coffee, it is not just the drinking activity and a taste of bitterness that are present in my perceptual awareness; my *self*, as the one tasting, is also present. Locke explains in light of this structure of consciousness that the continuity of one and the same "I" is established in the continuity of consciousness linked by memories: the "I" is aware of itself as the one having had all the remembered experiences. So, for Locke, we are intimately conscious of ourselves as subjects of thinking and perceiving in each moment, and as far as the continuity of consciousness is established through memory, we must be also constantly aware of our identity. However, since Locke explicitly distinguishes the notion of the self from that of substance, simplicity cannot be inferred simply from the continuing existence of one and the same self. It is unclear whether Locke considers the subject recognized in each mental act as a simple being.

However, neither Descartes' nor Locke's accounts satisfies the view of the self entirely that Hume attributes to some philosophers. Hume's description of their view is also unhelpful: it is unclear what he means when he says they "imagine . . . that we *feel* [the self's] existence and its continuance in existence" (T 1.4.6.1; SBN 252; my emphasis). This description might fit Descartes' *intuitive* grasp of the "I" in the *Cogito* result. Whomever Hume's target might be, he nonetheless quickly rejects the idea of the self as a simple and invariably persisting subject to which perceptions belong by arguing that there is no impression that could give rise to such an idea. He offers two types of arguments, one conceptual and the other observational.[10]

The first argument is a conceptual one: Hume argues that to count as an impression that would give rise to the philosophers' idea of the self, it must be *one simple* impression that is *invariably* and *constantly* present through the whole course of our lives. Moreover, it would also have to serve as a reference point for various perceptions that occur over time. So, it could not be a momentary impression; it must be a simple, yet somehow temporarily extended, single impression, which is absurd. All impressions are "fleeting and perishing," after all (T 1.4.2.20; SBN 195):

there is no impression constant and invariable. Pain and pleasure, grief and joy, passions and sensations succeed each other. . . . It cannot, therefore, be from any of these impressions, or from any other, that the idea of self is deriv'd; and consequently there is no such idea.

(T 1.4.6.2; SBN 251–252)

No impression can possibly be a candidate for an original impression of a simple, unchanging, persisting self. Therefore, the philosophers' idea of the self (and perhaps Descartes' idea of the mind/self/soul) is not intelligible.

Hume turns to another, observational argument:

For my part, when I enter most intimately into what I call *myself*, I always stumble on some particular perception or other, of heat or cold, light or shade, love or hatred, pain or pleasure. I never can catch *myself* at any time without a perception, and never can observe any thing but the perception.

(T 1.4.6.3; SBN 252)

Hume directly attacks the claim of Locke and possibly other philosophers that we are "intimately conscious of" a self in our experience Hume contends that our awareness in each moment is only of an object or a feeling presented in a perception, and it does not contain a subject at all. So, when I am drinking coffee, I am aware only of the bitterness of coffee; awareness of my*self* is not present along with the bitterness in that experience. Hume fails to find a simple impression of a subject in his own experience. His introspective finding suggests that the way *my* succession of perceptions looks to *me* is the same as the way it looks to someone else because there is nothing *first*-personal about those perceptions.

Hume not only finds the philosophers' idea of the self to be unintelligible but also holds that their claim about their intimate conscious acquaintance with a simple, continuing subject of experience is empirically false. All we are aware of are particular perceptions, say, of the computer screen, of the yellow clock, of the hardness of the keyboard, of the pain in the back, etc. that come and go "in a perpetual flux and movement" (T 1.4.6.4; SBN 252). *That* is all the scientist of human nature can confirm by introspective observation.

It is worth noting that those who engage in a contemporary debate over the phenomenal presence of a subjective center in perceptual experiences take Hume's observation very seriously. Zahavi, who is a strong advocate of the actual presence of an experiential self, argues that Hume is mistaken in concluding that he could not find a self in or among perceptions but only particular perceptions. Hume fails to notice a critical experiential feature of his perceptions: that is, their first-person givenness, which, according to Zahavi, amounts to a pre-reflective awareness of a self.[11] Dennett, on the other hand, considers Hume's observational finding of the non-existence of the self as a good piece of introspective discovery: he uses it to support his claim that a self is just like a center of gravity that no one has or will ever perceive as an object in experience.[12] The debate is far from being resolved.

Of the true idea of the self

Hume's first positive view of the self appears after he finds that there is no perception of a simple, continuing self through introspection. He concludes that the self is nothing but a bundle of particular perceptions. This assertion may seem reasonable, considering what Hume does and does not find introspectively. However, it seems to be a strong metaphysical assertion of what the self is. Having rejected the existence of a perception of a simple, continuing self on both conceptual and observational grounds, why would he not just stop there and dismiss the existence of the self as an "unintelligible chimera" (T 1.4.3.7; SBN 222) like substance altogether? Instead, Hume presupposes that something that we call the "self" *does* exist somewhere internally and claims that it *is* a bundle of perceptions. How should, or could, we understand the import of Hume's seemingly strong claim about the self?

I suggest that a strong parallel between Hume's accounts of the self and of objects sheds light on his stance on the existence of the self and the significance of his claim about what the self is. With regards to particular substances or objects like apples and hats, for example, Hume argues that we only perceive particular qualities, such as colors, sounds, and tastes (T 1.1.6). He then concludes that the idea of a particular object "is nothing but a collection of simple ideas, that are united by the imagination" (T 1.1.6.2; SBN 16). Later in the *Treatise*, tackling the question of the external existence of objects, Hume asks, "why we attribute a CONTINU'D existence to objects . . . and why we suppose them to have an existence DISTINCT from the mind and perception?" (T 1.4.2.2; SBN 188). He asks a similar question regarding the self: "What then gives us so great a propension to ascribe an identity to these successive perceptions, and to suppose ourselves possest of an invariable and uninterrupted existence thro' the whole course of our lives?" (T 1.4.6.5; SBN 253). These questions strongly suggest that Hume grants the existence of both objects and the self. Indeed, he explicitly affirms the existence of objects right before posing the questions quoted above: he writes, "We may well ask, *What causes induce us to believe in the existence of body?* but 'tis in vain to ask, *whether there be body or not?* That is a point, which we must take for granted in all our reasonings" (T 1.4.2.1; SBN 187). In light of the parallel, it is thus reasonable to think that Hume also takes the existence of the self in the same way as the existence of objects. The self is something in which ordinary people, or in Hume's terms, "the vulgar," naturally believe in the normal, practical course of their lives, just like external objects. Thus, Hume may also be thinking that "'tis in vain to ask" whether there is the self or not and that the existence of the self is also "an affair of too great importance" (T 1.4.21; SBN 187) and so it is unquestionable.

Furthermore, Hume's positive projects regarding objects and the self are also similar: they are neither to justify the continuity and independent existence of objects nor to demonstrate the simplicity and identity of the mind. Rather, his intention is to elucidate psychological propensities underlying the generation of our beliefs in objects and the self. He is not concerned with what objects and the self truly are. Therefore, his seemingly strong claim about what the self *is* should not be understood as a claim about what the true nature of the self *must be*, like Descartes' claim about the mind. Disagreeing with the philosophers and yet assuming that the self exists, Hume is only saying that the self is a bundle of perceptions as far as he can best confirm it within the stricture of his empiricist enterprise. His positive statement about the self is made from the perspective of the scientist of human nature as opposed to the metaphysically minded philosophers.

If I am right about the parallel between Hume's views of objects and the self, the belief in the self whose generation Hume attempts to explain later must be the belief that the vulgar naturally hold. However, up until the point where Hume raises the question about a psychological propensity for the identity-ascription to perceptions quoted above (T 1.4.6.5; SBN 253), he only discusses some philosophers' idea of the self, not the vulgar's specifically. Speaking of the identity and the uniting principle of a person earlier, Hume even says, "in common life 'tis evident these ideas of self and person are never very fix'd nor determinate" (T 1.4.2.6; SBN 189–190). He seems to think that the vulgar have no clear idea of themselves as persons, let alone as simple and continuing selves. This may suggest that the belief of the self at issue is the philosophers' rather than the vulgar's. But, if that were the case, the parallel between his accounts of objects and the self would break down. The belief in external objects that Hume is concerned with in T 1.4.2 is a belief held by both the vulgar and the philosophers. In fact, he argues that the belief in the continuity and independence of objects and the underlying psychological mechanism generating that belief are so rooted in human nature that even the philosophers cannot remove it when they recognize that objects are presented to us only by way of internal, mind-dependent perceptions and they are obviously interrupted and varied. As a result, the philosophers come to postulate the "double existence of perceptions and objects" in order to preserve the initial belief (T 1.4.2.44–55; SBN 210–217).

I suggest the belief of the self that Hume accounts for in T 1.4.6 is also a belief that both the philosophers and the vulgar naturally have, although it may not be as clear in the characteristics of the self for the vulgar as it is for the philosophers. Hume's description of the struggle that the philosophers go through in the ascription of identity to diverse objects is quite illuminating (T 1.4.6.6; SBN 253–255). He explains that at the level of "our common way of thinking," the feeling of the mind in considering a succession of related diverse objects is so similar to the feeling in contemplating an invariable and uninterrupted object that the former action is confounded with the latter. This propensity to confound is so great and strong that the philosophers cannot "take off this biass" even when they constantly try to correct themselves and keep an accurate understanding (i.e. diversity) of objects. Having failed to shake off the tendency, they "feign some new and unintelligible principle" like "the notion of a *soul*, and *self*, and *substance*" to disguise the obvious variation and interruption and justify the verdict of the initial, irresistible tendency (T 1.4.6.7; SBN 253). Having explained this process of reflective thinking that the philosophers undergo, Hume returns to the level of "daily experience and observation" to show "to every fair enquirer" that the identity-ascription is indeed induced by the feeling of a smooth transition of the mind over a succession of related objects (T 1.4.6.7; SBN 253–254). Then, after elaborating on different instances of our identity-ascription to changing compounded objects that we observe in everyday experience,[13] he moves on to his account of the identity-ascription to the self by stating that "the same method of reasoning must be continu'd" (T 1.4.6.15; SBN 259).

It is clear that the "fair enquirer[s]" are the philosophers. However, it would be strange if the belief of the self at issue were only the philosophers' when the psychological mechanism behind it is something that operates at the level of our "common way of thinking." Hume deems such a mechanism as universal and irresistible to the extent that even the reflective philosophers are subject to it and cannot resist it. It is difficult to think that only the philosophers have the belief of the self-generated by it, especially when the vulgar come to acquire the belief of persisting objects in the same way. To say that the vulgar do not have a fixed and determinate idea of the self is not to mean that they do not have a belief of the self at all. Even the vulgar would think, perhaps naively, that they are the same persons as themselves who were drinking coffee 10 minutes ago or that they did not pop into existence yesterday. They may not be thinking that they are simple in the sense that they are totally uncompounded or indivisible, but they would take themselves to be *single* persons. The vulgar may not understand the characteristics of identity and simplicity and thus may not be able to describe the general characteristics of themselves as persons (let alone the nature of the self) in the way that the philosophers and the scientist of human nature can. But it is quite reasonable to think that the vulgar take it for granted that they, as single persons, exist continuously throughout the course of their lives.[14]

In sum, a similarity between Hume's discussions of objects and the self is striking and illuminating. It helps us see that not only does he presuppose the existence of the self just as we ordinarily do, but also his positive view of the self as a bundle of perceptions is only about the self insofar as immediate observation of perceptions can confirm. What is more, it shows that the belief of the self whose origin Hume offers a psychological account for is anyone's naturally held belief, either the vulgar's or the philosophers.' It is indeed quite remarkable that Hume does not reject our ordinary belief of the self when it is not, strictly speaking, a correct one.

Of psychological account of the identity-ascription

Let us look closely at Hume's explanations of the workings of the mind behind the identity-ascription to the self. Clearly, the characteristic of identity that we normally believe ourselves to have cannot be an appropriate one for Hume, because, according to Hume, the self is just a collection of fleeting perceptions. It is not, therefore, surprising that Hume declares that the kind of identity ascribed to the self, as well as to objects, is not *perfect* but rather *imperfect* identity (T 1.4.6.9; SBN 256). A perfect identity can be properly attributed only to unchanging and uninterrupted objects. But these objects or the self are a mere succession of distinct, changing perceptions, which obviously lack the required characteristics of invariance and uninterrupt-edness. Thus, the identity ascribed is imperfect. It is, as Hume also alludes, "a fictitious one" (T 1.4.6.15; SBN 259).

Hume's general account of the psychological mechanism underlying the *imperfect* identity-ascription appeals to what he calls "a general rule" or "general maxim." According to this rule or maxim, the mind tends to mistake one idea for another when a disposition of the mind that arises in considering one idea is the same as or similar to its disposition in considering another idea (T 1.4.2.32; SBN 203). Applying it to the case of the identity-ascription, Hume explains that the disposition of the mind in viewing an object with perfect identity is a very smooth and easy one, that "the passage from one moment to another is scarce felt" and there is no effort felt continuing its viewing (T 1.4.2.33; SBN 203). When a disposition of the mind in surveying a succession of diverse objects becomes as smooth and easy as the mind's disposition in viewing a perfectly identical object, an idea of identity mistakenly arises in the mind when the idea of diversity should (T 1.4.2.34; SBN 204). Hume identifies relations among objects as what pro-duces such a disposition:

> The very nature and essence of relation is to connect our ideas with each other, and upon the appearance of one, to facilitate the transition to its correlative. The passage betwixt related ideas is, therefore, so smooth and easy, that it produces little alteration on the mind, and seems like the continuation of the same action.
>
> (T 1.4.2.34; SBN 204)[15]

There are two points to be noted. First, Hume must be talking about *natural* relation rather than *philosophical* relation,[16] which is introduced earlier as "that quality, by which . . . the one natu-rally introduces the other" (T 1.1.5.1; SBN 13). Hume identifies three kinds of natural relation: resemblance, contiguity in space and time, and causation. Second, association *is* a smooth passage of the mind facilitated by natural relation. When a relation of resemblance, for example, obtains between *objects* of perceptions because there is a similarity between the *objects*, an association comes to be formed between the two *perceptions*, that is, a smooth transition happens from one perception to the other. An imperfect identity is then ascribed to a succession of the objects.

Hume further secures association between perceptions by way of the three natural relations as the only connection available for the working of the mind by eliminating any *real*, necessary connection that might possibly bind various perceptions together.[17] If perceptions were neces-sarily connected to form the human mind, then that would make perceptions inseparable from each other. Of course, Hume could not allow them to be that way, since they are essentially "different, and distinguishable, and separable from every other perception" (T 1.4.6.16; SBN 259). Moreover, real connections, even of cause and effect, cannot be observed between objects, as he argues earlier in considerable detail. So, if there is no real connection among perceptions that are related by identity, he argues, identity does not exist among perceptions themselves but must only be a "quality" that the mind attributes to them. There is no uniting principle among perceptions that could ground the identity of the whole mind; there are only the associative workings of the mind generated by the three natural relations that prompt our identity-ascription to the mind.

Let us be clear about the particular sort of observation that is used in the case at hand. Hume is careful with the description of what the mind does with perceptions when an identity gets to be attributed to their succession: it is not that perceptions just occur in succession in the mind, but it *reflects* on "the train of past perceptions" (T App. 20; SBN 635). There are two questions I would like to consider here. First, why *past* perceptions? Second, how could the mind's act of reflection be described without introducing a mind as an actor? Since objects to which an identity is to be ascribed are perceptions themselves, the mind's gaze must be directed to perceptions taken *as* perceptions. Reflecting on a flowing succession of perceptions, objects of reflection at each moment must be past ones, some of which may be immediately past. Introspection is, therefore, strictly speaking, retrospection.

In Hume's system, where there are only impressions and ideas, reflection must also be some form of perception, like memory and imagination. Hume introduces a type of ideas that take other perceptions as their objects earlier in the *Treatise*: "As our ideas are images of our impressions, so we can form secondary ideas which are images of the primary" (T 1.1.1.11; SBN 6–7).[18] There are original impressions and their corresponding ideas, which are perceptions of objects such as apples, trees, and cups. I call these perceptions "primary perceptions" and their objects "primary objects." There are second-order ideas which take primary perceptions as their objects, which Hume calls *secondary ideas*. By way of primary perceptions, we are said to be aware of primary objects like apples, and we can be aware of primary perceptions of apples *as* perceptions by way of secondary ideas. However, secondary ideas should not be understood as *reflecting* ideas, but more properly as *reflected* ideas. Secondary ideas are not monitoring ideas extraneously related to primary perceptions, but rather, they are copied images of past primary perceptions. So, the occurrence of such secondary ideas *is* an instance of primary perceptions being reflected on, just as ideas of memory are copied images of past impressions so that the occurrence of those ideas is an instance of past impressions being remembered. Interestingly, Hume defines consciousness as "nothing but a reflected thought or perception" (T App. 20; SBN 635).

In the case of our identity-ascription to an apple, a smooth and easy transition among primary perceptions of similar apple-looking objects (i.e. primary objects) is produced due to a resemblance relation among the primary objects, as a result of which an identity is ascribed to the successively presented, similar apple-looking objects. Our ascription of identity to the self happens in an analogous way, but at a different level. A smooth and easy transition is produced among *secondary ideas* that are images of primary perceptions due to one or more of the three natural relations holding among the primary perceptions, as a result of which an identity is ascribed to the successively presented, naturally related primary perceptions. Thus, Hume says: "identity is . . . merely a quality, which we attribute to them, because of the union of *their ideas* in the imagination, *when we reflect upon them*" (T 1.4.6.16; SBN 260; my emphasis). He further reiterates the point in the Appendix: "the thought alone finds personal identity, *when reflecting on the train of past perceptions*, that compose a mind, *the ideas of them* are felt to be connected together, and naturally introduce each other" (T App.20; SBN 635; my emphasis). To say that a felt connection or union (i.e. association) develops through the ideas of perceptions is to say that a feeling of smoothness and ease appears among the secondary ideas. Consequently, a fiction of identity arises at the level of associated secondary ideas, and it gets to be attributed to the succession of primary perceptions. Strictly speaking, therefore, the idea of an identical mind or personal identity arises at the level of secondary ideas, that is, reflected thoughts or consciousness, which Hume considers as "a promising aspect" of his view (T App. 20; SBN 635).

Let us see how the relevant natural relations for the self, resemblance and causation, generate the mind's smooth and easy progress in reflection. The resemblance relation is prevalent among perceptions in the mind because it contains many memory-ideas of past perceptions. Hume illustrates how a number of resembling perceptions create a smooth passage of the mind in its reflecting of them by supposing a situation where we could look into someone else's mind to observe a succession of his perceptions. Hume's purpose seems to be to make us imagine what it is like to observe a succession of resembling perceptions and see how it feels: *my* mind, observing a succession of another person's resembling perceptions, slides so easily from one perception to another that it feels as if I am looking at "the continuance of one object." He then claims, "The case is the same whether we consider ourselves or others" (T 1.4.6.18; SBN 261).

Two important points that I have already made above are implicated in this illustration. First, perceptions do not include any personal perspective in themselves at all, which is why "the case is the same" whether I am reflecting on a succession of my own perceptions or I am looking at a succession of someone else's.[19] Second, a feeling of the smooth passage arises in my mind that is distinct from the other person's mind in which a succession of related perceptions is observed and to which an identity is ascribed by my mind. There are two sets of perceptions involved here: the other person's and mine. Resemblance relations obtain among the other person's perceptions, whereas associative connections (i.e. the smooth passage) are formed among my perceptions of his perceptions; thus, the idea of identity arises in my mind, which in turn attributes it to the other person's mind. Applying this structure to my own case, there must be also two sets of perceptions: a set of primary perceptions and a set of secondary ideas of primary perceptions. Resemblance relations obtain among my primary perceptions, which contribute to associative connections among my secondary ideas of them. The idea of identity then arises on the side of the secondary ideas (i.e. reflected thoughts or consciousness) and an identity is attributed to the set of the resembling primary perceptions.

Hume's illustration of the role of resemblance makes a crucial point clear: association does not play a role of uniting primary perceptions to which an identity is to be ascribed. There are only two new things that arise in the mind as a result of the operation of the associative principle of resemblance and the general maxim of confounding dispositions: a mind's smooth and easy passage among secondary ideas and an idea of an identical mind. It is therefore important to remember that Hume's associative mechanism is not intended to establish the production of any type of unity of the mind.

Hume recognizes that causation is even more ubiquitous among perceptions, so much so that he takes it as sufficient to ground the arising of the idea of an identical mind. Accordingly, he goes on to claim:

> we may observe, that the true idea of the human mind, is to consider it as a system of different perceptions or different existences, which are link'd together by the relation of cause and effect, and mutually produce, destroy, influence, and modify each other.
>
> (T 1.4.6.19; SBN 261)

The relation between impressions and their corresponding ideas is a causal one, which Hume already explained earlier: a constant conjunction of an impression and its copied idea is observed "in such an infinite number of instances" (T 1.1.1.8; SBN 4). It is also Hume's contention that we can observe a succession of different types of impressions and ideas giving rise to each other. An impression of sensation, say, of a peach, produces a copied idea of the peach, which can remain even after the original impression of the peach disappears; the idea of the peach in turn produces a new impression that he calls an "impression of reflection," say, of desire, which then gives rise to its corresponding idea, and so forth (T 1.1.2.1; SBN7–8). Hume uses an analogy to emphasize that changes in perceptions and characters of the mind do not make it lose its identity, just as the republic remains the same even when its members and its laws and constitution change. Parts involved in various changes in the mind are related by cause and effect. To be consistent, however, Hume's point about the extensive role of causal relation should not be understood to be about causal relation uniting all the changing parts to form a whole mind. Causal relation is just one of the two natural relations that generate the mind's smooth and easy progress and underlie the arising of the idea of the identical mind. It is not a uniting principle of perceptions to form the human mind.

In the penultimate, short paragraph, Hume finally begins his explanation of our *simplicity*-ascription to the self. It parallels his psychological account of our *identity*-ascription. Simplicity is uncompoundedness; thus, a perfectly simple object is indivisible. The mind, being a bundle of distinct perceptions, is complex. The simplicity attributed to the mind is, once again, fictitious. The same general maxim and the associative mechanism work together to trigger our simplicity-ascription to the mind. He observes that the disposition of the mind arising in its surveying coexistent, different perceptions at a moment is very similar to its observing a perfectly simple and indivisible object, because of a close relation obtaining among those coexistent perceptions. The mind confounds its dispositions involved in each instance due to their similarity. Consequently, a simplicity is mistakenly ascribed to a collection of multiple perceptions despite its complex nature. Just like the case of our identity-ascription to successive perceptions, the close relation among coexistent, multiple perceptions facilitates the mind's effortless, "not a much greater stretch of thought" (T 1.4.6.22; SBN 263). As a result, the idea of a simple mind or self arises in the mind.

According to Hume, both identity and simplicity, or continuity and singularity (as the vulgar might think of them), are fictions that the mind attributes to what we call a *self*. Emphasizing that an identical, singular self is a fiction, Hume indicates that it is a mere construct created out of distinct perceptions by way of the associative principles of resemblance and causation. Importantly, however, he also demonstrates that such a self arises naturally and irresistibly in the minds of both the vulgar and the philosophers in everyday dealings. These are critical and significant aspects of Hume's analysis of the self. Although Hume may seem to reject the existence of a self altogether, it is important to notice that he allows a self to have some presence in our life. A self exists *as* a fictitious construct throughout our mental life.

Hume's final verdict on the analysis of the self rightly connects his views to the narrative notion of the self in the contemporary discussion of the self. Gallagher notes at the beginning of his discussion of the narrative self: "The narrative theory of self is a contemporary reading of [Hume's] view" (2000: 20).[20] Dennett compares a self to a center of gravity, showing that a self is also "an abstract object, a theorist's fiction," rejecting the substantial notion of the self.[21] He argues that a self emerges as a fictional character of a narratively constructed story in human. Hume does not appeal to a narrative construction to account for the emergence of a persisting self in mind; however, the line of a psychological explanation that he takes is a precursor to the narrative theory. Hume's introspective findings and analysis of the self have generated an exceptionally heated interpretive debate. More significantly, they continue to influence the subsequent discussions of the self up to this day.

Notes

1 He uses the terms "self" and "mind" interchangeably. Although Hume uses "the mind" or "the human mind" more often than "self" in T 1.4.6, he also says, "'Tis the composition of [perceptions], therefore, which forms the self" (T App. 15; SBN 634).

2 Don Garrett (1981, 1997, and 2011) provides a good survey of different types of interpretations as well as his own. Garrett's interpretation is a version of the interpretation according to which the associative principles are inadequate to connect all the perceptions to produce a unified collection that could yield an idea of a single, unified self in the way Hume wants. Other commentators who take this line of interpretation include Patten (1976), Loeb (1992), and Stroud (1977). More recent works that discuss different lines of interpretations that have been offered as well as new ones; see Ainslie (2008), Baxter (2008), Butler (2015), and Ellis (2006).

3 According to the minimal self view, a pre-reflective, immediate experience at the most basic level is not just of an object, but an object is presented in the first personal mode; that is, an object is first-personally presented *to me*. This *to-me-ness* is an immediate experiential character of experience, and it points to a minimal sense of the self. Zahavi (2005), therefore, says that Hume "overlooked something in his analysis, namely the specific givenness of his own experiences."

4 The Copy Principle, according to which every simple idea is derived from a past corresponding impression, is a methodological principle that Hume uses in his investigation of the intelligibility and comprehensibility of an idea.

5 Baxter gives a thorough explanation of this passage by drawing on other passages where Hume appeals to these principles and by making a distinction within the scope of the Separability principle (Baxter 2015: 53–57).

6 Hume first introduces the notion of identity in T 1.1.5: *perfect* identity can be attributed only to an *invariable* and *constant* object.

7 Traiger (1985: 47) and Broackes (2002: 200) think one of Hume's targets is Descartes.

8 Traiger (1985: 47) points out that one of Descartes' goals of the Wax argument in Meditation 2 is to show that he is more intimately conscious of his mind than physical object he senses.

9 Ainslie (2001: 558–559; 2008:141–143) presents Locke's view of the self and his account of personal identity as the most likely views that Hume has in mind in his rejection and critique of "some philosophers" view.

10 Traiger (1985) argues that these two types of arguments are directed against two distinct of the self in order to make good sense of the order of Hume's arguments.

11 Zahavi (2005: 126).

12 Dennett (1992: 115).

13 The mind ascribes an identity to a changing composite if the change in its parts does not destroy a common end or purpose of the composite (e.g. a ship, animals, and plants) (T 1.4.6.11–12; SBN 257). Other instances are: when changes in the parts of objects are small or gradual in proportion to whole objects (e.g. a mountain) or changes do not destroy specific identities of objects (e.g. a voice and a church) (T 1.4.6.9, 1.4.6.10, 1.4.6.13; SBN 256–258).

14 Pitson (2002: 77–79) similarly argues against Ainslie (2001), who argues that it is the philosophers' belief of the self that Hume explains by showing the strong parallel between Hume's accounts for the generation of anyone's belief in continuing bodies in 1.4.2 and the belief in the self 9n 1.4.6.

15 See also T 1.4.6.16, SBN 260.

16 In T 1.1.5, "Of relation," Hume distinguishes two types of relation, natural and philosophical. Unlike natural relation, philosophical relation is perceived to hold between two ideas that the imagination voluntarily compares.

17 What Hume means by "something that really binds . . . perceptions together" and "some real bond among his perceptions" must be *necessary* connections, since in rejecting such a connection, he refers to his previous discussion of the question regarding necessary connection between cause and effect.

18 Ainslie (2001) initially brought my attention to the role of secondary ideas in Hume's account of personal identity. See also Ainslie (2008: 145–146) and (Butler: 2015: 177–178).

19 This point, which is assumed by Hume here, is a critical point that is, perhaps correctly, criticized by the proponents of the "minimal self" view in the contemporary debate of the self.

20 Some of the proponents of the narrative approach to the self include Dennett (1991), Flanagan (1992), Gallagher (2000), Damasio (1999), and Velleman (2005).

21 Dennett (1992: 105).

References

Ainslie, D. C. (2001) "Hume's Reflections on the Identity and Simplicity of Mind," *Philosophy and Phenomenological Research* 60: 557–578.

———. (2008) "Hume on Personal Identity," in E. S. Radcliffe (ed.), *A Companion to Hume*, Oxford: Wiley-Blackwell, pp. 140–156.

Baxter, D. L. M. (2008) *Hume's Difficulty: Time and Identity in the Treatise*, London: Routledge.

———. (2015) "Hume on Substance: A Critique of Locke," in P Lodge and T Stoneham (eds.), *Locke and Leibniz on Substance*, London: Routledge, pp. 45–62.

Broackes, J. (2002) "Hume, Belief and Personal Identity," in P. Millican (ed.), *Reading Hume on Human Understanding*, Oxford: Clarendon Press, pp. 187–210.

Butler, A. (2015) "The Problem of Believing in Yourself: Hume's Doubts about Personal Identity," in D. C. Ainslie and A. Butler (eds.), *The Cambridge Companion to Hume's Treatise*, Cambridge: Cambridge University Press, pp. 165–187.

Damasio, A. (1999) *The Feeling of What Happens: Body and Emotion in the Making of Consciousness*, San Diego: Harcourt.

Dennett, D. (1991) *Consciousness Explained*, Boston: Back Bay Books.

———. (1992) "The Self as a Center of Narrative Gravity," in F. S Kessel, P. M Cole and D. L. Johnson (eds.), *Self and Consciousness: Multiple Perspectives*, Hillsdale, NJ: Erlbaum Associates, pp. 103–115.

Descartes, R. (1985) *The Philosophical Writings of Descartes*, trans. and edited by J. Cottingham, R. Stoothoff and D. Murdoch, vols 1 & 2, Cambridge: Cambridge University Press.

———. (1991) *The Philosophical Writings of Descartes*, trans. and edited by J. Cottingham, R. Stoothoff and D. Murdoch, vol 3, Cambridge: Cambridge University Press.

Ellis, J. (2006) "The Contents of Hume's Appendix and the Source of His Despair," *Hume Studies* 32: 195–232.

Flanagan, O. (1992) *Consciousness Reconsidered*, Cambridge, MA: MIT Press.

Gallagher, S. (2000) "Philosophical Conception of the Self: Implication for Cognitive Science," *Trends in Cognitive Science* 4(1): 14–21.

Garrett, D. (1981) "Hume's Self-Doubts about Personal Identity," *The Philosophical Review* 90(3): 337–358.

———. (1997) *Cognition and Commitment in Hume's Philosophy*, New York: Oxford University Press.

———. (2011) "Rethinking Hume's Second Thoughts about Personal Identity," in J. Bridges, N. Kolodny and W. Wong (eds.), *The Possibility of Philosophical Understanding: Reflections on the Thought of Barry Stroud*, New York: Oxford University Press, pp. 15–40.

James, W. (1890) *The Principles of Psychology*, vol.1. Cambridge, MA: Harvard University Press.

Locke, J. (1690) 1975. *An Essay Concerning Human Understanding*, edited by P. H. Nidditch, Oxford: Oxford University Press.

Loeb, L. E. (1992) "Causation, Extrinsic Relations, and Hume's Second Thoughts About Personal Identity," *Hume Studies* 18(2): 219–232.

Patten, S. C. (1976) "Hume's Bundles, Self-Consciousness, and Kant," *Hume Studies* 2(2): 59–75.

Pitson, A. E. (2002) *Hume's Philosophy of Self*, London: Routledge.

Stroud, B. (1977) *Hume*, London: Routledge.

Traiger, S. (1985) "Hume on Finding an Impression of the Self," *Hume Studies* 11: 47–68.

Velleman, J. D. (2005) "The Self as Narrator," in J. Christman and J. Anderson (eds.), *Autonomy and Challenges to Liberalism: New Essays*, Cambridge: Cambridge University Press, pp. 56–76.

Zahavi, D. (2005) *Subjectivity and Selfhood: Investigating the First-Person Perspective*, Cambridge, MA: MIT Press.

11

HUMEAN NATURALISM AND SKEPTICISM

P. J. E. Kail

The supposed tension between Hume's naturalism and his skepticism has been with us from at least the time of Kemp Smith. What is striking is just how little work tries to understand quite what is "naturalistic" about Hume's philosophy. That is not to say that it is completely ignored, and, indeed, Barry Stroud's classic *Hume* (Stroud 1977) is little short of a book-length investigation into the topic. In this chapter, I shall explore some senses of naturalism and relate them to aspects of Hume's skepticism. I am, though, much more concerned with the naturalism side of the coin, since that is less treated than the skepticism, and so my remarks on skepticism will be brief.

An evident issue is the very slipperiness of "naturalism" in the first place. The editors of *Naturalism in Question* (De Caro and MacArthur 2004: 3) remind of us of Lawrence Sklar's observation that "naturalism means many different things to many different people" is now a "philosophical commonplace." So rather than starting with some contemporary, and possibility tendentious, definitions of naturalism,[1] it is better explore some aspects generally thought to characterize naturalism in the company of Hume's texts.

Methodological naturalism

One key sense of "naturalism" is a methodological one. The *Treatise*'s subtitle, of course, is "an attempt to introduce the experimental method of reasoning into moral subjects." In this, Hume is often styled as the Newton[2] of philosophy, and one uncontroversial sense in which this is the case is as follows. Hume's explorations are unconstrained by any *a priori* conception of the nature of the human mind. It "seems evident," he writes, "that the essence of the mind being equally unknown to us with that of external bodies, it must be equally impossible to form any notion of its powers and qualities otherwise than from careful and exact experiments" (T Introduction 8; SBN xvii). One key sense of Newton's famous dictum *hypotheses non fingo* ("I frame no hypothesis") is that in natural philosophy one is not to let one's data or generalizations be contaminated by *a priori* conceptions of the nature of physical body. Newton develops this thought in his early work on color and light when he began to realize that Cartesian interpretations of empirical data on light and color were distorted by the metaphysical conception of matter as pure extension. Instead, he counsels one should generalize to principles on the basis of experience only. Similarly, in the *Abstract* Hume reports that he "proposes to anatomize human nature in a regular manner, and promises to draw no conclusions but where he [i.e. Hume] is authorized by experience. He talks with contempt of hypotheses" (Ab. 2; SBN 646). The aim is to arrive at general principles by "tracing up our experiments to the utmost, and explaining all effects from the simplest and fewest causes" (T Introduction 8; SBN xvii). These principles (and subsequent explanations based upon those principles) are arrived at through "a cautious observation of human life" (T Introduction 10; SBN xix).

So one sense in which Hume's approach in the *Treatise* is methodologically naturalistic is the rejection of *a priori* claims in favor of observation. Notice also that such a methodological approach does not saddle Hume with any significant foundationalist assumptions about meta-epistemology. He starts with claims about perceptions and the principles of association, but the vindication of these claims rests in their empirical status, their explanatory roles rather than as independently justified foundations for the rest of his philosophy.

Substantive naturalism

Second, naturalism can be conceived ontologically. All that exists is natural, and what is natural is all and only that which is recognized by the relevant sciences.[3] But yoking Hume's naturalism to an ontological doctrine along these lines is problematic. We can say that he rejects the "super-natural," but this is only a relatively mild bite: we cannot appreciate what is rejected without the relevant conception of natural with which the supernatural is contrasted. Furthermore, if Hume does commit himself to some general conception of what is natural, its implausible to see him as holding an immodest view, namely one whereby some finished human science will be such as to characterize or delineate exhaustively the world. Hume's naturalism, it seems to me, is a modest kind, inasmuch as while the method of sciences will include some things in an ontology, and rule others out, there is no reason to think this will be exhaustive. We "cannot go beyond experience" (T Introduction 8; SBN xii), and we cannot "establish any principles which are not founded on that authority" (T Introduction 10; SBN xviii). A corollary of this is that explanation ultimately gives out because we cannot grasp ultimate causes:

> [The] ultimate springs and principles are totally shut up from human curiosity and enquiry. Elasticity, gravity, cohesion of parts, communication of motion by impulse; these are probably the ultimate causes and principles which we shall ever discover in nature . . . [t]he most perfect philosophy of the natural kind only starves off our ignorance a little longer.
>
> (EHU 4.12; SBN 31)[4]

These issues about ontological commitments of naturalism are not uppermost in Hume's mind, however. The substance of Hume's naturalism is instead best approached by considering the slogan "human beings are part of nature." This is a slogan with which Bernard Williams' last writings (e.g. Williams 2000) on naturalism were concerned. Williams put this in terms of a dilemma: if, on the one hand, we characterize nature as 'all that there is,' the slogan is vacuous, but if, on the other hand, we try to characterize nature by appeal to some threshold limit of the sciences, there is a danger that a proper understanding of the human being escapes the natural, so conceived. Hume navigates this dilemma, though the route he takes is not trumpeted at the beginning of the project. If we take animals to be (relatively) unproblematically natural creatures, and we can exhaustively explain what is apparently distinctive about the human being in terms of animal materials, there is genuine bite to the claim that human beings are part of nature. Human beings are nothing but complicated beasts.

We are rather used to the idea of human beings as nothing but grand beasts, but it was hardly a commonplace in the intellectual milieu informing Hume's thought. The ways of establishing a categorical difference between humans and animals (over which humans supposedly have dominion) are different and often subtle, and we shall look at one in particular presently. What is of first significance is that the materials Hume introduces early in the *Treatise* – impressions, ideas, and the association of those perceptions – are not Hume's inventions and constitute materials that the philosophical tradition, stretching back to at least Hobbes, thought to characterize exhaustively animal cognition. Hume does not mention this fact at the beginning of the *Treatise* but is much more explicit about it later, declaring, almost as if an afterthought, that the "whole sensitive creation . . . [e]very thing is conducted by springs and principles, which are not peculiar to man, or any one species of animals" (T 2.2.12.1; SBN 397). This amounts to a large-scale view that the mechanisms (in the non-technical sense of 'mechanism') underlying human thought and behavior are no different in kind from those underlying animal behavior. So if we take "human nature" to mean the fundamental "spring and principles" that guide thought and behavior, then human nature is no different in kind from animal nature.

This idea is set against Christian conceptions of human nature, which are never far from Hume's sights. Human beings are not exceptional creatures, made in the Image of God.[5] It also connects to a favorite trope of ancient skepticism of comparing human and animal cognition. As I have argued elsewhere (Kail 2012), there is a descriptive[6] and evaluative dimension to the trope. The descriptive dimension insinuates that there is no difference in kind in cognitive mechanisms between humans and animals. The evaluative dimension is, as it were, a view of humanity's own presumptuousness in thinking itself as apart from the rest of creation. Thus, in "Of the dignity or meanness of human nature," Hume describes one species of philosophers who "exalt our species to the skies, and represent man as a kind of human demigod, who derives his origin from heaven, and retains evident marks of his lineage and descent," and another that "insist[s] upon the blind sides of human nature, and can discover nothing, except vanity, in which man surpasses the other animals, whom he affects so much to despise" (EMPL 80–81). Hume is evidently no friend to the first species of philosophy, but thinks that the second also is mistaken. Both species of philosophy draw "a comparison between men and animals, the only creatures endowed with thought that fall under our senses" (EMPL 82). The vast differences can seem favorable to humanity, thus leading to the first quasi-God like conception of human nature. But those who press the similarities between humans and animals do not merely insist "upon the weakness of human nature" but do so by "forming a new and secret comparison between man and beings of the most perfect wisdom" (EMPL 82–83). Both species operate with the notion of some supernatural exemplar, which we are thought falsely to resemble or to fall woefully short of it. But shorn of this supernatural exemplar, the notion of the meanness of human nature no longer has any purchase.

Reason, naturalism, and skepticism

We have a sense in which Hume's philosophy is methodologically naturalistic, and what substance there might be to substantial naturalism. Hume's naturalism is also *explanatory*. He seeks to explain human thought, behavior, and culture in terms of these relatively minimally characterized natural materials. The central project of Book I of the *Treatise* is to explain the operations of the understanding, including our reasoning faculties, which he accounts for in terms of the principles of association. But this explanatory ambition is often seen as secondary to a skeptical one. Hume's main aim, on this view, is to offer a negative *evaluation* of reason's epistemic standing. In popular philosophical consciousness, Hume poses "the problem of induction," purporting to show that beliefs about the unobserved lack positive epistemic standing.

This view of Hume is out of favor, though it is not without its defenders (most recently Winkler 2016). Here I can only make a few compressed remarks about this issue and its connection to naturalism.[7] Recall that the substance in substantive naturalism is the appeal to materials used to explain animal cognition. As I have argued elsewhere (Kail 2007), Hume's account of probable reason is essentially what others thought constituted animal cognition. The following sequence of passages from Leibniz's *Mondadology*[8] is telling in this respect. Consider first:

§26 Memory provides souls with a kind of *connectedness*, which resembles reason but must be distinguished from it. For we see that animals which have a perception of something that strikes them, and which they have previously had a similar perception expect, from the representation of memory, that which has been conjoined in that previous perception, and are led to sensations similar to those they have had before. For example, when one shows a stick to dogs, they recall the pain, that it has caused them, and whine and run off.

This is evidently an associative account of the inference, which is of course fundamental to Humean probable reason. Leibniz continues and in doing so gives us the elements of Hume's account of belief:

§27 The potent imagination that strikes and moves them, comes either from the magnitude (*grandeur*) or from the number of the preceding perceptions. For often a forceful impression (*une impression forte*) has in a moment the effect of long *habit*, or of many moderate perceptions oft repeated.

A "forceful impression" "strikes and moves" the animal in a manner akin to Humean impressions. But Leibniz counsels that such inferences should not be dignified with the term "reason" or its cognates. In the *New Essays* he writes:

Beasts pass from one imagining to another by means of a link between them which they have previously experienced. . . . In many cases children, and for that matter grown men, move from thought to thought in no other way but that. This could be called "inference" or "reasoning" in a very broad sense. But I prefer to keep to accepted usage, reserving these words for men and restricting them to the knowledge of some reason for perceptions being linked together. Mere sensations cannot provide this: all they do is to cause one naturally to expect once more the same linking that has been observed previously.[9]

Notice that Leibniz claims that such inferences are not the domain of reason because of a lack of "knowledge of some reason for perceptions being linked together." We may gloss this as follows: such inferences are not mediated via a grasp of some of normative consideration in favor of that inference. They are not a matter of moving from the thought that *p* to the thought that *q* in light of the awareness of *r* as a support for the inference.

Consider now the negative element in Hume's discussion of probable inference. His quarry is the nature of the inference we draw from impression to idea, and whether we are "determin'd by reason" to make the transition or by "a certain association or relation of perceptions" (T 1.3.6.4; SBN 88–89). We know that Hume's answer that we are not "determin'd by reason" rests on the fact that reason cannot support what has become known as the Uniformity Principle, the claim that nature is uniform. Hume thinks that we cannot support that claim in any way. Notice, however, that knowledge of the Uniformity Principle would constitute "knowledge of some reason for perceptions being linked together." We could infer effect from causes in the light of knowing that nature is uniform, a fact that would justify that inference. However, since we cannot justify that assumption, our inference cannot be so guided. We are left instead with "mere sensation" which "cause[s] one naturally to expect once more the same linking that has been observed previously." Reason for Hume is "brute" in the sense both that it is not caused by our capacity to grasp reasons in its favor *and* that the causal mechanism is the same as that which guides animals. In effect, Hume argues that the narrow sense of "reasoning," which Leibniz claims as the accepted usage, does not exist, and so it is the very broad sense of "reasoning" which Leibniz extends to animals that governs us, too.

That Hume's negative *considerations* lead to a substantive claim about the nature of the inference is not the same as a negative *evaluation* of its epistemic standing. As I mentioned, there is a long tradition of thinking that Hume is arguing that the inferences distinctive of probable reason have no positive epistemic standing. But this is very difficult to square with the text. As Louis Loeb (2008) shows, Hume treats probable inference as having epistemically positive standing. The project of the *Treatise* relies upon the results of probable inference as Hume uses "experience" and "experiments" in support of its claims. Probable inference is connected with epistemic success, of its being able to "discover" objects (T 1.3.2.2; SBN 73) and "[bring] us acquainted with such existences, as . . . lie beyond the reach of" sense and memory (T 1.3.9.3; SBN 108). Hume further refers to instances of reasoning "justly" (e.g. T 1.4.4.1; SBN 225) and draws a favorable contrast between habits in line with probable reason and those that are "merely the offspring of the imagination" (T 1.3.9.4; SBN 108).

It is possible, then, to read Hume's negative arguments about probable inference as indirectly supporting a claim of substantive naturalism. What Leibniz takes to constitute reason is impossible, and the inferences we draw are best explained in terms of the materials and brute inferences typical of animals. At the same time, Hume treats such inferences as having positive epistemic standing. This positive epistemic standing is itself understood to express a form of naturalism, namely *epistemic naturalism*. At a first approximation, epistemic naturalism sees terms of epistemic appraisal as intelligible in terms of some relatively unproblematic "naturalistic" terms. As that statement stands, it is hopelessly uninformative since we haven't characterized what is meant by "naturalistic." More informatively, one could attempt to understand evaluative and normative notions in descriptive terms. So "some belief *p* is justified," in Humean terms, could be understood ultimately as the fact that the belief that *p* is *irresistible* (Kemp Smith 1941) or that it contributes to doxastic *stability* (Loeb 2002). There is an overarching question, however, as to just why these *doxastic* properties should have any *epistemic* value. It may or may not be intelligible why we might value irresistible or stable beliefs for pragmatic reasons, but it seems an open question at least why properties should be epistemically valuable. If, however, we interpret "the belief that *p* is justified" as its being the product of a reliable process or mechanism, where "reliable" is understood as producing a preponderance of truth beliefs over false ones, then we can understand the normativity naturalistically and in a way that makes *epistemic* sense.[10] It is readily intelligible just how this property is related to truth, which is the aim of belief. Without, of course, claiming that Hume has a project so characterized explicitly in mind, it is perfectly plausible to see him assuming that reason is a faculty that is truth-conducive, and that its authority rests on its truth-conduciveness. Hume writes that our "reason must be consider'd as a kind of cause, of which truth is its natural effect" (T 1.4.1.1; SBN 180), a statement that seems to underwrite epistemic naturalism.

Reading Hume as treating probable reason as presumptively reliable is perfectly consistent with his claims that we cannot *justify* our reliance on reason by reason. As Don Garrett has emphasized (Garrett 2004), Hume's rejection of "antecedent scepticism" in the *Enquiry Concerning Human Understanding* is a rejection of any role for *a priori* forms of skepticism, and with it demands for an *a priori* vindication of reason against it. Legitimate skeptical worries emerge after, or are consequent upon, enquiry. When introducing consequent skepticism, Hume describes it as the idea that skeptics "are supposed to have discovered, either the absolute fallaciousness of [human] mental faculties, or their unfitness to reach any fixed determination in all those curious subjects of speculation, about which they are commonly employed" (EHU 12.5; SBN 150). But although Hume thinks there is something to consequent skepticism about probable reason, his conclusion is *not* that it is shows "the absolute fallaciousness" of our faculties. Instead, it is the softer conclusion that the skeptic

> seems to have ample matter of triumph; while he justly insists, that all our evidence for any matter of fact . . . is derived entirely from the relation of cause and effect; . . . that we have no arguments to convince us, that objects, which have, in our experience, been frequently conjoined, will likewise, in other instances, be conjoined in the same manner; and that nothing leads us to this inference but custom or a certain instinct of our nature; . . . which, like other instances, may be fallacious and deceitful.
>
> (EHU 12.22; SBN 159)

This reveals "the whimsical condition" of humanity, who cannot "satisfy themselves concerning the foundation" of the operations of reason. But saying that, because it is instinct, the inference "may be fallacious" is far from demonstrating the "absolute fallaciousness" of our faculties. It merely shows that we cannot know what we presume, namely the truth-conduciveness of the faculty. Certainly, the lack of arguments for the Uniformity Principle would show that probable inference is epistemically unwarranted *if* Hume thinks that that such arguments are the only things that can warrant the inference: but nowhere does Hume make such a statement.

That Hume treats probable reason as an epistemically good source of belief relates to his skepticism about the external world laid out in T 1.4.2, "Of scepticism with regard to the senses." Hume's ostensible aim is to examine the causes of the belief in body, but, famously, towards the end of that section he declares that he is "inclin'd to repose not faith at all in my senses" (T 1.4.2.56: SBN 217). The awareness of the causal origins of that belief, in both its vulgar and philosophical forms, destabilizes that belief, leading to suspension of belief. A key reason for this suspension of belief is the fact that the causation of the belief is not intelligibly linked to truth-conductive sources. The beliefs, in other words, cannot be caused by reason (see Loeb 2002 and Schmitt 2014).

There is another, less straightforward connection between epistemic naturalism and Hume's skepticism. Hume's claim that our reason is a kind of cause, of which truth its natural effect, is made near the beginning of the section entitled "Of scepticism with regard to reason." In barest outline, the argument is as follows. We are aware of our fallibility, and, virtue of this awareness, a norm emerges whereby we "must . . . in every reasoning form a new judgment, as check or controul on our first judgment or belief" (T 1.4.1.1; SBN 180). In so doing, the second-order judgment introduces an element of doubt, which decreases the probability of the first-order judgment. However, the norm iterates: the second-order judgment is itself subject to a higher-order judgment, which then introduces a further element of doubt:

> When I reflect on the natural fallibility of my judgement, I have less confidence in my opinions . . . and when I proceed still farther, to turn the scrutiny against every

successive estimation I make of my faculties, all the rules of logic require a continual diminution, and at last a total extinction of belief and evidence.

(T 1.4.1.6; SBN 182)

Quite a lot of recent attention has been devoted to this argument, its status, and whether Hume endorses the conclusion, understood as a negative evaluation of the epistemic standing of all beliefs.[11] I cannot comment on this huge issue here, except to say that it is not difficult to see argument as a natural outgrowth of the assumption of reliabilism. An interest in truth, the assumption that reason is a source of true belief, and an awareness of its fallibility naturally give rise to the norm Hume uses to drive this argument.

Causation and subject naturalism

There is another distinction within the notion of naturalism, which, though a contemporary one, is of first significance in understanding Hume. This is a distinction, drawn by Huw Price (Price 2011), between "subject" and "object" naturalisms. At a first approximation, object naturalism orients itself around a particular ontological conception of the natural. Science determines the ontology of nature. *Object* naturalism comes into play when this ontology generates "placement problems," roughly speaking, problems regarding how to accommodate seemingly recalcitrant phenomena within that ontological framework. If we are physicalists, how are we to understand consciousness, intentionality, morality, and modality and their place in this austerely characterized nature? There are a number of familiar ontological strategies that the naturalist can take with respect to these phenomena, such as a reduction or property identity claims. *Subject* naturalism, by contrast, focuses not on the world but on the subject: the human being. It focuses on the empirical investigation, and explanation, of the subject's thought and talk with respect to some area of discourse. Rather than asking, say, what moral properties are and how they can be accommodated in a world of physical properties, subject naturalists seek to explain how human beings come to think and talk in terms of moral properties. As such, the approach has the potential to bypass the ontological issue by illuminating the character of thought and talk in the area and showing that that it is, in fact, innocent of ontological commitments.

It seems to me that the real originality in Hume's discussion of causation lies in his turn to a subject naturalist approach to the matter. To see this, and to illustrate better what is distinctive of subject naturalism, let us consider, not the fact that he offers two definitions of 'cause,' but the way in which he arrives at them. Notice that in both the *Treatise* and the *Enquiry* Hume's discussion is primarily a discussion of causal *inference*, and Hume's interest in the causal relation is introduced as subordinate to this end. Causation is the only relation that "can be trac'd beyond our senses, and informs us of existences and objects, which we do not see or feel," and so to understand the inference we make from the observed to the unobserved we must "endeavour to explain fully [the causal relation] before we leave the subject of the understanding" (T 1.3.2.3; SBN 74). But he does not start by explaining that relation; instead, Hume tells us of his "seemingly preposterous" method of "examining our inference from the relation before we had explain'd the relation itself" (T 1.3.14.31; SBN 169). The subject naturalist interpretation of this "preposterous" method is to see Hume eschewing questions about the metaphysics of causation and instead focusing on our cognitive life in order to illuminate the role causation plays in it. Once we understand *how* causation figures in inference, we then grasp better *what* we represent by the concept. So the definitions emerge from the account of the role causation plays in our inferential lives rather than a prior attempt to articulate a metaphysic of causation.

Hume notes, early in his discussion of causal inference, two observed relations of objects deemed causal, namely that cause and effects are contiguous, and causes are temporally prior to effects. These two relations are introduced on predominantly[12] empirical grounds. None of this is very surprising. But two further features reveal the subject naturalist shape of Hume's approach. First, Hume introduces the notion of necessary connection and, after noting that none is observable, he elects to drop the direct approach to examining the "nature of that *necessary connexion*" and instead "beat about all the neighbouring fields" (T 1.3.2.13; SBN 78). Rather than asking what necessary connection is, he instead asks "why we conclude, that such particular causes must *necessarily* have such particular effects" (T 1.3.2.15; SBN 78). This is a shift from *what* necessity is to *how* it is that we come to *think* in terms of necessity. I shall come to the significance of this fact presently. Second, the inclusion of constant conjunction in Hume's account of causation comes not from some independent metaphysical assumption, but because of its role in inference. In explaining the inference we draw from the impression of some cause to the idea of its effect, Hume notes that "contiguity and succession are not sufficient to make us pronounce any two objects to be cause and effect, unless we perceive, that these two relations are preserv'd in several instances" (T 1.3.6.3; SBN 87). Constant conjunction is causally necessary to explain the inference, and it is subsequently included in the definitions of 'cause' because of this. We have "insensibly discover'd" one constituent relation in causation while considering "another subject," namely causal inference (T 1.3.6.2; SBN 87).

Constant conjunction then is added to "cause" because it is required to explain causal inference. But what of necessary connection? We noted that Hume elected to "beat around the neighbouring fields," and in the section where he "insensibly discovere'd" constant conjunction to be a constituent, there is a hint dropped about the nature of necessary connection. He writes "perhaps 'twill appear in the end, that the necessary connexion depends on the inference, instead of the inference's depending on the necessary connexion" (T 1.3.6.3; SBN 88). We form a conception of necessity because of the inferences we make rather than making causal inferences in virtue of a grasp of necessary connection. So while some philosophers hold that we can make causal inferences by grasping necessary connections, Hume argues that in fact the very notion of necessary connection emerges because of the causal inferences we make. Hume is aware what the inference depending on the necessary connection would involve. Were we able to grasp the necessary connection between objects, we would be able to a) immediately infer what effect the cause must have, without having to experience its manifestation, and b) find it inconceivable that that cause be followed by any other effect. The "true manner" of conceiving the "real force or energy, by which such a particular effect necessarily results" involves one being "able to pronounce from a simple view of the one, that it must be follow'd or preceded by the other" (T 1.3.14.13; SBN 161). Since, however, the ideas of cause and effect are distinct and separable, then it impossible to "read off" effect from cause, and we can always conceive of any putative cause being followed by any effect, and so there is no such relation of necessary connection discoverable. The inference cannot depend on the necessary connection. The illusion, however, that such connections are perceivable is the *effect* of the inference. Having observed *A* being followed by *B*, and acquiring the habit of inferring *B* from the impression of *A*, the psychological character of the inference changes. By "long habit," there is "such a turn of mind, that, upon the appearance of the cause, [observers] *immediately* expect with assurance its usual attendant, and *hardly conceive it possible that any other event could result from it*" (EHU 7.21; SBN 69, my emphasis). This psychological effect – which is the impression of necessary connection that becomes projected onto objects – determines why we come to think of causation in the modal terms we do. We think in terms of modal content because we infer, and we do not infer because we detect a modal relation between the *relata* of causation. Hume, therefore, understands the relation in light of the inference, rather than starting with claims about the metaphysics of the relation and explaining the inference in light of those claims.

Conclusion

"Naturalism" is not a label that Hume applied to his own philosophy, but it is nevertheless firmly associated with him. I have tried to sketch some senses in which that term might be appropriate without, for the most part, availing myself of categories of our contemporary discussions of what naturalistic philosophy might be. The "experimental method" applied to "moral subjects" is methodologically naturalistic in its rejection of *a priori* conceptions of human nature, and its findings are empirical generalizations, which in turn are deployed in explanations of disparate phenomena. The substance in substantive naturalism lies in the fact that the materials that enter into such explanations are conceived to be applicable to non-human animals, and that Hume thinks that human nature can be understood in their terms. Included within his purview are the operations of *reason*, which Hume explains in terms of association, an explanation which, while showing the "whimsical condition of mankind," does not deprive it of epistemic merit or undermine his own methodological naturalism. Hume's focus on human nature also explains his "seemingly preposterous" method of approaching causation, not from a metaphysical perspective, but arriving at his definitions through an examination of causal inference. That is to say, turning away from questions of what causation is and rather to the role that the concept plays in our cognitive lives.[13]

Notes

1 Kevin Meeker (2013), chapters six and seven, discusses various versions of contemporary naturalism in the company of Hume.
2 It is, I think, important not to overestimate the extent to which Hume is influenced by Newton, and some are apt to read far too much into Hume's allusions to him. Kemp Smith, for example, thought that Hume's associationism was directly inspired by Newton. A slightly weaker version of this claim is advocated in Hazony and Schliesser (2016). It is quite true that Hume talks of "a kind of attraction" (T 1.1.4.6; SBN12) in connection with the principles of association, but associationism (even if not known by the name) was long established prior to Newton.
3 Generally, naturalism is connected with empirical science, but it need not be: Spinoza is a conspicuous example of a philosopher categorized as a naturalist who, while by no means antithetical to empirical science, nevertheless arrives at his conception of nature in an *a priori* fashion (though would not, I think, see this as unscientific).
4 Such a reading of Hume is contentious and goes under the thoroughly misleading label the "New Hume" or sometimes "realism." Elsewhere I suggest that such avowals are best read as indicating a certain kind of epistemic and metaphysical modesty on Hume's part. On this see my (2014).
5 On this see Craig (1987).
6 Note, however, that for the skeptics everything is couched at the level of appearance. So for them it *appears* that humans and animals operate on the same principles and that it *appears* that human beings are presumptuous. Hume is developing the trope here beyond the level of appearance.
7 Paul Russell offers his own view of the relation between naturalism and skepticism in Russell (2008). He claims, rightly to my mind, that the *Treatise* has a significant irreligious agenda, and this is the fact helps to solve the "riddle" of Hume's *Treatise*, namely the "inescapable conflict between [Hume's] naturalistic ambitions to advance human knowledge in the area of "the science of man" and his extreme skeptical (Pyrrhonist) principles" (2008: 3). The skeptical weapons are aimed at religion, and so the triangulation of irreligion, skepticism, and naturalism solves the riddle. Unfortunately, Russell leaves the "riddle," as he conceives it, unsolved. The fact that Hume may have had an irreligious target does nothing to prevent skepticism undermining non-religious belief, nor does it tell us any positive epistemic status for belief is possible, given Russell's conception of skepticism as embodying "extreme sceptical (Pyrrhonist) principles." For a similar view, beset by similar problems, see De Pierris (2015).

8 Rescher (ed.) *G. W. Leibniz's* Monadology, London: Routledge, 1991.
9 *New Essays on Human Understanding*, ed. Remnant and Bennett, Cambridge: Cambridge University Press, 1996, 143.
10 For an extended reading along these lines that is both textually rich and philosophically sensitive, see Schmitt (2014).
11 For two rather different views, see Meeker (2013) and Schmitt (2014).
12 Hume offers an *a priori* argument in favor of temporal priority but is rather insouciant about its persuasive power, writing that if "this argument appear satisfactory, 'tis well. If not, I beg the reader to allow me the same liberty, which I have us'd in the preceding case [i.e. contiguity], of supposing as such. For he shall find, that the affair is of no great importance" (T 1.3.2.8; SBN 76).
13 Many thanks to audiences in Belo Horizonte, Cambridge, Austin, Texas, and Rome for comments on earlier drafts, and to Angela Coventry for comments on the last draft of this chapter. I dedicate this chapter to the memory of my sister, Alix Clarke, who died preposterously young.

References

Craig, E. J. (1987) *The Mind of God and the Works of Man*, Oxford: Clarendon Press.
De Caro, Mario and MacArthur, David, eds. (2004) *Naturalism in Question*, Cambridge, MA: Harvard University Press.
De Pierris, G. (2015) *Ideas, Evidence, and Method: Hume's Skepticism and Naturalism Concerning Knowledge and Causation*, Oxford: Oxford University Press.
Garrett, D. (2004) "'A Small Tincture of Pyrrhonism': Skepticism and Naturalism in Hume's Science of Man," in Sinnott-Armstrong (ed.), *Pyrrhonian Skepticism*, New York: Oxford University Press.
Hazony, Y. and Schliesser, E. (2016) "Newton and Hume," in Paul Russell (ed.), *The Oxford Handbook of Hume*, Oxford: Oxford University Press.
Kail, P. J. E. (2007) "Leibniz's Dog and Humean Reason," in Emilio Mazza and Emanuele Ronchetti (eds.), *New Essays on David Hume*, Rome: Franco Angeli.
———. (2012) "The Sceptical Beast of the Beastly Sceptic," in Constantine Sandis and Mark J. Cain (eds.), *Human Nature*, Cambridge: Cambridge University Press.
———. (2014) "Hume on Efficient Causation," in Tad M. Schmaltz (ed.), *Causation Oxford Philosophical Concepts*, Oxford: Oxford University Press.
Kemp Smith, N. (1941) *The Naturalism of David Hume*, London: Palgrave Macmillan.
Loeb, L. (2002) *Stability and Justification in Hume's Treatise*, Oxford: Oxford University Press.
———. (2008) "Inductive Inference in Hume's Philosophy," in Elizabeth S. Radcliffe (ed.), *Blackwell Companion to Hume*, Oxford: Basil Blackwell.
Meeker, K. (2013) *Hume's Epistemology and the Fate of Naturalized Epistemology*, Basingstoke: Palgrave Macmillan.
Price, H. (2011) *Naturalism Without Mirrors*, Oxford: Oxford University Press.
Russell, P. (2008) *The Riddle of Hume's Treatise: Skepticism, Naturalism, and Irreligion*, New York: Oxford University Press.
Schmitt, F. (2014) *Hume's Epistemology in the Treatise: A Veritistic Reading*, Oxford: Oxford University Press.
Stroud, B. (1977) *Hume*, London: Routledge.
Williams, B. (2000) "Naturalism and Genealogy," in Edward Harcourt (ed.), *Morality, Reflection and Ideology*, Oxford: Oxford University Press.
Winkler, K. (2016) "Hume's Skeptical Logic of Induction," in Paul Russell (ed.), *The Oxford Handbook of Hume*, Oxford: Oxford University Press.

12

MIRACLES AND THE HUMEAN MIND

Michael P. Levine

The following passage in a letter from Hume to George Campbell (1719–1796), shows that Hume took his argument against the justified belief in miracles to be closely connected with his *Treatise*. It is a connection that most commentators, pro and con, have ignored.[1]

> It may perhaps amuse you to learn the first hint, which suggested to me that argument which you have so strenuously attacked. I was walking in the cloisters of the Jesuits College at La Fleche . . . engaged in conversation with a Jesuit . . . who was relating to me, and urging some nonsensical miracle performed in their convent, when I was tempted to dispute against him; and as my head was full of the topics of my *Treatise of Human Nature*, which I was at that time composing, this argument immediately occurred to me.
>
> – David Hume[2]

Preferring to treat "Of Miracles" as a "stand alone" essay, commentators suppose that the argument in Part I of the essay could be understood without reference to the *Treatise*, and more specifically to his theory of impressions and ideas which grounds his empiricism. But even those that do connect the argument to the *Treatise* do not do so in sufficient depth, or in the right way, to see just how close the connection is.[3]

Despite Hume's essay "Of Miracles" being one of the most widely read essays in philosophy of religion, it is notable (remarkable in fact) that there is no common agreement on just what his argument is – not even whether it is an *a priori* or *a posteriori* argument (Levine 2011).

Contrary to those who believe Hume's argument is more or less a stand-alone work, I argue that Hume's "Of Miracles" cannot properly be understood apart from his analysis of causation, *a posteriori* reasoning, and the most fundamental element of his empiricism – his analysis of "impressions" and "ideas" (T 1.1.1–7; SBN 1–25; EHU II.11–17; SBN 17–22). Given these intrinsic connections to his *Treatise*, it is easy to show why that argument is properly understood as an *a priori* argument against the possibility of justified belief in miracles, and to show that this argument is mistaken. By *a priori* I mean a conceptual argument that is not based on experience. One need only consider what the term "miracle" means – as discussed below. Hume's argument against even the possibility of justified belief in miracles on the basis of testimony (his *a priori* argument) is presented below. I then go on to argue that Hume's *a posteriori* arguments (four arguments based on experience) in Part II "Of Miracles" are not only important, but that relative to some plausible assumptions, they are successful.[4]

It is in part the lack of clarity of the young Hume that has resulted in so much disagreement, and such fundamental disagreement, as to just what he is claiming, let alone the nature of his arguments, in "Of Miracles." But the disagreement also indirectly supports Hume's insights in Part II regarding our (Freudian) orectic natures (driven by desire and wish-fulfilment).[5] We believe what we want to believe and our beliefs are driven by desire (usually in the service of ego-protection). And these insights in turn help explain why interpreters of Hume's essay have been split along the lines they have been, with the religious (mostly) claiming that Hume thought one could be justified in believing in a miracle, and the non-religious claiming that Hume argued one could never be so justified.[6]

I The Humean mind in relation to the argument against miracles

Let us' then examine Hume's argument against justified belief in miracles[7] in the context of his accounts of "impressions" and "ideas," causation, and *a posteriori* reasoning. This will explain (1) why Hume's argument (mostly in Part I but taken up in Part II as well) is and must be *a priori*; (2) why, for Hume, any interpretation of his argument in Part I as an *a posteriori* argument against justified belief in miracles must coalesce or reduce to his *a priori* argument; (3) why it makes no difference whether the alleged evidence for a miracle's occurrence is based on testimony as in Hume's examples, or first-person sensory experience – like seeing a miracle for oneself; and, finally, (4) why it is so easy to show why Hume's argument fails. Points 1–4 are all interconnected, and a consideration of any one of them leads to a consideration of the others. No one of them can be answered without answering the others.

As with so many (most) other arguments in philosophy, what makes "Of Miracles" interesting is why it fails. If we can be justified in believing a miracle has occurred (which does not mean that we are or ever have been), but Hume's account of causation, *a posteriori* reasoning, and theory of impressions and ideas (his empiricism) entail that such justification is impossible, then something is wrong with his empiricism. I write above "If we can be justified in believing a miracle has occurred . . .," and although the "if" looms large, it is fairly self-evident that under certain circumstances we could be. One can imagine many instances in which one would be justified in believing a miracle occurred. Suppose, for example, you are at the shore of the Red Sea with Moses, and Moses raises his staff and the Red Sea splits up the middle (no low tide but raging waters on both sides – as in the movie[8] version); and then suppose the Red Sea crashed to a close the moment the last Israelite was safe. Wouldn't one then be justified in believing a miracle occurred?

The received view is that "Of Miracles" was published posthumously, although formulated while he writing the *Treatise*, because of its content. Unsurprisingly Hume ran into difficulty from the religious and academic establishment because of his views about religion. He was denied chairs at both Edinburgh and Glasgow Universities. It is, however, worth at least considering (hypothesizing) whether Hume held off publication of "Of Miracles" because he knew his argument in Part I failed and he knew why.[9] On the one hand, his account of *a posteriori* reasoning ruled out justified belief in miracles. But on the other, Hume would have been aware of scenarios (like the Red Sea parting) where he would admittedly – and despite his account of *a posteriori* reasoning – have been justified in believing a miracle occurred.

The situation with regard to miracles is similar to his account of the "self," an account also based on his theory of impressions and ideas – which is the foundation of his empiricism – that he later in the *Treatise* expresses doubts about. The question is why he would have had the section on miracles appear even posthumously if he thought it to be mistaken? But again, one has only to look at the account of the self in the *Treatise* to note that he was disinclined to retract views that followed from his empiricism even when he had doubts about their validity. More than this, the failure of his central argument against justified belief in miracles may have intimated to Hume that the entire edifice on which the *Treatise* and *Enquiries* is built, his cornerstone theory of impressions and ideas, along with his account of causation and *a posteriori* reasoning, was mistaken.

The crux of Hume's argument is succinct. He says, "A miracle may accurately be defined, a transgression of a law of nature by a particular volition of the deity, or by the interposition of some invisible agent" (EHU 10.13; SBN 115–116).

> A miracle is a violation of the laws of nature; and as a firm and unalterable experience has established these laws, the proof against a miracle, from the very nature of the fact, is as entire as any argument from experience can possibly be imagined.
>
> (EHU 10.11; SBN 114)

This is the sentence that those who claim Hume's argument is not *a priori* (i.e. "from the very nature of the fact") have to explain.

Hume's argument appears to depend upon the premise that "a miracle is a violation of the laws of nature." However, the role such a premise plays in Hume's argument, and whether Hume meant to define a miracle as a violation of a law of nature, or merely to characterize a miracle as, in some epistemologically relevant sense, "contrary" to the ordinary course of nature, is controversial. Regardless of Hume's view, technically speaking miracles are not violations of such laws but are instead positive instances of those laws. This is because laws of nature do not and are not meant to account for or describe events with supernatural causes – but only those with natural causes. Once some event is assumed to have a supernatural cause it is, by that very fact, outside the scope of laws of nature altogether and so cannot violate them (Levine 1989: 65–74; Levine 2017). Only if one disregards the possibility of supernatural causes can known exceptions to laws possibly be regarded as violations of laws. However, in such a case, as Hume saw (with the example of the Indian discussed below), there might be better reason, experientially speaking, to suppose that the exception shows that what was taken to be a law is not a law, rather than that the exception is a violation of a genuine law of nature that otherwise universally holds.[10]

Hume thinks that all reasoning about matters of fact, any *a posteriori* reasoning, is a species of reasoning founded on the relation of cause and effect. Our judgments concerning the reliability of testimony, whether to ordinary or extraordinary events, should therefore be consistent with the principles of reasoning from experience that are based on the cause–effect relation.[11] Hume says:

> It being a general maxim, that no objects have any discoverable connection together, and that all the inferences, which we can draw from one to another, are founded merely on our experience of their constant and regular conjunction; it is evident that we ought not to make an exception to this maxim in favour of human testimony. . . . This species of reasoning, perhaps, one may deny to be founded on the relation of cause and effect. I shall not dispute about a word.
>
> (EHU 10.5; SBN 111–112)

Hume's analysis of the causal relation has allegedly shown that "the foundation of our inference [from cause to effect and vice versa] is the transition [in the mind, from the idea of an object to the idea of its usual attendant] arising from the accustomed union [of cause and effect]" (T 1.3.14.21; SBN 165). The inference that A will be followed by B will be warranted to the extent that our experience of B's following A's has been constant (and frequent). This is because the force of the "transition, in the mind, to pass from an object to the idea of its usual attendant," and the "strength" of that idea is ideally a direct function of our past experience with events "resembling" those present. The force fails to be a function of past experience to the extent that the transition is affected by ulterior motives such as desires. Hume says, "If you weaken either the union or resemblance, you weaken the principle of transition, and of consequence that belief, which arises from it" (T 1.3.12.25; SBN 142).

According to Hume, we should not believe any more (i.e. with a greater "strength") than we can justifiably infer on the basis of the mind's *natural* propensity to believe as a result of experience. To do otherwise would be to act "unnaturally" (Levine 1989: 7–12). To the extent to which we believe beyond our warrant for that belief, the belief is unjustified and should be rejected by the reasonable person.

Hume (EHU 10.5; SBN 111–115) relates the case of the Indian who refused to believe that water turned to ice. According to Hume, the Indian "reasoned justly" on the basis of his past experience. He refused, at first, to believe that water turned to ice, despite the fact that it was well attested to, because the event not only had the Indian's constant and uniform experience to count against it, but also because the event "bore so little analogy" to that experience. The Indian "reasoned justly," but he extended his judgments about the properties of water to cases where all the circumstances were not the same (the relevant circumstance here being tempera-ture). In certain situations in which we hear testimony to extraordinary events, we may be in a situation similar to that of the Indian, unaware of some relevant natural circumstance, and so suppose there is a naturalistic explanation for some extraordinary event. *On the basis of experience,* this is what we should suppose.

In the case of extraordinary events that are well attested to and for which we have suitable experiential analogies, Hume thinks that the most we are justified in believing is that the event did occur – not that the event is a miracle. We are to "search for the [natural] causes whence it might be derived" (EHU 10.37; SBN 128). Such cases may require us to reassess our estimation of what nature is capable of. Statements of laws of nature must sometimes be reassessed in light of new experience. Also, we must be careful not to extend our judgments as to what to believe or expect of nature to situations in which the relevant (natural) circumstances are different.

Indeed, according to Hume, if we justifiably believe that an extraordinary event did occur, then we *should* assume that we are in a situation like that of the Indian. We should assume this because there are logically compelling reasons why the consistent Humean, in accordance with the principles of *a posteriori* reasoning based on Hume's analysis of causation and his empiricism, can do nothing else. A naturalistic explanation must be opted for even if one has no idea what such an explanation might be. The extraordinary event should be judged "[not] contrary to uniform experience of the course of nature in cases where all the circumstances are the same" (EHU 10.11; SBN 114).

It is *on the basis of experience* – it is *experience* – that tells us that when we are justified in believing in an extraordinary event, we should liken ourselves to the Indian. That is why, in a case like the eight days of darkness, "we ought to search for the [*natural*] causes whence it might be derived." Experience demands it. When an extraordinary event is extraordinarily well attested to, we have two options according to Hume. One is to accept the testimony and look for the event's natural causes. The other is to reject the testimony on the grounds that the event testi-fied to bears no *significant* analogy to events as experienced. Hume thinks that testimony, no matter how reliable, *can never* establish the occurrence of a miraculous event, in accordance with the principles of *a posteriori* reasoning (EHU 10.5; SBN 111–112). One is constrained by the principles of *a posteriori* reasoning to reject any testimony to the miraculous as being justified.

Fogelin (2003: 18) says that Hume acknowledges "that under certain conditions it *could* be possible to establish the occurrence of a miracle based on testimony. The miracle in question concerns a worldwide interlude of eight consecutive days of darkness." Hume, however, never calls this darkness a "miracle," and he deliberately does not do so. Indeed, it is being juxtaposed with an imaginary event he does call miraculous – Elizabeth's resurrection – but one that he says he would "not have the least inclination to believe." Hume's point about the darkness is that insofar as we can accept the report of its occurrence we must also, in accordance with his principles of *a posteriori* reasoning, opt for a naturalistic explanation. And so Fogelin attributes to Hume a view that he did not hold, that the eight-day darkness could be regarded as miraculous.

Given his principles of reasoning about empirical matters and philosophical empiricism (his theory of "impressions" and "ideas"), supernatural explanation cannot be justified experientially. David Johnson (2002) argues that Hume begs the question by assuming that *uniform experience tells or must tell against miracles*. It may well seem that way unless one takes account of Hume's empiricism and account of *a posteriori* reasoning in the *Treatise* and the later *Enquiry*. Hume may be wrong, but it is not because he begs the question. It is because the views upon which his claim that uniform experience tells or must tell against miracles are themselves mistaken. Hume in effect assumes naturalism, and his naturalism is a result of his empiricism. His naturalism and empiricism may be mistaken, but they are not question-begging.

What is it about experience, in the sense of expectations about future events or judgments about past events, that could justify the positing of a supernatural cause? Positing such a cause is necessary if one is to justifiably believe some event to be a miracle. Hume would say that positing such a cause is speculative. It can have no basis in experience. Even if some event really were a miracle, whether it be a resurrection or "the raising of a feather, when the wind wants ever so little of a force requisite for that purpose" (EHU 10.12; SBN 114–115), we would not be justified in believing that it was anything more than an extraordinary event. Extraordinary (but natural) events are at the limits of our experience; the supernatural is beyond it.

For Hume, a "cause," insofar as it can be used as an item in reasoning from experience, can only be something that we can have an "impression" of. The cause of a miracle would have to be identified as something we could perceive, even if we were to posit some metaphysical "power" of this cause and attribute it speculatively to God. The "cause" of Lazarus' coming forth from the grave would have to be identified with Christ's beckoning – either his voice or some physical gesture – both of which we have "impressions" of and both of which are events "in the usual course of nature."

That a miraculous occurrence could never be judged relevantly similar to anything in experience – that there must be "a firm and unalterable experience" counting against belief in it – is something that on Hume's account we know, since we know that we cannot have an "impression" of a supernatural cause. *Impressions (sensations or their copies in ideas) are by their very nature empirical, and there is no ground for supposing them supernatural. The supernatural exceed the limits of our experience.*

If a resurrection were well enough attested to that it warranted belief, then that event could still only be assigned status as an extraordinary event with a natural explanation. Hume is thus constrained by his empiricism that had he been at the shore of the Red Sea with Moses; and had Moses raised his staff and the Red Sea split up the middle (no low tide but raging waters on both sides); and had the Red Sea crashed to a close the moment the last Israelite was safe – killing those in pursuit; and had Hume lacked grounds for assuming he was hallucinating or perceiving events in any way other than as they were actually happening – Hume would *still* be constrained by his principles to deny that what he was witnessing was a miracle. This suffices to show the unacceptability of Hume's argument. Indeed, assuming Hume had been there with Moses, and events transpired in a manner similar to the way just described, he would have (readily) agreed that he was justified in believing that a miracle occurred. Would there have been any more plausible explanation? If so, his argument against justified belief in miracles can be used as a *reductio ad absurdum*.[12]

Apart from a commitment to Humean empiricism, and his theory of *a posteriori* reasoning, cases like that of the Indian leave the question of whether there have ever been, or could be, cases that should not be likened to that of the Indian unanswered. Apart from such a commitment there is no reason to assume that either (i) there is natural explanation or else (ii) the alleged event did not happen. If, for example, the Red Sea did part (as in the movie) that would be such a case – at least for those present. And it would be a case in which it is more probable (by far) that the event was a miracle than that it occurred naturally.

Few philosophers argue that miracles are impossible, and those that do are in effect presupposing or arguing for a thoroughgoing naturalism (Levine 2011). Hume's empiricism commits him to naturalism, and although he explicitly says that miracles are possible, his empiricism commits him to the view that miracles are impossible.[13] But even allowing for the possibility of miracles, his empiricism and naturalism are at the core of his argument against justified belief in miracles. If one accepts his empiricism/naturalism, then one can be justified in believing in a miracle whether on the basis of testimony *or* first-hand experience.

We set out to answer the following four questions. (1) Why Hume's argument is and must be *a priori*; (2) why, for Hume, any interpretation of his argument in Part I as an *a posteriori* argument against justified belief in miracles must coalesce or reduce to his *a priori* argument; (3) why it makes no difference whether the alleged evidence for a miracle's occurrence is based on testimony as in Hume's examples, or first-person sensory experience – that is, seeing a miracle for oneself;[14] and, finally, (4) why it is easy to show why Hume's argument fails against the possibility of justified belief in a miracle fails. Points 1–4 are all interconnected, and a consideration of any one of them leads to a consideration of the others.

I believe we have addressed and answered all four questions, but it is worth being more explicit with regard to #2. Hume's *a priori* argument against justified belief in miracles coalesces with his *a posteriori* argument against such justified belief. On *a posteriori* grounds – because of Hume's empiricism – we could never justifiably believe testimony to the miraculous because we could never judge the occurrence of such an event to be similar, in relevant respects, to anything we have experienced.[15] However, that a miraculous occurrence could never be judged relevantly similar to anything in experience (that there must be "a firm and unalterable experience" counting against belief in it) is something that we can know *a priori*, since *a priori* we know that we cannot have an "impression" of a supernatural cause. It follows from this that on *a priori* grounds we can also rule out the possibility of justified belief in testimony to the miraculous.[16]

Testimony for a miracle would have to at least be regarded as a "proof," and then we have to weigh this proof against the evidence of "proofs" for laws of nature that the miracle is in violation of. But his empiricism rules out the possibility that could ever be such a proof. Experience rules out any impression of a supernatural cause. What is interesting is that I think Hume was aware of this conflict in his thought. He claimed miracles are possible but that on his account one could never be justified in believing one occurred. This is the reason for the (successful) *a posteriori* arguments in Part II of his essay. Even if, contrary to his empiricism, there could be a miracle (a supernaturally caused event), we still would not be justified in believing in it. There are, as a matter of fact, always going to be better explanations. Hume may be right. But the fact that there will always be better explanations for the allegedly miraculous event does not mean in principle that some event might occur for which there is no better, more plausible, explanation. Imagine standing at the shore of the Red Sea with Moses.

Buckle (2012: 45) is adamant that Hume's argument in Part I is an *a posteriori* argument. "The whole basis of Hume's case against miracle-reports is necessarily a posteriori, so interpretations that appeal to *a priori* considerations are ruled out." Hume's argument however is an *a priori* argument – albeit masquerading (or reducible to) an *a posteriori* argument. And oddly, the account of Hume's "core argument" Buckle (2012: 49–51) gives is itself an *a priori* one ("a miracle is necessarily at odds with the laws of nature"). It is the modal element ("necessarily") that makes it an *a priori* argument, and what underwrites (supports) the "necessarily" is ultimately Hume's empiricism as explained above. Buckle (2012: 49–51) says:

> A miracle is an event totally at odds with the normal stream of experience, that is, with otherwise uniform experience. Since the laws of nature are the codification of that uniform experience, a miracle is necessarily at odds with the laws of nature. Moreover, since the uniformity of that experience constitutes a proof – a conviction of the necessity of that pattern continuing – it implies (for us) that the experience is "firm and unalterable." (EHU 10.12 [SBN 114–115]) This makes it appropriate – indeed necessary – to describe the miracle as "a *violation* of the laws of nature." (EHU 10.12 [SBN 114–115]; emphasis added) The uniformity of experience constitutes, for us, a proof of the necessity of that pattern continuing, and so implies that an exception must be judged a violation of natural laws. This means that, even in the best possible case of the testimony – where the testimony itself is so fully reliable that it, too, is judged a proof – the testimony cannot suffice to produce belief in the object of testimony.

In other words, given that a miracle is a violation of a law of nature – *by that very fact* (conceptually – i.e. *a priori*) – given our "natural" reasoning about matters of fact – there can be no testimony whatsoever that can outweigh the evidence against a miracle. Buckle's allegedly *a posteriori* argument does not reduce to an *a priori* argument. It is an *a posteriori* argument.

Buckle tries to trace Hume's argument back to his account of *a posteriori* reasoning, but he does not trace it back far enough. Hume's account of *a posteriori* reasoning (casual reasoning) is based on his empiricism – his theory of impressions and ideas. And it is because of this that we *must* reason, if we reason naturally, that testimony to the miraculous or even first-hand experience is to be rejected.

II Part II of Hume's essay: not just much better, but right

If Hume's argument in Part I of his essay was successful, then the several arguments against justified belief in miracles in Part II would be superfluous. But it is worth hypothesizing that Hume recognized that Part I was either unsuccessful, or at least relied on his empiricism, his account of *a posteriori* reasoning, and causation, etc., that would make the success of that argument no more probable than the theories it rested on. Or he took it to be unsuccessful because it relied on his empiricism. If Hume knew or even had intimations that his argument in Part I was not successful (what would Hume have believed if he were standing at the shore of the Red Sea with Moses?), then he would have deployed other arguments as to why belief in miracles was not, under ordinary circumstances, justified.

This is what Part II of his essay is about. It is Hume without the (metaphysical) baggage (his theory of impressions and ideas; his empiricism; his account of *a posteriori* reasoning – all related) of Book I of the *Treatise*. None of the four principal *a posteriori* arguments in Part II of his essay

"Of Miracles" rely on the *Treatise* or corresponding parts of the *Enquiry* – nor, incidentally, do any of his successful arguments in his *Dialogues* (for example his against the argument from design). It is worth remembering that although Hume followed the lines of reasoning and various conclusions that the early chapters (theories) of the *Treatise* led him to – particularly the theory of impressions and ideas – he expressed degrees of dissatisfaction with his analysis of the self (personal identity), skepticism with regard to the external world, and by extension, though not always explicitly, his account of causation and inductive reasoning. Clearly Hume was not satisfied with some of the principal (some counterintuitive and some downright bizarre) conclusions in Book I of the *Treatise*.

In Part II of his essay, Hume (EHU 10.15–10.23; SBN 116–121) gives the following four reasons for rejecting testimony to the miraculous. Buckle (2012: 55) claims they "are a mixed bag," but I think they are all successful – including the fourth, given suitable background assumptions. First, no miracles have in fact been sufficiently well-attested to, to justify belief. "There is not to be found, in all history, any miracle attested by a sufficient number of men, of such unquestioned good-sense . . . as to place them beyond all suspicion." The quotation is, I believe self-evident. The evidence is not there.

Second, people's love of miracle stories undermines the way our usual and ordinary principles of reasoning on the basis of experience would ordinarily lead us to reject claims of the miraculous. "The passion of surprise and wonder, arising from miracles, being an agreeable emotion, gives a sensible tendency towards the belief of those events, from which it is derived." Though perhaps not as quite self-evident, this assertion, and the one below, is amply supported by our own experience.

Third, reports of the miraculous should be judged unreliable because of their sources. Their sources are invariably (experientially) unreliable – even if they are true!

> It forms a strong presumption against all supernatural and miraculous relations, that they are observed chiefly to abound among ignorant and barbarous nations . . . as we advance nearer the enlightened ages, we soon learn, that there is nothing mysterious or supernatural in the case, but that all proceeds from the usual propensity of mankind towards the marvellous.

Fourth,

> in matters of religion, whatever is different is contrary. . . . Every miracle, therefore, pretended to have been wrought in any of these religions . . . as its direct scope is to establish the particular system to which it is attributed; so has it the same force, though more indirectly, to overthrow every other system. In destroying a rival system, it likewise destroys the credit of those miracles, on which that system was established; so that all the prodigies of different religions are to be regarded as contrary facts, and the evidences of these prodigies, whether weak or strong, as opposite to each other.

Assuming there can be only one true religion and that miracles establish the truth of a religion (that its core contentions are true), then testimony to the miraculous that established the truth of any one religion, by that very fact, also counts against the truth of all others. Miracles are part of every revealed religion and are called upon to establish the truth of each religion. However, since the trustworthiness of the testimony in each case is about the same, any testimony to the miraculous that seeks to underwrite the truth of any religion thereby also undermines the grounds that we have for accepting testimony to the miraculous in any other religion.

Nothing in Hume's four arguments suggests that one could not be justified in believing in a miraculous occurrence – whether on the basis of testimony or first-hand experience. However, the fact that one *could be* epistemologically justified in believing that a miracle has occurred in no way suggests that anyone ever has been so justified objectively, on the basis of verifiably sound evidence – rather than as a result of other unjustified or false beliefs they may have. This is what Part II addresses. In particular, the fact that one *could be* epistemologically justified in believing a miracle occurred (standing there with Moses on the shore of the Red Sea) in no way supports the claim that anyone is or ever has been, or even could be, so justified in believing in miraculous occurrences in the objectively robust historical sense (on the basis of verifiably sound evidence) – at least not as testified to in scripture on the basis of historical evidence (for example, reports in the bible).

The interesting philosophical question about miracles, one addressed by Hume in Part II of his essay, is why so many people believe in such things (Levine 2011). One can quibble about a few of the reasons he gives, like whether testimony to the miraculous from different religions mutually undermine the truth claims of one another. However, the principle reasons he cites for people believing miracle stories are sound. These are wishful thinking, gullibility, authority (for example, belief in the claims of the bible literally understood), ignorance, and love of fantasy. To these should be added that a belief in miracles may be justified on the basis of other beliefs (whether justified or not) that a person may have; but that ultimately there is no good historical evidence for such a belief.

The reasons for believing miracles (why we believe) are also the basis of the four reasons Hume gives for rejecting testimony to the miraculous. Should we believe what the gullible tell us – especially in circumstances where we have good and ample reason to believe they are being gullible? Should we believe what those who are susceptible to wishful thinking tell us – especially in those circumstances where we have good and ample reason to believe that such beliefs are the product of wishful thinking?

Beckwith (2003: 227) says that "I do not see why the believer is not within her epistemic rights in believing that a miracle has occurred (based on a convergence of independent probabilities)." But he deftly leaves untouched the principal issue – that is, whether anyone has ever has been justified in believing in a miracle and particularly (in the current context) whether anyone ever has been justified in believing in miracles alleged in the Bible. This is the question of whether one can justifiably accept miracles stories as "historically accurate," which he simply drops as if it were of no concern. It is a perfect illustration of aspects of Hume's arguments in Part II. But despite Beckwith's passing assumption or intimation that one can be – or even that we are so justified – the answer is an emphatic and unequivocal "no."[17]

Nothing in this critique of Hume's argument suggests that miracles have ever occurred, or that we are justified in believing that any have occurred. But it would be most surprising if some people at some time and in certain circumstances have not been, and will not again be, justified in believing in the occurrence of a miracle given other (objectively unjustifiable) beliefs they have. However, nothing suggests that the evidence available for the occurrence of any alleged miracle warrants justified belief in miracles for most people – including those who do believe in them. Haldane (Smart and Haldane 1996), for example, mistakenly believes that the bible is an accurate source of information about alleged events it depicts. Does this mean he is justified in his belief in miracles in any interesting or epistemologically robust sense? Certainly not (Levine 1999). His belief in miracles is justified only via other unjustified and false beliefs he has. These other beliefs are unjustified because the objectively available evidence (including biblical scholarship!) not only does not support them but shows them to be groundless. Creationist views (Haldane holds these as well) may have been justifiable for some before the facts of evolution were so well established, but they no longer are. Similarly, belief in biblical accounts of miracles may have been justified in the relevant epistemic sense before the advent of modern canons of historical evidence and biblical scholarship, but they too no longer are.[18]

Notes

1 I have done my best to keep this as a "stand-alone" essay, and one in which I argue for things I have not said previously – at least not as said here. But for a useful and perhaps even necessary background to this essay, see Levine (2011; 2015; 1989: 1–86).

2 Cited in Burns (1981: 133) and Gopnik (2015). Campbell's (1762) *Dissertation on Miracles* was a reply to Hume. See Gopnik (2015) for an unrelated but interesting possibility regarding Buddhist influence on Hume while he was at *La Flèche*.

3 For example: Swinburne (1970); Beckwith (2003); Johnson (2002); Earman (2000); Fogelin (1990; 2003). Burns (1981 chapter 7) argues contrary to Flew (1967), that Hume's argument in Part I is *a priori*; and contrary to Gaskin (1978, p. 295, n120) that Hume's argument is as applicable to cases of seeing (first-hand experience) of a miracle as well as to belief based on testimony (295, n120)—despite Hume's focus on testimony alone. On all of these points I agree.

4 The most problematic of the four is the argument "from contrary religions," as it has come to be called. The relevant problematically unacceptable assumptions here are that (i) only one religion can be "true" and that (ii) a miracle establishes the truth of the religion in which (in the context of which) it occurs. So Jesus turning water into wine established the truth of Christianity and the falsity of all other religions.

5 I leave additional similarities between the Humean and Freudian minds to one side.

6 Tamas Pataki, "Racism, the Psychology of Racism and Envy," unpublished. Orectic prejudices are based on unconscious wishes or desires invoked as a means of psychological defense of the ego.

7 Hume speaks of "just reasoning" and a "just reasoner" rather than justified belief. But it is clear that a justified belief is the result of just reasoning according to Hume. Note, however, that "justified" is here being used in a relative sense given that according to Hume, none of our *a posteriori* beliefs are ever justified. See Levine (1989: 8–9).

8 *The Ten Commandments*. Directed by Cecil B. de Mille, 1956.

9 Buckle (2012: 53) disagrees. Hume "regarded his treatment of probability to be a cutting-edge application of the relatively recent application of the idea of probability to the miraculous, and for this reason was rather proud of the argument." By way of supporting this claim, Buckle (2012: 53n14) says: "His [Hume's] argument is a direct response to Locke's (1975) [1690] claim that precisely because they are 'contrary to ordinary Observation' miracles 'not only find Credit themselves' but 'give it also to other Truths, which need such Confirmation.'" But how does this support the claim that Hume "was rather proud of the argument"? And of course it is also the case that one can be proud of at least some arguments – even if they fail.

10 For a discussion of the Indian example as well as the case of the eight-day darkness that Hume contrasts with the alleged resurrection of Elizabeth I, see Levine (2011: 297–298; 1989 Part I). Understanding these examples is essential to understanding Hume's *a priori* argument against justified belief in miracles. Most commentators focus on Hume's distinction between proof and probable reasoning. While relevant, the examples Hume discusses are more important to understanding his argument.

11 See Hume (EHU 10.5; SBN 111–112).

12 In Part II, Hume discusses two allegedly miraculous events: (i) the resurrection of Queen Elizabeth and (ii) an eight-day darkness. A consideration of these two cases can help explain why Hume thought we can be justified in believing an extraordinary event occurred but not a miraculous one. It helps us to understand Hume's argument in Part I. For a discussion of these cases, see Levine (2015: 593–595).

13 Hume (EHU 10.36; SBN 127–128) says: "I beg the limitations here made may be remarked, when I say, that a miracle can never be proved, so as to be the foundation of a system of religion. For I own, that otherwise, there may possibly be miracles, or violations of the usual course of nature, of such a kind as to admit of proof of human testimony; though, perhaps, it will be impossible to find any such in all the records of history."

14 For a view to the contrary (that Hume thinks belief in a miracle can be justified on the basis of first-hand experience), see Buckle (2012: 46). Hume does say that he is only talking about testimony to

the miraculous. He does not say that one can be justified in believing in a miracle if one sees one for oneself. Nor, if my interpretation is correct, can Hume consistently say this.

15 Coady (1992) thinks that Hume underestimates the significance of testimony. But on the interpretation of Hume's argument that sees his *a priori* and *a posteriori* argument as essentially the same, it is clear that Hume at least thought he was doing no such thing, that he was giving testimony to the miraculous its complete due.

16 Buckle (2012: 53–54) says: "It is not known whether either man knew of the other, or indeed whether Hume ever became aware of Bayes's Theorem … However, there is no doubt that, if he had become aware of it would have given him, at least at first, a chastened sense of his argument's sophistication." See Levine (1998; 2011) for an argument that shows why Bayes' Theorem is completely inapplicable to Hume's argument because Hume's empiricism rules out certain types of evidence as evidence for the miraculous. The interpretation of Hume's argument I am offering here should make it clear that any attempt to apply a Bayesian calculus to the problem of justified belief in miracles as Hume saw it must be otiose.

17 See Levine (2015: 600–601) for discussion of the Catholic Church's attempt to establish miraculous occurrences. For a critique of Beckwith's position, see Levine (2011).

18 My thanks to the editors for their comments on an earlier draft. The chapter should be at least somewhat clearer as a result.

References

Beckwith, Francis (2003) "Theism, Miracles and the Modern Mind," in Paul Copan and Paul Moser (eds.), *The Rationality of Theism*, London: Routledge.

Buckle, Stephen (2012) "Understanding Hume on Miracles," *Ethics Education* 18(1 and 2): 45–60.

Burns, R. M. (1981) *The Great Debate on Miracles: From Joseph Glanvill to David Hume*, Lewisburg: Bucknell University Press.

Campbell, George (1762) *A Dissertation on Miracles*, Edinburgh. Reprinted, New York: Garland, 1983.

Coady, C. A. J. (1992) *Testimony: A Philosophical Study*, Oxford: Clarendon Press.

Earman, John (2000) *Hume's Abject Failure: The Argument Against Miracles*, New York: Oxford University Press.

Flew, Antony (1967) "Miracles," in Paul Edwards (eds.), *Encyclopedia of Philosophy*, vol. 5. New York: Palgrave Macmillan and Free Press.

Fogelin, Robert J. (1990) "What Hume Actually Said About Miracles," *Hume Studies* 16(1): 81–86.

———. (2003) *A Defense of Hume on Miracles*, Princeton: Princeton University Press.

Gaskin, J. C. A. (1978) *Hume's Philosophy of Religion*, London: Palgrave Macmillan.

Gopnik, Alison (2015) "How an 18th Century Philosopher Helped Solve My Midlife Crisis: David Hume, The Buddha, and a Search for the Eastern Roots of the Western Enlightenment," *The Atlantic*, October issue.

Johnson, David (2002) *Hume, Holism, and Miracles*, Ithaca, NY: Cornell University Press.

Levine, Michael (1984) "Hume's Analysis of Causation in Relation to Miracles," *History Philosophy Quarterly* 1(2): 195–202.

———. (1989) *Hume and the Problem of Miracles: A Solution*, Dordrecht: Kluwer Publishers.

———. (1998) "Bayesian Analyses of Hume's Argument Concerning Miracles," *Philosophy and Theology* 10(1): 101–106.

———. (1999) "Critical Study of J.J.C. Smart and J.J. Haldane 'Atheism and Theism'," *Canadian Journal of Philosophy* 29(1): 157–170.

———. (2011) "Philosophers on Miracles," in Graham Twelftree (eds.), *The Companion to Miracle*, Cambridge: Cambridge University Press.

———. (2015) "It's Part II that Matters: Hume on Miracles," in Paul Russell (eds.), *Oxford Handbook on David Hume*, Oxford: Oxford University Press.

——— (2017) "Laws of Nature and the Possibility of Miracles," in Graham Twelftree and Robin Parry (eds.), *The Nature Miracles of Jesus: Historical and Theological Perspectives*, Eugene, OR: Wipf and Stock Publishers.

Locke, John and Peter H. Nidditch, eds. (1975) [1690] *An Essay Concerning Human Understanding*, Oxford: Clarendon Press.

Mackie, John L. (1982) *The Miracle of Theism: Arguments for the Existence of God*, Oxford: Clarendon Press.

Smart, J. J. C. and J. J. Haldane (1996) *Atheism and Theism*, Oxford: Blackwell Publishers.

Swinburne, Richard (1970) *The Concept of Miracle*, London: Palgrave Macmillan.

13

HUME'S PSYCHOLOGY OF RELIGION

Willem Lemmens

1 Introduction

Hume's philosophy of religion is often interpreted as first and foremost an ingenuous skeptical critique on the rational foundation of religious belief, in particular the belief in the existence of the providential God of Christianity. However, in line with his naturalistic science of human nature, Hume was at least as much interested in religion as a *psychological* phenomenon. From this perspective, *The Natural History of Religion* (1758) investigates the "origin of religion in human nature" (NHR Intro). In this remarkable dissertation, Hume focuses not on the epistemology of religious belief, but on the causal explanation of the emergence of religious belief in the human mind and its relation to the passions as well as religious practices and institutions.

Hume was not the first to develop a psychological account of religion. We find traces of such an explanation in Lucretius and, closer to Hume's days, in the works of Hobbes and Spinoza. In England, John Trenchard was a precursor of Hume with his *The Natural History of Superstition* (1709). Hume's natural history of religion stands out, however, because it integrates some crucial findings of his philosophy of mind, developed in the *Treatise*, in a broadly psychological-cum-historical explanation of the origins of religion. Hume combines his explanatory intentions with an abrasive moral critique of religious beliefs and practices and the propagation of a secular naturalistic ethics (Streminger 1989; Malherbe 1995; Russell 2008; Holden 2010).

Among contemporaries, the *NHR* was received with mixed feelings, even hostility. Having read the essay before publication, a prominent member of the clergy, Bishop Warburton, warned Hume's editor that with his essay the author intended to "establish naturalism" in the study of religion, which came down to nothing less than the propagation of "atheism, instead of religion."[1] Other critics were more friendly, though a certain William Rose wrote that Hume's essay contained a few hidden insinuations against the legitimacy of Christianity. At the same time, Rose admitted that Hume proved to be an accurate observer of human nature.[2] In the intellectual culture of his days, Hume clearly stood not alone in using a historical narrative to question the morality and rationality of traditional Christianity: his approach mirrored the conviction of deists like Trenchard that the emergence of Christianity in fact meant a sort of perversion of natural religious belief and morality (Harris 2015: 291). In contrast with the Deists, however, Hume saw no ground for the hypothesis that a natural belief in the one supreme Deity (and a corresponding morality) could be found in primitive mankind.

In this chapter, I reconstruct the basic features of Hume's explanation of the origins of religious belief. This reconstruction can be understood as an account of Hume's *psychology of religion*, though one should keep in mind that psychology of religion as a separate scientific discipline emerged only at the end of the nineteenth century. Hume's psychological approach offers a special blend of its own: ingredients of the *Treatise* account of the role of belief and passions in human life are in the *NHR* interwoven with findings from early ethnographic studies and ancient historiography. The *NHR* thus foreshadows the contemporary cognitive science of religion (CSR) as well as the recent naturalist study of religion inspired by evolutionary psychology and cultural anthropology (De Cruz 2015).

Hume, as we will point out, had a very dismissive attitude towards religious belief and religious practices in general. The contention that religious beliefs are illusory and irrational stands out not only in the *NHR*, but also through many of Hume's publications, where it is a recurrent theme. It lies also at the heart of Hume's penetrating moral critique of religion in essays such as "Of Superstition and Enthusiasm," in the monumental *History of England*, and, last but not least, in the posthumous *Dialogues Concerning Natural Religion*. The multi-faceted design of the *NHR* mirrors the broadly practical scope of Hume's life-long interest in religion as a natural phenomenon. Therefore, one might read Hume's *NHR* not only as the key to a better understanding of his psychology of religion as such, but also as a major contribution to the secularizing ambition underlying his science of human nature in general (Kail 2007; Russell 2008).

2 The natural history of religion: a specific agenda

Why do people have religious beliefs? The answers on this question might be very divergent, depending on the point of view of the addressee. For example, a believing Christian might answer: "I believe in God, because He is my source of consolation and hope." A scientific-minded psychologist might say: "People believe in God because this belief alleviates their pain and sorrow by offering hope in a future life after death." While the second answer looks for a *causal* account of the religious belief in question by referring to some underlying passion (grief, pain, fear), the first explains why someone thinks, from a first person perspective, why he or she has good reasons to hold a specific religious belief (in this case the belief that there exists a God, source of consolation and trust, and that there is an afterlife).

At the outset, the *NHR* neatly distinguishes both approaches in the investigation of religious belief. In fact, Hume suggests that once we pose the psychological question, and thus take a third person explanatory perspective towards religion, religious belief appears in general to be whimsical and illusory: it contains some recurrent core, to wit, the "belief of invisible, intelligent power" (NHR Intro), but this belief can take different forms, depending on culture and personality. Moreover, religious belief goes hand in hand with a variety of sentiments and practices that also are widely divergent in time and place. Therefore, so Hume contends, religious belief or "the first religious principles must be secondary" (NHR Intro). Calling them secondary, Hume stresses that religious beliefs emerge in the human mind from more basic conditions and features of man's natural condition and life in society. At this point, Hume clearly distances himself from the view, widespread in his days, that religious belief, especially the belief in the existence of a supreme God or Deity, is innate in the human mind and as such identifiable as a natural belief.[3]

Hume has thus sketched the purpose of the *NHR*: he wants to develop a causal account of the primary principles and conditions that explain the emergence of religious belief. He also wants to understand why religion as it is found in the world has generally had such a bad influence on morality. Before we set on to reconstruct the agenda of Hume's psychology of religion, two further points should be mentioned. First of all, given its third person, explanatory perspective, Hume's *NHR* is clearly an example of a *reductionist* account of religion. In the spirit of eighteenth-century naturalism and materialism, such an account distances itself from any reliance on the supernatural for the explanation of the phenomenon at hand. In the line of his *Treatise of Human Nature*, Hume contends that religious belief, insofar it is not derivable from an original instinct or a natural cognitive capacity, must originate from more basic features and propensities of human nature. Moreover, Hume's approach is reductionist not only in the sense that it brings down the supernatural belief in God or a realm of deities to its natural constitutive causal components, but also insofar it aims at unmasking (almost) every instance of religious belief as a form of wishful thinking. In the *NHR*, Hume labels religious beliefs generally as forms of 'superstition': the superstitious mind is, in principle, in the grip of an illusion, the prey of irrational passions and delusive beliefs.

Second, Hume identifies his psychological account of religion as a form of *natural history*. Such a history functions in the eighteenth century as a systematic hypothetical explanation of the different aspects of a specific phenomenon – in this case religion – as it exists today and has evolved from the rude to the complex, as part of the gradual establishment of civilization. The *NHR* takes the Scottish Enlightenment paradigm of human development for granted: according to this paradigm, the improvement of society in general can be reconstructed through different stages (hunting and gathering, farming, commerce) in a so-called conjectural history.[4]

The *NHR* conjectural history of religion does not neatly distinguish historical stages of religious development, though Hume confidently defends the thesis that polytheism was the first religion of mankind, monotheism being a later development of it. The *NHR* teaches us that a pure monotheism has hardly, if ever, been established through history, and the traces of polytheism are still to be found in eighteenth-century Christianity. Whether Hume really thought popular religion could become more 'civilized' is doubtful. While he does make in the *NHR* a neat distinction between superstition and the principles of "genuine Theism and Religion," in the *DNR* he contends that such a 'true religion' is nowhere to be found in the world.

3 Religious belief: from anthropomorphic projection to deification

According to Hume, the belief in the existence of invisible, intelligent powers form the core of religion: this belief arose in the most primitive stages of human civilization because of fear and ignorance. Confronted with the "various and contrary events of human life" (NHR 2, 3), humans felt at a loss to understand and control the forces that cause them to suffer: storm and tempest, famine and sickness, but also war, conflicts and strife, or strange and terrifying natural phenomena, such as "a monstrous birth" (NHR 1, 6). At the outset of the *NHR*, Hume clearly borrows from his *Treatise* account of the human mind when he observes that already in the most primitive stages of human civilization "the ignorant multitude" wanted to get a grip on the "*unknown causes*" that disturb human existence, by forming, through the imagination, "some particular and distinct idea" of them (NHR 3, 2).

According to Hume, polytheism or the belief in the existence of a plurality of gods or deities here finds its origin. Driven by the passions of fear and uncertainty, the human mind invents some imaginary beings to alleviate the mental disturbances caused by the confrontation with a hostile, mysterious world. These imaginary beings are called gods or deities and function as the invisible and intelligent powers that explain why humans become the prey of the forces of nature and the whims of fate. The qualification of the gods as 'invisible powers' is a bit careless at first sight, because for Hume all power is in a way invisible (Garrett 2015: 284). Moreover, especially in polytheism, gods appear often with an extended form and are thus visible. However, what Hume means is roughly the following.

Deities or gods are invisible beings because the ways in which they produce effects in the empirical world are not discernable as forms of causal regularity (such as billiard balls that move and strike another, as Hume illustrates in the *EHU*). Apparently, the gods or deities remain hidden when they cause all sorts of natural processes to happen, or they do not change in an observable way when they interfere in human affairs, even when they are represented as a natural object (the sun, a stone, some idol or statue) (Garrett 2015: 285). Calling the deities 'invisible' might also allude to some essential features they share: deities have a whimsical and unpredictable character, exemplified also by the power to change their visible outlook.

Clearly, polytheistic beliefs somehow appease ignorance, but remain at the same time highly imaginative. Hume relies on this point on his account of *credulity* in Book 1 of the *Treatise*. Religious belief, so Hume suggests here, is a form of imaginative thinking, that stands closer to mythology and poetry than to the scientific understanding of the world (T 1.3.9.12–15; SBN 112–113; 1.3.10.6; SBN 121–122). Moreover, it is a form of thinking that has a huge impact on the passions and thus on human agency. This bond between imagination and action is one of the main factors that in Hume's eyes cause religious belief to be such a detrimental force for morality and political life. Implicitly, however, Hume acknowledges also a more constructive, positive dimension in religious belief: after all, this class of beliefs alleviates up to a certain extent the fear and uncertainty by which they are triggered.

Religious belief, so one could say, appears to have a homeopathic function: it emerges out of passions that are threatening and potentially destructive and creates an order of invisible powers that is equally mysterious and incomprehensible, but at the same time consoling and more manageable than the blind forces of nature. Merely destructive or negative passions are, through the imaginative mediation of religious belief, transformed into more positive ones: thus the mind copes somehow with the overwhelming reality of the natural world and the uncertainties of human existence. This constructive force of religious belief might also explain why religions, once emerged, maintained themselves through history and became part of human culture and civilization.

In the *NHR*, Hume borrows further from his *Treatise* when he delineates some deep-rooted propensities and features of the human mind that help us to understand this constructive role of religious belief (Yandell 1990: 11). Next to the propensity to believe in the existence of invisible, intelligent powers as such, Hume calls attention to the almost irresistible propensity of the human mind at personification or *prosopopeia*: the tendency to conceive of these powers as *somehow analogous to human beings* (NHR 3, 2). He observes:

> as the *causes*, which bestow happiness or misery, are, in general, very little known and very uncertain, our anxious concern endeavours to attain a determinate idea of them; and finds no better expedient than to represent them as intelligent, voluntary agents, like ourselves; only somewhat superior in power and wisdom.
>
> (NHR 5, 9)

Obviously, this propensity at anthropomorphic imaginative projection, so omnipresent in primitive culture, yields beliefs that are highly paradoxical in nature: deities are invisible, but at the same time human-like. As Hume suggests, the belief in the existence of deities probably emerged through the deification of exemplary humans: we see examples of this in hero-worship or the narratives of mythology. Hume also points at the practice of *apotheosis* in the ancient world, whereby an emperor received after his death the status of a god by political decree (NHR 5, 6–9). Sensitive to the history of religious traditions, Hume contends that the theogony of

Greek and Roman antiquity illustrates how deities are in fact "nothing but a species of human creatures, perhaps raised from among mankind, and retaining all human passions and appetites, together with corporeal limbs and organs" (NHR 3, 3).

This propensity at anthropomorphic projection is for Hume one of the most fundamental feature of religious belief. Not only the more primitive polytheistic religions of mankind bear testimony to this, but also the allegedly more civilized monotheism of Christianity. For the Christian God, so Hume makes clear through his *DNR*, is as such anthropomorphic in nature: He is conceived of in analogy to the human mind or presented as a Divine Father. The *NHR* further observes that in Medieval Europe ordinary believers not only shaped God to the image of man, but also believed God to intervene – on the basis of his particular providence – in everyday life with "the interposition of his angels and subordinate ministers" (NHR 4, 1). In other words, the medieval Christian mind conceived of God's particular providence by reminiscence to a quasi-polytheistic creed: the belief in the existence of a plurality of semi-divine, invisible beings with human-like features. Moreover, in the uncivilized middle ages the belief in God was generally combined with the opinion "that all nature was full of other invisible powers; fairies, goblins, elves, sprights; beings, stronger and mightier than men, but much inferior to the celestial natures, who surround the throne of God" (NHR 4, 1). Even in the era of Christian monotheism, the remnants of polytheism were part of ordinary culture.

4 Symbolic representation and worship

Religious belief, as found throughout history all over the world, in Hume's view not only hinges on anthropomorphic projection and imaginative representations but also necessarily depends on practice and devotion. In fact, to allow religion to properly fulfill its homeopathic function, this devotional and ritual dimension is essential, so we learn from the *NHR*. Hume discerns two further crucial propensities of the human mind that explain this practical impact of religion: the propensity to make visible representations of the deities and the propensity to pay them worship through rituals and prayers (what Hume calls *adulation*).

Hume appears throughout the *NHR* sensitive to the fact that religion is a cultural and social reality: religious belief is unavoidably embedded in and dependent on a web of cultural meanings and practices. For the belief in deities is fostered by 'visible' and tactile representations (through painting, stories, and statues), while rituals and sacrifices of all sorts, performed at holy places by priests or persons with sacral power, mediate between the gods and mortal humans. Only through this symbolic mediation religious does belief have such a huge impact on human passions and agency by establishing, as Geertz calls it, "powerful, pervasive, and long-lasting moods and motivations," while at the same time "formulating conceptions of a general order of existence" that shapes moods and motivations that are experienced as "uniquely realistic" (Geertz 1973: 90).

In the *NHR*, reference is especially made to the role of mythology and allegory in Ancient Greek and Roman culture, and to their custom of building temples and visualizing the gods in painting and sculpture (NHR 5, 3–9). These religious narratives and holy places were in turn part of a larger practice of worship that had a huge political impact. No Roman emperor, for example, would go to war without passing by the Temple and asking for the support of the gods. At the same time, as Hume reminds his readers, an emperor like Augustus, being himself a sort of demigod, could challenge the gods: after he lost his fleet twice in a storm, he forbade to bear around the statue of Neptunus, the god of the sea, in holy processions: "[he] fancied he had sufficiently revenged himself by that expedient" (NHR 4, 7).

Other cultures also knew this propensity at visual and tactile symbolization of the divine in order to establish a practical relation with the gods and thus shape human passions and agency. Hume observes:

> The CHINESE, when their prayers are not answered, beat their idols. The Deities of the LAPLANDERS are any large stone they meet with of an extraordinary shape. The EGYPTHIAN mythologists, in order to account for animal worship, said, the gods, pursued by the violence of earthborn men, who were their enemies, had formerly been obliged to disguise themselves under the semblance of beasts.
>
> (NHR 4, 3)

Closer to his own culture, Hume equally discerns these propensities at representation and active worship of the divine in European Christianity:

> The Virgin *Mary*, ere checked by the reformation, had proceeded, from being merely a good woman, to usurp many attributes of the Almighty: God and St NICHOLAS go hand in hand, in all the prayers and petitions of the MUSCOVITES.
>
> (NHR 6, 6)

The role of Mary and the saints in Catholicism is, so Hume suggests, similar to that of some minor deities in polytheism.

The mediation of religious belief through symbolic representation and worship forms an intrinsic ingredient of the imaginative attempt to overcome the fear and distress that causes religious belief to emerge. For on the basis of these propensities, a practical relation between humans and gods is established and becomes part of everyday life. In all polytheistic creeds, human beings can ask the gods for help or consolation through prayer and sacrifices, but the same goes for monotheistic religious traditions, where prayer and ritual are equally essential features of religious life. Through worship, the believer hopes to have the gods or God on his side, to gain their or his favors. Humans can thus become the object of the divine grace or wrath (if they ignore the gods' or God's will): this causes, so Hume points out, a constant restlessness in the religious mind, which goes often hand in hand with devotional rigor and all sorts of superstitious practices. Especially in monotheistic religions, so Hume contends in the *NHR*, this may lead to an obsessive form of "superstitious piety and devotion" (NHR 14, 7).

Through the *NHR* Hume reminds us that there is quite wide divergence between the central creeds of more primitive polytheism and monotheism: while polytheists especially hope to gain the favor of the gods in order to prosper and thrive in their earthly existence, in Christianity, Judaism, and Islam the core of religious belief concerns a longing to eternal salvation by joining the divine reality in the afterlife. In monotheistic faith, the realm of the divine is thus identified with divine perfection and pure love and with the promise of eternal bliss after death (what Hume calls in *EHU* "a future state"): as such the belief in God is seen as a consoling answer to the riddle of earthly existence.

Despite these divergences, both monotheism and polytheism establish a relation between the divine world and everyday life, between the sacred and profane, and thus shape human passions and agency in a very specific way. Hume's account of religious belief and practice recognizes, in fact, what Georges Santayana has identified as the capacity of religions to offer to the believer "another world to live in" by opening, so to say, specific vistas to this 'other world' (Geertz 1973: 112). This 'other world' – populated by a plurality of deities or spirits for the polytheist, by one

God and angels and saints in Christian monotheism – is across cultures understood as having a positive spiritual significance.

However, as Hume observes, in most religious traditions attitudes of hope and bliss wax and wane. For the threat of divine wrath may haunt the religious mind, under various circumstances doubts may bedevil the feelings of bliss and salvation. In fact, so Hume observes, the obsession with religious exercises often increases fear and terror, instead if relieving these passions: "it has been observed," says Hume, "that enormities of the blackest dye have been rather apt to produce superstitious errors, and increase the religious passion" (NHR 14, 7). Often, religious belief redoubles the fear and anxiety it is supposed to alleviate. The homeopathic medicine turns into a poison.[5]

This intrinsic instability of religious belief causes a sort of ambivalence among the passions and explains, so Hume contends, why religious belief is, in principle, unstable and intrinsically ambiguous. The ordinary religious mind seems up to a certain extent to be aware of the unreliable or even contradictory nature of the gods or God he or she worships. Especially in monotheistic traditions, he or she might also feel unsure about the exact outlook and nature of the future state of salvation that waits after death. In short, religious belief is difficult to sustain. Hume remarks:

> We may observe, that, notwithstanding the dogmatical, imperious style of all superstition, the conviction of the religionists, in all ages, is more affected than real, and scarcely ever approaches, in any degree, to that solid belief and persuasion, which governs us in the common affairs of life. Men dare not avow, even to their own hearts, the doubts which entertain on such subjects: They make a merit of implicit faith.
>
> (NHR 12, 15)

But how does religious belief then gain such a grip on the human mind? How to account for its homeopathic force, when it is at the same time inherently ambivalent and causes such an emotional instability? Famously, at the end of the *NHR* Hume sighs that the phenomenon of religion remains "a riddle, an aenigma, an inexplicable mystery" (NHR 15, 13). There is something unaccountable in the huge impact religious belief has on the human mind. However, already in his *Treatise*, Hume remarks how education and custom play a decisive role in the establishment of most of our beliefs (T 1.3.9.17; SBN 116). This might especially be the case with religious beliefs that hinge so much on religious discourses and the word of priests and clergy.

In fact, Hume suggests that religious belief gets inculcated from early childhood on and thus gains an ineradicable grip on the human mind. An adult or more enlightened person might question the received religious creeds, but, generally spoken, within a religious tradition a sort of collective 'will to belief' – as William James would call it – will prevail. Hume appears sensitive for the possibility that this will-to-believe goes hand in hand with collective pressure: therefore, the tendency to doubt or question one's religious belief might cause tensions and emotional ambivalence on the side of the faithful, which might further trigger a tendency at dissimulation and hypocrisy. Hume seems to consider this tendency a common feature of religious traditions, especially in monotheism. In the *Treatise*, he gives the example of the monotheistic belief in the afterlife, so eagerly propagated by "eminent theologians" and divines in his Christian culture: according to Hume, common people (the "vulgar") do not really have a strong confidence in this particular belief. So they are "infidels in their heart," while they at the same time continue their practices of devotion and hide their secret doubts (T 1.3.9.13; SBN 113–114). According to Hume, this tendency at dissimulation and hypocrisy is stronger among monotheist believers than in ancient polytheism.[6]

5 From polytheism to monotheism (and back)

This brings us to two crucial theses of the *NHR*: *first*, that monotheism, or the belief in 'one supreme Deity,' arose out of polytheism, and, *second*, that history shows how monotheism, once established, is prone to a "flux and reflux between polytheism and theism."

For Hume, it is beyond doubt that monotheism or "the doctrine of one supreme Deity, the author of nature" emerged quite naturally out of polytheism. As such, monotheism is "very ancient, has spread itself over great and populous nations, and among them has been embraced by all ranks and conditions of men" (NHR 6,1). Hume discerns two features of the human mind that account for this gradual emergence of the belief in one Supreme Deity.

A first derives from the propensity to worship as such. The primitive superstitious mind, while believing in the existence of "several limited deities," has a tendency to select a sort of favorite Deity as object of worship and adoration (NHR 6, 5). The more fear and distress haunt the human mind, the more eager humans search for divine assistance: thus the imagination almost naturally constructs the idea of a highest Deity that outdoes the other deities in power and grace. The passionate devotion to this Deity bears testimony to a self-fortifying religious enthusiasm: the religious person gains in self-confidence and exaltation, as if he or she shares through this devotion in the power and grace the Deity bestows on the believing mind.

A second feature or propensity of the human mind to which Hume alludes is more cognitive. The belief in invisible agents that are at the same time tangible and human-like remains deeply contradictory in nature. Therefore, so Hume observes, a tendency arises in all 'idolatrous nations,' to develop a quasi-*rational account of the divine*: hence emerges the idea of one supreme, invisible power that stands above all other gods and is the maker of the universe. This idea of a pure, spiritual Highest Being an "infinite Being, who exists from eternity to eternity" (NHR 7, 2) is pleasing to the mind because it derives from an abstract extrapolation on the natural idea of causality: God becomes the all-encompassing 'first cause' of everything that exists. According to Hume, polytheism thus gradually yields a purer theism.

The tendency or propensity to develop a rational account of the divine, to render religious belief more coherent and systematic, is a feature of the great monotheistic traditions (Judaism, Christianity, and Islam) that fascinated Hume. It explains the strong hold that theology had on religious life in the scholastic middle ages, notably among the 'very learned sect' of Catholicism (NHR 12.2). Here, philosophy or rational thinking became indeed the handmaiden of faith, an evolution with far-reaching consequences, as Hume highlights at various instances in his writings. For the alliance of philosophy with religion in Christianity caused also the perversion of the first: philosophy helped to 'rationalize' the doctrinal content of religion, but at the price of making philosophy itself doctrinal and scholastic. Hume sees in this zeal for doctrinal truth the source of intolerance and proselytism, which is in monotheism notoriously higher than in polytheism.

When philosophy and rational thinking thus become perverted, all sorts of intellectual disputes and doctrinal factions emerge within monotheistic traditions. Unable to obey to the principles of pure reason and common sense, the "devout votaries" desire at the same time to convince others of their 'Truth.' Thus a sort of collective self-deception finds its soil and religious sectarianism flourishes. Hume sees both in polytheism and monotheism this tendency to proselytism and religious indoctrination at work. But it is especially in monotheism that doctrinal rigor and stubbornness leads to fanaticism and zeal. Here lies according to Hume the origin of "that sacred zeal and rancour, the most furious and implacable of all human passions" (NHR 9.1).

Religious fanaticism among monotheists further fosters a vision on the Deity that remains in fact as anthropomorphic and contradictory as the credulous belief of polytheism. Hume illustrates this with reference to the Islam where the "Deity" is sometimes "painted in the most sublime colours, as the creator of heaven and earth": at other moments, however, this God is degraded to "a level with human creatures in his powers and faculties" (NHR 6, 12): like humans, the Deity of Islam has passions and all sorts of terrifying moral features.

Hume, with hardly hidden irony, contends that Christianity remains free of these sort of 'contradictions' (NHR 6, 12). Hume might have tried to appease here a bit his orthodox Christian readers, who could not but be provoked by the hypothesis that the belief in one Supreme Deity arose from polytheism. However, further in the *NHR*, Hume approves of a long citation by Chevalier Ramsey in which the doctrine of predestination, defended by some 'Christian sects,' is scorned: "all this makes God odious, a hater of souls, rather than a lover of them; a cruel vindictive tyrant, an impotent or wrathful daemon, rather than an all-powerful, beneficial Father of spirits" (NHR 13, 7 (footnote 87)). In short, the Judeo-Christian tradition as well as Islam, despite coming closer to a purer theism, is not free from the anthropomorphism of polytheism: both are instances of superstition.

According to Hume, this family resemblance between the belief in one Supreme Deity and the devotion towards a panoply of deities is further explained by a law-like characteristic of all religions to be found in history: the "flux and reflux of polytheism and monotheism."

In the *NHR*, Hume observes that the tendency to conceive of the divine in abstract terms of unity, purity, and spirituality conflicts with the equally strong tendency to dwell on vivid, more tangible representations of the divine. In other words, on the one hand, the monotheistic belief in a highest Deity, exemplifying pure transcendence and spirituality, emerges naturally from polytheism: on the other hand, once the mind loses itself in this abstract notion of the divine, a contrary tendency to make the divine more visible and tangible pops up again. Hence, specific features of polytheism regain their influence. Hume observes:

> Men's exaggerated praises and compliments still swell their idea upon them; and elevating their deities to the utmost bounds of perfection, at last beget the attributes of unity and infinity, simplicity and spirituality. Such refined ideas, being somewhat disproportioned to vulgar comprehension, remain not long in their original purity; but require to be supported by the notion of inferior mediators and subordinate agents, which interpose between mankind and their supreme deity. These demi-gods or middle beings, partaking more of human nature, and being more familiar to us, become the chief objects of devotion, and gradually recall that idolatry, which had been formerly banished by the ardent prayers and panegyrics of timorous and indigent mortals.
>
> (NHR 8, 2)

This dialectics between monotheism and polytheism form an ineradicable feature of *any* religion. For Hume, this restless movement is a specific psychological feature that haunts the mind of the ordinary believer, also in eighteenth-century Christianity. Hume observes:

> The feeble apprehensions of men cannot be satisfied with conceiving their deity as a pure spirit and perfect intelligence; and yet their natural terrors keep them from

imputing to him the least shadow of limitation and imperfection. They fluctuate between these opposite sentiments.

(NHR 8, 2)

Again, we see how religion's homeopathic force remains ambivalent: religious belief alleviates an original fear and uncertainty, but creates a new sort of terror and uncertainty. The religious mind longs to receive God's grace and seeks shelter under his guidance: at the same time, the believing mind is at loss to hold firm to his religious belief. He fears the God he does not know and seeks consolation in beliefs focused on more tangible representations of the divine. This tendency is only strengthened by the obsessive attention for religious practices and superstitious worship. For Hume, the clergy plays a decisive role in the cultivating of these tensed passions and beliefs, thus fortifying the impact of religious fear and melancholy on the minds of the faithful flock.

In the *Treatise*, Hume calls to attention how 'preachers' might succeed in having this impact: he observes how "in matters of religion men take a pleasure in being terrify'd" (T 1.3.9.15; SBN 115). For in religious discourse, like in dramatic performances, the preacher excites the "dismal and gloomy passions" that lie at the root of religious belief. While in everyday life these passions are experienced as threatening and unpleasant, both in tragedy and religious worship the very enactment of these passions (through imaginative play and narrative) invigorate a special sort of pleasure. In fact, Hume suggests that religious discourse and practice have something in common with tragedy: both function as mechanisms to mediate terrifying passions of fear and anxiety and transform them into more positive attitudes.

In his essay "Of Tragedy," Hume explains more in detail how classical drama triggers such a process of affective transformation. He observes that in attending tragedies, the spectator identifies with the strong and violent negative passions of the personages in the play, while at the same time enjoying the beauty of the performance. According to Hume, this posture of the mind causes the affective energy of the negative emotions to be transposed to the delicate *aesthetic* pleasure invigorated by the formal aesthetic features of the theatrical performance (E 216–225). By pointing, in the *Treatise*, to this analogy between dramatic performances and religious discourse, Hume suggests that a similar emotional transformation is achieved by religious discourse and practice.

Of course, there remains a huge difference between the fictions of tragedy and the belief on which religious discourse thrives. The second, as we have seen, concerns the belief in the real *existence* of 'invisible powers' or one Supreme Power that interferes in human existence in an effective though mysterious way. While this belief in the real existence of the divine remains more vague and loose in polytheism, in monotheism it becomes the core belief of a religious metaphysics that at the same time fosters religious intolerance and persecution.

6 'True religion,' superstition, enthusiasm

This brings us to Hume's moral critique of religion.[7] This critique concerns mostly the qualms and terrors of monotheistic traditions, in particular Christianity, less those of ancient polytheism. In general, so Hume remarks in the *NHR*, the "pagan religion" of the pre-Christian era was really "a true poetical religion" that remained strongly imaginative and "sat so easy and light on men's minds" (NHR 12, 18, 26). As a consequence, the ancient religious believer did not bother too much about the truth and rational consistency of his or her religious creeds. Polytheists, so Hume observes, could live better with the ambivalence and half-hearted character of religious belief and practice: and this made them less stubborn in their religious devotion.

Overall, so Hume thinks, polytheism is more tolerant towards other religious denominations than monotheism (NHR 9, 2). It is also, as we have seen, less preoccupied with salvation in an afterlife and closer to the messiness of everyday life. Hume therefore praises the morals of Greek and Roman polytheism, because here "the gods are conceived to be little superior to mankind": one can more easily address oneself to them in worship and try to emulate them in daily life. Hence, the moral superiority of polytheism: it invigorates "activity, spirit, courage, magnanimity, love of liberty, and all the virtues which aggrandize a people" (NHR 10, 2).

In contrast, the morals of Christian monotheism prove, according to Hume, the truth of the adagio that "corruption of the best things gives rise to the worst" (NHR 10, 1; 11, 1). In the essay "Of Superstition and Enthusiasm," written a few years before the *NHR*, Hume analyzes the pernicious moral effects of both forms of false religion on what he calls "true religion" (E 73). This is a short but significant essay that summarizes nicely the gist of Hume's penetrating moral critique of religion developed in more detail in his political essays, the *History of England*, and the posthumous *Dialogues*. Remarkably, in "Of Superstition and Enthusiasm," Hume understands by *superstition* a specific type of monotheistic religion, not, as in the *NHR*, all forms of religion to be found in history. At the same time, he introduces the term *enthusiasm* to refer to a specific feature of some forms of Christian belief. Thus borrowing from common terminology in seventeenth and eighteenth century religious discourse, he sees both as forms of 'false religion.'

Hume opens "Of Superstition and Enthusiasm" with the observation that "weakness, fear, melancholy, together with ignorance" lie at the roots of superstition, while enthusiasm is the fruit of "raptures, transports, and surprising flights of fancy." This observation clearly illustrates that both forms of religion rely on the passions to flourish. But while superstition is rather based on fear, enthusiasm thrives on hope. As a consequence, superstition fosters a submissive attitude towards the Deity and relies heavily on ritual devotion and the authority of the clergy, while enthusiasm leads to ecstatic zeal insofar it takes "the immediate inspiration" of the Divine Being as "object of devotion" (E 74).

We here clearly see the discourse of the *NHR* foreshadowed: Hume's characterization of superstition bears reminiscence to his account of the emergence of religious belief in general, with its strong reliance on symbolic and ritual mediation, while the rough sketch of the main features of enthusiasm reminds us of the propensities that lead to the emergence of monotheism: the tendency to make an imaginative projection of a Highest, All-Powerful Deity, with whom humans long to be united.

In fact, Hume suggests that both superstition and enthusiasm exemplify some core features of *all* religious belief: but some religious traditions tend more to superstition, while others have a more enthusiastic outlook.[8] In Christianity, for example, Catholicism is more superstitious in nature, while Protestantism exemplifies in the rule enthusiasm. Enthusiasm might be typical for modern religion (seventeenth- and eighteenth-century Christianity), for it is suspicious towards all forms of tangible representation and symbolic mediation of the Divinity: enthusiasm is therefore also less prone to the influence of priestly power and melancholic submission than Catholicism. But, as Hume observes, enthusiasm is generally in its first emergence more violent and furious and exemplifies, as the *NHR* points out, the intolerance and proselytism of monotheism.

Hope and self-confidence are attitudes typical for enthusiasm, while fear and melancholy characterize the spirit of superstition. Therefore, so Hume contends with reference to the religious fanatics of seventeenth-century England, "enthusiasm produces the most cruel disorders in human society" (E 77), while superstition leads to a blind and debilitating submission to "the authority of the priesthood" (E 75). Hume hopes that enthusiasm in his days may gradually become more calm and moderate, for the posture of religious ecstasy and self-aggrandizement cannot be long sustained. Moreover, enthusiasts are, in general, lovers of freedom.

This brings us back to the question whether Hume really believed some more civilized and morally harmless form of religion could ever be established. Remarkably, as Hume observes towards the end of the *NHR*, religion seems to take so deep root in the human mind and passions that it appears to be an ineradicable feature of the human condition. "Look out for a people, entirely destitute of religion: If you find them at all, be assured, that they are but few degrees removed from brutes" (NHR 15, 10). It seems that Hume was convinced that religious belief, thriving on both enthusiasm and superstition, on imaginative projection and ecstasy as well as devotional melancholy, will be part of human culture and society for a long time to come. Therefore, the possibly detrimental influence of religion on public life and morality will remain something to cope with for the civil magistrate.[9]

Sporadically, Hume refers to a form of 'true religion' or the principles of 'genuine theism and religion' that is free of the qualms and negative influences of superstition and enthusiasm. Hume's 'true religion' appears to derive equally from a core feature or propensity of the human mind: the capacity at wonder and amazement towards the order in Nature. At the outset of the *NHR*, Hume thus speaks enthusiastically about "the primary principles of genuine Theism and Religion" that reveal to every rational enquirer the belief in "an intelligent author" whose causal force is revealed by "whole frame of nature" (NHR Intro). Hume here appears to assent to the famous "argument from design" so exemplary for eighteenth-century Deism. However, as Hume further observes in the *NHR*, this form of wonder and rational piety could only emerge out of a scientific, detached view on the world, whereby abstraction is made from all too human passions and attitudes of fear and uncertainty. Moreover, as the posthumous *Dialogues* show, this form of rational theism should clearly be distinguished from Christian monotheism as it unfolded in history.

Irrespective of Hume's own well-considered views on the legitimacy of rational theism (which he appears not to consider philosophically solid), it is not the sort of religious belief that underpins the mainstream forms of religion to be found in human history. As Hume lets Philo testify at the end of his *Dialogues Concerning Natural Religion*, such a religion is nowhere to be found in the world but is rather a form of 'speculative Theism' that remains aloof of strong human passions and everyday life. It perhaps fosters a sort of rational contemplative piety, but remains elitist in nature: only a few will be thrilled by this philosophical ideal and will there find the solace and consolation that is offered to the masses by popular religion.[10]

Notes

1 Letter of Warburton to Andrew Millar (Hume's editor), quoted in Mossner (1980: 325).
2 Essay of William Rose in the *Monthly Review* of February 1757, cited in: Tweyman (1996: 219).
3 Some scholars contend that Hume in his investigation of the legitimacy of religious belief does himself leave some room for an "attenuated deism," which would mean that the belief in God is a 'natural belief.' For this view, cf. Butler (1960) and Gaskin (1988). For a critical reflection on this position, cf. Penelhum (2000).
4 The concept of 'conjectural history' comes from Dugald Stewart. Cf. his *An Account of the Life and Writings of Adam Smith* (1793), reprint in: Adam Smith (1980: 293).
5 In the *Dialogues* Hume remarks that "terror is the primary principle of religion, it is the passion which always predominates in it, and admits but of short intervals of pleasure" (D, 12, 29 (Coleman edition, 100)).
6 In the *NHR* Hume remarks: "The usual course of men's conduct belies their words, and shows, that their assent in these matters in some unaccountable operation of the mind between disbelief and conviction, but approaching much nearer to the former than to the latter" (NHR 12, 15).
7 For a more extensive overview of Hume's moral critique of religion, cf. Lemmens (2011).
8 In the *Dialogues*, Hume refers to a sort of dialectic between enthusiasm and superstition as typical for religious belief and devotion as such: "It is true, both fear and hope enter into religion; because both

these passions, at different times, agitate the human mind, and each of them forms a species of divinity, suitable to itself. [. . .] Not to mention, that these fits of excessive, enthusiastic joy, by exhausting the spirits, always prepare the way for equal fits of superstitious terror and dejection" (DNR 12, 29).

9 In the *Dialogues*, Hume sounds cynical about this difficult task: "Whence comes it then, that in fact, the utmost a wise magistrate can propose with regard to popular religions, is, as far as possible, to make a saving game of it, and to prevent their pernicious consequences with regard to society?" (DNR 12, 21).

10 "True religion, I allow, has no such pernicious consequences: But we must treat of religion, as it has commonly be found in the world; nor have I anything to do with that speculative tenet of theism, which, as it is a species of philosophy, must partake of the beneficial influence of that principle, and at the same time must lie under a like inconvenience, of being always confined to a few persons" (DNR 12, 22). For an interpretation of Hume's concept of true religion and his (alleged) appreciation of some form of enlightened monotheistic belief as expressive of this true religion, cf. Livingston (1998) and Willis (2014).

References

Butler, R. J. (1960) "Natural Religion and the Enigma of Hume," *Archiv für Geschichte der Philosophy* 42: 73–100.

De Cruz, H. (2015) "The Relevance of Hume's *Natural History of Religion* for Cognitive Science of Religion," *Res Philosophica* 92(3).

Garrett, D. (2015) *Hume*, London and New York: Routledge.

Gaskin, J. C. A. (1988) *Hume's Philosophy of Religion*, New York: Palgrave Macmillan.

Geertz, C. (1973) *The Interpretation of Cultures*, New York: Basic Books.

Harris, James A. (2015) *Hume: An Intellectual Biography*. New York, New York: Cambridge University Press.

Holden, T. (2010) *Spectres of False Divinity: Hume's Moral Atheism*, Oxford: Oxford University Press.

Kail, P. (2007) "Understanding Hume's *Natural History of Religion*," *The Philosophical Quarterly* 57(227): 190–211.

Lemmens, W. (2011) "Beyond the 'Calm Sunshine of the Mind': Hume on Religion and Morality," *Aufklärung und Kritik* 18(1): 214–240.

Livingston, D. W. (1998) *Philosophical Melancholy and Delirium: Hume's Pathology of Philosophy*, Chicago, IL and London: University of Chicago Press.

Malherbe, M. (1995) "Hume's *Natural History of Religion*," *Hume Studies* 21(2): 255–274.

Mossner, E. C. (1980), *The Life of David Hume*, Oxford: Clarendon Press.

Penelhum, Terence (2000) "Natural Belief and Religious Belief in Hume's Philosophy," in Terence Penelhum (ed.), *Themes in Hume: The self, the Will, Religion*, Oxford: Clarendon Press, pp. 204–221.

Russell, P. (2008) *The Riddle of Hume's Treatise: Skepticism, Naturalism and Irreligion*, Oxford: Oxford University Press.

Smith, A. (1980) *The Glasgow Edition of the Works and Correspondence of Adam Smith*, vol. 3, Oxford: Clarendon Press.

Streminger, G. (1989) "Religion as a Threat to Morality: An Attempt to Throw Some New Light on Hume's Philosophy of Religion," *Hume Studies* 15: 277–294.

Tweyman, S., ed. (1996) *Hume on Natural Religion*, Bristol: Thoemmes Press.

Willis, A. C. (2014) *Toward a Humean True Religion: Genuine Theism, Moderate Hope, and Practical Morality*, University Park, PA: Pennsylvania State University Press.

Yandell, K. (1990) *Hume's "Inexplicable Mystery": His Views on Religion*, Philadelphia: Temple University Press.

14

HUME ON RELIGIOUS LANGUAGE AND THE ATTRIBUTES OF GOD

Thomas Holden

1 Introduction

Hume is justly famous for his case that natural human reason licenses us to say nothing, or next to nothing, about the divine attributes, at least if we intend such talk to accurately describe the nature of the first cause of all. Given the weakness of our faculties and the indeterminacy of the evidence available to human inquirers, the actual nature of the original cause of all things is almost entirely beyond the reach of human reason. But there is also another side to Hume's treatment of talk about the divine attributes: his concession that we *are* justified in ascribing wisdom, thought, goodness, and, indeed, "every species of perfection" to the first cause of all (DNR 2.3), so long as we do not mean thereby to describe this incomprehensible being or principle, but merely express our reverence toward it in words employed not for their usual descriptive content but rather purely for their honorific connotations. This concession raises questions about Hume's religious position that go beyond the familiar issues of skepticism, belief, and the limits of human knowledge. Here I review the main contours of Hume's skeptical treatment of descriptive natural theology (that is, the attempt to establish facts about the being and attributes of the deity through natural human reason, without assistance from supernatural revelation). I also consider his purposes in permitting the ascription of attributes to the deity for their honorific value.

2 The critique of descriptive natural theology

Hume's skeptical assessment of the prospects of descriptive natural theology follows fairly directly from his general epistemological views regarding knowledge of matters of fact, here applied to the particular case of speculation about the nature of the first cause of all in light of the evidence presented by its causal productions. These skeptical consequences for natural theology are largely left implicit in the *Treatise*,[1] but they are developed explicitly in the *Enquiry Concerning Human Understanding* and especially in the *Dialogues Concerning Natural Religion*, in which Hume's arguments emerge in the course of a dramatic three-cornered dialogue and are most often (though not exclusively) presented by the "careless" skeptical character Philo, who can be regarded as a playful, ironic, and perhaps sometimes hyperbolic Humean alter ego (DNR "Pamphilus to Hermippus" 6).[2]

According to Hume's general epistemological principles, whatever is clearly and distinctly conceivable is possible, and since we can clearly and distinctly conceive of any event being followed by any other event whatsoever, it follows that we can have no *a priori* insight into what *must* follow from what. We can only learn from experience what kinds of events do *in fact* follow from one another, and even Adam, created in Eden with perfect human faculties of sense and reason, would be at a loss to predict future effects or judge of prior causes until he has had at least some experience of the regular patterns of constantly conjoined event-types that actually unfold in the empirical world – discovering that water quenches thirst, sunlight warms the skin, unsupported heavy objects accelerate toward the earth, and so on. So there are no *a priori* causal principles:

> If we reason *a priori*, any thing may appear able to produce any thing. [. . .] It is only experience, which teaches us the nature and bounds of cause and effect, and enables us to infer the existence of one object from that of another.
>
> (EHU 12.29; SBN 164; see also T 1.3.15.1; SBN 173, 1.4.5.30;
> SBN 247, EHU 4.6; SBN 27, DNR 2.12–13)

Although various philosophers and theologians have claimed to have some *a priori* insight into the causal structure of the world – to be able to rationally intuit that every event must have a cause, that matter alone cannot give rise to thought, that a complex adjustment of parts to an end can only arise from design and intelligence – in fact there can be no such *a priori* knowledge of matters of fact and existence, and the confidence that we have in our favored hypotheses about what causes what ought only to be as great as the accumulated evidence of experience and observation will support.

Persuaded of these principles, what havoc must we make? First, there can be no *a priori* insight into the nature of the first cause, nor indeed any *a priori* guarantee that that there even *is* a first cause of all. The universe might trace back to eternity, or have sprung into existence without external prompting: these sequences of events are conceivable, and hence must be regarded as possible. However, while Hume is firm that we cannot demonstrate the existence of a first cause of the universe *a priori*, throughout most of his critique of cosmological speculation he treats the existence of some sort of first cause of all as a given. In his *Letter from a Gentleman*, written to defend his earlier *Treatise* against charges of skepticism and irreligion, he insists that he never intended to question the principle "*that whatever begins to exist must have a Cause of Existence*," but only to show that our confidence in this principle properly rests on empirical rather than aprioristic grounds (LG 26; 426). And the debate between the three main characters in Hume's *Dialogues* proceeds on the shared assumption that (as Philo puts it) "nothing exists without a cause; and the original cause of this universe (whatever it be) we call GOD." The usually skeptical Philo even grants that the existence of some sort of first cause of all is "unquestionable and self-evident" (DNR 2.3). Still, while Hume does in practice grant the existence of an original cause of all, his insistence that we can establish neither its being nor any of its attributes *a priori* constitutes a rejection of the sort of natural theology of pure reason associated with Anselm, Descartes, and Samuel Clarke.

Second, any reasoning about the nature of the first cause of all, like any reasoning about any unknown cause of given effects, must proceed from the evidence of its observed effects together with what we have learned from experience about what kinds of things tend to cause what. Each of these points is important: we are limited to the humanly observable effects of the creation, and in making inferences from these effects to the likely character of the first cause must argue by analogy with reference to a background of other empirically confirmed cause–effect relationships. The crucial case here is 'the argument to design' (also known as 'the teleological argument,' and referred to by Hume's characters as the "argument *a posteriori*" and "the experimental argument" (DNR 2.5, 5.1)), that is, the argument that appeals to empirical facts about the high degree of order and apparently purposive organization in (at least parts of) the universe in order to infer intelligence and design in the first cause. In assessing this line of reasoning, Philo will apply the usual Humean logic and insist that

> order, arrangement, or the adjustment of final causes, is not of itself any proof of design; but only so far as it has been experienced to proceed from that principle. For ought we can know *a priori*, matter may contain the source or spring of order originally within itself as well as mind does.
>
> (DNR 2.14)

The argument to design is sometimes presented as an inference to the best explanation that has force independently of any analogical reasoning, as if we can 'just see' (or rationally intuit) that order and purposive organization are best explained by design. But for Philo the principle that order and purposive organization are best explained by design is only as plausible as the overall weight of empirical evidence from analogous observed cases suggests. Unless and until it is backed by suitable experience with analogous cause–effect relationships, the conviction that order and the adjustment of parts to an end is 'best explained' by design remains simply an *a priori* prejudice.

At first glance, this might not seem to be such a problem for a more properly empirical version of the argument to design. Do we not in fact have the necessary confirmation that order and purposive organization in an effect *are* reliably correlated with intelligence and design in their cause, given our experience of the production of machines, houses, ships, and other artifacts, which provide us with so many observed instances of order and purposive organization proceeding from design? And does the universe not exhibit order and purposive organization in at least some of its parts, suggesting by analogy with these observed cases of human artifice, intelligence, and design in its original cause?[3]

But as Philo shows in forensic detail, the evidence here is much weaker than might at first appear. First, we only have a very limited view of the overall universe, and it is rash to assume that the part we have seen is representative of the wider creation across space and time. Perhaps the order and organization we experience in our part of the universe is not the rule but the anomalous exception (DNR 2.20, 2.22). Second, the analogy at work in the argument to design is between the overall universe on the one hand, and one miniscule part of the universe (artifacts, which we observe to be produced by human designers) on the other. But experience shows us that the origin of a part is an unreliable basis for conclusions about the origins of a whole: "From observing the growth of a hair, can we learn anything concerning the generation of a man?" (DNR 2.18; compare also 2.19, 2.23). Third, where it does fall under our observation, the universe is *not* in fact so similar to a machine or a house, or to the other productions of human artifice. And the weaker the resemblance between the universe and the effects of human artifice, the less compelling any analogical reasoning we might mount upon this resemblance between effects to infer a resemblance between their causes. "Wherever you depart, in the least, from the similarity of cases, you diminish proportionably the evidence; and may at last bring it to a very weak *analogy*, which is confessedly liable to error and uncertainty" (DNR 2.7).

> Observe I entreat you, with what extreme caution all just reasoners proceed in the transferring of experiments to similar cases. Unless the cases be exactly similar, they

repose no perfect confidence in applying their past observation to any particular phenomenon. Every alteration of circumstances occasions a doubt concerning the event;
and it requires new experiments to prove certainly, that the new circumstances are of
no moment or importance.

(DNR 2.17; see also 2.17, 5.1–2)

For Philo, at least, this point is sufficient to eviscerate the argument to design, reducing its proba-
tive force to the level of "a guess, a conjecture, a presumption" (DNR 2.8). And, fourth, in what
is perhaps Philo's most damaging observation of all: while the universe could be said to bear
some resemblance to the productions of human artifice, it bears at least as much resemblance to
an animal or vegetable, the productions of sperm, egg, and seed. After all, animals and vegetables
exhibit no less order and purposive organization in their parts than artifacts do, and moreover
also exhibit rhythmic patterns of internal motion and self-repair in a manner at least somewhat
analogous to cyclical aspects of universe such as the revolution of the seasons and the motion of
heavenly bodies (DNR 6.3). And the production of order through generation and vegetation
appears more frequently in the observed world than the production of order through artifice
and design (DNR 7.13). So insofar as speculation backed by experience and analogy goes, there
is at least as much reason to conjecture that the universe arose from an organic principle of generation or vegetation as there is to conjecture that it arose from a principle of intelligence and
design (DNR 6.3–6, 7.3–17). If it is said that an organic process of generation and vegetation
itself requires a prior explanatory cause, and that in tracing the universe to something like an
egg or seed we invite a regress ('What produced the egg or the seed?'), the same point applies
no less forcefully to the processes of thought and intelligence and the tracing of the world to a
designing mind ('What produced the designing mind?') (DNR 4.6–11; see also 7.13). Further,
if experience is to be our guide, it suggests that intelligence and thought depends upon organic
processes and material embodiment rather than the other way around (DNR 6.6, 8.11). Philo's
point is not of course that it is *likely* that the universe in fact arose from organic principles of
generation or vegetation. Rather, his point is that these hypotheses are not *less* likely than the
hypothesis that the universe arose from principles of thought and design, and that the availability of these equally supportable hypotheses shows how flimsy the evidence we have to work
with really is. Given the narrow reach of our faculties and the limitations of our experience,
each of the numerous "imperfect analogies" we might draw between the universe and this or
that better-understood species of object is simply too tenuous to support any plausible speculation about the attributes of the first cause of all (DNR 8.1). In the round, "we have no *data*
to establish any system of cosmogony. Our experience, so imperfect in itself, and so limited in
both extent and duration, can afford us no probable conjecture concerning the whole of things"
(DNR 7.8; compare also 1.10, 2.24).

So, as Philo sees it, the argument to design is essentially worthless. But notice that he never
denies that there is *some* degree of resemblance or analogy between the principles of intelligence and design on the one hand and the cause of the universe on the other. In fact, in what is
sometimes thought to be a reversal of his previous skeptical position and an admission of some
residual form of deism, in the closing part of the *Dialogues* Philo explicitly admits "*that the cause
or causes of order in the universe probably bear some remote analogy to human intelligence*" (DNR 12.33).
But reports of Philo's reversal have been greatly exaggerated. All along his argument was that
we cannot establish that there is a *significant, meaningful* degree of resemblance between the first
cause of the universe and the intelligence responsible for human artifacts, not that there is no
degree of resemblance at all. Philo makes this last point very clear in DNR 12.7, using language
that provides the key to his famous 'concession' in DNR 12.33. There is, he says, no denying

that there is "*a certain degree* of resemblance among *all* the operations of nature." For instance, "the rotting of a turnip, the generation of an animal, and the structure of human thought [are] energies that *probably bear some remote analogy* to each other"; and even an atheist would have to concede that "it [is] probable, that the principle which first arranged, and still maintains order in this universe, bears [. . .] some remote inconceivable analogy to the other operations of nature, and among the rest, to the economy of mind and thought" (DNR 12.7, emphasis mine). So to assert *some* remote degree of resemblance between two kinds of object is really to say nothing distinctive about either, and the first cause bearing a remote analogy to a human mind is perfectly consistent with its bearing a closer and much more meaningful analogy to other empirical phenomena, such as, perhaps, organic generation, vegetation, or (borrowing Philo's parodic example) the putrefaction of a root vegetable. And so when Philo uses the same language in admitting a "remote analogy" between the cause of the universe and human intelligence in DNR 12.33, he may give the superficial appearance of meeting the proponents of the design hypothesis halfway, but in fact cedes them nothing worth contending. His skepticism regarding the ability of natural human reason to fathom the nature of the first cause remains as strong as it ever was throughout the *Dialogues*, and as strong as the skepticism regarding cosmological speculation that Hume endorses in his own voice in the *Enquiry* (EHU 12.25; SBN 162). If this is an "attenuated deism," it is attenuated to the point of meaninglessness.[4,5]

Philo makes one other crucial point about the limitations of the argument to design. Waive all the preceding objections and assume that the argument does go through, establishing that the first cause of all bears a significant, meaningful resemblance to a human mind (while perhaps being "possessed of much large faculties, proportioned to the grandeur of the work, which he has executed" (DNR 2.5)). Even so, this conclusion is still hopelessly under-specific for the purposes of traditional theism, and has no implications for moral or religious practice. It does not tell us that the original cause is an infinite being (DNR 5.5), or a perfect being (DNR 5.6–7), or even a single mind rather than a team of intelligences that worked on the world as a group project (DNR 5.8). Indeed, the more compelling one finds the analogy between the universe and the productions of human artifice, the more the logic of analogical inference would encourage one to expect the cause of the universe to closely resemble the cause of human artifacts – that is to say, to resemble beings that are not just intelligent, but also limited, imperfect, multitudinous, social, and even mortal, gendered, and bipedal (DNR 5.10–11). Nor would a successful argument to design tell us anything about the first cause's interest or lack of interest in human beings, or anything about its putative benevolence and justice, its moral sentiments or intentions. Moreover, as Philo argues, any other attempt to infer the deity's supposed moral attributes from the mixed and fragmentary evidence available to human inquirers will fail for the same sort of reasons that empirically motivated speculation failed in the case of the attributes of intelligence and design (DNR 11.2–4; compare also EHU 11.15–17; SBN 137–139; EHU 11.21; SBN 141). Our experience is simply too limited to support any responsible speculation about the distinctive character of the first cause of all, and so far as natural human reason goes, the first cause of all remains a permanent black box (DNR 8.12; NHR 15.13).[6]

3 Philo's expressivist treatment of the language of divine attributes

Hume devotes the bulk of the *Dialogues* to this scorching critique of traditional descriptive natural theology. But early in the work he also has Philo endorse an alternative way of talking about the divine nature, a positive approach that would validate the ascription of numerous attributes to the first cause of all, if only as an expression of our reverence toward it. Perhaps understandably, this brief moment of pious uplift has received little attention in comparison with the extensive, severe, and unremitting critique of descriptive natural theology that follows. However, it presents a radical move in the philosophy of religion and opens up questions about Hume's attitude to religious feeling that go beyond the more familiar issues of evidence and belief.

Philo rejects any attempt to describe the distinctive character of the first cause of all on the basis of the evidence available to natural human reason. But in his opening position statement in part 2 of the *Dialogues*, he also says that we *can* properly assign all manner of perfections to the first cause – speaking of it as wise, intelligent, and the rest – just so long as we do not thereby intend to describe it, but only to express our reverence toward it in words employed not for their usual descriptive content, but for their connotations of awe and respect. Here is the crucial passage:

> Nothing exists without a cause; and the original cause of this universe (whatever it be) we call GOD; *and piously ascribe to him every species of perfection.* [. . .] But as all perfection is entirely relative, we ought never to imagine, that we comprehend the attributes of this divine being, or to suppose, that his perfections have any analogy or likeness to the perfections of a human creature. *Wisdom, thought, design, knowledge; these we justly ascribe to him; because these words are honourable among men, and we have no other language or other conceptions, by which we can express our adoration of him.* But let us beware, lest we think, that our ideas anywise correspond to his perfections, or that his attributes have any resemblance to those qualities among men.
>
> (DNR 2.3, emphases mine; compare also Demea at DNR 3.13)

We ascribe these various attributes "justly" to the first cause of all, but only for their honorific value, in order to "express our adoration." To judge by the surface grammar of such talk, it might seem that we are making claims about the actual character of the original cause. But if we are speaking as Philo says we ought, our words will simply express our reverence and awe, not any attempt to pronounce on the nature of this incomprehensible being or principle.

Philo does not develop this positive account in any detail. But he does in practice avail himself of it in the later parts of the *Dialogues*, allowing him to bestow various traditional attributes upon the first cause of all while rejecting any meaningful analogy between, for example, human mercy and benevolence on the one hand, and divine 'mercy' and 'benevolence' on the other (DNR 10.24; see also 10.27, 11.16, 12.8). And when Philo adds that, given this approach to the divine attributes, the first cause "is more the object of worship in the temple than of disputation in the schools" (DNR 2.3), we might perhaps hear an echo of Hume's suggestion in the *Enquiry* that once we accept that human judgment is unable to determine the nature of ultimate cosmological realities, we should hand such "sublime topics" over to "the embellishment of poets and orators, or to the arts of priests and politicians" (EHU 12.25; SBN 162). That last suggestion might easily be read as sarcastic and irreligious in intent. But perhaps, in light of Philo's account of the proper function of talk about the nature of the first cause, it is also possible to read Hume as at least semi-serious in handing off such topics to the adornments of poets, orators, priests, and politicians. Is he? And is he serious in promoting this positive approach to religious language in the *Dialogues*? Or is the whole account just pious smoke?

First, a couple of points to help situate the proposed account. It is sometimes suggested that in adopting this account of talk about the divine attributes, Philo is simply reprising the tradition of 'negative' or 'apophatic' theology that runs back through Pseudo-Dionysius and Tertullian, and which was associated in Hume's day with the works of William King and Peter Browne.[7] According to this negative theology or 'via negativa' none of our human ideas or words can apply in any literal sense to God, and we can therefore speak of the divine attributes only in negative or highly figurative terms. But it is a mistake to see Philo's proposal as a form of negative theology. First, Philo's critique of literal, descriptive talk about the divine attributes is epistemological in character, not metaphysical or semantic. He does not argue that human ideas and words *cannot* apply to the first cause of all, but only that we cannot know which, if any, of them do. After all, as Philo sees it, the first cause *might* possibly be a mind much like the human, or an egg, or a seed, or of course something else again. (As Hume himself says, "to consider the matter *a priori* any thing may produce any thing" (T 1.4.5.30; SBN 247).) Philo even explicitly considers the possibility that the first cause is a mortal being with a human figure. So he has no truck with the view that human ideas and words could never accurately describe the attributes of the first cause. Philo's position is just that we lack the evidence needed to support any specific attempted description. Second, traditional negative theology *is* descriptive in intent, even if those descriptions are purely negative in character ('God is not finite,' 'God is not corporeal') and only specify attributes that God lacks (finitude, corporeality) rather than attributes he positively possesses. This is to describe God in some sort, if only by negation. But Philo's proposal is that in talking about the divine attributes we should not employ words for their usual descriptive content, positive *or* negative, but exclusively for their honorific, reverence-conveying value. Consider that for Philo the statement 'God is infinite' should simply convey our veneration for the first cause rather than describe it, in which case one can utter these words without ruling out the possibility that the first cause is in fact a finite, limited being. In this way, Philo can ascribe all the various traditional perfections to the first cause while keeping a completely open mind as to its actual nature.

So Philo's account is not a recapitulation of King or Browne, or the tradition of negative theology more generally. In fact, Hume's likeliest inspiration, and the only other major early modern philosopher to have advocated this expressivist treatment of talk about the divine attributes, is Thomas Hobbes. Much like Philo, Hobbes holds that statements about God's nature are properly "oblations rather than propositions." They display our desire "to praise, magnify, and honor God," and should not convey any claim about the actual nature of this indecipherable being (Hobbes 1976: Ch. 35 sec. 16).

> The nature of God is incomprehensible; that is to say, we understand nothing of *what he is*, but only *that he is;* and therefore the attributes we give him, are not to tell one another, *what he is*, nor to signify our opinion of his nature, but our desire to honour him with such names as we conceive most honourable amongst ourselves.
>
> (Hobbes 2012: 616)

For Hobbes, such talk is simply an act of homage or obeisance, a speech act displaying our humility and reverence before this indescribable being as best we can in human words. All of Hobbes' works addressing natural theology endorse this expressivist theory, and it is reasonable to suppose that Hume would have been familiar with it by way of *The Elements of Law* and *Leviathan* at least.[8]

There is another intriguing precedent or point of departure for Philo's proposed account, this time in Hume's own writings. Hume clearly holds that philosophers and philosophically minded theologians often *do* intend to describe God when they speak of his attributes. But when it comes to the unselfconscious speech of everyday believers, things are not so straightforward. Hume addresses this issue in his speculative genealogy of popular religious practices in the *Natural History of Religion* (a work that was published two decades before the *Dialogues*, though at a time when Hume already had an early draft of the *Dialogues* in hand). According to the *Natural History*, the accounts of God's nature that emerge in popular theistic culture are in large part a reflection of the hyperbolic language of pious flatterers who, desperate to please their divinity with most ostentatious praise they can pour forth, typically overtop their own imaginations and the limits of intelligibility. The devotees of popular religions

> will endeavor, by every art, to insinuate themselves into [their deity's] favour; and supposing him to be pleased, like themselves, with praise and flattery, there is no eulogy or exaggeration, which will be spared in their addresses to him. In proportion as men's fears or distresses become more urgent, they still invent new strains of adulation; and even he who outdoes his predecessor in swelling up the titles of his divinity, is sure to be outdone by his successor in newer and more pompous epithets of praise. Thus they proceed; till at last they arrive at infinity itself, beyond which there is no farther progress: And it is well, if, in striving to get farther, and to represent a magnificent simplicity, they run not into inexplicable mystery.
>
> (NHR 6.5)

> When more magnificent ideas are urged upon [the followers of popular theism], they esteem it dangerous to refuse their assent. Will you say, that your deity is finite and bounded in his perfections; may be overcome by a greater force; is subject to human passions, pains, and infirmities; has a beginning, and may have an end? This they dare not affirm; but thinking it safest to comply with the higher encomiums, they endeavor, by an affected ravishment and devotion, to ingratiate themselves with him. As a confirmation of this, we may observe, that the assent of the vulgar is, in this case, merely verbal, and that they are incapable of conceiving those sublime qualities, which they seemingly attribute to the Deity. Their real idea of him, notwithstanding their pompous language, is still as poor and frivolous as ever.
>
> (NHR 7.1; see also 8.2, 13.2)

So in popular theism, as in Philo's own prescription, we have talk about the divine attributes that is driven by the desire to express reverence rather than the desire to accurately describe, and in which words are pressed into service for their honorific connotations and may be detached from any descriptive content. The purpose of such talk is to laud the deity, and the specific words used largely incidental. Even so, it would be a mistake to see Philo as enjoining us to return to this sort of pre-philosophical religious speech, while perhaps also warning us against a sort of philosophical literal-mindedness when it comes to the interpretation of pious talk in the pews. Consider two significant differences between Philo's proposed religious language and the language of popular theism. First, in Hume's speculative genealogy, popular theism begins with a descriptive account of a deity – perhaps a chief god of the nation or tribe, a limited, anthropomorphic being with ideas and passions not so different from the human (NHR 6.5). That account is subsequently inflated with praise and flattery, but it never entirely sheds its descriptive core as the thoughts of believers, for all their transcendental panegyrics, are continually drawn back into "grosser and more vulgar conceptions" of an anthropomorphic divinity better suited to human imagination (NHR 8.2). So while popular theistic talk about the divine attributes does tend to range in the honorific, reverence-expressing direction that Philo recommends, it is not as purely non-representational as he would like. Second, in the *Natural History*'s account of popular theism, believers are motivated to employ hyperbolic flattering language out of an "anxious concern for happiness" and the hope of gaining rewards and avoiding divine displeasure (NHR 6.5, 7.1, 8.2). This is in contrast to Philo's proposed approach to talk about the divine attributes, in which our reverential language is prompted not by private hopes or fears, but rather a disinterested respect for the "adorably mysterious and incomprehensible" original cause of all (DNR 2.4). It also shows that the adulatory language of popular theism is premised upon the decidedly descriptive claim that, as Philo puts it, the first cause of all has "one of the lowest of human passions, a restless appetite for applause" (DNR 12.31; see also NHR 13.5).

So despite some points of similarity, Philo's proposed approach to talk about the divine attributes has neither the metaphysical conceit of negative theology nor the lowly motivation and anthropomorphic presuppositions of popular religious language. Like Hobbes before him, Philo is making no claims about the actual nature of the first cause of all, but simply asserting that humans ought to feel awe and reverence toward the mysterious source of the universe, and that those feelings should be conveyed by speaking of this incomprehensible being or principle using words "honourable among men," human language being all that we have to express our veneration (DNR 2.3). It is important to appreciate that this position is consistent with a strong form of religious skepticism and perhaps even atheism. We are all familiar with the twenty-first-century atheist who regards the theistic conception of God as totally unfounded but would be aghast to be mistaken for an emotional philistine who does not feel reverence and awe before the majesty of nature, the heavens turning above, and (since you asked) the mysterious source or sources of the universe, whatever they may be. Such a position is not so different from the one Philo is recommending, though the modern reader might perhaps question Philo's suggestion that reverence for the original cause of the universe is best expressed in the language of anthropomorphic perfections, with its convenient tendency to give us the verbal trappings of a personal, theistic God.

4 Hume's attitude toward the expressivist treatment of the language of divine attributes

Does Hume himself endorse the expressivist approach to talk about the divine attributes outlined in the *Dialogues*? As we have seen, such an approach is perfectly consistent with his strict skepticism regarding cosmological speculation that is descriptive in intent. But the suspicion might remain that Hume puts the Hobbesian account of religious language into the mouth of Philo simply to give himself a kind of pious cover as he goes on the offensive against the arguments of traditional descriptive natural theology. This sort of insincere reading can hardly be ruled out. And perhaps, if the underlying question here is whether Hume sincerely holds that we should feel reverence toward the first cause of all, or even whether he himself feels such reverence, it might seem unanswerable. Who knows the hearts of men?

However, there is another aspect of Hume's philosophy that might inform our interpretation. In addition to his doubts about religion of the understanding, Hume also has doubts about religion of the heart. According to his account of the psychological mechanisms controlling the human passions (that is, our feelings, emotions, and affective attitudes, including reverence, awe, fear, hope, love, and the rest), although we may experience passions such as reverence and awe directed toward the starry heavens above and the other parts of nature that fall under sense and imagination, it is not so easy to experience *any* passion directed toward a being as remote from human experience and abstract in human conception as the first cause of all. As Hume puts in a 1743 letter to his friend William Mure, the deity

> is no Object either of the Senses or Imagination, & very little of the Understanding, without which it is impossible to excite any Affection. [. . .] A man [. . .] may have his Heart perfectly well disposd towards every proper & natural Object of Affection, Friends, Benefactors, Countrey, Children, &c, & yet from this Circumstance of the

Invisibility & Incomprehensibility of the Deity may feel no Affection toward him. [...] Neither [the "turbulent Passions" nor "the calm Affections"] can operate without the Assistance of the Senses, and Imagination, or at least a more compleat Knowledge of the Object than we have of the Deity. In most Men this is the Case; & a natural Infirmity can never be a Crime.

(NL 13)

So the first cause "is not the natural Object of any Passion or Affection," meaning that we are unable to experience passions directed toward it, or, at the very least, that any such passions run against the grain of human psychology, are highly difficult to sustain, and "can not be requir'd of any Man as his Duty" (NL 13). Although many believers take themselves to experience passions directed toward the first cause of all, Hume is skeptical, and traces such claims to a combination of wishful thinking, the misinterpretation of private hopes and fears, and the confusion of the first cause with more readily imaginable religious forms and icons (NL 13; compare also E 73–74, NHR 8.2). For Hume, this limitation on our passions constitutes "an Objection both to Devotion and Prayer, & indeed to every thing we commonly call Religion, except the Practice of Morality, & the Assent of the Understanding to the Proposition *that God exists*" (NL 12). And plainly it would constitute an objection to the proposal that we should speak of the divine attributes in a language expressing any *genuine* reverence and awe. Although the works authorized by Hume for publication do not explicitly press this (potentially scandalous) thesis that the first cause is not a natural object of any human passion, the *Treatise* and the *Dissertation on the Passions* confirm that our passions are governed by sense and imagination, and are therefore constantly preoccupied with the concrete and immediate at the expense of the abstract and remote (T 2.3.6; SBN 424–427; DP 6.9–18). And other authorized writings point in a similar direction, as when the title character of Hume's essay "The Sceptic" states that, when it comes to the direction of the passions, "an abstract, invisible object, like that which *natural* religion alone presents to us, cannot long actuate the mind, or be of any moment in life" (E 167; compare also EHU 8.34; SBN 101–102).[9]

If Hume holds that human psychology blocks us from feeling any real reverence toward the first cause of all, or even that such feelings are impossible for "most Men," then it seems unlikely that he sincerely endorses the reverence-expressing approach to talk about the divine attributes that he puts into Philo's mouth. At best he might regard honorific talk about the divine 'perfections' as aspirational in nature, less a display of our actual passions than a display of the sort of passions we might like to feel toward the first cause of all, and which the rare contemplative sage can *perhaps* genuinely experience (NL 13; compare also E 167). Overall, however, Hume seems to regard pious avowals of reverence before the first cause of all as self-deceiving, in which case Philo's approach to talk about the divine attributes has all the comforts and convenience of a Potemkin village.

Notes

1 See Paul Russell (2008) for an account of the implicit irreligious agenda of the *Treatise*.
2 The identification of Philo as a (playful and sometimes ironic) spokesman for Hume remains controversial in some quarters. But as I see it, the point-by-point case for identifying Philo with Hume pressed by Kemp Smith (1947: 57–74) and expanded by Gaskin (1988: 209–218) is entirely conclusive and has yet to be adequately engaged, much less answered.
3 See the statements of this version of the argument to design at DNR 2.5 and 2.14.
4 Gaskin (1988: 219–229) presents Hume as accepting a form of "attenuated deism." I see this label as potentially misleading, insofar as Hume's position (as presented by Philo) is no less consistent with

similarly attenuated versions of the hypotheses of cosmological vegetation, generation, or putrefaction – the first cause bearing *some* remote analogy to each of these things – than it is with an appropriately attenuated version of the hypothesis of design. But perhaps this disagreement is, as Hume might say, "merely verbal" (DNR 12.7).

5 Those who read Philo as reversing himself and embracing some version of the design hypothesis in Part 12 of the *Dialogues* also point to his apparent concessions and respectful tone in DNR 12.2–5. But those apparent concessions may be simply a pious performance, and in any case must be read in the light of what follows in DNR 12.7 and Philo's final position statement in 12.33. And it may not be an accident that certain of Philo's superficially more respectful remarks admit of a sharper-edged double reading. For instance, "A purpose, an intention, a design strikes everywhere the most careless, most stupid thinker." Or: "no one [. . .] pays more profound adoration [than I, Philo, do] to the divine being, *as he discovers himself to reason* [TH: which is for Philo very little], in the inexplicable contrivance and artifice of nature" (DNR 12.2, emphasis mine) (Blackburn 1999: 16 note 15).

6 In addition to arguing that we *cannot* infer that the first cause has positive moral attributes, in three subsequent paragraphs Philo also gives the appearance of going further and arguing that, given the "mixed phenomena" of the world, we *can* infer that the first cause is most likely a morally indifferent being possessed of "neither goodness nor malice" (DNR 11.14–16). But in licensing this substantive conclusion about the divine attributes, Philo seems to be abandoning his usual skeptical attitude toward cosmological speculation and ignoring several of his own specific objections to empirically motivated natural theology. For this reason among others, I suggest that Philo is being ironic, and that in presenting this argument for divine indifference he is simply parodying the kind of argument one finds in traditional empirically motivated natural theology (Holden 2010: 168–178). For the rival, non-ironic interpretation, see Gaskin (1988: 72) and Tweyman (1987: 83–85).

7 On King's and Browne's versions of negative theology, see Berman (1982: 148–165).

8 On Hobbes's version of the expressivist account of religious language, see Holden (2015: 657–660). For evidence of Hume's familiarity with Hobbes's *The Elements of Law* and *Leviathan*, see Russell (2008: 61–69).

9 I examine Hume's claim that the deity is not the natural object of any human passion, the psychological theory underpinning that claim, and Hume's debunking analysis of emotions that are supposedly focused on the first cause of all in Holden (2010: 52–84).

References

Blackburn S. (1999) "Playing Hume's Hand," in D. Z. Phillips and Timothy Tessin (ed.), *Religion and Hume's Legacy*, New York: St. Martin's Press, pp. 3–16.

Berman, D. (1982) "Enlightenment and Counter-Enlightenment in Irish Philosophy," *Archiv für Geschichte der Philosophie* 64(1982): 148–165.

Gaskin, J. C. A. (1988) *Hume's Philosophy of Religion*, 2nd edn, Atlantic Highlands, NJ: Humanities Press International.

Hobbes, T. (1976) *Thomas White's De Mundo Examined*, trans. Harold Whitmore Jones, Bradford: Bradford University Press.

———. (2012) *Leviathan: The English and Latin Texts*, edited by Noel Malcolm, Oxford: Clarendon Press.

Holden, T. (2010) *Spectres of False Divinity: Hume's Moral Atheism*, Oxford: Oxford University Press.

———. (2015) "Hobbes' First Cause," *Journal of the History of Philosophy* 53: 647–667.

Kemp Smith, N. (1947) "Introduction," in D. Hume (ed.), *Dialogues Concerning Natural Religion*, Indianapolis, IN: Bobbs-Merrill, pp. 1–75.

Russell, P. (2008) *The Riddle of Hume's Treatise: Skepticism, Naturalism, and Irreligion*, New York: Oxford University Press.

Tweyman, S. (1987) "Hume's *Dialogues* on Evil," *Hume Studies* 13: 74–85.

PART IIB

Passion, morals, and taste

15

PASSIONS AND SYMPATHY IN HUME'S PHILOSOPHY

Alessio Vaccari

Sympathy is a key principle in Hume's theory of the passions.[1] The genesis, phenomenology, and causal properties of these states depend to a great extent on the "propensity to sympathize with others, and to receive by communication their inclinations and sentiments" (T 2.1.11.1; SBN 316). Hume's philosophy makes the emotions, and their capacity to be stabilized by sympathy, central to our social life.

My chapter examines the various interconnections between sympathy and the passions. After sketching the main elements of the theory of the passions and the principle of sympathy (sections 1 and 2), I consider three aspects of human sociality. First, I examine some characteristics of our relations with our family and friends (section 3). Second, I consider our evaluative practices in this context and how non-verbal behavior governs not only how other people think and feel about us, but also how we think and feel about ourselves (section 4). Finally, I explain how human beings not only behave benevolently within their families, but can also be sensitive to the suffering of strangers (section 5).

1 Humean passions: an outline

Hume's theory of the passions is set out in Book II of his *Treatise of Human Nature* and, later, in *A Dissertation on the Passions*. Despite characterizing these states as "simple and uniform impressions" with no inner components and therefore unsusceptible to definition (T 2.1.1.1; SBN 275; T 2.2.1.1; SBN 329), Hume develops a complex and innovative anatomical explanation, making these mental states the motor of human sociality. (Harris 2010). This explanation concerns the "circumstances" that accompany the occurrence of passions in the human mind (T 2.1.2.1; SBN 277). While illustrated by constant references to "common life" and "conversation" with our fellows (T 2.2.5.1; SBN 357), the circumstances are explained in the course of Book II by reference to complex theoretical ideas such as "cause," "effect," and "object" (T 2.1.1.3; SBN 276), drawn from Book I of the *Treatise* (see also Taylor 2015, for a similar point).

Hume classifies the passions as *secondary* or *reflective* impressions. Unlike *original* impressions, bodily sensations, and sense-perceptions, which arise in the mind "without any antecedent perception" (T 2.1.1.1; SBN 275), these impressions are caused by perceptions that produce them "either immediately" or through the "interposition of its ideas" (T 2.1.1.1; SBN 275). This distinction introduces the principal taxonomy of Book II and the *Dissertation*: that between *direct* and *indirect* passions. The casual factor common to both kinds of passions are *good* or *evil*,[2] which Hume identifies with pleasure and pain, stripping them of any reference to objective conceptions of human happiness (Cohon 2008; Kail 2007). In the case of the direct passions, good or evil immediately produce impressions of "desire" and "aversion." For the indirect passions to be aroused, however, a complex of ideas must be present.

The indirect passions – pride and humility, love and hate – are examined in the first two parts of Book II. Hume characterizes these mental states through two constituent elements: the feeling, which gives them their hedonic quality, and the object (T 2.1.2.2; SBN 277), that is, the idea towards which, the passions, once raised, "direct our view" or "turn our attention" (T 2.1.2.4; SBN 278). These are the axes on which Hume illustrates the resemblances and differences between the four basic indirect passions. The hedonic tone contrasts love and pride – both pleasant – with the painful states of hatred and humility. The other concerns the object, and distinguishes between pride and humility, which are self-directed, and love and hatred, which are directed towards others (T 2.2.2.3; SBN 333).

Indirect passions have varied causes, including both mental qualities and "bodily accomplishments [. . .] and [. . .] external advantages," such as possessions, family, and nation, and they are directed at a large variety of subjects. Every cause comprises two parts: a subject and a quality pertaining to it, arousing a pleasant or painful impression in those who consider it. Each subject can cause an indirect passion only if it has a double relation, with both the feeling and the object of that passion. More precisely, the idea of the subject – for example, our body – must be related to the idea of the object of the passion – the self or another person – and its quality, gymnastic agility, for example, must arouse an impression such as admiration and wonder, which is associated with the hedonic tone of the passion. In the light of these principles, a house, for example, is a source of pride to me on two conditions: it must possess some positive qualities (such as being bright, silent, beautiful) which arouse the admiration of those who see it, a sensation that resembles the feeling of pride, and it must have some kind of stable relation with me, such as ownership or the fact that I designed it.

As commentators note, the indirect passions are evaluative attitudes towards persons – ourselves and others (Ardal 1966; Cohon 2008; Taylor 2015). Unlike the direct passions, which simply motivate us to pursue or avoid objects, indirect passions fix our attention on persons, casting a positive or negative light on them. This clearly emerges if we consider once again the two constituent elements that characterize them: feelings and their object. Hume's use of "object" corresponds to the "intentional object" of a passion – that is to say, what the passion is directed at (Cohon 2008; Baillie 2000). The object always directs our attention to something different from its cause (though it is related to it). If I am proud of my child's success at school, my pride does not fix my attention on the 'merits of *my* child,' and still less on 'me *in the role* of father,' but on the whole of myself. As Rachel Cohon has rightly said, "when I feel pride, I am proud of something in particular [its cause] . . . But the attitude of pride is a pleasure or satisfaction not in that particular accomplishment or possession, but in myself in my entirety" (Cohon 2008: 166). Similarly, love and hate are directed at other persons and not at the particular qualities or behavior we admire them for.

Now consider the relevant feelings. Hume describes the peculiarity of sentiment directed at the person, pointing out its evaluative dimension. Pride makes us feel "elated" at ourselves, while humility makes us feel "dejected" (T 2.1.2.2; SBN 277; Taylor 2015, for a similar point). We feel pleasure in considering a quality of our own or of a person close to us, one that also increases or diminishes our overall sense of ourselves. This aspect is again brought out in connection with love and hate. Hume shows that these passions involve different kinds of evaluations of others (T 2.2.2.10; SBN 337): esteem and respect for qualities such as riches and power, contempt and anger for their opposite (T 2.2.2.10; SBN 337; T 2.2.5; SBN 357–365); love or kindness in proportion to the pleasure they procure us (T 2.2.3.2–4; SBN 348–349), to the degree of 'consanguineity' or 'acquaintance' (T 2.2.4.2–3; SBN 351–352), or to resemblance in behavior and character. Unlike pride and humility, these evaluations can accompany the direct passions, such as *benevolence* and *anger*, which play a considerable role in our relations with others.

Throughout Book II, Hume insists that these passions are deeply interconnected and that this link is the basis of a crucial aspect of our mutual interactions. Through pride and humility, we construct our self as an object of reflective approbation or disapprobation. This image, in turn, is reinforced through the love and hatred of others. The possibility of steady pride is therefore connected with being the object of love, just as a sense of dejection is connected with the contempt of others. Each of us, as an agent and a spectator, participates in this constant process of emotional construction and mirroring that constitutes a fundamental dimension of social life. One of the themes of Book II of the *Treatise* is that this process depends on our capacity to sympathize with our fellows. In the following sections, I shall explain how this fundamental principle of the human mind works and the various ways it interacts with our emotional life.

2 The mechanism of sympathy

Sympathy is a capacity to receive by communication the passions and sentiments of other persons. Hume accounts for sympathy by means of a psychological mechanism that has two successive steps (Ainslie 2005). First, we acquire the idea of another person's passion through a process of inference. Second, we convert this idea into its corresponding impression and feel it as our own. By association, the idea of another's passion is "inliven'd" (T 2.1.11.7; SBN 318–319) by the impression or the idea of ourselves, and is thus transformed into a genuine passion. In the second step, the subject of sympathy moves from having merely a lively idea or belief of the other's passion to experiencing a vicarious passion, which is of the same type as that originally felt by the other person.

As many commentators note, sympathy involves various processes that are more or less conscious and more or less immediate (Pitson 1996; Ainslie 2005; Waldow 2008). It can operate as a kind of emotional contagion when, in the presence of other persons, a "good-natur'd man finds himself in an instant of the same humour with his company" (T 2.1.11.2; SBN 316–317). The inference happens without the subject noticing it (Ainslie 2005), and the idea is converted, through the relation of contiguity, just as suddenly (T 2.1.11.3; SBN 317). In other situations, the process presupposes a voluntary effort and the active exercise of reason and imagination. The transmission of vivacity from the idea of ourselves to that of the passion of another operates not only when we are contiguous with the object of sympathy, but also when it is distant and we are linked to it through similar tastes or manners. These relations of ideas are not always immediately evident, but are discovered by examining the facts or by exercising "delicacy of imagination," allowing us to react emotionally even to the smallest nuances of situations. Finally, as we shall see, human beings can sympathize not only with the emotions that another is feeling at the moment, but, by an additional effort of the imagination, with those he might feel in the future as a result of his present condition.

The multiplicity of the sympathetic processes creates interpretive problems and worries about its consistency with Book I of the *Treatise*. I examine two questions. The first concerns whether the two-phase explanation Hume proposes in T 2.1.11 (SBN 316–324) accounts adequately for these different *processes* of transmission. The second concerns the role of the self. To explain the less automatic forms of sympathy, the impression of the self involved in the second step cannot be reduced to a mere medium of vivacity, but requires the subject to position himself at the right imaginative and emotional distance from the object of sympathy.

Let us start with the first question. Do the various sympathetic processes require different types of sympathy or, if they are all explicable through the two-phase explanation indicated above, do they all belong to one single type? Some claim there are at least two types of sympathy in Hume: one requiring the existence of the process of inference and one – so-called emotive contagion – that does not. Is this so? Consider first the role of inference in the first step of the mechanism of sympathy described in T 2.1.11 (SBN 316–324). True to his epistemology, Hume claims that the process of sympathy must start from perceptions. The impressions of sensation yield no direct knowledge of the passions and sentiments of other persons. Nevertheless, these produce effects that we can directly experience. The passions cause our actions and our non-verbal and verbal behavior ("countenance and conversation") (T 2.1.11.3; SBN 317; T 2.3.3.9; SBN 417–418). From these "external signs" (T 2.1.11.3; SBN 317) of affections, we infer the ideas of their causes – i.e. ideas of the passions that have produced them.

As commentators note, Hume here describes a special form of causal inference. Standard causal inference is based on repeated observation of the spatial contiguity and temporal succession between two classes of objects. Each time we have an impression of one object, we are spurred, by a sort of psychological necessity, to recall the idea of the other. The initial impression transfers some of its vivacity onto this idea, turning it into a belief. For this inferential process to be in place, we must have experienced directly both cause and effect and the relation of succession. This condition does not seem to be satisfied in the inference as to the content of other persons' minds, which, as Hume notes, are never the object of our impressions.[3]

We can, however, avoid this problem if we take into account the general resemblance between human beings and how this influences the sympathetic process. Anik Waldow, for example, argues that the fact that the passions of other persons are "imperceptible" does not thwart our ability to obtain an idea of them. The inference is the effect of "perception of the constant conjunction between our passions and our behavioural expressions" and of the "resemblance between the other's behavioural expressions and our own" (Waldow 2008: 63). We would be inclined to associate the ideas of our passions to the impressions of the conduct of other persons. Waldow's suggestion can be fully accepted. Some textual support for this thesis can be found in Hume's examination of the link between pride and the desire to be esteemed and admired by others. Hume claims that this connection would be inexplicable if the objects that cause pride were not also causes of the love and esteem that others feel for us. Hume notes that, though no philosophical system can offer a proof of this identity of causes, we have no fear of erring in their behavior as we are guided by a sort of *presensation* showing how other persons' minds work, starting from how one's own does (T 2.2.1.9; SBN 331–332). This peculiar impression explains that human beings are inclined to regard the minds of others as like their own.

Surprisingly, Hume does not examine this perception further, simply describing it as 'natural,' meaning common to all humans. However, one can expand this observation by examining his thoughts on the resemblance between human beings. In T 2.1.11.5 (SBN 318), Hume compares the resemblance of bodies and the resemblance of minds, claiming that, in both cases, "however the parts may differ in shape or size, their structure and composition are in general the same." The similarity between bodies and their movements is a "very remarkable resemblance, which preserves itself amidst all their variety" (ibid.). The resemblance between bodies is the object of our impressions and constitutes a shared belief. Furthermore, every human being has repeated experience of the link between his own mental states and his bodily movements, which brings about convictions as to the effects of his passions on his behavior (Decety and Meltzoff 2011).

It is plausible to regard *presensation* as the effect of these beliefs. On this, we develop a *presensation* that leads us to believe that the bodily movements of others have the same mental causes. It constitutes the principle underlying every inference from which each sympathetic episode arises. In other words, we are able to infer the idea of a passion from another person's behavior because we believe that our minds are similar and actuated by the same principles.

Having clarified the difficulties concerning the form of causal inference involved in grasping other people's emotions, we can return to the question we started from: is this kind of inferential process a constituent of the various sympathetic processes described by Hume? Some commentators reject this view, claiming that there at least two types of sympathy in Hume. The first does not involve inference, consisting of an immediate knowledge of the other person's emotions, while the other can be broken down into the two stages we have described (Baier 2008; Waldow 2008; Postema 2005). But this is not supported by the texts. The only passage in the *Treatise* seeming to confirm the existence of the first form of emotional contagion is in "Of the love of relations," where Hume discusses the effects of resemblance on sympathy (T 2.2.4.7; SBN 354). Hume imagines the case in which the person who sympathizes immediately feels the same emotion as another person. As they are similar, both react similarly in similar circumstances. But Hume adds an important qualification, reconciling this case with his standard explanation. These cases also require that we infer the idea of the other's emotions. The only difference is that the idea of the object of sympathy is not converted by its relation with our self, but is replaced, so to speak, by our impression of the same type. This case too, then, lends itself to explanation along the standard lines. Hume does not modify the constituent features of his two-step explanation, but he regards this methodological simplicity as a strong point in his theory: it allows him to explain complex forms in the light of small variations of a simple mechanism that is clearly confirmed in our experience.

What of the second question concerning the role of the self in the sympathetic communications of the passions? Hume claims that "the idea, or rather impression of ourselves . . . is always intimately present with us" (T 2.1.11.4; SBN 317–318). He adds that the presence of a relation of resemblance, causality, or contiguity between ourselves and the sympathetic communicant allows the "vivacity" of our impression of ourselves to be transferred onto the idea of the communicant's sentiment (T 2.1.11.4; SBN 317–318). The role of the self in sympathy poses two fundamental problems. The first, more basic one, concerns the nature of this impression and its capacity to be always present without monopolizing our attention, preventing us from attending to others. The second concerns the opposite problem: whether an impression of oneself that is too weak does not risk leaving the sympathetic agent trapped in the sentiments of the other. Without a clear perception of himself as separate from the person with whom he is sympathizing, the spectator might be unable either to understand or help.

What is the impression of the self that plays a role in sympathy? The problem springs from Hume's famous remark that "in sympathy our own person is not the object of any passion" (T 2.2.2.17; SBN 340–341). This qualification originated in the need to forestall a possible objection to sympathy. Hume claims that when the imagination dwells on a clear and lively idea it is unable to move on to less lively ideas related to it (T 2.2.2.16; SBN 339–340). Applied to sympathy, this means the idea or impression of the self – which mediates vivacity in the second step – could not be part of an episode of pride. If it were, the imagination would stop there, blocking the process of transforming the idea of another's passion into the passion itself. So if the idea of the self is not what pride fixes its attention on, what idea is it? And also: how can this idea be "ever present" without monopolizing all our attention on itself?

Some commentators, like Nicholas Capaldi, ignore this difficulty, claiming that the self is an impression that is part of an episode of pride or humility (Capaldi 1989). Others, like Don

Garrett, claim that in this context Hume is using the idea of the self in Book I and not in Book II (Garrett 1981). Garrett argues that every perception of the mind can function as a medium of vivacity as each one can stand in for the "abstract idea" of the self that Hume is using in the discussion of sympathy. Donald Ainslie tries to mediate between these positions, claiming perceptions always enter the mind in particular "patterns." These reflect the "peculiar point of view" on the world (T 3.3.1.15; SBN 581–582), of an embodied individual who has specific commitments occupying a specific social position (Ainslie 2005). According to Ainslie, the "idea or rather the impression of ourselves" in every episode of sympathy consists in the "manner of perception's appearances" (Ainslie 2005: 23) reflected in each of our perceptions. As the human mind is constantly thronged with perceptions, the impression of ourselves is, so to speak, "ever present" in the back of our mind.

Though Hume did not explicitly claim that perceptions succeed each other in specific "patterns" reflecting the agent's viewpoint, this thesis seems consistent with what Hume claims about the self in the context of sympathy (T 2.2.2.17; SBN 340–341). In speaking of the perceptions of external objects that are "contiguous to us" or resemble us, Hume clearly includes persons. He writes a few sections later of persons who are contiguous with us or resemble us as those who are intimate with us or with whom we have various forms of mutual interactions. They constitute our circle of persons with whom we interact frequently, and our perceptions concerning them constantly call up our character and social status. That is, in succeeding each other and in having one specific content rather than another, they constantly refer to our self – that is, to a specific embodied individual who occupies a specific social position, and who is related to those persons. Interpreted in this way, the impression of the self may exercise its role as part of the sympathetic mechanism without being at the center of an actual episode of pride, and so without risking blocking the exercise of the imagination.

This interpretation also solves the question of the distinction between oneself and others. As we shall see in the final section, it is a potential problem that concerns above all those complex sympathetic processes that are the basis of the passion of pity. An interest in the suffering of our fellows that can produce benevolence can only be generated if the sympathetic agent can distinguish between his condition and that of others – if, that is, he confuses his vicarious passion with the original one. Without it, the sympathizing subject might run the risk of remaining trapped in the other's suffering, losing sight of what he can do for the other.

3 Company, relations, cheerfulness

Humans tend to live in families and in a wide circle of friends and acquaintances. For Hume, this inclination, reinforced and stratified in ranks with the formation of complex commercial societies, constitutes an original feature of human nature. Contra Hobbes, who describes the natural human condition as solitary and animated by permanent conflict in the pursuit of power, Hume represents pre-social life as marked by relatively stable and peaceful interactions. Animated by sexual appetite and a "natural concern for the common offspring" (T 3.2.2.4; SBN 486; E 162), even before the formation of the state and the rules of property, human beings were already living in small communities in which the young gradually learned the advantages of the common life and corrected their anti-social tendencies.

In Book II of the *Treatise*, Hume several times examines these specific interactions and the passions that animate them: not only love within the family, but also esteem and mutual gratitude, which are the basis of friendship between similar persons. Hume shows that an exhaustive explanation of these relations and the fundamental impact they have on our individual happiness cannot fail to involve the principle of sympathy. Hume thus accounts for a fundamental characteristic of our life: human beings are social individuals as they are sympathetic individuals and as a life without company would be one without sources of interest.

Sharing the passions of others at an emotional level is an "agreeable" fact, without which our existence would be one of "solitude" and "despair" (T 2.2.4; SBN 351–357). Hume introduces this topic with some short general reflections on the human condition. Our mind is unable to sustain "its own entertainment" and therefore needs new sense impressions periodically to stop it from falling into a state of melancholy and apathy. These impressions are always accompanied by concomitant impressions of pleasure or pain – perceptions that, in turn, arouse our desires and our passions, and activate our will, exciting our interest in new objects (T 2.2.4.4; SBN 352–353). Hume claims that our fellow-men are the most appropriate external objects for performing this function. Human company communicates passions and feelings to those around (T 2.2.4.4; SBN 352–353). Compared with other perceptions, the ideas of other people's emotions transmitted by sympathy are immediately transmuted into genuine passions that confer "a more sensible agitation to the mind, than any other image or conception" (T 2.2.4.5; SBN 353). While not questioning the general principle that sympathy is a neutral mechanism for transmitting the emotions, Hume makes a significant addition to it in this context. As it communicates lively emotions that sustain the mind and prevent it from sinking into torpor, there is an important sense in which every operation of sympathy is "peculiarly agreeable" (T 2.2.4.5; SBN 353), quite apart from the type of passion communicated.

This aspect of sympathy explains the main features of our passional life in our mutual interactions with our friends and family. The particularly intense relations of resemblance and causality that we have with these persons guarantee that the communication of their emotions is particularly effective and, when they are not openly hostile towards us, communicates a strong pleasure to us that derives precisely from our capacity to feel a wide range of vicarious emotions. It also explains the peculiar aspects of 'love' and 'kindness' that we have for our blood relations, as well as our good-will towards them. Unlike other forms of love, they arise even when their objects have no distinctive admirable quality and arouse no pleasant impression. To arouse this form of love requires no more than the relation of ideas that binds us to our families. This facilitates the operations of sympathy, arousing a concomitant pleasure that is associated with love. Similarly, the resemblance of inclinations and manners between persons explains the strong tie of friendship that is created between persons and the strong desire we have for their company.

In both cases the indirect passions, their causes, and the desires that accompany them are explained by sympathy and the associationist principles that govern it. As we have emphasized, it includes various processes, and this allows this principle to account for the various phenomena we have mentioned. Sympathetic communication with one's blood relations and friends involve more immediate forms of transmission, closer to emotional contagion. Through this principle Hume gives an account of the various kinds of ties within our closest emotional circle and their impact on our individual happiness.

4 The indirect passions, self-evaluation, and national characters

In Book II of the *Treatise*, Hume introduces the mechanism of sympathy to account for the genesis of pride and humility. Together with love and hate, these two passions constitute the 'indirect' passions, whose distinctive characteristic, as we have indicated, is to express a complex positive or negative evaluation of selves. Without sympathy, these passions would be ephemeral emotional episodes at the mercy of our changing and conflicting judgments. Sympathy makes it possible to stabilize these opinions, turning the resulting indirect passions into stable judgmental dispositions.

This process can be best understood if we think in terms of two levels at which sympathy operates. The first concerns the ways in which evaluative opinions are transmitted within circles of families or friends on the qualities of the components of those circles, while the second concerns the role of sympathy in disseminating forms of behavior and shared qualities within large societies or nations. Hume discusses this second level cursorily in Book II of the *Treatise* and in more detail in the essay "Of National Characters," where he examines the fundamental role that our imitative capacity and our inclination to company have in spreading certain types of character within a community. As we shall see, though they are connected, the two levels should be distinguished. While in the latter sympathy is required to account for the "great uniformity" (T 2.1.11.2; SBN 316–317) in our judgments on persons, which is the basis for the possibility of conversing and judging each other, in the former Hume also uses sympathy to explain the dissent that can arise between individuals and in the sphere of their most intimate relations. Hume shows that sympathy may not only boost the positive opinions we have of ourselves (and contribute to our happiness), but also increase our shame and unhappiness to the point of separating us from those who are best known to us.

We begin by considering the first level of enquiry. Hume claims that pride and humility are not impervious to the opinions of others, but are influenced at various levels by the reactions of admiration or disapprobation that are aroused in others when they consider our qualities and our behavior. In the section "Of the love of fame," Hume claims that, apart from the *original causes* of pride and humility, there is a secondary cause in the "opinions of others" (T 2.1.11.1; SBN 316). He adds that the "vast weight and importance" of this cause depends on a characteristic that distinguishes it from the other causes. The opinions that others have of us, which form our "reputation" and our "name," are not only an independent cause of pride and humility, but also the condition that makes the other causes effective. Without the support of the opinions of others, such causes would have "little influence" on those passions.

In the *Treatise*, and later in the *Dissertation on the Passions*, Hume explains this fact, claiming that our judgments "of our own worth and character" (T 2.1.11.9; SBN 320–321; but see also T 2.1.8.9 SBN 303) are particularly shaky and in need of confirmation. On the one hand, they are frequently disturbed by various passions that make them unstable, driving us to constantly embrace different opinions (T 2.1.11.9; SBN 320–321; Diss. 2.10). On the other, as human beings are also partial to themselves, they always seek views that confirm "the good opinion" they have of themselves (ibid.). To give stability to our ideas on what we regard as the causes of our pride, human beings therefore need to receive confirmation from others. But why is sympathy required rather than there being a simple original instinct to seek a good name and reputation?

Sympathy is required to explain why our desire for reputation is highly selective: we grant our preference to those we "esteem and approve of" (T 2.1.11.11; SBN 321) and with whom we have "long and intimate acquaintance" (T 2.1.11.12; SBN 321–322). This is explained by the associative principles that govern sympathy. As our companions and friends have a closer relation to us than mere resemblance, the conversion of our idea of their esteem will be simpler and more complete than that of strangers, communicating a strong passion of approbation of our qualities. As this sentiment has a double relation of impressions of ideas with our pride, it constitutes a complete cause of this passion – a cause that will add its force to the ones that originate from our positive opinions of ourselves, making our pride more agreeable and stable, and counterbalancing our contrary opinions, which might weaken it.

As emerges from this reconstruction, when Hume refers to the crucial role that the "opinions of others" have in the process that generates pride, he is clearly referring to the sentiments that our qualities arouse in those who are exposed to them. More precisely, they are the "praise" (T 2.1.11.9; SBN 320–321) and "approbation" (T 2.1.11.11; SBN 321) or the "blame" (T 2.1.11.9; SBN 320–321) and "contempt" (T 2.1.11.17; SBN 323) felt by those within their circle. More than the opinions themselves and their verbal expression, what plays a fundamental role in this particular explanatory context are the pleasant (or, in the case of humility, unpleasant) passions they express. It is these that are communicated by sympathy to the subject of pride (or humility), and have a crucial role in stabilizing the evaluation of oneself.

Sympathy's fundamental role is repeated in the examination of love, where Hume expounds a more detailed description of the series of sympathetic reflections that are pride's basis. In his famous statement that the minds of human beings are "mirrors to one another," Hume shows that a standard episode of pride is interwoven with the esteem of others in a dynamic process that entails at least two waves of mutual support. So the ease and joy that characterize, for example, the rich man's life arouse esteem in those who come into contact with him. This is transmitted by sympathy to the "possessor," who receives a "second satisfaction" of his wealth. In turn, this second pleasing sensation, "once more reflected," becomes a new form of esteem in the observer (T 2.2.5.21; SBN 365).

The esteem of those who comprise our personal circles can reinforce and support, but never constitute, our evaluative ideas that produce pride. These can activate pride only when they confirm our opinions of our qualities and the value they have (T 2.1.11.13; SBN 322). The evaluation of oneself produced by pride is, therefore, never merely the effect of the approval of others. While our opinions depend to an extent on what society regards as appropriate to our profession or our membership of certain institutions, the evaluations of others cannot gain a purchase on us when they conflict with what we are disposed to regard as the qualities we actually possess and that are appropriate or useful to our style of life.

The effect of sympathy on self-evaluation does not, of course, only concern positive emotions like pride. Hume underlines the consequences for our distress and shame derived from sympathizing with the members of our circles that disapprove of us. This distress is all the more intense when the persons communicating it to us are related to us in ways stronger than resemblance. This distress can become so unbearable as to drive us away from our family sphere and prefer the company of strangers to that of our friends and those best known to us (see T 2.1.11.14; SBN 322 and Waldow 2012 for further discussion). In this way, the separation of the relation of contiguity with those closest to us thwarts the operations of sympathy. Deprived of sympathetic support, our shame becomes less unbearable.

There is also a second level to the role of sympathy in propagating forms of behavior and shared ways of judging it in a society. Hume says that "to this principle [i.e. sympathy] we ought to ascribe the great uniformity we may observe in the humours and turn of thinking of those of the same nation" (T 2.1.11.2; SBN 316–317). On various occasions in Book II of the *Treatise*, Hume mentions the *uniformity* in human passions and their dependence on contingent cultural factors. Of pride, for example, he claims that "power, riches, beauty or personal merit" (T 2.1.3.4; SBN 280–281) are causal factors of "pride and vanity" in every period, and what these ideas include depends on the "effects of the 'art,' 'industry' and 'caprice' of men" (T 2.1.3.5; SBN 281–282). Hume adds that these processes tend to become stable in a country, indicating the difficulties that one meets in seeking to interact with the inhabitants of a foreign country with forms of behavior different from our own (T 2.1.6.9; SBN 293–294).

Despite these comments, Hume does not examine in the *Treatise* how sympathy operates in this process. His discussion in "Of National Characters" is illuminating. Rejecting the view that attributes uniformity to physical causes such as climate and territory, Hume explains it in terms of "moral causes" including forms of government and state, the relations with neighboring countries, the economic condition of its components, and how widespread religion is. It is interconnection of these various causes that explains the frequency of certain professions rather than others, and has the effect of developing or impeding the liberal arts, science, and trade – factors that, in turn, are "fitting" to make some qualities and forms of behavior more useful, or simply more widespread, than others. It is sympathy that allows "moral causes" to work in the way they do. It explains the uniform presence of forms of behavior in a society, and the possibility of passing them on to the next generation (E 202–203). In the course of this enquiry, new aspects of sympathy emerge, showing its explanatory flexibility. Hume underlines more clearly, for example, the importance of conversation as a means of transmitting sentiments. Without contradicting his thoughts on the ease with which sympathy operates in friendship and family relations, Hume shows how conversation between people who share the same tongue or interests, facilitated by trade or by defense of their territory from external threats, fosters the discovery of new forms of resemblance, facilitating sympathy between persons outside the circle of friends and family, which may potentially include the whole body politic (E 202–203). Considering the effects that the main institutions of society have on its interactive dynamics, Hume explains the gradual extension of sympathy and the inclination to company, and the gradual propagation of shared behavior and the value that is attributed to them through the indirect passions.

This dynamic and expansive dimension coexists with the partial dimension of sympathy. A society can consist of small communities, which are united by a shared language or religion ("Turks," "Greeks" E 205) or which are held together by a "similitude of manners" making them closer to other communities of other nations than their fellow-citizens ("Jews" E 204–205). These ties encourage closer forms of sympathy that may weaken the more extended forms or enter into conflict with them.

5 Compassion, imagination, extensive sympathy

The previous sections showed how the combination of sympathy and the passions accounts for two important aspects of our social life, the desire to form close personal relationships and how our non-verbal communication governs how other people think and feel about us, and how their opinions affect how we think and feel about ourselves. Hume adds a third important aspect: our capacity to be moved by the suffering of others even when we have no tie of affection or friendship with them.

Hume discusses compassion *or* pity, a passion that consists in a particular expression of our "desire of happiness to another, and aversion to his misery" (T 2.2.9.3; SBN 381). Unlike benevolence, which is an original instinct (T 2.2.6.3; SBN 367; T 2.2.7.1; SBN 368–369), pity is a form of interest for others that derives from "secondary principles" (T 2.2.7.1; SBN 368–369). Specifically, it arises as a reactive passion when another's pains are communicated to us by sympathy (T 2.2.7.1; SBN 368–369).

Hume regarded sympathy-based pity as fundamental to altruism, allowing us to feel interest in the condition of others even when they have no tie to us. This is possible by a special characteristic of sympathy Hume highlights in this context. This transmission mechanism is affected more strongly by painful emotions than pleasant ones, and that is why it can also be activated when the relation between agent and sympathetic communicant does not go beyond species resemblance (T 2.2.7.2; SBN 379). As a result, when the suffering of others comes into play, species resemblance, along with a relation of contiguity with the object of sympathy, is sufficient, to give us not only an idea of these sensations but also, above all, a direct experience that others can feel, which may produce in us concern for their condition. Unlike benevolence, compassion can extend its range of action beyond those who are the object of our esteem and love, precisely because it is activated by sympathy with suffering.

Hume initially presents compassion as a natural and unintentional reaction to sympathetic sentiments. Nevertheless, he adds two qualifications that show that this passion is not produced automatically but requires one to assume a particular perspective on people. This provides an opportunity for Hume to explore sympathy again and the roles that imagination and his idea of the self play in this mechanism and in the human passions generally. He focuses on how comparison and association – the two principles that, along with sympathy, govern human passions – can thwart the budding or full blooming of compassion. Let us start with association. As we have seen, impressions tend to associate with those that have a similar hedonic nature. Applying this rule to the present case, since compassion is painful, it will tend to associate with hatred or anger rather than the pleasant sentiment of good will. Therefore, though sympathy produces compassion, it will be a passion that is useless for others, tending to produce an immediate desire to distance oneself from the source of suffering, rather than generating concern.

The second objection questions the very capacity of sympathy to produce compassion. Hume insists that human beings "always judge more of objects by comparison than from their intrinsic worth and value" (T 2.2.8.2; SBN 372; T 2.1.6.4; SBN 291–292). This principle plays a crucial role in the examination of pride, being the basis of the second limitation on its genesis. Pride's causes must be "not only closely related, but also peculiar to ourselves, or at least common to us with a few persons" (T 2.1.6.4; SBN 291–292). Hume once again evokes the principle of comparison ("original quality of the soul," T 2.2.8.2; SBN 372) in examining pity, giving it a similar function. He makes clear that pity is not the only emotional response possible to suffering. The pain of others might increase our awareness of our own happiness or the perception of the value of our qualities or external advantages. Should that happen, the sympathetic agent would not feel pity, but malice, joy or pride. Pity for suffering is not the inevitable outcome, then. Despite the powerful impact that pain has on sympathy, we might also use this suffering to reinforce the perception of our pleasure rather than be led to alleviate it.

What circumstances determine pity rather than, say, pride, and how far do these circumstances depend on the sympathetic agent or remain beyond his control? Feeling pity or malice in the face of suffering depends on the perspective with which our imagination considers the other's suffering – particularly if it dwells on the suffering or on our condition in relation to that suffering. In the first case we will feel pity, in the second malice and joy or pride. (T 2.2.9.1; SBN 381). Surprisingly, Hume does not seem interested in indicating if there are circumstances in which the agent willingly "enters deep into [. . .] the sentiments of others" other than for purposes of comparison.

Hume claims that sympathy with pain is only associated with anger rather than with a genuine interest in the condition of others when sympathy is weak. When it is intense, it is not restricted to the present pain of the other person but extends, so to speak, to (our ideas as to) his future condition. This process, dubbed "extensive sympathy" (T 2.2.9.14; SBN 386), produces a shift in our attention: we no longer consider the other's suffering in relation to the present time and place it in the overall context of our ideas concerning the other's life. The change of perspective gives us an interest in that life that in some cases may even lead us to act in his favor. In this way, sympathetic pain will tend to be no longer associated with anger, but benevolence, which, though its hedonic character is the opposite of pity, will share with it the overall direction of our concern: towards others rather than towards our own momentary pain.

Both of Hume's suggested solutions draw on the crucial role played by the agent's imaginative perspective. The imaginative perspective that allows a sympathetic spectator to feel emotionally involved in the suffering of others and feel an interest in their condition is marked by two factors. First, the suffering of others must be considered in itself and not in relation to the person sympathizing. Second, it must be considered in relation to the future condition of the sympathetic communicant and not just in the present context. This dual constraint explains how compassion is associated with good will, and how sympathy avoids comparing the sentiments of others to our own, resulting in malice. Examining present suffering in the light of an overall condition of life is the most effective way of assuming that perspective which, Hume says, "enters deep" into the "sentiments of others" and "makes us sensible . . . of grief or sorrow."

How does this relate to the sympathetic processes we have considered? The process of communicating the impressions that produce pity is certainly only loosely connected with that of emotional contagion. Sympathy requires the spectator to be aware that the sentiments he feels do not originate in himself but are from the sympathetic communicant. If he did not have this awareness, as in the case of emotional contagion, the spectator could not develop any interest in other persons. This awareness often requires reason and imagination, which are indispensable for reconstructing the circumstances of other people's lives and simulating their passions. However, this does not falsify the hypothesis we have been trying to sustain in this essay: all these processes are explicable through a single, simple, explanatory schema. As for the delicate role that "extended sympathy" is required to play in the impression of oneself, we have already indicated the main issue in section 3.

This question is at the center of the contemporary philosophical debate on empathy, whose main lines can provide a cue for measuring the feasibility of Hume's solution to these problems. According to one fairly widely held and plausible position, the self-involved in the extended sympathetic imagination must assume a midway place that avoids the twin dangers of solipsistic detachment or merging with the other. Amy Coplan argues sympathy is based on an imaginative process that is other-oriented rather than self-oriented (Coplan 2011). We set up an authentic sympathetic relation with the other when we no longer imagine how we would feel in the other's place but we learn to simulate what it actually means for the other to be in that situation. However, as Hoffman, Stocker, and Hegemon, and Coplan herself show, the other-oriented process is insufficient to characterize the perspective of sympathy. We might be able to simulate the passions of others and, for this very reason, fall into the opposite error, which consists in merging with another's perspective (Hoffman 2000, 2011; Stocker and Hegemon 1996; Coplan 2011). In other words, sympathy requires more than imagining what it means for another person to be in a certain situation. Once we have assumed that perspective, we must also avoid remaining trapped in the sympathetic communicant and losing that sense of ourselves that is clearly indispensable for taking an interest in the suffering of others.

Where does the role Hume attributes to the self fall in these contemporary debates? As noted in section 3, Hume successfully carves out a role for the self that allows the sympathetic agent to assume this midway perspective between detachment and merging. On the one hand, Hume underlines that pride cannot itself be a part of episodes of sympathy. This guarantees we are actually concentrating on the other and not on ourselves. On the other hand, what Ainslie calls the "modes of our perceptions," which transfers vivacity to our ideas of the other, is strongly connected to the social and embodied self that is the object of pride. So, although we are not concentrating on ourselves when we sympathize, the self is in some sense in the background of every episode of extended sympathy, guaranteeing the separation between ourselves and the sympathetic communicant.

As we have seen, Hume builds his account of this sophisticated form of sympathy from an explanatory schema that is also at work in the more automatic forms of sympathy. The more complex forms of human social interaction can be described as a gradual development of simpler and more immediate forms that humans share with the non-human animals (De Waal 2009).[4] The explanatory power of Hume's account is one of its virtues.

Acknowledgement

I am grateful to Peter Kail for indispensable comments on previous drafts of this chapter. I am also grateful to Angela Coventry for helping me identify some redundant parts and to Anik Waldow for very helpful discussions.

Notes

1 See Abramson (2001): 45–80 and Debes (2007) for a discussion of the relationship between the account of sympathy in the *Treatise* and in the second *Enquiry*. Kirby (2003) focuses on a treatment of sympathy as a source of aesthetic evaluation and Mercer (1972) provides an extended treatment of the philosophical difficulties of Hume's account of sympathy. Waldow (2013) discusses the relationship between Hume's account of sympathy and the activity of the mirror neurons, and finally, Waldow (2009) treats the role of sympathy in the formation of the belief that human minds are similar to each other.

2 However, a few direct passions do not come from good and evil, such as "the desire of punishment to our enemies, and of happiness to our friends; hunger, lust, and a few other bodily appetites" (T 2.3.9.8). Hume regards them as original impulses.

3 According to some, Hume did not actually consider the ascription of mental states to others as the result of an inferential process. According to Tony Pitson, for example, the first step of sympathy is "an instance of those beliefs, which, for Hume, might be classified as 'natural.'" Like belief in the existence of external objects, this belief too is not "capable of being vindicated by reason," but is still an "unavoidable" fact for human beings (Pitson 1996; Ferreira 1994; Postema 2005).

4 Boyle (2003) provides a treatment of Humean sympathy towards non-human animals.

References

Abramson, K. (2001) "Sympathy and the Project of Hume's Second Inquiry," *Archiv für Geschichte der Philosophie* 83(1): 45–80.

Ainslie, D. (2005) "Sympathy and the Unity of Hume's Idea of Self," in J. Jenkins, J. Whiting and C. Williams (eds.), *Persons and Passions: Essays in Honor of Annette Baier*, Notre Dame, IN: University of Notre Dame Press.

Ardal, P. (1966) *Passion and Value in Hume's Treatise*, Edinburgh: Edinburgh University Press.

Baier, A. C. and Waldow, A. (2008) "A Conversation Between Annette Baier and Anik Waldow About Hume's Account of Sympathy," *Hume Studies* 34(1): 61–87.

Baillie, J. (2000) *Hume on Morality*, London: Routledge.

Boyle, D. (2003) "Hume on Animal Reason," *Hume Studies* 29(1): 3–28.

Capaldi, N. (1989) *Hume's Place in Moral Philosophy*, New York: Peter Lang.

Cohon, R. (2008) "Hume's Indirect Passions," in E. S. Radcliffe (ed.), *A Companion to Hume*, London: Blackwell Publishing.

Coplan, A. (2011) "Understanding Empathy: Its Features and Effects," in A. Coplan and P. Goldie (eds.), *Empathy, Philosophical and Psychological Perspectives*, Oxford: Oxford University Press.

Debes, R. (2007) "Humanity, Sympathy, and the Puzzle of Hume's Second Enquiry," *British Journal for the History of Philosophy* 15(1): 27–57.

Decety, J. and A. N. Meltzoff (2011) "Empathy, Imitation, and Social Brain," in A. Coplan and P. Goldie (eds.), *Empathy, Philosophical and Psychological Perspectives*, Oxford: Oxford University Press, pp. 58–81.

Ferreira, M. Jamie (1994) "Hume and Imagination," *International Philosophical Quarterly* 34(1): 39–57.

Garrett, D. (1981). "Hume's Self-Doubts about Personal Identity." *The Philosophical Review* 90(3): 337–58.

Harris, James A. (2010). "Hume on the Moral Obligation to Justice." *Hume Studies* 36(1):25–50.

Hoffman, M. L. (2000). *Empathy and Moral Development: Implications for Caring and Justice*. Cambridge, UK: Cambridge University Press.

———.(2011) "Empathy, Justice, and the Law," in A. Coplan and P. Goldie (eds.), *Empathy, Philosophical and Psychological Perspectives*, Oxford: Oxford University Press.

Kail, P. (2007) *Projection and Realism in Hume's Philosophy*, Oxford: Oxford University Press.

Kirby, B. (2003) "Hume, Sympathy, and the Theater," *Hume Studies* 29(2): 305–325.

Mercer, P. (1972) *Sympathy and Ethics: A Study of the Relationship Between Sympathy and Morality with Special Reference to Hume's Treatise*, Oxford: Clarendon Press.

Postema, G. J. (2005) "Cemented with Diseased Qualities: Sympathy and Comparison in Hume's Moral Psychology," *Hume Studies* 31(2): 249–298.

Pitson, T. (1996) "Sympathy and Other Selves," *Hume Studies* 22(2): 255–271.

Stocker, Michael and Hegeman, Elizabeth (1996). *Valuing Emotions*. Cambridge: Cambridge University Press.

Taylor, J. (2015) *Reflecting Subjects: Passion, Sympathy, and Society in Hume's Philosophy*, Oxford: Oxford University Press.

Waal, F. B. M. de. (2009) *The Age of Empathy: Nature's Lessons for a Kinder Society*, 1st edn, New York: Harmony Books.

Waldow, A. C. (2009) "Hume's Belief in Other Mind," *British Journal for the History of Philosophy* 17: 119–113.

———. (2012) "Sympathy and the Mechanics of Character Change," *Hume Studies* 38(2): 221–242.

———. (2013) "Mirroring Minds: Hume on Sympathy," *The European Legacy* 18(5): 540–551.

Waldow, A. C. and A. Bair (2008) "A Conversation Between Annette Baier and Anik Waldow About Hume's Account of Sympathy," *Hume Studies* 34(1): 61–87.

16

HUME ON MOTIVES
AND ACTION

Rachel Cohon

Hume is renowned for saying that "reason is perfectly inert": that reason alone, or of itself, is not a motive to the will. In this chapter, I explain his position on motivation to action in general, and I try to resolve some controversies about the meaning of this famous claim. I also show some of its connections to Hume's view that moral evaluation depends upon sentiment and not on reason alone.[1]

The passions and intentional action

According to Hume's theory of the mind, the passions (what we today would call emotions, feelings, and desires) are impressions rather than ideas: vivid and lively perceptions that are not copied from other perceptions. Hume classifies passions as impressions of reflection or secondary impressions, in that they are caused by impressions or ideas in the mind, unlike the primary impressions such as sensations of color or heat, whose causes are not evident to introspection. The direct passions, which include desire, aversion, hope, fear, grief, and joy, are those that "arise immediately from good or evil, from pain or pleasure" that we either experience or think about in prospect (T 2.1.1.4; SBN 276; T 2.3.9.2; SBN 438). Hume also enumerates several instincts, among them the bodily appetites (hunger, thirst, lust) and the desires for the good of those we love and the harm of those we hate, which do not proceed from thoughts or sensations of pain or pleasure (T 2.3.9.7; SBN 439) but give rise to direct passions independently of such thoughts – though the instincts tend to lead to pain or pleasure. What Hume calls the indirect passions, most importantly pride, humility (shame), love, and hatred, are generated in a more complex way, but still one involving either the thought or experience of pain or pleasure, whether physical or psychological. If pleasure or pain (also called uneasiness) are removed from the human mind, "there immediately follows a removal of love and hatred, pride and humility, desire and aversion, and of most of our reflective or secondary impressions" (T 2.3.9.1; SBN 438). Intentional actions are caused by the direct passions (including those that arise from the instincts). Regarding the indirect passions, Hume says that pride, humility, love, and hatred do not directly cause action, though they can play a mediated role in its production by reinforcing a direct passion (T 2.3.9.4; SBN 439). It is not clear whether he thinks this true of all the indirect passions.

In discussing Hume's approach to the springs of intentional action, we do best to avoid the verb 'to motivate' and the noun 'motivation(s)' where possible, because in present-day Hume scholarship, no doubt influenced by present-day philosophy of action, they are used very differently by different authors, leading to confusion. Sometimes a motivation is taken to be a rational or seemingly rational ground of action – a reason in one sense; sometimes a psychological influence or inclination, which either competes with other influences or plays the dominant role in directing action; and sometimes a cause of action, which may be conceived either as a contributing or complete cause, the proximal cause only, or also a remote causal factor. Often the meaning is not specified. Hume never uses these terms at all, though he uses the word 'motive.' His account of intentional action is unapologetically causal, so we will speak of the causes of intentional actions, and try to distinguish proximal causes from those farther back in the causal chain, and contributory from complete causes.

According to Hume, an intentional action is the immediate causal product of one or more direct passions, generated either by feeling or thinking of "good or evil" (pleasure or pain/uneasiness) or by the instincts. Sometimes Hume speaks of the instincts as themselves being desires or aversions, other times as sources of them. Though he does not argue for this, Hume does not appear to allow that any sort of mental state other than a passion could give rise to an intentional action as its immediate effect. So another kind of mental state, such as a sense perception or a belief, if it were to play a causal role in generating intentional action, would have to do so either by first causing a passion (which would in turn cause action) or by partnering with a passion brought into being in some other way or already present in the mind. Those passions that cause action proximally, without causal intermediary, I call *motivating passions*.

The motivating passions, such as desire and aversion, hope and fear, in their turn have their own causes. These are identified early in the *Treatise* where Hume first explains the distinction between impressions of sensation and impressions of reflection:

> An impression first strikes upon the senses, and makes us perceive heat or cold, thirst or hunger, pleasure or pain, of some kind or other. Of this impression there is a copy taken by the mind, which remains after the impression ceases; and this we call an idea. This idea of pleasure or pain, when it returns upon the soul, produces the new impressions of desire and aversion, hope and fear, which may properly be called impressions of reflection, because derived from it.
>
> (T 1.1.2.2; SBN 7–8)

Thus, ideas of pleasure or uneasiness are the causes of these direct passions, all of which can proximally cause action under the right conditions. Not just any ideas of pleasure or pain give rise to passions that actually prompt action, however, but only ideas of those pleasures or pains we believe exist or will exist (T 1.3.10.3; SBN 119). More generally, the motivating passions of desire and aversion, hope and fear, joy and grief, and a few others are impressions produced by the occurrence in the mind either of a *feeling* of pleasure or pain, whether physical or psychological, or of a *believed idea* of pleasure or pain to come (T 2.1.1.4; SBN 276, T 2.3.9.2; SBN 438). These passions, together with the instincts (hunger, lust, and so on), are all the motivating passions that Hume discusses.

The will, Hume claims, is an immediate effect of pain or pleasure (T 2.3.1.2; SBN 399) and "exerts itself" when either pleasure or the absence of pain can be attained by any action of the mind or body (T 2.3.9.7; SBN 439). The will, however, is merely that impression we feel when we knowingly give rise to an action (T 2.3.1.2; SBN 399); so while Hume is not explicit (and perhaps not consistent) on this matter, in the *Treatise* he does not commit himself to the will being itself a (separate) cause of action, though he seems to do so in the *Enquiry Concerning Human Understanding* (EHU 7.9–10; SBN 64–65). In the *Treatise*, the only causes of action he describes are those already identified: the instinctually produced and the other direct passions; his talk of "the will" seems merely to indicate that the actions in question are intentional. It is possible that in any particular case of intentional action Hume would identify the will or a volition with the direct passion such as a desire that proximally causes that action.

"Reason is perfectly inert": three arguments and some extreme consequences

Hume famously sets himself in opposition to most moral philosophers, ancient and modern, who talk of the combat of passion and reason and who urge human beings to regulate our actions by reason and to grant it dominion over our passions. He claims to prove that "reason alone can never be a motive to any action of the will," and that reason alone "can never oppose passion in the direction of the will" (T 2.3.3.1; SBN413). His view is not, of course, that reason plays no role in the generation of action; he grants that reasoning provides information, in particular about means to our ends, which makes a difference to whether we act in one way or another (T 2.3.3.3; SBN 415). His point is that reason *alone* cannot move us to action; passion is necessary. Hume's doctrine that reason alone is merely the "slave of the passions," i.e. that reason pursues knowledge of abstract and causal relations in order to achieve passions' goals, and provides no ends or motivating passions of its own, is systematically defended in the *Treatise*, but not in the second *Enquiry*, although in the latter he elegantly articulates the doctrine and supports it with some examples (EPM App.1.18–21; SBN 293–294). Hume gives three famous arguments in the *Treatise* for the "inertia" of reason alone.

The first is a largely empirical argument based on the two rational functions of the understanding. Call it the Demonstrative and Causal (DC) Argument. The understanding, according to this argument, discovers the abstract relations of ideas by engaging in demonstration, a process of comparing ideas and finding congruencies and incongruencies between them; it also discovers the causal (and other probabilistic) relations of objects that are revealed in experience by forming a habit-guided connection between an impression or believed idea of a cause and the idea of its effect (or vice versa). (Even though Hume denies in Book 1 that causal inference is an activity of reason (e.g. at T 1.3.6.12; SBN 92 and T 1.3.7.6; SBN 97), he also talks of causal inference as an activity of the understanding and as reasoning (e.g. T 1.3.6.14; SBN 93 and T 1.3.7.6; SBN 97), and he groups it with reasoning throughout Books 2 and 3. Demonstrative reasoning, the argument goes on, is never the cause of any action by itself, because it deals in ideas rather than realities. We only find it useful in action when we have some purpose in view and can use the outcome of demonstration (such as the sum we arrive at by adding up some numbers) to "direct[] our judgment concerning causes and effects" (T 2.3.3.2; SBN 414). Probable or cause-and-effect reasoning does play a role in determining what we do, but we see that it only functions as an auxiliary, and not on its own. When we anticipate pain or pleasure from some source, we "feel a consequent aversion or propensity, and are carry'd to avoid or embrace what will give us" the pain or pleasure (T 2.3.3.3; SBN 414). Our aversion or propensity makes us seek the causes and effects of the expected source of pain or pleasure, and we use causal reasoning to discover what they are. Once we do, our desire or aversion naturally extends itself to those causes, and we act to avoid or embrace them. Plainly, the impulse to act does not arise from the casual reasoning but is only directed by it. "'Tis from the prospect of pain or pleasure that the aversion or propensity arises" (ibid.). Probable reasoning is merely the discovering of causal connections, and knowledge that A causes B never interests us if we are indifferent to A and to B. Thus, neither demonstrative nor probable reasoning alone causes action.

This argument coheres with Hume's Book 1 explanation of the origin of the direct passions. Once more the prospect of pain or pleasure (that is, the idea that one or the other is forthcoming) is the cause of a desire or aversion. This Book 2 argument adds that once "reasoning takes place to discover" a means to get or avoid the pleasure or pain, we come to desire the means as well, which causes action. "The prospect of pain or pleasure from any object" is presumably a believed idea that one or the other is in store for us; call this a *hedonic belief*. Note that Hume asserts that hedonic beliefs cause motivating passions in one of the very arguments he gives for his thesis that reason alone is not a motive to the will. Given this, we can see that he does not take the initial passion-production by a hedonic belief to be an instance of reason alone acting as a motive to the will. Later we will see how these two things can be different.

The second argument, which we may call the Opposing Impulse Argument, is intended specifically to show that reason of itself cannot *oppose* passion in controlling the will (T 2.3.3.4; SBN 414–415). It is a corollary of the DC Argument. It takes as a premise the conclusion of that argument, that reason alone does not produce any impulse to act. What is requisite to stop a volition or retard the force of an existing passion is a contrary impulse, Hume claims. If reason alone were to resist a passion, it would need to give rise to just such a contrary impulse. But if reason alone were able to put up such resistance, it would have an original influence on the will (a capacity to cause a motivating passion of itself, when unopposed), which, according to the previous argument, it does not have. Therefore, reason alone cannot resist any impulse to act. Therefore, whatever it may be in the mind that offers resistance to our passions and controls them, it cannot be reason of itself. Hume proposes that when we exercise restraint over our imprudent or immoral desires, the contrary impulse that does so comes also from passion, but often from a passion so "calm" that we confuse it with reason (T 2.3.3.8; SBN 417).

The third or Representation Argument is different in kind. Hume offers it initially (in T 2.3.3.5; SBN 415) only to show that a *passion* cannot be opposed by or be contradictory to "truth and reason"; later (T 3.1.1.9; SBN 458), he repeats and expands it to argue that volitions and actions as well cannot be so. It looks as if Hume means to give another argument to show that reason alone cannot provide a force to resist passion or volition. Yet the Representation Argument is not empirical and does not talk of forces or impulses. Passions (and volitions and actions), Hume says, do not refer to other entities; they are "original existence[s]" (T 2.3.3.5; SBN 415), "original facts and realities" (T3.1.1.9; SBN 458), not mental representations of other things. Hume here understands representation in terms of copying, and so he says that a passion has no "representative quality, which renders it a copy of any other existence or modification" (T 2.3.3.5; SBN 415).[2] Contradiction to truth and reason, however, consists in "the disagreement of ideas, consider'd as copies, with those objects, which they represent" (ibid.). Therefore, a passion (or volition or action), not having this feature, cannot be opposed by truth and reason. Hume says the argument, as applied to actions, proves two points. First, it shows that actions cannot be reasonable or unreasonable. Second, it shows that "reason cannot immediately prevent or produce any action by contradicting or approving of it" (T3.1.1.10; SBN 458). The point here is not the earlier, empirical observation that the rational activity of the understanding does not generate an impulse in the absence of an expectation of pain or pleasure. It is rather a conclusion about the relevance of reason to action, or whether passions and actions are capable of being inherently reasonable or unreasonable. Because passions, volitions, and actions have no content suitable for assessment by reason, reason cannot classify prospective motives or actions as rational or irrational; and therefore reason cannot, by so assessing them, create or obstruct them. By contrast, reason *can* assess a potential opinion as rational or irrational by comparing it with the original of which it is meant to be a copy; by endorsing the opinion (finding it true), reason can induce us to adopt it, while by contradicting the opinion (finding it false), reason can destroy our credence in it. The Representation Argument, then, makes a point *a priori* about the relevance of the functions of the understanding to the generation of actions.

Interpreters disagree about exactly how to parse this argument and about its importance to Hume's project. Some take him to say here that passions have no representational content at all, and infer from this that they have no intentionality or directedness to objects. This thought has led some to dismiss the argument as overzealously stated and not what Hume really means (Baier 1991: 160ff.), and indeed the argument is absent from the *Dissertation on the Passions* and (like the other arguments that reason is inert) from the *Enquiry Concerning the Principles of Morals*. Some think Hume is committed to the view that passions must contain representations in order to have intentionality (Weller 2002). Hume writes explicitly that both direct and indirect passions have objects (see, for example, T 2.1.2.4; SBN 278; T 2.2.2.24; SBN 344–345; T 2.2.11.6; SBN 396), so he certainly regards passions as intentional in some fashion, whether or not his philosophy gives him a way to attribute representational content to them (which it may well provide in causal terms).[3] At the same time, in the *Treatise* Hume attributes great weight to the Representation Argument, stating it twice at length and using it to ground his moral anti-rationalism, so it is unlikely that it was a momentary slip.

Most likely, he does not intend his claim there that passions have "no representative quality" to deny that they have intentional objects. His purpose is different. Perhaps part of his purpose is to deny that passions such as desires are to be identified with beliefs, such as beliefs to the effect that something is good, a view held by various predecessors.[4] According to Hume's theory of the mind, beliefs are ideas rather than impressions, and so are copies of impressions or are composed of copies of impressions, while passions, as impressions, are original perceptions as distinct from copies. The crucial assumption in the Representation Argument is that the only kind of item that can conform to reason is one that reasoning can discover to be true by comparing it with its original, and likewise, the only kind of item that can be contrary to reason is one that reasoning can discover to be false. Hume sees reasoning as the comparing of ideas and the finding of correspondences, and holds a correspondence theory of truth (as at T 2.3.10.2; SBN 448). Conformity to reason, in this argument, is correspondence to an original. Consequently, only something that is truth-apt can be assessed as reasonable or against reason. Hume can consistently claim that passions, even though they are directed toward objects (in that I am proud of *myself*, I fear *injury*, and so on), are nonetheless not truth-apt, and so cannot be assessed as conformable or contrary to reason in these senses. And actions, of course, clearly are not truth-apt (a point he makes against Wollaston 1991 [1724]), so also are not evaluable by reasoning.

Hume allows that, speaking imprecisely, we often do say a passion is unreasonable because it arises in response to a mistaken judgment or opinion, either that something (a source of pleasure or uneasiness) exists, or that it may be obtained or avoided by a certain means. In just these two cases, a passion may be called unreasonable, but strictly speaking even here it is not the passion but the judgment that is so. Furthermore, he says, once we abandon the mistaken judgment, "our passions yield to our reason without any opposition," so there is still no combat between passion and reason (T 2.3.3.7; SBN 416). And no other sort of passion can be described as contrary to reason. Hume notoriously declaims,

> 'Tis not contrary to reason to prefer the destruction of the whole world to the scratching of my finger. 'Tis not contrary to reason for me to chuse my total ruin, to prevent the least uneasiness of an Indian or person wholly unknown to me. 'Tis as little

contrary to reason to prefer even my own acknowledg'd lesser good to my greater, and have a more ardent affection for the former than for the latter.

(T 2.3.3.6; SBN 416)

The first example denies that there is anything contrary to reason about a preference that is stunningly selfish, the second denies there is anything unreasonable about a preference for extreme (and disproportional) altruism, and the third denies the unreasonableness of a preference that is known to be imprudent. All such attitudes were and still are commonly called unreasonable, but according to Hume this is a mistake.

Many philosophers talk of practical reason – a faculty that not only plays a role in deciding what to do but also evaluates our actions as rational or irrational. Interpreters disagree as to whether Hume is an instrumentalist or a skeptic about practical reason. Either way, Hume denies that reason can evaluate the ends people set themselves; only passions can select ends, for Hume, and reason cannot evaluate passions. Instrumentalist interpreters understand the claim that reason is the slave of the passions to allow that reason not only discovers the causally efficacious means to our ends (a task of theoretical causal reasoning) but also requires us to take them. If Hume regards the failure to take the known means to one's end as contrary to reason, then on Hume's view reason imposes genuinely practical norms, albeit rather minimal ones: it classifies some actions (or failures to act) as unreasonable.[5] Skeptical interpreters (Hampton 1995; Millgram 1995; Korsgaard 1997) read Hume, instead, as denying that reason imposes any requirements on action whatsoever, even the requirement to take the known, available means to one's end. They point to the list of extreme actions that are not contrary to reason, and to the Representation Argument, which denies that any passions, volitions, or actions can be contrary to reason. Hume never says explicitly that failing to take the known means to one's end is or is not contrary to reason: it is not one of the extreme cases in his list, though it could be argued that selecting one's known lesser good might incorporate it. The Representation Argument's point about truth-aptness makes Hume sound like a skeptic about practical reason, holding that no action whatsoever is reasonable or unreasonable.[6]

Some scholars have argued that while Hume does not allow reason, as he understands it, to evaluate motivating passions, actions, or ends, he allows the moral sentiment to do so, yielding a moral analog of standards of practical reason (Radcliffe 1997; Setiya 2004). On this view, while it is not, strictly speaking, against *reason* to fail to take the known and available means to my end (given that Hume restricts reason to demonstration and probable inference), on reflection an observer would feel moral disapproval of one who is not prompted to do so, which means that such a failure of motivating passion and action exhibits a vice – presumably in this case the vice of imprudence or inconstancy.

Interpreting the conclusions of the arguments for the inertia of reason alone

The three arguments in the *Treatise* set out above do not all have the same conclusion. The conclusion of the DC Argument is that we do not find that either demonstrative or causal reasoning acts as the sole (and proximate) cause of action; in addition to reasoning, there is always a role for the prospect of pain or pleasure and the motivating passion sparked by this expectation. The conclusion of the Opposing Impulse Argument is that reason alone (presumably this means the two processes described in the DC Argument) cannot stop a passion from moving us to action. The Representation Argument concludes both that passions and actions cannot be assessed as either reasonable or unreasonable (they are of the wrong category for this) and that reason (therefore) "can never immediately prevent or produce any action by contradicting or approving of it" (T 3.1.1.10; SBN 458).

For this and other reasons, the claim that reason alone cannot influence action is devilishly tricky to interpret. But it is central to Hume's thinking about the springs of action and provides a crucial premise in one of his main arguments against moral rationalism, the rejection of which forms the basis of his entire ethical theory. So it matters a great deal what the claim means.

One natural way to understand it is as saying that the *capacity* for reasoning cannot by itself cause new motivating passions without help from another capacity or faculty (see, for example, Setiya 2004: 370). Another natural interpretation is that a process of reasoning or inference is not sufficient to cause a new passion without help from another kind of process (Cohon 2008: chs. 2 and 3). Note that the interpretation of "reason" determines the meaning of 'reason *alone*' or 'of itself.' If reason is a faculty, 'alone' means without another faculty. If 'reason' designates inferential processes, 'alone' means without another sort of process.

Many interpreters since the middle of the twentieth century, however, have assumed or argued that what Hume means or must mean by the inertia of reason is not only that the faculty of reason or the activity of reasoning alone cannot cause a new passion or action, but also that a *belief* cannot produce a motivating passion, either. Some interpreters seem merely to assume this or think it obvious,[7] though Hume never explicitly says it. Some suppose that Hume conceives of reason as a set of beliefs or propositions, an assumption that entails this view (Stroud 1977: ch. 7). Others give a variety of arguments for their interpretation (for example Radcliffe 1999). Probably the best reason to embrace this interpretation is that it is hard to see how a belief that was reached by reasoning could prompt a new desire or aversion once we have established that the faculty or process of reasoning that produced the belief had no such power. Is a belief about cause and effect not simply the output of the faculty of probable reason or the conclusion of a process of causal inference? If so, and if the faculty or process by itself cannot prompt a new passion, it seems that its product cannot do so, either (Radcliffe 1999, 2008). This interpretation of Hume's inertia claim, which we may call the Inertia of Belief position, must of course specify what 'alone' means in the claim that beliefs alone cannot cause motivating passions. After all, its advocates agree that for Hume beliefs about means *contribute* to the causation of actions. Perhaps because Hume describes passion as an active principle and reason as an inactive one ('principle' here meaning origin or cause), advocates of the Inertia of Belief reading maintain that no belief can cause a motivating passion without the help of a passion not caused by that belief – a passion of independent causal origin.

The main reasons we might reject the Inertia of Belief position are that it requires us to read Hume as contradicting himself at many points in his account of passions and motives and as making some weak (even irrelevant) arguments. Below I summarize two of those difficulties and lightly sketch an alternative interpretation that does not saddle Hume with so much error. (See Cohon 2008 for more detail.)

Problematic consequences of the Inertia of Belief interpretation

The Representation Argument does not attempt to prove that belief alone, or even reason alone, cannot cause any motivating passion. Its conclusion is that reason cannot endorse or contradict any passion or action. The closest it comes to mentioning causation is where it says that reason "can never immediately *prevent or produce* any action *by* contradicting or approving of it" (T 3.1.1.10; SBN 458, my emphasis). This, of course, only rules out one possible method of production, not causation in general (by reason or by belief).

Only the DC Argument actually tries to show that reason alone does not cause action without aid, so Hume's support for the Inertia of Belief thesis, if he gives any, would have to lie there. Now, the Inertia of Belief claim is either a necessary thesis known *a priori* or a contingent, empirical thesis. If the former, then the DC Argument would have to prove that, of necessity, no belief *can* cause a motivating passion or action without the help of a causally independent passion. (And this is usually what advocates of this interpretation take Hume to mean, given the way they read his later argument about the power of morality to influence action.) But the DC Argument clearly does not attempt to do any such thing; all it does is describe our experiences. And as Hume argues in Book 1, in setting out his views of causation, in principle no causal relation holds necessarily or is discoverable by demonstrative reasoning: "anything can cause anything. Creation annihilation, motion, reason, volition; all these may arise from one another" (T 1.3.15.1; SBN 173). And he reaffirms in Book 3 that "there is no connexion of cause and effect . . . which is discoverable otherwise than by experience, and of which we can pretend to have any security by the simple consideration of the objects" (T 3.1.1.22; SBN 466). So the DC Argument could not prove that either reason or belief alone *cannot* cause passions or actions, which would require a demonstration. At best it would have to prove that reason or belief *does* not do so.

As an empirical argument for the claim that belief never does cause motivating passion without contribution from some independent passion, however, the DC Argument fails. First, it gives very limited evidence and does not take into account what philosophers over the millennia have considered evidence to the contrary. It certainly seemed to them, and seems often to Hume's readers, no doubt, that on many occasions, beliefs about what is good or bad to do frequently *are* conjoined with motivating passions so to act. This happens to us again and again, even when our heart's desire is to act otherwise. True, Hume explains away one kind of situation of that kind: when I judge that some action would be an efficacious means to what I desire, that means-judgment alone does not make me desire to take the means – I typically have a desire for the end already in place. What he does not show is that my desire for the end is never prompted solely by a belief. In fact, he twice (within this argument) says just the reverse: that my desire for an end is prompted by my expectation of pleasure or pain from an object, which is surely a belief that some object has pleasure or pain in store for me. He does say that the mere recognition that A causes B (a causal belief) will not move us to act "where the objects themselves do not affect us" (T 2.3.3.3; SBN 414). But if B is a source of pleasure or pain for me, then it does affect me. And it is not just within the DC Argument that Hume talks of hedonic beliefs as causes of desires and aversions; as noted above, he says so in Book 1, and makes similar remarks in two other places (T 2.3.3.6–7; SBN 416 and T3.1.1.12; SBN 459). So were he to intend to argue in the DC Argument that no beliefs cause motivating passions, he would thereby contradict a claim he espouses consistently.

The other problem with the Inertia of Belief thesis is that if hedonic beliefs (or any beliefs) can never spark any new desires or aversions but can only channel existing ones, Hume needs some account of where those independent passions come from that are being channeled. The instincts could explain some of them: presumably instincts cause desires that simply assail us, as when hunger comes over us as the result of a bodily condition and not in response to any beliefs. But what is the origin of the other motivating passions that do not arise from instinct but arise from "good and evil," considered either simply or together with opinions about their likelihood (T 2.3.9.5–7)? Hume says that they arise from pleasure or pain in the form of an impression or an idea in the mind, and those arising from an idea become motivating when the idea is believed. In the latter case, if the hedonic belief by itself is not sufficient to cause a new desire or aversion for the source of pleasure or pain, but needs help from an independent passion, then where does *that* passion come from? It must, somehow, already be there, to be activated by the belief, which presumably informs us of the means to satisfy *it*. This requires that we attribute to Hume the view that the mind is already furnished with a set of more general desires and aversions to which our hedonic beliefs provide direction. But for Hume, desires and aversions are impressions, and so we would have to feel at all times that we have them, or at least to do so when we attend to them and are not distracted. If they are always in the mind, then we would be able to feel them at all times if we paid attention to them. If they develop at certain points in response to our experiences, they would nonetheless have to be available to introspection from that moment on, throughout the time they are not activated, before we acquire a belief about the likelihood of satisfying them.[8] This, however, is not something Hume ever says. He does not claim that we feel a desire for pleasure as such, for example, at all times, not even a calm one; nor that if I taste something delicious once I feel a desire for that tasty food continuously until my next opportunity to eat it. And this is a strength in his view, for introspection reveals no such feelings or urges in residence in our minds over protracted periods or our whole lives.

There are those who interpret Hume as having an unofficial commitment to desires that we do not actually feel, desires that are, instead, dispositional properties to feel and act in certain ways rather than impressions of longing or craving.[9] Desires that are dispositional properties could be present at times when they were not felt. The trouble with this reading is that (to put it very tersely) first, dispositional properties lack independent causal efficacy, and second, for Hume their attribution could only be a consequence of an already-established causal relation between hedonic beliefs and motivating passions (see Cohon 2008; 52–61). So this is not a promising way to salvage the Inertia of Belief position.

An alternative: the process interpretation

The Inertia of Belief interpretation cannot be ruled out entirely; of course, Hume may contradict himself or postulate the existence of desires and aversions whose presence he cannot account for within his theory of the mind. But a more promising interpretation is this one: Hume allows, as he seems to, that hedonic beliefs spark new direct passions in the human mind without assistance from independent passions.[10] Then what does he claim in saying that reason is impotent or inert? By 'reason,' he means the process of comparing perceptions and finding them to be true or false. All three Books of the *Treatise* provide ample evidence that this is how he understands reason: he means by it *reasoning*, this process of comparing and linking different perceptions in the mind and coming to believe some of them as a result (Book 1 passim, e.g. T 1.3.7.3; SBN 95; T 1.3.4 entire; T 2.3.3.3 "reasoning takes place"; T 3.1.1.4; SBN 457). By its nature, it is a process that increases the evidentness and so the vivacity of ideas, regarded as representations.[11] The outcome of this process is a believed idea; it is not the kind of process that yields an impression. This comparing and finding true or false is what happens in demonstrative reasoning and in cause-and-effect reasoning as well, which is some grounds for calling them both operations of reason. By its nature it is not a process that generates new passions. Of course, given Hume's understanding of causation, a reasoning process could *cause* anything; whether it does or not depends on what constant conjunctions we observe. But if it causes a passion, *that* causal process is not one of reasoning, but some other kind of process.

According to the process interpretation, when Hume says that reason is inert his claim is that no reasoning process can produce motivating passions or actions without the occurrence of a further, different kind of process. The central idea is that the process of motivation to action is not inferential, even though inference and its results sometimes play a role in it.

On this interpretation, we can take Hume at his word that hedonic beliefs spark new desires and aversions and other motivating passions, even in those cases in which the hedonic beliefs themselves are the product of causal inference (as when, for example, my belief that swimming in the Caribbean now will cause me pleasure is inferred from my having observed past constant conjunctions between swimming in tropical seas and pleasure).

This interpretation makes good sense of the DC Argument, which observes that reasoning processes alone do not typically spark motivating passions, but only seem to do so if the items about which we reason have some effect on us. It coheres with his other observation that the discovery that a pleasure-producing object is available to us can engender desire (T 1.3.10.3; SBN 119). And it gives a central role to the Representation Argument. Since reasoning can only find ideas to be true (and so generate our belief in them), it cannot of itself provide warrant for or contradict any passion or action, since they are not ideas and are not truth-apt. This does not mean that ideas cannot cause passions at all.[12]

The relation between reason and moral distinctions

Hume claims that moral distinctions are not derived from reason but rather from sentiment. His rejection of ethical rationalism is at least twofold. Moral rationalists tend to say, first, that moral properties are discovered by reason, and also that what is morally good is in accord with reason (even that goodness consists in reasonableness) and what is morally evil is unreasonable. Hume rejects both theses. Most of his arguments are directed against the first thesis, though some attack the second, and it is not always clear which he means to attack in certain places.

In the *Treatise*, he argues against the epistemic thesis (that we *discover* good and evil by reasoning) by showing that neither demonstrative nor probable/causal reasoning has vice and virtue as its proper objects. Demonstrative reasoning discovers relations of ideas, and vice and virtue are not identical with any of the four philosophical relations (resemblance, contrariety, degrees in quality, or proportions in quantity and number) whose presence can be demonstrated. Nor could they be identical with any other abstract relation; for such relations can also obtain between items such as trees that are incapable of moral good or evil. Furthermore, were moral vice and virtue discerned by demonstrative reasoning, such reasoning would have to reveal their inherent power to produce motives in those who discern them; but no causal connections can be discovered *a priori*. Causal reasoning, by contrast, does infer matters of fact pertaining to actions, in particular their causes and effects; but, Hume argues, the vice of an action (its wickedness) is not found in its causes or effects, but is only apparent when we consult the sentiments of the observer. Therefore, moral good and evil are not discovered by reason alone.

Hume also attempts in the *Treatise* to establish the second anti-rationalist thesis, that virtue is not the same as reasonableness and vice is not contrary to reason. He gives two arguments to this end. The first he says follows directly from the Representation Argument, whose conclusion was that passions, volitions, and actions can be neither reasonable nor unreasonable. This "direct" argument is quite short. Actions, he observes, *can* be laudable or blamable. Since actions *cannot* be reasonable or against reason, it follows that "laudable and blameable are not the same with reasonable or unreasonable" (T 3.1.1.10; SBN 458). The properties are not identical.

So far he does not appeal to the inertia of reason. The second and more famous argument, though, makes use of the conclusion he defended earlier that reason alone cannot produce passions or actions. As we have seen, reason alone "can never immediately prevent or produce any action by contradicting or approving of it" (ibid.). Morals, however, "excite passions and produce or prevent actions" (T 3.1.1.6; SBN 457). Therefore, morals are not the product of reason alone. Here is another way he states this argument: because (premise 1) morals (or moral distinctions) "have an influence on the actions and affections," and (premise 2, the inertia of reason) "reason alone can never have any such influence," "it follows, that [morals] cannot be derived from reason" (ibid.). Hume formulates it some five times in T 3.1.1.

This argument about morality and motives (call it Argument M) is first introduced as showing it impossible "from reason alone . . . to distinguish betwixt moral good and evil" (T 3.1.1.4; 547) – that is, as defending the epistemic thesis that we cannot discover the difference between moral good and evil by reasoning alone, and this may be its main purpose. But Hume also says that, like the little direct argument above about property non-identity, Argument M proves that "actions do not derive their merit from a conformity to reason, nor their blame from a contrariety to it" (T 3.1.1.10; SBN 458), the second anti-rationalist thesis. In addition, Argument M is thought by some to reach a general causal conclusion, as we shall see.

Hume supports premise 1, that morals (or moral good and evil) "excite passions and produce or prevent actions," by observing that we regard morality as a practical subject, we take the trouble to teach it with the expectation that it will influence behavior, and experience shows that this sometimes works: "men are often govern'd by their duties, and are deterred from some actions by the opinion of injustice, and impell'd to others by that of obligation" (T 3.1.1.5; SBN 457). He does not claim that moral opinions always or necessarily cause motivating passions, nor that they do so without intermediary.

Scholars have offered many conflicting interpretations of Argument M. I shall discuss just three.

A promising way to interpret Argument M is that Hume mainly intends it to attack the moral rationalist thesis that "morality . . . is discern'd merely by ideas, and by their juxta-position and comparison" (T 3.1.1.4; SBN 456–457), advocated by such predecessors as Samuel Clarke (1706/1991) and John Balguy (1734/1991: 399). The argument is intended to show that such a comparison of ideas (whether in demonstration or in probabilistic inference) is not sufficient to enable us to grasp moral good and evil. First, we should understand 'moral distinctions' here as the activities of making moral discriminations, acts of distinguishing virtue from vice. Where he says 'morals have an influence' or 'good and evil' or 'the merit and demerit of actions' do, he means that moral properties, insofar as we become aware of them, "frequently contradict, and sometimes controul" our motivating passions (T 3.1.1.6; SBN 457). Premise 2 we interpret as above to say that the process of reasoning, without another process, cannot produce passions or actions. Therefore the process of discovering moral good and evil or distinguishing between them is not a process of reasoning alone (without another process), and the rationalists are wrong to say it is. Whatever we do in finding things to be good or evil, we do more than merely compare ideas and find some of them true. Often, we also feel a motivating passion, something that cannot be created by inference.

This interpretation makes good sense of Argument M and shows the relevance to it of the Representation Argument. It also enables Hume to reject both aspects of moral rationalism: the claim that we use reasoning alone to discover good and evil and that the goodness of an action consists in its being reasonable.

Some read this argument quite differently. There are two main possibilities, though scholars have discussed others.[13] The first interprets Argument M roughly thus:

1   Moral judgments excite passions and produce actions.
2   Reason alone cannot do this.
3   Therefore, moral judgments are not the products of reason alone.

This, however, is not valid. Premise 2 says that reason alone cannot cause passions. The conclusion follows only if we also assume that therefore reason alone cannot cause anything that *in turn* causes passions. If we do, we rely on an unstated (and undefended) assumption that causation (or non-causation – not being the cause of) is transitive: that what cannot cause A cannot cause any cause of A. But non-causation is not transitive in this way, as many counterexamples show;[14] and there is no evidence that Hume accepts this false principle. It is a bad strategy for interpreters to attribute to him a tacit commitment to a false rule of transitivity that he himself never mentions.

Advocates of the Inertia of Belief interpretation read the argument in another way. They construe it as being all about the *products* of reason. It is natural to suppose that the products of reason alone are beliefs, and so we could substitute 'belief' for 'product of reason alone' everywhere that the latter expression occurs. (Hume does not actually think that all beliefs result from the workings of reason: some come from sensation and others from sympathy. But let us disregard that for now. He does think that believing some ideas is the result of the workings of reason.)

Then we read the argument roughly as follows:[15]

1   Moral judgments cause passions and actions.
2   Beliefs (the products of reason) alone cannot do this.
3   Therefore moral judgments are not beliefs.

This version does not rely on causal transitivity and is valid if we assume that in premise 1 Hume means to say that moral judgments *alone* cause passions and actions. But, first, it is very different from anything Hume says, since he talks about reason and never mentions beliefs in any version of this argument. Second, as we have seen, the Inertia of Belief position in premise 2 conflicts with much else that Hume says. Finally, this reconstruction makes the Representation Argument irrelevant to Argument M. Hume could simply have omitted it and relied solely on the DC Argument. But Hume appeals to it explicitly as providing crucial support for Argument M. So this interpretation is also far from ideal.[16]

No interpretation of this influential and fascinating argument is perfect. Clearly, though, I favor the process interpretation as most faithful to Hume's text and the historical context in which he was moved to argue against the moral rationalists. On that interpretation, Argument M sweeps away the moral rationalist notion that the vice of an action consists in its failure to be fitting to its circumstances, something that, were it true, could be discovered entirely by comparing our perceptions to one another. It opens up the option that so appeals to Hume, that virtue and vice are characteristics we discover "by means of our . . . impressions" (T 3.1.1.3; SBN 456) – "matters of fact [that are] the object of feeling, not of reason" (T 3.1.1.26; 469). Our sentiments discover good and evil, and this influences our motives and actions.

Notes

1   Our main source is Hume's *Treatise of Human Nature*, with a few references to his *Enquiry Concerning the Principles of Morals* and *Dissertation on the Passions*.
2   It is possible that Hume countenances other forms of representation besides being a copy of something. Apparently he regards representation-as-a-copy as a prerequisite for truth-aptness. But he might allow that an item could be representational in some weaker sense without being truth-apt, and so a passion could be representational in some other way. One hopes so, since it is clear that many signs and symbols represent the world without being copies.
3   Páll S. Árdal (1966/1998) and others argue that when it comes to passions, Hume accounts for their directedness to objects by specifying their causes and effects, including their effect of turning our attention to certain objects.
4   According to Radcliffe (2012: 121), this is the position of Descartes and Leibniz. But Hume may have in mind the Stoic view that desires incorporate beliefs that something is good, or other historical views of the passions according to which they incorporate mental representations with a propositional structure.
5   This view is usually attributed to Hume in passing by philosophers who are not explicating Hume's texts but advocating instrumentalism (which they call "Humeanism") in their own right (e.g. Michael

Smith 1994: ch. 4, and Bernard Williams 1980). But Millgram (1995) suggests that Hume shows signs of holding the instrumentalist view in EPM Appendix 1, though not in the *Treatise*.

6 One may also wonder whether Hume sees incoherence of ends or desires as contrary to reason, as present-day choice theorists do. (An example: preferring A to B, B to C, yet C to A.) Setiya (2004) construes the claim in the Representation Argument that a passion has no "reference to any other object" to indicate that a passion is not to be rationally evaluated with respect to any other passion, thus denying that coherence of desires is a requirement of reason.

7 Harrison (1976: ch. 1), Mackie (1980: ch. 3), Snare (1991: chs. 2 and 3), Bricke (1996: ch. 1), Shaw (1998: ch. 2).

8 This seems to be Radcliffe's position (2012). We experience an object with a certain characteristic that gives us pleasure. This stimulates a desire for more things with that characteristic. When we learn that another instantiation of the characteristic is available, our desire is channeled toward that new object. Her example is seeing a movie by a certain director that has features I enjoy. The pleasure I experience creates a desire in me to see more movies with those features – perhaps humor and a touch of surrealism (my examples). When I learn that this director has a new movie out that is funny and slightly surrealistic, my desire is then channeled toward seeing the new movie. What this requires is that from the time I saw the first movie until the time I hear about the new movie, I have a desire to see more funny and slightly surrealistic movies. This could be so. But it is hard to attribute to Hume the view that it must be so. Given his position that desires are impressions, I would have to feel some sort of urge or longing to see more humorous and slightly surrealistic movies continuously, perhaps forever after, until I perhaps had a bad experience with one. Now, I might; some experiences leave us with a longing that never goes away, I suppose. But that sounds rather pathological, like an addiction. What more often happens is that our thoughts turn to other things and we have no introspectable desire for those features for quite some time. But when a new opportunity to encounter them comes our way, it kindles a desire to pursue it. Or not – it will depend on our mood and preoccupations at the time.

9 Shaw (1998: ch. 2) explicitly interprets Hume as ultimately holding a dispositional account of desire and aversion.

10 Baier (1991: 158–159) points out that hedonic beliefs actuate the will and argues that they influence our passions, but does not explicitly conclude that they cause entirely new passions. Karlsson (2000 and 2001), Sturgeon (2001), and Cohon (2008) argue for this view.

11 This interpretation of Hume's conception of reason(ing) is influenced by Garret (1997: ch. 1) and Owen (1999, chs 5–8). As Owen notes, this conception of reason has its roots in Locke's view Owen (1999: ch. 2).

12 Another alternative to the process interpretation is the faculty interpretation, that what Hume means by saying reason is inert is that the faculty of reason cannot produce actions or passions. Its disadvantage is that, although Hume uses the language of faculties of the mind, his empiricism does not allow him to identify a faculty first and then observe what it does. The only evidence we have that there is such a thing as the faculty of reason or the faculty of desire is the sequence of our impressions and ideas. What we observe is a series of perceptions in the mind. We can observe that some interact by way of comparison and finding true and others interact in other ways, but we do not observe any faculties. Once we have discovered different types of interactions, we can then attribute some to one faculty and others to another, but we cannot start with faculties.

13 Other reconstructions, some close to those offered here and some very different, can be found in Capaldi (1975: ch. 7), Cohon (1997), and Botros (2006).

14 Here is one: greenhouse gases do not of themselves cause flight delays, but they do cause climate change, which causes more severe storms, which do cause flight delays.

15 I cannot figure out what the scope of 'alone' should be in this argument: whether 'belief' replaces 'product of reason alone,' or instead 'belief' replaces 'product of reason' and then belief *alone* does not cause passions or actions. Maybe advocates of this interpretation see 'alone' playing both roles.

16 It has had great appeal for some who interpret Hume as an ethical emotivist, because of its conclusion that moral judgments are not beliefs, which they take to say that moral thoughts and utterances do not make statements and are not truth-apt but simply give vent to emotions. However, we should be cautious about reading Hume as an emotivist. He certainly regards moral sentiments as the foundation of virtue and vice, good and evil. But he does not offer an account of the meaning or lack of meaning of moral language (something that becomes far more pressing after the "linguistic turn" of the twentieth century), and there is room in his theory of the mind for moral impressions to be sentiments while

moral judgments would be ideas that purport to represent them and correspond or fail to correspond to those sentiments, and so are true or false.

References

Árdal, Páll S. (1966/1998) *Passion and Value in Hume's Treatise*, 2nd edn, Edinburgh: Edinburgh University Press.

Baier, Annette (1991) *A Progress of Sentiments: Reflections on Hume's Treatise*, Cambridge, MA: Harvard University Press.

Balguy, John (1991/1734) "The Foundations of Moral Goodness," excerpted in D. D. Raphael (ed.), *British Moralists 1650–1800*, vol I, Indianapolis, IN: Hackett Publishing.

Bricke, John (1996) *Mind and Morality*, Oxford: Clarendon Press.

Botros, Sophie (2006) *Hume, Reason and Morality: A Legacy of Contradiction*, London and New York: Routledge.

Capaldi, Nicholas (1975) *David Hume: Newtonian Philosopher*, Boston: Twayne Publishing Company.

Clarke, Samuel (1991/1706) *A Discourse Concerning the Unchangeable Obligations of Natural Religion and the Truth and Certainty of the Christian Revelation*, excerpted in D. D. Raphael, *British Moralists 1650–1800*, vol i, Indianapolis, IN: Hackett Publishing.

Cohon, Rachel (1997) "Is Hume a Noncognitivist in the Motivation Argument?" *Philosophical Studies* 85: 251–266.

——— (2008) *Hume's Morality: Feeling and Fabrication*, Oxford: Oxford University Press.

Garret, Don (1997) *Cognition and Commitment in Hume's Philosophy*, Oxford: Oxford University Press.

Hampton, Jean (1995) "Does Hume Have an Instrumental Conception of Practical Reason?" *Hume Studies* 21(1): 57–74.

Harrison, Jonathan (1976) *Hume's Moral Epistemology*, Oxford: Clarendon Press.

Karlsson, Mikael M. (2000) "Rational Ends: Humean and Non-Humean Considerations," *Sats – Nordic Journal of Philosophy* 1(2): 15–47.

———. (2001) "Cognition, Desire, and Motivation: 'Humean' and 'Non-Humean' Considerations," *Sats – Nordic Journal of Philosophy* 2(2): 30–58.

Korsgaard, Christine M. (1997) "The Normativity of Instrumental Reason," in G. Cullity and B. Gaut (eds.), *Ethics and Practical Reason*, Oxford: Oxford University Press, 1996, pp. 43–76.

Mackie, John L. (1980) *Hume's Moral Theory*, London: Routledge.

Millgram, Elijah (1995) "Was Hume a Humean?" *Hume Studies* 21(1): 75–93.

Owen, David (1999) *Hume's Reason*, Oxford: Oxford University Press.

Radcliffe, Elizabeth S. (1997) "Kantian Tunes on a Humean Instrument: Why Hume Is Not Really a Skeptic About Practical Reasoning," *Canadian Journal of Philosophy* 27: 247–269.

———. (1999) "Hume on the Generation of Motives: Why Beliefs Alone Never Motivate," *Hume Studies* 25(1–2): 101–122.

———. (2008) "Reason, Morality, and Hume's Active Principles: Comments on Rachel Cohon's *Hume's Morality: Feeling and Fabrication*," *Hume Studies* 34(2): 267–276.

———. (2012) "The Inertness of Reason and Hume's Legacy," *Canadian Journal of Philosophy* 42(S1): 117–133.

Setiya, Kieran (2004) "Hume on Practical Reason," *Philosophical Perspectives* 18: 365–389.

Shaw, Danial (1998) *Reason and Feeling in Hume's Action Theory and Moral Philosophy*, Lewiston, NY: Edwin Mellen Press.

Smith, Michael (1994) *The Moral Problem*, Oxford: Blackwell Publishers.

Snare, Francis (1991) *Morals, Motivation and Convention*, Cambridge: Cambridge University Press.

Stroud, Barry (1977) *Hume*, London: Routledge.

Sturgeon, Nicholas (2001) "Moral Skepticism and Moral Naturalism in Hume's *Treatise*," *Hume Studies* 27(1): 3–83.

Weller, Cass (2002) "The Myth of Original Existence: The Content of Passions in Hume's *Treatise*," *Hume Studies* 28: 215–249.

Williams, B. A. O. (1980) "Internal and External Reasons," in *Moral Luck*, Cambridge: Cambridge University Press, 1981, pp. 101–113.

Wollaston, William (1991 [1724]). "The Religion of Nature Delineated," in D. D. Raphael (ed.), *British Moralists 1650–1800*, vol i, pp. 237–258.

17

HUME ON MORAL RESPONSIBILITY AND FREE WILL[1]

Tamás Demeter

Introduction

Hume devotes two focused and extensive discussions to the questions of liberty and necessity in human action in the *Treatise* (Book 2, Part 3) and the first *Enquiry* (Section VIII). In both places the discussion is conceptual: in what sense can we talk about the freedom and causal determination of human action, and what are the consequences of our understanding for morality and religion? These problems are closely related to various areas of Hume's interests in metaphysics, ethics, and religion. Hume's account of liberty and necessity relies on how he derives from experience the idea of 'causation' and its chief conceptual ingredient, i.e. the necessary connection of two logically distinct events (see e.g. EHU Section VII). As we shall see, his views on the causal determination of action provide the foundation of his account of moral judgment by emphasizing our moral sensitivity to motivations and character traits while evaluating actions arising from them. And he also puts constraints on drawing theological inferences from moral evaluations, or relying on theological considerations in them. So the questions of moral responsibility and free will are embedded in a network of distinctively Humean philosophical commitments.

There is a voluminous literature reconstructing and commenting on various aspects of Hume's account and its development from the *Treatise* to the *Enquiry*. Its significance is frequently perceived from the angle provided by contemporary arguments surrounding compatibilism and incompatibilism. This debate is focused on the question of whether free will and moral responsibility are compatible with the causal determination of action. One could understand this debate as revolving around how to fit moral responsibility into a world where every event is determined by initial conditions (facts of the past) combined with the laws of nature. Some see Hume as a historically important contributor to this debate. George Botterill (2002), for example, argues that Hume gives up the position of an incompatibilist determinist in the *Treatise* for the sake of a compatibilist determinist stance in the *Enquiry* while strenuously rejecting the libertarian option as incoherent in itself and incompatible with the facts. Accordingly, contra-causal freedom, i.e. freedom for action that does not fit the causal chain of events, is not a matter of freedom but "is the same thing with chance; which is universally allowed to have no existence" (EHU 8.25; SBN 95–96). In the same vein, the concept of causation and necessity as elaborated by Hume is presupposed by moral responsibility and is compatible with political freedom, i.e. freedom from external constraints and coercion.

There are commentators who point out that such actualizations of Hume's contributions entail misrepresentations. One could point out that the problems of compatibilism and libertarianism do not arise for Hume, because taking a stance in this debate would commit him in questions of metaphysics that he would rather try to avoid. William Morris' diagnosis can be invoked here:

> Many of Hume's readers miss what is so distinctive about his approach to philosophy because they are interested in metaphysical questions and take him to be interested in these questions in the way they are. In doing so, they fail to see that part of Hume's attack on traditional approaches to philosophical questions consists in shifting the ground of discussion from what he regards as incoherent metaphysics to the only area where he believes we can have a fruitful discussion – where we have a clear understanding of the cognitive contents of the central ideas involved.
>
> (Morris 2008: 473 f.)

Historical interpretations are more sensitive to the question as to what Hume's project might be and to the context in which it took shape. James Harris (2005), for example, situates Hume, primarily the *Enquiry*, in the aftermath of Samuel Clarke's and Anthony Collins' debate. Here Collins argues that the cause of an action always necessitates the action itself, but Clarke insists that while the motivations of an agent are causes, the possibility is always given to act otherwise. This debate can be seen as revolving around the meaning of words, as 'cause' cannot mean the same in the two arguments: for Clarke, contrary to Collins, a cause does not necessitate its effect. Hume solves this problem by a revision of the received meaning of 'cause,' inherited from Hobbes and others, that equates causal and logical necessity. Hume replaces this received meaning by a new analysis of 'cause' that reduces the concept to constant conjunction instead of (logical) necessitation, and this move makes the two positions reconcilable.

Paul Russell's (2009) historical contextualization introduces Hume's position in the *Treatise* as contributing to an agenda of irreligion against the background of which Russell reads the whole work. Russell reads the *Treatise*'s discussion of liberty and necessity as it struck his contemporaries and concludes that Hume sides with Collins' view in the debate, accepting all its irreligious implications (Russell 2009: 235). Hume's argument in this context is interpreted as contributing to a "project to establish a secular, scientific account of moral life" (Russell 2009: 238).

In the present chapter, I intend to shed a somewhat different light on Hume's argument. While not challenging the widely held view that the first *Enquiry* reworks many of the central arguments in the *Treatise*, I suggest that they differ in their agendas and that the difference is reflected by the discussions of liberty and necessity in the two works.

The project of the *Treatise* is to provide an overarching theory of human nature by exploring natural human cognitive and affective functioning and their implications for sociability. As announced in the subtitle, Hume's aim is to apply the "experimental method of reasoning" to find the principles underlying psychological and social phenomena and thereby provide an explanatory framework for phenomena characteristic to moral beings *qua* moral beings. The project is thus to delineate an autonomous "anatomy of the mind" (see L 1:32; T 1.4.6.23; SBN 263; T 2.1.12.2; SBN 325–326; T 3.3.6.6; SBN 621; Ab. 2; SBN 646; EHU 1.13; SBN 13) that has no recourse to the physiological constitution or transcendent aspirations of human beings. The project of the *Enquiry* is to clarify the legitimate aims of inquiry in natural, moral, and theological matters, their foundational concepts, and the prospects and limitations of their methods. Hume's aim here is to remove abstrusity preventing epistemic progress by cultivating "true metaphysics with some care, in order to destroy the false and adulterate" (EHU 1.12; SBN 12–13). The *Enquiry* has a more focused and narrower scope than the *Treatise*, as it devotes attention primarily to the issues of systematic inquiry, and it discusses common cognitive functioning in relation to systematic inquiry.

In what follows, I will present Hume's account of the will and moral responsibility as opening up three perspectives on human action. The *first person perspective of introspection* provides a phenomenology of action and its causal sources as they become manifest to the agent. The *second person perspective of participation* offers an insight into human action as it is present to us while taking part in various processes of interpersonal coordination and social interaction. This is the field of practical inference and everyday moral judgment, but not of philosophical reasoning that belongs to the *third person perspective of observation*. Exploring the principles and explaining action is possible from this perspective, and this is the stance that properly belongs to the science of human nature.

While these perspectives are present in both the *Treatise* and the *Enquiry*, they are present with different emphasis in accordance with the general projects of the two works. In the *Treatise*, the will is discussed along with the passions, and the discussion there is focused on the phenomenology of will and necessity as perceived in common ways of acting. And this is what one should expect given the project of the *Treatise* aiming at an overarching theory of human psychological and social functioning. In the *Enquiry*, the same problems are discussed along with those of understanding, and the focus is placed on reasoning and inferences in moral matters. This discussion comes right after the problems of causation in Section VII and is also organically connected to it: it concerns inferences in and about the social world and the continuity of everyday and philosophical inferences. This shift in emphasis from the perspectives of introspection and interaction to that of observation is consonant with the discussion of the *Enquiry* being focused on the problems of systematic inquiry into matters of nature, morality, and theology.

Introspection and participation in the *Treatise*

The discussion of the will in the *Treatise* begins with an italicized definition: "by the *will*, I mean nothing but *the internal impression we feel and are conscious of, when we knowingly give rise to any new motion of our body, or new perception of our mind*" (T 2.3.1.2; SBN 399). This is a curious definition, as the will emerges here emphatically as a sensation and not as, one might expect, a faculty of the mind. While Hume likes to refer to the understanding, imagination, reason, or moral sense as "faculties" or even as "organs" of the mind (e.g. T 2.3.3.4; SBN 414–415; T 2.1.5.6; SBN 287), he refrains in his official definition from similar terms, however natural that might seem. Unlike of the will, we do not have impressions of faculties; if we had, there would be no need for Hume's "anatomy of the mind," as our "mental geography" would be easily accessible introspectively. But an anatomy is required here, precisely because we can only see the causes and effects of their functioning, and only on this basis can we infer their principles (T 1.3.14.34; SBN 171).[2]

If the will is an impression, talking about its freedom sounds like a category mistake. A faculty could be understood on analogy with some model of agent causation, but an impression cannot: a faculty could be free in the sense of standing outside the chain of causes and effects, and could be seen as initiating new causal chains without the instances of its doing so being caused – but it makes no sense to say that an impression of reflection, such as the will, is free in this sense. An impression of reflection cannot arise independently of a chain of causes, because they are by definition caused by ideas (T 1.1.2.1; SBN 7–8 and T 2.1.1.1–2; SBN 275–276), and it is even introspectively clear that the impression of the will has significant causal pre-history, as it arises "when either the good or the absence of the evil may be attained by any action of the mind or body" (T 2.3.9.7; SBN 439).

The will, from the agent's *first person* point of view, is thus an impression arising in those cases when we ascribe the authorship of a piece of behavior or a thought to ourselves – and not to external coercion, or some physiological process, involuntary movement, or spontaneous psychological activity – in order to achieve some good or avoid some evil consequence. In these cases of acting knowingly, we are prompted to imagine that *liberty as indifference* prevails in our actions (T 2.3.2.2; SBN 408–409) – i.e. that our willingness to do something is not part of a chain of causes and effects. But this feeling quickly turns out to be problematic, because it arises only while performing actions, but when we contemplate them or take part in social interaction, a contrary impression arises. This impression is that of causal *necessity*, by which Hume means the constant conjunction of motivations and actions, and what they foster: the corresponding inferences we draw concerning them (T 2.3.2.4; SBN 409–410).

Given the constant conjunction between motivations and actions, his position can easily be seen as an *epiphenomenalist* stance:[3] the will is an impression that arises when we act knowingly. But our inferences concerning the causes of actions invoke motivations, reasons, character traits, etc. as causes. Invoking the will in itself would not amount to an informative explanation of action, and given sufficient motivation, its addition would be superfluous. Actions lacking sufficient conjunction with motivations, even if voluntary, are not considered free but random, and random behavior cannot be free, because, as is well known, "mad-men have no liberty" (T 2.3.1.13; SBN 404).[4] And this is why the impression of liberty as indifference is a *"false sensation or experience"* (T 2.3.2.2; SBN 408): only a confused idea can be derived from it that removes our actions from the chain of causes and effects, and thus it does not fit our inferential practices. However, we cannot easily accept the insight that liberty as indifference is an illusion, because its prevalence, as Hume sees it, is supported by three mistaken commitments.

First, we cannot convince ourselves that the action we decided to take has been necessitated by various factors, and we could not have acted otherwise. This is due to our lacking as we act the impression of "force, and violence, and constraint" (T 2.3.2.1; SBN 407) implied by the idea of causal necessity. Yet, the lack of this impression justifies only liberty as *spontaneity*, i.e. the liberty to act without coercion and violence, but does not imply indifference in the sense of standing outside the chain of causes and effects. Second, while lacking an impression of coercion, we do have, as we have seen above, the opposite impression: "We feel that our actions are subject to our will on most occasions, and imagine we feel that the will itself is subject to nothing" (T 2.3.2.2; SBN 408–409). As we have this illusory feeling, we can easily imagine performing some other action instead of the one that we actually performed. But imagining entails only logical possibility here, and not the actual possibility of performing the alternative action itself – just as imagining the malleability of the bars by touch (a logical possibility) does not entail the actual possibility of escaping the prison (T 2.3.1.17; SBN 406–407 and EHU 8.19; SBN 90–91). And third, the idea of liberty as indifference persists for religious and ethical reasons, because it is often claimed "that necessity utterly destroys all merit and demerit either towards mankind or superior powers" (T 2.3.2.7; SBN 411–412). But if 'necessity' is analyzed in terms of constant conjunction and inferential practices, as Hume suggests, then necessity turns out to be presupposed in moral evaluation: without a constant conjunction between motivation and actions, there would be no way of inferring passions, principles, character traits (virtuous and vicious) from actions, and there would be nothing to pass moral judgment on. As we will see, this argument is further elaborated in the *Enquiry*.

Proclaiming the impression of liberty as indifference a "false sensation" is consonant with Hume's reluctance to invoke introspection as a reliable source of insight and justification while exploring psychological processes (T Intro. 10; SBN xviii–xix and EHU 1.13; SBN 13). His distrust is due to the tendency of introspection to distort the processes it is directed at, while publicly accessible observations tend to be more reliable. So an alternative route to explore liberty and necessity in human action is to consider the *second person* perspective and see what our participation in everyday social interactions reveals about human action.

Given our inferential practices, there is no way to avoid the conclusion that our motivations and actions are part of a network of causes and effects. Our actions are subject to the same kind of necessity as events in the physical world: the connections between "motives, volitions and actions, or figure and motion" (T 2.3.1.17; SBN 406–407) have the same character, because physical necessity and moral certainty have the same foundation in our sensitivity to regularities and ability to get used to them that give rise to an impression, a feeling of necessity (T 2.3.1.16; SBN 405–406). This is the source of causal inferences in general, but this is also the foundation of conventions, institutions, and the legitimacy of political power.

Due to this homogeneity of natural and moral causes, they can enter into the same chain of reasoning, as the example of the prisoner shows whose fate is equally doomed because of the physical properties of his prison and the "obstinacy of the gaoler" (T 2.3.1.17; SBN 406). Thus, from the second person (participant) perspective, unlike from the first person (introspective) perspective, it is natural to assert continuity between the world of human action and the natural world (T 1.3.14.12; SBN 632–633). We infer the workings of men just as the workings of nature, and just as the course of nature arises from "natural and necessary principles," "human society is founded on like principles" (T 2.3.1.8; SBN 401–402). This continuity provides the basis of methodological continuity between moral and natural philosophy, and of the continuity between the second and third person (observer) perspectives – as we will see shortly in the context of the *Enquiry*.

The idea of a necessary connection emerges in the beholder's eye with respect to both moral and natural phenomena: there is no need for the agent to be sensible of the necessity that connects his motives to his actions. It is enough if he as a participant or an observer can feel the necessity in the cases he attends to – just like with respect to physical objects:

> The necessity of any action, whether of matter or of the mind, is not properly a quality in the agent, but in any thinking or intelligent being, who may consider the action, and consists in the determination of his thought to infer its existence from some preceding objects.
>
> (T 2.3.2.2; SBN 408–409)

Therefore, with sufficient background knowledge, an actual spectator usually can infer our actions in advance, but an ideal spectator "acquainted with every circumstance of our situation and temper, and the most secret springs of our complexion and disposition" (T 2.3.2.2; SBN 409) can surely tell how an agent will act, even if the agent himself feels that he could have acted otherwise. He falls prey to a "false sensation" – as any spectator can tell.

The main source of Hume's argument against trusting this sensation at face value comes from everyday social practices and inferences. The "common course of human affairs" (T 2.3.1.5; SBN 401) provides the "moral evidence" we rely on in these cases:

> moral evidence is nothing but a conclusion concerning the actions of men, derived from the consideration of their motives, temper and situation. . . . The same kind of reasoning runs throu' politics, war, commerce, œconomy, and indeed mixes itself so entirely in human life that 'tis impossible to act or subsist a moment without having

recourse to it. A prince, who imposes a tax upon his subjects, expects their compliance. A general, who conducts an army, takes account of a certain degree of courage. A merchant looks for fidelity and skill in his factor or super/cargo. A man, who gives orders for his dinner, doubts not of the obedience of his servants. In short, nothing more nearly interests us than our own actions and those of others, the greatest part of our reasonings is employ'd in judgments concerning them. Now I assert, that whoever reasons after this manner, does *ipso facto* believe the actions of the will to arise from necessity, and that he knows not what he means, when he denies it.

(T 2.3.1.15; SBN 404–405)

Our interactive behavior and expectations reflect that we are committed to the doctrine of necessity, as Hume understands it: our volitions are taken to arise as parts of a chain of causes and effects, and for this reason we can make reliable predictions concerning prospective actions, and draw inferences concerning motivations for moral evaluation.

Hume's focus in the *Treatise* is largely on this participant perspective and not on speculative reasoning concerning actions; however, the two are continuous as we "both in speculation and practice proceed upon" (T 2.3.1.15; SBN 405) the same kind of moral evidence. The difference between practice and speculation can be explained by invoking the distinction between "natural" and "philosophical relations." In natural relations, "two ideas are connected together in the imagination, and the one naturally introduces the other" (T 1.1.5.1; SBN 13–14), by means of the principles of association. In philosophical relations, ideas are "subject of comparison, without a connecting principle" (T 1.1.5.1; SBN 14), and then they belong to the realm of reasoning (T 1.3.2.2; SBN 73). When directed at matters of fact, reason by the aid of experience can discover the connection between causes and effects (T 1.3.6.12; SBN 92 and T 3.1.1.12; SBN 459–460), which is to say that the philosophical relation of cause and effect presupposes the corresponding natural relation.[5] Hume's summary account of causation here (T 2.3.1.16; SBN 405–406) invokes only the natural relation of cause and effect with respect to motivations and actions, but not the philosophical relation required for causal reasoning. So this inference belongs to the imagination and not reason (T 2.3.1.12; SBN 403), just like our everyday inferences concerning physical causes and effects.

Observation and causal reasoning in the *Enquiry*

In the *Enquiry*, Hume repeats his diagnosis: from the first person perspective "we imagine we feel that the will itself is subject to nothing." This is "a false sensation or seeming experience" that we feel while doing something, but a spectator, given sufficient knowledge of the circumstances, could fairly securely infer what action to expect despite our feeling of "looseness and indifference" (EHU 8.22n18; SBN 94). This impression has no practical or philosophical relevance for two reasons. First, the idea we derive from this impression is inconsistent with the facts that are accessible from external observation and the common course of action (8.24). Second, this idea of liberty is inconsistent in itself, because it suggests that actions can stand outside the chain of causes and effects, which means "the same thing as *chance*": a "mere negative word, and means not any real power" (EHU 8.25; SBN 95–96).

The *Enquiry* also shares the lessons the *Treatise* drew about the participant perspective (EHU 8.17; SBN 89). Causal inference relies on the idea of a necessary connection that is grounded in constant conjunctions, i.e. the regular experience of one event following another (T 7.28; SBN 75–76). Without "necessity, according to the sense, in which it is taken here," no causal inference is available for human beings, and Hume thinks that its practical and speculative relevance had not been and cannot be effectively denied (T 8.21; SBN 92–93). With respect to human actions,

> we acquire this idea from the insight that actions . . . have a regular conjunction with motives and circumstances and characters, and as we always draw inferences from one to the other, we must be obliged to acknowledge in words, that necessity, which we have already avowed, in every deliberation of our lives, and in every step of our conduct and behavior.
>
> (EHU 8.22; SBN 93–94)

When navigating the social world, we rely on such empirically grounded practical inferences whose principles are not reflected on, but philosophical inquiry makes them explicit.

The attention Hume devotes to the *observer perspective*, i.e. to detached philosophical inquiry into moral matters, gives one distinctive flavor of his discussion in the *Enquiry*. This perspective has a double focus: the first is on the exploration of the participant perspective, and the second is on the methodological role historiography plays in moral philosophy. Inquiries into moral matters begin "at the wrong end" when they start from the appearances of the first person perspective "by examining the faculties of the soul, the influence of the understanding, and the operations of the will" (EHU 8.22; SBN 93). What we can access introspectively is not validated by careful observation and analysis; it is not reflected in our social practices and in history. So, instead of hypotheses ungrounded in observable phenomena, moral inquiry should rely on regularities as found in publicly accessible experience (EHU 8.22; SBN 93–94, see also EPM 1.10; SBN 174).

In this vein, the *Enquiry* reasserts the continuity of moral and natural philosophy. Inquiry in both fields of study is based on the same idea of a necessary connection that copies the impression of expectation that arises due to experiencing constant conjunctions. The natural relation of causation is based on this idea of necessary connection, and this is the foundation of all causal reasoning concerning both the moral and the natural world (EHU 8.5; SBN 82). We cannot "penetrate farther" than to observe the phenomenal properties of things and the regularities in their behavior (EHU 8.21; SBN 92–93). The uncertainty in our inferences concerning human affairs are largely due to unknown complexities, that are equally characteristic to our inferences concerning physical matters (EHU 8.12; SBN 86 and EHU 8.20; SBN 91). There is thus no reason to believe that the two fields of study should be methodologically different (EHU 8.19; SBN 90–91 and EHU 8.35; SBN 102–103). Character traits (virtues or vices) and motivations as causes are regularly linked to behavior as effect, and the necessity is of the same kind as the one on which reasoning about natural phenomena depends. Thus, it supports the same kind of reasoning.

In accordance with the idea of a philosophical relation of cause and effect that relies on the corresponding natural associative relation, reasoning in moral philosophy and everyday practical inference are continuous, because they have the same foundation in the experience of constant conjunctions between actions and motivations. With this kept in mind, the philosopher's task begins with observable regularities, continues with tracing them back to their causal sources, and ends with explaining phenomena by the principles thus reached. By doing so she does not go beyond the limits of everyday inferences because "this experimental inference and reasoning concerning the actions of others enters so much into human life, that no man, while awake, is ever a moment without employing it" (EHU 8.17; SBN 89). Philosophical speculation only transfers the matter from the realm of imagination to that of reason, from the association of ideas to their careful comparison: it is a systematic extension of everyday inferences concerning the common course of action as well as the common course of nature (EHU 8.13–15; SBN 86–88).

The observer perspective is thus continuous with the participant perspective: it is a methodologically conscious refinement of existing inferential practices. From the observer perspective, a moral philosopher can describe human actions, and by comparing them can arrive at conclusions concerning their underlying principles that guide our actions and expectations in the social world, and thereby explain them. So, moral philosophy also provides the means for understanding the participant perspective on taking part in social practices. The principles are founded on past experience, which teaches us that the world of human action and interaction, just like the natural world, is full of detectable regularities, and participation in social interaction tacitly relies on them (T 8.17; SBN 89). If there were no necessity in this sense for us to rely on in these matters, then it would be "almost impossible . . . to engage, either in science or action of any kind" (EHU 8.18; SBN 90).

Beside the participant perspective, the other source of observations that the moral philosopher can rely on while searching for the principles of human nature is history, whose

> chief use is only to discover the constant and universal principles of human nature, by showing men in all varieties of circumstances and situations, and furnishing us with materials from which we may form our observations and become acquainted with the regular springs of human action and behavior. These records of wars, intrigues, factions, and revolutions, are so many collections of experiments, by which the politician or moral philosopher fixes the principles of his science, in the same manner as the physician or natural philosopher becomes acquainted with the nature of plants, minerals, and other external objects, by the experiments which he forms concerning them. Nor are the earth, water, and other elements, examined by Aristotle, and Hippocrates, more like to those which at present lie under our observation than the men described by Polybius and Tacitus are to those who now govern the world.
>
> (EHU 8.7; SBN 83–84)

So the significance of historiography in moral philosophy is methodologically analogous with that of natural history and experimental natural history for natural philosophy in an important way: they present their objects in various situations and furnish us with empirical findings to theorize on. If our focus is on human nature, then human history provides us with the variation of circumstances in which the principles of human nature can be established. "The observation of several parallel instances" (EHU 8.13; SBN 86–87) and finding analogies between them gives the chance of reducing phenomena to the underlying principles productive of them (EHU 4.12; SBN 30–31). Same effects must be traced back to some similarity in their causes – a conviction that is extended to the study of human nature, too: "human nature remains still the same, in its principles and operations. The same motives always produce the same actions: The same events follow from the same causes" (EHU 8.7; SBN 83–84).

In the *Enquiry*, Hume also clarifies how to use the experimental basis so as to arrive at the principles of human nature, and then at the explanation of moral phenomena. The method here is a kind of *analysis and synthesis*:

> By means of this guide [i.e. historical and everyday observations of human behavior, we mount up to the knowledge of men's inclinations and motives, from their actions, expressions, and even gestures; and again descend to the interpretation of their actions from our knowledge of their motives and inclinations. The general observations treasured up by a course of experience, give us the clue of human nature, and teach us to unravel all its intricacies.
>
> (EHU 8.9; SBN 85)

Though the exact terms 'analysis' and 'synthesis' do not figure here, in the context of early modern philosophy the terms 'mounting up' and 'descending' belonged to the same family of methodological concepts as 'analysis' and 'synthesis,' and they were applied especially in the context of searching for causes (see Jardine 1974: 249). Later in Section XI Hume puts a constraint on how far we can reach while analyzing the causes of particular effects:

> We can never be allowed to mount up from the universe, the effect, to Jupiter, the cause; and then descend downwards, to infer any new effect from that cause. . . . The knowledge of the cause being derived solely from the effect, they must be exactly adjusted to each other; and the one can never refer to anything farther, or be the foundation of any new inference and conclusion.
>
> (EHU 11.14; SBN 137)

Analyzing causes from effects cannot proceed arbitrarily: particularly, we cannot be justified in analyzing phenomena into the characteristics of some deity. What we can do is to collect relevant phenomena, find analogies between them and ascribe those analogies to similar causes, thereby reducing a variety of phenomena to regular principles underlying them. But our knowledge cannot transcend what we can infer proportionately from the effects themselves.

The methodological considerations in the *Enquiry* highlight that Hume's question concerns the limits of knowledge about human actions and how they can be reached. This question does not belong to the metaphysics of the freedom of the will, but to the epistemology of practical knowledge and inferences as manifested while navigating the social world, and of philosophical knowledge based on reasoning from causes to effects and from effects to causes. Thereby Hume transmutes a question traditionally belonging to the realm of transcendent metaphysics into an empirical one – a move that can be aptly called Newtonian: Newton frequently turns traditional metaphysical questions, like, for example, those concerning space or God, into empirical ones, and so transfers them from the field of speculative metaphysics to experimental natural philosophy (Stein 2000: 261–262, 269–270, 277). Hume treats foundational concepts (e.g. causation, necessity etc.) in a like manner: the genealogy and content of these concepts are not explored as *a priori* metaphysical issues, but as questions pertaining to an experimental science of man.[6]

With his commitment to the authenticity of the observer and participant perspectives as opposed to the first person perspective, Hume endorses the primacy of a scientific image of human nature as opposed to its manifest image that introspection provides, because it is not reflected in social practices, and not vindicated by philosophical reasoning. This argument can only be conclusive if one admits that the proper method of inquiry into moral matters is experimental. And as Hume sees it, we cannot begin elsewhere. Particularly, we cannot presuppose the truth of the manifest image, because it is inconsistent with plain fact and with itself. No inquiry into human action should begin with the first person perspective which contradicts our natural commitments and supplies a confused idea.

Moral responsibility and theodicy in the *Enquiry*

As we have seen, the relation of necessity and moral responsibility emerges in the *Treatise*, but a more detailed treatment is offered in the *Enquiry*, and it adds another distinctive flavor to its discussion. Ignoring the false sensation of liberty as indifference does not threaten liberty in the sense in which it "concerns us to preserve," namely liberty as opposed to "force, and violence, and constraint" (T 2.3.2.1; SBN 407 and EHU 8.25; SBN 96). This liberty is the "*power of acting or not acting, according to the determinations of the will*" (EHU 8.23; SBN 95), and this is the kind of freedom we need for the possibility of moral evaluation. External constraints abolish responsibility, because

> actions are objects of our moral sentiment, so far only as they are indications of the internal character, passions, and affections; it is impossible that they can give rise either to praise or blame, where they proceed not from these principles, but are derived altogether from external violence.
>
> (EHU 8.31; SBN 99)

Therefore, Humean moral evaluations also presuppose Humean necessity, because it is possible to infer causally from an action to its internal motivation only if constant conjunction underpins the inference. Moral evaluation of an action is possible only if we deny liberty as indifference and affirm independence from external constraint.

In the second part of Section VIII of the *Enquiry*, Hume does two things. First, he illustrates that the practice of moral evaluation is based on the experience of constant conjunction, and thus it is continuous with philosophical inquiry. Moral evaluation springs from the action's motivation, which is inferred on the basis of previously observed conjunctions between actions and motivations. Were there no such conjunctions, actions could not provide evidence for motivation, and consequently for moral evaluation (EHU 8.30; SBN 98–99). Inferences from action to motivation presuppose a constant conjunction between types of action (virtuous or vicious) and relatively stable types of motivation (virtues, character traits, passions), a conjunction that gives rise to the impression of necessity in moral phenomena. Thus, Hume shows that our moral practice is founded on the same idea of necessity as our reasoning about moral (and natural) matters.

Second, the lesson he offers about moral practice leads to the problem of *theodicy* and thus to a possible objection to Hume's theory of necessity – at least in moral matters: if, relying on Humean necessity, actions are traced back to their motivations, and motivations to the circumstances influencing them, and the circumstances to other preceding circumstances, then we eventually arrive at "the Creator of the world" (EHU 8.32; SBN 100). Once there, two things can be said: either our actions cannot be wrong because ultimately they spring from a good cause, *or* they can be wrong, but then the Creator must share in the blame. As both horns of this dilemma are impossible, Hume's doctrine of necessity is untenable – so argues Hume's imagined opponent (EHU 8.32–33; SBN 100–101). But Hume rejects the dilemma altogether.

On the one hand, he argues that the perspective of moral evaluation is much narrower in practice than to be sensitive to the entirety of this alleged causal chain. It is possible to argue that some particular wrong could arise from general laws that are otherwise right if considered from the perspective of the whole; or that some morally wrong action fits into the causal texture of the world so that it prevents something even worse or facilitates some future good. Yet, these arguments cannot alter our natural moral sentiments that respond to particular actions. Moral judgments are founded on "the natural sentiments of the human mind" (EHU 8.35; SBN 102), and our moral sense, which responds naturally to character traits in relation to their contribution to sociability, is not susceptible to the conclusions of such abstract reasoning.

On the other hand, *prima facie* it might seem as if Hume could not find an effective argument against the second horn of the dilemma. Well, says Hume, if the Deity is the distant cause of our actions, then it is unavoidable that the Deity be the cause of our vicious actions, too. But the point of real importance comes only after this:

> These are mysteries, which mere natural and unassisted reason is very unfit to handle; and whatever system she embraces, she must find herself involved in inextricable

difficulties, and even contradictions. . . . Happy, if she be thence sensible of her temerity, when she pries into these sublime mysteries; and leaving a scene so full of obscurities and perplexities, return, with suitable modesty, to her true and proper province, the examination of common life; where she will find difficulties enow to employ her enquiries, without launching into so boundless an ocean of doubt, uncertainty, and contradiction!

(EHU 8.36; SBN 103)

Thus, Hume's response to the second horn is that reason is simply unequipped for solving the problem of theodicy, and the problem is therefore placed outside the appropriate realm of philosophy, at least as it is defined by Hume's standards of experimental reasoning. And this is the note on which this section ends: on the basis of our social practices and philosophical reasoning, it is impossible to answer questions about the Deity and the Deity's relation to the world. That is to say, these problems are unsolvable from a human point of view, because the solution, if there is any, lies outside the boundaries of human understanding.

Hume thus addresses a question of central importance in then-contemporary natural philosophy from the perspective of moral philosophy. This question pertains to the possibility of *natural theology*. Natural philosophical inquiry was largely driven by the conviction that God is the author of two books, namely the Bible and the Book of Nature. Natural philosophers frequently thought about themselves as studying God and God's intentions through the latter work (Shapin 1996: 104–105, 138–139). While discussing theodicy, Hume considers the possibility of this kind of inquiry based on the study of human nature: to what extent, if at all, can God and his intentions be known from human actions? The question whether this kind of knowledge is possible is analogous with the question about the possibility of deriving a natural theology from our knowledge of nature – but the answers to the two questions are logically independent.

By declaring the problem of theodicy unsolvable and moral philosophy unfit for the questions of transcendence, Hume articulates an ideology of natural and moral knowledge that circumscribes the limits of their legitimate aspirations: he detaches the questions of knowledge of nature and human nature from questions of knowledge and knowability of God and his purposes. In the context of the *Enquiry*, the problem of theodicy is relevant in this epistemic guise, as a component of the "religious hypothesis" (see EHU 11.18; SBN 103, EHU 11.27; SBN 146). The closing of Section VIII gestures toward some of the epistemic lessons drawn in Section X and XI of the *Enquiry* on miracles and particular providence. Taken together, these Sections drive toward a secular ideology of knowledge that distinguishes the modern natural and social sciences from the religious aspirations of early modern natural and moral philosophy.[7]

Conclusion

Hume sketches three possible perspectives on discussing moral phenomena in general, and the problem of free will and moral responsibility in particular. He considers the participant and the observer perspectives as continuous: if it is reached by the proper philosophical method, theoretical knowledge about human phenomena is congruent with our implicit practical knowledge about human matters as is exhibited in everyday social practices. At the same time, he denies the adequacy of an introspective perspective, which leads us to conceptually and factually defective ideas about moral phenomena.

The moral philosopher's aim is to explore from the observer perspective the principles of moral phenomena. This inquiry shares the methodology as well as the epistemic aims and limitations of natural philosophy. It must be consistent with the common course of action – just as natural philosophy must answer to the course of nature. Hume argues that moral philosophy should be constrained on mundane matters and should avoid transcendent aspirations. There is no justification for inferences drawn from human phenomena that allegedly lead us to knowledge about how things stand outside this world, and there is thus no problem of theodicy that can be meaningfully addressed. Moral evaluation concerns human affairs only, so its workings and functions can be accounted for in terms of causal relations. This is the only knowledge available to us from a human point of view, so moral philosophy, just like natural philosophy, is a human enterprise that belongs exclusively to the realm of human experience.

Notes

1 This chapter is part of a research program of MTA BTK Lendület Morals and Science Research Group.
2 Bricke (2008: 205) 'suggests volition' would be more appropriate in the official definition, which seems to reserve the place of the will as a faculty responsible for producing volitions. Similarly, Garrett (2014: 109) suggests "'The will' is his term for the faculty of producing bodily movements or perceptions by means of such volitions." Indeed, in T 2.3.4.9; SBN 422 Hume passingly mentions the will as a faculty, but I stick to the official definition, mainly for the reason just given. I consider the will/volition, just as Garrett, an impression of reflection not produced by a specific faculty, but by reflection, the same mechanism that produces passions in general.
3 Something similar is suggested in Harris (2015: 113).
4 If the will has no proper causal role to play in the production of action, what role could it play? Lacking textual evidence, only a speculative, but perhaps Hume an answer can be sketched here. By reminding us of the authorship of our action, the impression of the will reminds us of our moral responsibility. We can acquire this impression by observing others ascribing the authorship of many of our actions, and then we get used to ascribing them to ourselves and feel morally responsible. For a similar contemporary account, see Wegner (2002: 325 ff.), who argues that the will can be seen as an affective shadow of some physiological processes (a somatic marker), which reminds us that some events are attributable to us.
5 For a similar reading of natural and philosophical relations in Hume, see Owen (1999: 149–154) and de Pierris (2015: 86–88).
6 Schliesser (2011) calls this move Newton's Challenge to philosophy in which Hume seems to be an ally.
7 I discuss the questions of method and ideology of knowledge in Demeter (2016).

References

Bricke, J. (2008) "Hume on Liberty and Necessity," in E. Radcliffe (ed.), *A Companion to Hume*, Oxford: Wiley-Blackwell, pp. 201–216.
Botterill, G. (2002) "Hume on Liberty and Necessity," in P. Millican (ed.), *Reading Hume on Human Understanding: Essays on the First Enquiry*, Oxford: Clarendon Press, pp. 277–300.
Demeter, T. (2016) *David Hume and the Culture of Scottish Newtonianism: Methodology and Ideology in Enlightenment Inquiry*, Brill: Leiden.
de Pierris, G. (2015) *Ideas, Evidence, and Method: Hume's Skepticism and Naturalism Concerning Knowledge and Causation*, Oxford: Oxford University Press.
Garrett, D. (2014) *Hume*, London: Routledge.
Harris, J. (2005) *On Liberty and Necessity*, Oxford: Clarendon Press.
———. (2015) *Hume: An Intellectual Biography*, Cambridge: Cambridge University Press.
Jardine, L. (1974) *Francis Bacon and the Art of Discourse*, Cambridge: Cambridge University Press.
Morris, W. (2008) "Hume's Epistemological Legacy," in E. S. Radcliffe (ed.), *A Companion to Hume*, Oxford: Wiley-Blackwell, pp. 457–476.
Owen, D. (1999) *Hume's Reason*, Oxford: Clarendon Press.
Russell, P. (2009) *The Riddle of Hume's Treatise: Skepticism, Naturalism, Irreligion*, Oxford: Oxford University Press.

Schliesser, E. (2011) "Newton's Challenge to Philosophy: A Programmatic Essay," *HOPOS: The Journal of the International Society for the History of Philosophy of Science* 1: 101–128.

Shapin, S. (1996) *The Scientific Revolution*, Chicago, IL: University of Chicago Press.

Stein, H. (2000) "Newton's Metaphysics," in I. B. Cohen and G. E. Smith (eds.), *The Cambridge Companion to Newton*, Cambridge: Cambridge University Press, pp. 256–307.

Wegner, D. (2002) *The Illusion of Conscious Will*, Cambridge, MA: MIT Press.

18

HUME'S MORAL SENTIMENTALISM

James Baillie

Sentimentalism grounds morality in naturally formed benevolent feelings towards others. It emerged in eighteenth-century Britain in opposition to both *egoism*, which grounded all action, including purportedly moral behavior, in self-interested motives; and *rationalism*, which based morality on reason alone. Hume's sentimentalist predecessors were the moral sense theorists the Third Earl of Shaftesbury (Anthony Ashley Cooper) and Frances Hutcheson. His most illustrious successor in a sympathy-based sentimentalism was Adam Smith.

The main presentations of Hume's sentimentalism are in Book 3 of the *Treatise* and in the *Enquiry Concerning the Principles of Morals*, which I will call the '2nd *Enquiry*.'[1] The *Treatise*'s moral theory emerges within a complex empiricist–naturalistic theory framed around an associationist psychology. The central place given to the associative nature of our thinking and feeling is the most revolutionary feature of the Humean mind, as presented in the *Treatise*. While the 2nd *Enquiry* does not explicitly employ this associationism, it is not rejected. The 2nd *Enquiry* has a much narrower focus, with its main text primarily devoted to the virtues: discovering the character traits that elicit approval and identifying common characteristics among them. Conclusions are derived from observations of common life together with introspection and wide historical learning.

The *Treatise* is subtitled 'An Attempt to Introduce the Experimental Method of Reasoning into Moral Subjects.' This can be paraphrased as 'an application of scientific methods to human nature.' He does not employ experiments in the now standard sense in which nature is manipulated to reveal mechanisms that are normally obscured. Rather than contriving artificial settings, Hume derives his data from ordinary social interactions. In his opinion, the fundamental flaw of previous studies of human nature is that the theoretical tail wagged the experiential dog. They would start with some ideal picture of our psychology and then struggle to squeeze the facts into line with it. In contrast, Hume urged not to engage in speculation beyond what is required by a parsimonious explanation of the empirical data.

Since Hume's account of morality in the *Treatise* emerges from his theory of human nature, I briefly discuss some features of his system to show how sentimentalism emerged from his account of the passions, sympathy, and motivation.

Background: passions, sympathy, motivation

Hume makes a fundamental distinction among mental states, i.e. *perceptions*, between *impressions* and *ideas*. *Ideas* are thoughts. *Reason*, or the *understanding*, is Hume's name for our capacity to

236

work with ideas. *Impressions* are of two main kinds: *original*, comprising bodily sensations and sensory data; and *secondary*, emotions that he calls the passions.[2] All ideas are grounded in impressions, being 'copies' of impressions, or composites of such copies.

Hume's main criterion of individuation among perceptions, whether in distinguishing ideas from impressions, or among different kinds of either, is phenomenal. Each kind of perception has a *quale*, a distinctive experiential quality that differentiates it from every other kind. Experientially, the main difference between impressions and ideas is the former's greater intensity, i.e. 'force' or 'vivacity.' However, Hume downplays this phenomenal criterion in his treatment of *calm passions*, which play a key role in his moral theory. These "produce little emotion in the mind, and are more known by their effects than by the immediate feeling or sensation" (T 2.3.3.8; SBN 417). This remark shows that, in addition to his 'official' phenomenal account, Hume employs a *functional* taxonomy of perceptions deriving from their typical causal relationships within human psychology.

Hume distinguishes *direct* and *indirect* passions. *Direct* passions are proximate causes of action. They are identified as *desire, aversion, grief, joy, hope,* and *fear*, along with *volition*. The will had commonly been viewed as independent of all passions, and capable of overruling them to cause or prevent action. Hume rejects such a faculty, taking volition as the impression that immediately precedes deliberate movement. Other than volition, the direct passions comprise pairs of reactions to events that are associated with pleasure or pain – either as present impressions, or the belief that some such event will occur. The fact that direct passions are prompted by events seen as to-be-pursued or to-be-avoided explains their motivational power.

The basic *indirect* passions are pride, humility, love, and hatred. Whereas the direct passions concern situations *per se*, the indirect passions concern *people*. Pride and humility consist, respectively, in pleasure or pain on seeing oneself in a good or bad light. Love or hatred involve taking these attitudes to someone else. More precisely, the *object* of pride or humility is *oneself*, and that of love or hatred is another person. The *cause* of pride or humility can be a mental or physical trait, or anything that I take to be related to me. These same causes produce love or hatred when possessed by others.

Apart from phenomenal intensity, one important difference between ideas and impressions is that ideas represent some factual matter, or formal relationship, and so can be true or false, and in that sense be reasonable or unreasonable. So error consists in *misrepresentation*, a lack of fit between the idea and what it purports to depict. Impressions lack this representational quality. Hume's point is easy to misunderstand. Surely, one might say, if I am angry over your rude behavior, my anger does represent you – it's about *what you have done*. But Hume would respond that this intentional content holds only for an *idea* that accompanies the impression. More precisely, the notions of truth and falsity apply only to *beliefs*, which make a claim as to how things stand. So when I am angry at you, it is not this passion, but an associated thought, e.g. 'You are being obnoxious,' that is about you, and can be true. So beliefs and passions are different kinds of perceptions in that whereas beliefs operate around the dualism of Yes or No, acceptance or rejection, true or false, passions fall under the non-representational polarity of pleasure or pain, like or dislike, attraction or repulsion. Passions can be considered false only in a loose sense, if they are caused by or lead to false beliefs. But strictly, the error lies in the belief.

Hume extends his claim about non-representationality to *actions*, as illustrated in his hyperbolic provocation that "'Tis not contrary to reason to prefer the destruction of the whole world to the scratching of my finger" (T 2.3.3.6; SBN 416). But he is not denying that the person is unreasonable in the broader sense, since any beliefs that would accompany such an act or preference would, if expressed, expose the utterer as a lunatic.

Sympathy is a mechanism by which passions are communicated, enabling one to replicate aspects of another's experience.[3] Sympathy is not something that we *do*, such as intentionally inferring or imaginatively reconstructing another's inner state. Rather, it is an involuntary associative process through which observing or considering someone's behavior causes an idea of what she is experiencing; this then causes an idea of myself undergoing such an experience; finally, this idea is converted into an impression of the same kind as I originally ascribed to the other person. Key to this process is the fact that we always have a vivid awareness of ourselves – not of a substantive self, but our own perceptions. When I form an idea of someone's inner state, it connects to this sense of myself, leading to the idea of my being in that state. The vivacity of my impression of myself is transmitted to this idea, which is transformed into an impression, so that I feel the passion.

While our common humanity allows some degree of sympathy between any of us, the amount that is naturally generated is governed by the principles of association – the extent of one's identification with this person, as determined by the three dimensions of association, namely some subjectively relevant resemblance, contiguity in time or place, and, most importantly, the closeness of the causal relationship between us.

Hume describes sympathy as a 'secondary' source of pride and humility. That is, I do not experience these passions only in response to my traits or possessions considered in themselves. I can also feel pride through detecting the positive regard that others show towards me.

Some important groundwork for the *Treatise*'s sentimentalism is laid in T 2.3.3, 'Of the influencing motives of the will.' This brilliantly compact statement lays out the picture that Hume targets for demolition:

> Nothing is more usual in philosophy, and even in common life, than to talk of the combat of passion and reason, to give the preference to reason, and to assert that men are only so far virtuous as they conform themselves to its dictates.
>
> (T 2.3.3.1; SBN 413)

In this deeply entrenched view, humans are essentially rational beings, and passions are disruptive forces that take possession of one, so that any resulting behavior is not so much *acting* as *being acted on* by them. In this rationalist picture, reason and passion are inevitably at odds, and virtuous action emerges when reason is victorious. Hume denies the underlying assumption that both reason and passion are individually capable of initiating behavior, arguing that while reason and passion play necessary and complementary roles, passion holds all the executive power, with reason operating in a merely advisory capacity. In that sense, "Reason is, and ought only to be the slave of the passions" (T 2.3.3.4; SBN 415).

While action requires input from both reason and passion, Hume gives the latter a structural priority in setting ends rather than means. Given this division of labor, the two cannot be at odds with each other. Reason cannot initiate action, as this requires seeing the prospective action in terms of some pleasure or pain – something we want to acquire or to avoid. It follows that any inquiry, from the most mundane to the most rarified, is partly grounded in passion, since inquiring is a doing, and all action is responsive to pain or pleasure.[4]

Here I should stress that Hume's psychological explanations are always on the level of the perceptions themselves, and the mechanisms operating on them. So, for example, to say that *reason* cannot initiate action is to say that no *ideas* have that motivating power. Likewise, talk of *passion* causing actions really refers to the work of secondary impressions.

Hume holds that the role of the understanding, reason, is restricted to making inferences among 'relations of ideas' or 'matters of fact.' That is, it can discover truths, either through demonstrative proofs or causal inferences grounded in observation. But, he insists, none of this can make us *do* anything. Relations of ideas affect action only through assisting deliberation about causal relations. This, in turn, will only make us act when the situation *matters to us* by being related to some pain or pleasure. For example, reason can determine the precise nature of means–ends relationships, such as the consequences of some proposed action, the probability of such an outcome, or the best ways of bringing it about. But then reason is working on behalf of the goal-setting passions. So when he says that reason "can never oppose passion in the direction of the will" (T 2.3.3.1; SBN 413), he does not mean that reason cannot advise passion against some action – indeed, that is precisely what reason *can* do. Reason can influence action only indirectly, through assisting a desire.

Hume concedes the *prima facie* plausibility of the rationalist view of the 'combat of passion and reason,' but reinterprets it within a more convincing psychology. The *calmness* of certain passions causes them to be mistaken for ideas, which share this relative lack of vivacity. Calm passions are often embedded in character traits, rendered invisible to consciousness by their constant presence.[5] Their stable role in our mental economy allows them to overrule the clamor of our violent passions. So, rather than between passion and reason, the real motivational conflict takes place between passions – particularly between forceful demands directed to immediate stimuli, and cooler desires regarding what to do, all things considered. The role of reason in this struggle is to undermine the appeal of the immediate craving, and promote the calm passions.

Anti-rationalism

We now have the context with which to consider Hume's sentimentalism, which I will introduce by showing how it emerges from his critique of the moral rationalism of Samuel Clarke, William Wollaston, and John Locke.[6] Hume frames the central issue in terms of ideas (the province of the understanding) and impressions by asking "*Whether 'tis by means of our ideas or impressions we distinguish betwixt vice and virtue, and pronounce an action blameable or praise-worthy?*" (T 3.1.1.3; SBN 456). Rationalism held that the understanding could identify an action as morally required or forbidden and cause one to act on that knowledge. Suppose I see you fall off your bicycle, and come to your aid. A rationalist might say that I act from my general, standing belief that *one ought to help those in need*, and seeing that *you need help*.

Hume, by contrast, holds that moral distinctions are primarily the product of our sentiments, with the understanding only working in their service. As in T 2.3.3, he grants that the rationalist position has some initial credence. It seems that we can observe the wrongness of a cruel act, for example. Likewise, it seems obvious that we can do the right thing because it is right. Surely we have all experienced the struggle between what we know we *ought* to do, and what we *want* to do, and even to have succeeded in doing the former. But, Hume insists, this account cannot withstand scrutiny. Recall that he established that merely *recognizing* that some situation held could not induce one to *act* on it. Rather, the condition had to matter, through having some implications for pain or pleasure. That is, relations among ideas only influence action when they relate to matters of fact, which only motivate when some passion is invoked. Passions, as pains or pleasures, are intrinsically motivational. This earlier argument was utterly general: if mere reason cannot cause *any* action, then it cannot produce *moral* action.

Hume's application of his motivational arguments to morality is stated with admirable brevity: "Morals excite passions, and produce or prevent actions. Reason of itself is utterly impotent in this particular. The rules of morality, therefore, are not conclusions of our reason" (T 3.1.1.6; SBN 457). The first sentence states that moral considerations motivate because they cause passions that, being pleasures or pains, are intrinsically motivational. The second sentence affirms his earlier thesis that the resources of the understanding cannot, by themselves, provide motivation to act. The conclusion follows that something other than reason is involved in grasping, and acting on, moral distinctions or judgments.

Hume had already established that the role of the understanding is restricted to comparing ideas or discovering facts.[7] Hence, if the discovery of moral distinctions was the work of reason, "the character of virtuous or vicious must either lie in some relations of objects, or must be a matter of fact, which is discovered by our reasoning" (T 3.1.1.18; SBN 463). Hume gives a set of powerful arguments that neither option holds. I will discuss Hume's criticisms of the two rationalist lines of argument in turn.

If moral distinctions were discoverable *a priori*, then they would have to concern *relations of ideas:* resemblance, contrariety, degrees of quality, and proportions in quantity and number. To show that an action is wrong, the vice would have to be derived from some such relation ascribable to that action. But a fatal problem with such a proposal is that it cannot restrict the attribution of moral properties to *persons*, since these relations, being formal, would apply in any case in which the relation held. Absurdity beckons, as "inanimate objects may bear to each other all the same relations which we observe in moral agents; though the former can never be the object of love or hatred, nor are consequently susceptible of merit or iniquity" (EPM App.1.17; SBN 293). Hume has fun at the rationalists' expense here, giving analogues to incest and patricide in the vegetative realm: "A young tree, which over-tops and destroys its parent, stands in all the same relations with NERO, when he murdered AGRIPPINA; and if morality consisted merely in relations, would, no doubt, be equally criminal" (EPM App.1.17; SBN 293).

Of course, a rationalist would not surrender so easily, stressing the crucial difference that only we can *apprehend* that an action is immoral. But Hume has a ready reply, that the rationalist has moved away from the original claim that the wrongness was grounded in the relation being instantiated. To say that an elk or an aubergine is blameless because it lacks the intellectual wherewithal to *recognize* wrongness is to grant that the wrongness is already there, prior to any identification of it. Furthermore, even if Hume has failed to give a complete inventory of 'relations of ideas,' any new relation would require an improbable combination of features: to be only applicable to humans, and such that apprehending it would necessarily motivate one to act on it.

The second rationalist option is to derive moral distinctions from matters of fact. Hume notes that such a move equates blameworthiness with factual error, to which he makes the decisive objection that not all errors are immoral. The diner who mistakes a habanero pepper for fruit is an object of amusement or pity, not blame. A second criticism, again as easy as effective, is that the distinction between truth and falsity is strict and binary, whereas moral properties can hold to varying degrees. Some acts are much more blameworthy than others. So rationalism wrongly makes all wrong actions equally wrong.

Hume notes that while the rationalist may reply that immorality is not based on just any error, but in 'mistakes about *right*,' such a move would be question begging. To mistake something as right is to assume the existence of some right-making properties, that were erroneously ascribed in that case, so that "'tis impossible that such a mistake can ever be the original source of immorality" (T 3.1.1.14; SBN 460).

Hume argues that moral distinctions are not grounded in factual matters of the kind that reason can detect on its own. He makes his point in this famous passage:

> Take any instance allow'd to be vicious: Wilful murder, for instance. Examine it in all lights, and see if you can find that matter of fact, or real existence, which you call *vice*. In which-ever way you take it, you find only certain passions, motives, volitions and thoughts. There is no other matter of fact in the case. The vice entirely escapes you, as

long as you consider the object. You never can find it, till you turn your reflexion into your own breast, and find a sentiment of disapprobation, which arises in you, towards this action. Here is a matter of fact; but 'tis the object of feeling, not of reason. So when you pronounce any action or character to be vicious, you mean nothing, but that from the constitution of your nature you have a feeling or sentiment of blame from the contemplation of it. Vice and virtue, therefore, may be compar'd to sounds, colours, heat and cold, which, according to modern philosophy, are not qualities in objects, but perceptions in the mind.

(T 3.1.1.26; SBN 468)

Hume does not deny a factual basis for moral distinctions, but only that the understanding can detect such a base. We *do* detect wrong-making features, but only because our engagement with the world involves passion as well as understanding. Hume knows that on witnessing a murder, I would take it to be gravely wrong. But this passage presents a thought experiment in which I consider murder using all and only the resources of reason. In *that* case, the vice would escape me. But this does not mean that morality is not grounded in matters of fact – he explicitly says "here is a matter of fact" – but that some of these facts are detected by our sympathetically transmitted feelings. I will return to these matters later on.

The passage ends with an analogy between virtues and vices and secondary qualities. Locke regarded these as powers within objects to cause sensations in us, where these 'ideas' did not resemble the qualities themselves. So Locke distinguishes the qualities from the ideas, or, in Hume's terms, the sensory impressions they cause. Berkeley, on the other hand, took secondary qualities to be 'in the mind,' and Hume appears to be agreeing in this passage. On the other hand, an analogy with the Lockean position fits better with Hume's view that vices and virtues are character traits possessed by persons, recognition of which produces passions in us that can be transformed into moral sentiments.[8]

Moral sentiments and judgments

Having shown that moral distinctions cannot be derived from reason, Hume concludes by elimination that they are revealed "by means of some impression or sentiment they occasion," and that morality "is more properly felt than judg'd of" (T 3.1.2.1; SBN 470). Hume is often classified with Shaftesbury and Francis Hutcheson as a *moral sense theorist*. Indeed, naming a *Treatise* chapter "Moral distinctions derived from a moral sense" (T 3.1.2) would seem to settle the matter. However, while there are some points of resemblance between Hume and these earlier philosophers, there are some importance differences.[9]

Recall Hume's question: "*Whether 'tis by means of our* ideas *or* impressions *we distinguish betwixt vice and virtue, and pronounce an action blameable or praiseworthy?*" (T 3.1.1.3; SBN 456). Moral sense theorists take the latter option, holding moral judgments to be secondary impressions, sentiments produced in response to traits of character. Hutcheson proposes a sense through which we detect virtue or vice by seeing behavior as expressing certain motives. This moral sense is innate and operates involuntarily. Just as the sense of vision automatically causes sensations of redness when we see a ripe tomato, so a feeling of approbation is generated on taking actions as signs of *benevolence*, the disinterested concern for another's well-being. Hutcheson takes benevolence as intrinsically good, and regards our approval of it as basic, with no deeper explanation possible or needed, except to say that our capacity to reliably detect and approve of it is a sign of God's benevolence.

While Hume agrees that we regularly feel a distinctive kind of pleasure and pain in response to certain character traits, for him a 'moral sense' consists in this ability to sense virtue or vice.

That is, this capacity is not *explained* in terms of some faculty of 'moral sense.' Rather, the 'moral sense' is a *description* of the capacity, where all the explanatory work takes place on the level of the perceptions themselves, and the associative mechanisms governing them.

His rejection of a Hutchesonian moral sense rests, in part, on giving virtue a far more diverse base than Hutcheson allows, with several grounds of moral approval that are irreducible to benevolence. Hence, one same domain-specific sense would not detect virtue in all its diversity. On the other hand, positing a set of specialized senses, corresponding to each source of virtue, would be unparsimonious. Hume's solution is to reject any faculty of sense, while giving a unified account of our moral responses based on sympathy. The pleasantness or usefulness of a trait explains our approval of it, which attunes us to the effect of the trait on its bearer or others affected by it.

As I will describe shortly, moral sentiments are refined responses to character traits. The virtues are the traits that elicit moral approval, whereas the vices cause disapproval.[10] So Hume must identify these virtues and vices, and provide a sound taxonomy for them. His most extensive treatment of this matter is in the 2nd *Enquiry*.[11] Rather than derive the virtues and vices from the *Treatise*'s psychological system, he relies on introspection, observations of common life, historical examples, and moral vocabulary. All languages, he claims, contain expressions that denote admirable traits, and others that involve a negative evaluation. Furthermore, anyone competent in the use of these words distinguishes them from terms expressing mere personal preference:

> When someone bestows on any man the epithets of *vicious* or *odious* or *depraved*, he then speaks another language, and expresses sentiments, in which he expects all his audience are to concur with him. He must here, therefore, depart from his private and particular situation, and must choose a point of view, common to him with others.
>
> (EPM 9.6; SBN 272)

These methods reveal four bases of moral approval: "Personal Merit consists altogether in the possession of mental qualities, *useful* or *agreeable* to the *person himself* or to *others*" (EPM 9.1; SBN 268). A virtue is intrinsically pleasing or useful, either to oneself or others. Of these four kinds, the most important is *social utility*, traits that benefit society as a whole.

The *Treatise* lists the socially useful virtues as including "meekness, beneficence, charity, generosity, clemency, moderation, equity" (T 3.3.1.11; SBN 578), to which the 2nd *Enquiry* adds "fidelity, justice, veracity, integrity" (EPM 3.48; SBN 204). The virtues useful to oneself include "*prudence, temperance, frugality, industry, assiduity, enterprize, dexterity, . . . generosity* and *humanity*" (T 3.3.1.24; SBN 587). Whereas wit, eloquence, ingenuity, decency, and decorum are pleasant to behold in others, a person enjoys her own serenity, cheerfulness, and contentment. As this partial list indicates, Hume makes no distinction between character traits, on the one hand, and talents or pleasing attributes that one has acquired. Such a division, in his opinion, assumes a false account of the will and voluntary action.

One notable difference in Hume's presentations of the virtues in the *Treatise* and the 2nd *Enquiry* is that the later book does not employ the *Treatise*'s distinction between natural and artificial virtues, where the former are traits we naturally approve of, and the latter require a social convention in order to emerge and be approved of. I see this as a difference in presentation rather than of substance, resulting from the 2nd *Enquiry*'s more informal manner, in contrast to the *Treatise*'s complex architectonic system.

In developing his sentimentalism, Hume realized the need to confront the influential view that our actions are all rooted in 'self-love,' and that the distinction between morality and self-interest is a social conditioned illusion, so that all *benevolence* is mere hypocrisy, friendship a cheat, public spirit a farce, fidelity a snare to procure trust and confidence; and that while all of us, at bottom, pursue only our private interest, we wear these fair disguises, in order to put others off their guard, and expose them the more to our wiles and machinations.

(EPM App. 2.1; SBN 295)

Egoism claims that we are naturally self-centered, and that the ultimate ground of our conformity to moral codes is recognizing the long-term benefit of curbing our short-term desires when others reciprocate. For example, Bernard Mandeville argued that all of morality was rooted in 'education,' i.e. social conditioning, where 'politicians,' i.e. experts in manipulating public opinion, grasp our inability to admit our selfish nature to ourselves and see that we must be tricked into promoting the common good by being taught that suppressing our selfish desires is a sign of moral superiority.

Hume's objections to egoism are of a very different character to those aimed at rationalists, where his arguments are intended to show that rationalism is fundamentally flawed, so that it *cannot* be correct. By contrast, his critique of egoism is empirical, in that it fits the facts far less well than his own theory. In reducing all motivation to a single factor, egoists fail to do justice to the complexity of moral phenomena. As we have seen, he made a similar criticism of Hutcheson's exclusive reliance on benevolence. It is evident to Hume that we are significantly motivated by self-interest, but also by the good of others, albeit in a limited and partial manner. Adopting the moral stance involves not only expanding our natural circle of concern, but also decentering the realm, as we move towards a more impersonal perspective.

Hume takes his sympathy-based theory to have far more explanatory power than egoism, and gives numerous examples of acts that egoism strains to accommodate. For example, we can morally approve of attitudes or behavior that have no clear causal relation to ourselves or our interests, such as remote historical events. While Hume can admit a place for 'education,' he grounds it not in a Mandevillean conspiracy theory, but in sympathy. Without the sympathetically grounded capacity to detect and respond to morally salient considerations, such 'education' would not take hold. Furthermore, even when we morally approve of something that happens to benefit us, we easily distinguish the two species of pleasure that we feel. But, he says, the egoist would be unable to grasp moral concepts in the first place.

Had nature made no such distinction, founded on the original constitution of the mind, the words, *honourable* and *shameful, lovely* and *odious, noble* and *despicable*, had never taken place in any language; nor could politicians, had they invented these terms, ever have been able to render them intelligible, or make them convey any idea to the audience.

(EPM 5.3; SBN 214)

Hume's own positive view of moral judgment involves the assessment, from a "steady and general point of view" (T 3.3.1.15; SBN 581) of character traits that we approve of because of their pleasantness or usefulness, or that prompt disapproval due to their unpleasantness, uselessness or harmfulness.[12] In the process of reaching this moral stance, our sympathetically induced reactions undergo a multi-faceted process of correction, which may involve the deployment of imagination, reason, or reframing the situation in distinctively moral vocabulary.

The moral sentiments of approbation and disapprobation are the analogues, from the general point of view, of the indirect passions of pride and humility, love and hatred. One difference emerges when we recall Hume's distinction between *cause* and *object*. The *cause* of an indirect passion is some feature relating to a person, and its *object* is that individual. However, the object of a *moral* sentiment is a character trait type rather than an instance of it. I may be caused to hate someone on account of his cruelty, but I morally condemn *cruelty*, not just *his* cruelty. "'Tis only when a character is considered in general, without reference to our particular interest, that causes such a feeling or sentiment, as denominates it morally good or evil" (T 3.1.2.4; SBN 472). If I feel irritation towards a student texting during class, my response is not yet moral, as it is too much about me. I need to abstract away from the individuals involved to get at the general structure of the situation. If I manage to transform my feeling into a moral response, its object becomes not *this student's* disrespect towards *me*, but the character trait that produces ill-mannered behavior.

As with all passions, Hume distinguishes the moral sentiments from other impressions in two ways. First is his 'official' criterion based on phenomenal 'feel.' Second, he notes that the moral sentiments have a unique causal profile within the mind, namely the process of refining the verdicts of sympathy, as we enter into the general point of view. I will now go into this in a little more detail.

As discussed above, the natural operation of sympathy is partial, in that its force depends on one's degree of identification with another person, whereas moral sentiments and judgments are essentially impartial. So sympathy is both a bridge to the moral perspective and also a barrier to it. Hume recognized that coming to the moral viewpoint involves amending the verdicts of sympathy, and showed how reason can contribute to this process by revealing inconsistencies between our goals, or by drawing inferences about the likely outcomes of actions, and their prospects of fulfilling our ends. For example, reason, alongside imagination, can reveal the potentially disastrous consequences of directly drawing judgments about someone's character from our emotional reactions. One means of correcting our initial responses is to imagine what we *would* feel, were we in various other positions relative to the person in question. I may not initially be moved on reading about some far-off tyrant, but when I imagine what it would be like to have to deal with such a person, I sympathize with the plight of the victims and am brought to a more reliable assessment of the tyrant's character. By these techniques, we enter into the general point of view, which we can potentially share with everyone, in that anyone applying these methods will converge in their assessments of character.

With all this in mind, we can revisit the famous 'wilful murder' case (T 3.1.1.26; SBN 468), and see that Hume's motive in employing it is primarily negative, attacking one strain of rationalism. It does not bring out the complexity of Hume's positive theory, as the moral judgment would be immediate in such an extreme case. No adjustment would be required.

So, to sum up, there are two main aspects of attaining the general point of view. One is to distance myself from my immediate partial sympathetic responses. The other is to sympathetically enter into the perspective of those directly affected by the person whose acts and attitudes are being assessed.

These considerations reveal the ways in which Hume thinks that our judgments about someone's character can be erroneous. One way is when we mistake indirect passions for moral judgments. For example, you might fail to sufficiently compensate for personal involvement, and the partiality of sympathy. So, in my example above, I may mistake my annoyance with the texting student for a fully moral response. Here it is not that a moral judgment is mistaken, but that you never make the transition from indirect passion to moral judgment, and do not realize this fact. This failure of recognition would be the fault of reason, whose job it is to eliminate such distorting factors, and determine the extent to which the 'general point of view' is achieved. However, this is not to say that the moral viewpoint is infallible. It is not the God's-eye view, but a human perspective that we can actually inhabit or at least approximate.

Hume compares our adoption of the moral viewpoint to the way in which we can distinguish an object's 'real' shape from the way it appears to us. A little care should be taken here, as this comparison should not be drawn with the constant recalibration of our visual representations as we negotiate our environment, since this process is utterly automatic. Rather, the analogy is stronger for the special case when I suspect that appearances may be deceptive, and so actively figure out how things would look from a number of perspectives. In that way, I step back from my actual position, which may be epistemically sub-optimal, and construct a more satisfactory picture through synthesizing perceptions from a set of hypothetical viewing positions.

In a similar manner, then, coming to a moral judgment requires stepping back from our own involvement, and our automatic reactions, and making a determination about someone's character that is sensitive to how one might perceive it under a variety of conditions. Our initial judgment is not excluded from this process, but neither does it have any presumed authority. Rather, it is one source of information among others, engaged in the mutual correction of reflective equilibrium, as we move towards the general viewpoint.

This use of imaginative counterfactuals to revise our reactive judgments is illustrated in cases of 'virtue in rags' (T 3.3.1.19; SBN 584). If moral judgments were equated with the automatic deliverances of sympathy, they would be restricted to cases where the moral sentiments were actually generated. However, we can approve of those who cannot exercise their virtues due to circumstances beyond their control. In such cases, we adjust the variables in thought, keeping the person's character constant while eliminating the disruptive circumstances. We sympathetically grasp what one would feel when encountering her under these imagined conditions, which generates moral approbation.

In describing moral judgments in terms of the general point of view, Hume conveys that while our emotional responses can greatly diverge, given our various interests and situations, our positions converge as these reactions are replaced by calm passions. While our selfish interests often conflict, each person's occupancy of the general viewpoint tends to be in harmony with that of any other. So, within a society, our combined moral sentiments have greater power than all the self-interest of individuals.

We can now return to the issue as to whether Hume takes moral judgments to be factual and truth-apt. Since a virtue is "whatever mental action or quality gives to the spectator the pleasing sentiment of approbation" (EPM App.1.10; SBN 289), is it not a straightforwardly factual matter as to whether someone possesses these traits? Hume would grant that systematic observation would reveal a strong correlation between traits we regard as virtuous and their capacity to produce a distinctive kind of pleasure in those who encounter them, whereas consideration of traits deemed vicious causes an unpleasant experience. However, he would add that this knowledge does not yet constitute a moral judgment, since these have motivating power that is lacking in facts of the kind accessible to the understanding. Hence a sentimental input is also required.

We must also recall that Hume denies passions any representational function, so they cannot be true or false. But, while disapproving of a cruel act is not truth-apt, the accompanying thought 'That is a cruel act' can be a true judgment about a matter of fact. So Hume should grant that moral judgments are true or false. A claim that someone is cruel is made true by that person having a settled tendency to maliciously harm others, a trait that causes moral disapprobation when considered from the general point of view.

Now that we have set out the main points of Hume's moral sentimentalism, we can show his reinterpretation of what I might call 'rationalism's Exhibit A,' the notion of *acting from duty*.[13] Rationalists hold that to recognize some action as morally right, and hence that we have a duty to perform it, can cause us to do it. Hume denies this, arguing that "*no action can be virtuous, or morally good, unless there be in human nature some motive to produce it, distinct from the sense of its* morality" (T 3.2.1.7; SBN 479). So, since moral rightness is always grounded in some non-moral features, no one does something merely because it is good, without reference to these underlying factors. As before, Hume will argue that our sense of duty, moral obligation, is rooted in the passions. Furthermore, rather than taking 'acting from duty' as the central and paradigm moral phenomenon, Hume regards it as a derivative matter.

Suppose that a man notices that he lacks some virtue, and wants to acquire it. He can deliberately act as that virtue would demand, in order to establish a habit of acting in such a manner, and thereby acquire the virtue. Hume considers a neglectful father, who recognizes that he has no natural concern for his children, and no direct motive to address their needs. However, he knows that this absence of paternal love is widely abhorred. By sympathetically seeing himself through the disapproving eyes of others, he feels ashamed, which makes him want to acquire parental feeling. This higher-order desire leads him to act in accordance with what his obligations require, that is, as someone with natural parental sentiments would do, so that this behavior eventually becomes second nature. In this way, the sense of duty emerges from self-hatred, the shame-fueled condemnation of one's lack of naturally benevolent tendencies. So Hume's account is a reversal of Kant's (1785) famous example of one whose empathetic and generous nature causes him to help those in need. Kant notoriously held that this person's actions only attain moral worth once his natural affections are blocked through depression or self-pity, but he continues to assist others from duty alone. By contrast, Hume's man does what duty would recommend, in order to eventually respond naturally, from a benevolent passion. Only then, Hume would say, does his action have true moral worth.

Finally, Hume confronts the question of how such a plausible and pleasing theory as his own has escaped the notice of so many people. His answer presents him at his most mischievous, turning the tables on the austere Presbyterianism of the day. These Calvinists held that Original Sin, and the subsequent fallen world, brought about the intellectual and emotional corruption that prevents us from grasping the true nature of reality, including ourselves. On the contrary, Hume suggests that adherence to the 'monkish virtues,' whether Calvinist or Catholic, perverts the mind and heart so that a more accurate study of human nature is rejected. Religion is a cause of our corruption.

Hume's sentimentalism is an important contribution to moral psychology. It made devastating criticisms of the moral rationalism of its day. It gave a more accurate account of the sources of moral motivation than egoism offered. It sets the agenda for much contemporary work in philosophy and psychology.[14]

Notes

1 The '1st *Enquiry*' being *An Enquiry Concerning Human Understanding* (EHU).
2 For a groundbreaking treatment of the passions, and their place in Hume's moral philosophy, see Ardal (1966).
3 Vitz (2016) gives a detailed account of the roles of sympathy in Hume's theory.
4 For Hume's theory of motivation, see Radcliffe (1999). For an influential statement of the contemporary 'Humean' theory, see Smith (1994).
5 See Radcliffe (2015).
6 For an excellent account of the key debates in moral theory in seventeenth- and eighteenth-century Britain, see Gill (2011).
7 This distinction is most succinctly described in EHU 4.1–2; SBN 25.
8 For a clear discussion of contemporary developments of the analogy between moral and sensory qualities, see McNaughton (1988: chs. 4 & 5).
9 See Harris (2015: chs. 1 & 2); also Gill (2011).
10 For a recent discussion of Hume as a virtue ethicist, see Swanton (2015: Part II).

11 See Taylor (2009).
12 See Sayre-McCord (1994) and Cohon (2008, ch. 5).
13 See Cohon (2008: ch. 6).
14 For a survey of some of this work, see Antti Kauppinen, 2014, "Moral Sentimentalism," *Stanford Encyclopedia of Philosophy*.

References

Ardal, P. (1989 [1966]) *Passion and Value in Hume's Treatise*, Edinburgh: Edinburgh University Press.

Cohon, R. (2008) *Hume's Morality: Feeling and Fabrication*, New York: Oxford University Press.

Gill, M. (2011) *The British Moralists on Human Nature and the Birth of Secular Ethics*, Cambridge: Cambridge University Press.

Harris, J. (2015) *Hume: An Intellectual Biography*, Cambridge: Cambridge University Press.

Kant, I. (2002 [1785]) *Groundwork of the Metaphysics of Morals*, trans. M. Gregor and J. Timmermann, Cambridge: Cambridge University Press.

Kauppinen, A. (2014) "Moral Sentimentalism," *Stanford Encyclopedia of Philosophy*. https://plato.stanford.edu/entries/moral-sentimentalism/

McNaughton, D. (1988) *Moral Vision*, Oxford: Wiley-Blackwell.

Radcliffe, E. (1999) "Hume on the Generation of Motives: Why Beliefs Alone Never Motivate," *Hume Studies* 25: 101–122.

———. (2015) "Strength of Mind and the Calm and Violent Passions," *Res Philosophica* 92(3): 1–21.

Sayre-McCord, G. (1994) "On Why Hume's General Point of View isn't Ideal – and Shouldn't Be," *Social Policy and Philosophy* 11: 202–228.

Smith, M. (1994) *The Moral Problem*, Oxford: Wiley-Blackwell.

Swanton, C. (2015) *The Virtue Ethics of Hume and Nietzsche*. Chichester, West Sussex; Malden, MA: Wiley/Blackwell.

Taylor, J. (2009) "Hume's Later Moral Philosophy," in D. Fate Norton and J. Taylor (eds.), *The Cambridge Companion to Hume*, 2nd edn, Cambridge: Cambridge University Press.

Vitz, R. (2016) "The Nature and Functions of Sympathy in Hume's Philosophy," in P. Russell (ed.), *The Oxford Handbook of Hume*, New York: Oxford University Press.

19

JUSTICE AND CONVENTION IN HUME'S PHILOSOPHY

Eléonore Le Jallé

Hume begins his enquiry into justice by asking explicit questions about its nature and sources. *Is justice a natural or an artificial virtue? In what sense are the rules of justice artificial, and in what sense can they be called natural? For which motives is it instituted? What is the source of its approbation?* Those questions and the answers which Hume gives them are at the core of the present chapter. But Hume's conception of justice and convention also answers other questions that he did not ask explicitly. These include: is there an antecedent and independent criterion of justice? What would be the best system of property distribution, and what should be its foundation: equality, merit, need, or another criterion? Is it rational to be just? He also ignored other questions that have come to been seen as central to the topic, such as the fairness of the rules of justice themselves (or their system) (Rawls 2000: 64–65; Harrison 1981: 42).

As Hume's conception of justice is intertwined with his views on convention, property, and social order, I shall examine how he linked them, thus showing that justice and property appear together, how their introduction enables the maintenance of social order in certain conditions without the invention of government, and how the adoption of each fundamental rule of justice involves a convention but not a promise. While explaining Hume's arguments on such matters, I shall also illuminate them using the formulations of some contemporary philosophers, e.g. Brian Barry's idea of "justice as mutual advantage" (Barry 1989) and David Lewis' definition of convention, for which Hume's definition served as a model (Lewis 2002).

Justice as an artificial or conventional virtue

The main contents of Hume's theory of justice are set out in the second part of the third book of *A Treatise of Human Nature*. Hume's enquiry about justice is twofold, first about the origin of the institution of justice (from which motives and circumstances does it come?), and second about the source of its moral approbation ("*Why we annex the idea of virtue to justice, and of vice to injustice?*" [T 3.2.2.23; SBN 498]). This twofold question is itself based on a previous result that the virtue of justice is not natural: since no "original motive" moves us to behave justly, one must admit that "*that those impressions, which give rise to this sense of justice, are not natural to the mind of man, but arise from artifice and human conventions*" (T 3.2.2.21; SBN 496).

In order to establish that "the sense of justice and injustice is not deriv'd from nature" (T 3.2.1.17; SBN 483), Hume claims to rely on the following "short" and decisive argument: a just action must come from a virtuous motive, necessarily distinct from "a regard to the [justice or] honesty of the action" (T 3.2.1.9; SBN 480); but men "have naturally no real or universal motive for observing the laws of equity" (T 3.2.1.17; SBN 483).

The first part of this reasoning is simply proved by excluding circular reasoning: "A virtuous motive is requisite to render an action virtuous. An action must be virtuous, before we can have a regard to its virtue. Some virtuous motive, therefore, must be antecedent to that regard" (T 3.2.1.4; SBN 478). Hume does not deny that a regard to the honesty of an action (i.e. a sense of its "morality") may induce someone to behave justly. Thus, her "sense of duty" can make a person repay her loan or abstain from the property of others. However, Hume warns, such a consideration of duty only concerns man "in his civiliz'd state, and when train'd up according to a certain discipline and education" (T 3.2.1.9; SBN 479). Hume introduces for justice a distinction between man "in his civiliz'd state," and man "in his rude and more *natural* condition" (ibid.).

Hume does not mean by the latter phrase "the suppos'd *state of nature*," which in his eyes "never had, and never cou'd have any reality" and is "a mere philosophical fiction" (T 3.2.2.14; SBN 493). By evoking the "rude condition" of men, Hume in fact refers to their "natural uncultivated ideas of morality." But, as Hume explains, those uncultivated ideas conform themselves to our common affections. Thus, they incline us to treat others *unequally*, according to the "*unequal* affection" which we feel for them: one owes kindred the most attention and favor, whereas strangers are owed much less attention, especially in cases where there is an "opposition of interest" (T 3.2.2.8; SBN 488; cf. T 3.2.1.18; SBN 483–484). Therefore, our uncultivated ideas of morality would induce us to repay a loan, or procure an estate to his rightful possessor, only in *some* circumstances, and never *inflexibly*. Justice, whose laws are "universal and perfectly inflexible," cannot come from such a flexible source (T 3.2.6.9; SBN 532). Thus, thanks to a distinction among our ideas of morality, between those uncultivated, original, or "common," and those which follow a certain "discipline," Hume succeeds in showing that the sense of justice is not instinctive. A regard to the honesty of an action can certainly be a motive when justice has already been instituted. But, for justice to be considered as natural, a natural inclination must lead us to it directly and inflexibly.

However – and this is the second step of Hume's argument – human nature does not offer such an inclination. To begin with, self-interest cannot immediately be "the legitimate motive to all honest actions." Indeed, when one observes its "*natural* movements" – and not its corrected and more "reflected" movements which are indeed, as we shall see, the source of the institution of justice and its interested obligation – one realizes that this motive is so far from drawing men to honesty, that it is indeed "the source of all injustice and violence" (T 3.2.1.10; SBN 480). Other motives have the appropriate direction but their *reality, universality,* or *inflexibility* are dubious. Thus "the *regard to public interest*" is a motive "too remote and too sublime to affect the generality of mankind" (T 3.2.1.11; SBN 480). Besides, as Hume affirms, each application of justice does not directly serve public interest: justice fosters it in a more *indirect* way. The "love of mankind" is rejected because man never loves mankind as such, without a "cause" or "relation" linking persons (T 3.2.1.12; SBN 481–482, cf. T 2.2.1.4; SBN 330). To end with, "*private benevolence, or a regard to the interests of the party concern'd*" gives rise to honest but *intermittent* actions. To take the example of the loan again, my motive to repay it would be suspended whenever the interests of the creditor do not seem to me to demand this payment.

Having shown that "we have naturally no real or universal motive for observing the laws of equity, but the very equity and merit of that observance," and that the sense of duty is not an original motive, but only a secondary one, one must admit that "the sense of justice and injustice is not deriv'd from nature, but arises [. . .] from education, and human conventions" (T 3.2.1.17; SBN 483).

Now the result that the sense of justice comes from a human artifice calls for the two questions which govern Hume's enquiry about justice. Indeed, it implies that it is first necessary to discover the "nature" and "origin" of the artificial rules of justice, before asking why a sense of virtue and vice is annexed to justice and injustice. Those questions are in fact interlocked. Notably, Hume, in the third section of *An Enquiry Concerning the Principles of Morals* dealing with justice, does not examine those two questions separately. This is because the "utility" of justice, i.e. its interest for men, turns out to be at the same time the *reason* why justice is *instituted* and the *quality* of it which is morally *approved*. Thus, thanks to his twofold approach, Hume's theory of justice succeeds in explaining an essential characteristic of justice: the fact that it is both an institution and a virtue, a fact which Hume captured by his qualification of justice as an "artificial virtue."

Three clarifications must be given about this artificiality of the virtue of justice. First, even though Hume thinks that "our sense" of the virtue of justice appears "by means of an artifice or contrivance" (T 3.2.1.1; SBN 477), he does not think that the sentiment by which we approve justice – a particular kind of pleasure – is (or can be) artificially produced. Indeed, for Hume approving an action or a character is feeling a particular pleasure, whereas disapproving them is feeling a particular kind of pain: only such "feelings or sentiments" make us "denominate" a character as virtuous or vicious (T 3.1.2.4; SBN 472). But Hume also maintains that "we can naturally no more change our own sentiments, than the motions of the heavens" (T 3.2.5.4; SBN 517). New sentiments cannot be created at will. Consequently, no artifice or contrivance can produce such a pleasure and moral approbation alone, so that the artificiality of the justice is compatible, in Hume's mind, with the naturality of its approbation, once it is instituted.

Second, Hume does not even exclude the possibility that justice can be, in a sense, qualified as natural. Indeed, once we leave the opposition between natural and artificial but rather use the opposite meanings of "natural" and "rare and unusual," we realize that justice is an invention so "necessary" to mankind and "inseparable" from it (T 3.1.2.9; SBN 474), that no virtue is more natural in that sense than justice, and that its rules can also be properly denominated "laws of nature" (T 3.2.1.19; SBN 484). In this sense, the extension of the "first rudiments of justice" within the family, to its general rules in the entire society, can also be viewed as a *natural* progression, i.e. a *necessary* and *non-accidental* one (T 3.2.2.14; SBN 493).

Third, though justice is not, in the above sense, less natural than other virtues, Hume nevertheless insists that man is *not directly* induced to it, inasmuch as the positive influence of justice is *not direct* either. Thus, men behave honestly only with "reference" to the actions of others, from whom they expect a fair behavior in return (T 3.2.2.10; SBN 490); whereas, by contrast, men act benevolently by a direct impulse, without asking "whether any other person in the universe were ever before actuated by such noble motives, or will ever afterwards prove their influence" (EPM App. 3.2; SBN 303). Besides, the virtue of justice is not adopted because of its immediate utility – an isolated application of justice can be disadvantageous to individuals or the public – but thanks to its global (systematic) utility. By contrast again, "every particular act of generosity [...] is beneficial to a particular person" (T 3.3.1.13; SBN 580). A twofold *obliquity* thus characterizes justice: it is neither directly adopted nor directly beneficial. Thus, the specificity of justice compared to other virtues is due less to the conjunction of the passions and reflection which it requires (a conjunction which is indeed as natural as those two elements), than to the fact that each person acts honestly only because, having observed "like passions and reflections" in others, *he expects the same behaviour from them* (EPM App. 3.9; SBN 307). Justice is then a reciprocal and *conventional* virtue, if one adopts Hume's meaning of *convention*: "*a sense of interest, suppos'd to be common to all, and where every single act is perform'd in expectation that others are to perform the like*" (T 3.2.2.22; SBN 498, my emphasis).

The "circumstances" of justice

Looking for the origin of justice, Hume shows that the rationale of this virtue is to be found in certain "circumstances," which are both subjective and objective (to quote John Rawls), i.e. in Hume's terms, due to human nature and to the "external objects" which men need and covet. One can name those circumstances, after Rawls, the "circumstances *of justice*," for "unless these circumstances existed there would be no occasion for the virtue of justice" (Rawls 1999: 110). Hume refers to those circumstances when he reveals the true origin of justice: "'*tis only from the selfishness and confin'd generosity of men, along with the scanty provision nature has made for his wants, that justice derives its origin*" (T 3.2.2.18; SBN 495). In a longer but more precise formulation, Hume enumerates four circumstances at the source of justice and explains that they are to be viewed as "inconveniences" to be remedied by the conventions of justice:

> Justice takes its rise from human conventions; and [. . .] these are intended as a remedy to some inconveniences, which proceed from the concurrence of certain *qualities* of the human mind with the *situation* of external objects. The qualities of the mind are *selfishness* and *limited generosity:* And the situation of external objects is their *easy change*, join'd to their *scarcity* in comparison of the wants and desires of men.
>
> (T 3.2.2.16, SBN 494)

The *selfishness* and *confin'd generosity* of human nature, the *mobility* and *scarcity* of the external objects, are thus the four main circumstances from which justice derives its origin.

Hume also evokes other conditions in the absence of which justice would have been impossible or useless. He names first the love between the sexes, this principle from which family comes, and which is in fact implied by the existence of a confin'd generosity. Thus, "the natural appetite betwixt the sexes" is "the first and original principle of human society" inasmuch as it gives rise to a familial union, itself preserved by benevolent parental government.[1] This familial union gives men an "early education in society," which make them "sensible of the infinite advantages that result from it" (T 3.2.2.4, 3.3.2.9; SBN 486, 489). It is also within the family that men invent the first and most fundamental rule of justice, the rule for the stability of possession, "that every parent [must establish], in order to preserve peace among his children" (T 3.2.2.14; SBN 493). By insisting on the existence of rudiments of justice within the family, Hume also underlines the obviousness of the first law of justice, thus eventually showing how absurd it is to consider as a durable state (the so-called state of nature) the disorders produced by the "blind motions" of the passions (ibid.).

Another condition belonging to the original context of justice is the rough equality of men's bodily and intellectual capacities, a circumstance which Hume highlights in *An Enquiry Concerning the Principles of Morals*:

> Were there a species of creatures, intermingled with men, which, though rational, were possessed of such inferior strength, both of body and mind, that they were incapable of all resistance [. . .] we should be bound, by the laws of humanity, to give gentle usage to these creatures, but should not, properly speaking, lie under any restraint of justice with regard to them.
>
> (EPM 3.18; SBN 190)[2]

Indeed, such an inequality between two groups or species would produce the domination of the stronger over the weaker, and not to this mutually advantageous association which is at the core of Hume's conception of convention.

The inconveniences which characterize man in isolation can also be viewed as a condition of justice, inasmuch as they explain why society – and thus justice – is advantageous to him. Indeed, while the social troubles due to the incommodity of our affections and our outward circumstances are the very *inconveniences which justice must overcome*, it is because *society palliates other inconveniences* that it is advantageous to preserve it, by means of justice. Thus, justice is necessary to man because society is necessary to him. This is why the *Treatise's* section on the origin of justice begins with the traditional Lucretian picture of man as a creature with fewer assets but more needs than other animals, a creature in which an "unnatural conjunction of infirmity, and of necessity, may be observ'd in its greatest perfection" (T 3.2.2.2; SBN 485).

The four main circumstances of justice, and other conditions *sine qua non*, depict the origin of justice as "the normal conditions under which human cooperation is both possible and necessary" (Rawls 1999: 109). But Hume has more to say concerning this origin. Inquiring into "the manner in which the rules of justice are establish'd among men," Hume, first, identifies the motive which induced men to invent and adopt them; second, determines the content of the fundamental law of justice – the rule for the preservation of property; and third, explains why this rule is stable. With the first and the third developments, Hume explains why men behave justly. The second point makes him identify justice with rules on property: an identification which we shall discuss in the last section of the present chapter.

Justice as a result of the self-regulation of the love of gain

As already shown, Hume considers no natural motive is "real or universal" enough to induce men to behave honestly constantly: the love of humanity as such does not exist, the concern for the interests of the injured person is too intermittent, the concern for personal interest most frequently leads, *at least in its "natural* movements," to injustice. By stressing *natural* movements, Hume indicates the possibility that a *correction* of these movements might be a cause of justice, but he has still to discover which motive might be at the origin of such a correction. He finds this motive in the *Treatise's* section on the origin of justice, in which "the love of gain" (a passion also designated as "the avidity of acquiring goods and possessions for ourselves and our nearest friends," "the passion of self-interest," "self-interest," "jealousy of interest," "interest") is presented in two steps. First it is described "when it acts without any restraint, and gives way to its first and most natural movements" as the most destructive passion of society (T 3.2.2.12; SBN 492). Then, it appears as the only passion capable of controlling its most natural movements and preserving society. "The origin of society" is thus explained by an "alteration of direction" of the passion of interest (T 3.2.2.13; SBN 492). But this spontaneous change of direction of the love of gain turns out to explain at the same time the origin *of justice*. Indeed, "'tis by establishing the rule for the stability of possession, that this passion restrains itself" (T 3.2.2.14; SBN 492). This rule is the remedy of the principal cause of *social* disorder, but it is also the most fundamental of the "laws of nature" or "rules *of justice*." Justice then ultimately appears as a product of the love of gain. Justice is the result of the inventivity of the human species,[3] specifically the inventivity of our passions[4] and, more precisely, of the inventivity of the most dangerous *and* cautious of all the passions, i.e. the love of gain. Besides, as the change of direction of the love of gain "[takes] place upon the least reflection" (T 3.2.2.13; SBN 492), the role of reason in the invention of justice appears to be instrumental and not directly impulsive: as always, reason can only be the slave of passions.[5]

While viewing the passion of interest as the origin of the institution of the rules of justice, Hume considers at the same time that the manner in which those rules are instituted involves a "sense of common interest." Such a reference to the sense of common interest corresponds to a second way of explaining the adoption of a just behavior: not by discovering the motive which induces men in general to invent the rules of justice, but by revealing the particular motive which makes each person conform to justice as a collective and reciprocal system of actions. Seen in this manner, justice appears to be *a convention of coordination*.

The conventions of justice and their stability: justice as mutual advantage

As Rawls observed in his lecture on Hume's theory of justice, Hume holds that a convention of justice has two aspects: first, its *content* (given by a rule of which we shall give examples below), and, second, "the shared awareness of a common interest, which all members of society express to one another, [and which] leads all to regulate their conduct by the rule" (Rawls 2000: 60). In fact, Hume is more radical than this interpretation suggests because he identifies the convention with the second aspect: "it is only a general sense of common interest [. . .] which induces [men] to regulate their conduct by certain rules" (T 3.2.2.10; SBN 490, cf. EPM App. 3.7; SBN 306). Hume explains how men adopt a collective and reciprocal behavior through convention by conforming themselves to a rule – the stability of property, its transference by consent, the obligation to keep promises – thanks to their sense of the general interest in conforming to this rule rather than abstaining from it. In this way, Hume is very close to the contemporary definition of conventions of coordination, especially the one given by David Lewis in his seminal book *Convention: A Philosophical Study*. Lewis favorably cites Hume's definition and also borrows some of his examples: the rowers, the division of property, the agreement on gold, and a common language (Le Jallé 2012: 253–254). Lewis produces a definition "along the lines of Hume's":

> A regularity *R* in the behavior of members of a population *P* when they are agents in a recurrent situation *S* is a *convention* if and only if, in any instance of *S* among members of *P*,
>
> (1)   everyone conforms to *R*;
> (2)   everyone expects everyone else to conform to *R*;
> (3)   everyone prefers to conform to *R* on condition that the others do.
>
> (Lewis 2002: 42)

Here I quote Lewis' first "rough definition," which seems to me closer to Hume's since it focuses on "a regularity in behavior, a system of mutual expectations, and a system of preferences" (Lewis 2002: 58). It does not include the condition of a "common knowledge" of (1), (2), and (3): a cognitive condition present in Lewis' "amended definition" and which constitutes Lewis' proper concept and insight on the nature of a convention (Lewis 2002: 58).

Taken in its own polemical context, Hume's definition of convention as "a general sense of common interest," first enables him to make a distinction between a convention and a promise, thus implicitly criticizing Hobbes' identification of a covenant and a promise. Furthermore, this very distinction opens up the possibility of explaining the institution of promising as one of the most fundamental conventions of justice: it is, Hume thinks, the third "law of nature."

Second, thanks to this definition of convention, Hume also explains conformity to justice. Indeed, the convention for the stability of possession

> is only a general sense of common interest; which sense all the members of the society express to one another, and *which induces them to regulate their conduct by certain rules*.
>
> (T 3.2.2.10; SBN 490; my emphasis)

Every member of society is sensible of this interest: Every one expresses this sense to his fellows, along with the resolution he has taken of squaring his actions by it, on condition that others will do the same. No more is requisite *to induce any one of them to perform an act of justice*, who has the first opportunity.

(T 3.2.2.22; SBN 498, my emphasis)

Thus, it is the expectation (and not the promise) of a reciprocal behavior which induces men to behave justly. We already noted that, according to Hume, the virtue of justice is unusual in that its beneficial influence only appears when it is systematically applied. One can see now that it is precisely the expectation of such a *general* conformity which produces the *particular* conformity of each participant. And one also understands why, in Hume's opinion, *it is rational to be just*. If, Hume admits, each "[has] reason *to wish*, that with regard to [such] single act, the laws of justice were for a moment suspended in the universe," it is not rational *to act* in a way that constitutes an exception to this scheme (T 3.2.2.22; SBN 498, my emphasis). Indeed, one of Hume's answers to the sensible knave who thinks that "[he] conducts himself with most wisdom, who observes the general rule, and takes advantage of all the exceptions," is that his injustice cannot remain secret for long (EPM 9.22; SBN 283). His detection – a highly probable one – shall automatically exclude the knave from the social and juridical system which he thought – wrongly – he could take advantage of without conforming to it *systematically* (see EPM 9.24; SBN 283).

Third, Hume's definition of a convention as a general sense of common interest enables him to account for the *stability* of justice, produced by a general conformity of behavior. As Hume shows, the conformity to the rules of justice increases as each becomes *more confident* in the general sharing of the sense of interest. Hume tackles this "assurance problem" (as Rawls calls it) and also formulates an argument which shall later be developed by Mancur Olson[6] and John Rawls.[7] According to Hume as well as to those writers, mutual confidence in a collective agreement can prevail without coercion whenever the social group is of a small size, whereas coercion becomes necessary within large groups. Indeed, Hume thinks, it is only "in large and polish'd societies" (T 3.2.8.5; SBN 543) that the mutual confidence in others' conformity disappears:

You have the same propension, that I have, in favour of what is contiguous above what is remote. You are, therefore, naturally carried to commit acts of injustice as well as me. Your example both pushes me forward in this way by imitation, and also affords me a new reason for any breach of equity, by shewing me, that I should be the cully of my integrity, if I alone shou'd impose on myself a severe restraint amidst the licentiousness of others.

(T 3.2.7.3; SBN 535)

It is also in those large societies that the institution of a government becomes necessary. By contrast, within small and uncultivated societies, the interest which men find in conforming to the rules of justice is sufficiently evident to make them conform without a coercion:

I observe, that it will be for my interest to leave another in the possession of his goods, *provided* he will act in the same manner with regard to me. He is sensible of a like interest in the regulation of his conduct. When this common sense of interest is mutually express'd, and is known to both, it produces a suitable resolution and behavior.

(T 3.2.2.10; SBN 490)

Then justice appears as a stable convention, at least in small uncultivated societies. Just as *two* rowers succeed in making their boat go on "by an agreement or convention" but without giving promises to each other (T 3.2.2.10; SBN 490), *two* neighbors "may agree to drain a meadow, which they possess in common; because 'tis easy for them to know each other's mind" (T 3.2.7.8; SBN 538), the members of a small society only have to rely on the sense of common interest which they feel, express, and observe in others, to behave justly. This is the reason why, according to Hume, society may be preserved "for some time" on the sole foundation of justice, "without having recourse to [the] invention [of government]" (T 3.2.8.1; SBN 539).

The moral obligation to justice

As already said, the explanation of the moral approbation of justice counts as the second part of Hume's enquiry on justice, once the origin of its institution is established. This explanation simply consists in showing that justice, by means of sympathy, is qualified as virtuous:

> When the injustice is so distant from us, as no way to affect our interest, it still displeases us; because we consider it as prejudicial to human society, and pernicious to every one that approaches the person guilty of it. We partake of their uneasiness by *sympathy*; and as every thing, which gives uneasiness in human actions, upon the general survey, is call'd *vice*, and whatever produces satisfaction, in the same manner, is denominated *virtue*; this is the reason why the sense of moral good and evil follows upon justice and injustice.
>
> (T 3.2.2.24; SBN 499)

Here Hume applies to just or unjust behavior the explanation which he generally gives of the moral approbation of characters (or of the actions which *signify* them). For this reason, Brian Barry is not wrong in maintaining that, according to Hume, adopting a moral point of view involves a shift towards impartiality. However, Barry goes further when he maintains that Hume, when basing the *moral approbation* of just behavior on an exigence of impartiality, admits at the same time the existence of *a moral motive irreducible to interest*, able by itself to account for the adoption of just behavior (Barry 1989: 167). Hume considers that the approbation of justice involves a moral obligation which makes up for interest when society "has become numerous, and has encreas'd to a tribe or nation" (T 3.2.2.24; SBN 499). However, the moral obligation to justice is only, in Hume's eyes, a *supplement* to interest (its function is thus similar to the institution of government). Hume is so far from considering this moral obligation as a motive irreducible to interest, that he rather considers it as a supplementary motive, which can itself be reinforced by other motives, such as private or public education, and the interest of our reputation (see T 3.2.2.25–27; SBN 500–501). Hume in fact describes unambiguously the "close connexion" between the moral obligation and the obligation of interest: as the latter "gives rise to" the former, their connection is to be considered as a *causal relation* (T 3.2.8.7; SBN 545).

Justice, property, and social order

It is now time to consider Hume's identification of the conventions of justice to rules of property, as it is at the core of Hume's theory of justice, as well as a subject of criticism from many scholars (with the notable exception of Friedrich Hayek). Hume is often accused of having reduced justice to rules governing property (Harrison 1981: 42). Moreover, Hume does not question the justice or fairness of such rules: their interest to the public, i.e. to quote Rawls, the fact that they form the "practically best scheme," is sufficient to legitimize them (Rawls 2000: 64). Finally, Hume considers that a distribution of property which applies these rules as just by definition. Let us now show how such a "reduction" is achieved in his system. Let us show how *he justifies it philosophically*, far from adopting it under the influence of an unfortunate conservative prejudice.

From Hume's point of view, this so-called reduction of justice to the rules of property consists in revealing their *co-implication*, which he makes when determining the content of the most fundamental rule of justice, the first "law of nature." Since, on the one hand, the main obstacle which justice must overcome is the mobility of external goods joined to their scarcity, and because, on the other hand, scarcity cannot be overcome institutionally, it follows that the *instability* of the possession of those goods is to be compensated by human conventions. Thus, the first law of nature is directly deduced from the circumstances which Hume carefully identified: it is the convention for the *stability* of possession of external goods. Here is its obvious justification: preserving society implies the elimination of the main social "disturbances," and this "can be done after no other manner, than by a convention to bestow stability" to goods whose possession is naturally precarious (T 3.2.2.9; SBN 489). *Property* – which Hume defines as "*a constant possession*" – thus appears with the institution of this convention, which means that it is introduced with justice:"the same artifice gives rise to both," as well as to the ideas of"*right*" and "*obligation*" (T 3.2.2.11; SBN 490–491). The reason why justice and property are identical, or rather imply each other, is thus simply that *they appear together*.

Now Hume insists that this coextensivity of justice and property directly contradicts the "vulgar definition of justice" as "*a constant and perpetual will of giving every one his due*" (T 3.2.6.2; SBN 526).[8] Indeed, what is *due* to someone is what is *proper* to him, what he has a *right* to, and that others *ought to* respect, so that the vulgar definition in fact presupposes that the notions of *right*, *property*, and *obligation* are antecedent to justice (see T 3.2.2.11; SBN 490–491).[9] For Hume the reverse is true: human conventions – i.e. justice – determine those notions.

It is thus the necessity of preserving social order which justifies in Hume's eyes the content of the most fundamental law of justice, namely the establishment of property. By the same argument, he also shows that no consideration other than legitimate possession can govern the application of justice.

Thus, the role of the rules "which determine property" is to apply the fundamental rule for the stability of possession by separating and attributing possessions. In the *Treatise*, Hume seems to define the complete set of those rules, showing that present possession (at the first formation of society), then first possession, long possession, accession, and succession are five "circumstances [giving] rise to property" to which men naturally agree (T 3.2.3.5; SBN 505). However, he does not qualify those five rules as "laws of nature," a probable sign that he was not dogmatic in enumerating them. Indeed, according to Hume, the relevant fact is that an *agreement* has been made on such criteria (or others), either because they were patently *useful* to the public, or because of the *salience* of such characteristics, which makes people's imaginations converge on them.[10] Thus, to show that some of those rules are useful, Hume observes that by designating the first possessor of a good as its rightful proprietor, people have reached the advantage of never "leav[ing] property in suspence" (T 3.2.3.6; SBN 505); as far as the institution of the rule of succession is concerned, it usefully fosters human industry (see T 3.2.3.11; SBN 510–511). At the same time, those very rules also prove to be attractive to the imagination;"the first possession always engages the attention most" and by "the association of ideas,""we are naturally directed to consider the son after the parent's decease" (ibid.). Thus, utility and imaginative association sometimes reinforce each other. In a skeptical gesture, Hume endeavors to show that the more "frivolous" of those two causes of selection can also operate alone. However, the essential reason of the choice of the circumstances which determine property, whether directly useful to the public or only suggested by the imagination, is their ability "to cut off all occasions of discord and contention" (T 3.2.3.2; SBN 502). This is the ultimate consideration which, according to Hume, explains their selection.

It is thus the maintenance of public order which justifies in Hume's eyes the selection of the rules which determine property. By the same argument, Hume rejects other criteria which might be used in this determination. Hume shows that justice would be a source of dissention if it took into account in its decisions "the fitness or unfitness of objects to particular persons" (ibid.), i.e. their needs or desires (see T 3.2.4.1; SBN 514). The rejection of such a criterion seems to Hume indispensable to the *impartiality* of justice on the one hand (needs are always appreciated with partiality and passion) and to the *equal consideration* of persons answerable to the law, on the other hand: "whether a man be generous, or a miser, he [. . .] obtains with the same facility a decision in his favour, even for what is entirely useless to him" (T 3.2.3.2; SBN 502). For the same reason, a rule assigning property proportionally to *merit* should also be rejected. Indeed, Hume thinks, such a rule, though apparently useful in theory, would be much controversial in practice, "so great is the uncertainty of merit, both from its natural obscurity, and from the self-conceit of each individual" (EPM 3.2; SBN 193). An equal distribution of property seems to Hume as *impracticable* as the former, pace a few exceptions such as the agrarian laws in Greece and Rome, and highly *pernicious* if put into practice (see EPM, 3.25–26; SBN 193–194). Indeed, Hume shows, the natural difference of industry would destroy the initial equal share of property, and, if human industry was authoritatively prevented, a decrease of general welfare would ensue. Not to mention, he adds, that no power could be entrusted the charge of leveling all possessions. Indeed, the leveling of property eventually produces the leveling of power, which definitely shows how impracticable such a measure would be.

To end, Hume proves that a determination of property which aims at fostering *directly* the public interest would also be pernicious. Indeed, though a seditious bigot or a miser be more pernicious to the public than an industrious father, justice cannot favor the latter at the cost of the former. Indeed, to pursue in each case the largest public utility would imply *particular* judgments of justice, depending on *circumstances* and *characters*, whereas the public order demands *impersonal*, *general*, and *inflexible* principles. The direct maximization of the overall utility of the group is thus to be rejected, because it amounts in practice to applying a "*particular* view" of public interest, which takes circumstances into account (T 3.2.6.9; SBN 532). By contrast, the connection of justice with utility is, Hume thinks, "somewhat singular" (T 3.2.2.22; SBN 497). Indeed, the indispensable rigidity of the rules of justice inevitably entails some ills, not only to singular individuals but to the public itself. However, those "temporary" ills are largely compensated by the utility of the "whole plan or scheme" formed by the acts of justice. The utility of the rule, or rather of the "system," thus compensates in Hume's eyes for the utility of the (single) act, a thesis which he illustrates in comparing justice to a "vault" which is supported only by the "mutual assistance" of the stones which compose it, and where each stone, apart from those convergent forces, would "fall to the ground" (EPM, App. 3.5; SBN 305). Now, once again, the utility of the system is but the fact that it is "absolutely requisite, both to the support of society, and the well-being of every individual" (T 3.2.2.22; SBN 497).

As we saw, Hume considers that the fitness of possessions to persons should not be a criterion for justice, because it cannot be judged impartially. Nevertheless, he also thinks that *this problem of inadaptation* is a paramount one, and that *justice* has to remedy for it. Indeed, to leave men resolving it directly would amount to allowing "every man to seize by violence what he judges to be fit for him," which "*would destroy society*" (T 3.2.4.1; SBN 514, my emphasis). The same argument thus enables Hume to reveal the content of a second law of nature which aims at relaxing, by institutional means, the "rigid stability" introduced by the first law of nature. The rule of "the *transference* of property by consent," which is a ruling exception to the rule of stability, is thus indispensable "to render [men] mutually advantageous" thanks to the legal exchange of possessions (T 3.2.5.8; SBN 520).

As for *the third (and last) law of nature*, namely the rule of the obligation of promises, it makes "the commerce of mankind" extend, first, to the goods which cannot be immediately delivered (goods that are "*absent* or *general*"), and second to "services and actions" (ibid.). As it is the case for the two preceding laws, this third law proves to be absolutely necessary "to the support of society" (T 3.2.6.1; SBN 526). Indeed, without the commerce of services which the institution of promises introduces, every man would be confined to its *private* work, which Hume had shown, at the beginning of his enquiry concerning justice, how *inefficient* it is. Without the commerce of services, human society viewed as a *community* would thus be eventually lost. Besides, the consideration of the obligation of promises as a third law of nature shows that justice, in Hume's eyes, does not in fact reduce entirely to rules of property: it rather involves the establishment of an extended intercourse between men, which is both *mutually advantageous* and based on *trust*. Indeed, for Hume, the "interest" of the obligation of promises for society is not only to extend exchange to absent or general possessions, nor is it only to preserve or increase possessions *by means of* services: it is mainly "*to beget mutual trust and confidence in the common offices of life*" (T 3.2.8.5; SBN 544, my emphasis). For this reason, Hayek's characterization of the rules of justice as "rules of just conduct" seems to fit Hume's perspective rather well: it implies that not all those rules concern property, but that they aim more generally at "establishing a good correspondence among men" (T 3.2.6.1; SBN 526).[11] "The well-being of men," as Hume writes in the same place, is thus the ultimate end of society, which the rules of justice support. Besides, just as the fidelity to promises encourages many *collective actions*, thanks to the *security* it offers, those actions can also be extended to the entire society on a larger scale, by means of government (see T 3.2.7.8; SBN 538–539).

Conclusion

Even though Hume's theory of justice has reduced the realm of justice by focusing intensely – though not exclusively – on property, it also offers some strong and convincing aspects which the present chapter has endeavored to underline. Those aspects are mainly the following.

First, the force of Hume's theory of justice is to explain how justice appears both as an institution and a virtue. This explanation seems to me coherent (and not composed of two "irreconcilable" approaches, as Brian Barry thinks; Barry 1989: 152), since the rationale of this institution – i.e. its utility for mankind – is also the very quality which makes it appreciate as a virtue.

Second, this theory succeeds in explaining the stability of justice in small societies and the necessity of supplementary devices in large and refined societies. This observation enables Hume to describe the functioning of justice in a manner that is independent of the institution of a State, which differentiates his approach from Hobbes' one.

Third, Hume's analysis of justice as a convention is another original aspect of his approach. His definition of convention as a "sense of common interest" and its description in terms of expectations, beliefs, and reciprocal actions based on a mutual confidence form a strong conceptual insight, which was plainly revealed by David Lewis and underlined by John Rawls in his lectures. By applying such a conception of convention to justice, one may find some determinations of it other than the rules concerning property. Hume himself has only discovered one of those other conventional (but not property-depending) determinations, namely the obligation to promises. It remains permissible to imagine others.

Notes

1 Though Hume views family as an origin of society, he does not view parental government as a model of society: it is neither (obviously) the model of society *without government*, which is only supported by the rules of justice, nor of the society *with a government*. Indeed, Hume overtly criticizes patriarchalism at T 3.2.8.2; SBN 541.

2 Here Hume has principally in mind the inequality between men and animals, thus depriving the latter from any right claims to our justice (but only to our compassion and benevolence). This claim is repeated by Rawls (1999: 441, 448).

3 "Mankind is an inventive species; and where an invention is obvious and absolutely necessary, it may as properly be said to be natural as any thing that proceeds immediately from original principles, without the intervention of thought or reflection" (T 3.2.1.19; SBN 484).

4 "Nothing is more vigilant and inventive than our passions; and nothing is more obvious, than the convention for the observance of [the three fundamental laws of justice]" (T 3.2.6.1; SBN 526).

5 On Hume's theory of reason as an instrument of the passions, see in particular T 2.3.3. The correction of the natural and unreflected movements of the love of gain corresponds to the second of the two ways in which, according to Hume, reason may (indirectly) influence action, namely "when it discovers the connexion of causes and effects, so as to afford us means of exerting any passion" (T 3.1.1.12; SBN 459).

6 Mancur Olson (2002) shows that collective goods can be obtained automatically within small groups (no enforcement, nor even an informal agreement, are needed), whereas the success of a collective action within large groups necessitates coercion or an external enticement.

7 Rawls agrees with Olson in thinking that "in a large community the degree of mutual confidence in one another's integrity that renders enforcement superfluous is not to be expected" (Rawls 1999: 237). Rawls signals in his lectures that Hume had anticipated this argument (Rawls 2000: 63).

8 As the Norton edition of Hume's *Treatise* indicates, this definition can be found in Plato, Cicero, Justinian, Pufendorf, etc.: see the annotation to T 3.2.6.2 in vol. 2 of the *Treatise*, p. 923.

9 By criticizing the vulgar definition of justice, Hume thus also implicitly refutes Locke's thesis that, in the state of nature, man has a *property* on his life, his liberty, and his estate, and has *an obligation* to respect the law of nature which commands to preserve oneself and, as far as possible, the rest of mankind.

10 The locus classicus on coordination by salience is Schelling (1960: chaps. 3–4).

11 See Hayek (1982). The reference to Hume and his three fundamental laws of nature is pervasive in this book, e.g. vol. 2, p. 40.

References

Barry, B. (1989) *Theories of Justice*, London: Harvester-Wheatsheaf.

Harrison, J. (1981) *Hume's Theory of Justice*, Oxford: Clarendon Press.

Hayek, F. (1982) *Law, Legislation and Liberty*, London: Routledge.

Le Jallé, É (2012) "La convention: ce que Lewis doit (ou non) à Hume," *Klésis, Revue philosophique* 24: 239–271.

Lewis, D. (2002) *Convention: A Philosophical Study*, Oxford: Blackwell Publishers.

Olson, M. (2002) *The Logic of Collective Action*, Cambridge, MA: Harvard University Press.

Rawls, J. (1999) *A Theory of Justice*, Cambridge, MA: Harvard University Press.

———. (2000) *Lectures on History of Moral Philosophy*, Cambridge, MA: Harvard University Press.

Schelling, T. (1960) *The Strategy of Conflict*, Cambridge, MA: Harvard University Press.

20

HUME AND THE TWO TASTES

Bodily and mental

Christopher Williams

1. It is a significant datum for philosophical aesthetics that the concept of taste is used to characterize both a sensory modality – the palate – and certain appreciative responses to art and natural beauty. Some writers in the eighteenth century, such as Hume and Burke, were also sufficiently impressed by the parallel applications of the concept as to hope that uncontentious claims about the palate could serve to clarify, and indeed vindicate, claims made in the more contentious domain of appreciative response. Hume spoke of a "great resemblance between mental and bodily taste," and he supposed that it would enable us to learn something about the judging of literature from the judging of wine (E 235). In particular, he wanted to exploit the putative resemblance in order to show that "the taste of all individuals is not upon an equal footing" (E 242), and recruited an episode concerning Sancho Panza's wine-tasting kinsmen (from Cervantes' *Don Quixote* [1963]) for that purpose. My topic in this chapter will be Hume's "great resemblance." Much philosophical attention and ingenuity have been devoted to explicating Hume's thoughts about the standard of taste, how the standard is supposedly arrived at, and whether there can even be a standard. But the exact relationship, for him, between bodily and mental taste has been neglected by comparison.

If the contrast between two kinds of taste is intuitively clear enough for us to ask how similar or dissimilar the two kinds are, then one possible view – Hume's – is that these two distinct activities parallel one another in the sense that whereas bodily taste is literally perceptual, mental taste is to be understood in quasi-perceptual terms. This is not the only possible view, and it is not a popular view nowadays. The reasons why such a view is out of favor are perhaps suggested by the very terminology to which Hume is drawn, the language of "mental" versus "bodily" taste. For it is an equally significant datum for aesthetics that the expression 'mental taste' has not caught on, and it may be that the expression promises more philosophy of mind than it can deliver. And as for the object of this mental taste, there has been mounting resistance to any proposal that an activity modeled on the sense of taste could begin to explain the value of art (or natural beauty). On a view currently more in fashion, we may speak of judging wines and judging poems, if we please, but there will be no deep parallel between the activities; and so the sense of taste will simply be a bad model for criticism. Thus, in an article critical of Hume's account, Jerrold Levinson speaks of "The British Objection" to Hume, and the focus of the objection is such a model.[1] As Roger Shiner bluntly puts the point, "Hume begins his actual discussion of the standard of taste with what will turn out to be a deeply misleading analogy – that between aesthetic taste and gustatory taste."[2] Skepticism of this sort naturally encourages neglect of the body–mind resemblance on which Hume so notably insisted.

In what follows, I shall first try to sharpen the sense of misgiving that people have about taste and then examine Hume's appeal to the palate in more detail. There is a problem with his investigative procedure, but it is not what the taste skeptics might think it is, namely, the mere appeal to the palate as such. Hoping to allay their misgivings, as well as to address the real problem with Hume's procedure, I shall then turn to a simple proposal about how best, on Hume's behalf, to think about the two tastes.

2. Skepticism regarding taste has two shapes. On the one hand, too much might be expected of any mental capacity that is analogous, but only analogous, to the sense of taste and whose job is to issue judgments concerning beauty. Burke was evidently unembarrassed to refer to such a capacity as "this delicate and aerial faculty," but however natural it is for a *sensory modality* to be reborn as a *mental faculty* if we are impressed by suggestive analogies, it is precisely the notion of a faculty, made unavoidably explicit and meant seriously, that seems to be nothing more than a quaint relic of the eighteenth century.[3] It is not problematic to identify a sensory modality because modalities have dedicated sensory organs, but if a merely mental faculty of taste is called upon to do the work of a modality without the benefit of an organ, its deliverances suddenly appear out of thin air. We thus confront the *mysteriousness objection*, to mental taste, and it is similar to the old objection to construing the imagination as the mind's eye.

On the other hand, mystery may not be the problem. Those who do not wince at a faculty of taste may nevertheless dispute the point of insisting on a parallel between taste as a sensory modality and whatever we are doing when we carefully examine, and are seriously engaged with, poems and the like. The center of gravity for the new objection is not the furniture of the mind and what it must not or cannot contain, but the arts and the sort of importance that they are supposed to have. The suspicion here, which can be directed at the whole subject of taste, has often been voiced since the so-called century of taste came to an end. Wordsworth voiced the essential irritation, in 1802, when he derided those

> who talk of Poetry as of a matter of amusement and idle pleasure; who will converse with us as gravely about a *taste* for Poetry, as they express it, as if it were a thing as indifferent as a taste for Rope-dancing, or Frontiniac or Sherry.[4]

Wordsworth's thought is that if taste did have anything to do with the real concerns of poets and their readers, then a taste for a particular poem would be of no greater moment than a bare liking or disliking. This is the *triviality objection* to mental taste. Its force may depend on our taking the arts to be a non-trivial business, as in Wordsworth's case, and a business whose ulterior aim may be that of goading people into having valuable aesthetic encounters outside their comfort zones (and hence outside the sphere of whatever bare likings they happen to have). The objection will be especially attractive to theorists who believe that the satisfactions of the arts are only superficially perceptual in character,[5] since colors, sounds, (bodily) tastes, and smells furnish obvious paradigms of items that people just like or dislike – merely personal tastes, which may be perfectly (but uninterestingly) idiosyncratic.[6]

But the triviality objection will also attract those who suspect that the conventional satisfactions, at any rate, are just plain superficial. For if we suppose (say) that class prejudice best explains aesthetic judgments, then, grave talk about discriminating tastes notwithstanding, these judgments quickly degenerate into the equivalent of a taste for "Frontiniac or Sherry."[7] If class interests, including aspirational desires to belong to an admired demographic, serve to show why people really enjoy what they profess to enjoy, then exercises of discrimination do no heavy lifting in the explanation. But since tastes appear to do real lifting, if taken at face value, they are little more than window dressing. The starting point here is different from Wordsworth's, but the end point is the same.

These two objections do not make it easy, at this late date, to accord Hume's "great resemblance" a hearing, and indeed it might be thought that Hume's treatment of taste has itself conspicuously given substance to them. Let us now look more closely at the details of Hume's intended analogy to see whether such a thought is correct. And to get a better grip on the analogy, let us begin by considering what Hume regards as *good* taste in each of the two domains.

3. Hume starts from the presumption that there is such a thing as good bodily taste, an ability to perform, by means of the palate, a certain kind of action, which can be done better or worse. To have good bodily taste is to be good at tasting (with one's body). At a basic level, it is the ability to discriminate differences of flavor, but at the higher level that interests Hume it is the ability to make fine discriminations of tasted ingredients in a compound of multiple flavors. Hume moreover takes it for granted that the discrimination of a given flavor consists in the identification of the flavor-cause via the palate.

The Cervantes episode, which has become exceedingly familiar to philosophers because of Hume's retelling, illustrates this conception of good taste.[8] Sancho Panza's two kinsmen report that wine drawn from a certain hogshead has a slightly disagreeable taste, while disagreeing about what that taste is: one of them thinks that the wine tastes like iron and the other that it tastes like leather. A key with a leathern thong, however, is found in the emptied hogshead, thereby showing that the subtlety of each kinsman's palate was not pretended, despite the opposing explanations the kinsmen gave of the flavor that spoiled the wine. The kinsmen's tasting prowess, so understood, provides Hume with his model for mental taste. And because it is a model, the next task on Hume's agenda is to find, for good mental taste, suitable counterparts to flavors and flavor-causes.

In place of fine discriminations of different flavors in compounds, we have fine discriminations of beauty and deformity in compositions, and there will be degrees of difference between them in order for the exercise of fine discrimination to gain a plausibly comparable foothold. (For Hume, as for other eighteenth-century writers, the standard contrast is between beauty, and deformity, and not, as it usually is for us, between beauty and ugliness: deformity is de-formity, loss of form, and a bodily disfigurement, for instance, would involve some such loss.)[9] Now, it might be thought that a determination of deformity (in a work of art) corresponds more aptly to the pronouncement that the wine is *spoiled* by the taste of iron or leather than to the tastes themselves. Owing to an ambiguity in the concept of beauty, there is doubtless room for some argument here. We often think of beauty in broadly perceptual terms, which would align beauty (or deformity) with the counterparts to winey tastes. But we equally think of beauty in broadly verdictive terms – an item judged to be beautiful is judged to possess a superlative degree of excellence and is attractive for that reason – and here the alignment of beauty (or deformity) is with the counterparts to, roughly, wine ratings. This ambiguity in the concept is not the offspring of Hume's fancy, and since it is not especially puzzling that Hume's casual presentation preserves the ambiguity, it may not be especially important to resolve it. Yet whatever the preferred categories for thinking about beauty are, a more important issue concerns the mental counterpart of the key with the leathern thong.

Hume speaks of "rules of beauty" (or "rules of art") in connection with the proper discernment of beauties, and these rules are exhibited in "established models" of artistic excellence. Usually the rules appear to be ancillary to, or derivable from, the models; sometimes it is a little difficult to tell the rules apart from the models. At any rate, the rules can be stated. And so, according to Hume, "to produce these general rules or avowed patterns of composition is like finding the key with the leathern thong" (E 236). These rules, then, are the official counterpart to flavor-causes.

Because rules of art are rules of beauty, we need to know something about beauty if we are to see the point of the rules. In the *Treatise*, Hume maintains that pleasure and pain "are not only the necessary attendants of beauty and deformity, but constitute their very essence" (T 2.1.8.2; SBN 299). He is not too explicit about the kind of pleasure or pain – that is, about how that which is beautiful "pleases after such a particular manner" (T 3.1.2.3; SBN 471) – but clearly he does think that the pleasure we take in beautiful objects is connected to their perceived fitness, which can be a fitness for a certain kind of life (as in cases concerning animal beauty):

> In judging of the beauty of animal bodies, we always carry in our eye the oeconomy of a certain species; and where the limbs and features observe that proportion, which is common to the species, we pronounce them handsome and beautiful.
>
> (T 3.2.1.18; SBN 483)

Or, as is more usual with Hume, the fitness can be a fitness for an end that someone or other can have.[10] That person is neither necessarily nor primarily myself, as he emphasizes when estimating the comparative beauties of a plain overgrown with useless furze and a hillside covered with profitable grapevines or olives (T 2.2.5.18; SBN 364). This observation about fitness occurs in a section where Hume is making the argument that sympathy, not self-interest, is the reason we esteem the rich and powerful, and that context is revealing: when Hume adverts to beauty (or its opposite), it is often to stress its distinctness from self-interested gain (or loss), however easy it might be to confuse the two pleasures (or pains) in particular instances. But although this anti-Hobbesian motivation preoccupies him, it is his identification of beauty with pleasure that is fundamentally relevant to the rules of art.

In the essay on taste, Hume is better at broaching examples of works that violate or observe rules than at saying what the rules themselves are. Ariosto's poetry, his central example, offers both rule-violations that displease and rule-observances that please. One thing Hume mentions, to the discredit of Ariosto, is "his bizarre mixture of the serious and comic styles" (E 231), and this blemish in Ariosto provides a clue to Hume's general understanding of these rules. Owing to an unexpected mention of rules in the *Treatise*, it is an important clue.

At the close of a section on the passions of malice and envy, in Book Two, Hume says that if an author composed a treatise that combined serious and humorous elements, the author would be accused of "the neglect of all the rules of art and criticism" (T 2.2.8.18; SBN 379). The explanation is that the rules depend on facts concerning human nature, and in particular "the quality of human nature, which requires a consistency in every performance," for it is this quality that makes it difficult for the mind to pass abruptly from one passion to another that is very different from the first. Hume develops the idea further by saying that although passion-mixtures displease, a volume of poetry can contain two poems of opposite character without causing displeasure, and likewise two paintings of opposite character on the walls of a room. In these cases, the absence of a suitable imaginative relation that links the poems or paintings precludes the feeling of inconsistency.

It is not implausible to speculate that *consistency*, understood liberally in terms of an imagination-friendly succession of passions, is Hume's master rule of art, informing all others. In his observations on the rules that determine property, Hume showed a keen interest in the ostensible irregularity of ownership practices, as exhibited, for instance, in the custom of allowing a person who occupies a small island to claim the entire island as his possession, but denying the claim if the island is the size of Great Britain. The two appropriative actions represent important imaginative differences, despite their equivalence from the standpoint of a general rule that assigns ownership to a first possessor, and so the irregularity of the custom is ultimately a matter of rational inscrutability only. Embedded in this discussion (which addresses such ownership rules in concrete detail) is a long footnote in which Hume remarks that if there is a "natural affinity" between objects no other reason is needed for the imagination to join them (and only a strong counter-reason can make us "over-look" the affinity). He adds:

> This we shall have occasion to explain more fully afterwards, when we come to treat of beauty. In the mean time, we may content ourselves with observing, that the same love of order and uniformity, which arranges the books in a library, and the chairs in a parlour, contributes to the formation of society, and to the well-being of mankind, by modifying the general rule concerning the stability of possession.
>
> (T n71; SBN 504)

Of all Hume's asides on beauty (and Hume on beauty is always an aside), this remark is the most tantalizing. We shall never know the detailed explanation that Hume would have given had he seized the "occasion," but probably enough of his hand was shown for us to hazard some guesses about the relationship between beauty and the rules of art, and its implications for the great-resemblance thesis.

Philosophers have often accorded rules of art (sometimes under the label "principles of taste") a cool reception.[11] Kant forthrightly denied their existence, and his position has seemed sensible and advanced, whereas Hume's unembarrassed references to them have seemed retrograde. And evidence is certainly lacking, to say the least, that critics ever approach works of art with rules in tow. But if rules of art, for Hume, are at all similar to rules that determine property, as Hume's delphic footnote suggests, then we should conclude that the rules of art are not prospective and regulative in their application, but retrospective and explanatory. For it is not as though Hume supposes that the hypothetical discoverer of Great Britain would be violating an antecedent rule of property by claiming the whole island; he is instead trying to explain why we would feel the discoverer's ownership claim to be much more limited. Similarly, Ariosto's mixing of serious and comic styles is felt to be jarring, and the difficulty of changing passions on the spot, in a poem whose parts are imaginatively joined, explains the feeling. Each rule captures the explanation.

On this picture, the exercise of mental taste will register a beauty or deformity, which, if genuine, will conform to a rule of art. The reference to genuineness needs to be made, because the good mental taster, let us recall, has got to be good at what she does; and the possibility of a good exercise necessarily allows for a bad. Hume, too, recognizes the distinction, inasmuch as he wanted to contrast (in his essay "Of the Simplicity and Refinement of Writing") the false or superficial beauty of "twenty insipid conceits" with the "one thought which is really beautiful" (E 193). Conformity to a rule of art (not the bare formulation of a rule, independently of a conforming instance) validates the detection of an authentic beauty, but in this context it is easy to speak of a rule when a rule-conformity is meant. Hume does this when he says that to "produce" a rule is like finding the key. But rule-conformity is the item that needs to be "produced," and rule-conformity is the true counterpart, for mental taste, to finding the key.

4. The mapping of Hume's intended parallel between bodily and mental taste now being complete in outline, let us consider how far Hume has succeeded in placing mental taste on a gold standard vouchsafed by the palate. To begin with, it may be thought that a difficulty arises from the in-built conservatism of Hume's version of beauty (resting as it does on a "love of order and uniformity"), and it might be thought that Hume's rules of art will unavoidably be ill-equipped to deal with art that is more self-consciously adventurous or transgressive (as is often the case with the farther reaches of our contemporary avant-garde) than the art of Hume's day. But this is not so much an objection to the modeling of mental taste on bodily as an objection to taste as such (or to tasteful-ness, if received, socially respectable tastes should receive special emphasis). For the conservatism of the mental palate may have an opposite number in the conservatism of the palate itself, which not uncommonly has to be accustomed to certain flavors before a person can enjoy them. And just as sour or bitter or spicy flavors can become acquired tastes, so too might the shocks of the avant-garde be accommodated by a more developed mental taste.

Nevertheless, the existence of novel art, or difficult beauty, does help to pinpoint a more potent objection. If a poet mixes styles, the mixture may be distastefully "bizarre," though it need not be, and time may be needed for people to grow accustomed to possible hidden charms. The type of uncertainty that the exercise of taste confronts in such situations can be redescribed as uncertainty about whether a perceived beauty conforms to a rule or not. This uncertainty cannot be dispelled.

For bodily taste, the corresponding doubts are dispellable. Sancho's kinsmen report the flavor of iron or leather, and the key with the leathern thong is the flavor-cause. Emptying the hogs-head and finding that key verifies the flavor-cause, and verification occurs because although tongues are employed to report flavors, tongues are not employed to empty hogsheads and locate keys. This procedure thus presents a contrast with mental taste, where the exercise of taste is required in order to verify rule-conformity – and this is to say that "verification," in the sense that finding the key provides it, does not occur at all.

Consequently, when Hume suggests that unless beauties are "methodized" as rules, it will not be "so easy to silence the bad critic," his optimism about resolving disputes of taste is extraordi-narily insouciant. It is not merely *difficult to silence* the bad critic, using reasonable procedures on a reasonable discussant, but *impossible*. As reason-givers in a dispute, opposing tastes are mutually opaque: the taste of one person (or perhaps the taste of many, whether now or in the fullness of time) merely opposes the taste of another person. Reasons of a different kind will have to be found in order to make progress with such an impasse.

Even though Hume does not mention this crucial difference between identifying a rule-conformity and identifying a flavor-cause, it is not surprising that his attention subsequently shifts from mental taste to the characteristics of the persons who, in matters of taste, are worth listening to: someone who displays the five marks of the true judge could offer testimony that might supply a more indirect reason for judging one author superior to another. In making that shift, however, Hume seems to be effectively, if unintentionally, conceding that the sense of taste is a bad model for taste in art, as well as giving aid and comfort to taste skeptics. If the good critic putatively aspires to silence the bad by adducing rules, the attempted verification of taste by taste will be naturally viewed as verification in name only (hence trivial), or as opaque in its deliverances (hence mysterious).

Yet the fortunes for the "great resemblance" may not be as dire as they seem. For a decent argument can be made that rather than getting aesthetic judgment wrong by relying on a ques-tionable analogy, Hume failed to do adequate justice to the sense of taste itself, prior to relying on the analogy, and that the thesis has more encouraging prospects once Hume's real mistake, or oversight, is corrected.

5. On this proposal, talk of a resemblance between bodily and mental understates the relationship between the two tastes. There is indeed a difference between them, and an obvious one, namely, that whereas bodily taste depends on a dedicated bodily organ, mental taste has no special tie to any part of the body. And so, at most there will be a resemblance. However, if we think of the *action* performed in tasting, it is possible that the same action of the mind could be performed with or without a specialized bodily part. From the standpoint of the action, we could speak of an identity, not just a resemblance.

To make this option available, Hume's picture of the kinsmen's performance needs to be revised. The kinsmen should not be regarded as identifying flavor-causes when they taste the wine. It is the supposition that they were doing so that dooms the sense of taste as a model for aesthetic characterizations; and rejection of that supposition greatly improves its plausibility.[12]

We most typically name flavors after their causes, a practice that arises from the usual way in which acquaintance with the flavors is secured. As Hume recognized, to teach someone the taste of a particular fruit we present the fruit, and the same word is used for both the flavor and the cause (and for a reason that is similar to the one that guides our use of demonstrative pronouns to individuate shades of color). "To give a child an idea of scarlet or orange, of sweet or bitter, I present the objects, or in other words, convey to him these impressions" (T 1.1.1.8; SBN 5). Hume's 'in other words' readily points up the flavor-cause coalescence in ordinary thought and speech.

The flavor and its cause should not be tied too closely, however. A beverage that is orange flavored may not contain any orange juice, but may owe its taste to artificial flavorings. An epistemologist may say that, in that case, the beverage is only *apparently* orange flavored; but to make this inference, here, is to make a substantive assumption about tasting, that it aims at getting facts right about the world where the facts do not concern the qualitative character of the tastes. On this assumption, tasting plays a similar role to vision in one of its common employments, that of establishing knowledge claims about items that are not themselves irreducibly perceptual. Yet other roles for tasting (and, for that matter, seeing) are possible, and one role for tasting is to make discriminations of flavor, irrespective of causal facts. If we approach the exercise of taste free of preconceptions drawn from the sphere of perceptual epistemology, this other role will be more clearly visible as the important one. A concoction that is contrived without real oranges may still be the bearer of a real orange flavor, if "orange flavor" is not only orange-*derived* flavor but orange-*like* flavor; and a good taster will typically be good at telling whether a hard-to-describe flavor is "like" an orange. Much of the time that which is X-like will also be X-derived, but that empirical connection is not enough to carry the assumption that the only true X-like taste is a taste of X.

To return now to Hume's hogshead. In the light of these observations, it is not right to say that the key is the true object of the kinsmen's taste, albeit provisionally concealed by the inaccessibility of the key; rather, the object is a key-like taste, and the key merely confirms the attribution of the taste to its cause. The tasting and the identification of the cause are distinct activities. And the second activity is not what we think of as the skill at which wine critics excel. Very obviously, a taster who detects a hint of vanilla in the chardonnay is not implicitly hazarding a prediction about the likelihood of hidden vanilla beans, but is attempting an apt description of the quality of the flavor, to pin it down in words, which are usually metaphorical, and sometimes highly so. After all, at the simplest level, to say what a flavor is merely like is already to enter the space of metaphors and similes, and not all levels of description are so simple. Some florid descriptions may startle by their fancifulness, but the results of creative fancy can be less apt or more apt to the object being described. In his occasional inclination to treat 'delicacy of imagination' as a synonym for 'delicacy of taste,' Hume may have had this capacity of the taster in mind. At any rate, he should have. To taste a wine and describe the flavor of the taste is naturally to call upon metaphors, and these are the work of imagination.[13] (By contrast, are metaphors ever identical to the *causes* that scientific investigators hope to find, whatever the heuristic value of the metaphor?)

If attributing tastes to their causes were the critic's province, the critic would be performing the same kind of action that a cookbook author and a spice importer once attempted when they jointly sampled a Moroccan spice mixture, *ras el hanout*, and concluded that the powder contained 26 separate spices (including some quite exotic and unfamiliar ones, by Anglo-American cultural standards, such as grains of paradise).[14] The author having brought back a packet of the stuff from Fez, she and her coadjutor arrived "after a long analysis" at a determination of its contents; and their presumed expertise would lead one to expect a successful analysis, more or less. If, as in this example, the spices are numerous and uncommon, the ability to make such determinations requires considerable training and patience, and exercising the ability can plainly be better or worse. But it would be misleading to say, without technical commentary, that those who have this ability are good at tasting; it would be better to say that they are good at relying on taste – their taste buds – to ascertain facts that might be ascertained, in principle, in some other fashion (by chemical analysis of the powder, or by relying on the testimony, if reliable, of the maker of the stuff). Those alternatives may be cumbersome or hugely inconvenient, but they *are* alternatives. With the wine critic's hint of vanilla, on the other hand, no approach to the identified quality other than the art of description is remotely doable.

These two skills, attribution of flavor-causes and description of flavors, both involve the palate and so fall within the ambit of the sensory modality. The skills are perhaps easily elided for that reason, and an ambiguity in Hume's thought reflects the risk of elision. Hume writes that "a good palate is not tried by strong flavours, but by a mixture of small ingredients" (E 236). A strong flavor could be a strongly *pronounced* quality, one that is especially salient and arresting, or a strongly *present* flavor, in the sense that its cause is present in undiluted abundance. A first pass at interpretation might give the edge to the qualitative conception of a strong flavor, but that mild conviction is jeopardized by a closer look at the second half of Hume's statement: a 'mixture of small ingredients' looks like a reference to a compound of numerous but tiny causes. Or, yet again, the second half just might be a reference, somewhat picturesquely stated, to an ensemble of subtly detectible characteristics. It all depends on whether the ingredients are taken literally to be the ingredients of a thing that has flavor or taken figuratively to be the perceived "ingredients" of a flavored thing (with emphasis on the adjectives, not the nouns). Hume's text wavers inconclusively.[15]

The ambiguity here moreover corresponds to two opposing notions connected to perceptual simplicity in empiricism, and it is possible to elide these notions, too.[16] On the one hand, there is the idea of a "uniform appearance" (in Locke's words), not further analyzable and for that reason unimaginable without first-hand acquaintance. Although the taste of pineapple offers an easy illustration of a uniform appearance, global qualities attaching to complexes or more elusive, less readily nameable qualities in a complex provide other illustrations. On the other, there is the Berkeleyan idea of the *minimum sensibile*, the least perceivable unit, and hence that which would suffice, at the margin, to secure acquaintance. "A taste of leather" could be a distinctive flavor, like that of pineapple, or just the faintest trace of something, like a dash of salt. The use to which Hume puts Cervantes depends on the latter conception, but the practice of critics, not to mention Hume's account of the virtues of critics, is better represented by means of the former.

6. An objection to the foregoing attempt to bridge the gap between the palate and aesthetic discrimination would be to say that all that these remarks show is that the boundary of mental and bodily taste is not where we initially supposed it to be, between our responses to art and everything we do with our tongues, but lower down the scale, between the art responses and the more highly imaginative flavor-describing activities that happen to involve the palate, together on one side, and the quotidian, less sophisticated engagements of the palate on the other. This could be said, one suspects, by a defender of the thesis that wine-tasting is itself to be reckoned a minor art, and so we could really be just considering two kinds of art appreciation. This upgrade of wine connoisseurship may coexist with a much less exalted estimate of the prospects for, say, the tasting of canned beans, which, on this showing, would be the truer bodily objects of taste.[17]

However much the wine aficionado might welcome a principled distinction between wine and beans as objects of appreciation, the objection is beside the point. The difference between wine and beans is surely a matter of their comparative importance, prestige, or *de facto* degree of artisanal craftsmanship that has been expended on their behalf during their production. We may not think that beans are worth the sustained effort of cultivating connoisseurship, and perhaps there are grounds for not making the effort. But this is not to erect a boundary between two kinds of tasting activity for wine and beans.

What is clear is that the art of description, as we have called it, and the science of causal attribution, as we may for the sake of rhetorical contrast call it, are different things, and that two kinds of activity do go with each. But this is not the distinction between mental and bodily taste that we supposedly started with, nor does it give reason to relegate the palate, or those actions of the mind that might be modeled on it, to a domain peripherally relevant to the arts. A clear-eyed awareness of the real difference can also remind us that causal attribution is peripherally relevant not only to the palate but also to artistic judgment. Although art connoisseurs such as Bernard Berenson have identified the provenance of paintings merely by looking, it would be eccentric in the extreme to generalize from this specialized competence to the mundane virtues of the critic.

The upshot of these reflections is that a single activity of tasting can be discerned in both gustatory and non-gustatory settings. To be good at tasting in either setting is to be good at noticing aspects, and the limits of the noticeable are the limits of a person's imaginative perception, which (as Hume's acknowledgment of the relative rarity of true judges attested) is a capacity that is very unevenly distributed across persons. But if "every convert to the admiration of the true poet or orator is the cause of some new conversion" (E 243), and if the original "conversion" requires the imaginative ability to articulate what the less imaginatively gifted can recognize and apprehend, the only available defense of a judgment in this area is ultimately the sense of fittingness that a description elicits. In view of the various influences to which the feeling of fit is subject, it is not surprising that defenses of this sort are less than decisive, if regarded as proofs, than those furnished by emptied hogsheads.

7. This discussion began by canvassing the mysteriousness and triviality objections to mental taste, and considered how Hume's assumption that a "great resemblance" obtains between the mental and bodily taste does not, on its own, give sustenance to those objections. However, bodily taste itself needs to be understood differently from the way in which Hume, some of the time, seems to understand it if his invocation of the resemblance is to be credibly exonerated of

the charges brought against taste. Nevertheless, even if mental taste and bodily taste are the same taste – the same action of the mind, whether or not a bodily organ is further involved – the two objections might be pressed by someone who is skeptical not merely about a mental taste that is different from (though modeled on) the palate, but about a single taste as well. To come full circle, we might ask how the two objections look in the light of the revised Humean account of the two tastes.

The mysteriousness objection gains traction from the thought that a quasi-perceptual faculty has privileged access to quasi-perceptual aesthetic qualities. That is, the traction comes from the respect in which aesthetic taste is oddly parallel to, or coordinate with, the sense of taste (a "seventh sense," as one history of early modern aesthetic theory puts it).[18] Such a faculty is not obviously an improvement on the fitness-detecting reason that the moral rationalist Samuel Clarke supposed to exist (and which Hume, by a stronger light of reason, rejected).[19] If we exchange that picture for one in which the ordinary senses may be informed by ordinary imagination, the troublesome parallelism disappears. It is true that Hume himself called the imagination a "kind of magical faculty of the soul" (T 1.1.7.15; SBN 24), whose workings can be explicated only so far, and so one might think there is plenty of mystery remaining in the imagination. But at least there is no *new* mystery for Hume as a result of the exchange.

Little headway, however, seems to have been made against the triviality objection; indeed, the explanation of good taste in terms of being good at tasting, in whichever domain we please, may seem rather specially to invite it. To a suitably sober judge of human life, any object of concentrated imaginative perception may seem a waste of time, attention, and energy, whether it is art in one of the accredited media, the wines that aficionados prefer, or canned beans. If distinctions on the list of items that can be tasted should be made, then we need some account of the scale of value that the different items occupy: (most) art higher than (most) wine, probably, and (most) wine higher than (most) beans, perhaps.[20] To make these distinctions we do not have to suppose that the occupants of the scale represent lesser or greater degrees of a single value that renders them all commensurable; the differences are akin to Mill's higher and lower pleasures (which signify a distinction not consistent with the utilitarian scale, but which can have an independent recommendation). Once the need for such an account such becomes evident, it also becomes clear that what is meant by good taste is often something other than being *good at tasting*; it is often, so to speak, *tasting the good*. If this second meaning of good taste is not to attract a mystery accusation of its own, a general characterization of the place that these good things have in our lives is in order, and how it is that these things are such that we feel drawn to tasting them. The triviality objection can be answered, in principle, to the extent that any target of appreciation is judged to be worth the effort to appreciate it. But that sort of judgment is not a judgment of taste itself.

Notes

1 See Levinson (2002), pp. 229 and note 8. Levinson includes references to writers who voice this objection – Anthony Savile (1993), Roger Shiner (1996), and others. (The "British Objection," however, is not Levinson's own "Real Problem.")
2 Shiner (1996: 240).
3 Burke and Boulton (ed.) (1968: 11).
4 Wordsworth, Coleridge, Brett (ed.) & Jones (1963: 251).
5 The work of Arthur Danto provides a spectacular illustration of the way in which taste, and aesthetic considerations more generally, can be relegated to a relatively trivial role in the arts. See *The Transfiguration of the Commonplace* (1981), among many other writings.

6 This statement may mislead because there is a sense in which all tastes are arguably personal tastes. But some tastes are more expressive of a person than others. A wholesale aversion to celery does not reveal much of interest about the character of a person who has the aversion.

7 For a view with some affinity to this option, see Richard Shusterman (1989: 211–229). Shusterman thinks that the eighteenth century ignored, or suppressed, the class determinants of taste and that the result has been "elitist and oppressive" (226), but does not say that people have been oppressed by superficial art admired by elites.

8 Cervantes 1963: 589–590. Hume's retelling (the language of which I retain) in "Of the Standard of Taste" is at pp. 234–235.

9 In Hume's philosophical writings, the word 'deformity' occurs 61 times and 'ugliness' not at all (though 'ugly' does occur six times).

10 Glenn Parsons and Allen Carlson (2008) include historical material on the connection between beauty and fitness, although Hume (as a thinker who connects beauty more narrowly, in their view, to "utility") has only a cameo role.

11 Mary Mothersill (1984) presents an excellent guide to the topic, and includes a chapter on Hume.

12 The causal motif is even more salient in Cervantes' original text than in Hume's retelling. Sancho boasts, "Would you believe me, Sir Squire, I have such a great natural instinct in this matter of wines that I have but to smell a vintage and I will tell you the country where it was grown, from what kind of grapes, what it tastes like, and how good it is, and everything that has to do with it" (589). To back up his claim, Sancho says that this prowess runs in his father's family, instancing his kinsmen, one of whom could make causal identifications of wine "with the tip of his tongue," while the other "merely brought it up to his nose" (590). Given the sheer preposterousness of Sancho's braggadocio, the anecdote concerning the kinsmen is a virtual *reductio ad absurdum* of the alleged prowess.

13 My picture of the wine-taster's skill is indebted to Frank Sibley (2001). The general spirit of my proposal concerning the relationship between mental and bodily tastes owes much to Sibley's magisterial paper.

14 Wolfert (1987: 24–25).

15 Hume is not alone. Anthony Savile (1993) wants to "advise Hume not to say in the explication of his anecdote that it is the key and the leather that the tastevins taste. Rather, it is the taste of leather and iron that has *infiltrated* the wine" (78, my emphasis). The taste is being contrasted with its cause – but is also being characterized as causally active.

16 For Hume on *minima sensibilia* (not in the context of aesthetic theory), see Don Garrett (1997).

17 The example of canned beans is due to C. I. Lewis (1946), who suggested that it might be possible to exercise "equal discrimination" on wines and beans. The passage is quoted by Mothersill (1984: 260).

18 Kivy (2003).

19 The extent to which Hume improves on Clarke – or might not improve (when the subject is aesthetics) – is considered by Christopher Williams (2007).

20 The notion of a "scale of value" was broached by Lewis and appropriated by Mothersill. Mothersill's point is that the Taj Mahal may be more beautiful than a violet without making the violet a borderline instance of beauty; it may be a central instance, but of lesser value (261). My own use of the notion does not confine the scale to aesthetic values, however delimited.

References

Burke, E. (1968) *A Philosophical Enquiry into the Origin of Our Ideas of the Sublime and Beautiful*, ed. J. T. Boulton, Notre Dame, IN: University of Notre Dame Press.

Cervantes Saavedra, M. D. (1963) *The Ingenious Gentleman Don Quixote de la Mancha: A New Translation from the Spanish*, trans. S. Putnam, New York: Viking Press.

Danto, A. C. (1981) *The Transfiguration of the Commonplace: A Philosophy of Art*, Cambridge, MA: Harvard University Press.

Garrett, D. (1997) *Cognition and Commitment in Hume's Philosophy*, New York: Oxford University Press.

Kivy, P. (2003) *The Seventh Sense: Francis Hutcheson and Eighteenth-Century British Aesthetics*, Oxford: Clarendon Press.

Levinson, J. (2002) "Hume's Standard of Taste: The Real Problem," *The Journal of Aesthetics and Art Criticism* 60(3): 227–238. doi:10.1111/1540-6245.00070.

Lewis, C. I. (1946) *An Analysis of Knowledge and Valuation*, La Salle, IL: Open Court.

Mothersill, M. (1984) *Beauty Restored*, Oxford: Clarendon Press.

Parsons, G. and A. Carlson (2008) *Functional Beauty*, New York: Oxford University Press.

Savile, A. (1993) *Kantian Aesthetics Pursued*, Edinburgh: Edinburgh University Press.

Shiner, R. A. (1996) "Hume and the Causal Theory of Taste," *The Journal of Aesthetics and Art Criticism* 54(3): 237–250. doi:10.2307/431625.

Shusterman, R. (1989) "Of the Scandal of Taste, Social Privilege as Nature in the Aesthetic Theories of Hume and Kant," *Philosophical Forum* 20(3): 211–229.

Sibley, F. (2001) "Tastes, Smells, and Aesthetics," in F. Sibley, J. Benson, B. Redfern and J. Roxbee Cox (eds.), *Approach to Aesthetics: Collected Papers on Philosophical Aesthetics*. Oxford: Oxford University Press.

Williams, C. (2007) "Some Questions in Hume's Aesthetics," *Philosophy Compass* 2(2): 157–169.

Wolfert, P. (1987) *Couscous and Other Good Food from Morocco*, New York: Harper & Row.

Wordsworth, W., S. T. Coleridge and R. L. Brett and A. R. Jones, eds. (1963) *Lyrical Ballads: The Text of the 1978 Edition with the Additional 1800 Poems and the Prefaces*, London: Methuen.

21

FLUCTUATIONS

Manners and religion in Hume's "Of the Standard of Taste"

Emilio Mazza

Hume's "Of the Standard of Taste" still excites different and contrary readings.[1] Since Hume is very reserved, if not elusive, about the origin of the *Standard*, I first outline the circumstances of its composition and its possible connections with Ramsay's dialogue and Gerard's essay on taste. Hume's dissertation on the standard of taste reveals some structural similarities with his *Dialogue* on the standard of morals: they are both examples of Hume's mature and limited (so to speak) skeptical writings, where the tension is concealed but still operating. They both reveal a skeptical process of limitation of unlimited skeptical views. Notwithstanding his conclusion for the possibility of a standard, Hume acknowledges two unavoidable sources of variation: the internal condition and the external situation of the true critics. However, the true critics should free themselves from their personal prejudices as well as from those of their age and country.

The *Standard* also reveals a process of limitation of the unlimited toleration attending unlimited skepticism. Indulgence towards the peculiar and innocent (morally uninfluential) manners of other ages and countries appears to be an important feature of Hume's view. While his attitude towards the manners of the ancients (simplicity and ferocity), and their literary representations from Homer to Wilkie, is subject to some variations, Hume's aversion to any kind of influential religion remains a constant feature: active religion can disfigure beauty as well as virtue. Hume's methodical recommendations can still be useful today: when we judge the writings of other ages and countries, we should not forget our personal and social or historical prejudices.

A great variety of opinions

At the very beginning of his literary career, Hume "seek[s] out some new Medium, by which Truth might be establisht" in philosophy and criticism (L I, 13; cf. L I, 13): the "Of the Standard of Taste" is one of the last philosophical pieces he composed. It is also one of the most disputed, both with regard to its interpretation and its contribution to aesthetic theory. A great variety of opinions prevails on Hume's *Standard*, in his and our own days. An "ingenious" piece on a "controverted subject," the *Monthly Review* announces (Fieser 1757/2005: 264, 268). Very disappointing, the *Literary Magazine* answers (Fieser 1757/2005: 293). Hume does not fix any standard, but shows that "he is himself possessed" of a delicate elegant taste, the *Critical Review* observes (Fieser 1757/2005: 284). The *Bibliothèque des Sciences* wishes he "would occupy himself only with this kind of compositions" (1757: 132). Nothing "new," nothing "interesting," the

Bibliothèque Impartiale replies: Hume does not establish any "true rule" (1757: 435). The English are "very little advanced" in matters of taste, the *Mercure de France* concludes (1759: 102).

"The most engaging and ingenious essay in the history of aesthetic thinking," a true "work of literature," a contemporary scholar says (Ginsberg 1987: 234, 200). "The finest piece [...] on the theory of criticism," another agrees (Fogelin 2002: 147). "A brilliant success [...] against the sceptic's charge," a third one adds (Blackburn 2008: 106). Other voices object: an ironic, "quite puzzling" piece (MacLachlan 1986: 18, 23, 34), almost a failure in establishing a standard (Rowe 2012; 349). More modestly, it is defined as "the most complete statement of the method for contemplating and judging a work of art that had appeared up to the time of its publication" (Cohen 1958: 270); Hume's "most sustained contribution to general aesthetic theory" (Laird 1932: 275); his most "sustained and foundational" (Garrett 2015: 28), "interesting" (Jones 1982: 106), "important" (Jones 2009: 430), and "definitive" (Costelloe 2004: 87) piece on matters of criticism. The *Standard*, the expert observes, "has inspired a literature the size of which is rivaled only by the bewildering number of competing interpretations" (Costelloe 2013: 52).

The dialogue, the dissertation, and the essay

In February 1757, Hume spends few general words on the *Four Dissertations*, where the *Standard* was originally printed: "some [of them] are Attempts to throw Light upon the most profound Philosophy: Others contain a greater Mixture of Polite Literature, & are wrote in a more easy Style & Manner" (Hume 2014: 40–41). In 1772, 15 years afterwards, he accounts for the *Standard* transaction:

> I know not if you were acquainted with this Transaction. [...] I intended to print four Dissertations [...]. I sent them up to Mr Millar; but before the last was printed, [...] Lord Stanhope [...] convincd me, that [...] there was some Defect [...]; and I wrote to Mr Millar, that I woud not print that Essay [...], and I sent him up these two [...]. They were printed; but it was no sooner done than I repented; and Mr Millar and I agreed to suppress them [...], and I wrote a new Essay on the Standard of Taste, to supply their place.
>
> (L II: 253)

An accurate scholar lately sums up: it is "a late makeweight" (Stewart 2005: 47).

In 1754, Ramsay reads the manuscript of Hume's *History of Great Britain* and makes some corrections to the "Character of Shakespeare" (Ramsay 1756; cf. H V: 151). In February 1755, Ramsay publishes the *Investigator* (Ramsay 1755, cf. L I: 221), later entitled a *Dialogue on Taste*. In March, the Edinburgh Society proposes a gold medal for "the best essay on Taste" (*Scots Magazine* 1755: 129b), and the *Monthly Review* pronounces the verdict on Ramsay's piece: "the subject [...] is treated with no great accuracy" (*Monthly Review* 1757: 238). Yet in April Hume informs him: "Your 'Investigator' [...] has met with a very good reception." Hume plays a joke on the dialogue: "in vain did I oppose myself, and assert it was not just metaphysics" (L I: 221). In February 1756, the Society repeats the proposal (*Scots Magazine* 1756: 106a), and Gerard is "determined to enter on his enquiry" (Gerard 1759: i). In March, possibly when Hume is writing the *Standard*, Ramsay tells him with pride: "I am still satisfied with my own Dialogue" (Burton 1849: 33). Ramsay's *Dialogue* could have been a pretext for Hume's *Dissertation*.

In August 1755, together with Hugh Blair and Adam Smith, Hume is appointed member of the Committee for "Belles Lettres & Criticism" (Select Society 1754–1763: 64), which must "take into consideration all Essays [...] relating to the Arts," and "receive and examine every thing offered to the Society" (Select Society 1754–1763: 60). In January 1757, before the publication of the *Standard*, the Society announces that the premium "is not yet determined," but presumably something has been "produced" (*Scots Magazine* 1757: 49b), since in March the essay on taste is not mentioned any more (*Scots Magazine* 1757a: 160b). Finally, in January 1758, the Society adjudges the medal to Gerard (*Scots Magazine* 1758: 43a). In 1756 – so he declares – Gerard had submitted only the "general principles," but in 1759 he publishes "the whole, as it was at first composed" (Gerard 1759: i). His *Essay on Taste*, it is said, was "corrected" by Hume "through the press" (Nichols 1812, II: 326n.) and, Hume says, was "very well received" in Paris (H I: 308). If Hume was one of the judges "appointed" for that purpose (Gerard 1759: i; Norton and Norton 1996: 28 n.45), if Gerard did submit his "general principles" before the 1756 "spring or summer," when, it is said, the *Standard* was "finished," (Mossner 1950: 43a; 1980: 325), Hume could have read Gerard during the composition of his piece (cf. Jones 2009: 431–432; Harris 2015: 363–364; Mock 2012).

Hume quotes neither his "friend" Ramsay, "a painter of eminence and a man of Merit" (Hume 1766: 38n), nor his "friendly adversar[y]" (H I: 376) Gerard. Gerard quotes Hume's *Treatise* (Gerard 1759: 20–22) and refers to the *Delicacy of Taste* (Gerard 1759: 200). In 1754, while composing the *Dialogue*, Ramsay makes a portrait of Hume. In his writings, Ramsay Humeanly shows "the necessity of experimental reasoning in philological and moral enquiries" (Ramsay 1753: i; cf. T frontispiece), and welcomes that philosophy which "is nothing but common sense and experience methodised" (Ramsay 1755: 28; cf. EHU 12.25; SBN 162; DNR 1.10, 134). Ramsay and Gerard were closer to Hume than Hume to them.

Fluctuations: the virtuous dialogue and the tasteful dissertation

"Morals, their Standard"; "Taste, its Standard." More precisely: "Morals, not fluctuating" (Hume 1758: 536, 539) and – we could add – "Taste, not fluctuating." This is Hume's Index for the 1758 edition of the *Essays*. The "morals" entry refers to the *Dialogue*, where the skeptic maintains that we cannot "fix a standard" of morals (EPM, D.25; SBN 333); in the *Standard*, the skeptical philosophy maintains "the impossibility of ever attaining any standard of taste" (E 229). In both pieces, manners and tastes fluctuate for a while (cf. Herdt 1997/2008: 137–141). Some sympathetic readers seem satisfied. "Why can't you always write in this manner?," Elliot asks Hume in 1751, leading into the "maze" of skepticism "with no other view, than to point out [. . .] more clearly the direct road" (Burton 1846, I: 323). From difference and opposition, the skeptic concludes: no reconciling rule; only uncertainty, fashion, custom, and original sentiments. With the sanction of a proverbial common sense (*to everyone his own custom, no dispute about tastes*), the skeptic denies any standard. This unlimited denial is itself denied and the existence of some (loose) uniform standard asserted: in the *Dialogue*, the qualities of a good character and the four sources of approbation (qualities useful or agreeable to the possessor or to others) (EPM, D.37, 42; SBN 336, 337–338); in the *Standard*, the five qualities of the rare good critics and their joint verdict:

> A true judge in the finer arts is observed [. . .] to be so rare a character: Strong sense, united to delicate sentiment, improved by practice, perfected by comparison, and cleared of all prejudice, can alone entitle critics to this valuable character; and the joint verdict of such, wherever they are to be found, is the true standard of taste and beauty.
>
> (E 241)

Yet some unavoidable sources of variation remain in the *Standard* as well as in the *Dialogue*: the different customs, manners, and situations of different ages and countries, and the different dispositions and ages of different individuals (E 243–245; EPM, D.37–38, 51; SBN 336, 340–341; cf. E, 163), namely the personal and social or historical prejudices of the critics (Cohen 1958: 272, 276–277, 282). But, the *Dialogue* says, these sources of variation cannot "vary [...] the original ideas of merit [...] in any very essential point" (EPM, D.39, 42–43, 51; SBN 337–338, 341), nor can "confound all the boundaries of beauty and deformity" (E 243), the *Standard* echoes.

Briefly, *A Dialogue* could be a dissertation entitled "Of the Standard of Morals," and *Of the Standard of Taste* could be put into the form of "A Dialogue". They both loudly bespeak a close liaison with each other and with the moral *Enquiry*. They both go back to Hume's 1734 starting point: "to seek out some new Medium, by which Truth might be establisht" in criticism (H I: 13). They both appear either as the limitation of an unlimited skepticism or the loosening of a too rigid standard. In both cases, religion can hurt virtue and beauty: in the 1750s, the party of Calvinist traditionalists are attacking Hume and the Moderates (Harris 2015: 353–354). As Hume writes to Ramsay in 1755: "I am preparing for the Day of Wrath. [...] They did not propose to burn me because they cannot" (H I: 224). And Hume starts a new open campaign against religion in general. The *Dialogue* and the *Standard* pull down the curtain in a similar militant manner: "Active religion? No thanks!"

Skeptical limitations of skepticism: the process

"Doubts stole in, dissipated, return'd, were again dissipated, return'd again" (H I: 154). This is Hume's progress of thought on religion before planning the *Treatise*, and the *Treatise* (with Horace) remembers that the philosophical doubt "must return upon us every moment, however we may chace it away" (T 1.4.2.57; SBN 218; cf. E 567). Hume's "just" observations – a review of the *Natural History* observes – are mixed with a "sceptical spirit" and "some insinuations [...] against the Christian religion" (Fieser 1757/2005: 263). The *Standard* reveals the same mixture. It is really more skeptical than Hume's mature artful writing suggests (Taylor 2009: 312, 337, 339).

No sooner does Hume grasp the "true standard" – the "joint verdict" (E 241) – than he calls it into question:

> *But* where are such critics to be found? By what marks are they to be known? How distinguish them from pretenders? These questions are embarrassing; and *seem* to throw us back into the *same* uncertainty, from which, during the course of this essay, we have *endeavoured* to extricate ourselves.
>
> (E 241, italics mine)

What a wonderful emblem of skeptical ambiguity. Are these questions really embarrassing? Do they simply seem to throw us back? Is it really the same uncertainty? Have we simply endeavored to extricate ourselves from it? Again, when Hume finally seems to have reached an established position, his doubts announce their return: "*But* notwithstanding all our *endeavours* to fix a standard of taste, [...] there *still remain* two sources of variation, [...] and we seek in vain for a standard" (E 243–244, italics mine).

The dissertation displays a succession of skeptical stances leading to a mitigated denial of a standard of taste. The first skeptical stance (E 229) is taken as something existent, and recalls Ramsay's *Dialogue*: it is the unlimited skepticism of the natural equality of tastes (all sentiment is right). The second (E 232, 234, 241) and the third (E 241) connected stances admit of an easy solution: it is the weak limited skepticism of the imperfection of our faculties and of the embarrassing questions (the qualities and the rarity of the critics). The fourth (E 243) is the only legitimate stance: it is the Humean limited skepticism of the two sources of variation (the dispositions and ages of different individuals and the manners of different ages or countries). This skeptical "but"-dissertation, written by "the foremost philosopher of 'but'" (Ginsberg 1987: 202, 207), reveals a skeptical process in four steps, leading from the unlimited skepticism of sentiments to the limited skepticism of innocent peculiar dispositions and manners.

Like the *Dialogue*, the *Standard* provides us with a Humean "sceptical solution" to Hume's "sceptical doubts" (cf. EHU 5; SBN 40). It recalls that mitigated skepticism which is the "result" of excessive skepticism, when its "undistinguished" doubts are, "in some measure," corrected by "common sense and reflection" (EHU 12.24; SBN 161).

Prejudice-free critic: into the others and out of himself

By good sense, the good critic preserves his mind free from "all" prejudice and considers "nothing [. . .] but" the very object under examination. Someone influenced by prejudice "obstinately" maintains his "natural" position. But every work must be examined from a "certain" point of view, and the examiner's situation must be "conformable" to that required by the work, so that the work can produce the "due" effect on the examiner and the examiner can "fully" be pleased by the work (E 239). The critic must depart from his own situation, either by being someone else or by not being himself.

Judging a work of a different age (or nation), he must put himself in the situation of a particular audience. The orator – says Hume following Dubos (Dubos 1719, 2.36: 507–508) who was following Quintilian (Quintilian 1996, I, 3.7.23–24: 474–477) who in turn followed Aristotle (Aristotle 1926, 1.9.29–31, 1367b7: 96–99) – addresses himself to a "particular" audience and must have a "regard" to their "particular" interests, opinions, and prejudices (E 239). The critic of a different age (or nation) must have "all these circumstances in his eye" and place himself "in the same situation as the audience": he must make "allowance for their peculiar views and prejudices" (E 239).

Judging a work of his own age (and nation), the critic must put himself in the impersonal situation of "a man in general." He must suspend his interests as a "friend or enemy" of the author, imposing the "proper violence" on his own imagination and forgetting himself "for a moment" (E 239–240). Hume shifts to the first person (cf. Mason 2001: 66b, 70b n.36): "I must depart from this [particular] situation" and "I must [. . .] forget, if possible, my individual being and my peculiar circumstances" (E 240).

Sources of variation: personal dispositions and manners of the age

The different "humours" of men and the different "manners and opinions" of our age and country: these are the inextinguishable "sources" of variation and often produce "a difference in the degrees" of approbation. This diversity is "entirely blameless" and there is no "just" reason for approving one taste and condemning the other. A "certain degree" of diversity in judgment is "unavoidable" and "we seek in vain for a standard" (E 243–244).

The first source of variation lies in our different age and disposition (the "internal frame") (E 244). Every individual's age has its favorite author from a "conformity" of dispositions: Horace may be the favorite author at 40 (cf. L I: 401; EPM 5.30; SBN 222; Dubos 1719, 1.49: 684–685). We have a "peculiar sympathy" with the writer who "resembles" us: we vainly endeavor to "divest" ourselves of our "natural" propensities and "enter into" the sentiments of others. A certain disposition is more pleased by a certain species of writing, quality, and beauty. It is "almost impossible" not to feel a preference for what "suits" our particular disposition, and such preferences are "innocent and unavoidable" (E 244). The second source of variation lies in the manners of our own historical age and country (the "external situation") (E 244). We are more pleased with representations of characters and manners which "resemble" ours. We can "reconcile" ourselves to the manners of another age only by "some effort" (E 244–245; cf. Ramsay 1755: 57–58). We may "allow in general" that their representation is no "deformity" in the work and no "fault" in the author, but we are not "so sensibly" touched with them. A common audience can "never divest" themselves of their usual sentiments so far as to relish pictures which "no wise resemble" them; only the men of learning and reflection can "make allowance for" these different peculiar manners (E 245).

Being more pleased with what does resemble us, can we excuse any representation of peculiar manners on account of the manners of the age? Hume distinguishes between innocent and blameable manners. The representations of innocent peculiar manners "ought certainly to be admitted" (to be "shocked" with them is a "false" delicacy): we can and should "make allowance" for the "continual revolutions" of manners and admit also what is not "suitable to the prevailing fashion" (E 245–246). The representations of vicious peculiar manners, which are not blamed, "disfigure" the work and are a "real" deformity or a considerable diminution of merit: where the ideas of morality and decency "alter" from one age to another, "I cannot, nor is it proper I should, enter into such sentiments" (another shift to the first person); we can "never" relish the work, even though we may excuse the author on account of the manners of his age (E 246).

Homer and Fénelon: roughness, simplicity, and ferocity

By "some effort" we can "reconcile" ourselves to the innocent peculiar manners of another age. We can reconcile ourselves to the "simplicity" of ancient manners and behold "princesses carrying water from the spring, and kings and heroes dressing their own victuals" (E 245). – This is Homer (*Iliad*, IX 206–221; *Odyssey*, VI 77–104; X, 102–105), possibly thinking of Madame Dacier and her disputes with La Motte and Pope, but Hume does not say it.[2] Yet the Homeric heroes go beyond simplicity and show some roughness (E 246), if not some ferocity (E 228).

In 1751, Hume observes that Homer paints a "full, natural, undisguis'd Picture of ancient Manners" (L I: 152). His ethics (of courage), the moral *Enquiry* adds, are "well suited" to their age and "very different" from those painted by his "elegant Imitator," Fénelon. Courage is the "predominant excellence" among all those "uncultivated" nations who "have not, as yet, had full experience of the advantages attending the social virtues" (EPM 7.15; SBN 155), even though the partiality for military honors "appears so natural in the mind of man" (EPM 7.25; SBN 259).

The *Standard* does not overlook a "durable admiration": "the same Homer, who pleased at Athens and Rome [. . .], is still admired at Paris and at London" despite "all" the changes (E 233). Yet, the variety of tastes is still greater "in reality than in appearance" and the "seeming" unanimity vanishes when the critics come to "particulars" (E 227). "From Homer down to Fénelon," in all nations and ages poets praise the "same" virtues, but their "seeming" harmony disintegrates when they paint "particular" pictures of manners. In representing Achilles' heroism or Ulysses' prudence, Homer puts a "greater degree" of ferocity or fraud than Fénelon would admit of (E 227).

We should excuse "any seeming absurdity" in the ancients "from the manners of the age," say their supporters, like Dacier; these manners can excuse "only" the author, reply their adversaries, like La Motte (E 245). Hume advances a modern balanced solution: we must admit any representation of peculiar innocent manners, and reject any representation of vicious disfiguring ones. In the latter case we may excuse the author "on account of the manners of his age," but we can "never relish" his work (E 245–246).

"Sometimes" even Homer paints his characters with such a "conspicuous" want of humanity and decency that diminishes "considerably" the merit of his work and gives a "great advantage" to Fénelon (E 246; cf. Taylor 2015: 180–182). We are not "interested" in the sentiments of such "rough" ancient heroes; we are "displeased" to find the limits of vice and virtue "so much confounded." Again: we may give indulgence to the author on account of his "prejudices," but we "cannot prevail on ourselves" and enter into his sentiments or "bear an affection" to blameable characters (E 246). As men of learning (E 245) we can relish Homer's innocent simplicity, not his blameable-and-not-blamed ferocity. This is Hume's moral standard of taste.

In a couple of years he will declare himself more easily pleased by Homer's simplicity and less displeased by his roughness. The "tediousness" of Spenser is usually ascribed to the "change of manners," the *History* observes, but manners have "more changed since Homer's age," and Homer "remains still the favourite of every reader of taste and judgment." Homer "copied true natural manners, which, however rough or uncultivated, will always form an agreeable and interesting picture" (HOE III: 386).

Wilkie's "wonderful" *Epigoniad* may "bestow an Air of Novelty on the Imitation of Homer." Wilkie himself betrays something Homeric: "that Simplicity of Manners, so common to great Men, & even [. . .] that Rusticity [. . .] which serve[s] to abate the Envy." Hume shows "so much Love for Arts, & for [his own] native Country, as to be very industrious in propagating the Fame" of the poem (L I: 253). Following Wilkie, in a letter to the *Critical Review*, Hume does not stop at simplicity. Like Fénelon, Wilkie is a "great [. . .] imitator of Homer" (Hume 1759: 324); unlike him, he carries his "boldness of copying antiquity beyond the practice of many, even judicious moderns": he paints the characters with "all the simplicity of the Grecian heroes" and "some degree of their roughness, and even of their ferocity" (Hume 1759: 331). A "mere modern" – Hume remarks – is "apt to find fault with" this in Homer and, "perhaps, he will not easily excuse it" in Wilkie. The ideas of manners are "so much changed since the age of Homer": the reader is "now almost always" on the side of the Trojans, and "much more interested for [their] humane and soft manners [. . .] than for the severe and cruel bravery" of the Greek heroes. Sensible of this "inconvenience," Fénelon "softened extremely the harsh manners of the heroic ages" and "contented himself with retaining that amiable simplicity" (Hume 1759: 331–332).

Wilkie does not follow Fénelon's modern French model or even Hume's *Standard*. However "displeased," the reader must allow that Wilkie paints "a more exact and faithful copy of antiquity" and makes "fewer sacrifices of truth to ornament" (Hume 1759: 332). Is Hume changing his view of Homer's ferocity? Does he only affect a preference for Fénelon's humanity? Is he flattering the modern reader? Or is he simply reluctant to forget his interests as a friend of a Scotchman, who is delivering "perhaps [. . .] one of the ornaments of our language" (Hume 1759: 324)? A Scottish biographer observes: "those who knew Mr. Hume's taste, friendship, or sincerity will be best enabled to determine whether he is serious" (Chalmers 1810: 111). Whatever uncertainty we may have concerning his preference and sincerity, it is however certain that Hume takes the opportunity for another serious anti-religious stroke: "the christian religion [. . .] is unfit for the fabulous ornaments of poetry" (Hume 1759: 332).

A disfigured Racine: religion, morals, and criticism

"Bad influence of most popular religions on morality" (NHR 14.1: 81): this added clarifying title to *Natural History* (L I: 250; Hume 2014: 43) announces Hume's final retortion. "Morality hurt by popular Religions" (Hume 1758: 536), the 1758 index echoes. The last part of the *Standard* could be entitled "Bad influence of active religion on morality and beauty."

The *Standard* makes three distinctions among (absurd) "peculiarities" (of manners). It distinguishes between innocent manners and vicious manners not "marked with the proper characters of blame" (E 246; cf. Dubos 1719, 1.15: 109). The former require a little effort to be entered into (E 245); the latter "disfigure" any work (E 246, 248): we cannot and should not enter into them, and we can be indulgent to the author only (E 246). Second, it distinguishes between speculative or religious principles, which are extremely changeable, and moral principles, which are more constant (E 246). Where they are very different from ours, a little effort is required to enter into the former, a violent one into the latter (E 246–247). Finally, it distinguishes between mere religious principles, which are always innocent, and active religious principles, which are but dangerous (E 247). Like blameable manners, active religious principles disfigure the work by making it hateful or ridiculous: bigotry "disfigured" Corneille's and Racine's tragedies; superstition rendered "ridiculous" Boccaccio's and Petrarca's writings (E 247–249). When religious principles take "such strong possession" of the writer's heart, they "confound" the sentiments of morality and "therefore are eternal blemishes": "the prejudices and false opinions of the age are [not] sufficient to justify them" (E 247).

Traditionally active religious principles are supposed to improve the beauty of a work. Dennis, for example, celebrates the "Dependence" of great poetry on religion (Dennis 1704: 22). Dubos apparently joins him: "the miracles of our religion have something marvellous [. . .] with what a success they are treated by Corneille in the *Polyeucte* and Racine in the *Athalie*" (Dubos 1719, 1.23: 170–171). And we would certainly blame, he adds, any impious "brutal discourse [. . .] against professed religion" (Dubos 1719, 1.15: 110). Addison asserts that "in the Old Testament we find several passages more elevated [. . .] than any in Homer" (Addison 1711, II, 160, 3 September: 298). Dubos quotes the sentence and adds: "actually in the *Athalie* Mr. Racine [. . .] appears a greater poet [. . .] because the subject, being drawn from the Old Testament, entitled him to adorn his verses with the most audacious images of the Holy Scripture" (Dubos 1719, 2.39: 528). Ramsay disagrees: "the spirit of controversy [. . .] rose so high" that Milton introduced "the Almighty discoursing like a school-divine, and the devils amusing themselves in hell with metaphysical cunnundrums" (Ramsay 1753: 52). The "detestable influence of [. . .] scholastic jargon" produced a "hodge-podge" in his brain (Ramsay 1755: 66). In 1755, Ramsay had read the *Natural History* (L I: 223) and corrected the first volume of Hume's *History* (so he says) (Smart 1952: 98); in the 1757 second volume, Hume seems to follow Ramsay on Milton: not even the *Paradise Lost* appears "wholly purged" of the fanatical "cant" (H VI: 150).

The *Standard* is clear: active religious principles should be "imputed" as a "blemish" to the work and as a "fault" to the author (E-ST: 247–248). The unity of God, the *Natural History* informs us, is a pretense for representing the adversaries as the "objects of divine as well as human vengeance" (NHR 9.1: 60). Catholic religion, the *Standard* adds, inspires a "violent hatred" and represents "all" the adversaries as the "objects of divine [. . .] vengeance." The catholic zeal elevates these "blameable" sentiments to a virtuous kind of "divine heroism" (E 247).

Hume loves Racine. In 1742 he celebrates him as the "Favourite of the Fair Sex, as well as of the best Judges" (E 537). In 1751 he laments that John Home "never read Racine" (L I: 150). Then he revises his view: as the author of the *Douglas*, Home "appears a true disciple of Sophocles and Racine" (L I: 204). In Paris, Hume even imagines Madame de Boufflers "along the banks of the same beautiful river, [. . .] with the same books in [her] hand, a Racine," he supposes (L I: 449). Religion can corrupt even Hume's beloved authors.

Actually, the *Standard* maintains, bigotry "disfigured" two "very fine" tragedies. In Corneille's *Polyeucte* and Racine's *Athalie*, "an intemperate zeal [. . .] forms the predominant character of the heroes" (E 248). – In every religion, the *Natural History* admonishes us, the votaries seek divine favor by their "intemperate zeal" (NHR 14.1: 81). Hume shows the beautiful *Athalie* disfigured by religion and makes her more shocking by his peculiar translation: "Why comes that enemy of God hither to poison the air, which we breathe, with his horrid presence?"[3] (E 248; cf. Ginsberg 1987: 225–226). Voltaire considers *Athalie* as Racine's "most admirable work" (Voltaire 1753 III, 29: 80): in Paris it was "received with enthusiasm" (Voltaire 1753 II, 27: 342). But in London, Hume objects, "the spectators would be full as much pleased to hear Achilles tell Agamennon, that he was a dog in his forehead, and a deer in his heart" (E 248). Homer's rough simplicity is still preferable to Racine's disfiguring bigotry.

Traffic and limits of indulgences

"Toleration naturally attends Polytheism" (Hume 1758: 539): since tradition "could not possibly be reduced to any standard" (NHR 12.17: 72), the *Natural History* argues, it was "absolutely impossible to fix a preference" among many contradictory reports all supported by "equal authority" (NHR 11.2: 65). Does toleration naturally attend skepticism with regard to taste? Dubos seems to be positive: everyone should "continue in his own opinion without blaming that of others." It does not depend on a palate, "so formed as to receive a greater pleasure from Champaign than Spanish wine, to change his taste and prefer Spanish wine" (Dubos 1719, 1.9: 683). Colonel Freeman, Ramsay's spokesman in the *Dialogue*, prefers "Canary to Champaign." As an "entire friend to toleration," Freeman makes his cheeky comparison: "to compel any man to swallow what goes against his stomach, on pretence of preserving unity in public drinking [. . .] [is] little better than [. . .] the inquisition" (Ramsay 1755: 7–8).

Hume allows that the skeptical equality of tastes may imply toleration: where "the taste of all individuals" is "upon an equal footing" (E 242), every individual "ought to acquiesce in his own sentiment, without pretending to regulate those of others" (E-ST: 230). If we reject this equality, how can we save toleration? By indulgence and allowance. We are "naturally apt to be [. . .] dogmatical" and do not have "any Indulgence for those who entertain opposite Sentiments" (EHU 12.23; SBN 161), the *Philosophical Essays* establish. In all the questions of fact, the *Standard* recommends, we should acknowledge "a true [. . .] standard to exist somewhere" and have "indulgence to such as differ from [us] in their appeals to this standard" (E 242). Only "extreme ignorance," the *History* observes, may render us "utterly incapable of [. . .] indulgence to the opinions of others" (H III: 407).

The *Enquiry* brings indulgence into morals. The "deformity" of Vitellius' death – he was prolonging his ignominy from a "wretched Love of Life" – "banished all compassion," Tacitus asseverates. Hume instructs us that, "to enter thoroughly into this method of thinking, we must make allowance for the ancient maxim, that no one ought to prolong his life after it became dishonourable" (EPM 7.9 and n.41; SBN 253 and n.41).

Tyrannicide used to be praised; history and experience convinced us that it increases the cruelty of princes, and now those who killed a tyrant are "very improper models for imitation." Yet, Hume observes, they are "treated with indulgence on account of the prejudices of their times" (EPM 2.19; SBN 180–181; cf. EPM, D.8, 31; SBN 326, 334–335; Dubos 1719, 1.14: 106). The Athenian man of merit, says the skeptic in the *Dialogue*, today would pass for a vicious character. The narrator, mistaking his skeptical aim, replies: "you have no Indulgence for the Manners [. . .] of different ages. Would you try a Greek or Roman by the common law of England?" (EPM, D.18; SBN 330). There are "no manners so innocent or reasonable, but may be rendered odious or ridiculous, if measured by a standard, unknown to the persons" (EPM, D.19; SBN 330).

The *History* insists on the point. Freedom of speech, as well as religious toleration, used to be esteemed "incompatible" with good government. Today we enjoy it "in the utmost latitude":

no people "had ever set an example of such an indulgence," and any severity against seditious authors will "naturally, to us, appear enormous." Yet, Hume remarks, "it seems unreasonable to judge of the measures, embraced during one period, by the maxims, which prevail in another" (H V: 240). Surveying Cromwell's character "with that indulgence, which is due" to the infirmities of our species (H VI: 109), the *History* meets the *Dialogue*. If we consider "the passions and the prejudices of that period," the murder of the King "was to [Cromwell] covered under a mighty cloud of republican [. . .] illusions": "he might believe it, as many others did, the most meritorious action" (H VI: 109–110).

Indulgence or allowance play their role in the *Standard*. We should be indulgent to the absurd and innocent religious principles of another age (or country), hoping that our descendants will be indulgent to ours (E 247). Denouncing the Catholics, the *Natural History* warns all the Christians:

> it will probably become difficult to persuade some nations, that any human, two-legged creature could ever embrace such principles. [. . .] these nations themselves shall have something full as absurd in their own creed, to which they will give a most [. . .] religious assent.
>
> (NHR 12.5: 68)

We should be indulgent to a work containing religious principles, provided that they are "excusable" mere principles, like those of the Pagans. Speaking to them, the *Standard* addresses itself to the Christians: "all the absurdities of the pagan system of theology must be overlooked by every critic; [. . .] our posterity, in their turn, must have the same indulgence to their forefathers" (E-ST: 247; cf. Dubos 1719, 1.15: 112). This is what Dubos – following Fontenelle ("someday we shall be ancients too, and [. . .] our posterity in its turn [will] correct and surpass us") (Fontenelle 1825 IV: 243) – says of philosophy: "our grandchildren will one day reproach us for similar errors" (Dubos 1719, II: 323). While a man of reflection "can make allowance for" the innocent peculiar manners of the past (E 245), a critic influenced by prejudice "makes no allowance" for the peculiar views and prejudices of the persons of another age (E 239); and a critic of false delicacy "makes no allowance" for the continual revolutions of manners and customs (E 246).

The *Standard* displays a procession of indulgence and skepticism: an unlimited indulgence attends the natural equality of tastes; an indulgence to the peculiar views and prejudices of the audience attends Hume's answer to the imperfection of the five qualities; an indulgence to the different appeals to the standard attends the answer to the embarrassing questions; and a limited indulgence to the works representing the peculiar innocent manners of another age (and to the authors of the works representing blameable manners) attends the two sources of variation.

Even indulgence shows its own limits: no indulgence (no sympathy, no pleasure) for a work which represents blameable peculiar manners not "marked with the proper characters of blame" (E 246–247). No indulgence for a work where active religious principles "alter the natural boundaries of vice and virtue" (E 247). Exactly where indulgence is one of the family ("the sale of indulgences seems [. . .] no more criminal than any other cheat of [. . .] any other church") (H III: 472), Hume is less inclined to be indulgent. Religion has a bad influence on morals, declares the first of the *Four Dissertations*; and therefore even on taste, the last one adds. The *Natural History* condemns the vicious religionist, the *Standard* the religionist of bad taste. The virtuous atheist has met the true critic.

Conclusion: what is the *Standard* for?

The *Standard* is a skeptical process of limitation. It restrains the first unlimited skepticism, which confounds "all the boundaries" of beauty and deformity, and leads us into a limited skepticism, which allows "a difference in the degrees" of approbation and blame. A persistent (calm and measured) return of skeptical doubt and solution. Philosophers ask themselves "what the standard of taste is to be used for" (Taylor 2015: 113; cf. Mothersill 1989)? I would ask: what use can be made of Hume's dissertation "Of the Standard of Taste"?

A minimal use for example. We can take it as a model of reasoning (cf. Cohen 1958: 288), if our disposition and age, manners, and views allow us to enter with pleasure into its sentiments. We can take it as the author's instructions for reading his work. Sometimes we lose our standard. Sometimes we show little taste. When we run over Hume's writings, do we use our good sense to free us from all our prejudices? To survey all the parts and compare them together? Do we have a long practice and all the delicacy that Hume's writing demands? Do we put ourselves in the situation required by the work? Do we consider its particular audience and place ourselves in their situation? When we run over Hume literature, do we suspend our enmity or friendship with other scholars? Do we make allowance for the peculiar unblameable manners of different ages and nations? When we are inclined to forget it, and admit only what fits well with the fashion, we should repeat our mantra: "Academic religion? No thanks!"

Notes

1 Some of the most important scholarship includes Guyer1993 (on Hume and Kant and Hume's theory of beauty); Carabelli 1995 (on the connection between "Of the Standard of Taste," the *Essays*, and their structure); Dickie1996; Towsend 2001 (a systematic enquiry on the connection between Humean aesthetics and philosophy); and Costelloe 2007 (on the connection between Humean aesthetics and moral philosophy, the "Of the Standard of Taste" and general rules).
2 Madame Dacier speaks of princesses, kings, and heroes (Dacier 1741, I: xxiv–xxv). Accounting for her view, Du Resnel refers to princesses, princes, and kings (Resnel 1730: 20–21), and quotes Lord Roscommon's 1684 "Essay on Translated Verse" ("And chuse an *Author* as you chuse a *Friend*, / United by this *Sympathetick Bond*") (Resnel 1730: 6), which is evoked by Hume: "We choose our favourite author as we do our friend, from a conformity of humour and disposition" (E-ST 244).
3 "De quel front cet ennemi de Dieu / Vient-il infecter l'air qu'on respire en ce lieu?" (*Athalie*, vv. 1025–1026; Ginsberg 1987: 236 n.24).

References

Addison, J. (1711) *The Spectator*, 6 vols, London: J. and R. Tonson and S. Draper.
Aristotle (1926) *The "Art" of Rhetoric*, LOEB, London: W. Heinemann.
Blackburn, S. (2008) *How to Read Hume*, London: Granta.
Burton, J. H. (1846) *Life and Correspondence of David Hume*, 2 vols, Edinburgh: W. Tait.
———. (1849) *Letters of Eminent Persons Addressed to David Hume*, edited by J. H. Burton, Edinburgh and London: W. Blackwood.
Carabelli, G. (1995) *On Hume and Eighteenth-Century Aesthetics: The Philosopher on a Swing*, New York, Peter Lang.
Costelloe, T.M. (2007) *Aesthetics and Morals in the Philosophy of David Hume*, London: Routledge.
Cohen, R. (1958) "David Hume's Experimental Method and the Theory of Taste," *English Literature History* 25(4): 270–289.
Chalmers, A. (1810) "The Life of William Wilkie," in *The Works of the English Poets, from Caucher to Cowper*, 21 vols, London: J. Johnson *et alii*, vol XVI, pp. 110–121.
Costelloe, T. M. (2004) "Hume's Aesthetics: The Literature and Directions for Research," *Hume Studies* 30(1): 87–126.

———. (2013) *The British Aesthetic Tradition. From Shaftesbury to Wittgenstein*, Cambridge: Cambridge University Press.

Dacier, A. (1741) "Préface," in *L'Iliade d'Homère, traduite en François [. . .] Avec Quelques Reflexions sur la Préface Angloise de M. Pope*, 2 vols, Paris: G. Martin *et alii*, pp. i–lxx.

Dennis, J. (1704) "The Proposal," in *The Grounds of Criticism in Poetry*, London: G. Strahan, pp. 11–29.

Dickie, G. (1996) *The Century of Taste: The Philosophical Odyssey of Taste in the Eighteenth Century*, Oxford: Oxford University Press.

Dubos, J-B. (1719) *Reflexions Critiques sur la poesie et sur la peinture*, 3 vols, Paris: J. Mariette.

Fogelin, R. (2002) *Walking the Tightrope of Reason: The Precarious Life of a Rational Animal*, Oxford: Oxford University Press.

Fontenelle (1825) "Digression sur les anciens et les modernes," in *Œuvres*, 5 vols, Paris: Salmon, pp. 235–254.

Garrett, D. (2015) *Hume*, London and New York: Routledge.

Gerard, A. (1759) *An Essay on Taste with Three Dissertations On the Same Subject by Mr. De Voltaire. Mr. D'Alembert, F.R.S. Mr. De Montesquieu*, London: A. Millar; Edinburgh: A. Kincaid and J. Bell.

Ginsberg, R. (1987) "The Literary Structure and Strategy of Hume's Essay on the Standard of Taste," in R. Ginsberg (ed.), *The Philosopher as Writer: The Eighteenth Century*, London and Toronto: Associated University Press, pp. 199–237.

Guyer, P. (1993) "The Standard of Taste and the 'Most Ardent Desire of Society'," in T. Cohen, P. Guyer, and H. Putnam (eds.), *Pursuits of Reason; Essays in Honor of Stanley Cavell*, Lubbock: Texas Tech University Press: 37–66.

Harris, J. A. (2015) *Hume: An Intellectual Biography*, Cambridge: Cambridge University Press.

Herdt, J. A. (1997/2008) *Religion and Faction in Hume's Moral Philosophy*, Cambridge: Cambridge University Press.

Hume, D. (1758) "Index," in *Essays and Treatises on Several Subjects*, London: A. Millar; Edinburgh: A. Kincaid and A. Donaldson.

———. (1759) "Review of *The Epigoniad: A Poem*," *The Critical Review: Or, Annals of Literature* London: A. Hamilton VII (April, art. 4): 323–334.

———. (1766) *A Concise and Genuine Account of the Dispute Between Mr. Hume and Mr. Rousseau with the Letters That Passed Between Them During Their Controversy*, London: T. Becket and P.A. De Hondt.

———. (2014) *Further Letters of David Hume*, edited by F. Waldmann, Edinburgh: Edinburgh Bibliographical Society.

Jones P. (1982) *Hume's Sentiments: Their Ciceronian and French Context*, Edinburgh: Edinburgh University Press.

———. (2009) "Hume on the Arts and 'The Standard of Taste': Texts and Contexts," in D. F. Norton and J. Taylor (eds.), *The Cambridge Companion to Hume*, 2nd edn, Cambridge: Cambridge University Press, pp. 414–446.

Laird, J. (1932) *Hume's Philosophy of Human Nature*, London: Methuen.

MacLachlan, C. (1986) "Hume and the Standard of Taste," *Hume Studies* 12(1): 18–38.

Mason, M. (2001) "Moral Prejudice and Aesthetic Deformity: Rereading Hume's 'Of the Standard of Taste'," *The Journal of Aesthetics and Art Criticism* 59(1): 59–71.

Mock, J. W. (2012) "Possible Influences by and Upon David Hume and the Writing 'Of the Standard of Taste'," *Southwest Philosophy Review* 27(1): 83–91.

Mossner, E. C. (1950) "Hume's *Four Dissertations*: An Essay in Biography and Bibliography," *Modern Philology* 48(1): 37–57.

———. (1980) *The Life of David Hume*, 2nd edn, Oxford: Clarendon Press.

Mothersill, M. (1989) "Hume and the Paradox of Taste," in G. Dickie, R. Sclafani and R. Roblin (eds.), *Aesthetics: A Critical Anthology*, 2nd edn, New York: St. Martin's Press.

Nichols, J. (1812) *Literary Anecdotes of the Eighteenth Century: Comprizing Biographical Memoirs of William Bowyer*, 6 vols, London: Nichols and Bentley.

Norton, D. F. and M. J. Norton. (1996) *The David Hume Library*, Edinburgh: Edinburgh Bibliographical Society.

Quintilian (1996) *Institutio Oratoria*, 3 vols, LOEB, London: Harvard University Press.

Ramsay, A. (1753) *An Essay on Ridicule*, London: A. Millar.

———. (1755) *The Investigator: Number CCCXXII*, London: A. Millar.

———. (1756) "A. Ramsay to D. Hume," 13 March 1756, Edinburgh NLS, MS 23156, n. 103, ff: 79–82.

Resnel, J. F. du Bellay du (1730) "Discours du Traducteur," in A. Pope (ed.), *Essai sur la Critique*, Paris: T. Le Gras *et alii*, pp. 5–36.

"Review of Hume's *Four Dissertations*," *Bibliothèque des Sciences et des Beaux Arts (1757)*, January–February–March, 1757, 7(1), La Haye: P. Gosse, art. V: 109–132.

"Review of Hume's *Four Dissertations*," *Bibliothèque Impartiale (1757)*, May–June, 1757, 15(1), Göttingue and Leide: E. Luzac, art. XI: 431–435.

"Review of Hume's *Four Dissertations*," *The Critical Review (1757)*, February, in *Early Responses to Hume's Writings on Religion I*, 2005, edited by J. Fieser, London: Continuum: 270–287.

"Review of Hume's *Four Dissertations*," *The Literary Magazine: Or Universal Review (1757)*, December, in *Early Responses to Hume's Writings on Religion I*, 2005, edited by J. Fieser, London: Continuum: 288–295.

"Review of Hume's *Œuvres philosophiques*," *Mercure de France*, December, 1759, Art. II, 'Nouvelles Litteraires': 87–102.

"Review of Ramsay's *Investigator*," *The Monthly Review (1755)*, March, art. XXVI: 238.

Rose, W. (1757/2005) "Review of *Four Dissertations*," *The Monthly Review (1757)*, February, in *Early Responses to Hume's Writings on Religion I* (2005), edited by J. Fieser, London: Continuum, pp. 253–268.

Rowe, M. W. (2012) "'Of the Standard of Taste': Decisions, Rules and Critical Argument," in A. Bailey and D. O'Brien (eds.), *The Continuum Companion to Hume*, London: Continuum, pp. 349–363.

The Scots Magazine, March 1755, 17: 126b–130b.

The Scots Magazine, February 1756, 18: 105b–108a.

The Scots Magazine, January 1757, 19: 49b–52a.

The Scots Magazine, March 1757, 19: 160b–163b.

The Scots Magazine, January 1758, 20: 43a–46b.

Select Society (1754–1763) "Minutes of the Procedure of the Select Society," Edinburgh NLS, Adv. Mss. 23.1.1, ff: 13–182.

Smart, A. (1952) *The Life and Art of Allan Ramsay*, London: Routledge & Kegan Paul.

Stewart, M. A. (2005) "Hume's Intellectual Development 1711–1752," in M. Frasca-Spada and P. J. Kail (eds.), *Impressions of Hume*, Oxford: Clarendon Press, pp. 11–58.

Taylor, J. (2009) "Hume's Later Moral Philosophy," in D. F. Norton and J. Taylor (eds.), *The Cambridge Companion to Hume*, 2nd edn, Cambridge: Cambridge University Press, pp. 311–340.

———. (2015) *Reflecting Subjects: Passion, Sympathy, & Society in Hume's Philosophy*, Oxford: Oxford University Press.

Towsend, D. (2001) *Hume's Aesthetic Theory. Taste and Sentiment*, London: Routledge.

Voltaire, F. M. Arouet de (1753) *Le siecle de Louis XIV*, 3 vols, Francfort: Veuve Knoch and J.G. Eslinger.

PART IIC

History, politics, and economics

22

HUME THE HISTORIAN

Mark G. Spencer

I Creating a *History of England*

Should those who want to know Hume bother with his *History*? It is vital they do so, Duncan Forbes argued. Hume's *History* "is a masterpiece; it is essential and vintage Hume. No one can say he knows Hume who is ignorant of the *History*" (Forbes 1970: 8).[1] Any worthwhile attempt to define "The Humean Mind" needs to incorporate Hume's *History*. Moreover, doing so is not task-reading. The *History* may be the most engaging of all of Hume's books. It sold exceedingly well during Hume's lifetime and he became rich from its sales. In the nineteenth century, its popularity rose to even greater heights. As a general readership for the *History* fell off in the late nineteenth and twentieth centuries, scholars, at least, showed a renewed interest. Even today, debates rage about how best to read Hume's challenging – but highly readable – *History of England*. This chapter will sketch its creation, basic contents, and meaning, in part by reference to its reception and by asking what it was that Hume aimed to accomplish as an historian.

The first of the six volumes that comprises what we have come to know as Hume's *History of England, from the Invasion of Julius Caesar to the Revolution in 1688* was published in November 1754 as *The History of Great Britain, Volume I. Containing the Reigns of James I and Charles I.* That book took as its subject matter the period of the reigns of the early Stuart kings, encompassing the turbulent rule of James I (1566–1625; ruled 1603–1625), the rise of Parliament, and the destructive English civil wars (1642–1651) that brought Charles I's rule (1625–1649) and life (1600–1649) to an abrupt end by execution at age 49. This volume also traced "a more free and independent genius in the nation" (H 5:19) and in some ways remained at the center of Hume's historical enterprise. In "My Own Life," written toward the end of his life, Hume wrote about his intention in his *History* and the reception with which it met:

> I thought that I was the only historian, that had at once neglected present power, interest, and authority, and the cry of popular prejudices; and as the subject was suited to every capacity, I expected proportional applause. But miserable was my disappointment: I was assailed by one cry of reproach, disapprobation, and even detestation; English, Scotch, and Irish, Whig and Tory, churchman and sectary, freethinker and religionist, patriot and courtier, united in their rage against the man, who had presumed to shed a generous tear for the fate of Charles I, and the earl of Strafford.
>
> (H 1: XXX)

The early reception of Hume's *History* has important things to tell us about Hume the historian. But to see more clearly how this is so and what it shows requires additional context.

Hume's first Stuart volume was published only two years after he had been elected (in 1752) Keeper of the Advocates' Library in Edinburgh. That post gave Hume ready access to a fine collection of books, totaling almost 30,000 volumes (Harris 1966; Hillyard 1989). In "My Own Life" (which was attached to the first posthumous edition of the *History*, in 1778, and printed in most editions thereafter), Hume wrote:

> In 1752, the Faculty of Advocates chose me their Librarian, an office from which
> I received little or no emolument, but which gave me the command of a large library.
> I then formed the plan of writing the History of England.
>
> (H 1: XXX)

But, Hume probably took the post because he had already formed the plan of writing England's history, as other historians have convincingly argued (Todd 1983; Emerson 2009). It is also certain that Hume's *History* contained a vast amount of scholarship mined from the shelves of the Advocates' Library, and elsewhere; from his reading as a child and young man, to the library of the British Museum, to private papers he sought out in Scotland, England, and France (Emerson and Spencer 2014).[2]

With the assistance of the Faculty of Advocates' book collection, the second volume of Hume's *History* was published shortly after the first, in 1757. In *The History of Great Britain. Vol. II. Containing the Commonwealth, and the Reigns of Charles II and James II*, Hume looked forward from the perspective of the earlier Stuarts. The volume covered Oliver Cromwell (1599–1658; Lord Protector, 1653–1658), the Restoration (1660), Charles II (1630–1685; ruled 1660–1685), and James II (1633–1701; ruled 1685–1688), bringing Hume's eighteenth-century readers to the Glorious Revolution of 1688–1689 and to the dynastic claims of the now displaced Stuarts. Hume described "a continual struggle" that was "maintained between the crown and the people." These were times in which "privilege and prerogative were ever at variance" (H 6: 530). Whig and Tory historians, whose works he aimed to supplant, had argued hotly over how to interpret these events. But Hume recommended that "extremes of all kinds are to be avoided; and though no one will ever please either faction by moderate opinions, it is there we are most likely to meet with truth and certainty" (H 6: 533–534). He would be an arbitrator between political factions, but one who found the Tories' history often right.

His next installment was published in two volumes in 1759. In *The History of England, Under the House of Tudor*, Hume looked backward from the early Stuarts to the reigns of the Tudor monarchs, including Henry VII (1457–1509; ruled 1485–1509), Henry VIII (1491–1547; ruled 1509–1547), and Elizabeth I (1533–1603; ruled 1558–1603). She was a figure in Hume's account whose "qualities as a sovereign, though with some considerable exceptions, are the object of undisputed applause and approbation" (H 4: 353). While Hume's *History* (like those published before it) was largely framed by the reigns of England's kings and queens, he made an effort to incorporate – often in Appendixes, such as that for Elizabeth – periodic summaries and asides related to government, economics, commerce, law, religion, wars, learning, and the general manners of the times. It might not strike us today as an effort to produce social or cultural history, but Hume incorporated more of that than what was then standard.

In 1762, Hume published his final two volumes, *The History of England, from the Invasion of Julius Caesar to the Accession of Henry VII*. There, he sketched England's medieval and ancient history, ranging all the way back to "remote ages" that were "involved in obscurity, uncertainty, and contradiction" (H 1:3). Many of his heroes here were "powerful, innovative, and aggressive kings who created the rule of law out of chaos" (Suderman 2013: 137–138) – Alfred (849–899; ruled 871–899), William I (1028–1087; ruled 1066–1087), and Edward I (1239–1307; ruled 1272–1307). Other noteworthy aspects to Hume's approach, contemporaries found curious. Writing his *History* by going further and further back in time, as Hume did, led one of his earliest critics to comment in a line that has been often quoted since: "as witches use to say their prayers," so David Hume wrote his history, "*backwards*" (Mossner 1980: 302). Hume's method of looking backward mystified many of his readers in the eighteenth century and thereafter, but it was key to his understanding of the past. Only by excavating the deep and often tangled roots of later historical events and by thinking historically about those who had brought those events about could the past be meaningfully understood.

Having completed his *tour de force*, all of his material could now be integrated and packaged together in a "complete" quarto edition of the *History of England* in 1762. By 1763, an octavo edition, in eight volumes, was also available for those whose preferences or budgets dictated a cheaper format. During his lifetime, new editions followed in various sizes and styles, from "Royal Paper" to "Small Paper" (Todd 1983: XX). They were often "corrected," as Hume fiddled with his text till the end (Slater 1992; van Holthoon 1997; van Holthoon 2000). Posthumous editions numbered in the hundreds by the end of the next century (Norton and Popkin 1965).[3] Hume had a much better run than most historians. Hume's success depended upon his political stance, his methods, and the brilliance of his writing. It also mattered that he gave his readers better and new-modeled historical explanations.

II Hume on history before the *History*

One cannot hope here to give a complete account of Hume's aims and accomplishments as historian in those six volumes covering a span of more than 1600 years and totaling well over a million words. But we can cast a bit of light on Hume's historical outlook and his argument. Hume consistently maintained that he aimed to write a history that was balanced in its approach to the past and entertaining in its delivery. "The first Quality of an Historian," wrote Hume to a friend, "is to be true & impartial; the next to be interesting" (L 1: 210).[4] He was keen to present England's history from the perspective of an enlightened observer; his preferred perch was not an identifiable agenda linked to a particular sectarian or political party – that was the perspective from which English history was regularly written before Hume. In neglecting "present power, interest, and authority, and the cry of popular prejudices," Hume aimed to be, and was, novel. He also saw that his innovative approach would cast new light on England's past, and present, and that doing so allowed the historian to attract more and different sorts of readers.

The study of Hume's thought – historical, but also philosophical, economic, political, and otherwise – has begun to benefit from scholars turning some of their attention from Hume's works to the early reception of those works.[5] It is not that Hume's eighteenth-century readers offer a privileged interpretation of Hume. Indeed, the *History*'s earliest readers were not always perceptive – although they sometimes were (Charles Carroll or Carrollton [1737–1832] offers a good example of one who was). But even Hume's less perceptive early readers help illuminate the contexts in which Hume wrote (Fieser 1996; Spencer 2002; Jones 2005; Spencer 2005; Allan 2013; Spencer 2013; Towsey 2013). We have begun to right the imbalance that one commentator identified a decade ago: "In spite of its great popularity, the early responses to Hume's *History* have been among the least explored areas of Hume scholarship" (Fieser 2005: xiii).[6] We have begun to see more clearly that with his *History*, "Hume was partly creating, partly responding to, a new market" (Wootton 2009: 447) for enlightened histories. Looking forward from the text of Hume's *History* to its early reception, then, has important things to tell us about Hume's aims as historian. Let us begin, however, by first looking backward – backward to some of what Hume wrote about the subject of history before any of the volumes of his own *History* were published, written, or even formulated, let alone purchased or read. That gaze tells us things worth learning about this historian.

In his pre-*History of England* published writings and surviving correspondence, Hume at several places addressed the aims of historians. That makes sense because he lived in a world in which history mattered (Emerson 2009: 104–115). One place he did so was in "Of the Study of History," a short essay first published in the *Essays, Moral and Political* of 1741 and included in the *Essays and Treatises on Several Subjects* through 1760, after which it was withdrawn. This essay closely linked the historian's craft to his audience, linking an historian's concerns with a history's readers. Hume concluded "Of the Study of History" in these words:

> The writers of history, as well as the readers, are sufficiently interested in the characters and events, to have a lively sentiment of blame or praise; and, at the same time, have no particular interest or concern to pervert their judgment.
>
> (E 568)

The balance to which Hume referred in 1741 – one between "lively sentiment" on one hand and "no particular interest" on the other – informed his developing historical attitude and the histories he wrote.

In his *Enquiry Concerning Human Understanding*, first published in 1748 at a time when Hume had begun to think more seriously about his *History*, he again linked writers and readers of history. Here, he remarked on the importance of presenting to a history-reading audience an historical story that was a connected chain of events. Hume wrote that a historian's narrative was to be led by a "connecting principle." He elaborated:

> the most usual species of connexion among the different events, which enter into any narrative composition, is that of cause and effect; while the historian traces the series of actions according to their natural order, remounts to their secret springs and principles, and delineates their most remote consequences. He chooses for his subject a certain portion of that great chain of events, which compose the history of mankind: Each link in this chain he endeavours to touch in his narration.
>
> (EHU 3.9)

Approaching history in that way was not always easy: "Sometimes unavoidable ignorance renders all his attempts fruitless: Sometimes, he supplies by conjecture, what is wanting in knowledge" (EHU 3.9) There is no evidence to suggest precisely when Hume began to write his *History*, but one might conjecture that these reflections in EHU were written from the perspective of one who had begun to know such difficulties first-hand – a possibility reflected in his letters. In 1748, Hume wrote to James Oswald of Dunnikier (1715–1769), showing that he had begun to look at life through the eyes of an historian:

> I got an invitation from General St Clair, to attend him in his new employment at the Court of Turin, which I hope will prove an agreeable if not a profitable jaunt for me. I shall have an opportunity of seeing Courts & Camps; & if I can afterwards, be so happy as to attain leisure and other opportunities, this knowledge may even turn to account to me, as a man of letters, which I confess has always been the old object of my ambition. I have long had an intention, in my riper years, of composing

some History; & I question not but some greater experience of the Operations of the Field, & the Intrigues of the Cabinet, will be requisite, in order to enable me to speak with judgement upon these subjects.

(L 1: 109)

Hume concluded his account in EHU: always the historian "is sensible, that the more unbroken the chain is, which he presents to his reader, the more perfect is his production" (EHU 3.9).[7]

Part of what enabled historians to construct their chains, according to Hume, was that basic human motives were constant over time. How else could one make sense of events and people of the past or present? Hume wrote:

> Mankind are so much the same, in all times and places, that history informs us of nothing new or strange in this particular [human actions and motives]. . . . Would you know the sentiments, inclinations, and course of life of the GREEKS and ROMANS? Study well the temper and actions of the FRENCH and ENGLISH: You cannot be much mistaken in transferring to the former *most* of the observations, which you made with regard to the latter.

(EHU 8.7; SBN 83)

The emphasis on "*most*" was Hume's.

Several questions come to mind: Was Hume's *History* impartial in the way he wanted it to be? How did his *History* balance "lively sentiment" on one hand and "no particular interest" on the other? What was the "connecting principle" providing links of the chain that was Hume's *History of England*? How was England's ancient history connected to recent times? Over the years, Hume's readers have put these and related questions to the *History*. Their answers have been surprisingly wide-ranging but also provide useful context.

III Looking backward, history, and historiography

Many of Hume's contemporaries and near contemporaries, especially in eighteenth-century Britain, saw the "connecting principle" of Hume's *History of England* in negative terms. Some saw Hume's work as being suspect because Hume's narrative was thought to be connected by a principle of religious skepticism – history written by "The Great Infidel." What else could be expected from the philosopher who wrote against miracles?

For many of those critics, and also others, Hume's story was thought to be one dictated by a political bias towards Toryism. They viewed Hume as an apologist for the early Stuarts. He was the historian who had dared to shed a tear for Charles I, denied the existence of the ancient Saxon constitution and the Norman yoke, and downplayed the historical importance of Parliament. Hume was accused of "Tory" leanings in Roger Flexman's (1708–1795) review of his first volume, published in *The Monthly Review* in 1754. William Rose (1757–1828) said something similar in his review of the second volume published in the same journal in 1757. Thomas Birch (1705–1766), the Rev. Daniel MacQueen (d. 1777), and Owen Ruffhead (1723–1769) all criticized Hume for producing a partial Tory account unsympathetic to religion.

With the publication of the complete quarto edition of the *History* in 1762, more and more commentators saw Toryism as Hume's connecting principle. That was the case in works such as Joseph Towers (1737–1779), *Observations on Mr. Hume's "History of England"* (1778); John Pinkerton (1758–1826), *Letters of Literature* (1785); John Millar (1735–1801), *An Historical view of the English Government* (1787); and Joseph Priestley (1733–1804), *Lectures on History and General*

Policy (1788), among others. There were important exceptions to these contemporary readings of a Tory Hume. In early America, for instance, Hume was more often read – at least before 1800 – not as a Tory but as one who provided a story of the slow growth of constitutional liberty. That was amenable to many American liberals. But by the early years of the nineteenth century – in Britain and America – Hume was most commonly portrayed as a Tory historian who falsely aimed to defend Charles I. That is the way that George Brodie (1786–1867) came to read the *History*, as did many who read Brodie's *A History of the British Empire* (1822), including Thomas Jefferson (1743–1826), Francis Palgrave (1788–1861), Thomas Babington Macaulay (1800–1859), and John Stuart Mill (1806–1873), to name a few influential accounts.

Still, the *History* was constantly in print during the nineteenth century, coming out in edition after edition, some illustrated, continued, enlarged, or otherwise embellished. Others were abridged and even expurgated, such as *Hume's History of England Revised for Family Use* (1816) or the *Student's Hume* (1858), books which suggested the unsettled nature of Hume's nineteenth-century reception. The *History's* immense popularity was not missed by its many critics, who were convinced that Hume's success was largely to be explained by his smooth writing. As a result, several critics thought it best to offer guidance to young and otherwise unwary readers of Hume, taking them by the hand to lead them safely through Hume's text, lest they too be lulled in by his beauties.

One who did so was John Baxter (dates unknown). Thomas Jefferson praised Baxter's *A New and Impartial History of England* (London, 1796) and aimed to have it reprinted in America in 1807; at the same time, Jefferson aimed to have Hume's *History* banned from the University of Virginia Library. Jefferson wrote that Baxter "has performed a good operation" on Hume.

> He has taken the text of Hume as his ground work, abridged it by the omission of some details of little interest, and wherever he has found him endeavoring to mislead, by either the suppression of a truth or by giving it a false coloring, he has changed the text to what it should be, so that we may properly call it Hume's history republicanised.
>
> (Spencer 2005: 253)

Others followed the illustrious censor.

William Smyth (1765–1849) sought to educate the naive general readers of Hume's *History*, protecting them from its sophistry. As Smyth put it, he would follow Hume,

> step by step, through the whole of his account; and showing what were his fair, and what his unfair inferences; what his just representations, and what his improper colourings; what his mistakes, above all, what his omissions; in short what were the dangers, and what the advantages, that must attend the perusal of so popular and able a performance.
>
> (Smyth 1848 1: 128)

In other words, Smyth, Baxter, and the others tampered with Hume's text and aimed to circumvent what they took to be Hume's connecting principle of Toryism. By the end of the nineteenth century – as the historical part of our story slips into the historiographical – there were *few* dissenting voices to the chant of a Tory Hume.

Early twentieth-century scholars saw things in similar ways. In 1926, J.B. Black wrote:

> Hume's idea of impartiality was peculiar. It did not consist in establishing truth of fact – the sense in which we should use the word to-day – so much as truth to certain

philosophical convictions from which he started as first principles. The conclusion is not that he falsified history either intentionally or involuntarily, but that he was bold enough to measure characters and events against a more or less absolute standard. . . . It is not the method a modern historian would, for a moment, think of employing; but it was the way in which the eighteenth century *philosophe* envisaged his task.

(Black 1965: 93–94)

It was against that entrenched reading of Hume that Ernest C. Mossner felt compelled to deliver "An Apology for David Hume, Historian" (Mossner 1941). Mossner's defense appeared at first to have little impact. For the next 30 years, descriptions of Hume's supposed partiality became even more elaborate and continued to be wrapped up with criticisms of Enlightenment historiography as a whole. In 1946, R.G. Collingwood dismissed Hume's *History* as "polemical and anti-historical." Hume's and other Enlightenment histories were mere "tracts for the times" (Collingwood 1946: 77).

Since the 1970s, however, more scholars have become dissatisfied with interpretations of Hume's *History* as a routine Tory tract or one that measured unthinkingly with absolute standards.[8] They have proposed other connecting principles. For Duncan Forbes, Hume was not a Tory historian but a "scientific" or "sceptical Whig," a voice of political moderation (Forbes 1975). For Victor Wexler and John J. Burke, Hume strove to attack the Whig myth of an ancient constitution, to "Wake the English from a Dogmatic Slumber"; Hume was anti-Whig, not Tory (Wexler 1977; Burke 1978). For J.C. Hilson, Hume in the *History* was a "Man of Feeling" (Hilson 1978); for Donald Siebert, he "refashioned the familiar sentimental character into a new type one might term 'the hero of feeling'" (Siebert 1989). For Philip Hicks, Hume was a neoclassical historian who "went to great lengths to observe ancient protocols" that he aimed to mirror in his own for historical writing (Hicks 1996: 170). Several others see the connecting principle of Hume's *History* to be its account of the growth of modern constitutional liberty. That is the collective case made by the essays in Nicholas Capaldi and Donald Livingston's *Liberty in Hume's "History of England,"* as it is with J.G.A. Pocock's account of Hume's *History* in his *Narratives of Civil Government* (Capaldi and Livingston 1990; Pocock 1999). Others have attempted to emphasize aspects of Hume as philosophical historian (Norton and Popkin 1965; Wertz 2000; Schmidt 2003), looking to Hume's philosophy as a systematic guide to his history, or, more recently, driving a wedge between the two (Harris 2015).[9] The *History* has been seen as a conservative text (Livingston 1984; Livingston 1995), as a liberal one (Stewart 1963; Stewart 1992), and one that touted the Magna Charta as a "turning point" establishing a "constitutional fundamental" (Sabl 2012: 152). Others see a historical narrative held together by imagination (Long 2013; Costello 2013). All of these are somewhat persuasive.

Several scholars have also problematized our understanding of Hume's understanding of historical distance. Two notable accounts that do so are by Nicholas Phillipson and Mark Salber Phillips. On the final page and concluding paragraph of his influential book on Hume in the "Historians on Historians" series, Phillipson wrote that Hume had shown "human beings":

how to distance themselves from their past and devote themselves to the peaceful pursuit of their interests in the material world in which they found themselves. For it was as important for the philosophical historian to liberate human beings from the priestcraft of historians as it was to liberate them from the clerics.

(Phillipson 1989: 141)[10]

There are good reasons to think differently, as we will see, but that has not stopped others from interpreting Hume's *History* in similar ways to Phillipson.

For Phillips, Hume's *History* shared the limits of other Enlightenment accounts. Phillips identified a tension between what he called "engagement" and "disengagement" in Enlightenment historiography in general and in Hume's *History* in particular (Phillips 2000: chapter 2, *passim*). Hume the historian, he wrote, was "looking back over an epochal divide" (Phillips 2000: 76). Like Phillipson, Phillips argued that Hume's past was a world distant and remote from the present.[11] To support that reading, Phillips quoted Hume's summary of the manners of England's political parties as they appeared after the polarizing effects of the English civil wars:

> No people could undergo a change more sudden and entire in their manners than did the English nation during this period. From tranquility, concord, submission, sobriety, they passed in an instant to a state of faction, fanaticism, rebellion, and almost frenzy. The violence of the English parties exceeded any thing which we can now imagine. No social intercourse was maintained between the parties; no marriages or alliances contracted.... The manners of the two factions were as opposite as those of the most distant nations.
>
> (H 6: 141)

Arguing that for Hume these seventeenth-century factions "served as a constant reminder that those days were very different from his own" (Phillips 2000: 74), Phillips concluded:

> The only way to understand the profound transformations of the past century, [Hume] seems to be saying, is to work in the very widest terms available, to adopt, in fact, the anthropological framework with which Enlightenment writers had learned to understand remote civilizations or barbaric tribes. How else to think about a habit of violence that he finds beyond present imagination? How else to imagine a social divide so deep that the English seemed split not merely into two nations, but distant ones at that?
>
> (Phillips 2000: 76)

That interpretation of Hume's historical intentions is helpful, but only to a point. Reading Hume's account of the English civil wars within the wider context of his discussion of faction suggests a different reading. Hume strove to see the English civil war factions in the contexts of their times. By doing so, he came to recognize that even barbaric manners were not as remote as he wished (after all, he lived with tribal Highlanders) or as distant as Phillips – and others who see Hume as distancing himself from the past – supposed.

IV Hume's *History* and historical context

In his *History of England*, Hume was not "distancing" himself or his readers from the past. Neither was he writing a party history nor judging events and actors from an a-historical perspective against an "absolute standard." Rather, Hume strove to delve into the past to bring it into a sharper and more intimate focus. Only then could one find a truly historical perspective from which to judge it in the context of its own time. He aimed to unite a "lively sentiment" with "no particular interest." He did not aim to demonstrate an "epochal divide" between those who lived in the seventeenth century and earlier times on one hand and readers of his eighteenth-century history on the other. He aimed instead to show that understanding the English civil wars, or any other past event or person, meant looking forward, and backward, in an effort to situate the event and its agents in a layered historical context. It meant looking at things and people from highly contextualized and even shifting points of view. It required giving credence to unintended consequences and being aware of idiosyncrasies. Hume's approach aspired to judge historical characters, their decisions and actions, within the realm of the limits and possibilities of the times, insofar as those might be reconstructed with the imperfect and incomplete records from which historians worked, or drew reasonable conjectures. And he invited his readers to make up their own minds about the story he presented.

This way of seeing things sits well with Hume's take on judging in other circumstances. Hume often showed himself to be comfortable living with uncertainties that appear to have troubled others in his world. He was even able to rest content when the judgments rendered from various points of view did not seem to agree. Hume's character sketch of Sir Robert Walpole (1676–1745) comes to mind:

> As I am a man, I love him; as I am a scholar, I hate him; as I am a BRITON, I calmly wish his fall. And were I a member of either house, I would give my vote for removing him from ST. JAMES'; but should be glad to see him retire to HOUGHTON-HALL, to pass the remainder of his days in ease and pleasure.
>
> (E. 576)

Hume was aware that his contemporaries were not always up to judging in this way. Some called for Walpole's impeachment; others for his execution.

Hume's letters contain many references to the goals of the *History*, as he saw them, as well as a surprising number of comments on the reception of the work. Often his sentiments were delivered to close friends to whom he had no reason to lie. Hume wrote to John Clephane (d.1758) in 1753: "You know that there is no post of honour in the English Parnassus more vacant than that of History. Style, judgment, impartiality, care – everything is wanting to our historians; and even Rapin, during this latter period, is extremely deficient" (L 1:170). (French historian Paul de Rapin-Thoyras' [1661–1725] history of England was one of those Hume aimed to supersede.) In 1754, Hume wrote to a friend, Mrs. Dysart of Eccles (d. 1789), sending her a copy of volume one of the *History*: "Whether am I Whig or Tory? Protestant or Papist? Scotch or English? I hope you do not all agree on this head; & that there [are] disputes among you about my principles" (L 1: 196). Hume's correspondence, then, suggests that Hume strove, actively, to make sure that the connecting principle of his *History* was not dictated by the interests of any particular party, religious persuasion, or national interest. Rather, if we take Hume at his word, he aimed to challenge the agendas that historians of various parties, sects, and countries had typically brought with them to their telling of the history of England. Indeed, it was for that historiographical reason that Hume began the *History* where he did. He wrote in "My Own Life": "I commenced with the accession of the House of Stuart, an epoch when, I thought, the misrepresentations of faction began chiefly to take place" (H 1: XXX). And it was precisely because Hume had aimed to write as an impartial spectator, taking no party line, that he was so perturbed by the early reception of the *History* and persistent attempts to cast him as an unthinking party writer. Those early responses to Hume's *History*, many of which are cited above, help us to see just how foreign and strange Hume's enlightened approach appeared to his contemporaries.

This chapter has argued that Hume aimed to judge historical actors and actions from within the historical context of their times. But as the details of the story Hume aimed to tell from the perspective of no particular present interest became clearer, Hume the historian became concerned that his readers would see his measured judgments as being a contrived middle ground. Hume worried that "moderation" would be seen as his "particular interest." In 1753 he confided to his good friend, James Oswald:

> The more I advance in my undertaking, the more am I convinced that the History of England has never been written, not only for style, which is notorious to all the world,

but also for matter; such is the ignorance and partiality of all our historians. Rapin, whom I had an esteem for, is totally despicable. I may be liable to the reproach of ignorance, but I am certain of escaping that of partiality: The truth is, there is so much reason to blame and praise alternately King and Parliament, that I am afraid the mixture of both in my composition, being so equal, may pass sometimes for an affectation, and not the result of judgement and evidence.

(L 1: 179)

Hume did not intend actively to stake out a political middle ground, as Duncan Forbes, Nicholas Phillipson, and others would have it. Rather, his evidence led him there.

To conclude, what does our perspective suggest about the first Stuart volume that was at the heart of Hume's story and has been at the heart of attempts to see Hume as a Tory historian or as one who aimed to distance himself from the historical past? For Hume, James I did not grasp for monarchical powers when he claimed to command "as an *absolute* king" (H 5: 17). James was only speaking in a language to which the English "had already been somewhat accustomed from the mouth of Elizabeth" (H 5: 17). Moreover, the House of Commons in "the former periods of the English government" had been "of so small weight in the balance of the constitution, that little attention had been given, either by the crown, the people, or the house itself, to the choice and continuance of the members" (H 5: 13–14). James' political troubles, as characterized by Hume, were not brought on by his supposed attempts to expand the powers of the monarchy as the Whig historians would have it, but largely resulted from the king's over-bearing personality, a character trait Hume fleshed out, and by the dispersal of wealth after the monasteries were suppressed, as Harrington had argued. The "leading members" of the house were "men of an independent genius and large views" who

> began to regulate their opinions, more by the future consequences which they foresaw, than by the former precedents which were set before them; and they less aspired at maintaining the ancient constitution, than at establishing a new one, and a freer, and a better.

(H 5: 42)

During James' reign, "the constitution of England was, at that time, an inconsistent fabric, whose jarring and discordant parts must soon destroy each other, and from the dissolution of the old beget some new form of civil government, more uniform and consistent" (H 5: 60).

Charles I inherited that same "ambiguous" English constitution. Hume aimed to judge Charles' conduct and reign from within this messy historical process, not from an illusionary context of an ancient, unchanging, and well-defined English constitutional settlement. That was the attitude that allowed Hume to shed a tear for Charles. It also informed the perspective from which he viewed the reign of Elizabeth, when he looked backward to it. There, he summed up in the form of a question, buried in a footnote, as he was apt to do with important passages:

> I shall only ask, whether it be not sufficiently clear from all these transactions that in the two succeeding reigns [of James I and Charles I] it was the people who encroached upon the sovereign, not the sovereign, who attempted, as is pretended, to usurp the people?

(H 4: 403)

The historical context offered by looking back further yet only confirmed Hume in his judgment. In September 1757, he wrote, again to Clephane:

I believe a man, when he is once an author, is an author for life; for I am now very busily engaged in writing another volume of History, and have crept backwards to the reign of Henry VII. I wish, indeed, that I had begun there: For by that means, I should have been able, without making any digression, by the plain course of the narration, to have shown how absolute the authority was, which the English kings then possessed, and that the Stuarts did little or nothing more than continue matters in the former tract, which the people were determined no longer to admit. By this means I should have escaped the reproach of the most terrible *ism* of them all, that of Jacobitism.

(L 1: 264)

While that is a statement about England's constitutional development over time, it is also a statement about the value of historical context for understanding and assessing actors and events of the past. We might even say that the links in the chain of Hume's enlightened *History of England* were fashioned from the connecting principle suggested by that context. As Hume put it succinctly in the first volume of history that he published, "it seems unreasonable to judge of the measures, embraced during one period, by the maxims, which prevail in another" (H 5: 240). But readers of the *History* will find that there is also much more to it than that. I wish to acknowledge the assistance of the volume's editors, as well as Roger L. Emerson, Marc Hanvelt, and David R. Raynor, for offering improvements to various drafts of this essay. My work on Hume as historian has benefited from financial support provided by the Social Sciences and Humanities Research Council of Canada.

Notes

1 Since Hume clearly also had his female readers in mind when he wrote the *History*, one should add a "she" to the "he" of Forbes's statement.

2 Including among the Classics, as recent work is making clearer (Baumstark 2010; Box and Silverthorne 2013). As M.A. Box and Michael Silverthorne have shown, in his essay "Of the Populousness of Antient Nations,""Hume makes use of all the well-known classical historians and a great number of other writers" (234).

3 See their "Appendix A: Posthumous Editions of *The History of England*," compiled in part from the work of T. E. Jessop.

4 Hume's letter, sent in October 1754, was to William Mure of Caldwell (1718–1776).

5 Others (Mazza and Ronchetti 2007: 12) have noted that trend.

6 At the same time, scholars have also begun to tap the "book history" side of Hume, including for what it tells us about his work as historian (Slater 1992; Norton and Norton 1996; van Holthoon 1997; Sher 2006; Emerson and Spencer 2014).

7 Hume used the language of links of a chain with reference to history in the *Treatise* as well (T 1.3.4.2; SBN 83).

8 But not all. Some (Okie 1985) aimed to hold on to the Tory Hume. See F. L. van Holthoon for a discussion of some of the historiographical trends identified in this paragraph (van Holthoon 2013).

9 Hume as historian figures prominently in Harris' account and is the primary subject of chapter 6, "The Start of a History of Great Britain," and chapter 7, "The Completion of a History of England."

10 In 2011, Phillipson's book was reissued in a revised version as *David Hume: The Philosopher as Historian*, London, Penguin Books.

11 Phillips presented that position more recently, too, writing: "As Francis Palgrave put it in a comprehensive attack on Hume, 'The historian should consider himself as an interpreter, standing between two nations, and he cannot well execute his tasks, unless he has lived with both' (Palgrave 1844: 557). This was not, needless to say, the way in which Hume or the other historians of his time had conceived their role, and their work was sure to fail its requirements" (Phillips 2005: 310). My contention in this chapter is that Hume as historian in fact intended and achieved something close to what Palgrave and Phillips found most lacking.

References

Allan, David (2013) "Reading Hume's *History of England*: Audience and Authority in Georgian England," in Mark G. Spencer (ed.), *David Hume: Historical Thinker, Historical Writer*, University Park, PA: Pennsylvania State University Press.

Baumstarke, Moritz (2010) "Hume's Reading of the Classics at Ninewells, 1749–1751," *Journal of Scottish Philosophy* 8(1): 63–77.

Black, J. B. (1926) *The Art of History: A Study of Four Great Historians of the Eighteenth Century*, New York: Russell & Russell, reprinted 1965.

Box, M. A. and Michael Silverthorne (2013) "The 'Most Curious & Important of All Questions of Erudition': Hume's Assessment of the Populousness of Ancient Nations," in Mark G. Spencer (ed.), *David Hume: Historical Thinker, Historical Writer*, University Park, PA: Pennsylvania State University Press.

Burke, John J., Jr. (1978) "Hume's *History of England*: Waking the English from a Dogmatic Slumber," *Studies in Eighteenth-Century Culture* 7: 235–250.

Capaldi, Nicholas and Donald Livingston, eds. (1990) *Liberty in Hume's "History of England,"* Dordrecht, Boston and London: Kluwer Academic Publishers.

Collingwood, R. G. (1946) *The Idea of History*, Oxford: Clarendon Press.

Costello, Timothy M. (2013) "Fact and Fiction: Memory and Imagination in Hume's Approach to History and Literature," in Mark G. Spencer (ed.), *David Hume: Historical Thinker, Historical Writer*, University Park, PA: Pennsylvania State University Press.

Emerson, Roger L. (2009) "Hume's Intellectual Development: Part II," in Roger L. Emerson (ed.), *Essays on David Hume, Medical Men and the Scottish Enlightenment: "Industry, Knowledge and Humanity,"* Farnham: Ashgate.

———. and Mark G. Spencer (2014) "A Bibliography for Hume's *History of England*: A Preliminary View," *Hume Studies* 40(1): 53–71.

Fieser, James (1996) "The Eighteenth-Century British Reviews of Hume's Writings," *Journal of the History of Ideas* 57: 645–657.

——— (2005) *Early Responses to Hume's "History of England,"* vols 7–8 in *Early Responses to Hume*, 2nd edn, 10 vols, Bristol: Continuum.

Flexman, Roger (1754) "Review of *The History of Great Britain, Vol. 1. Containing the Reigns of James I and Charles I,*" *The Monthly Review* 12: 206–229.

Forbes, Duncan (1970) "Introduction," in David Hume (ed.), *The History of Great Britain: The Reigns of James I and Charles I*, Harmondsworth: Penguin Books.

——— (1975) *Hume's Philosophical Politics*, Cambridge: Cambridge University Press.

Harris, James A. (2015) *David Hume: An Intellectual Biography*, Cambridge: Cambridge University Press.

Harris, Michael H. (1966) "David Hume: Scholar as Librarian," *The Library Quarterly: Information, Community, Policy* 36(2): 88–98.

Hicks, Philip (1996) *Neoclassical History and English Culture: From Clarendon to Hume*, Houndmills: Palgrave Macmillan.

Hilson, J. C. (1978) "Hume: The Historian as Man of Feeling," in Hilson et al. (eds.), *Augustan Worlds*, Bristol: Leicester University Press.

Hillyard, Brian. (1989) "The Keepership of David Hume," in Patrick Cadell and Ann Matheson (eds.), *For the Encouragement of Learning: Scotland's National Library 1689–1989*, Edinburgh: HMSO.

Jones, Peter, ed. (2005) *Hume's Reception in Europe*, London and New York: Continuum.

Livingston, Donald W. (1984) *Hume's Philosophy of Common Life*, Chicago, IL: University of Chicago Press.

———. (1995) "On Hume's Conservatism," *Hume Studies* 21(2): 151–164.

Long, Douglas (2013) "Hume's Historiographical Imagination," in Mark G. Spencer (ed.), *David Hume: Historical Thinker, Historical Writer*, University Park, PA: Pennsylvania State University Press.

Mazza, Emilio and Emanuele Ronchetti (2007) "Forward," in Emilio Mazza and Emanuele Ronchetti (eds.), *New Essays on David Hume*, Milan: FrancoAngeli.

Mossner, Ernest Campbell (1941) "An Apology for David Hume, Historian," *Modern Language Association Publications* 16: 657–690.

——— (1980) *The Life of David Hume*, 1st edn, Oxford: Clarendon Press, 1954.

Norton, David Fate and Mary J. Norton, eds. (1996) *The David Hume Library*, Edinburgh: Edinburgh Bibliographical Society.

——— and Richard H. Popkin, eds. (1965) *David Hume: Philosophical Historian*, Indianapolis, IN: Bobbs-Merrill.

Okie, Laird (1985) "Ideology and Partiality in David Hume's *History of England*," *Hume Studies* 11(1): 1–32.

Phillips, Mark Salber (2000) *Society and Sentiment: Genres of Historical Writing in Britain, 1740–1820*, Princeton: Princeton University Press.

———— and Dale R. Smith (2005) "Canonization and Critique: Hume's Reputation as a Historian," in Peter Jones (ed.), *Hume's Reception in Europe*, London and New York: Continuum.

Phillipson, Nicholas (1989) *Hume*, New York: St. Martin's Press. [Reissued in 2011 as *David Hume: The Philosopher as Historian*, London: Penguin Books.]

Pocock, J. G. A. (1999) *Narratives of Civil Government*, vol 2 of *Barbarism and Religion*, Cambridge: Cambridge University Press.

Rose, William (1757) "Review of *The History of Great Britain. Vol. 2. Containing the Commonwealth and the Reigns of Charles II and James II*," in *The Monthly Review* 16: 36–50.

Sabl, Andrew (2012) *Hume's Politics: Coordination and Crisis in the "History of England*," Princeton: Princeton University Press.

Schmidt, Claudia M. (2003) *David Hume, Reason in History*, University Park, PA: Pennsylvania State University Press.

Sher, Richard B. (2006) *The Enlightenment and the Book: Scottish Authors & Their Publishers in Eighteenth-Century Britain, Ireland, & America*, Chicago, IL: University of Chicago Press.

Siebert, Donald T. (1989) "The Sentimental Sublime in Hume's *History of England*," *The Review of English Studies* 40(159): 352–372.

Slater, Graeme (1992) "Hume's Revisions of the *History of England*," *Studies in Bibliography* 45: 130–157.

Smyth, William (1848) *Lectures on Modern History*, 2 vols, London.

Spencer, Mark G., ed. (2002) *Hume's Reception in Early America*, Bristol: Thoemmes Press.

————. (2005) *David Hume and Eighteenth-Century America*, Rochester: University of Rochester Press.

————., ed. (2013) *David Hume: Historical Thinker, Historical Writer*, University Park, PA: Pennsylvania State University Press.

Stewart, John B. (1963) *The Moral and Political Philosophy of David Hume*, Westport: Greenwood Press.

————. (1992) *Opinion and Reform in Hume's Political Philosophy*, Princeton: Princeton University Press.

Suderman, Jeffrey M. (2013) "Medieval Kingship and the Making of Modern Civility: Hume's Assessment of Governance in *The History of England*," in Mark G. Spencer (ed.), *David Hume: Historical Thinker, Historical Writer*, University Park, PA: Pennsylvania State University Press.

Todd, William B. (1983) "Foreword," to vol. 1 in David Hume (ed.), *History of England: From the Invasion of Julius Caesar to the Revolution in 1688*, 6 vol, Indianapolis, IN: Liberty Fund.

Towsey, Mark (2013) "'The Book Seemed to Sink into Oblivion': Reading Hume's *History* in Eighteenth-Century Scotland," in Mark G. Spencer (ed.), *David Hume: Historical Thinker, Historical Writer*, University Park, PA: Pennsylvania State University Press.

van Holthoon, F. L. (1997) "Hume and the 1763 Edition of His *History of England*: His Frame of Mind as a Revisionist," *Hume Studies* 23: 133–152.

————. (2000) "An Historian at Work [Editor's Introduction]," in F. L. van Holthoon (ed.), *David Hume: A History of England*. A variorum edn, Charlottesville: InteLex Corporation.

————. (2013) "Hume and the End of History," in Mark G. Spencer (ed.), *David Hume: Historical Thinker, Historical Writer*, University Park, PA: Pennsylvania State University Press.

Wertz, Spencer K. (2000) *Between Hume's Philosophy and History, Historical Theory and Practice*, Lanham, MD: The University Press of America.

Wexler, Victor G. (1977) "David Hume's Discovery of a New Science of Historical Thought," *Eighteenth Century Studies* 10: 185–203.

Wootton, David (2009) "David Hume: 'The Historian'," in David Fate Norton and Jacqueline Taylor (eds.), *Cambridge Companion to Hume*, 1st edn, New York: Cambridge University Press, 1993.

23

HUME'S HISTORY AND POLITICS

Andrew Sabl

As Hume scholars often note, Hume in his own age was better known as a historian and essayist than as a philosopher. Moreover, the main subject of his *History of England*, as well as many of his essays, is – to the discomfort of those who might expect philosophical (or "social" and "cultural") history (e.g. Forbes [1975]) – politics. Thus, a chapter on history and politics in Hume must be selective. I will focus on the ways in which Hume's political thought not only is best sought in his *History* but also is, in several crucial though unusual senses, deeply historical. It is essentially bound up with the way that actions and events appear in time and with the development of institutions and habits of constitutional allegiance over time. I will then say something about how the (perhaps singular) instance of a first-rate philosopher drawing general conclusions from his own historical narrative can provide political thinkers with distinctive insights and help correct some of our gravest professional vices.

I Politics as history: dynamic coordination and learned conventions

It is no longer respectable to claim that Hume's major contributions were all negative or Pyrrhonian, a matter of calling existing certainties into question. No serious scholar now doubts Hume's seminal contributions not only to philosophy but also to historiography and several of what came to be called the moral (later "social") sciences. This chapter will focus on a set of insights in political theory – that is, insights about politics – that are still commonly neglected for the same reason that they are still valuable, indeed crucial: because they show the ways in which the standards for evaluating political institutions and practices cannot avoid serious and continuous engagement with history. (Here is meant not the history of ideas but actual history, i.e. things that probably happened – or, as a genre, connected accounts of things that probably happened.) Hume's insights on this matter are neglected, partly because they appear in his massive *History*, which few contemporary political thinkers read, but also because they frustrate both sides of the usual divide in political theory. Against practitioners of standard "normative" political theory, Hume suggests that a wide range of political and constitutional structures are all legitimate (or, to use Hume's slightly archaic word, "legal"). No single structure can be derived from pure reason or subjective predictions regarding what agents in an ingeniously constructed, imaginary condition would agree to. On the other hand, against the Cambridge School of the history of ideas, or at least its most uncompromising and radical adherents, Hume suggests both that the words we use to describe political phenomena are of limited importance and that we can speak of institutions and practices being objectively better in one time or place than in another. In particular, we can expect a certain limited kind of progress. On average and in the long run, crude constitutional institutions and practices will tend to become ever better at effectively serving a wide range of human interests because their working parts, as opposed to the stories that sustain them, are essentially technological: subject to experiment, borrowing, and piecemeal improvement.[1]

As other contributions to this volume discuss, *conventions* are central to Hume's account of society and politics (for the same reason, I would claim, that artificial virtues are central to his moral theory: each virtue corresponds to a convention). The *History of England* deepens and complicates this story by showing how conventions, above all conventions of authority, are *dynamic*: they arise slowly through historical experience, solidify in the face of challenges through repeated reassertion, and adapt (or fall because they fail to adapt) to new circumstances and new social interests. Authors such as Baier (1991: esp. Chapter 10; 2010: Chapter 6) and Hardin (2007) have stressed how Hume is in the same broad family as Hobbes in seeing government in general, and governmental authority in particular, as an artificial contrivance formed to serve human – and fully secular – interests. While that is true, a focus on his *History* reveals that Hume (at least in a later phase, after his immersion in historical research and writing) differs profoundly from Hobbes in decoupling authority from sovereignty. Put differently: authority for Hume is the product not of will but of historical experience – and fortunately so.

Authority is not like other conventions: it is both ultimate and dynamic. Disagreements over the meaning of other conventions, or over proposals that they be changed or adapted to new circumstances, can often be settled by appeals to authority, which does not establish the lesser conventions but can adjudicate regarding them (see esp. EPM 3.33–34, SBN 196–197). Disputes regarding authority, however, can appeal to no higher judge; they are settled not by "lawyers and philosophers" but by "the swords of the soldiery" (T 3.2.10.15, SBN 562). This fact renders authority conventions simultaneously crucial and unstable. Those who want reforms in conventions of property, or who want to switch (as Sweden did in 1967) from driving on the left to driving on the right (Hardin 2007: 90–91), can accomplish incremental and peaceful change through government. But those who want to change the structure of government in fundamental ways must, it seems, wait for the kind of massive imbalances between politics and social or economic forces that will lead a great many people simultaneously to risk toppling an old equilibrium in the expectation of finding a new one.

The big questions of politics are thus fights over *dynamic conventions of authority*: what Hume called "the confusions incident to all great changes in government" (H 2.338). These are treated in Hume's *History* and nowhere else in his work. Hume's morals and jurisprudence may be all about consensus, about discovering and articulating the foundations for virtues, sentiments, and institutions whose substance could in Hume's time (and in his view) be taken for granted. Hume's *History* is all about disagreement, misjudgment, misunderstanding, unnecessary enmities that thwart potential cooperation, and the struggle for power. What most interests Hume in the *History* are cases in which conventional solutions to coordination games are theoretically possible but not yet present: "The convulsions of a civilized state usually compose the most instructive and most interesting part of its history" (H 1.3).

A *From coordination to convention*

Consider the "coordination games" put forth by Thomas Schelling (1980 [1960]: Chapter 3). To adapt to contemporary circumstances, one of his examples is as follows:

> You are supposed to meet someone in New York on a certain day. But you have forgotten the time and place and have no way of communicating with the other person (an outage or hack has disabled cellphone service). You know that the other person faces the same situation. Where do you meet?

Almost everyone, after some reflection, settles on 12 noon; those familiar with New York often settle on Grand Central station (or a handful of other possible landmarks). Another Schelling example; "Write some positive number. If you all [among respondents in a room] write the same number, you win." A large plurality of most groups writes down, on reflection, the number 1.

The meeting-in-New-York and write-a-positive-number problems exemplify problems of coordination. The stylized games or puzzles represent, inadequately, a much deeper and fundamental human state. Human beings have certain interests in common (we can put aside, for current purposes, what they are). But since the social and political institutions that we have an interest in supporting are advantageous not individually but collectively, which institutions deserve our support depends on which institutions everyone else believes, or can be brought to believe, deserve *their* support. Many great problems of high politics can thus be seen as problems of coordination. There are many ways of solving them, including what Schelling called "focal points" (e.g. "12 noon" and "the number 1"); charismatic leadership, whereby the leader is trusted to set a direction that others will follow; or the "common knowledge" whereby people in direct sight of one another can settle on a single action by looking at others and attuning themselves, in real time, to the crowd (Chwe 2001). The problem with most of these methods is that they are suitable for short periods, or among local groups united by common experiences, but wholly unsuitable to creating peace and prosperity throughout the kind of large unit where we do modern politics. Reliance on focal points, local leadership, or common knowledge is likely to result not in peace or prosperity but in warlordism and strife, as each of many small groups settles on one way of acting, or one person to follow, in ways that place that group at direct odds with others.

The only coordination method that stands a chance of being durable, uncontroversial, and capable of adoption throughout large societies is constitutional convention: rough agreement on a method of decision-making and a procedure for choosing public officials, rather than the substance of a course of action (Hardin 1999). In complex modern societies, this agreement is not – except in crisis circumstances that are too dangerous for any sane person to wish for – a matter of actors choosing, or even explicitly consenting to, which conventions they will live under. (Hume stressed the point in his famous *Essay* "Of the Original Contract"; the entire *History of England* could be said to illustrate it.) But this absence of control and responsibility cuts both ways. I cannot change our conventions of authority *for precisely the same reason that the powerful cannot flout them.* In both cases, conventions – at least in the short term and the typical case – frustrate every individual agent's desire to exert substantial control over social outcomes. One should not assume that conventions always serve the powerful. They embody authority rather than power, and potentially against power: they enable those who are willing to accept a convention to repel attempts by the powerful to dictate their own chosen terms of association.

B *Authority and allegiance*

One gangster in the film *Miller's Crossing* (1990) advises another, whose authority is slipping, "You don't hold elected office in this town. You run it because people think you do. They stop thinking it, you stop running it." That is essentially Hume's theory of authority. Government not only stands or falls with the opinion of the governed; it is *constituted* by the opinion of the governed. Authority and allegiance – which appear within 100 words of each other 25 times in Hume's work – are, at least roughly, two ways of describing the same thing. Hume repeatedly portrays a high level of one as going with a high level of the other; a government that governs by authority is one that has earned allegiance, and vice versa. While Hume already suggests this link in "Of the Original Contract,"[2] the fact that authority and allegiance are not all or nothing but a matter of degree and development – that they can rise or fall, be gained and lost – is most fully apparent in the *History*, a book about change. To say that a polity's authority has been established is to say that people have come to follow a durable custom or convention of doing as the magistrates say. To say that it is fragile is to say that people have begun to question and sometimes flout that convention. To say that it is limited means that the people have a convention of obeying government in many matters but not all. The last point is crucial in the English context. Hume says that Magna Charta began a constitutional order based on "limited . . . authority" and "conditional allegiance" (H 2.6–7). Of course for Hume, authority is always limited: since the magistrate's power is founded on opinion, it "can never subvert other opinions, equally rooted with that of his title to dominion" (E 40). But the example of Magna Charta makes much clearer how constitutional structures embody this "limited authority" and "conditional allegiance" as two ways of seeing the same thing. Put more analytically, "The government could not get people to cooperate with its officials when it ordered X" (limited authority) is equivalent to "the people chose not to cooperate with their magistrates when they tried to bring about X" (conditional allegiance).

The implications of seeing government authority as merely a shorthand for citizen allegiance are many, in fact staggering. Here I can suggest only a few.

First, authority is *necessarily* dynamic or historical. Even so-called conceptual questions require an account of stability and change. Since the main title to allegiance is "long possession" (which grounds the custom of allegiance [T 3.2.10.4, SBN 555]), what counts as possession – not to mention what counts as long – bears not just on allegiance's effects but on its content, its definition. Hume tells us that these questions defy "sound reason and philosophy": they depend on "general opinion" (or when that is divided, "the swords of the soldiery," "war and violence" T 3.2.10.15, SBN 562–563; E 483, 486). Since government is "an invention of men," and "the origin of most governments is known in history" (T 3.2.8.4, SBN 542), the substantive content and actual development of Humean allegiance are likewise matters not of logical deduction but of politics and experience.

Second, allegiance is always particular. Nobody swears allegiance, or feels allegiance, to "some Queen" or "a constitution." The hoary political-theory question of whether and why one should "obey the State" is badly posed: the members of actual polities feel "attachment" to a *particular* form of government – usually the "ancient" one (E 32; compare E 512). When Hume writes, "I must confess, that I shall always incline to their side, who *draw the bond of allegiance very close*" (E 490), he is not endorsing not an aspiration to "obey the law" in the abstract, or to make one's obedience conditional on whether government is observing or transgressing some allegedly objective (or rational) normative principle. The "bond of allegiance" involves a habit of mutual attachment between a particular polity's citizens or subjects and their constitutionally chosen government officials, and a set of mutually comprehensible actions that express this attachment.

Examining an abstract duty would be beside the point in a world of convention, because what we ought to do depends on what we can suppose others will durably do – and there is no reason to suppose that what they will durably do includes seeking out rational justifications of things.

On the contrary, what others will durably do, with important exceptions in crises, is live by the conventions to which they are accustomed. Political actors properly aware of this will adapt their proposals and preferred innovations so that they can be fitted – or at least seem to be fitted – within those conventions:

> It is not with forms of government, as with other artificial contrivances; where an old engine may be rejected, if we can discover another more accurate and commodious, or where trials may safely be made, even though the success be doubtful. An established government has an infinite advantage, by that very circumstance of its being established; the bulk of mankind being governed by authority, not reason, and never attributing authority to any thing that has not the recommendation of antiquity. To tamper, therefore, in this affair, or try experiments merely upon the credit of supposed argument and philosophy, can never be the part of a wise magistrate, who will bear a reverence to what carries the marks of age; and though he may attempt some improvements for the public good, yet will he adjust his innovations, as much as possible, to the ancient fabric, and preserve entire the chief pillars and supports of the constitution.
>
> (E 512–513)

C Fundamental conventions in history: contingency and progress

Politics is thus a deeply historical enterprise. The reasons for this are neither mystical nor linked to the claim that each age exhibits a peculiar consciousness. It is just that the advantages of common action – and for that matter, common inaction, the political quiescence with respect to most daily matters without which no one could pursue private projects – cannot be gained unless most people most of the time adopt the conventions of authority to which they and others have become accustomed over decades or generations. The ultimate reason for abiding by these conventions, however, is neither ineffable nor historically contingent but the unvarying fact that doing so benefits, loosely speaking, everyone. Hume's oft-used "utility" means no more or less than this.

Hume thus teaches us to embrace constitutional contingency and diversity for reasons that still respect normative universality. Put more simply: Hume is deeply historical without being even slightly relativist. Any constitutional structure is, for perfectly good reasons, better than none. Much of the *History* is about how codified and recognized rules of royal succession represented a giant constitutional advance – the achievement of a "*principle* of authority" (H 1.464; emphasis added) – compared to the dynastic struggles that had kept the Anglo-Saxon kingdoms in a constant state of civil and inter-kingdom war, and kept post-Conquest England before the Tudors under periodic threat of dynastic war. Moreover, no single constitutional structure is uniquely justified by reason. This is why "examples and precedents, uniform and ancient, can surely fix the nature of any constitution. . . . There is indeed no other principle by which those land-marks or boundaries can be settled" (H 5.583, note KK). The fact that fundamental conventions get baked into what might be called political identity solidifies their appeal and is to that extent to be welcomed. Historically contingent and apparently "irrational" attachments to particular national constitutions thus have a universal and rational basis.

If the Humean story about constitutions renders them both universally useful and historically contingent – it is always and everywhere the case that people have strong reasons to respect any existing institutions that durably specify and limit authority – it is also historical in another sense: once established, constitutional structures tend to become better over time. Constitutions become better able to secure liberty and good government as they gradually incorporate new political technologies and the findings of a political science that is ever more accurate for drawing on better data, and as they stretch themselves to accommodate new interests that arise with social and economic change and come to demand recognition. It is very fortunate, Hume thinks, that Magna Charta – one of England's fundamental conventions, the other being monarchy – gave a limited and contested power to parliament and in particular to the House of Commons. The Commons' unquestioned, though originally slight, constitutional role provided a "pretence" for new social powers, i.e. non-noble landowners, to make their opinions and interests felt ever more strongly over time (E 35). Much of the Stuart volumes of the *History* consists of a tragic tale of how poor political thinking, religious fanaticism, and accidents of personality rendered violent a clash between monarchical authority and parliamentary assertiveness that might otherwise have ended quite peacefully. With the aid of political experience after Hume's time, we can generalize the lesson: representative assemblies are astonishingly flexible, capable of accommodating and negotiating a whole range of interests and demands that cannot be predicted ahead of time.

In Hume's view, the constitutional settlement of 1688, the result of a century of strife between monarchs and parliaments (and the bitter experience arising from it), provided much clearer constitutional boundaries, and more security under law for individuals, than had existed in earlier ages. While Hume never denied that English institutions had ancient origins, he devoted much of the *History* to refuting the "ancient constitution" thesis that we could seek in those origins an ideal state of public or private liberty (Forbes 1975). The authority of hereditary (and increasingly constitutional) monarchy solidified over time, as did the limitations of authority embodied in Magna Charta. Both conferred great public benefits, given that the alternative to constituted authority is an appeal to greater force, and the alternative to limited authority is tyranny (a word Hume freely uses regarding Tudor rule, which for a century or so placed the Great Charter to one side). These two fundamental conventions were even more salutary taken together: they combined to form a productive, if tense, equilibrium between monarch and parliament that constituted "if not the best system of government, at least the most entire system of liberty, that ever was known amongst mankind" (H 6.531). But this took time. The longer these constitutional conventions lasted, the more perfect they became. In the American context, we might draw similar conclusions. While US politics is immeasurably strengthened by our current ability to assert against injustices and abuses of power the permanent validity of our own founding conventions – the Constitution and the Declaration of Independence – it does not follow that those conventions at their origin, as they worked in the eighteenth century, furthered everyone's interests perfectly or even adequately.

D Liberty and equality: late achievements, not states of nature

One great puzzle facing scholars of Hume's political thought is that while he places great value on liberty, he never clearly defines it. One thing that seems clearly true, however, is that liberty for Hume is not the absence of law but on the contrary requires law as the guarantee of individual security against private violence. The kind of liberty that can be truly and durably enjoyed is always "settled" liberty or a system of liberty. (See Capaldi and Livingston 1990; in this Hume was in rough accord with Montesquieu, whose own model for a polity embodying liberty was of course England.) Hume certainly thinks that many constitutional schemes, including modern "civilised," law-governed monarchies like that of France in his day, can further liberty imperfectly (E:"Of Civil Liberty"). But again, this does not prevent normative comparison. Liberty is more secure under a well-developed and codified constitution than under a rougher one in which redressing violations of liberty requires private violence. As noted above, it is particularly secure – at a potentially non-trivial cost in stability and efficiency – in countries that codify conflict between an executive and a separately elected legislative body. Equality – admittedly not a large and explicit topic raised by Hume himself, though we can read it back into his work – is likewise a late, historical achievement. We are entitled to read Hume's story of how non-noble landowners' economic gains ultimately resulted in their winning greater power for the Commons as an advance in social equality that rested on and required a certain level of economic development. Going beyond Hume's analysis, and his time, we might see other social groups as having gained equal status through similar means: social and economic power eventually give rise to demands for political power and equal legal status. In terms of coordination theory, one might see both liberty and equality as challenges to the power that otherwise accrues to those in a position to solve coordination problems. Those in a position to grant, or withhold, the decision-making power necessary for common action are in a position to tyrannize over others by reserving special powers, privileges, and rights for themselves. Or they can reward certain groups over others, secure in the knowledge that those relatively worse off are still much better off than under anarchy and therefore unwilling to risk, through rebellion, a return to that state. Separation of powers helps prevent the first abuse. Legislative power dispersed widely (ultimately equally) among the population helps prevent the second.

For the purpose of this chapter, one might flesh out a different set of claims concerning the difference between a static liberalism of dignity and a dynamic Humean liberalism of enlargement.[3] What might be called the liberalism of dignity, characteristic of the dominant, neo-Kantian form of normative political thought, insists that the hallmark of a liberal society, and the standard by which to judge its citizens, is a universal tendency on behalf of citizens to treat one another with respect. (This is often cashed out in rationalist terms: we show respect for others not so much through courtesy or decent treatment but by not seeking to employ coercive laws against them unless we can justify those laws with reasons that they could not reasonably reject.) Hume, who famously denied the distinction between moral and non-moral virtues,[4] also refused to separate out dignity and respect as trumping other ethical and social considerations.

Let us translate respect into Humean language (following Krause 2008: 108 and chapter 3 *passim*) as a civilized form of the passion known as vanity, and translate dignity as a durable state of being respected by oneself and others. We can then observe that vanity – the desire to be respected, to have dignity – is only *one* of the common springs of human action. Others include "ambition, avarice, self-love, friendship, generosity, public spirit" (EHU 8.7.14, SBN 83). A variegated and urban society provides plenty of opportunities for the complex, corrected, or productively channeled satisfaction of vanity (aka dignity) and for actions that satisfy others' vanity (aka respect). But it also provides for complex, corrected, or productively channeled satisfactions of ambition, friendship, generosity, public spirit, and of course, but not uniquely, avarice. Surely the most "liberal" position is not to say that satisfying these other passions lacks a value comparable to satisfying vanity, but to seek out a society in which peace, prosperity, and the advantages of scale render less and less frequent the necessity to choose among them. To demand that people sacrifice opportunity, friendship, public service, and community life to the academic's favorite activity of exchanging abstract reasons is arbitrary and narrow. It is also a recipe for missing one of the greatest attractions of modern societies (when they are working well): a sense of social excitement and general progress, the feeling that we are constantly providing individuals with new choices and opportunities, partly by creating ways – through exchanges of services, ideas, and information – in which projects that I find fulfilling can also further yours.

For current purposes, the main point is this: a historical examination of politics, including claims of political authority and political right, allows us to imagine – more precisely, re-imagine – politics as a matter of serendipity and invention. As technological and social change and the accidents of human interaction produce new problems and new sources of conflict, they also provoke agents to suggest innovative solutions and new opportunities for fruitful interaction (within an actually or fictively constant framework of unchanging conventions and distinct national institutions). And history, by gathering and synthesizing knowledge not just of what was learned but under what circumstances and to what beneficial or harmful purpose, lets the members of each society profit from the ingenuity, as well as the tragic but instructive mistakes, of other societies.

The Platonic view of moral truth sees it as a recollection of the eternal, a victory over the distractions of common life. The Kantian view, moralizing that, sees it as consisting of a victory of the practical reason within each of us over the accidental passions that distract us from the clear teachings of that Reason. It is well known that Hume describes ethics as a science, linked to other "liberal" and "practical" arts and sciences in an "indissoluble chain." Discoveries in one art or science both enable and rely on discoveries in all others, and on the restless activity and interaction that prompt all such discoveries (E 271). Hume's *History* shows us, in a detail that is dazzling but also somehow comforting, what this means. We should not judge "the measures, embraced during one period, by the maxims, which prevail in another" (H 5.240) because later political wisdom, being the distillation of experience, is bound to be more sophisticated than what counts as wisdom in previous ages, regardless of past actors' virtues or good intentions (Sabl 2002). Political theory and political science are progressive sciences; the insights of geniuses like Machiavelli must be, and are, integrated into later knowledge of institutions about which those earlier thinkers could not have known (E 88). Where the Platonist or Kantian distrusts history as a source of distraction or corruption, the Humean should – and Hume did – embrace it as the chronicle and distillation of experience, and as such the only source of the limited wisdom and knowledge of which human beings are capable.

II Philosophical narrative as political theory: the uses of discourse

As noted above, Hume's *History* takes the outward form not of cultural or social analysis but of a narrative history focused on political, military, and diplomatic events. At the same time, no one would mistake it for an attempt at a neutral or objective account. Hume constantly inserts into his narrative moral and political evaluation, insights regarding human nature, examples of (and warnings against) partisan bias, and general lessons to be drawn regarding political institutions and practices. This means, for one thing, that Hume's general insights can draw on the reader engagement that comes from recounting the acts of vividly painted characters. Here I shall suggest that Hume's method makes deeper, distinctive contributions, though not ones that are easy to replicate.

That method is essentially that of the "discourse": the philosophical or theoretical reflection on an extended historical narrative. The discourse most familiar to us is probably Machiavelli's *Discourses on the First Ten Books of Titus Livius*, his most systematic work and his most famous besides *The Prince*; John Adams' *Discourses on Davila* (1805) might have won similar fame had its author not been a poor writer. Discourse might at first seem a weak method, guaranteed to yield neither new historical material nor systematic philosophical or theoretical insight. However, without at all slighting the virtues of professional history or systematic philosophy, we should recognize the distinctive merits of the discourse method – and Hume's *History* provides an excellent occasion for doing so. In particular, a discourse on *political* history, like

Hume's (and Machiavelli's, and Adams'), is capable of reminding us of what kinds of things political actors and institutions are. And it is one of the few methods capable of yielding new and productive political concepts, not through analysis but through synthesis.

Political events are, by definition, instances of change. It is hard to forget that fact (though the truth of it so worries some political theorists, subject to what might be called gignophobia or fear of becoming, that we end up determined never to study actual political events. Seeking eternal truths, we resent the persistent tendency of events to fidget too much while we are trying to paint them). Not just events, however, but political actors, situations, and structures are also instances of change. They embody past change and promise future change. That is much easier to forget.

Consider the coordination problems mentioned above. How is it that we can often solve them? Schelling himself thought that the immediate solutions to coordination games – focal points – could not be derived mathematically. This is because discerning prominence or salience often involves intuition, guessing, or even whimsy more than logic and calculation. In Schelling's words, "Poets may do better than logicians," and the game is "more like 'puns and anagrams' than like chess" (Schelling 1980 [1960]: 57–58). Neo-traditionalist philosopher Alasdair MacIntyre's claim (1984: 102) that the meeting-in-New-York game properly illuminates our political and social circumstances presumably reflects a similar conviction: we solve coordination games not by calculating but by *sharing intuitions* or creatively deriving new ones from what we do share.

But these anti-quantitative paths were not taken. "Coordination games" became one branch of game theory, and subject to game theory's proviso that the payoffs the players are seeking must never contain proper names on pain of losing mathematical precision and generalizability. But this means that the "theory" of how agents coordinate has come to rule out the only mechanisms through which actual agents do coordinate: the substantive traditions, perceptions, or intuitions – circumstantial, cultural, visual, linguistic, historical – that agents have in common. It is as if someone making lemonade considered citric acid an impurity and filtered it out.

A work like Hume's *History* makes us stop and smell the lemons. It does not just tell us but also shows us, through beautiful and witty prose that effortlessly thwarts skimming, that, and why, politics in any regime with even a little bit of common history behind it necessarily bears very little resemblance to the non-political "political analysis" of the payoff matrix (though we can learn something from the thought experiment of asking why it bears no resemblance). The lesson might be called methodologically elusive but psychologically crucial. If we do not read old-fashioned, narrative history, accounts of what identifiable people have done and why, we may forget the difference between the attractive falsehood that a stylized example teaches us what actually happens and the useful truth that, on the contrary, it instructs by teaching us what does not happen. After reading Hume's three-million-word story about how conventions of political authority arise, change, improve by various measures, are threatened with destruction, and often rise again in new forms, one can forget many things, but not that these conventions *exist*. We are not disembodied agents but people with histories, endowed with common knowledge and historically laden habits. We know that hour 12 is in the middle of the day, that certain places in New York are more natural meeting places than others, that people start counting at the numeral 1 – and that Americans profess allegiance to a republican Constitution; Britons, to a constitutional monarch.

Narrative history also reminds one of what politics is: not a museum containing a series of frozen structures, some more praiseworthy or legitimate than others,[5] but a series of events. This is a truth not only about human experience – life presents itself to us as happenings, not tableaux – but also about the preconditions of normative evaluation. A mathematical theorem can be *proven* true or false. A political institution can only be *acknowledged* by certain people to be valid or authoritative (a judgment almost always under the pressure of an event that calls mere habit into question, else the question would not even arise), or illegitimate and tyrannical, or something in between. Again, while this might seem theoretically obvious, it is psychologically easy for political inquiry to under-stress it. To the extent that academic inquiry tends to portray, and evaluate, political conditions as if they were static, a discourse on history can educate both empirical political scientists and political theorists.

It has been said that economics is about equilibria. Schelling (2006 [1978]: 26) describes it as being about what happens "after the dust has settled," and writes that disequilibrium is interesting only if one "is particularly interested in *how* dust settles." (Jurisprudence, one might add, is much the same way, as is what has come to be called ideal theory, which sets forth standards for what a just or legitimate regime ought to look like while leaving to others the task of bringing actual, so-called non-deal regimes closer to the ideal.) But if seeing the world from the perspective of jurisprudence and economics entails focusing on equilibria, seeing the world *politically* entails seeing the unsettled dust: politics is not always a dust storm but is never a mopped floor. Politics is a story of incessant, often deliberate disturbances in our common life. To study politics is to study the disturbances. And to do political theory by trying to make sense of political narrative is to avoid the easy slippage that occurs between *positing* regularities for analytic purposes and mentally assuming for an instant – or a lifetime – that real politics might ever stand as still as the ink on our pages.

As a further contribution, history – again, not the "history of ideas" but history in the prosaic sense, a connected account of things that probably happened – is also a source, and arguably a unique source, of *synthetic insight*. Much contemporary philosophy and political theory is analytic. It operates by distinguishing one concept from another that is, or at least seems, closely related. One might even describe much of the history of ideas, in the "Cambridge" mode, as being analytic *in the broadest sense*. The work of Quentin Skinner and his followers, for instance, may be described as determined to point out that there is a "republican" way of talking about liberty less familiar than the familiar, liberal sense but worth taking note of (Skinner 1998). One should never disparage either the analytic project of drawing distinctions or the historical project of unearthing neglected concepts (and forgotten meanings of familiar concepts). Both, however, presuppose the existence of an existing conceptual vocabulary that is taken to be sufficient for describing and evaluating our experiences. Where do such concepts come from in the first place, and how can we produce more adequate ones if the ones we have are not, in fact, sufficient?

One common answer is "constructivism" and is essentially subjunctive: by asking what we would think if we filtered out biases and power relations from our social situation, we arrive at new concepts.[6] Another common answer stresses "conceptual change": new concepts employ the same words but use them to such different effect that those accustomed to prior usages would have trouble recognizing them (see e.g. Ball and Pocock 1998). But for those who seek to discover new and useful concepts, not just to chronicle past changes, and who doubt that our moral intuitions remain reliable guides once we try to imagine them in abstraction from the experiences from which they are derived, synthesis grounded in history is one of the few ways forward.

Let us stipulate that most of us are nominalists who believe that concepts arise through organizing experience in ways our minds find useful. The concepts used in politics and political theory, both descriptive and normative, concern political experience. That being so, one of the most easy or efficient ways to produce new concepts – and here the word "concept" is evolutionary, and normatively laden; nothing will survive as a concept unless it strikes many as useful – is through reflection on a series of political events, so arranged that they are already primed for meaning and significance. In other words, new descriptive and, in particular, normative concepts can most plausibly be produced through a deliberate theoretical discourse on an artful political history. In reading and rereading accounts of political events, a mind primed for theory may discover acts, institutions, practices, and characters that seem worthy of praise and blame, but that same mind may have no sufficient way of synoptically describing what these historical entities have in common or *why* we should praise or blame them. Thus are political concepts born.

In this way Machiavelli, reading and rereading his volumes of Livy, realized that there was something in these relations of Roman events that his contemporaries had missed: they told a tale of actors who did not have to wait on divine grace, Providence, or the Second Coming but could achieve a partial mastery of events through their own skill and initiative. As Pocock (1975) has put it, Machiavelli rehabilitated secular time. We might equally say that he discovered *virtù*: not the word, which is just Italian for virtue, but the concept, which we still cite in Machiavelli's Italian to mark its originality and distinctively useful meaning. Similarly, though less famously, Adams, through reading Davila on the French civil wars, discovered the concept (though not the word) "emulation": a passion to excel and be noticed that can, when present in political figures, motivate civil war – or, when channeled through constitutional forms, public service (Adams 1805; compare Arendt 1963). *Convention*, an old word that Hume made into a new concept, can be seen as a similar, happy instance of conceptual distillation from a historical base.

One last element must be mentioned. Hume, as perhaps the unique Western case of a single figure who was at once his country's (and his age's) greatest philosopher, its greatest historian, and one of its greatest stylists, was not only a discourser but what might be called an auto-discourser: he provided *both* the sweeping narrative and the philosophical reflection. It is as if Livy's historical works had been written by Aristotle, or Tacitus' by Hobbes. The oft-observed doubleness of Hume's *History*, which combines an older, "Tacitean" history (narration plus insights into character, and wry observation) with an eighteenth-century philosophical history of social, economic, political, and intellectual trends (Pocock 1999: 207–208; for further discussion see Sabl 2012: 12–17, and on Hume's assuming the mantle of "English Tacitus," Hicks 1996), is one small sign of this singular and fruitful combination. One might posit that Hume's skeptical philosophy, which pointed him towards empiricism and away from partisan myths and Providential or Reason-affirming master narratives, made the combination of philosophy and history both possible for Hume to sustain – most philosophers, but not Hume, hold the grit of historical fact in contempt – and less dangerous in his hands than in those of more doctrinaire thinkers such as Voltaire, of whose forays into history Hume thought little.

Contemporary students of politics will rarely if ever be able to follow Hume's example. But there are three things we can learn from it. One Hume stressed himself and applies to us as readers: philosophizing via history can produce the proper level of engagement, one that moves us more than dry philosophizing but less than partisan or ideological politics, which provides too much engagement at the cost of pervasive bias (E 563–568). Two others are lessons that we as readers can draw after the fact.

The first of these contemporary lessons concerns earworm control. An earworm (the word is originally German, though now respectable English) is an unwelcome but catchy tune that sticks in one's head. In political theory the earworm is neo-Kantianism. Neo-Kantians concerns with "practical reason," "autonomy," "regulative ideals," and a rationalist "legitimacy" based on pervasive presentation of un-rejectable reasons are, in fact, wholly contemporary – none of these was widely considered an indispensable or even a useful category of political theory before Habermas and Rawls – yet not easy to dispel. Dispelling the neo-Kantian earworm requires not just advocating a rejection of these categories but also continually *working through* political theories that do not use them and do not need them. Hume's *History* shows that one can give an account of politics, and one that is "critical" in the sense of allowing for ethically driven criticism of existing structures, using terms and tools that preceded all the Kantian ones. But Hume's *History* does more than show this to be possible; it draws us in through the narrative in ways that can retrain our mental pathways.

Crediting Hume with dispelling Kantian categories is obviously anachronistic: that effect benefits us but could not have been intended by Hume.[7] But there is another kind of lesson that we can not only credit to Hume but also experience in common with him. Military thinkers say that no battle plan survives contact with the enemy (a reformulation of Moltke 1993 [1871]: 92). For political theorists, the enemy, too often, is facts. We do not like them; we try to construct them out of existence; we bristle at Arendt's (1968) renegade claim that we can't make them up, that facts – here she is alluding to Adams! – are "stubborn." We know that every theory oversimplifies experience. But we typically apply this insight in a judgmental, jeremiad form: others' theories should be contested or subverted so that they come to embody the truths present in our own.

An extended, years-long engagement with history forces stubborn facts on us in ways that multiplications of theories are unlikely to do. One can see this as having happened to Hume himself: the bookish young man who wrote the *Treatise* found that the philosopher's assumptions could not survive contact with 17 centuries of English history. For instance: in the *Treatise* Hume took property to be the essential convention that needed explaining, and treated government as little more than a minor invention, useful for safeguarding property. In the *History*, Hume was forced to confront the centrality of political *authority* to human experience, the way in which contests over authority drive human history. He wrote a book that can be read as being all about shifts in conventions of authority: not because that is the book he intended to write, or was initially prepared to write, but because that is where the phenomena, the stubborn facts, drove him. In the process he was forced to grapple, as he did not have to when philosophizing in his closet, with the problems of common people who lacked property, with the pathos of physical insecurity and the fear of death. He came to appreciate, and strove to explain, the slow progress of conventions that allowed the weak some protection against the strong.

Hume was also forced to deal more fundamentally with what came to be called unintended consequences: the fact that in collective contexts there is usually no particular reason to believe that a single agent's aiming at a goal has any causal effect on bringing it about unless that agent can reliably predict (or bring about) the actions of others (see esp. Whelan 2015). At the end of Volume 2 of the *History* – the last one Hume wrote, so this is a kind of valediction – Hume proclaimed a final lesson that was hardly that of a philosopher who had the world all figured out: "the great mixture of accident, which commonly concurs with a small ingredient of wisdom and foresight, in erecting the complicated fabric of the most perfect government" (H 2: 525). When done well, perhaps above all when done with the aid of true philosophers to whom nothing human is alien, history teaches us not the comfortable lesson that others' theories fail to grasp all of political reality, but the uncomfortable lesson that our own do.

Notes

1 The following draws throughout on Sabl 2012.
2 "A small degree of experience and observation suffices to teach us, that society cannot possibly be maintained without the authority of magistrates, and that this authority must soon fall into contempt, where exact obedience is not payed to it. The observation of these general and obvious interests is the source of all allegiance, and of that moral obligation, which we attribute to it" (E: "Of the Original Contract," 480).
3 The word enlarged meant in Hume's time something like tolerant, broad-minded, free of bigotry: what we would now call "liberal."

4 "Who did ever say, except by way of irony, that such a one was a man of great virtue, but an egregious blockhead?" (EPM, App. 4.2.23–25, SBN 314).
5 On one reading, Hegel portrays history this way: as a series of historical stages, with different truths contained in each, leaving out the transition between them. See Dienstag (1997).
6 Or, in Rawls' (1971) terminology, new "conceptions": it is not that we learn for the first time what justice means, but that we realize for the first time that a particular understanding of justice, e.g. "justice as fairness," may be the best one.
7 Although: as often pointed out, what Hume called false philosophy, an alliance between quasi-religious fervor and non-empirical philosophy, could be seen as proto-Kantian in form; Kant shared many Christian forbears with the moralisms of Hume's own time.

References

Adams, J. (1805) *Discourses on Davila*, Boston: Russell and Cutler.
Arendt, H. (1963) *On Revolution*, New York: Viking Press.
———. (1968) "Truth and Politics," in *Between Past and Future*, New York: Penguin Books.
Capaldi, N. and D. W. Livingston, eds. (1990) *Liberty in Hume's History of England*, Dordrecht and Norwell, MA: Kluwer Academic Publishers.
Chwe, M. S. (2001) *Rational Ritual*, Princeton: Princeton University Press.
Baier, A. C. (1991) *A Progress of Sentiments: Reflections on Hume's Treatise*, Cambridge, MA: Harvard University Press.
———. (2010) *The Cautious Jealous Virtue: Hume on Justice*, Cambridge, MA: Harvard University Press.
Ball, T. and J. G. A. Pocock, eds. (1998) *Conceptual Change and the Constitution*, new edn, Lawrence, KS: University Press of Kansas.
Dienstag, J. (1997) *Dancing in Chains: Narrative and Memory in Political Theory*, Stanford, CA: Stanford University Press.
Forbes, D. (1975) *Hume's Philosophical Politics*, Cambridge: Cambridge University Press.
Hardin, R. (1999) *Liberalism, Constitutionalism, and Democracy*. New York, NY: Oxford University Press.
Hardin, R. (2007) *David Hume: Moral and Political Theorist*, Oxford: Oxford University Press.
Hicks, P. (1996) *Neoclassical History and English Culture: From Clarendon to Hume*, Houndmills: Palgrave Macmillan.
Krause, S. (2008) *Civil Passions: Moral Sentiment and Democratic Deliberation*, Princeton: Princeton University Press.
MacIntyre, A. (1984) *After Virtue*, Notre Dame, IN: University of Notre Dame Press.
Miller's Crossing (1990), Directed by Joel Coen, Circle Films. Motion Picture.
Moltke, H. K. B. (1993) [1871] *Moltke on the Art of War: Selected Writings*, edited by D. J. Hughes, Novato: Presidio Press.
Pocock, J. G. A. (1975) *The Machiavellian Moment: Florentine Political Thought and the Atlantic Republican Tradition*, Princeton: Princeton University Press.
———. (1999) *Barbarism and Religion, Vol. 2: Narratives of Civil Government*, Cambridge: Cambridge University Press.
Rawls, J. (1971) *A Theory of Justice*, Cambridge, MA: Harvard University Press.
Sabl, A. (2002) "When Bad Things Happen from Good People: Hume's Political Ethics of Revolution," *Polity* 35(1): 73–92.
———. (2012) *Hume's Politics: Coordination and Crisis in the History of England*, Princeton: Princeton University Press.
Schelling, T. C. (1980 [1960]) *The Strategy of Conflict*, Cambridge, MA: Harvard University Press.
———. (2006 [1978]) *Micromotives and Macrobehavior*, with a new preface, New York: W. W. Norton.
Skinner, Q. (1998) *Liberty Before Liberalism*, Cambridge: Cambridge University Press.
Whelan, F. G. (2015) "'Contrary Effects' and the Reverse Invisible Hand in Hume and Smith," *The Political Thought of Hume and His Contemporaries* 2: 84–147, New York: Routledge.

24

HUME

The science of man and the foundations of politics

Christopher J. Berry

In the Introduction to *A Treatise of Human Nature*, Hume declares that an explanation of the "principles of human nature," or the formulation of "the science of man," is the "only solid foundation" for a "compleat system of the science" (T Intro., 4,6; SBN xv, xvi). Among the sciences mentioned by Hume, along with logic, morals, and criticism, is politics, which (he states) has a "close and intimate" connection with human nature (T Intro., 5; SBN xv). Hume covered the first two of this quartet in the *Treatise* and reprised them in the two *Enquiries*, but he never systematically analyzed the latter pair.

An intimation of his approach to criticism can be found in some of his Essays, especially "Of the Standard of Taste," which, in line with the *Treatise*'s prefatory intent, was concerned to elicit "rules of criticism" based on universal principles such that "it is natural" to seek a standard (E 229). In comparison, "politics" receives a fuller treatment. Not only is there extensive discussion in *Treatise* Book III but it is also the subject matter of many of his *Essays*. The title of the *Political Discourses* of 1752 is, however, somewhat misleading inasmuch as its contents deal principally with what we would now call "economics." However, I want here to co-opt the approach that Hume himself adopts and self-consciously outlines in the preamble to the first essay in that collection ("Of Commerce").

In line with the distinction drawn in that preamble I here deal primarily with "universal propositions" rather than "particular deliberations" (E 254–255). This means that I will not consider in any detail either his early post-*Treatise* writings on contemporary politics and debates or the concrete exemplifications of political principles that abound in the *History of England*. Hence, rather than politics in the sense of politicking or policy formulation and implementation, my focus is upon what can pretend to be "universal propositions," that is, politics in the sense of the principles and institution of "government or political society" (to give the title of a chapter in the *Second Enquiry*). This itself is an elaboration of what Hume himself in the Introduction to the *Treatise*, defines as the subject matter of "politics," namely, that it "consider[s] men as united in society and dependent on each other" (T Intro.5; SBN xv: repeated verbatim Ab.3; SBN 646 cf.; EHU 8.18; SBN 90).

Given the explicitly foundational link between the science of man and politics, I here investigate what are the foundations of politics. These are the "universal propositions." In this chapter, I will claim that two supporting but not independent pillars – artifice and custom – constitute the foundations of politics.

Nature and artifice

In order for its foundations to have the necessary solidity, the "science of man" has to attend carefully to experience. This attention is not to be spent on simply cataloguing phenomena but is, rather, via observational "experiments," to be devoted to uncovering universal principles and, in an implicitly Newtonian fashion, to explaining "all effects from the simplest and fewest causes." But, still in a Newtonian vein, this endeavor should not "go beyond experience." This latter prescription, importantly, imposes the self-denying ordinance that it is "presumptuous and chimerical" ("unscientific," in other words) to attempt to "discover the ultimate original qualities of human nature" (T Intro.8; SBN xvii).

For Hume, humans are part of the natural world, and most of the chimeras that infect the human world are rooted in ignorance or unjustified presumptions, deriving in a large measure from not appreciating that humans are, *generically*, natural beings. But this is consistent with the recognition that the human world, that of moral subjects as the subtitle of the *Treatise* identifies them, is *specifically* distinct. Hume is centrally concerned with correcting the still largely prevalent "philosophical" misconceptions of that specific distinctiveness.

As we will see, precisely because it is chimerical, Hume judges that much current political speculation rests on faulty foundations. The exposure of these faults is a key part of what accounts for the superior utility of the experimental science of man (T Intro.10; SBN xix). One expression of this usefulness when discussing politics is ending the confusion that comes from recourse to those presumptive "original qualities." Hume is explicit that humans possess no "peculiar original principles" to order their affairs (T 3.2.6.1; SBN 526 cf. T 3.2.2.8; SBN 489). To say with Aristotle that man is naturally a political being is chimerical; it rests on a view of (final) causality that Hume's science is concerned to replace.[1] This replacement means, as we will see in section IV, that there is a strong polemical element in Hume's analysis (a key theme in Stewart 1992). Hume's science of politics is not a neutral *Wertfrei* exercise but, as the military metaphors in the Introduction to both the *Treatise* and *First Enquiry* indicate, an engagement seeking victory.

Hume opposes Aristotle's teleological naturalism with a naturalism of his own. In his careful delineation of the meanings of "natural," he says that when an "invention is obvious and absolutely necessary," then "artifice" may "properly be said" to be natural (T 3.2.2.19; SBN 484).[2] Hume is here setting up his account of justice as an artificial virtue. Given my claim that artifice is the first foundational pillar of politics, then, as a first step, there is a need to outline briefly his general account of convention and artifice.

Justice, convention, and expectation

Hume opens his pivotal chapter on the 'origin of justice and property' in Book III of the *Treatise* by comparing the situation of humans to that of other animals. He notes, from observation, that, compared to lions, sheep, and oxen, whose needs and the means to satisfy them are in balance, humans experience an "unnatural conjunction of infirmity and necessity" (T 3.2.2.2; SBN 485). To deal with this conjunction, humans need society. The root of this need is "the natural appetite between the sexes" (T 3.2.2.4; SBN 486). Clearly there is nothing distinctive to the human species in the possession of this "appetite," but even here its expression differs in humans (cf. Berry 2003). More generally for Hume, the "circumstances of human nature," in particular the selfishness in "our natural temper," when compounded by the incommodiousness of "outward circumstances" has, in implicit contrast to the natural facts about sheep and other animals, the consequence that human social/group life is naturally unstable.

This instability arises "necessarily" from the concurrence of two facts: it is a uniform fact of human nature that humans have only a "limited" or "confin'd generosity" and that, in fact, "external objects" are scarce relative to the desire for them (T 3.2.2.16; SBN 494). The only remedy to this instability is an artificially or conventionally induced stability. This is what justice provides. Hume is emphatic: "without justice society must immediately dissolve" (T 3.2.2.22; SBN 497 cf.; EPM 3.38; SBN 199). Since justice is necessary to prevent societal dissolution, then it is crucial to Hume's claims to establish a new foundation to account for its presence and operation in way consonant with the science of man. Not being provided by nature with ready-made solutions, humans have had to "invent" a solution. This represents no departure from Hume's naturalism, since inventiveness is part of human nature (T 3.2.1.19; SBN 484).

Social "order" is conventional, a contrived human artifice. In the case of justice, these conventions take the form of inflexible general rules. In the guise of "fundamental laws of nature," understood as being what is "inseparable from the species" (T 3.2.1.19; SBN 484), Hume itemizes three rules (T 3.2.6.1; SBN 526). The key one is stability of possession through the creation of property, followed by its transfer by consent which, in turn, requires promise-keeping in order to permit "interested commerce." I will return to these three rules and their inflexibility, but for the present want to highlight the common underlying message. This is encapsulated in his comment that only these rules can give us a "confidence" in the "future regularity" of the conduct of others, where "every single act is performed in *expectation* that others are to perform the like" (T 3.2.2.22; SBN 498, my emphasis).

Such confidence is a learned experience, not some natural instinct. Hence the rule/convention establishing stability of possession "arises gradually and acquires force by a slow progression and by the repeated experience of the inconveniencies of transgressing it"; it is "*only on the expectation* of this, that our moderation and abstinence are founded" (T 3.2.2.10; SBN 490, my emphasis). Similarly, regarding promises, it is the lesson of experience that "I foresee that he will return my service in *expectation* of another of the same kind and in order to maintain the same correspondence of good offices with me or others" (T 3.2.5.9; SBN 521, my emphasis).

Human society coheres then, for Hume, because expectations are not arbitrarily dashed but are sustained by the presence of uniform or regular behavior. This regular uniformity is based on the constancy of the conjunction between motives and actions. Like any other human endeavor, this applies to politics. Hume captures the nub issue when he observes that, "a prince who imposes a tax upon his subjects *expects* their compliance" (T 2.3.1.15; SBN 405, my emphasis). Underpinning the prince's expectation are the two foundational pillars. His rule relies on his 'artificial' status as a governor whereby he enforces compliance to the equally artificial laws of justice. It also relies on the power of custom in socializing individuals into habitual obedience. I will consider the second pillar in the section "Time, custom, and legitimacy", but in the next two parts I pursue the first pillar.

Origin and role of government

While the mutually beneficial conventions of justice have their origin in the coincidence of self-interest, that very same natural disposition is always potentially liable to generate free-riding (on Hume as a proto-game theorist, see Hardin 2007: 99), especially the more social relations develop beyond the clan. This liability generates a need for government. To say this is 'generated' is also to say that justice and government are not coeval; the former is temporally prior to the latter. On the "first formation of society" (essentially small tribal kin groups), mutual, interested coordination is "sufficiently strong and forcible" to self-police (as we might say) (T 3.2.2.24; SBN 499). Justice must nonetheless still be contrived even in these groups (parents, for example, need to enforce stability of possession in order to preserve peace among their off-spring [cf. T 3.2.2.14; SBN 493]).

When he turns explicitly to the origin of government in the *Treatise*, Hume's argument is of a piece with his account of the artificiality of justice. In the same way that justice is a contrived artificial convention, so government or political society is a contrived convention to resolve a similar shortfall in the human condition. Hence it is that artifice constitutes the first foundational pillar of politics. At the heart of what I have called a "shortfall" is Hume's declaration that it is a "quality of human nature" to prefer the contiguous to the remote (T 3.2.7.4; SBN 535). This "narrowness of soul" is a given for the science of man – humans "cannot change or correct their nature" (T 3.2.7.6; SBN 537). This preference for the immediate or contiguous is, he says, a "dangerous" quality because it makes humans prefer trivial "present advantage" to the more distant maintenance of justice. Since, *ex hypothesi*, everyone has an "interest" in justice, then this dangerous "infirmity of human nature" becomes a remedy to itself (T 3.2.7.5; SBN 535), as humans create the artificial institution of government or "persons whom we call civil magistrates, kings and their ministers, governors and rulers" (T 3.2.7.6; SBN 537).

By the means of this artifice, the observance of justice is made the task or "immediate interest" of a few magistrates who "inforce the dictates of equity thro' the whole society" (T 3.2.7.6; SBN 535). Enforcement is necessary, because that "dangerous quality" to prefer the present to the remote is ever-present, but it is effective if organized or institutionalized in a magistracy. Its efficacy reposes on the constancy of human nature, as elicited by the science of man. Fear is a case in point; it is a powerful motive. Hume observes dramatically that fear of the civil magistrate is as powerful a restraint on a potential perpetrator as if he were in chains (T 2.1.10.5; SBN 312). This is not to say fear is the only factor. Hume is no Hobbesian, as the second of the two foundational pillars will demonstrate.

Since Hume declares that these "few" enforcers are "satisfy'd with their present condition" (T 3.2.7.6; SBN 537) and are "indifferent to the greatest part of society," then, he infers, they can act equitably (T 3.2.7.7; SBN 538). While in his posthumously published (1777) essay "On the Origin of Government," he seemingly acknowledges the inherent complacency of that view by remarking that governors may "often" be "led astray by private passions" yet, nonetheless, they are still said to have a "visible interest in the impartial administration of justice" (E 39). We can reasonably read this last phrase to indicate Hume's commitment to the principle of the rule of law. By this "administration" (and enforcement), security is enhanced and complex constructive interactions can ensue, all the more requisite the more society develops. Hence under its care "bridges are built; harbours open'd; ramparts rais'd; canals form'd; fleets equipp'd; and armies disciplin'd" (T 3.2.7.8; SBN 539).

Hume's references here to the "interest" of the magistrates means that governance does not rely on the magistrates having some special public-spirited virtue (cf. Moore 1977). Hence, in this same passage in the *Treatise*, he avers that government is "compos'd of men subject to all human infirmities." Elsewhere, in an early essay, he declares the maxim that "everyman must be supposed a knave" to be false "in fact," while it is "true in politics" (E 43). However, this is no insuperable barrier. Governments do maintain order. In practice this is variable, but Hume's theoretical explanation for this in the *Treatise* lies, once more, in his claim that since these governors have an "immediate interest" in their role and are "indifferent" or impartial, this enables them to promote the interests of "any considerable part of their subjects." In addition, with the sanctions at their disposal, they can police free-riding and thus prevent a collapse of cooperative endeavors or public goods, like building bridges (T 3.2.7.8; SBN 539).

Hume is all too aware that actual governments have scarcely embodied impartiality. Rather, the evidence returns the verdict that rulers exploit their position to aggrandize themselves materially and overawe their subjects with trappings of majesty and invocations of the sacred (cf. T 2.1.10.5; SBN 312). In an oblique manner, this realism reinforces a major Humean theme. While the need for government, its utility, or its promotion of the common good is thus evident (to use one of Hume's favorite terms), it does not follow that it was deliberately set up with great forethought. In the *Treatise*, he observes that the laws of justice themselves, though in the public interest, were not "intended for that purpose by the inventors"; their interest was for themselves (their "self-love," as Hume calls it) (T 3.2.6.6; SBN 529).

This same insight recurs when the *Treatise*'s abstract formal treatment is subject to more concrete investigation in his later *Essays*. There Hume remarks that while the emergence of government looks "certain and inevitable," it actually commences "more casually and imperfectly." Appealing to the evidence that warfare is endemic in "savage tribes," he conjectures that its "long continuance" at that time gave to the strongest and most prudent a leadership role (E 40). The people being "enured" to their submission come to accept the leader's decisions as an arbiter during peace-time disputes. (I will return to the role of enurement.) It was in this way, as an unintended consequence, that government commences; it "cannot be expected that men should beforehand be able to discover them [principles of government] or foresee their operation" (E 39). This is in outline exactly the case that Hume drew upon to account for the emergence of conventions to regulate property, establish money, and form languages (T 3.2.2.10; SBN 490). Once initiated, these conventions become self-supporting as (to re-quote) "the sense of interest has become common to all our fellows and gives us a confidence of the future regularity of their conduct." I obey because you obey (and vice versa), and the beneficial effect of obedience gives us an interest in obeying.

When Hume in his later work deals with politics less abstractly, what he is detailing is how over time, especially in fortunate places like Britain, government increasingly acts in accord with the rule of law. As Hume's acute awareness of unintended consequences indicates, this development is hardly one of a seamless progressive march, even while it is susceptible to causal explanation (H 2: 602–603). There is a polemical dimension to this discussion. One of the central features of Hume's entire philosophy is the downgrading of "reason," in the sense of treating appeals to rationality as a motivational explanation for social institutions. The most celebrated expression of this in Hume's political writing occurs in this context as he undercuts the theory of the "original contract," especially in its Lockean form (see Buckle and Castiglione [1991]).

Critique of contract and natural rights

Hume's critique of contract takes both a philosophical and historical form. The heart of the 'philosophy' of contract was that the ruler promised he would govern equitably in exchange for obedience and, reciprocally, the subjects promised that they would obey in exchange for fair, stable rule. Hume's philosophical rejection turns on a distinction in moral duties (E 479–480). One category of duties emanates directly from a "natural instinct or immediate propensity" and operates independently of any ideas of obligation or utility. His examples are love of children, gratitude to benefactors, and pity to the unfortunate. When humans reflect on the social advantages of these propensities, they "pay them the just tribute of moral approbation and esteem." The duties in the other category do not emanate immediately from instinct; they operate only after experienced-based reflection upon their necessity for social intercourse. His examples are justice, fidelity, and, crucially for the present argument, allegiance. Although Hume no longer calls these "artificial" virtues, the basic argument is the same as that spelt out in the *Treatise*. From the basis of this distinction in duties, he now proceeds to argue that the Contractarian claim to base the duty of allegiance on the duty of fidelity (promise-keeping which – recall – is the third rule of justice) does nothing to explain our allegiance. We keep our promises and also obey our rulers because both are necessary for social life. That necessity is sufficient explanation – in either case, "we gain nothing by resolving one into the other" (E 481).

Hume's historical critique cites the available evidence; the claim that government originated in a contract is "not justified by history or experience in any age or country of the world" (E 471). The actual origins do not correspond to a Lockean-type story of free, equal individuals contracting with each other. Hume allows that the effective equality of individuals does mean that an element of consent was involved in the establishment of government. However, he denies that in practice this amounted to any more than falling in behind an originally temporary war-leader; it is clear, he maintains, that there was "no compact or agreement . . . expressly formed for general submission" (E 474).

If the Contractarian account of origins is empirically invalid, it is even less tenable when it claims the legitimacy of current government rests on consent. Neither rulers nor subjects believe their relationship is the effect of some prior pact, something "unknown to all of them" (E 469, 470). Hume reinforces the argument by also pointing out the implausibility of any notion of "tacit consent." According to Locke, those who enjoy the protection of the laws (even by only traveling on the highway) are tacitly giving their consent, and it is a signal of withdrawal of consent if they leave the jurisdiction (Locke 1965: II, §§119, 121). Hume asks rhetorically how serious is any account that claims a "poor peasant or artisan" who knows no foreign language and has no capital has a "free choice to leave his country" (E 475). This is analogous, he claims, to remaining aboard ship and freely consenting to the captain's rule even though one was carried aboard asleep and the only alternative is leaping overboard and drowning.

Locke had claimed that in order to understand the "true, extent and end" of civil power, it was necessary to identify its origins (Locke 1965: II §1). The immediate source is the contract, but its purpose was to protect and preserve the rights already enjoyed in the pre-civil state of nature. These natural rights for Locke were encapsulated in "property," which he capaciously defined as "Lives, Liberties and Estates" (Locke 1965: II §124) as well as more narrowly as that with which a person has "mixed his Labour" (Locke 1965: II §27).

For Hume, Locke's entire rights-based approach, and what it generically represents, exemplified an unscientific approach in that it went beyond experience; in effect, it relied on the "chimerical" presumption that it embodies the "ultimate original principles of human nature" (T Intro.8; SBN xvii). As we have seen, Hume has traced the necessity of justice, and subsequently government, to the imperative to contrive stability in human intercourse because of the "unnatural conjunction" of partiality and scarcity (T 3.2.2.2; SBN 485). To subscribe to what he calls the "the vulgar definition of justice," namely, giving each his due, also means subscribing to the view that "right and property [are] independent and antecedent." This view, which the Lockean account embodies, is fallacious. What it supposes is a "natural" social condition or, in other words, it is the unscientific product of posited "peculiar original principles" in human nature (T 3.2.6.1.2; SBN 526).

However, the experiments in the science of man reveal that humans are naturally moved by their passions to the preclusion of their satisfaction, but by artifice they restrain these passions by establishing the rules of justice so that they may be satisfied. To subscribe to natural provision is to undermine that restraint. The vulgar (or Lockean-rights) account effectively makes justice flexible and thereby destroys its "public utility," its ability to ensure stability (T 3.2.6.8; SBN 531; cf. EMP 3.12; SBN 188). This is why Hume has a narrow conception of justice and for which, on those grounds, he has been frequently criticized (see for example Harrison 1981). Because, for Hume, property is an artificial/moral and not a natural relation, then to conceive of it as a "natural right," as "antecedent, and independent" of justice, as an ingredient of a "natural morality," would "produce an infinite confusion in human society" (T 3.2.6.9; SBN 532).

The reason he supplies for this conclusion is the inconstancy of our natural morality.[3] To illustrate this, we can use his example of the miser who justly receives a great fortune. Hume admits that a "single act" of justice like this may "in itself be prejudicial to society" (the money could have done more good elsewhere) but, nonetheless, the "whole plan or scheme" is "absolutely requisite" (T 3.2.2.22; SBN 497; cf. T 3–3–1.12; SBN 579). Though there may be an agreement that it be would just, on this occasion, to deny this miser his bequest, this concurrence is contingent on the particulars; there is no "natural" necessity here because on other occasions there might be disagreement. This contingency is a recipe for flexibility. Indeed, Hume takes the very inflexibility of justice as proof that its source lies in artifice (T 3.2.6.9; SBN 532). Social cohesiveness demands that the miser inherits securely, in line with rules of just transfer, and without any hint of insecurity derived from some "external" moral assessment. He might be subject to moral censure if he chooses not to act charitably (exercise a natural virtue) with the proceeds but that is not, for Hume, a matter of justice (cf. T 3.3.1.12; SBN 579). Justice, to repeat, is inflexible and thus confined or narrow.[4]

This same language, and argument, is retraced in his analysis of political allegiance in the *Treatise*. An interest in stable government is paramount in the same way that it is necessary that possession be stable. In the latter case it would "perpetuate confusion" if particular persons, in line with some claimed-for principle of "natural justice," were assigned particular properties (as when the money is not given to the miser but to a charity). In the former, it would involve "endless confusion" if allegiance (obedience) to government were determined by either "private" or "public interest." Here confusion would follow because private interest necessarily differs as one individual's own interests diverge from those of another. It would also follow if the public interest was appealed to, because that too is indeterminate since, Hume claims, individuals have different opinions as to its content. The way to avoid confusion in both property and allegiance is to "proceed by general rules" (T 3–2–10.3; SBN 555), and these are the work of artifice, not nature. To have explanatory recourse to 'natural rights' is to invoke chimeras, which is to say (again) it is unscientific. This recourse invites confusion rather than the useful clarity that Hume believes the foundational science of man will provide.

To summarize thus far: artifice is the first foundational pillar of politics because humans have to establish conventions in order that they can be "united in society and dependent on each other." Since it is human nature to develop conventions (cf. T 3.2.2.19; SBN 484), then politics is seamlessly incorporated into the overarching science of man.

Time, custom, and legitimacy

We now turn to custom, Hume's second foundational pillar of his science of politics. In the critique of Contractrarian political thinking, he points to the fact that all existing governments were originally founded on usurpation or conquest (E 471). This does not mean he is condoning violence (there is nothing – he says elsewhere – more dangerous to liberty than an authority acquired from usurpation [E 374]), but he is committed to demonstrating how illegitimate origins (force) can produce legitimate allegiance; how might can change into right. (Against the backdrop of the "abdication" of James II, the "invitation" to William and Mary to accept the throne in 1688 and the Hanoverian succession of 1714, the practical purchase of this entire line of enquiry was clear, and Hume referred to it in the *Treatise* [T 3.2.10.17–19; SBN 564–566] and later (1752) published his essay "On the Protestant Succession.")

How might becomes right pivots on the effect of time – it is "time alone," he says in the *Treatise*, that "gives solidity" to the right of rulers to govern (T 3–2–10.4). A few pages later he repeats the observation with a significant refinement: "time *and custom* give authority to all forms of government and all successions of princes; and that power which at first was founded only on injury and violence becomes in time legal and obligatory" (T 3.2.10.19; SBN 566 my emphasis). As this statement makes explicit, this link between time and custom has a direct bearing on political legitimacy. For Hume, it is a "wonder" how easy it is for a few to rule over the many, especially since strength (of numbers) must always lie with the latter. All the governors (the few) can rely on is "opinion" (E 32 cf. E 51, E 40, H 3 395). Hume proceeds, in "Of the First Principles of Government," to distinguish between "opinion of interest," based on "the sense of advantage reaped from government," and "opinion of right," which is subdivided into "right to power" and "right to property" (E 33). He takes the latter of these two subdivisions to be well-established, and his chief example of the former is attachment to "ancient government" since, and this the point of current moment, "antiquity always begets the opinion of right" (E 33). The key role played by "opinion" demonstrates Hume's divergence from Hobbes. Hume is explicit that fear is a "secondary" principle, although, of course, it has a role to play (E 34).

Recalling the role of "enurement" mentioned above, this sway or authority conveyed by antiquity is the effect of habit: "men once accustomed to obedience never think of departing from that path in which they and their ancestors have constantly trod" (E 39). Obedience or allegiance is an habitually induced (artificial) virtue, the source of which is the "general and obvious interests" in maintaining the authority of magistrates as they function to restrain "our primary instincts to indulge ourselves in unlimited freedom" (E 480). Here the two foundational pillars come together, both of them sunk in the bedrock of the science of man. It is human nature to contract habits (T 1.3.16.9; SBN 179; EHU 5.5; SBN 43; E 39 etc.) and to contrive conventions (cf. T 3.2.2.19; SBN 484). Humans form socially necessary habits, but given the (unnatural) conjunction of human nature and circumstances, then, ineluctably, conventions are generated which acquire "force by a slow progression" and by "repeated experience" (T 3.2.2.10; SBN 490).

Hume is here extending to political legitimacy the established legal principle of prescription. In the *Treatise* in his discussion of property, Hume had defined prescription or long possession as conveying title "to any object" (T 3.2.3. 9; SBN 508). This principle is a standard component in the jurisprudential account of property, but Hume knowingly gives it a radical twist (cf. H 3: 394). In its received reading, prescriptive title to property presupposed that it was obtained in "good faith." However, Hume argued that subjects originally obeying a ruler out of "fear and necessity" come, in time, to consent willingly "because they think that from long possession he has acquired a title" (E 475). Hume here has reversed the order of normative cause and effect. People consent *because* they think (opine) their rulers entitled to their obedience; they do not think that entitlement is the effect of an act of consent on their part (E 478). This prescriptive principle is independent of any assessment of the regime to which allegiance is given; it applies as equally to "the most despotic and most military" as it does to the "most free and most popular" (E 32).

This conclusion about legitimacy is consonant with the gleaned moral evidence that humans routinize their behavior. Of course, it is also experientially evident that they can break from custom, but even this rupture – if persisted with – can in turn lead to a new comforting pattern of behavior; it is part of the power of custom that it can turn pain into pleasure (as in, say, physical exercise) (T 2.3.5.1; SBN 422). While this can apply on an individual level (as I grow to appreciate modern art), the real impact derives from the fact that habits and customs are mutually reinforcing; the human mind "is wonderfully fortified by an unanimity of sentiments" (E 60).

As an implicit supportive fact of this fortification, Hume refers to the imitation of "Roman manners" by the conquered Gauls as weaning them (over about a century) from their "ancient prejudices" (E 61–62n).

This interaction is also at the heart of Hume's notion of sympathy. He claims that sympathy is a better explanation for the "great uniformity in the humours and turns of thinking of those of the same nation" than "any influence of soil or climate" (T 2.1.11.2; SBN 316). It is depicted as sort of contagion (E 203; EPM 7.2; SBN 251). This has a political import. Because we are naturally more sympathetic to those with whom we have most contact (EPM 5.42; SBN 229), then it can abet factionalism. Hence, notwithstanding that sympathy can underwrite a uniform national character, it can, given that humans have a "propensity to divide into personal factions" (E 56), also fuel internal partisanship to the detriment of good government (E 55). The seeming solution to this, on both a personal and societal level, is to enlist in the "party of humankind," to adopt "social and public principles" that are indeed universal (EPM 9.9; SBN 275). Here we can detect what Duncan Forbes called Hume's "scientific Whiggism" as he sought in his philosophy to "rise above party and prejudice" (Forbes 1975: 136 cf.91). This is a running thread in the early 1741–1742 essays.

A custom is necessarily a creature of time; usurpers do not suddenly become endowed with legitimacy. In order that a routine or a set of stable beliefs can be established, there has to be some fixity or constancy in the experience. Habits are repeated responses (associations) to a stable set of circumstances; custom is "the guide of life" (T Abs. 16; SBN 652). This guidance stems from the fact that repetitiveness of behavior leaves its mark and is especially significant regarding political authority. In a strong passage that reflects, once again, Hume's downplaying of human autonomy in its rationalistic individualist guise, he remarks that human societies are comprised of continually changing populations so that to achieve any stability it is necessary that "the new brood should conform themselves to the established constitution and nearly follow the path which their fathers, treading in the footsteps of theirs, had marked out to them" (E 476–477). The "brood" conforms not as a consequence of any deliberate (or as we might say with the metaphor, "adult") decision, but because there is a pre-existent path. This path they follow routinely. Humans, to repeat, become "accustomed to obedience." This is why, as quoted above, the prince can expect obedience and why custom is the second foundational pillar of politics.

Habits or customary ways of behaving not only stabilize but also constrain by circumscribing the range of effective or discernible options. This delimiting of options applies to institutions as well as to individuals. Governments, for example, do not operate on a blank canvas; they are constrained by the inertial weight of received "opinion," and customary way of doing things. The 'wise magistrate' will be aware that "habits more than reason" are "in everything . . . the governing principle of mankind" (H 3: 116). Implicit here is Hume's account of political change.

In his *History*, Hume refers to a "secret revolution of government," the crux of which is the institution of the rule of law, or, as he terms it, the emergence of "general and regular execution of laws" (H 2: 603). This arose causally from a two-stage process (see Berry 2006). The first cause was the loss by the barons of their localized power bases. They spent their surplus on the now available personal luxury goods and released their retainers, which in so doing removed the key obstacle to central authority. The second stage was the growth of the Commons, composed of the middle rank, constituted by the now independent former retainers. As the wealth of this rank increased *pari passu* with the growth of commerce (and cities), they accreted financial power. These tradesmen and merchants "covet equal laws" and, in so doing, they constitute the "best and firmest basis of public liberty" (E 277–278), because their business requires the security that comes from the consistent and predictable (regular) operation of law, without which "markets" will not function (see further below). Since this fundamental shift occurred gradually (secretly), Hume sees little positive in violent or sudden revolution.

While no advocate of passive obedience, Hume's lodestone is to counsel against de-stabilizing upheavals, the costs of which rarely outweigh the benefits. It is precisely because government relies on opinion, and because it serves to "restrain the fury and injustice of the people," that it is "dangerous to weaken . . . the reverence which the multitude owe to authority" (H 3: 395). "Secret" revolutions by their very nature are not disruptive and by the same token they account for significant or fundamental political change. Hume strives to make the eviction of James II and accession of William and Mary consistent with this. Though he never quite says this, it was James who was the "revolutionary" because it was his desire (and that of the Stuart heirs) to re-introduce Catholicism, which was "contrary" to that "established amongst us" (E 506 cf. H 3: 765). Again reading between the lines, 1688 was an exception to the "violence, tumult and disorder" that "commonly" attends revolutions (H 3: 771), because by decisively settling the power of royal prerogative it confirmed, or institutionalized, the "new plan of liberty" that had begun under Henry VII (H 2: 602).

Nonetheless, this emphasis on stability and habit should not be interpreted to mean that government should forebear from principled action. Often these actions will be negative in the sense of removing obstacles, such as ending absurd and pernicious restrictions on trade and employment, though more positive action can be justified in order to encourage trade and manufactures (E 293). It is a mistake to identify Hume's politics with conservatism (Berry 2011; also Sabl 2012).

Modern politics

Hume's "experimental" science of man has to be rooted in careful observation of human life "in the common course of the world" (T Intro 10; SBN xix). And to be capable of establishing a new foundation, this science has, at the very least, to draw some of its evidentiary base from the contemporary world and not rely solely on the reports of classical and medieval historians or the ethnographic reports of, among others, Amerinds or Polynesians. It would lack its claimed-for usefulness if this science was unable to offer a convincing explanation of the operation of the decisive and distinguishing feature of the contemporary world, the emergence of a commercial society (Berry 2013).

As an example of this operation, and picking up terminology already encountered, we find Hume remarking in the *First Enquiry*,

> [the poorest artificer] *expects* that when he carries his goods to market and offers them at a reasonable price, he shall find purchasers and shall be able, by the money he acquires, to engage others to supply him with those commodities which are requisite for his subsistence. In proportion as men extend their dealings and render their intercourse with others more complicated, they always comprehend in their schemes of life a greater variety of voluntary actions which they *expect*, from the proper motives, to cooperate with their own.
>
> (EHU 8.9; SBN 89, my emphasis).

As society develops into a commercial era and becomes more complex, an increased premium is placed on stability of expectation. In a commercial society, confidence that the future will be like the past is crucial. A merchant or artificer invests or manufactures *now* in the expectation of *future* return. The system of justice, the rule of law, operates to underwrite the solidity of that expectation. In "Of the Origin of Government," Hume is categorical that government "ultimately . . . [has] no other purpose but the distribution of justice." And the point is elaborated in the closing paragraph of that same essay: "government . . . must act by general and equal laws that are previously known to all the members and to all their subjects," which is the definition of "a free government" and of liberty as "the perfection of civil society" (E 37, 41).

This understanding of the role of government as upholding justice further underlines why he stresses the inflexibility of its rules. If the rules operated flexibly, or occasionally, thus forfeiting their generality, then justice in the form of expectations that "everyone will perform the like" will break down and "confusion" will reign. Hume counsels against evaluating single transactions as unjust if they seem clearly contrary to the public interest (as when a miser justly inherits a fortune). On the contrary, what needs to be considered is the "general point of view," seeing not a series of discrete transactions but a "whole plan or scheme." Once so viewed, it will be appreciated that this general perspective is "highly conducive or indeed absolutely requisite both to the support of the society and well-being of every individual" (T 3.2.2.22; SBN 497).

If social interactions are based or founded on reliable expectations and associated beliefs, then the effect of flexibility is to undermine those foundations. Moreover, these are genuinely foundations such that the superstructure is jeopardized if they are meddled with – while *fiat iustitia ruat coelum* is a false maxim (E 489), and short of extreme circumstances, when the "rules of equity and justice" are suspended (EPM 3.6; SBN 186),[5] it is better to let the miser inherit than to thwart established expectations in the name of some particularly favored or superstitiously invoked principle.

Contemporary critics of commerce judged this reliance on predictability and expectation to be its Achilles heel; a commercial society is fundamentally unsound since it seemingly rests on nothing more substantial than a tissue of beliefs and opinions. While on occasion, as with public debt (see "Of Public Credit"), Hume appears to share some qualms along these lines, the basic thrust of his account is consistent. The source of this consistency remains the commitment to a science of man. The whole of Hume's philosophy, his account of politics included, is about building an edifice on the solid foundations of that science. The scientific foundations of politics rely on the naturalistic premises of artful contrivance and the contraction of habits to deal with the way the world just happens to be for humans.

Notes

1 Writing to Francis Hutcheson, Hume declares "Consideration" of "final Causes" to be "unphilosophical" and relying on a meaning of "Natural" that merely raises "endless" questions (L. I,33). Of course, for all his claims for novelty, Hume is scarcely a lone voice here. Hobbes (1991), though not mentioned in a footnote that lists predecessors (T Intro. n; SBN xviin), is resolute in dismissing Aristotle and seeing justice and politics as "artificial." While he clearly departs from Hobbes on many points, it nonetheless takes little effort to see his presence in aspects of Hume's own argumentation.

2 That Hume's "positive philosophy" is naturalistic, see Whelan (1985). That Hume's epistemological skepticism is not "applied" to his political thought, see McArthur (2007).

3 To adopt the expansive vulgar definition of justice (Hume is implicitly citing Ulpian) is to make it, in effect, the code of conduct suffusing all human relationships. This broader sense was a central presence in classical, Christian, and Natural Law ethics, as recently expressed by Hutcheson. In Hutcheson's account of the "public interest," an individual can "be deprived of his acquisitions" when such a deprivation is deemed appropriate by the "moral sense," the determinant for Hutcheson of "natural morality" (Hutcheson 2005: I, 254,53ff). But this reliance on natural morality, as we have noted, is conducive to indeterminacy, and it is exactly that looseness that the science of man is policing; this is a central part of its usefulness, as identified in the Introduction to the *Treatise*.

4 That Hume in his post-*Treatise* work enlarged his conception of justice is argued, with particular reference to the *History*, by Annette Baier (2010). While Hume's view is not static, the stress on predictability

remains, as when he reaffirms in the *Second Enquiry* that the utility of the "rules of equity or justice" derives from their "strict and regular observance." But this is consistent with their suspension in times of necessity (EPM 3.8; SBN 188).

5 Note that this is a "suspension" (see n.4). Hume has no separate extensive discussion of "equity" – it is often a synonym of justice. For example, he explicitly refers to "rules of justice and equity" and elides them as "that virtue" (EHM 3.6; SBN 186). This synonymity is a residue of Roman jurisprudence.

References

Baier, A. (2010) *The Cautious Jealous Virtue*, Cambridge, MA: Harvard University Press.

Berry, C. (2003) "Lusty Women and Loose Imagination: Hume's Philosophical Anthropology of Chastity," *History of Political Thought* 24: 415–433 (Now in Berry Essays Ch. 10).

———. (2006) "Hume and the Customary Causes of Industry, Knowledge and Humanity," *History of Political Economy* 38: 291–317 (Now in Berry Essays Ch. 11).

———. (2011) "Science and Superstition: Hume and Conservatism," *European Journal of Political Theory* 10: 141–155 (Now in Berry Essays Ch.14).

———. (2013) *The Idea of Commercial Society in the Scottish Enlightenment*, Edinburgh: Edinburgh University Press.

———. (2018) *Essays on Hume, Smith and the Scottish Enlightenment*, Edinburgh: Edinburgh University Press.

Buckle, S. and D. Castiglione (1991) "Hume's Critique of Contract Theory," *History of Political Thought* 12: 457–480.

Forbes, D. (1975) *Hume's Philosophical Politics*, Cambridge: Cambridge University Press.

Hardin, R. (2007) *Hume's Moral and Political Theory*, Oxford: Oxford University Press.

Harrison, J. (1981) *Hume's Theory of Justice*, Oxford: Clarendon Press.

Hobbes, T. (1991) *Leviathan (1651)*, edited by R. Tuck, Cambridge: Cambridge University Press.

Hutcheson, F. (2005) *System of Moral Philosophy (1755)*, 2 vols, London: Continuum.

Locke, J. (1965) *Two Treatises of Government (1689)*, edited by P. Laslett, New York: Mentor Books.

McArthur, N. (2007) *David Hume's Political Theory: Law, Commerce and the Constitution of Government*, Toronto: University of Toronto Press.

Moore, J. (1977) "Hume's Political Science and the Classical Republican Tradition," *Canadian Journal of Political Science* 10: 809–839.

Sabl, A. (2012) *Hume's Politics*, Princeton: Princeton University Press.

Stewart, J. (1992) *Opinion and Reform in Hume's Political Philosophy*, Princeton: Princeton University Press.

Whelan, F. (1985) *Order and Artifice in Hume's Political Philosophy*, Princeton: Princeton University Press.

25

HUME'S POLITICAL ECONOMY

Carl Wennerlind

Introduction

Commerce was rapidly transforming Europe and the world in the eighteenth century, sparking a vibrant debate about its manifold implications for society, politics, and morality. Hume was an ardent proponent of the on-going commercial modernization process. He was confident that it generated higher standards of living by multiplying the variety of goods available and by raising people's real wages. He even believed that the commercial world had a built-in dynamic that ensured that all trading nations would eventually be lifted out of poverty. As much as he considered the improvement in material wealth as most advantageous to human happiness, what Hume really valued about commercial society was that it had the capacity to promote the refinement of virtues. While many eighteenth-century philosophers insisted that commerce promoted selfishness and greed, and therefore that wealth and virtue were mutually incompatible, Hume argued forcefully that people in commercial societies develop more finely tuned moral sentiments and thus have the capacity to cultivate more pleasing and agreeable social virtues. In claiming that commerce promotes both material and moral improvement, Hume was a far more enthusiastic champion of commercial society than most Enlightenment philosophers, including his friend Adam Smith.[1]

Hume's insistence that commerce was essential for moral refinement meant that his political economy played an integral role in his moral philosophy (Wennerlind 2011). Hume presented his vision for the ideal institutional framework of a modern society in part III of the *Treatise of Human Nature*, the spirit of which he retained in the *Enquiry Concerning the Principles of Morals*. He argued that the institutions of property, markets, and money are best equipped to facilitate the interactions between people who can be described as exhibiting only "limited generosity" towards others and who live in a world characterized by nature's "scarcity" (T 3.2.2.16; SBN 494).[2] These three institutions were preferable in that they best promoted industry, commerce, and the arts. While these pursuits are directly productive of material abundance, they also contribute to the refinement of people's intellects, manners, and customs, as he described in the *Political Discourses*. He maintained that people are more likely to develop a sound moral foundation by engaging in diligent industry, honest commerce, and the refinement of the liberal and technical arts, than by adhering to reason or listening to moral sentiments alone (EPM 1.3; SBN 170).

This chapter begins by explaining how, in Hume's opinion, everyday practices carried out by people in commercial societies contribute to the refinement of the human mind and the enhancement of people's moral psychology. Next, I explore the importance of consumption as an incentive for people to become industrious, commercial, and ingenious. For Hume, consumption is the most consistent force operating on the bulk of humanity, providing the fundamental impetus of a commercial society. For this reason, it is crucial to remove all moral and political limitations on consumption and allow commodities and money to circulate freely within and between countries. The freer the trade, the more commodities enter circulation and the richer everyone – people and nations – becomes. To Hume's great dismay, statesmen governing the "mercantile system" did not embrace this spirit of liberty.[3] Hume therefore set out to reeducate statesmen and the public in sound economic principles. Indeed, as I show in the second half of this chapter, the *Political Discourses* were designed to convince the legislator to refrain from interfering with trade, money, prices, wages, and interest rates. Such interventions suffocate productive pursuits and bring the improvement process to a halt. For Hume, the government's only role was to protect the basic institutions of commercial society – property, markets, and money – and provide for the nation's defense. Industry, commerce, and the arts should be allowed to thrive and prosper in liberty and perfect security. Only then will a commercial society ensure both moral and material advancement.

Virtue in commercial society

Bernard Mandeville's scandalous framing of the relationship between wealth and virtue sent philosophers scrambling to find ways to rescue the idea that virtue could thrive in a society in which selfishness and greed were recognized as essential to the wealth creation process.[4] Reason, conscience, moral sense, and politeness were proposed as mechanisms that might check people's self-interest and facilitate the formation of an affluent, yet morally agreeable society. Hume was not convinced by these arguments. He acknowledged that reason and sentiments for the most part provide people with proper moral guidance, but he saw no guarantee that they would always promote behavior beneficial to the stability, prosperity, and morality of society. Social virtues, such as benevolence, sociability, friendship, generosity, and humanity, while universally cherished, did not always promote the "happiness of human society" and the "interest of our species" (EPM 2.22; SBN 181). For example, while giving alms to the poor might be a laudable act, "when we observe the encouragement thence arising to idleness and debauchery, we regard that species of charity rather as a weakness than a virtue" (EPM 2.18; SBN 180). In the same sense that Mandeville proclaimed that "Bare Virtue can't make Nations live" (Mandeville 1988: 37), Hume argued that a different criterion than virtue must provide the foundation for society.

Hume argued that public utility should be the primary standard whereby human actions are judged (EPM 3.1; SBN 183). He considered a number of different ways in which people can make themselves useful to society and concluded that the most publicly useful actions are industry, commerce, and the refinement of the arts. These activities consistently contribute to the "happiness of society" and the "interest of the species" by promoting material affluence, political stability, and moral refinement. He argued that something profound happens to the human mind in the process of engaging in industry, commerce, and the arts. People operate both on nature, to produce material wealth, and on their own minds, to generate more polished moral sentiments. It is in the very process of engaging in industry, participating in commerce, and acquiring new knowledge that the mind is transformed in a manner that enables it to develop the capacity for greater humanity, benevolence, and sociability. These virtues, in turn, partly supplant and partly polish people's self-interest and desire for simple pleasures, thus creating a more refined moral psychology that eventually contributes to a more convivial moral atmosphere. It is, therefore, Hume insisted, not just possible for material affluence and moral improvement to coincide – moral refinement is altogether inconceivable without commercial prosperity.

Industry is the first and most fundamental component of the moral and material improvement process. The pursuit of systematic, diligent, and ingenious labor both makes people happier and promotes the refinement of their minds. Hard work contributes to happiness, not only by enabling people to consume more, but also because people ultimately "enjoy . . . the occupation itself." Moreover, when people engage in diligent and productive pursuits, "the mind acquires new vigour; enlarges its power and faculties" (E 270). Industrious people thus tend to be happier because they possess more active minds, and as a consequence are capable of experiencing higher-order pleasures. Hume also noted that the industrious stay clear from the kinds of deleterious appetites and pursuits that are "nourished by ease and idleness" (E 270).

In societies where industry becomes a habit, a culture of ingenuity takes root. Hume described how the "same age, which produced great philosophers and politicians, renowned generals and poets, usually abounds with skilful weavers, and ship-carpenters" (E 270). In a particularly vivid description of the power of industry to serve as a catalyst for moral improvement, Hume wrote,

> In order to cure most of the ills of human life, I require not that man should have the wings of the eagle, the swiftness of the stag, the force of the ox, the arms of the lion, the scales of the crocodile or rhinoceros; much less do I demand the sagacity of an angel or cherubim. I am contented to take an increase in one single power or faculty of his soul. Let him be endowed with a greater propensity to industry and labour; a more vigorous spring and activity of mind; a more constant bent to business and application.
>
> (DNR 11.10; SBN 208)

Commerce constitutes the second ingredient in Hume's recipe for material and moral improvement. As the conduit whereby merchants, "one of the most useful races of men," move goods through society, commerce not only facilitates a higher standard of living, it also generates a more refined material culture and triggers an advancement in knowledge.[5] As commerce brings different regions into conversation, people come across new commodities, making their material culture more diverse and sophisticated. New culinary delights, more splendid dress, and increasingly sophisticated manufacturers become available to a growing portion of the population. As people develop a more refined taste, they come to appreciate, in subtle ways, the finer pleasures in life. The "middling sorts" in commercial societies "flock into cities; love to receive and communicate knowledge; to show their wit or their breeding; their taste in conversation or living, in clothes or furniture" (E 271). He added that "it is impossible but they must feel an encrease of humanity, from the very habit of conversing together, and contributing to each other's pleasure and entertainment" (E271). In the spirit of Joseph Addison and Richard Steele's claim that commerce promotes peace and conviviality by making people pay less attention to political, national, ethnic, and religious difference, Hume argued that commercial sociability promotes more amicable social relations. He famously concluded,

> Thus industry, knowledge, and humanity, are linked together by an indissoluble chain, and are found, from experience as well as reason, to be peculiar to the more polished, and, what are commonly denominated, the more luxurious ages.
>
> (E 271)

Through an exposure to foreign commodities, people acquire a deeper understanding of how material goods are produced. As soon as they come into contact with new commodities, domestic manufacturers seek to emulate and copy foreign production processes. "Imitation soon diffuses all those arts," Hume noted, "while domestic manufactures emulate the foreign in their improvements, and work up every home commodity to the utmost perfection of which it is susceptible" (E 264). Had it not been for such emulation and imitation, Great Britain would still have been stuck with an "extremely rude and imperfect" material culture. Furthermore, there is, according to Hume, a sense that knowledge was enhanced simply by the fact that it was transmitted between nations. Where there is "great intercourse of arts and commerce, [people's] mutual jealousy . . . makes them examine every work of art with the greatest care and accuracy" (E 120). Suspicion and jealousy thus meant that people were even more likely to learn and further refine knowledge as part of its migration between nations.

Knowledge, both of the liberal and technical arts, constituted Hume's third pillar of the material and moral improvement process. Once a society commits itself to the pursuit of intellectual advancement, a contagious spirit unites different epistemic spheres. Hume described:

> The spirit of the age affects all the arts; and the minds of men, being once roused from their lethargy, and put into a fermentation, turn themselves on all sides, and carry improvements into every art and science. Profound ignorance is totally banished, and men enjoy the privilege of rational creatures, to think as well as to act, to cultivate the pleasures of the mind as well as those of the body.
>
> (E 271)

A more vibrant intellectual culture inspires people to bring a problem-solving approach to all areas of life. In the economic sphere, creativity and ingenuity are employed to navigate obstacles, leading to a continuous development of new technologies and techniques. Once breakthroughs are made and the producers are able to expand production and become more competitive, other producers are forced to emulate, imitate, and further innovate, generating a dynamic of knowledge-driven improvement that ultimately brings great benefits to society.

Advancements in the arts and sciences are also essential to the refinement of people's moral sentiments. By engaging in reading, mathematics, and science, a person's mind is strengthened and acquires the capacity to "form juster notions of life" (E 6). In the same way that the *process* of partaking in industry, not the fruits thereof, brings about moral refinement, it is the *act* of engaging the mind in the study of the arts that produce the capacity for social virtues. Hume wrote,

> It is certain, that a serious attention to the sciences and liberal arts softens and humanizes the temper, and cherishes those fine emotions, in which true virtue and honour consists. It rarely, very rarely happens, that a man of taste and learning is not, at least, an honest man, whatever frailties may attend him. . . . He feels more fully a moral distinction in characters and manners; nor is his sense of this kind diminished, but, on the contrary, it is much encreased, by speculation.
>
> (E 170)

Hume called this the "chief triumph of art and philosophy" (E 171).

Public utility is thus best promoted by industry, commerce, and the arts. While they mutually reinforce each other, their joint flourishing depended on justice being upheld at all times. For Hume, this meant that private property had to be inviolable and that the auxiliary institutions of markets and money had to be jealously protected against anyone who might violate its rules.

Consumption as the engine of progress

The "insatiable perpetual, [and] universal" desire to consume was one of the most powerful passions embedded in the human chest. While it has the potential to become "directly destructive of society," Hume believed that the desire for consumption, with a few restraints, has the capacity to serve as a beneficial force (T 3.2.2.12; SBN 492).[6] As long as the desire for consumption does not cause people to violate other people's property rights, bankrupt themselves, lose their appreciation of "the pleasures of ambition, study, or conversation," or fail to leave ample time, energy, and resources to provide for friends and family, Hume had nothing against it (E 269). While philosophers from Aristotle onward had condemned the pursuit of bodily enjoyment through consumption as a moral failing, Hume believed that the energy unleashed by this desire could be harnessed for beneficial purposes. As Hume famously pointed out, "every thing in the world is purchased by labour; and our passions are the only causes of labour" (E 261).

Hume specified in the *Treatise* that that are three types of pleasures: "the internal satisfaction of our mind, the external advantages of our body, and the enjoyment of external goods we have acquir'd by our industry and good fortune" (T 3.2.2.7; SBN 487). While the consumption of "worthless toys and gewgaws" constitute the greatest inducement to industry for most people, Hume argued that as people become more refined and sophisticated by engaging in industry, commerce, and the arts, they will gradually shift their attention towards the finer and higher pleasures in life, such as art, music, and poetry. As sentiments develop, a person is "more happy by what pleases his taste, than by what gratifies his appetites, and receives more enjoyment from a poem or a piece of reasoning than the most expensive luxury can afford" (E 271). Similarly, he argued elsewhere,

> the unbought satisfaction of conversation, society, study, even health and the common beauties of nature, but above all the peaceful reflection of one's own conduct; what comparison, I say, between these and the feverish, empty amusements of luxury and expense?

These pleasures, he argued, "are really without price; both because they are below all price in their attainment, and above it in their enjoyment" (EPM 9.25; SBN 284).[7] Hume thus argued that while commerce itself is not a catalyst for moral improvement, it creates incentives for industry, commerce, and the arts, which *are* directly responsible for the refinement of people's minds. Once their minds become more polished, they are able to move beyond simple pleasures derived from consumption and derive greater enjoyments from more sophisticated pursuits.

For people to be able to engage in the consumption of their choice, they must enjoy the liberty to do so. This means that people have to be able to freely dispose of their property and labor, and be able to undertake purchases in markets unencumbered by arbitrary restrictions. Trade has to be open and free, both within and between nations. Unfortunately, there were "innumerable barriers and obstructions" erected throughout the European trading landscape, motivated by a combination of fears – the fear of losing goods, the fear of importing too many goods, and the fear of money draining into neighboring nations (E 309–310). In short, the prevailing "jealousy of trade" was suffocating international commerce. Hume argued that this jealously was based on the "narrow and malignant opinion" that the flourishing of one country must always occur at the expense of one of its neighbors. No policy could be more shortsighted. All nations would be better off if their leaders realized that

> the encrease of riches and commerce in any one nation, instead of hurting, commonly promotes the riches and commerce of all its neigbours; and that a state can scarcely

carry its trade and industry very far, where all the surrounding states are buried in ignorance, sloth, and barbarism.

(E 328)

This led Hume to famously proclaim,

I shall therefore venture to acknowledge, that, not only as a man, but as a BRITISH subject, I pray for the flourishing commerce of GERMANY, SPAIN, ITALY, and even FRANCE itself.

(E 331)

Although Hume was not known for his devotion to prayer, he genuinely believed that the world would be a more prosperous and happy place if "ministers" adopted a "more benevolent sentiment" towards other nations. (E 331)

Spreading universal opulence

A free and vibrant trade not only contributes to an expansion in the volume of commerce throughout the world, it also sets in motion a dynamic whereby the world's growing wealth would become more equitably distributed among trading nations. Hume articulated a powerful analytical framework for this idea, by which he described how economic growth in rich countries would, slowly but surely, benefit poor countries. Hume explained that in rich nations where industry, commerce, and the arts flourish, production increases, putting a downward pressure on prices. As the nation's commodities become cheaper, it does not take long before exports begin to increase (E 329). This sets off a complex adjustment process. As the exporting merchants and manufacturers receive the additional revenues from abroad, they immediately seek to invest the revenues in order to expand production further. As they begin to hire more workers, they are soon forced to pay higher wages. This, in turn, forces them to raise their prices. This process will continue until the initial price advantage is erased and the prices of the commodities sold by the exporting merchants are back at the international level. At this point, there are no further incentives for foreign consumers to keep buying these goods, at least not until the thriving industry, commerce, and arts of the rich country generate additional improvements that allow its merchants to once again undersell the foreign competition.

This dynamic captures only part of the story. Hume also traced what happens to the rest of society as money flows in and triggers first an increase in wages and then an increase in prices. The workers who receive the wage increase will soon enter the marketplace, where they find "every thing at the same price as formerly" (E 287) – apart from the goods they themselves produced. They are able to buy more goods than before, which generates higher revenues for the producers. These producers, seeing their inventories fall, will increase their production by asking their workers to increase their industry. Soon, however, the producers need to hire additional workers, which will push up wages in that sector, too. These workers, in turn, can now buy more and better goods because as they enter the market they too encounter commodities that have yet to increase in price. This process continues from sector to sector, gradually increasing wages and prices throughout the country. "It is easy to trace," Hume suggested, "money in its progress through the whole commonwealth; where we shall find, that it must first quicken the diligence of every individual, before it encreases the price of labour" (E 287).

In sum, the rich country's superior industry, commerce, and arts attract money from abroad through increasing exports. As the money flows in, it gives a further boost to industry, increases wages across the nation, and pushes prices upwards. Exports will continue to outstrip imports as long as the rich country enjoys a price advantage. But when prices in the exporting sectors are back at par with that of surrounding nations, exports will taper off. This will not necessarily put an end to the rich country's prosperity. Most likely, the customs and habits of people in rich countries are such that they will continue to generate improvements in technique and technology. When they do, production will increase and once again give them a competitive advantage.

Thus far, the discussion has focused on the sectors in which the general progress in industry and the arts have favorable effects on the level of production. However, all sectors do not benefit equally from improvement in the mechanical arts. Sectors that rely less on skill, capital, and technology do not experience the same secular downward pressure on prices. However, because all sectors of the economy experience a proportional increase in demand following an inflow of money, wages tend to increase at the same rate across the board. All producers are therefore forced to raise their prices. The less-technologically advanced sectors will thus see its prices rise above the international level. This gives producers of more rudimentary goods in poor nations, where wages are lower, a distinct advantage over their rich-country analogues. As they take advantage of their competitive advantage, the benefits of industry, commerce, and the arts will spread across the trading world.

To Hume, this was a favorable dynamic. He pointed out that there "seems to be a happy concurrence of causes in human affairs, which checks the growth of trade and riches, and hinders them from being confined entirely to one people" (E 283). He described this fortuitous process:

> Manufactures, therefore gradually shift their places, leaving those countries and provinces which they have already enriched, and flying to others, whither they are allured by the cheapness of provisions and labour; till they have enriched these also, and are again banished by the same causes.
>
> (E 283–284)

The rich country loses some of its business and employment, but as long as "the spirit of industry be preserved," there was no danger of the nation falling into decay. The industry can "easily be diverted from one branch to another; and the manufacturers of wool, for instance, be employed in linen, silk, iron, or any other commodities, for which there appears to be a demand" (E 330). Hence, as long as the rich country continues to develop new knowledge that it applies in the production process and keeps its commercial and industrious habits, it will be able to stay ahead of other nations and continue to enjoy gradual progress. The poor country will take over the less technologically sophisticated and capital-intense sectors. In terms of the example used above, the poor country will gain an edge in the production of coarse woolen textile, which will provide industrial employment and opportunities for the population to learn manufacturing skills and productive habits. Soon, through a process of contagion, the poor nation will see its industry, commerce, and arts flourish. The nation will eventually start exporting goods, money will flow in, and wages will begin to rise. Through this process, the poor nation will be incorporated into the march of opulence and will not remain poor for very long. The key for Hume was not whether countries would converge, or whether poor countries would overtake the rich, but rather that they all be incorporated into a universal march of progress, in which all nations enjoy both material and moral refinement.[8]

Decentering money

Hume argued that if governments uphold property, markets, and money, people's desire for consumption propels them to engage systematically in industry, commerce, and the arts. These activities, in turn, not only generate widespread improvements in the standards of living of the world's population, they also, as pointed out above, contribute to the refinement of people's moral sentiments, making the world more peaceful and convivial. This process did not rely on the discretionary actions of statesmen and governments, but operated according to its own internal logic. In fact, the best form of government was one that limited its involvement to the safeguarding of justice. Unfortunately, the contemporary commercial world was not governed on the basis of these principles. In addition to erecting "innumerable barriers and obstructions" to trade, derailing the progression of universal opulence, governments actively experimented with various ways to manipulate the money stock. Many statesmen were laboring under the misconception that it was always in the interest of the nation to have a great deal of money within its borders. While Hume acknowledged that more gold and silver are advantageous to the government in its diplomatic and military affairs, he insisted that every nation is ultimately better off having the quantity of money that the specie-flow mechanism dictates.[9] No industrious nation should ever worry about its money draining into neighboring nations. "I should as soon dread," he noted, "that all our springs and rivers should be exhausted, as that money should abandon a kingdom where there are people and industry" (E 309). Inasmuch as statesmen should not worry about the possibility of money leaving a productive nation, they also should not be focused on trying to artificially expand the quantity of money in the nation. It was actually detrimental to the nation's commerce to increase the money stock beyond its natural proportion to economic activity. And, since a thriving economy is ultimately the best foundation for a strong and powerful government, it is better for statesmen to allow the quantity of money to freely fluctuate in accordance with the nation's economic activity and to refrain from using artificial instruments to manipulate the size of the nation's money stock.[10]

Yet, having posited this most fundamental lesson regarding money, Hume acknowledged that it was more favorable to have an increasing rather than a decreasing quantity of money. This essentially meant that it was better to have a thriving and prosperous economy that attracted money from abroad, rather than vice versa. Hume's discussion raised the then-contentious question of whether the government should try to generate the same effect through an expansion in publicly issued paper money.

Hume described money as a socially constructed convention. It is a behavioral and discursive device that enables people to agree on the exchange of goods, in the present and in the future. The essential ingredients of this convention are that people make credible promises, uphold their obligations, and foster a culture of trust.[11] The object used to represent money is of secondary importance. Consequently, paper money, as long as it meets certain standards, is fully capable of mediating commerce. Hume's view on the feasibility of non-metallic money, combined with his discussion of the multiplier effect, suggest that he might have been in favor of the government issuing paper money to stimulate industry and commerce. However, this was not the case. He objected to the artificial expansion of money through the issuance of public paper money on three grounds. First, while an artificial increase in the money stock has the capacity to spark the multiplier process, it also causes wages and prices to rise, and thus undermines the nation's international competitiveness. While an inflow of money from trade generates the same effects, it is an unavoidable consequence of prosperity. As Hume noted,

> that provisions and labour should become dear by the encrease of trade and money, is, in many respects, an inconvenience; but an inconvenience that is unavoidable,

and the effect of that public wealth and prosperity which are the end of all our wishes.

(E 284)

But to artificially expand the money stock through the use of paper money and thus bring about a worsening of the nation's competitiveness when it was entirely avoidable constituted, for Hume, an inadvisable policy.

His second objection to the use of publicly issued paper money was that the new currency would drive out gold and silver from the nation. If the quantity of paper money was increased by £10 million, there would be an outflow of gold and silver coin of the exact same amount. While this would not have an immediate effect on the nation's commercial vibrancy, it would tarnish the government's capacity to engage in diplomacy and war. Over the long haul, however, the substitution of paper money for metallic money might become a problem for the nation's commercial vibrancy, too. A paper currency was more precarious and might even be subject to collapse "as must happen upon any violent shock in public affairs" (E 317).

The third major problem Hume had with publicly issued paper money was that there were neither intrinsic, nor extrinsic, limits to how much money the government could create.[12] Hume probably would not have been opposed to an occasional government-engineered increase in the money stock, but he was convinced that no government would be able to resist the temptation of using the printing press whenever it encountered an obstacle, which would eventually undermine the stability of both the polity and the economy.[13] Hume thus concluded that even though publicly issued paper money can circulate without a problem and even has the capacity to spark industry, on balance these publicly issued instruments bring more harm than good.[14] It should also be added that Hume was staunchly opposed to those who argued that a government-induced expansion in the money stock lowers the interest rate. For him, the only development that triggers a fall in the rate of interest is an overall expansion in economic activity (E 295–307).

Hume remained firmly opposed to paper money in the first few editions of the *Political Discourses*. However, in the 1764 edition he revised his thinking on this issue and opened up to the possibility that paper money – at least, privately issued paper money – might be beneficial. He announced that it must be

confessed, that, as all these questions of trade and money are extremely complicated, there are certain lights, in which this subject may be placed, so as to represent the advantages of paper-credit and banks to be superior to their disadvantages.

(E 318)

He still insisted that paper money, regardless of type, banishes specie from the nation and that anyone who looks at the issue solely from this point of view is certainly entitled to condemn non-metallic money. But, he added, "specie and bullion are not of so great consequence as not to admit of a compensation, and even an overbalance from the encrease of industry and of credit, which may be promoted by the right use of paper-money" (E 318).

Hume noted the benefits of the circulation of private debt instruments, whereby merchants were able to monetize their debts and thus expand their investments faster. This was not only beneficial to the merchants, but also "favourable to the general commerce of a state" (E 319). He also described how banks in Edinburgh had come up with the "ingenious" idea of creating a system of bank-credit, or what in modern terminology would be called running check-credit. Depending on a merchant's reputation and wealth, he could go to a bank and receive a credit line that he could draw on as needed. He could withdraw any amount, payable in notes, whenever he chose, and only pay interest on the money he had "in his hands" (E 319). There were multiple advantages to such a system:

> as a man may find surety nearly to the amount of his substance, and his bank-credit is equivalent to ready money, a merchant does hereby in a manner coin his house, his household furniture, the goods in his warehouse, the foreign debts due to him, his ships at sea; and can, upon occasion, employ them in all payments, as if they were the current money of the country.
>
> (E 319)

Not only is the merchant able to monetize the debts owed to him, he is able to transform his entire net wealth into liquid capital, which enables him to put it to work right away in his business. Hume was enthusiastic about this innovation and used it as an example of "the right use of paper-money."

The 1764 revision reveals that Hume made a strict demarcation between publicly and privately issued paper money.[15] While both types of money were certainly capable of mediating transactions, only privately issued credit money – because of the explicit limitation that notes could only be issued on sound security – were safe and had the capacity to contribute positively to the nation's commercial vibrancy. Hume's revision might have appeared surprising to some of his contemporaries. However, if the 1764 edition of the *Political Discourse* is situated in the context of his broader thinking on money as a symbol, as articulated in the *Treatise* and *Enquiry*, the revision appears less jarring and, in fact, follows his philosophical deliberations rather seamlessly.

Frugal governance

Hume insisted that the government should not interfere with money or trade. Apart from its responsibility to safeguard these institutions and institute occasional trade restrictions to protect the nation's infant industries, Hume advised statesmen to leave people alone in their pursuit of industry, commerce, and the arts (E 324). Yet, he recognized fully that a nation would not be able to uphold justice and maintain its defense without a well-functioning government. The government has to have access to enough resources to adequately finance its activities. The greater the nation's commercial prosperity, the easier it is to siphon off some of the wealth to the government. The challenge is therefore to tax people in a manner that has the least impact on industry and commerce, or ideally in ways that actually encourage these activities. The most important lesson of all, however, which Hume sought to instill in statesmen, is that the government has to bring in enough tax revenues to be able to pay for all its expenditures. In other words, the government should not be allowed to finance its activities by borrowing and running up a substantial national debt. Not only did he view the national debt as a giant drain on the nation's commercial revenues, it fueled warfare on a scale that threatened the future of civilization.

Hume argued that the best way to tax the population is in a manner that actually encourages industry. If taxes are moderate and not levied on necessities, the result is often that it serves "to excite the industry of a people, and render them more opulent and laborious" (E 343). Taxes on luxury consumption could be designed to appear voluntary, "as a man may chuse how far he will use the commodity which is taxed" (E 345). They might even appear invisible, if "confounded with the natural price of the commodity" (E 345). The worst kinds of taxes are those that are arbitrary. As they fall differently on different people, they serve as "punishments on industry" (E 345). In general, Hume argued, taxes belong to the set of political phenomena in which "the consequences of things are diametrically opposite to what we should expect on the first appearance" (E 347). The general rule, therefore, is to keep it simple, and to try to align the tax with the interest of the people paying them.

Most of Hume's discussion of fiscal matters focused on the national debt. While not ordinarily prone to rhetorical hysteria, Hume was remarkably alarmist about the dangers that a runaway debt posed for Great Britain, as well as the rest of Europe. The most fundamental problem was that the national debt had been very successful in that which it was designed to accomplish, namely, in facilitating large-scale warfare. Wars are of course incredibly destructive on their own, leading to a "loss of men, encrease of taxes, decay of commerce, dissipation of money, [and] devastation by sea and land" (E 351). When wars are financed by credit, the destruction becomes all the greater. Hume argued that the national debt creates imbalances in the economy and puts pressure on prices. The biggest drawback, however, is that the interest payments fall into the hands of idle people and thus encourages their "useless and unactive life" (E 355). The redistribution of wealth from the industrious commercial classes to idle bondholders saps the commercial system of its energy and brings the progression of universal opulence to a halt. Having no direct interest in industry, commerce, or the arts, the idle bondholders "sink into the lethargy of a stupid and pampered luxury, without spirit, ambition, or enjoyment" (E 357–358).

Hume insisted that the government had to find a speedy solution to the ballooning national debt. Unfortunately, there were no easy solutions. Great Britain was faced with a stark choice: "either the nation must destroy public credit, or public credit will destroy the nation" (E 360–361). There were a number of different ways whereby the debt could be euthanized. First, Great Britain could repeat the experience of 1720, when the debt was first absorbed by the South Sea Company and subsequently erased with the company's bankruptcy. Hume labeled this way of eliminating the debt, to *"die of the doctor"* (E 361). The second and most likely scenario whereby the British debt would be erased was through a paralysis of "national faith." Hume argued that the "wars, defeats, misfortunes, and public calamities" fueled by the national debt would eventually undermine people's faith in both the government and its bonds (E 362). When this happens, the "whole fabric, already tottering, falls to the ground, and buries thousands in its ruins" (E 363). This Hume called the *"natural death"* of public credit. The third possible way in which the national debt might be erased was also the most damaging to society. If the government continued to honor its growing debt, eventually so much of the nation's wealth would be transferred from the industrious middling sorts to the idle annuitants that the nation would become economically and politically weakened and would easily fall prey to a foreign power. Once conquered, not only would people's property be at the mercy of the invading power, the public debt would certainly never be paid. This, Hume suggested, constituted "the *violent death* of our public credit" (E 365).

As far as Hume was concerned, this left Great Britain with only one option, to unilaterally declare bankruptcy. He recognized that a voluntary default on the national debt constituted a massive violation of property rights and would have a negative impact on bondholders. However, since the annuitants constituted nothing but a drain on society *and* the bonds they held would inevitably become worthless anyways, the government might as well pronounce the debt dead and be through with it, before a host of other, much more detrimental, consequences materialized.

Conclusion

Hume articulated an intricate, yet rigorously consistent, political economic framework that has wide-ranging implications for morality, politics, and history. He argued that as long as people are able to operate freely in a world of strict property rights, liquid markets, and stable money, their irrepressible desire for consumption propels them to dedicate their lives to industry, commerce, and the arts. As the bulk of the population commits themselves to these activities, they transform both nature and their own minds. Industriousness and ingeniousness, combined with a willingness to emulate and innovate, will not only generate a more refined material culture, but will also produce generations of people equipped with more polished moral sentiments. As the human mind develops and people become more refined, society will be more convivial, politics more sophisticated, and international relations more peaceful. While this idealized historical vision has yet to materialize, Hume's analytical framework provides posterity with a taxonomy of necessary conditions for commercial prosperity to translate into material and moral refinement.

Notes

1 For a discussion, see Hont and Ignatieff (1983), Sakamoto and Tanaka (2003), Robertson (2005), Schabas (2012), Berry (2013), and Rasmussen (2017).
2 For a discussion of Hume's conventions, see Haakonssen (1981) and Wennerlind (2001).
3 In the lead up to his discussion of the "mercantile system," Adam Smith noted that Hume is the "only writer" who had taken notice of how "commerce and manufactures gradually introduced order and good government, and with them, the liberty and security of individuals" (Smith 1976: 433).
4 For a discussion, see Force (2003), Tolonen (2013), and Sheehan and Wahrman (2015).
5 For further discussion, see Phillipson (1989) and McArthur (2007).
6 For further discussion, see Rotwein (1970), Berry (1994), and Susato (2015).
7 For further discussion, see Schabas (2014).
8 For further discussion, see Hont (1983) and Hont (2008).
9 For a recent discussion, see Harris (2015).
10 Hume famously pointed out that the "greatness of a state, and the happiness of its subjects, how independent soever they may be supposed in some respects, are commonly allowed to be inseparable with regard to commerce" (E 255).
11 For a discussion, see Gatch (1996) and Wennerlind (2001).
12 For a discussion, see Caffentzis (2008).
13 Hume suggested in a footnote that when it is time for a recoinage of the metallic currency it was better to remint the coin with a slightly smaller silver content (E 287–288).
14 Hume also acknowledged that government bonds can serve as a circulating medium of exchange – the bonds have "with us become a kind of money, and pass as readily at the current price as gold or silver" (E 353).
15 As Loren Gatch points out, "it was not credit *per se*, . . . but public credit that had earned Hume's opprobrium" (Gatch 1996 177).

References

Berry, C. (1994) *The Idea of Luxury: A Conceptual and Historical Investigation*, Cambridge: Cambridge University Press.
———. (2013) *The Idea of Commercial Society in the Scottish Enlightenment*, Edinburgh: Edinburgh University Press.
Caffentzis, G. (2008) "Fiction or Counterfeit? David Hume's Interpretations of Paper and Metallic Money," in Wennerlind and Schabas (eds.)
Force, P. (2003) *Self-Interest Before Adam Smith: A Genealogy of Economic Science*, Cambridge: Cambridge University Press.
Gatch, L. (1996) "To Redeem Metal with Paper: David Hume's Philosophy of Money," *Hume Studies* 22(1).
Haakonssen, K. (1981) *The Science of a Legislator: The Natural Jurisprudence of David Hume and Adam Smith*, Cambridge: Cambridge University Press.
Harris, J. (2015) *Hume: An Intellectual Biography*, Cambridge: Cambridge University Press.
Hont, I. and M. Ignatieff, eds. (1983) *Wealth and Virtue: The Shaping of Political Economy in the Scottish Enlightenment*, Cambridge: Cambridge University Press.

Hont, I. (1993) "The Rhapsody of Public Debt: David Hume and Voluntary State Bankruptcy," in N. Phillipson and Q. Skinner (eds.), *Political Discourse in Early Modern England*, Cambridge: Cambridge University Press.

———. (2008) "The 'Rich Country – Poor Country' Debate Revisited: The Irish Origins and French Reception of the Hume Paradox," in C. Wennerlind and M. Schabas (eds.), *David Hume's Political Economy*, London: Routledge.

Hont, J. (1983) "The 'Rich Country – Poor Country' Debate in Scottish Classical Political Economy," in Hont, I. and Ignatieff, M. (eds.) *Wealth and Virtue*.

Mandeville, B. (1988) *The Fable of the Bees, or Private Vices, Publick Benefits*, edited by F. B. Kaye, Indianapolis, IN: Liberty Fund.

McArthur, N. (2007) *David Hume's Political Theory: Law, Commerce, and the Constitution of Government*, Toronto: University of Toronto Press.

Phillipson, N. (1989) *Hume*, London: Weidenfeld & Nicolson.

Rasmussen, D. (2017) *The Infidel and the Professor: David Hume, Adam Smith, and the Friendship That Shaped Modern Though*, Princeton: Princeton University Press.

Robertson, J. (2005) *The Case for the Enlightenment: Scotland and Naples, 1680–1760*, Cambridge: Cambridge University Press.

Rotwein, E. (1970) "Introduction," in E. Rotwein (ed.), *David Hume: Writings on Economics*, Madison: University of Wisconsin Press.

Sakamoto, T. and H. Tanaka, eds. (2003) *The Rise of Political Economy in the Scottish Enlightenment*, London: Routledge.

Schabas, M. (2012) "Hume on Economic Well-Being," in A. Bailey and D. O'Brien (eds.), London: Continuum.

———. (2014) "'Let Your Science Be Human': David Hume and the Honourable Merchant," *European Journal of the History of Economic Thought* 21(6).

Sheehan, J. and D. Wahrman (2015) *Invisible Hands: Self-Organization and the Eighteenth Century*, Chicago, IL: University of Chicago Press.

Smith, A. (1976) *An Inquiry into the Nature and Causes of the Wealth of Nations*, edited by Edwin Cannan, Chicago, IL: University of Chicago Press.

Susato, R. (2015) *Hume's Sceptical Enlightenment*, Edinburgh: Edinburgh University Press.

Tolonen, M. (2013) *Mandeville and Hume: Anatomists of Civil Society*, Oxford: Voltaire Foundation.

Wennerlind, C. (2001) "The Link Between David Hume's *A Treatise of Human Nature* and His Fiduciary Theory of Money," *History of Political Economy* 33(1): 139–160.

———. (2011) "The Role of Political Economy in Hume's Moral Philosophy," *Hume Studies* 37(1): 43–64.

26

CUSTOM IN HUME'S POLITICS AND ECONOMICS

John Christian Laursen

David Hume recognized that virtually all of history is a history of customs, almost all of personality is rooted in habits, and much of public opinion, politics, and economics is a matter of custom and habit. This chapter will explore the role of custom in Hume's politics and economics. It will emerge that understanding custom is fundamental for understanding our social life.

Hume described himself as some sort of skeptic, at least concerning some issues, and it is much contested as to exactly what sort of skeptic he was. In the absence of truth, skeptics often claim that they can live adequately well by going along with customs, habits, and the prevailing opinions. Analyzing politics and economics in terms of custom and habits is one way of learning how to live without dogmatic truths and knowledge.

The new "science" of custom and habit

In *A Treatise of Human Nature*, Hume wrote that he was following the path of Locke, Shaftesbury, Mandeville, Hutcheson, and Butler, who had "begun to put the science of man on a new footing" (T Intro. 5; SBN xvii). In order to understand how Hume went beyond them, we will review some of what they said about custom and habit. In his *Essay Concerning Human Understanding*, John Locke wrote that our ideas come from our "customs and manner of life" (Locke: 432–433). Regrettably, they are often wrong: "Education, Custom, and the constant din of their Party" are the causes of "the greatest, I had almost said, of all the errors in the World" (400–401). He observed that "'Tis not easy for the Mind to put off those confused Notions and Prejudices it has imbibed from Custom, Inadvertancy, and common Conversation" (180). Custom is often "a greater power than Nature" (82), too often stronger than divine and civil law (357). But Hume saw beyond the negative and brought out the positive in custom and habit.

Joseph Butler relied on the power of custom in defense of religion. In *The Analogy of Religion*, he wrote that human beings are capable "of getting a new facility in any kind of Action, and of settled alterations in our temper of character" through the "power of habits" (Butler 1828: 110–111). By "accustoming ourselves to any course of action, we get an aptness to go on, a facility, readiness, and often pleasure, in it," he noted (113). Thus, "moral and religious habits" can improve our "virtue and piety" (116). A "constant regard to veracity, justice, and charity, may form distinct habits of these particular virtues" (125; see Wright 1994).

Butler analyzed the place of habit in philosophical psychology. He pointed out that "apprehension, reason, memory . . . are greatly improved by exercise" (112). It

> may be hard to explain the faculty, by which we are capable of habits. . . . But the thing in general, that our nature is formed to yield, in some such manner as this, to use and exercise, is matter of certain experience.
>
> (113)

Hume generalized Butler's argument about religion to show that almost all important aspects of life take place in the realm of habit and custom.

By Hume's account, man is a habit-forming animal. In the *Treatise*, he wrote that the "greatest part of our reasonings with all our actions and passions can be deriv'd from nothing but custom and habit" (T 1.3.10.1; SBN 118). He returned to the point often, writing of "custom, to which I attribute all belief and reasoning" (T 1.3.9.16; SBN 115), that "custom be the foundation of all our judgments" (T 1.3.13.9; SBN 147), and that "all reasonings are nothing but the effects of custom" (T 1.3.13.11; SBN 149). Explaining the *Treatise* in the *Abstract*, he wrote that "'Tis not, therefore, reason, which is the guide of life, but custom" (Ab. 16; SBN 652). It may not be possible to overestimate the role of custom in Hume's philosophy.

Hume admired Frances Hutcheson, but rather than following him on custom and habit, Hume endeavored to refute him. Hutcheson always tried to establish a natural human ethical and aesthetic sense that was prior to habit. Section VII of his *An Inquiry into the Original of Our Ideas of Beauty and Virtue* (1725) argues against custom and habit:

> Custom, Education, and Example are so often alleged . . . as the occasion of our relish for beautiful objects, and for our approbation of, or delight in a certain conduct of life in a moral species, that it is necessary . . . to make it appear that there is a natural power of perception, or sense of beauty in objects, antecedent to all custom, education, or example.
>
> (Hutcheson and Downie 1994: 38)

Hutcheson wants a "natural power of perception" in order to have a fixed and universal foundation for aesthetic and moral judgments. His basic purpose is justifying Christianity in the face of theories that undermine it such as those of Hobbes and Mandeville. Hume does not share that purpose, and for him what Hutcheson calls a "natural power" and an irreducible "natural" sense of beauty are founded in custom and habit.

It is not that custom and habit are unnatural. As Hume puts it in the *Treatise*, habit "is nothing but one of the principles of nature, and derives all its force from that origin" (T 1.3.16.9; SBN 179). Animals are said to live by instinct, where we live by reason, but "reason is nothing but a wonderful and unintelligible instinct" (T 1.3.16.9; SBN 179) based on custom and habit. Habits are part of human nature: in judgments concerning cause and effect "our imagination passes . . . by a natural transition, which precedes reflection, and which cannot be prevented by it" (T 1.3.13.8; SBN 147). The ideas of cause and effect "can never operate upon the mind, but by means of custom, which determines the imagination to make a transition from the idea of one object to that of its usual attendant" (T 1.3.14.31; SBN 170).

Hume repeated the point in the *Enquiry Concerning Human Understanding*: custom or habit is a natural instinct, a "principle of human nature," and the "ultimate principle, which we can assign, of all our conclusions about experience" (EHU 5.8, 9.5–6, 5.5; SBN 47, 108, 43). We cannot go any deeper to give "the cause of this cause" (EHU 5.5; SBN 43). "Custom, then, is the great guide of life. It is the principle alone which renders our experience useful" (EHU 5.6; SBN 44). It is even a matter of survival: it is "necessary to the subsistence of our species" (EHU 5.21; SBN 55).

Ordinary life, politics, and economics are dependent on custom. As Hume says in the *Treatise*, custom or repetition creates "a *facility* in the performance of any action or the conception of any object; and afterwards a *tendency* or *inclination* towards it" (T 2.3.5.1; SBN 422). It motivates us: "Nothing causes any sentiment to have a greater influence upon us than custom, or turns our imagination more strongly to any object" (T 3.2.10.4; SBN 556). A "constant perseverance in any course of life produces a strong inclination and tendency to continue for the future" (T 1.3.12.6; SBN 133).

Hume even turned to psychophysiology to explain the power of custom and habit in the *Treatise*. This was the speculative theory of "animal spirits" used by Hume's predecessors, such as Descartes, Locke, and Malebranche, to account for the ability of the soul to move the body. Animal spirits are something that can run through the various paths in the brain, and repetition or habit makes them more likely to follow certain channels. Belief is "*more properly an act of the sensitive than of the cogitative part of our natures*," Hume writes (T 1.4.1.8; SBN 183). An "imaginary dissection of the brain" gives us a mechanical model of the association of ideas: "the animal spirits run into all the contiguous traces, and rouze up the other ideas, that are related to it" (T 1.2.5.20; SBN 60). Later, Hume omitted reference to animal spirits in the *Enquiry*, perhaps because he realized that their existence was wholly speculative, or perhaps because he did not need them in order to describe the effects of custom and habit.

If so much of our make-up is a product of custom and habit, the history of politics and economics will be one chapter in the larger history of custom and habit. We shall now turn to one element of that chapter.

Opinion as a habitual way of thinking

Although some of his contemporaries were what we now call rationalists, who believed that life should be guided by reason, rationality, and truth, Hume thought that in fact we base most of our life on opinion, prejudice, belief, judgment, and even taste and sentiment. None of these can claim the high epistemological status of truth, which for Hume is limited to "the discovery of the proportions of ideas" and "the conformity of our ideas of objects to their real existence" (T 2.3.10; SBN 448). All of them are forms of custom and habit. For Hume, ordinary life, politics, and economics take place within a larger and constantly fluctuating history of custom. It can be expressed in the terms of his philosophical psychology. "An opinion or belief is *nothing but a strong and lively idea deriv'd from a present impression related to it*," he wrote in the *Treatise* (T 1.3.8.15; SBN 105). Custom and habit give force to these ideas and create beliefs by "invigorating an idea" by repetition (T 1.3.9.16; SBN 115).

In Hume's vocabulary, "judgments," "principles," and "taste" are terms for types of opinion. Judgments are "connected by custom"; judgment "peoples the world, and brings us acquaintance with such existences, as by their removal in time and place, lie beyond the reach of the senses and memory" (T 1.3.9.4; SBN 108). Those who claim to rely on "principles" will not like Hume's frequent response to them. Their principles are never more than a matter of opinion, and are often harmful: "Parties from principle, especially abstract speculative principles, . . . are, perhaps, the most extraordinary and unaccountable phenomenon, that has yet appeared in human affairs," he observed in his essay "Parties in General" (E.60). Judgments of taste, too, which for Hume apply to both beauty and morals, are no more than social customs. In "Of the

Standard of Taste," Hume wrote that "though the principles of taste be universal . . . few are qualified to give judgment" (E 241). His standard is elitist: "Strong sense, united to delicate sentiment, improved by practice, perfected by comparison, and cleared of all prejudice, can alone" justify a judgment of taste, "and the joint judgment of such, wherever they are to be found, is the true standard of taste" (E 241). The point seems to be that the assessment of morality, and thus of political and economic systems, will never be more than a matter of the opinion of those who are recognized by their peers as good judges.

Custom and opinion in *The History of England*

In *The History of England*, Hume based many explanations on his theory of custom and habit and the contagion of opinion. A "torrent of general inclination and opinion ran so strongly against the court" in 1640 that the king was deprived of his power (H 5: 284). The "spirit of mutiny and disaffection" was "communicated from breast to breast" (H 5: 294). So "strong was the current for popular government in all the three kingdoms, that the most established maxims of policy were every where abandoned" (H 5: 336–337). These metaphors of currents and torrents are constant reminders of the non-rational behavior of public opinion: London was a "furious vortex of new principles and opinions" when the smaller cities were still peaceful (H 5: 378). The "force of popular currents over those more numerous associations of mankind . . . gave, there, authority to the new principles" (H 5: 387). Elections to Parliament could become "one of those popular torrents, where the most indifferent, or even the most averse, are transported with the general passion, and zealously adopt the sentiments of the community, to which they belong" (H 6: 135). This vocabulary provides Hume with his explanations for a great deal of political behavior.

In the *History*, Hume observed that the rise of absolutism at the time of the Tudors and early Stuarts was the product of a "great revolution in manners" (H 5: 80). In the age of Queen Elizabeth, the nobility "still supported, in some degree, the ancient magnificence in their hospitality, and in the numbers of their retainers" (H 4: 381–384). The political meaning was that each of the nobles maintained what amounted to a private army (Hume calls it 'hospitality'), which was a constant threat to the queen. She ordered them to limit the number of their retainers and required them to spend down their fortunes entertaining her. They began to transfer their ambitions and resources from supporting bands of retainers to other forms of ostentation: they acquired "a taste for elegant luxury; and many edifices, in particular, were built by them, neat, large, and sumptuous" (H 4: 383). Opinions changed. This meant a "decay of the glorious hospitality of the nation," but it also "promoted arts and industry; while the ancient hospitality was the source of vice, disorder, sedition, and idleness" (H 4: 383). Commerce and luxury had democratizing effects: they "dissipated the immense fortunes of the ancient barons; and as the new methods of expense gave subsistence to mechanics and merchants, who lived in an independent manner on the fruits of their own industry, a nobleman . . . retained only that moderate influence which customers have over tradesmen" (H 4: 384). Changes in manners and opinion meant changes in the distribution of political power.

The revolution in opinion that Elizabeth's policy created in turn fortified her power and then early Stuart power. It was followed by another revolution in ideas, the Puritan rejection of luxury, rites, and ceremonies. "From tranquillity, concord, submission, sobriety, [the English] passed, in an instant, to a state of faction, fanaticism, rebellion, and almost phrenzy" (H 6: 141). And then the Puritan customs and habits were replaced by yet another set of customs and habits: the Restoration. "By the example of Charles II, and the cavaliers, licentiousness and debauchery became prevalent in the nation. The pleasures of the table were much pursued. Love was treated more as an appetite, than a passion." Charles' French manners and opinions made him a "model of easy and gentleman-like behaviour" who "improved the politeness of the nation" (H 6: 539–540). These changes in public opinion created a political atmosphere that accommodated much more personal liberty than the previous Stuart or Commonwealth regimes.

Note that Hume was well aware that custom and habits could change and often did change, at times quite rapidly. It has sometimes been asserted that living in accordance with customs and habits means stagnation and quietism. But sociologists of custom and habit like Edward Shils know better. Shils' *Tradition* describes both the endogenous and the exogenous factors that lead to changes in customs (Shils 1981, esp. chs. 5 and 6). Endogenous factors may be divided into at least two kinds. One is deliberate rationalization and correction of elements of a tradition that do not conform to professed ideals. Traditions may include sub-traditions of critical self-correction that are always at work. One such tradition was behind the Puritan rebellion that Hume chronicles, pursuing a time-honored ideal of holiness. This tradition of rebellion broke out from within a larger tradition – but it was still a tradition.

Some changes in customs and habits are not deliberate. Elizabeth probably did not deliberately set out to change the habits of her nobles exactly as she did. It seems likely that she was nervous about rebellion and wanted to keep an eye on them, so she made state visits to do so. But that had the effect of changing their customs and opinions.

The rise of Puritan customs and opinions, and their replacement by Restoration customs and opinions, were probably not predictable. As Shils points out, ideals and values can change by their own internal dynamics. He believes that much of modern history is about an increase in the value assigned to wealth and liberty and a decrease in the value assigned to obedience and conformity. Modern history is about changes in the individuals' sense of responsibility for their own well-being, which can be observed in long-term secular trends in opinion and habit (Shils 1981: 219). The changes in English customs and opinions recorded by Hume contributed to these trends, even if they were not intended to do so, and even if no one foresaw that they would.

Exogenous sources of change in customs and opinions can include the reception of foreign traditions, the movement of traditions in either direction between center and periphery, and the addition or blending of previously heterogenous traditions. In Shils' exposition, these forces are constantly at work. There has never been a static and settled tradition that never changed. For his part, Hume knew that England was constantly absorbing French, Dutch, and even German customs and opinions, both religious and secular. Some of English history was the product of the contest for superiority of competing exogenous traditions.

Custom and opinion in politics

Hume is aware that in politics, opinion does not guarantee moral truth, as admirers of public opinion sometimes seem to think it does. Rather, Hume uses words like "ferment," "clamor," "currents and tides," and "torrents" to describe the behavior of opinion. It is a product of sympathy, which is more a product of mechanical influences from others than of reasoning. We learn of another's opinion from "external signs in the countenance and conversation" of another person, which "convey an idea of it." That idea "is presently converted into an impression, and acquires such a degree of force and vivacity" as to equal the other person's opinion. "We never remark any passion or principle in others, of which, in some degree or other, we may not find a parallel in ourselves." This "resemblance must very much contribute to make us enter into the sentiments of others" (T 2.1.11.3, 5; SBN 317–318). It is contagion of ideas, not reason, which gives us most of our opinions and customs.

Hume provides remedies for the contagion of opinion. In one essay, he proposed the dispersion of people into small groups for the purposes of making political decisions because then they "are more susceptible both of reason and of order," and "the force of popular currents and tides is, in a great measure, broken" (E 36). Newly established customs may help: "it is to be hoped, that men, being every day more accustomed to the free discussion of public affairs, will improve in the judgment of them" (E 605). Customs can be self-correcting.

In "Of the First Principles of Government," Hume wrote that politically significant opinion can be distinguished into "two kinds, to wit, opinion of interest, and opinion of right" (E 33). Opinion of interest is "the sense of general advantage which is reaped from government; together with the persuasion that the particular government, which is established, is equally advantageous with any other that could easily be settled" (E 33). Opinion of right consists of two kinds, concerning power and property. All governments are founded upon opinions about the public interest and the right to power and property (E 34).

Opinion of interest is not the same as self-interest in the narrower sense of "the expectation of particular rewards" (E 34). No government can reward everyone individually. Those who are not rewarded must believe that the government guarantees "general protection" and "general advantage" (E 33–34). In the *Treatise*, Hume pointed out that the general advantage we expect from government is that it will protect property and maintain "peace and order" (T 3.2.8.6–7; SBN 544–546).

Authority is founded in opinion of right to power. In the *Treatise*, Hume observed that custom or "*long possession*" gives "authority to almost all the establish'd governments of the world." Like any other custom, it is the product of repetition, "operating gradually on the minds of men." "Time alone" reconciles them to "any authority" (T 3.2.10.4; SBN 556). Accordingly, Hume's advice to the "wise magistrate" is to "bear a reverence to what carries the marks of age" and "adjust his innovations, as much as possible, to the ancient fabric, and preserve entire the pillars and supports of the constitution" (E 512–513).

It should be clear that opinion of right to power does not exclude change. It can even retroactively justify changes and new governments. When time and custom give authority to a government now, the mind does not "rest there; but returning back upon its footsteps, transfers to their predecessors and ancestors that right. . . . [Thus,] the present king of *France* makes *Hugh Capet* a more lawful prince than *Cromwell*" (T 3.2.10.19; SBN 566–567). The endogenous and exogenous factors discussed by Shils can shift opinion of right from one person or dynasty to another, especially over time.

The influence of opinion of right to power was an important explanatory factor in Hume's *History*, as we have already seen. Queen Elizabeth was "the most popular sovereign that ever swayed the scepter" because "the maxims of her reign were conformable to the principles of the times, and to the opinion generally entertained with regard to the constitution" (H 4: 145). Later, the Stuart family relied wholly upon opinion. Its "authority was founded merely on the opinion of the people, influenced by ancient precedent and example. It was not supported, either by money or by force of arms," unlike what the realists like Machiavelli and Harrington would expect (H 5: 128). When opinion deserted Charles I, he lost his head; when it supported Charles II, he regained the throne, and the last of the line, Queen Anne, came to the throne on nothing but opinion (H 5: 128).

"It must be owned," Hume wrote, "that the opinion of right to property has a great influence" on the "foundation of all government" (E 33–34). Unlike his predecessor, James Harrington, Hume stressed that property was mostly a matter of opinion, and that opinions about right to power and right to property could counteract each other. This explained Harrington's failure to predict the Restoration. A

> government may endure for ages, though the balance of power, and the balance of property do not coincide. This chiefly happens, where any rank or order of the state has acquired a large share in the property; but from the original constitution of the government, has no share in the power.
>
> (E 35)

There was no support in public opinion for changing the form of government to better reflect the ownership of property.

Public habits and opinions were also a standard for evaluating ancient politics. The "scurrility," "vanity," and "common licentiousness" in the writings of the Romans suggests that "the arts of conversation" were not refined (E 127). The custom by which "a Roman always named himself before the person to whom . . . he spake" (E 130) and the "illbred custom of the master of the family's eating better bread, or drinking better wine at table, than he afforded his guests, is but an indifferent mark of the civility of those ages" (E 132n.). If the political liberty of republics could not provide that civility, Hume was prepared to find it in monarchies. "Civility" and "mutual deference" lead us to "resign our own inclinations to those of our companion, and to curb and conceal that presumption and arrogance, so natural to the human mind" (E 126). If monarchies teach such habits, so much the better for social and political harmony.

Custom and opinion in economics

In "Of Commerce," Hume observed that

> Man is a very variable being, and susceptible of many different opinions, principles, and rules of conduct. What may be true, while he adheres to one way of thinking, will be found false, when he has embraced an opposite set of manners and opinions.
>
> (E 255–256)

And it is not that people's opinions can be easily changed: sovereigns "must take mankind as they find them, and cannot pretend to introduce any violent change in their principles and ways of thinking" (E 260). Hume uses these principles to argue that commerce is the best way to enrichen a state. It makes men work. So, for example, it is "impracticable, to oblige a labourer to toil, in order to raise from the land more than what subsists himself and family. Furnish him with manufacturers and commodities, and he will do it himself": that is, raise more than his own subsistence in order to buy those commodities (E 262). "Afterwards you will find it easy to seize some part of his superfluous labour, and employ it in the public service" (E 262). The key is that by that time, "being accustomed to industry, he will think it less grievous, than if at once you obliged him to an augmentation of labour without any reward" (E 262). By encouraging the cultivation of the appropriate work habits, the state benefits. The habits of commerce make both the individuals and the state "richer and happier" (E 263).

In "Of Refinement in the Arts," Hume observed that "education, custom, and example, have a mighty influence in turning the mind to any . . . pursuits" (E 270). He used the language of customs and opinion to reject the republican critique of luxury and defend commercial society, as Mandeville had done before him. Luxury is part of a package: "Laws, order, police, discipline; these can never be carried to any degree of perfection before human reason has refined itself by exercise, and by an application to the more vulgar arts, at least, of commerce and manufacture" (E 273). "Thus, industry, knowledge, and humanity, are linked together by an indissoluble chain, and are found . . . to be peculiar to the more polished, and . . . more luxurious ages" (E 271). Hume makes it clear that what counts as desirable is a matter of custom. "The value, which all men put upon any particular pleasure, depends on comparison and experience," and the people around them (E 276). They only want "pleasures, such as men are accustomed to" (E 276). In modern times, they want the pleasures of commercial society, not those of the more warlike and patriotic past, exemplified by republican Rome. In the long run, this is actually better for political liberty: rich peasants and tradesmen who have acquired property "submit not to slavery" (E 277). The customs and habits of commercial society are the foundation of modern liberty.

Hume's economics treats the value of money as determined in part by customs. Some people think the scarcity of money will keep the prices of things low. But in "Of Money," Hume observes that "the effect, here supposed to flow from the scarcity of money, really arises from the manners and customs of the people" (E 290). If there is not much money and not much industry, prices will be low. If people begin to work harder and produce more, competition will increase and prices will fall. Of course, by the scarcity theory the flood of silver into Europe from America ought to have caused prices to increase substantially. But they had only increased modestly. As Hume puts it, "no other satisfactory reason can be given, why all prices have not risen to a much more exorbitant height, except that which is derived from a change of customs and manners," which meant more production and thus more price competition (E 292). So it was not abundance or scarcity of money that mattered most, but customs and manners that we might understand as work habits.

The point of Hume's essay "Of Interest" is the same: "a consequence is ascribed to the plenty of money; though it be really owing to a change in the manners and customs of the people" (E 294). Some people think that where the landed interest dominates and borrows a great deal of money to splurge on luxury, the rate of interest will necessarily be high. But in fact, different rates of interest depend "not on the quantity of money, but on the habits and manners which prevail" (E 298). It is the "habits and way of living of the people" which determine the availability and demand for loans (E 298). It is the "manners and customs" which determine whether there will be sufficient capital available, and thus low interest rates, or not enough, and thus high rates (E 299).

Hume's economics also treats property as a matter of custom and opinion. Different forms of government distribute honors in different ways, in order to maintain their control. "Birth, titles, and place, must be honoured above industry and riches" in monarchies, he explains in "Of Civil Liberty," because "subordination of ranks is absolutely necessary" in them (E 93). In republics men work for ever greater wealth and power, but in monarchies they work in order to buy titles and retire. Different opinions of the value of property determine different customs and different regimes of property.

Wealth has its virtues, but there can be too much. In "Of the Balance of Trade," Hume pointed out that if a rich state hoarded up large amounts of money, it would be tempted into "dangerous and ill-concerted projects" (E 321). Money is not as much the real essence of wealth as the habits of the people. Those too-ambitious projects might "dissipate its wealth . . . and probably destroy, with it, what is much more valuable, the industry, morals, and numbers of its people" (E 321).

Hume worried a great deal throughout his career about the growing public debt. In "Of Public Credit," he admitted that one of its benefits was "a greater consumption [which] quickens the labor of the common people and helps to spread arts and industry" (E 353). But he also worried about "a strange supineness, from long custom" in the acceptance of public credit (E 360). He feared the collapse of credit and bankruptcy, ruining thousands, or its weakening of the country to the point that it would easily be conquered. But he had to admit that the system had survived far beyond previous predictions of its demise (E 365). Our habits may be generated by economic conditions and our interests, but then they take on a life of their own that may not track those conditions and interests. It is possible that Hume simply could not fully understand, or at least could not reconcile himself to, the logic of the customs and opinions about property in modern commercial society. So, for example, his predictions of the coming disaster in Britain because of the growing public debt turned out to be off by centuries: in fact, the debt financed great prosperity throughout the nineteenth century, and only led to significant problems in the mid-twentieth century (Laursen and Coolidge 1994).

Custom and opinion in religion

Hume also thought that religion, which can never be entirely separated from politics and economics, was largely a product of customs and opinion. In his analysis, it was largely pathological. In "Of Superstition and Enthusiasm," he argued that the words in the essay title describe the two "corruptions of true religion" that constitute the vast majority of all actual religion (E 73). Superstition consists of "unaccountable terrors" which are placated by "ceremonies, observances, mortifications, sacrifices, presents," and more (E 74). Enthusiasm is an "unaccountable elevation and presumption, arising from prosperous success, from luxuriant health, and from strong spirits," such that "the inspired person comes to regard himself as a distinguished favourite of the Divinity" (E 73–74). In "Idea of a Perfect Commonwealth," he asserted that "we know not to what length enthusiasm, or other extraordinary movements of the human mind, may transport men, to the neglect of all order and public good" (E 528–529).

Superstition gives power to the priests and fears civil liberty: it is a synonym for Catholicism. Enthusiasm rejects priest craft and ceremonies, and encourages liberty. He did not like it, but Hume had to admit that the English owed their liberty to the fanatic enthusiasts of the Civil War. The "precious spark of liberty had been kindled, and was preserved, by the puritans alone; and it was to this sect, whose principles appear so frivolous and habits so ridiculous, that the English owe the whole freedom of their constitution" (H 4: 145–146). Hume often described the power of religious opinion as "supernatural and unaccountable" (e.g. H 5: 67), but he also expended considerable effort on understanding it and tracing its influence in politics.

Hume is sometimes considered a "conservative," which of course is a much-contested term. But many of Hume's writings are efforts to change people's opinions about religion. He knew it would not be easy because of the accumulated weight of religious custom in both practice and opinion. But if he had succeeded – and maybe he did in the long run, in self-described, more enlightened circles in modern times – it would have been a revolution in opinion, not at all a matter of conservatism.

All of the above should make it clear that for Hume, no one in politics is making judgments on the basis of truth and knowledge, and thus no one can be sure that they hold the higher epistemological ground from which to judge others. Hume's critique of religious and political opinion, part of his philosophy of custom and habit, can be read as a contribution to the critique of moralism in politics. Posturing from the moral high ground, which is often based on an assumption of direct access to God or the truth, will almost never be justified by anything more than opinion and habit in Hume's analysis. If moral truths and religions are only customs and habits, they lack the epistemological certainty and stability that they claim.

Living with skepticism

Up to this point, we have reviewed Hume's analysis of human action and belief in terms of custom and habit and explored his vocabulary of opinion. Now we shall see how it fits into the tradition of skepticism as a theory of how to live in the absence of truth and knowledge. Almost every scholar believes that Hume is some sort of skeptic, so it will not be necessary to prove that here. There has been some debate about whether he is best understood as a Pyrrhonian or an Academic skeptic, or an early modern skeptic different from the ancient traditions (Junqueira Smith 2011). It is probably true that all early modern philosophers were different in some ways from their ancient predecessors, just by virtue of the changes in way of living and in the overall framing of philosophical, religious, political, and scientific issues. I do not mean to intervene here in debates over precisely what sort of skeptic Hume was, but only to draw attention to the way Hume's philosophy of custom and habit can be seen as an answer to the eternal question of the anti-skeptic: "how are you going to live if you cannot live by truth and knowledge?" The answer, of course, is to live by custom and habit.

In ancient times, Sextus Empiricus gave an account of the life of the skeptics that observed that in the absence of truth and while suspending judgment, the skeptics live "a life conformable to the custom of our country and its laws and institutions" (Sextus Empiricus, PH I 17). This was explicated by four "rules for life," which a skeptic could follow, not dogmatically and as a truth, but as a practice. They were: 1. follow the guidance of nature, 2. live subject to the "constraint of the passions," 3. and in accordance with "the tradition of laws and customs," and 4. learn a skill (PH I 23). Much of what Hume wrote about custom and habit is an explication of what it means to live by the general statement quoted above, and by rule number 3. His philosophy can be read as a specification of the details of living with custom and habit in the absence of knowledge.

Ever since Sextus Empiricus, critics have charged the skeptics with philosophical inconsistency or contradiction, and with moral turpitude (Laursen 2004). Yet imagine what it would be like if we had to make rational philosophical decisions concerning every aspect of life. It would be a nightmare if we had to reason out new ways of living and make conscious decisions at all times. All of what Hume says about custom and habit helps us avoid this nightmare. Rather, life in accord with customs and habits both saves us a lot of time and effort and does not pin us down to a single behavior at any one time. For Hume as for the ancient skeptics, the rule which calls for living in accordance with custom and habit is as good a guide to life as any we will ever have.

Hume's philosophy of custom and habit can be compared to later philosophers of custom and habit, such as John Dewey. The first part of his book, *Human Nature and Conduct*, is on "The Place of Habit in Conduct" (Dewey 1922: 14–88). "All virtues and vices are habits," he observes (16). They are who we are: "we are the habit" (24). We are not enslaved to them: there is such a thing as "intelligently controlled habit" (28). But intelligence and ideas do not stand on their own: "an idea gets shape and consistency only when it has a habit back of it" (30), and "reason pure of all influence from prior habit is a fiction" (31). There is no moral standard outside of custom: "for practical purposes morals means custom, folkways, established collective habits" (75). And habits are not necessarily conservative: there are just as many progressive habits (66). In addition to ordinary habits, there are habits of change (69). The real opposition, Dewey writes, is between routine, unintelligent habit, and intelligent habit (77). It is clear that Hume knew this, and put it in his own words. Most of what is quoted above from Hume would not have been out of place if lightly modernized and rephrased in Dewey.

Dewey explores the interaction of custom with two other factors: impulse and intelligence. Impulse would seem to correspond to the ancient skeptical rules of living in accord with nature and subject to the constraint of the passions. Dewey had more confidence in the second of his factors, intelligence, than the ancient skeptics. It is arguable that Hume did, too. His skepticism did not require us to eschew all intellectual effort: in fact, of course, Hume spent his life dedicated to it. But he played the game within constraints. For one, he recognized that "reason is, and ought only to be the slave of the passions" (T 2.3.3.4; SBN 415). For another, he wrote that he deliberately tried to "compose my temper" in order to obtain an "easy disposition" and study "philosophy in this careless manner," all ways of saying that we should not take our philosophy too seriously (T 1.4.7.14; SBN 273). The best philosophy does not take itself too seriously.

In the texts we have reviewed, Hume brought out the importance of custom and habit in politics and economics. By his account, the fact that we live largely by habit is not something to worry about. It is a way of living with a deep skepticism about knowledge. We may not often know what is really and positively true, but that is not necessary in order to figure out how to live. Hume shows us that in politics and economics we regularly get by, and even prosper, by relying on custom and habit. Most of life is a matter of living with custom and habit, and such a life is not by any means the worst life.

References

Butler, Joseph (1828) *The Analogy of Religion* in *Works*, London.

Dewey, John (1922) *Human Nature and Conduct: An Introduction to Social Psychology*, New York: Holt.

Hutcheson, Francis and R. Downie, eds. (1994) *Philosophical Writings*, London: Dent.

Junqueira Smith, Plinio (2011) "Hume on Skeptical Arguments," in D. E. Machuca (eds.), *Pyrrhonism in Ancient, Modern, and Contemporary*, Dordrecht: Springer.

Laursen, J. C. (2004) "Yes, Skeptics Can Live Their Skepticism and Cope with Tyranny as Well as Anyone," in J. R. Neto and R. H. Popkin (eds.), *Skepticism in Renaissance and Post-Renaissance Thought: New Interpretations*, Amherst: Humanity Books.

———. and G. Coolidge (1994) "David Hume and the Public Debt: Crying Wolf?" *Hume Studies* 20(1): 143–149.

Locke, John and P. H. Nidditch, ed. (1975) *An Essay Concerning Human Understanding*, Oxford: Oxford University Press.

Sextus Empiricus and R. G. Bury, ed. (1933) *Sextus Empiricus*. 1, 1. (*Outlines of Pyrrhonism*), Cambridge, MA: Harvard University Press.

Shils, Edward A. (1981) *Tradition*, Chicago, IL: University of Chicago Press.

Wright, John P. (1994) "Butler and Hume on Habit and Moral Character," in M. A. Stewart and J. P. Wright (eds.), *Hume and Hume's Connexions*, State College, PA: Penn State University Press.

27

HUME AND THE PHILOSOPHY OF LAW

Neil McArthur

Hume never devoted a single book or treatise to the law. But he comments extensively on the topic throughout his works.[1] We cannot identify any Humean school among modern legal philosophers, nor place him squarely within one of the major traditions of legal philosophy. However, when we examine the relevant texts, we can see that Hume made a major contribution to the development of legal thought, one that has not been fully recognized. Hume offers an account of the nature and origins of our sense of justice, which he sees as rooted in our awareness of the utility it provides to society. He also emphasizes the importance of the rule of law to a modern commercial society and analyzes the development of English law towards a system that is stable and predictable. His influential *History of England* helped turn legal thinkers away from the fruitless search for some "original contract" between king and people and encouraged them to attend to the more complicated process of evolution that created the constitution of his day. And he provides the first systematic analysis of the law as a system of conventions to which people adhere in order to reap the benefits of social cooperation.

Hume's acquaintance with the law

We cannot say for certain the extent of Hume's background in the law, since he never underwent any systematic program of training. But we know that this background was significant. Hume's father Joseph Home was a lawyer, who trained at the University of Utrecht, at that time the center of learning for Roman law, on which the Scottish legal system was based. Joseph died when Hume was 2. As a young man, Hume, in need of a profession, was pushed towards a career in law by his family, who felt that his "studious disposition," "sobriety," and "industry" ideally suited him to it. It was in any case a natural choice for the son of an advocate. At that time an aspiring young lawyer trained by attending trials and other court sessions, and, most importantly, read on his own. Hume tried to work through the standard textbooks and may have sat in on the Courts of Session in Edinburgh. But the teen-ager ultimately found that he had at the time "an unsurmountable aversion to everything but the pursuits of philosophy and general learning," and he abandoned his legal studies. (L 1: 1.)

Despite this early failure, Hume remained closely connected to the world of the law. His circle of intimates included two of the country's most brilliant legal minds. Hume's cousin Henry Home was a prominent lawyer, raised to the bench in 1752 as Lord Kames. Fifteen years older than Hume, Kames was a man of broad philosophical interests. Kames mentored his younger cousin and helped promote his ideas. Hume was also close to Alexander Wedderburn, who defended Hume from charges of heresy before the Scottish kirk, and who ultimately became Britain's Lord Chancellor.

Hume was fluent enough with the law to be appointed a Judge Advocate in the military during the Seven Years War, charged with presiding over courts martial. And he spent several years as Librarian to the Faculty of Advocates at Edinburgh, a job that made him superintendent to Scotland's finest library. The library was established in the late seventeenth century to provide lawyers with access to both legal and non-legal texts, and Hume spent his time reading deeply in the library's collection. It was during this period that he did the bulk of his research for his *History of England*.

The virtue of justice and the emergence of law

Any discussion of Hume's contribution to the philosophy of law must begin with his original, and controversial, account of justice. Hume uses the term "justice" in slightly different ways at different points in his writing, but he uses it primarily to describe the trait of character that disposes us to respect the society's rules regarding the possession and transfer of property. Hume aims to provide an explanation of how such rules arise, and why we are generally, even if not invariably, disposed to obey them. Hume's account is original in several respects. First of all, he thinks that the rules of justice, which later become formalized as laws, emerge gradually, as the result of a slow evolution. He thus rejects the notion of an "original contact" between the people and their governors that establishes a society's legal framework. Second, he thinks these rules emerge to protect property, and that remains their primary purpose. Third, he denies that justice is an innate feature of the mind. To use Hume's (somewhat idiosyncratic) terminology, it is an artificial rather than a natural virtue. Finally, he thinks that people's allegiance to the legal system comes from their awareness of the utility of this system, rather than a fear of sanctions.

To understand Hume's originality, we can contrast his account of justice with that of one of his most influential predecessors, Thomas Hobbes. Hobbes begins by imagining people living in a state of nature, where everyone is alone and fends for him or herself. However, these solitary creatures realize they are better off living together under a system of rules, with people empowered to enforce them, and so they agree to form a society. Certain people are designated as magistrates, and they lay down laws which the people are obliged to obey. While Hobbes' account was itself original and highly controversial, the idea that the laws owed their origin to a contract between ruler and people was axiomatic among the Whigs of Hume's day, and it had carried currency since the middle ages. For Hume, the contract accounts ignore the crucial, intermediate stages of social development. He insists that the basic rules governing people's behavior precede the appearance of magistrates and of formal sanctions.

Hume thinks that, because people are inherently social, there was never any stage in our history where we lived as isolated individuals. Instead, we first lived together in family units. But our experience with such small units convinced us that we benefit from cooperation, and so we naturally tended to expand our social circle outwards, into ever-larger groups. Hume speculates on how a legal system might emerge from these early forms of society. As people moved from family units to larger social groups, they saw that life in such larger groups had distinct benefits. But it also created the potential for conflict. People thus realized that it was necessary for continued coexistence that there be divisions between "mine" and "yours" – or in other words an idea of property. They established rules for exchange and transfer. The rules of property thus emerge before any formal laws, and before anyone is given any powers of enforcement. Hume thinks that a society can reach a stage of considerable complexity, and can remain quite stable, without a formal system of laws or government. People follow the rules of property due to their fear of social disapproval, and due to their awareness that these rules are necessary for maintaining a society that delivers benefits to everyone in it.

At some point, rulers and magistrates emerge, and the laws become formalized and enforced. Hume is not willing to say definitively how this happens, and he provides different explanations for how it might. He speculates that magistrates might emerge as divisions in wealth become more pronounced, increasing the temptation for lawlessness. Or it might be that they establish themselves as the society faces the threat of foreign attack. In any case, once people have experienced strong rulers who can enforce the rules of property, they see the benefits of having such rulers. As time goes on, these rulers appoint lesser magistrates to administer justice, and they begin to refine and revise the established rules. A legal system has emerged.

In asserting that legal systems emerge from the need to protect property, Hume departs from predecessors such as Hobbes, Pufendorf, and Hutcheson, who all argue that societies need laws at least partly due to people's propensity to do harm to one another. Hume is aware that the scope of the law extends significantly beyond the governance of property relationships. His essays and *History of England* discusses a wide variety of constitutional, criminal, and civil laws. But he thinks that it is the law's ability to guarantee the stable possession and transference of property that explains both its emergence and its on-going legitimacy. Our sense of justice is rooted in our understanding that a system of stable property rules is in our long-term best interest.

Though Hume is more or less alone among philosophers in focusing exclusively on property as the foundation of law, he offers only the most cursory defense of his view. He says that there is little reason to rob people of life or security, since we gain nothing by doing so, and so there is no reason to think that when people first established the rules of justice, they were motivated by the desire for personal safety. Property, by contrast, is ever in short supply and is easily hijacked, and so it makes sense to believe that people have always needed rules to secure it.

Thomas Reid, among others, remarked critically on Hume's property-based account of justice, and few historians would be convinced by Hume's argument in its defense. No one would deny that what he calls "avidity" – the desire for material possessions – has long been an important source of social disorder. However, even a cursory glance at the historical record seems to give ample evidence for the thesis that humans are willing to engage in violence for a wide variety of reasons, beyond the mere hope of material gain. Scholars have yet to give a fully satisfactory account of why Hume thinks the rules of justice are rooted entirely in our desire to protect our property.

Hume also departs from his predecessors in arguing that justice is, as he puts it, an artificial, rather than a natural virtue. This too earned him criticism from Reid and others, not all of whom understood clearly what he meant. It is not surprising that Hume's view was seen as provocative. Johnson's *Dictionary* gives one definition of "artificial" as "fictitious," and Hume's description of virtue as artificial would have reminded some readers of Bernard Mandeville, who notoriously argues that society's moral and legal rules are mere artifices devised by cunning politicians to manipulate people into behaving in the ways they deem desirable. When Hume says that justice is artificial, he does not mean that the rules of property are arbitrary, nor does he think they may be traced to specific artificers, who have deliberately developed them to serve their own ends. By claiming justice is an artificial virtue, he means to say rather that it is the product of education, socialization, and reflection. We can contrast his view with the position of Francis Hutcheson, who believes that the rules of justice originate from an innate principle of the mind – what Hume calls "a simple original instinct in the human breast" – and that such an instinct can explain our allegiance to them.

Hume does not think, as Hobbes does, that people act entirely out of self-interest. He recognizes that we have naturally benevolent motives. Indeed, he thinks that, ultimately, people's "kind affections, taken together . . . over-balance all the selfish" ones (T 3.2.2.5; SBN 487). However, he thinks that our natural benevolence cannot be the basis of our sense of justice, and thus Hutcheson's account cannot be right, for two reasons. First of all, Hume does not think that a system that relied on our natural benevolence would be stable enough to act as the basis for a lasting social order. For Hume, the problem is not that we lack benevolence. It is that, in individual cases, we are easily overwhelmed by self-interest, or by a force at least as potent: partial sympathy for those closest to us. Both of these emotions would lead us into behavior that is destructive to society, were they not tempered by our willingness to follow the more impartial rules of justice.

Second, and more importantly, even when benevolence is strong enough to cause us to act, it does not invariably lead us in the direction that justice demands. Hume notes something that few others before him had seen clearly: that benevolence and justice are in fact quite distinct. The acts we esteem as just are very often neither intrinsically praiseworthy in themselves, nor immediately beneficial to the parties involved. If we had only our instinctive benevolence to guide us, the society's rules would look very different than they in fact do – if it were able to implement a stable system of rules at all. Benevolence causes us to make judgments based on individual cases, whereas the benefits of a system of justice come from the functioning of the system as a whole. Indeed, many just judgments look distinctly unpraiseworthy when viewed merely through the lens of benevolence. As Hume says:

> If we examine all the questions, that come before any tribunal of justice, we shall find, that, considering each case apart, it would as often be an instance of humanity to decide contrary to the laws of justice as conformable them. Judges take from a poor man to give to a rich; they bestow on the dissolute the labour of the industrious; and put into the hands of the vicious the means of harming both themselves and others. The whole scheme, however, of law and justice is advantageous to the society.
>
> (T 3.3.1.12; SBN 579)

Hume thinks that we can explain people's obedience to the law by attending to the advantageousness of the legal system as a whole. While we do not follow the laws from any natural desire to do good, neither do we act merely from a fear of the sanctions attached to their violation. This could not be the motive, since the rules of justice pre-exist the presence of formal sanctions. We also do not follow them because of any promise, explicit or tacit, to do so. Hume insists that our willingness to keep our promises has the same source as our fidelity to the law. He argues that our on-going obedience is rooted in our understanding of the utility provided by the overall system of rules. He says:

> Justice arises from . . . a sense of common interest; which . . . each man feels in his own breast, which he remarks in his fellows, and which carries him, in concurrence with others into a general plan or system of actions, which tends to public utility.
>
> (EPM, App. 3.7; SBN 306)

Hume thinks that the utility of the legal system is obvious enough, so that anyone who reflects on the rules of society easily sees the advantages that come from following them. But he does not think that it is necessary for each and every person to reflect on the law and understand its utility in order to acquire a sense of obedience to it. Our sense of justice is in practice created by an on-going process of socialization. Hume asserts that we are turned into law-abiding members of society by the work of our parents and our teachers in instilling good behavior, by the moral exhortations of politicians urging us to be good citizens, and ultimately by the force of habit.

General laws and Britain's legal development

Hume's *Treatise* provides a highly abstract and speculative discussion of how legal rules emerge in a society. In his essays and his *History of England*, however, he offers a different sort of analysis – one that draws on concrete examples and cases. Despite this more practical focus, he remains faithful to the basic ideas he develops in the *Treatise*. In his later works, Hume focuses on the conditions necessary to establish what we now call the rule of law. He does not use this phrase, though he does speak of "a government of laws" – which has a similar meaning, and which he invariably contrasts with a government "of men." Hume identifies both the key features of such a government of laws and the conditions necessary for its establishment, and he argues that, once established, it has broad-reaching impacts on society as a whole. For Hume, the key features of a government of laws are, first of all, that it places limits on the discretionary power of magistrates, and, second, that it applies the laws to the magistrates themselves.

Hume argues there are two stages in a society's legal development: an early, imperfect one, in which the magistrates govern using broad discretionary powers, and a more advanced state in which they enforce, and are restricted by, what he calls "general laws." Hume tells us in the *Treatise* that a stable property regime depends on "general rules, which must extend to the whole society, and be inflexible either by spite or favour" (T 3.2.3.3; SBN 502). As he explains in his later writings, this means that monarchs or central authorities must watch over what he calls "the lesser magistrates" to ensure that these magistrates are not exercising discretion in their judgments. He says it is a virtue of the British government of his day that it must "maintain a watchful jealousy over the magistrates, to remove all discretionary powers, and to secure every one's life and fortune by general and inflexible laws" (E 96; cf. EPM Appendix 3.6; SBN 305). And he says it is characteristic of "all civilized nations" that they restrict such judicial discretion (EPM Appendix 3.10; SBN 308). Hume also emphasizes the importance of applying the laws to the magistrates themselves. He says that "a scene of oppression and slavery" is the inevitable result of any legal system "where the people alone are restrained by the authority of the magistrates, and the magistrates are not restrained by any law or statute" (E 118).

Hume paints a dire picture of societies where a government of laws has not been established. He calls such societies "barbarous," and says that the inadequate legal regime "debases the people, and for ever prevents all improvements." Because property is not secure, the economy cannot flourish. The arts and sciences also stagnate. However, the situation is not entirely hopeless. A gradual process can take place, driven by chance events and by talented monarchs, whereby the society can progress to a state of "civilization." Once an adequate system of laws begins to emerge, the economy, science, and the arts will begin to improve as well, and this in turn will further stimulate legal development. This is precisely what he thinks happened, over the course of several centuries, in England.

Hume's analysis of England's legal history begins with the Norman conquest. He dismisses the views of certain "common law" thinkers of his era, who insisted that English law was rooted in the immemorial past and that it was the task of the jurist to learn and preserve these timeless traditions. For Hume, the Normans founded English law as we know it when they seized all of the nation's land by right of conquest, and then bequeathed it to the most powerful aristocrats among the conquerors. These barons held the land as vassals of the king and granted land to their own followers on the same terms – thus inaugurating the feudal system.

Hume speaks in scathing terms of this feudal system, which he sees as dangerously unstable and unproductive. First of all, the lords retained the right to administer justice on their estates, ensuring that judgments were determined by discretion rather than general laws. Second, he thinks there was constant struggle between the king and his "unruly barons." The outcome depended on the talents of the individual monarch. A strong king could rule as a tyrant, while a weak one allowed rebellion and lawlessness among the nobles to thrive.

Hume argues that it is only during the Tudor era that this conflict was resolved decisively, on the side of the monarchs. The Tudor rulers were able "to pull down those disorderly and licentious tyrants [i.e. the aristocracy] ... and to establish [a] regular execution of the laws" (H 2: 525). This triumph, though it benefited the people, came at a cost, however. The crown established itself through the use of royal prerogative, which, though it served a useful purpose, nevertheless brought a danger that soon became apparent, that of royal oppression. The nation required a second stage, when the monarchs themselves were brought under the control of law. Hume praises the Long Parliament for finally abolishing the Star Chamber, an act which he thinks effectively made Britain "a government of laws." "The parliament justly thought," he says,

> that the king was too eminent a magistrate to be trusted with discretionary power, which he might so easily turn to the destruction of liberty. And in the event it has hitherto been found, that, though some sensible inconveniences arise from the maxim of adhering strictly to law, yet the advantages overbalance them, and should render the English grateful to the memory of their ancestors, who, after repeated contests, at last established that noble, though dangerous, principle.
>
> (H 5: 329–330)

Hume thinks that, after this great breakthrough, England's legal and political system continued to evolve in the direction of liberty, with the crown's power further restricted by gradual stages. He speaks warmly of the effects of the Glorious Revolution, which he says was "attended with consequences ... advantageous to the people." "By deciding many important questions in favour of liberty," he concludes, "and still more, by that great precedent of deposing one king, and establishing a new family, it gave such an ascendant to popular principles, as has put the nature of the English constitution beyond all controversy" (H 6: 531).

Hume expresses great admiration for Britain's modern constitution, which he thinks has achieved a near-ideal balance of liberty and authority – in other words, protections for the rights of citizens alongside effective central authority. However, he thinks that this balance is a fragile one, and events could always tip things too far in one direction or the other. Late in life, he took a decided turn towards pessimism concerning Britain's political future, believing that popular disorder might necessitate an assertion of strong central power in order to keep the peace.

Hume and the critique of natural law

Modern debates in the philosophy of law have turned on the distinction between positivist and natural law approaches to the law. While Hume cannot be defined as a legal positivist, Bentham and other positivist thinkers drew on his arguments in their effort to demolish the natural law tradition. Natural law theory was the dominant mode of legal thought during Hume's era, and his contribution to its eclipse should not go unnoticed.

As I have said, Hume thinks that justice is in one sense natural, and he uses the term "laws of nature" to describe the basic rules of property, which govern "the stability of possession" and "its transference by consent." These rules arise in any human group that has reached a certain level of size and complexity, and they address needs that are universal to creatures like us. Despite his use of the term "laws of nature," however, Hume departs dramatically, and quite deliberately, from conventional conceptions of what such laws were. His views on the law are consistent with his general philosophical project, which involves explaining human phenomena by appeal to principles of human nature, and without recourse to the supernatural. Thus he rejects any suggestion that the laws might be the product of divine will, or might serve some larger providential purpose. He also denies that the proper exercise of human reason leads us towards the good, as Aquinas believes. Hume famously declares something no natural law thinker in the Aquinian tradition could endorse, that "it is not contrary to reason to prefer the destruction of the entire world to the scratching of one's little finger" (T 2.3.3.6; SBN 157).

I have said that for Hume, our obedience to the laws may be traced to their utility, and it is perhaps not surprising that Hume exercised an influence on Jeremy Bentham, who is sometimes seen as the founder of legal positivism. In his *Fragment on Government*, published in 1776, Bentham says that when he read David Hume's *Treatise of Human Nature* (which appeared in 1739), he felt "as if the scales had fallen from my eyes." It was from Hume, he claimed, that he "learned to see that utility was the test and measure of all virtue" (Bentham Burns, J. H. and Hart 1977: 440–441). However, there is reason to believe that, in this text, Bentham over-states Hume's actual impact on him. There are no references to Hume in Bentham's surviving correspondence of the time, and he directly cites Hume's idea of utility nowhere else. Bentham seems to have come across appeals to utility and to the greatest happiness in a number of authors he read during his youth, including Helvetius, Beccaria, and Priestley. It would be a mistake to give Hume exclusive credit for inspiring Bentham's adoption of utility as the measure of all value. And Bentham's energetic project to reform Britain's laws, and those of all nations, is foreign to Hume's conservative temperament. Hume uses the notion of utility primarily as an explanatory one, to provide an account of how the laws in fact emerge. He is willing to praise historical figures such as King Edward I, who reformed England's laws for the better. But he could never have endorsed a project such as Bentham envisaged, of completing rewriting the existing legal codes of every country, in order to ensure they conformed to the demands of utility.

Even if we determine that, in formulating his notion of utility, Bentham's debt to Hume is a limited one, the English reformer also attributes to Hume another important insight that became central to positivism's critique of natural law theory. Bentham credits Hume with first observing

> how apt men have been, on questions belonging to any part of the field of Ethics, to shift backwards and forwards, and apparently without their perceiving it, from the question, what has been done, to the question, what ought to be done.
>
> (Bentham and Bowring1843: 8, 128)

Bentham is referring to the passage in the *Treatise* where Hume argues that moral conclusions can never be derived from non-moral premises (See T 3.1.1.27; SBN 469–470). Natural law theory is, as we have seen, premised on the derivation of normative propositions from facts either about the nature of reality or the nature of human reason. Bentham thinks Hume dispenses with the possibility of any such derivation, and, taking this insight on board, Bentham divides jurisprudence into two separate provinces:

> To the province of *Expositor* it belongs to explain what, as he supposes, the Law *is:* to that of the *Censor,* to observe to us what he thinks it *ought to be.* The former, therefore,

is principally occupied in stating, or in inquiring after *facts:* the latter, in discussing *reasons.*

(Bentham Burns, J. H. and Hart 1977: 397)

While Bentham had no qualms about acting as censor, later positivists have placed themselves staunchly in the role of expositor, insisting that they are providing a sociological analysis of the law and its functioning.

Hume also deserves recognition for anticipating another important theme within modern legal positivism: its emphasis on convention. It is a great insight of Hume's that rules for social cooperation can emerge without any explicit agreement among the parties involved, and that people will continue to follow these rules in a stable and predictable way. Though modern legal conventionalism draws its immediate inspiration from the work of Thomas Schelling (1963) and David Lewis (1974), it may nevertheless be seen as broadly Humean in spirit. Gerald Postema has written influentially on both modern legal conventionalism and on Hume's legal theory, and his work makes conventionalism's debt to Hume clear (Postema 1982; Postema 1986).

Modern legal conventionalism begins from the view that the legal system depends on a particular kind of social fact, namely the cooperative behavior of those involved, rather than on some abstract set of principles. Scott Shapiro, for instance, describes legal practice in Humean terms, as a joint activity, the goal of which is the "creation and maintenance of a unified system of rules." Shapiro says that the legal officials are obliged to "mesh" their actions with those of others because they participate in an on-going process of cooperation, "not because of the principles of morality" (Shapiro 2002: 437).

Legal conventionalism has been criticized for its exclusive focus on the law's coordinating function (Green 1999). There has been debate among scholars whether, for his part, Hume sees the law purely in terms of social coordination, or whether he endorses specific normative criteria according to which we may judge different legal systems as better or worse relative to one another. Russell Hardin (2007) offers the most thorough interpretation of Hume as a conventionalist who abjures all normative evaluation. This stands in contrast to the reading of Hume offered by Stewart (1992) and McArthur (2007), who both argue that he puts forward a set of normative criteria that allow him to recommend certain forms of political and legal society over others, not just as more effective forms of social coordination but as preferable on moral grounds. On their reading, Hume is not merely a social scientist who analyzes the conditions under which a society develops legal and political institutions and who seeks to explain why citizens retain an on-going allegiance to these institutions. He is also a committed reformer who wants to promote certain kinds of institutions – specifically those that foster individual freedom and commercial development.

Conclusion

While philosophers have long acknowledged the importance of Hume's analysis of justice and his critique of the social contract, he is not normally given a place in the canon of major legal philosophers. I have argued that his contributions to the field are significant, and extend beyond what many people recognize today. We can find in his work a pioneering analysis of what we now call the rule of law, as well as anticipations of important themes within modern legal positivism.

Note

1 K. Mackinnon, ed., *Hume and Law* (2012) provides an authoritative collection of article on all aspects of Hume's legal thought. Other important works include Harrison (1981), Haakonssen (1981), and

Postema (1986). My monograph *David Hume's Political Theory: Law, Commerce, and the Constitution of Government* (2007) discusses Hume's distinction between barbarous and civilized governments, and the role played by the law in the evolution of modern commercial society.

References

Bentham, J. and J. Bowring, eds. (1843) *The Works Volume 8 Chrestomathia*, Edinburgh: William Tate.

————., J. H. Burns and H. L. A. Hart, eds. (1977) *A Comment on the Commentaries and a Fragment on Government*, London: University of London Athlone Press.

Green, L. (1999) "Positivism and Conventionalism," *Canadian Journal of Law and Jurisprudence* 12(1): 35–52.

Haakonssen, K. (1981) *The Science of a Legislator: The Natural Jurisprudence of David Hume and Adam Smith*, Cambridge: Cambridge University Press.

Hardin, R. (2007) *David Hume: Moral and Political Theorist*, Oxford: Oxford University Press.

Harrison, J. (1981) *Hume's Theory of Justice*, Oxford: Clarendon Press.

Lewis, D. K. (1974) *Convention: A Philosophical Study*, Cambridge, MA: Harvard University Press.

Mackinnon, K., eds. (2012) *Hume and Law*, London: Routledge.

McArthur, N. (2007) *David Hume's Political Theory: Law, Commerce, and the Constitution of Government*, Toronto: University of Toronto Press.

Postema, G. (1982) "Coordination and Convention at the Foundations of Law," *Journal of Legal Studies* 11(1): 165–203.

————. (1986) *Bentham and the Common Law Tradition*, Oxford: Clarendon Press.

Schelling, T. (1963) *The Strategy of Conflict*, Oxford: Oxford University Press.

Shapiro, S. (2002) "Law, Plans and Practical Reason," *Legal Theory* 8(4): 387–441.

Stewart, J. B. (1992) *Opinion and Reform in Hume's Political Philosophy*, Princeton: Princeton University Press.

References

PART III

Hume's reception

PART IIIA

Eighteenth–early twentieth century

28

HUME AND THE SCOTTISH INTELLECTUAL TRADITION

Gordon Graham

Hume's philosophical writings have long been studied closely for the elegance with which they articulate an enduringly appealing philosophical position, and they have been mined intensively for the contribution they can make to contemporary philosophical debate and inquiry. They have also been studied in historical context – both the context of Hume's less obviously philosophical writings and the cultural milieu within which they arose. So extensive has the literature on Hume become, we may wonder whether there is any prospect of genuinely fresh illumination. A topic that exercised commentators and interlocutors in Hume's own day, and for a good part of the nineteenth century as well, was Hume's place in a much larger context – the Scottish intellectual tradition. Was his version of the "science of man," despite its skeptical implications, an inevitable development of this trajectory of thought, or was it an aberration born of the fact that Hume had, intentionally or by default, relinquished something fundamental to it? Interest in the subject faded, but the fact that it was once so keenly debated gives us reason to think that it might be worth returning to now.

A problem confronting anyone who wants to resuscitate that debate is that intellectual traditions are generally easier to allude to than to articulate clearly or analyze cogently. What sustains the identity of an intellectual tradition over time? How much consistency and coherence must it have? How much of this coherence must it retain before we have to say that it has turned into something else? So intractable can these questions be, it is sometimes hard to avoid the suspicion that "intellectual tradition" is just a rather grand way of referring to a conventional clustering of authors and/or ideas which may, or may not, benefit from being read and examined together. Since the difficulties these questions raise are not easily resolved and cannot legitimately be circumvented, we may be tempted to abandon talk of "intellectual traditions" altogether.

To do so, however, is to give up on an important possibility. By placing writers in a much larger historical context, we may come to a better appreciation of both their originality and their dependence on frameworks of thought from which, initially, they seem to break away. Novelty can only be evaluated against the background of continuity. It is the potential of just such illumination that makes the questions worth persisting with in the case of David Hume, the depth and originality of whose philosophical ideas have been debated almost from their first appearance.

There is a case to be made for thinking that if we confine ourselves to Scotland, we can indeed identify an intellectual tradition within which we might plausibly seek to relate to

Hume. The identification of this tradition rests upon solid, if rather less than conclusive, grounds. To begin with, somewhat unusually, there is an identifiable institutional base that may be said to have sustained Scottish intellectual life over a very long time, namely the universities of Scotland. From the foundation of St Andrews in 1411–1413 until their relatively rapid integration into the state-sponsored British-wide system that came into existence after World War I, the Scottish universities took a lead in Scotland's intellectual life. This is an unusually long period, possibly unmatched elsewhere. Second, these institutions – five eventually – were remarkably integrated. Though geographically dispersed, they pursued the same curriculum (more or less) and amended it in tandem, and educated each other's teachers. In response to both religious reformation and new intellectual trends, they underwent similar re-organizations. Third, they were all expected to play the same social role in their vicinity, namely the education of the professional classes, chiefly clergy, but also (especially later) lawyers and physicians, and they generally did so. Consequently, the intellectual leadership of the country was, for the most part, university educated. Fourth, across these many centuries, philosophy played a strikingly prominent role in the curriculum and in the scholarly agenda of these universities. Scotland's most prominent and influential intellectuals were either philosophers themselves – from John Mair (?1465–1550) through Adam Smith (1723–1790) and Thomas Reid (1710–1796) to Edward Caird (1835–1908) and Alexander Bain (1818–1903) – or they were theologians, social theorists, and educationalists grounded in philosophy – from John Knox (?1513–1572) and Andrew Melville (1545–1622) through Lord Kames (1696–1782) to Herbert Grierson (1866–1960). Finally, the tradition was linked, not by unanimity of doctrine, but by self-consciousness. The expression "Scottish philosophy" may be said to have been coined late in the day (when James McCosh published *The Scottish Philosophy* in 1875), but this simply signals the fact that historical continuity is primarily to be recognized with hindsight. "The Scotch Metaphysics" had been the subject of criticism and defense long before that.

There is reason, then, to hold that over five centuries or so, there existed in Scotland an intellectual tradition shaped by philosophical thinking, sustained by educational institutions, and realized in the wider community through the role of those institutions. It is easy to exaggerate, and to romanticize this idea, as arguably George Davie did in his celebrated book *The Democratic Intellect* (1961). Over these same centuries there was radical disagreement between figures who may, on equally good grounds, be said to be members of the tradition. This is especially true in the aftermath of the Protestant Reformation and during the period of (what came to be known as) the Scottish Enlightenment, when theological and philosophical debate was intense. Furthermore, the universities were almost continuously subject to political manipulation, and even at the best of times the success with which they fulfilled their appointed social role varied greatly. Still, the idea of a Scottish intellectual tradition is not groundless, and easier to lend substance to than in many other contexts. The question here is whether it is substantial enough to provide a context that casts additional light on the intellectual endeavors and achievements of Hume.

From Reformation to Enlightenment

On the face of it, the answer, it seems, must be "No." The institutional and educational dimensions that appear to sustain the idea of a centuries-long intellectual tradition are real enough, but they fail to take account of a radical break within its history. This break may be marked, without too much distortion, as concurrent with the Act of Union in 1707, when Scotland and England became one country. This was the point at which an intellectual shift from Reformation to Enlightenment thinking took place. However uncertain the precise boundaries between

"Reformation" and "Enlightenment" may be, it is highly plausible to think that the change they constituted is so significant that the idea of their being transcended in a single intellectual tradition sustained by the Scottish universities becomes almost fanciful.

This rupture, it is to be noted, is not between pre- and post-Reformation Scotland, where, given the intensity of the conflict between Catholic and Protestant, the continuities are perhaps surprising. The ancient Scottish universities were characteristic foundations of the medieval Christian Church, devoted to the seven liberal arts of the medieval curriculum. Their purpose was the teaching of theology as preparation for priesthood, as well as supplying experts in canon and civil law, and their method was that of Aristotelian scholasticism. The Reformation brought great changes, including the addition of two more self-consciously Protestant universities (Edinburgh and Marischal College in Aberdeen) and "new" foundations for the other three. Nevertheless, a great deal stayed the same – the teaching of theology and the education of the clergy remained central. After a flirtation with the logic of Ramus, Aristotelianism reasserted itself in Protestant scholasticism, and the universities generally resisted the innovations of Cartesianism that were proving popular elsewhere. As institutions, both the old and the new universities, small though they all were, continued to be politically and socially important.

This is a simplified picture, but it serves to underline how very much more radical the differences were that came about at the time of the Enlightenment. Under the influence of Gersholm Carmichael, George Turnbull, and especially Francis Hutcheson, moral philosophy, reconceived along (vaguely) Baconian/Newtonian lines and shaped by ideas of "the law of nature and nations," took center stage in place of dogmatic theology, whose key topics were no longer debated by the leading professors. The heterodox Presbyterians in the first half of the eighteenth century (of whom Hutcheson was a leading light), and the "Moderates" of the second half (led by the historian William Robertson), sidelined the ardent Calvinists and generally ignored the theological issues by which they were animated. As the eighteenth century wore on, there was an astonishing outburst of intellectual activity in the study of mind and society in all their aspects, alongside the flowering of both conjectural history and historical studies. None of this has any very evident foundation, or even precursor, in the life of the medieval and reformed universities.

If a distinctive tradition may be said to have developed out of all this intellectual ferment, it was the "Scottish School of Common Sense," inspired by Thomas Reid's *Inquiry into the Human Mind* (1764), and first identified as such by Joseph Priestly, Reid's arch critic. It was Reidian common sense, subsequently defended first by Dugald Stewart and then by Sir William Hamilton, that spread to America, and was identified in France as the "philosophie ecossaise" by Victor Cousin. Once again this is a simplified picture, but accurate enough so far as it goes. Its adequacy for present purposes is a matter to be returned to.

If we are persuaded that, contrary to the unifying factors cited earlier, there is good reason to regard Scottish intellectual history as importantly divided in this way, it seems relatively easy to make a case that leaves Hume out of both halves. With respect to the intellectual culture of the pre- and post-Reformation universities, there is the obvious fact that in a lifetime of authorship, Hume shows no interest at all in the content of the theological debates that animated intellectual debate in Scotland right up to the time he was born. Though he wrote extensively about religion and cannot be classified unqualifiedly as an atheist, his most enduring interest is in its nature and effects. His posthumously published, and subsequently famous *Dialogues Concerning Natural Religion*, deals directly with theological questions, but these are the questions of *natural*, not *revealed*, theology. His essays show a familiarity with the Bible but no inclination to use it. The most we can say by way of continuity is that they also show Hume shared his Presbyterian contemporaries' distaste for "Romish" religious practices.

Hume was a student at Edinburgh University in the second decade of the eighteenth century. He was only 11 years of age (possibly as young as 10) when he entered the university, and this fact alone raises a question about how much induction into an intellectual tradition he could have received. In any case, the curriculum and teaching were still largely as they had been in the seventeenth century, and had little connection with the study of human nature that subsequently interested him. According to M A Stewart, "the mission of education in Hume's day was to train students for virtuous living in a society regulated by religious observance" (Stewart 2005: 12). The educational method was largely rote learning, and even the "logic" course was geared to "the chief end of man" as specified by the Shorter Catechism and amplified by the Westminster Confession. We are largely ignorant about Hume's studies at Edinburgh, but if this is true, there seems little reason to suppose that he absorbed anything that might have shaped or even colored his thought in later life. More importantly, perhaps, his own comments, published and unpublished, suggest that his view of his time as a student in Edinburgh was largely negative. In 1735, he advised a young friend not to bother going to college, writing in a letter,

> There is nothing to be learnt from a Professor, which is not to be met with in Books ... I see no reason why we shou'd go to an University, more than any other place, or ever trouble ourselves about the Learning or Capacity of the Professors.
>
> (quoted in Harris 2015: 32)

In the *Treatise* he gives voice to a similar sentiment.

> Our scholastic head pieces and logicians show no such superiority above the mere vulgar in their reason and ability, as to give us any inclination to imitate them in delivering along system of rules and precepts to direct our judgment, in philosophy.
>
> (T 1.3.15.11; SBN 175)

It seems reasonable to conclude then that uncovering a meaningful intellectual continuity between Hume and Scottish philosophy before the Enlightenment is a doubtful enterprise. Initially, finding such a connection with Scottish intellectuals after the Enlightenment seems rather more promising. Hume, after all, has been heralded in many quarters as the archetypal thinker of the Scottish Enlightenment. Here too, though, problems arise. The chief difficulty is that the style of thinking peculiarly identified with Scottish philosophy – "the School of Common Sense" – was founded as, and widely conceived to be, an *answer* to Hume. It can hardly, then, have incorporated him. Kant, too, sought to answer Hume, and famously held that the Scottish philosophers had completely failed to appreciate the deep challenge the *Treatise* represented. "It is positively painful to see how utterly [Hume's] opponents, Reid, Oswald, Beattie and lastly Priestly missed the point of the problem" (Kant 1783/1980: 6) This is more evidence of a gulf between Hume and his Scottish philosophical contemporaries, whose appeal to "common sense" Kant dismissed as the means by which "the most superficial ranter can safely enter the lists with the most thorough thinker and hold his own" (ibid.: 7). One hundred years later, in 1882, when Andrew Seth gave some influential lectures entitled "On the Scottish Philosophy," he expressly subtitled them "a comparison of the Scottish and German answers to Hume." James McCosh, in *The Scottish Philosophy* (1875) takes a broader view of the Enlightenment phase and does not confine it to "common sense," but he still sees Hume as essentially a skeptical thinker operating outside the broad parameters of Scottish philosophy.

The conclusion seems to be that, despite first appearances perhaps, there is no single "Scottish intellectual tradition" within which philosophy had a central role. Scottish intellectual history clearly divides into two – 300 years of theological education which a training in philosophy was intended to serve, followed by 150 years during which philosophy was transformed into the study of mind and society guided by a conception of "common sense." We cannot plausibly say that Hume's thought owed much, if anything, to either phase. And indeed, Hume's distance from the Scottish intellectual tradition could be said to be increased by his relationship to a wider world of letters. In a well-known footnote to his Introduction to the *Treatise*, Hume mentions five philosophers whose work he means to capitalize on. Only one of them – "Mr Hutchinson" – is a Scottish professor; the others are all English men of letters. It is here, indeed, that James Harris finds an important clue to Hume's intellectual biography. Hume's life-long aim, Harris contends, was to be a man of letters, someone who, after the fashion of Addison but with a little more rigor, would bring a "philosophical" voice to the public discussion of the topics of the day. This, however, should not be thought "philosophical" as we currently mean the term. The "philosopher" for Hume, if Harris is right, is someone who deliberately eschews partisanship in intellectual debate, drops all the rhetoric that goes with it, and strives to create an intellectual milieu in which profound disagreement is compatible with the free and easy exchange of ideas, all in the pursuit of truth and understanding.

On the strength of these considerations, it seems that there is little to be gained by trying to consider Hume against the background of something called "the Scottish intellectual tradition." Yet the prospect of doing this to some real purpose is not as hopeless or pointless as the argument so far suggests. On the contrary, it is possible to find the roots of Hume's ideal of "the philosopher" as Harris depicts it in the theological debates that exercised the Scottish universities in the seventeenth century, thereby forging a connection with the intellectual tradition that preceded him. Second, and looking to the trajectory of Scottish philosophy in the nineteenth century, there is a good case to be made for thinking that the "skeptical" consequences of Hume's "science of mind" which prompted Reid's *Inquiry*, represent one side of a tension within the philosophy of the Scottish Enlightenment. This tension gradually played itself out in such a way that certain of its later proponents could with plausibility claim Hume as their true precursor. The aim of the next two sections is to explain and defend both these contentions, and thereby rescue the idea that setting Hume in the context of a long Scottish intellectual tradition has some illumination to offer us.

'True religion' and 'philosophy'

Any attempt to do this needs to be aware from the outset that in the history of ideas what most evidently appears to be the case is not wrong exactly, but nevertheless misleading. Deeper continuities that run counter to widely received wisdom can be discovered in surprising places and ways. Consider, for instance, the Cartesian origins of modern philosophy.[1]

Descartes is generally hailed as the founder of modern philosophy in virtue of the break he makes with the long medieval scholarly tradition in which theology is the queen of the sciences and philosophy its handmaid. While it is true that he mentions God and gives him a role in his thought, his great accomplishment is to reverse the order of importance and put theology in a subservient role to philosophy, thereby establishing a new focus on intellectual accomplishment instead of spiritual formation. Before too long, of course, theology drops out of the picture entirely; philosophy comes back into its own and resumes (so to speak) where Plato and Aristotle left off.

This is something of a caricature, but not wholly mistaken, and there is some clear sense in which Descartes does indeed mark the start of "modern philosophy." Against this background, however, it is startling to discover just how closely Descartes' *Meditations* follow the pattern of the meditations of the mystics, notably the *Interior Castle* of St Theresa of Avila (which there is reason to think he knew). They even employ some of the same devices, the contrast between sleeping and waking, for instance, and satanically inspired illusion. We now think of the "evil demon" of Descartes' "First Meditation" as just a kind of thought experiment, but there is no reason actually to suppose that Descartes himself lent the idea any less substance than Theresa. Similarly, when in the "Fourth Meditation" he fears that he might fall into "both error and sin," the spirit of "modern philosophy" discounts the second, or treats it as a *façon de parler*, and concentrates on the first. But once again there is no reason to suppose that Descartes thought in this way, and good reason to think that he did not.

The same kind of observation can be made about Hume. While it is true that his writings self-consciously strike out in new directions and are easily read today as making a clear break with what went before, there are some striking continuities that are evident only when we look a little more closely. Hume, the previous section argued, had no interest in the theological issues that had dominated the world into which he was born. Given the existence of the *Dialogues*, with which he seems to have tinkered over many years, this cannot be quite right, though these were published posthumously, of course. More to the point for present purposes, however, are some of his other writings on religion. The essay "Of Superstition and Enthusiasm," published in 1741, opens with this memorable sentence. "That *the corruption of the best of things produces the worst*, is grown into a maxim, and is commonly proved, among other instances, by the pernicious effects of *superstition* and *enthusiasm*, the corruptions of true religion" (E 73). The threefold classification in the last part of this sentence is not Hume's invention, but well-known and widely used in the theological debates of the seventeenth century. Moreover, his concern here – to distinguish and analyze corruptions of religion – is the same concern that we can find among Scottish intellectuals writing 70 years before. Thus, *The Life of God in the Soul of Man*, a lengthy letter composed by Henry Scougal, Professor of Divinity at Kings College Aberdeen, first published in 1677, opens with precisely this aim, and broadly speaking the same ambition – to distinguish between true religion on the one hand and manifestations of religion that are mistakenly taken to be religion proper on the other.

Of course, there are unmistakable differences between Scougal and Hume, not least their tone. Scougal is a devout Christian wishing to offer others spiritual guidance. He quotes the Scriptures with reverence and verges on religious mysticism. There is no trace of Christian devotion in Hume, none of his writings are intended to offer spiritual guidance, and when he makes express mention of religious practices it is often with an element of mockery. Yet, once again, the gap between the two writers is not as wide as these evident differences would lead us to suppose. Scougal is interested in clarifying the nature of true religion so that he can commend it, and this, we might think, makes his endeavor radically different to Hume's. Yet, though in this short essay Hume is far more concerned to uncover the invidious consequences of "superstition" and the only slightly less iniquitous nature of "enthusiasm," and says almost nothing positive about "true religion," in the *Enquiry Concerning Human Understanding* he declares that religion is a "species of philosophy." This remark appears in the same section in which he seems to contrast religious believers with religious philosophers, and reserves his criticism for the latter.

> The religious philosophers, not satisfied with the tradition of your forefathers, and doctrine of your priests (in which I willingly acquiesce) indulge a rash curiosity, in trying how they can establish religion upon the principles of reason; and they thereby excite, instead of satisfying, the doubts which arise from diligent and scrutinous enquiry.
>
> (EHU 11.10)

Scougal, at the outset of his little book, discounts those who place religion in "the understanding, in orthodox notions and opinions," thereby rejecting just the kind of intellectualism in religion that Hume is also discounting.

How does this passage about religious philosophers square with the description of religion as a "species of philosophy"? Hume's own view of religion, a subject by which he was fascinated throughout his life, will never be determined for sure; he was too cautious to be emphatic about this. We may suppose that the parenthetical remark in this passage about acquiescing in Christian doctrine is not to be taken seriously, but there are other places where a similar judgment would be much less certain. Commentators on the *Dialogues Concerning Natural Religion* who identify Hume with the skeptical Philo have often been puzzled by the *volte-face* that Philo seems to make at the start of the final section. But we might see this as another warning against the presumption of reason in matters religious. James Harris has made an impressive case for thinking that Hume's purpose in the *Dialogues* is not primarily one of advancing a (negative) conclusion about God (Harris 2015: 445–456). Rather, the *Dialogues* are a literary illustration, a demonstration perhaps, of how, in an ideal world, philosophical discussion would go. Differences of opinion, even of the deepest kind, would not be converted into point scoring, or lead to personal animus and division. In the *Dialogues*, we might say, we find civility dramatized. On this account, to be a "philosopher" is to engage in a certain style of thought and discussion, one that is marked by humility and open mindedness, and may therefore be contrasted with both unthinking "superstition" and dogmatic "enthusiasm."

Hume means to commend philosophy so conceived, and since he describes religion as a "species of philosophy" he can be seen to be far closer in thought to Scougal than first appearances suggest. The "true religion" Scougal means to commend is also to be contrasted with both the unreflective practicality of mere conformity to religion and the enthusiasm of the zealot. In his thought on these matters, Scougal seems to have drawn on the Cambridge Platonists, who strove, against the more ardent Puritans of their time, to create a space within Christian orthodoxy where untrammeled philosophical reflection and debate could take place. But Scougal had Scottish forebears also in this matter. Half a century before his time, the "Aberdeen Doctors," most notably John Forbes of Corse, had taken just such a position against the zealotry of the Covenanters, and while they lost the battle and were deposed from their posts at Aberdeen, they cannot be said to have lost the argument. Just a generation or so later, their successors, of whom Scougal was the most gifted, sought to occupy similar ground. It does not seem an abuse of language to describe this as claiming a rightful place for "philosophy."

There is no doubt that the Scottish philosophers and theologians of the later seventeenth and early eighteenth centuries were orthodox Calvinists, where Hume was not even a Christian. It is also true what they taught and studied was directed at knowledge of God, whereas his philosophical orientation was to human nature, history, and society. But even here, the difference is not as radical as it might seem. Scougal, like Calvin before him, believes that human nature as we encounter it in experience is oriented to the divine, and is interested in how the natural basis of religion is related to the light of revealed truth and free grace. Consequently, he thinks it essential to devote two short sections to "What the Natural Life Is" and "The Different Tendencies of the Natural Life." At the start of the *Natural History of Religion*, Hume identifies two distinct questions about religion as being of "the utmost importance," the first being its "foundation in reason" and the second "its origin in human nature." Hume thinks that religion is rooted in more basic emotions, chiefly hope and fear, while the Calvinists believed that religious sentiments are themselves basic to human nature. The difference is important, but it is nonetheless easy to see that both sides are parties to the same debate.

Anyone reading Scougal and Hume could not fail to be struck by the great differences of tone and content. These are undeniable, and we should be wary about overestimating the continuities between Hume and the Scottish thinkers of the seventeenth century. There are the similarities I have detected, and they are not inconsequential, but little, if any, direct link can be established. Scougal's book went through a great many editions and was widely read for a hundred years or more, but I know of no evidence that Hume read it, or even knew of it, still less that he was acquainted with the contest between the Covenanters and the Aberdeen doctors. At the same time, it is impossible to prove a negative. Ideas are often "in the air" and transmitted by means that may not lend themselves to documentation. The main point here, however, is to counter another assumption that is too easy to make – that Hume's writings constitute a radical break with an intellectual tradition to which they owed nothing.

After the Enlightenment

Let us turn now to the question of Hume's relationship to the post-Enlightenment Scottish intellectual tradition. As was observed earlier, the general presumption has been that he was importantly out of step with his philosophical contemporaries in Scotland. His relationship with Adam Smith, who found in him an inspiration, was cordial, while for others, notably James Beattie, Hume was a *bête noir*, a dangerous skeptic and infidel. Smith's alliance and Beattie's hostility were both atypical. The most influential responses came from those who admired his "genius" but were both deeply critical of the assumptions underlying his philosophical writings and resistant to their implications. Relatively early on, Francis Hutcheson expressed his reservations and declined to support Hume's candidature for the Chair of Moral Philosophy in Edinburgh. Twenty years later, George Campbell subjected Hume's arguments to close scrutiny in a *Dissertation on Miracles* (1762) that Hume himself described as "ingenious." In 1764, Thomas Reid published his *Inquiry in the Human upon the Principles of Common Sense*. Neither writer exhibited anything like the hysteria of Beattie's *Essay on the Nature an Immutability of Truth*, first published in 1770. Reid, in fact, openly acknowledged his intellectual debt to Hume. Nevertheless, together with his later two sets of *Essays*, Reid's *Inquiry* came to be widely regarded as having produced a definitive answer to Hume, and as a consequence to have set mental philosophy on a path that could leave the puzzles and problems of the *Treatise* behind.

Regardless of the merits of the arguments Hume's critics brought against him, in succeeding decades their intellectual triumph seemed complete. In the universities Reid's deployment of common sense was taken as standard, and in Edinburgh especially it found hugely influential champions, first in Dugald Stewart, who had studied under Reid for a year, and then in Sir William Hamilton, who produced the first complete edition of Reid's works in 1848. In America, Samuel Stanhope Smith, President of the College of New Jersey (subsequently Princeton University) established Reid's works as the main philosophical texts in liberal arts colleges, and in France, as noted earlier, Victor Cousin gave an influential series of public lectures on *Philosophie Ecossaise* in which Reid was the key figure. In all these places, the dominant themes identified with "the Scottish School" were those of Reid and Common Sense.

Meanwhile, Hume as a philosopher virtually disappeared. His *History of England* was reprinted multiple times, in innumerable abstracts and editions, but no fresh editions of his philosophical works appeared for most the nineteenth century. The *Treatise* was reprinted in London in 1811, but had to wait a further 70 years before Selby-Bigge's edition was published in 1888. The *Enquiries* disappeared for even longer. A second edition having been published in 1751, they were not reprinted until 1861, and a scholarly edition, again edited by Selby-Bigge, only came out in 1892. The *Dialogues* in their proper form were effectively out of print for 130 years. (See

Jessop 1938). Hume may be said to have been restored to the Scottish intellectual pantheon by his inclusion in the "Famous Scots" book series, but these did not start to appear until 1898. This was more than a century after his death. The celebrated Blackwood's Philosophical Classics series followed suit with a volume devoted to him in 1901, but this was 20 years after the volume devoted to William Hamilton had been published.

Today, Hume is by far the most famous of the Scottish philosophers and studied much more widely than Reid, while Hamilton and Dugald Stewart are virtually unknown. All the evidence suggests that this is a major reversal. Within a short time of his death, Hume ceased to stimulate much interest within the world of Scottish intellectual debate at home and abroad, except as Reid's chosen foil. Still less, it might seem, did he influence the direction those debates took. Once again, however, this is not as straightforward a matter as it appears. The hegemony of Reid and Common Sense was neither as comprehensive nor as secure as its proponents sometimes claimed. At the turn of the nineteenth century, Dugald Stewart, who held the Chair of Moral Philosophy in Edinburgh, was the doyen of Scottish intellectual life, highly regarded and well known across Europe, and a protagonist of the philosophy of Reid and Common Sense. In 1810, however, he was succeeded in the Chair by Thomas Brown, and somewhat to Stewart's consternation, Brown departed significantly from the orthodox camp.

It was Brown who observed, in a memorable remark, that the difference between Hume and Reid, though widely thought to be very great, could actually be interpreted in a way that made it very small.

> Reid bawled out that we must believe in an outward world; but added in a whisper, we can give no reason for our belief. Hume cries out we can give no reason for such a notion; and whispers, I own we cannot get rid of it.
>
> (quoted in Brown 2010: 19)

Brown's own lectures took up themes from Hume, and though he was not uncritical, he was sufficiently in sympathy with their general thrust, that James Mill could later describe him as a "direct successor of Hume" (ibid.: 16). Brown argued that Reid and his followers had radically misunderstood Hume on causality, and indeed, so critical was he of Reid, that his posthumously published lectures incurred the wrath of Sir William Hamilton. The second of three hugely influential papers that Hamilton published in the *Edinburgh Review* – "Philosophy of Perception" – was a ferocious attack on Brown's criticisms of Reid. Hamilton's defense of Reid was by no means slavish. He identified deficiencies in Reid that he took it upon himself to remedy. But when, some years later and relatively late in his career, he was appointed to the Chair of Logic and Metaphysics at Edinburgh, his enormous prestige made a version of Reidian common sense the philosophical orthodoxy once more – though not in every quarter.

In 1848, Hamilton's edition of *Reid's Collected Works* came out and was reviewed by, among others, Hamilton's protégé James Frederick Ferrier. Ferrier, who is plausibly regarded as the most brilliant Scottish philosopher of the nineteenth century, held the Chair of Moral Philosophy at St Andrews. In his review, Ferrier was highly complementary about Hamilton's editorial labors but scathingly critical of Reid, the philosophy of common sense, and by extension Dugald Stewart. In attacking Reid, however, Ferrier did not mean to endorse Hume. On the contrary, he rejected the associationist psychology that Brown thought to be a strength of Hume's account of mind. Ferrier himself aimed to turn the clock back to Berkeley, whose philosophical idealism, he claimed, Reid had blunderingly misunderstood. He also looked forward with enthusiasm to the lengthy "Supplementary Dissertations" which Hamilton appended to his edition of Reid as a place where real illumination was to be secured.

371

It is hard to say whether Ferrier was sincere in his assessment of Hamilton's potential contribution to the philosophical topics of mind and knowledge. However this may be, not long after Hamilton's death, criticism of his philosophical writings arose from three different quarters. These included some of Hamilton's own students who were sympathetic to the "Scottish School," proponents of the Hegelian Idealism that was arriving from the continent, and most famously, John Stuart Mill, whose *Examination of Sir William Hamilton's Philosophy* (1865) dealt a blow from which Hamilton's great reputation never recovered (see Graham 2014a). The point about Mill's *Examination*, however, is that it brought back into play one of Hume's most important ideas – the association of ideas.

Mill, of course, is a major contributor to philosophical debate in the nineteenth century, and Cairns Craig has set out a very strong case for regarding him as essentially educated in, and continuing to work with, the Scottish intellectual tradition. "Mill's method," Craig contends, "can be seen to derive from Reid, even though his means – the association of ideas – derive from Hume. Mill's achievements are thus built upon the foundations of eighteenth-century Scottish philosophy" (Craig 2015: 100). At the same time, *contra* Brown, the opposition between Reid and Hume was a real one, so that Mill's combination of Reid and Hume had an important tension within it. In a departure from Cartesian rationalism, both Reid and Hume applied Baconian empiricism to the problems of philosophy. This was key to the progress they expected to make. But unlike Reid, Hume, Brown, and Mill were, we might say, on their way to positivism, a trajectory, it can be argued, that was finally completed by Mill's friend and collaborator, Alexander Bain. Bain held the Chair of Logic at the (newly united) University of Aberdeen from 1860 to 1880, and quite intentionally took psychology in a strictly associationist (and materialist) direction. Through Bain, via Brown and the Mills, it may be said, Hume's continuing influence in the Scottish intellectual tradition showed itself in this more obviously positivistic version of the project of the "science of mind."

Hume's complete rehabilitation, by some accounts, was the work of another Scottish philosopher – Norman Kemp Smith. In a subsequently famous and highly influential two-part paper entitled "The Naturalism of Hume," Kemp Smith exorcized Hume's reputation as a skeptic by interpreting him as having advanced a wholly naturalized conception of reason. According to this interpretation, human reason is not opposed to feeling and instinct, as it is in Kant, but grounded in them. This is the fundamental insight of both Hume and "the science of human nature," and if we understand it properly, it does not result in the skeptical paradoxes to which Reid thought Hume's *Treatise* inevitably led.

Kemp Smith's interpretation has been widely accepted. The difficulty with it is that Hume's naturalism, on Kemp Smith's account, does not simply resolve a longstanding tension within the Scottish intellectual tradition; it puts an end to that tradition. Effectively, Bain transforms psychology from a branch of philosophy into a positive science. Arguably, though, this is only one example of a recurrent phenomenon – the emergence of a number of social sciences that asserted their autonomy as the years went by.[2] Thus, Adam Smith was both Professor of Moral Philosophy and a (possibly *the*) founding figure in positive economics,[3] while Adam Ferguson's *Essay on the History of Civil Society* (1767) had a significant role to play in the development of sociology. In certain important respects, philosophy as Reid pursued it continued the pre-Enlightenment tradition more fully and faithfully than Hume. As these more strictly Humean sciences of human nature emerged, the philosophers of Scotland did not return to Reid or Hamilton; they turned elsewhere.

Should we conclude from this that it was Hume, finally, who had the last word in the debate with Reid and the Reidians? The answer turns on the adequacy of Kemp Smith's interpretation, and here a doubt arises. Does the emergence of the social sciences represent the final vindication of naturalism, or its abandonment? In *Hume's Naturalism*, H O Mounce makes a strong case for thinking that Kemp Smith failed to see that eighteenth-century naturalism could not be combined with the robust empiricism that Hume's philosophy claimed to endorse.

> The naturalist has no problem about the existence of the independent world, since the existence of such a world provides the setting for his whole philosophy. The empiricist, having characterized the mind, has great difficulty in showing how it can know an independent world.... The naturalism to which Kemp Smith refers is really present in Hume's philosophy and constitutes its most profound aspects. But empiricism is also present and is incompatible with the naturalism.
>
> (Mounce 1999: 6–7)

According to Mounce, the metaphysical naturalism Hume shared with his contemporaries cannot be made consistent with the epistemological or scientific naturalism that we find a century later in Comte and Mill. The empirical method of "observation and experiment" to which Reid no less than Hume subscribed is not positivistic, but implicitly relies on a teleological conception of nature. It is just such a conception that underlies the Scottish intellectual tradition over many centuries, rooted in Christian theism. To study the way the mind works is to study the way it is *meant* to work. On Mounce's interpretation, Hume did not (even if he wanted to) break free of it. If this is true, then Hume's ultimate influence did not lead to the fulfillment of the project of the Scottish Enlightenment, but to its demise.

Notes

1 I owe this example to Christia Mercer, "Feeling the Way to Truth: The Real Story about How Early Modern Philosophy Developed," The Inaugural Margaret Dauler Wilson Occasional Lecture delivered at Princeton University, February 12, 2016.
2 The classic study of this subject is Gladys Bryson (1945).
3 For a discussion of how the one emerges from the other, see Gordon Graham (2014b).

References

Bryson, Gladys (1945) *Man and Society*, Princeton: Princeton University Press.
Craig, C. (2015) "Alexander Bain, Associationism, and Scottish Philosophy," in Gordon Graham (ed.), *Scottish Philosophy in the Nineteenth and Twentieth Centuries*, Oxford: Oxford University Press.
Davie, George. (1961) *The Democratic Intellect*, Edinburgh: Edinburgh University Press.
Dixon, T. (2010) "Introduction," in *Thomas Brown: Selected Philosophical Writings*, Exeter: Imprint Academic.
Ferrier, J. F. (1883) *Collected Works*, vol III, Edinburgh: William Blackwood and Sons.
Graham, G. (2014a) "Hamilton, Scottish Common Sense, and the Philosophy of the Conditioned," in W. J. Mander (ed.), *The Oxford Handbook of British Philosophy in the Nineteenth Century*, Oxford: Oxford University Press.
———. (2014b) "Adam Smith as a Scottish Philosopher," in David F. Hardwick and Leslie Marsh (eds.), *Propriety and Prosperity: New Studies on the Philosophy of Adam Smith*, New York, NY: Palgrave Macmillan.
Harris, J. (2015) *Hume: An Intellectual Biography*, Cambridge: Cambridge University Press.
Jessop, T. E. (1938) *A Bibliography of David Hume and of Scottish Philosophy from Francis Hutcheson to Lord Balfour*, Oxford: Oxford University Press.
Kant, I. (1783/1980) *Prolegomena to Any Future Metaphysics*, edited by L. W. Beck, Indianapolis, IN: Bobbs-Merrill.
McCosh, J. (1875) *The Scottish Philosophy*, London: Palgrave Macmillan.
Mounce, H. O. (1999) *Hume's Naturalism*, London: Routledge.

Scougal, H (1677/1948) *The Life of God in the Soul of Man*, edited by W S Hudson, Philadelphia: The Westminster Press.

Seth, A. (1882), *On the Scottish Philosophy*, Edinburgh: William Blackwood and Sons.

Smith, N. K. (1905) "The Naturalism of David Hume," *Mind* xiv: 54–55.

Stewart, M. A. (2005) "Hume's Intellectual Development 17–11–1752," in Marina Frasca-Spada and P. J. E. Kail (eds.), *Impressions of Hume*, Oxford: Clarendon Press.

29

HUME AND GERMAN PHILOSOPHY

Anik Waldow

Hume famously argues that the human mind is best understood as a bundle of perceptions:[1] mental episodes come and go as a result of associative processes that organize which kinds of mental contents attract one another. When Hume speaks of the mental world in this way, he conceives of the mind as organized by principles similar to those found in the "natural world" (T 1.1.4.6). Thus, for him, habitual associations constitute a "force" (EHU1.15) that is similar to Newtonian gravity and describable by the causal laws of motion (Schliesser 2007).

Through this analogical treatment of the forces of the mind and the forces of nature, Hume naturalizes the concept of thought: instead of invoking a special set of explanatory resources exclusively reserved for the explanation of specifically *mental* phenomena, the study of the mind is approached through the same causal framework that is also typically employed in the study of nature. (It is in this sense that I will use the concept of naturalization in what follows.) Importantly, once this methodology is in place, the mind no longer counts as constituting an extra realm of its own, but instead as being fully integrated into the causal network that organizes processes of change and development in nature.

Hume's philosophy, including his conception of the mind as a bundle of causally associated perceptions, had a significant impact on the German debate of the eighteenth century. "By 1755 Hume is referred to as a well-known author," Manfred Kühn notes, "who no longer needs any introduction" (Kühn 2005: 103). During this time, Hume's works also began to appear in German and French translations, and "the first *Enquiry* was, as soon as it came out in German, 'in everyone's hands'" (ibid.). The *Treatise* which contains Hume's discussion of personal identity, and the controversial claim that the mind is a bundle of perceptions, appeared anonymously, however. It is therefore not clear if the readers of the *Göttingische Anzeigen von gelehrten Sachen* that reviewed Hume's *Treatise* in 1740 indeed made the connection between the philosophical topics discussed in this work and Hume's name.[2] Despite these problems of tracing Hume's earliest influences on the German debate, what seems to be evident, however, is that by the 1770s Hume's theory of the mind as a bundle of causally interacting mental episodes was widely known. Much of this knowledge reached Germany via James Beattie, who gave generous citations from the *Treatise* to ridicule Hume's conception of the mind.[3]

To many philosophers in Germany, Hume's conception of the mind as a bundle of causally interacting mental episodes did not only seem to be false for its failure to explain the real unity of thought;[4] it also provoked a fierce dispute over the more general question of the status of the human being and its place in nature. A good example of this latter debate can be found in the controversy between Immanuel Kant, Johann Gottfried Herder, and Johannes Nikolaus Tetens.[5] While all of them conceived of themselves as Humeans in their rejection of occult powers, they reached very different conclusions about what it is that can justifiably be derived from experience.

Kant sharply distinguished between the empirical world, in which experience informs us about what is contingently the case, and the realm of the mental, in which *a priori* considerations about the possibility of thinking point us to a form of necessity that establishes that the mind cannot be comprehended through the same methodological framework as nature. By contrast, Herder wholeheartedly embraced Hume's experimental method and added a developmental twist to the idea that experience informs our thoughts about the world. Claiming that the cognitive structure through which the world becomes intelligible to us arises through our interactions with specific environmental patterns, he argued that the human capacity for rational thought evolves out of nature itself. Tetens agreed with many aspects of Herder's experience-grounded developmental psychology, but he thought that Herder did not go far enough. Thus, he argued that Herder's claim about the necessity of the emergence of language and reason had to be dropped, since, strictly speaking, it is a contingent fact whether or not humans actualize themselves as rational and free agents.

Through this debate, as I will argue below, two things became clear: first, with the German uptake of Hume's acknowledgment of experience as a crucial influence on the shaping of cognitive structures, pressing questions about the unique status of the human being as a rational creature emerged and called for decisive answers. More precisely, the thought was this: if it holds that humans were able to develop the capacity for thought and reason through their experiential engagement with contingent environments, it becomes conceivable that one day animals too will morph into creatures with human-like capacities. Second, because this was an altogether untenable conclusion for many German thinkers – even for those who defended a developmental model of human reason – the attempt to provide a naturalized theory of the human mind led to the incorporation of explanatory resources that clearly go against the anti-metaphysical spirit of Hume's experimentalism.

In Section One of this chapter, I discuss how the controversy between Kant and Herder about our ability to know causal powers spilled over into a debate on the origin of the human capacity to think. Section Two discusses Herder's methodological push for a comparative analysis of humans and animals. It will here become clear that there are important parallels between Hume's treatment of reason as an instinct and Herder's claim that reason develops as a way of compensating humans for their scant natures. Section Three looks at the question of whether or not the emergence of the human species was understood as a contingent or rather necessary development. For this purpose I will turn to the discussion of Tetens, a figure who crucially influenced Kant and Herder, but who also directly responded to Herder's theory of language formation. Here I will mostly focus on Tetens' response to Herder in order to highlight the connection between the attempt to understand human reason as something that develops gradually, rather than is simply given, and the pressing need for a defense of the conception of humans as indisputably unique creatures. So what will provide us with the focus of our discussion is Teten's concrete attempt to deal with some of the implications of Herder's theory of language acquisition, rather than just general questions of influence.

1 The experimental method and the forces of nature

Kant famously stated that it was Hume who awoke him from his dogmatic slumber (4:260, 57).[6] What is less well known is that, for Kant, thinking about the forces of nature, and our inability to know them, was tightly connected with his conception of nature as constituting a realm that is very different from the realm within which human thought takes place. That Kant drew these connections becomes clear if we turn to his controversy with Herder, a former student of his with whom he fell out after his 1785 review of Herder's *Ideas for a Philosophy of the History of Humanity* (1784).[7] In this work, Herder develops the thesis that processes in nature are driven by forces that not only make it possible for nature to create life, but also the human capacity for language and reason. Kant forcefully rejected Herder's theory:

> But now as pertains to that invisible realm of effective and self-sufficient forces, it is difficult to see why the author [Herder], after he has believed he is able safely to infer from the organic generations to its existence, did not prefer to make the thinking principle in the human being pass immediately to it, as a merely spiritual nature, without raising it up out of chaos through the structure of organization.
>
> (8: 53, 131–132)

The chaos to which Kant refers here is the realm of matter where entirely random constellations of causes determine what happens next. The specific problem that Kant discerns is that Herder takes "the thinking principle," so the capacity for the kind of thought we find in human beings, to develop just the way in which life is taken to have originally developed. Noting the lack of evidence for the truth of this claim, Kant asks:

> What is one to think in general about the hypothesis of invisible forces, effecting organization, hence about the endeavor to want to explain *what one does not comprehend* from *what one comprehends even less*. At least with respect to the former we can become acquainted with its laws through experience, although their causes will remain unknown; but with respect to the latter we are deprived of all experience.
>
> (8: 53–54, 132)

On the face of it, Kant here seems to be very Humean. He objects to the belief in principally unobservable forces, warning that "the rational use of experience also has its boundaries": it can teach us that "something is so-and-so," but it cannot reveal that something "*could* not at all *be otherwise*" (8:57, 134). In order to know that something could not be different, we need to be acquainted with the forces in question, but this, as Kant and Hume agree, is not possible.

To better understand what is at stake in Kant's conception of experience as being concerned with factual claims alone, it is useful to remember that for him – as for many other eighteenth-century thinkers – the concept of necessity stands for the logical derivability of consequences. What this exactly means can be illustrated through some short reflections on Kant's concept of systematicity. For Kant, systematicity is a feature of thoughts that have been generated through the application of *a priori* principles and, because of this, occur as part of a systematic whole (20:195–196, 3–4 and 20: 209, 13). An important feature of these thoughts is that their location within the relevant system is deducible, which in turn means that the connections that hold together the system in question are necessary (A832–833/B861–862, 691–692). The system itself thus qualifies as having unity, since its elements are necessary and cannot be exchanged.

The contrast case is provided by empirically generated collections of data: such collections, Kant notes, emerge "haphazardly" and "like maggots, by a *generatio aequivoca* from the mere confluence of aggregate concepts, garbled at first but complete in time" (A835/B863, 692). Kant here takes issue with the empirical methods practiced in eighteenth-century natural history and the experimental sciences. A major fault with these methods is, Kant argues, that their practitioners never know where they are heading, given that they lack the ability to predict *a priori* the connections between the individual elements in the resulting collection of data.[8] Since, for Kant, unity arises through the ability to deduce (or predict with necessity) the location of the relevant elements within a system, collections of data count as aggregates that lack unity and necessity (A832/B860, 691).

We can thus see that, for Kant, necessity and unity come with the mind's capacity to draw *a priori* inferences. In this sense, necessity does not reside in nature; rather, it resides in the mind's activity that leads us to see what is necessarily the case. For this reason, stipulating that there are forces in nature that make it necessary for certain developments to take place means imbuing nature with something that is in fact a feature of our practice of drawing logical inferences. It also means ontologizing logical necessity: what is stipulated is the existence of a force, the knowledge of which would make it possible for us to deduce *a priori* the consequences of this force. Since Kant thinks that we cannot know that such forces exist, he rejects Herder's metaphysics of forces as purely speculative.

Although Kant's critique of Herder clearly resonates with Hume's skepticism concerning our knowledge of causal powers, both thinkers could not be further apart when it comes to their conception of the mind. As mentioned above, for Hume, the mind is a bundle, or, to invoke a Kantian term, an "aggregate" of different perceptions that lack real "unity." After all, what organizes the mind's individual perceptions are processes of association, so rather loose ties that contingently bring together mental episodes of certain types. It is at exactly this point that Kant parts company with Hume. For Kant, the mind has real unity, and since this is so, a Humean form of causation that amounts to no more than conjunctions of loosely associated perceptions cannot be the principle that organizes our thinking.

Without being able to give an exhaustive account of Kant's concept of mind, I want at least to briefly flag how the claim that the mind has real unity is developed. As Patricia Kitcher has noted, Kant almost repeats the passages from Hume in which he denies that an introspective investigation of the mind can reveal anything other than the fact that the mind's representations are in a perpetual flux. Kant writes:

> The consciousness of the self, according to the determinations of our state in inner perception, is merely empirical and always changing. There can be no permanent and continuing self in this flux of inner appearances. . . . *What has necessarily to be represented as numerically identical cannot be thought as such through empirical data.* To render such a transcendental presupposition valid, there must be a condition which precedes all experience, and which makes experience itself possible.
>
> (A107, emphasis mine)

Kant here makes the point that empirical investigation fails to deliver insights into that which is *necessarily* the case. For this reason, the empirical investigation of the mind that only introspectively observes what happens in our thoughts is doomed from the start. All it can show is that things within the mind are thus and so, but not that they could not be otherwise; however, exactly this would need to be shown if the mind should turn out to be unified, in the sense of being necessarily connected. So, from Kant's point of view, Hume's failure to "explain the principles, that unite our successive perceptions in our thought or consciousness" (T App. 20; SBN 636) – as Hume puts it in the Appendix to the *Treatise* – is primarily methodological, as it relies on empirical observation.

Of course, Kant himself turns his back on the empirical method and tries to meet the challenge of explaining what it is that unites the mind by offering a transcendental argument: one that does not engage with what is the case, but seeks to determine the "condition which precedes all experience" and "makes experience possible." More concretely, he argues that the possibility of having cognitive states requires that these states stand under what he calls "the original synthetic unity of apperception" (B135). Apperception here refers to being conscious of oneself as having cognitive states, while synthesis stands for the "act of adding different cognitive states [or their contents] to each other and of comprehending their diverse elements in a single representation" (A77/B103, quoted in Kitcher 1990). Differently put, one can say that the "I" here emerges *through* the act of synthesis and for this reason cannot be seen as distinct from what is represented in the mind. Kitcher writes:

> The 'unity of apperception' refers to the fact that cognitive states are *connected* to each other through syntheses *required* for cognition. 'Apperception' does not indicate any awareness of a separate thing, a 'self', or even that different cognitive states belong to a separate thing, a 'self'. Rather, they belong to the unity of apperception in being connected by syntheses to each other.
>
> (Kitcher 1990 105)[9]

With this in mind, we can see that more is at stake in Kant's critique of Herder's *Ideas* than a defense of Hume's skeptical approach towards causal powers.

From Kant's perspective, Herder's metaphysics of forces blurs the border between the realm of contingent existences, the knowledge of which can be approached through the empirical method, and the realm of *a priori* necessity that underlies the possibility of drawing *a priori* inferences. To Kant's mind, Herder ignores this distinction, for his metaphysics of forces attributes to nature the kind of necessity that Kant only accepts when dealing with the logical structure of *a priori* arguments, and the structure of thought more generally. Approached from this angle, the discussion of whether or not there are forces in nature leads over to the attempt to distinguish the methodological repertoire used in the study of nature from that used when dealing with the principles that underlie our thinking. By employing this methodological distinction, Kant thus undoes what Hume sought to establish: a conception of the human mind as something that is organized by the same causal principles that also structure the realm of nature.

In the next section, we will see that Herder's engagement with Hume takes him in the opposite direction. While Kant sharply differentiates between the principally experientiable realm of nature and the realm of logical necessity that underpins his reflections on the unity of the human mind, Herder aligns himself with Hume by approaching an understanding of the human mind through the experimental method. He also follows Hume when conceiving of the capacity for reason as something that is functionally similar to animal instinct, in that both enable successful adaptation to the demands of specific environmental milieus. By choosing this approach, Herder demonstrates that, for him, understanding the human place in nature is indispensable for his conception of what the human mind is.

2 From animal cognition to human reason

For Herder, like Hume, it is our way of being in the world that crucially impacts, not only on the way in which we form our habits, but also on the formation of those cognitive structures that enable us to render the world intelligible to us. Thus, the Humean mind can infer that fire produces smoke only because it is acquainted with many instances in which it could be perceived that this was the case. "Custom," based on the habitual perception of two events accompanying one another, thus acts as a force that determines "the imagination to make a transition from the idea of one object to that of its usual attendant" (T 1.3.14.31; SBN 170). Within Herder's theory, we find a similarly tight connection between experience and the emergence of our structures of thought that enable us to comprehend the world. However, on Herder's account it is not simply custom, but custom in combination with our capacity to acquire language that establishes this connection. Herder, as we will see in this section, develops this account by comparing animals with humans, thus following Hume, who uses reflections on the cognition of animals in order to explain human thought (T 1.3.16.1–9; SBN 176–179).

Herder's engagement with Hume through the concept of habit and custom resonates with much of Johann Georges Hamann's Humean account of human nature as essentially driven by sentiment. Yet this should not lead us into thinking that Herder stands for what Isaiah Berlin has termed the "Counter-Enlightenment," which resorts to sentiment where Enlightenment proponents invoke reason as the defining feature of human nature. Drawing on this distinction, Stuart Hampshire, for instance, writes:

> Berlin has argued with great force that Enlightenment thinkers that looked forward to men and women becoming citizens of an undivided world were deceived. Herder, Hamann and Hume were, in their different ways, right to represent persons as governed in their thoughts and sentiments by the habits and the customs in which they were nurtured, and not by rational principles demanding universal agreement.
>
> (Hampshire 1991: 128)

Herder, as we will see below, defends a conception of reason that is *grounded* in sentiment and sensation. He thus seeks to bring *together* what Berlin's distinction between the Enlightenment's emphasis on reason and the Counter-Enlightenment's commitment to sentiment tears apart. Moreover, Herder is firmly committed to the belief that the progress of the human species can and ought to be achieved through an experience-grounded form of learning. Given that this belief lies at the heart of the enlightenment project, and was shared by many of the authors that Berlin identifies as figures of the official enlightenment canon, his distinction turns out to be too coarse to capture the nuanced views that stand for Herder's (and Hamann's) Humeanism.

In the essay *Treatise on the Origin of Language* (1772), Herder argues that, compared with all other animals, it appears that humans possess relatively few instincts and are deprived of senses fitted to the environmental conditions that constitute their sphere of life (FHA 1, 770; F 128). Lacking in instincts, they find themselves in a precarious situation, as nature does not, as in the case of other animals, direct them to perform actions conducive to their survival. Yet Herder also conceives of humans as able to compensate themselves for this lack that fundamentally characterizes their situation. The idea here is that instincts tie an animal's attention to the outward world, while humans who lack instincts are aware of what is going on within their minds. Endowed with this form of reflective awareness (*Besonnenheit*), humans can stand back from their experiences and single out marks to name what, in the animal case, must be taken to be perceived as intermingling sensations, images, and sounds (FHA 1, 722; F 87). Through this process of "taking-awareness," human language emerges, not as a contingent development that depends on the coming together of various accidents and circumstances, but as a necessary consequence of the way the human animal is constituted: as lacking in instincts and endowed with awareness (DeSouza 2012: 227). I will return to this aspect of Herder's theory of language acquisition in the next section, when discussing whether the emergence of the human species must be regarded as a necessary or contingent development in nature. Before this, however, we need to become clearer on the connection between experience and the formation of language and reason.

For Herder, the act of taking-awareness expresses itself in a process of naming. He gives the following example: "White, soft, woolly – his soul operating with awareness, seeks a characteristic mark – the sheep bleats!" (FHA 1, 723; F 88). The sounds of the world here turn into signs that stand for all those mental episodes typically experienced when we are presented with sheep. Being in a place with specific features of that place (in our example, these features are sheep) thus directly impacts on the human capacity to form language, not only in the sense that it provides us with the contents of our concepts, but also with the sounds that become our first words. Once linguistic signs have been instituted in this way,[10] Herder claims, reason is able to evolve. This is because, for him, reason arises through the mind's ability to structure its thought linguistically (FHA 1, 770; F 128),[11] which in turn brings with it the ability to organize commingling sensations into a linear "succession of ideas" (FHA 1, 773; F 130).

It is important to note at this point that Herder presents us with an account that systematically undermines the conception of reason as an innate universal capacity. After all, language and reason are taken to emerge when we respond to the features of a given environmental pattern, while it is clear that places and times change, so that the environmental patterns that inform the development of language and reason also change. To stress this situatedness of human reason, Herder speaks of this capacity as a culturally and historically situated "manner of thought" (FHA 1, 149; F 247) that is responsive to the natural environmental features as much as to the customs of the people that surround us once language has evolved.

With the emergence of linguistically structured human thought, Herder argues, humans acquire the capacity to self-organize their thinking and acting. Thus, he claims that the fox fails to escape the cunning of its hunter, since the hunter can devise novel action strategies in line with his understanding of the situation, while the fox's thoughts and actions remain conditioned by its previous experiences (FHA 1, 772; F 130). A similar point is made in relation to the ape, who, deprived of many of its instincts, is taken to be closest to the human being, but still seen as different in kind, since all it can do is "process a thousand combinations of ideas of sense" (FHA 6, 117) without being able to go beyond the mere imitation of the previously experienced. To illustrate this point, Frederick Beiser helpfully notes that, for Herder, reason

> is an active self-realizing energy, and one that adapts to all kinds of circumstances. What we should mean by reason is not a kind of thing but *a way of acting*, and indeed a *second-order* way of acting that organizes, directs and unifies all of our particular activities.
>
> (Beiser 2011: 124)

We can here see that Herder agrees with Hume that animals can draw simple inferences based on previous experiences, but he stresses more than Hume that what separates humans from animals is the human capacity to think in language, which in turn enables humans to organize their thoughts in a self-determined way. Despite this difference, however, Herder remained faithful to the Humean spirit in a more general sense. As we have seen, Herder starts his analysis with a comparison between animals and humans, and the claim that humans lack instincts, so that it becomes necessary for them to develop language and reason. Reason is here thought of as *compensating* humans for their lack of instincts, which means that human reason can be regarded as a *quasi* instinct that fills the void left by human nature. Moreover, for Herder reason is a cognitive capacity that grows out of the human engagement with specific environmental conditions. As such, language and reason develop as ways of adapting the human being to the particular situation within which it finds itself, similar to the way in which specialized instincts and sense organs adapt the animal to the demands of its environmental niche. Herder's approach to reason thus clearly resonates with Hume's claim that "reason is nothing but a wonderful and unintelligible instinct in our souls, which carries us along a certain train of ideas, and endows them with particular qualities, according to their particular situations and relations" (T 1.3.16.9; SBN 179).

More generally, we can conclude that Herder is as committed to the empirical method as Hume: *qua* animal existence, he locates the human being in the natural world and derives his account of how reason emerges from an examination of the manner in which humans experiences shape their cognitive structures. Herder's methodology thereby clearly distances himself from the Kantian conviction that, in order to explain human thinking, empirical methods are useless. As we have seen in the previous section, this conviction led Kant to develop a transcendental, *a priori* argument that conceives of the mind as something that is unlike anything else in nature, given that it must be conceived of as necessarily unified. In the next section, I will show that with the attempt to see the human being as equally dependent on environmental conditions as animals, questions about our unique status of the human species had to be answered. Herder's claim that for the human being it was necessary to acquire language and reason is a response to this question, and provoked Tetens to radicalize Herder's claims about the developmental character of human reason.

3 The status of the human being: contingent or necessary?

As we have seen, in his review of Herder's *Ideas*, Kant straightforwardly rejected Herder's claim that nature, which, according to Kant, cannot be known to act with necessity, should be responsible for the emergence of the principle of human thought; for him, it was more plausible to think of this principle as an original endowment.[12] Why it was important for Herder to claim that the emergence of language and reason was natural and, at the same time, necessary, becomes clearer if we turn to the positions he targeted.

On one side of the debate, there were Rousseau and Condillac, who argued that human language developed out of the language of animal cries, which can be interpreted as suggesting that it is in principle conceivable that animals can acquire human-like reason if they meet with the right kind of circumstances. On the other side, we find Süssmilch, who claimed that human language was divinely ordained, and who thus cemented the border between animal and human cognition by invoking supernatural explanatory resources. Herder distanced himself from both positions: by arguing that it was not due to contingent developments that humans acquired language and reason, he blocked the worry that, one day, animals could morph into humans as a consequence of changing circumstances; yet, by treating nature as the ground that contains everything needed to enable the emergence of the human species, he stressed his commitment to naturalistic explanatory strategies.

What crucially underlies Herder's claim about the necessity of the emergence of language and reason is his conception of precisely those forces that every good Humean would find difficult to accept: active principles in nature responsible for large-scale evolutionary processes, such as the formation of geographical and climatic conditions and the emergence of life (FHA 6, 21–32; cf. Sloan 2002: 243). The emergence of the human species is here seen as a relatively late development, one that became possible when the forces, which had given rise to and sustained animal life, reorganized themselves, so that humans could assume an upright posture and become aware of what is happening within their own minds (FHA 6, 127).

Even though Herder acknowledges that we cannot perceive the forces of nature, he thinks that we need to stipulate them in order to explain what is perceptible: namely, that there are uniform processes of development in nature that underlie the emergence and decay of individuals and entire species.[13] Importantly, the forces at stake are conceived as *necessitating* developments in the sense that it is impossible that these developments could not take place. This conception of forces reflects the common seventeenth- and eighteenth-century idea that if we knew the essential forces of nature, we could predict *a priori*, and without engaging in empirical investigations, what happens next.[14] Now, since Herder stipulated that such forces exist, he was left with the view that nature can in fact act with necessity, for instance when organizing itself in such a way that the first humans were caused to stand up and become aware of their mental contents. Herder's claim that human language and reason emerged with necessity at precisely the point at which humans found themselves endowed with awareness thus entails the claim that, due to the way the forces of nature acted, it was not possible for humans not to possess these capacities.

Tetens was sympathetic to Herder's developmental account, but strongly objected to his claim that language and reason develop with necessity. To his mind, humans are no more than predisposed to develop language, as he writes in his response to Herder's *Treatise on the Origin of Language* in the eleventh essay of his main work, *Philosophische Versuche* (1777). By dropping claims about necessity, Tetens in principle moved away from the idea that language and reason are what *essentially* defines humans as members of the human species.[15] After all, as much as environmental circumstances can be conducive to the formation of language and reason, they can also prevent their emergence, a claim that Tetens supports by invoking the case of feral children. Stressing the fundamental openness of human development, he writes:

> Could every imbecile have become a clever person, every brute a sensitive soul, every villain a righteous man under different circumstances? I answer that there could not be any doubt about this if all external circumstances had unified their influence under this opposite form.
>
> (Tetens 1777, II: 593)

Tetens' works were studied by Kant and Herder and, as many believe, provided Kant with inspiration for the critical turn (Kühn 1989). Tetens knew Hume's *Enquiry* and *Treatise* well and his discussion brought into contact central principles of Leibniz's and Wolff's metaphysics with the methodological framework of British experimentalism (Stiening 2007/2008). Like Kant, Tetens struggled with Humean skepticism, but nevertheless defended the belief that the empirical study of the human being is essential for the endeavor of providing the sciences with an appropriate foundation.[16] Unsatisfied with the prospect of conceiving of causation as a mere projection of the mind where the link between cause and effect counts as invented, he sought to provide an argument that grounds the existence of causal laws in reflections on the forms of thinking (*Denkform*), rather than in the analysis of the contents of our thoughts.[17] This argument, as many commentators have noted, ultimately failed, as it assumed that which had to be shown: namely, that objective necessity follows from subjective necessity (*Denknotwendigkeit*).[18] Despite this, it is clear, however, that the fact that Tetens attempted to solve Hume's challenge in this particular way suggests that, to him, Herder's uncritical embrace of a conception of nature as acting with necessity must have looked as suspicious as it did to Kant.

With this in mind, we can see that Tetens' position sits some way in the middle between Kant's and Herder's engagement with Hume. On the one hand, Tetens remains as critical towards the belief in unobservable forces as Kant and, like him, also looks to the mind and its structure of thought in order to salvage a notion of necessity. On the other hand, Tetens remains committed to the empirical method in the analysis of the human being when arguing that comprehending the emergence of human reason requires an understanding of the empirical circumstances within which this capacity has formed.

It is important to note that although the analysis of the circumstances of human life play a crucial role in Tetens' explanation of human cognition, he does not approach the human being through a deterministic explanatory model. For him, being human and having reason means being self-determined in one's actions, so that it becomes possible to actively create environmental conditions that positively impact on the flourishing of individuals and societies, which for Tetens includes a strengthening of the human physiological constitution (Sommer 2014: 294–296). In all of this, Tetens firmly holds in view the connection between mental and bodily realm. Thus, it is the "whole man," including physiological constitutions and biological dispositions, that must be addressed as a vehicle of human self-actualization. As John Zammito has pointed out, Tetens here comes very close to Herder's own attempt to work out a physiological psychology, in which bodily sensations, affect, desire, and imagination are not seen as inferior animal capacities, as for instance Remarius held together with many other proponents of traditional Wolffian faculty psychology (Remarius 1760: 396), but as integral parts of regular processes of cognition. Herder writes:

> All these forces [of imagination, wit, memory, and cleverness] are at bottom only a single force if they should be human, good, and useful – and this is *understanding, intuition* with inner *consciousness*. Let one remove this from them, and the imagination is illusion, the wit childish, the memory empty, the cleverness a cobweb.
>
> (FHA 4, 357; F 210–211)

We here find a conception of the human mind that understands excellence of thought in terms of a smooth interplay between different affective and cognitive capacities. So, similar to Hume, who acknowledges the intermingling character of affect and thought and even demands that reason be lively when we assent to it (T 1.4.7.11; SBN 270), Herder also thinks of reason as a capacity that ought to be carried out in such a way that it integrates affect.

Tetens agreed with all of this. Where he went further than Herder was in his claim about the contingency of the development of human language. This claim drew even more attention to the importance of the specific quality of our experiences as affective, embodied creatures when interacting with the world. After all, for Herder *any* kind of circumstances are sufficient for the actualization of language and reason, given that it is necessary for humans to develop them. Not so for Tetens, whose decision to drop claims about necessity meant that it truly matters *what* it is that we sense and feel when being affected by the circumstances within which we find ourselves. To establish conditions conducive to the actualization of human language and reason thus becomes paramount.

Although Herder agreed with Tetens' methodological program as much as with his developmental account of embodied cognition, Tetens was of course right to claim that, in principle, Herder's developmental thesis can stand without the claim about the necessity of the emergence of language. For what is sufficient for the purpose of guarding the species border between animals and humans – a concern that was important to Herder – is the claim that humans possess the disposition to develop language and reason, while animals do not. A strict Humean would of course leave open what it is that establishes this difference at the metaphysical level; and this would mean acknowledging that, ultimately, we do not know if animals *necessarily* lack the disposition for human language and reason and cannot, at some point, develop these capacities. Tetens rejected this possibility as much as Herder did. Yet while Tetens remained rather traditional in thinking that it is the human soul that accounts for the unique status of humans as beings who have the disposition to develop language and reason (Tetens 1777, I: 738–740),[19] Herder ventured into new territory. He offered an explanation that presented the human capacity for rational thought as emerging out of the forces of nature, thereby pushing further Hume's attempt to see the mind as something that is organized by the same principles as nature.

Conclusion

The aim of this chapter was to reveal that the eighteenth-century German engagement with Hume's causal skepticism interlinked with a debate about the human place in nature, and the question of how it was possible that humans acquired the rational capacities that distinguish them from other animals. Accepting Hume's belief that we fail to penetrate into the powers of nature, Kant believed that it is impossible to derive a conception of the features that render us human from the empirical study of nature. Moreover, he thought of empirical observations as principally unsuitable for providing us with insights into the workings of the human mind. Invoking transcendental *a priori* arguments instead, Kant introduced a fundamental divide between the realm of nature and the realm of thought. He thereby undid Hume's effort to see the mind as something that is organized by the same causal principles that also underlie the unfolding of processes in nature.

By contrast, Herder, whom Kant attacked for his unruly metaphysical speculations about very un-Humean forces, remained faithful to Hume's belief that "a cautious observation of human life" (T Intro. 10; SBN xix) is what is required if we want to understand the human being. Together with Tetens, he argued that it is through the study of the concrete empirical circumstances of human existence, and of the languages that are developed within these circumstances, that we can explain human thought. Of course, this account comes with a wrinkle: Herder's metaphysics of forces makes unjustified assumptions about hidden forces. However, in principle this metaphysical grounding is not needed, as Tetens' account shows: it dispenses with Herder's metaphysics of forces and yet advocates the study of empirical circumstances as a means of comprehending human cognition.

With this emphasis on the factual conditions of human existence and the way in which our experience nourishes our self-conception as humans, we find much of what will later figure in Schopenhauer's and Nietzsche's critique of a universally unfolding history that leaves no room for contingencies (Schnädelbach 1984; Kail 2016). Hume's influence on German philosophy should therefore not be seen as ending with Kant's professed "solution" of Hume's skepticism, but as extending far beyond it into the attempt to see human nature as fundamentally shaped by the sphere of human life.

Notes

1 What is at stake here is the idea of our mind, rather than claims about the nature of the mind; see Alanen (2014) for a discussion of this distinction.

2 See Mossner (1947: 43) for the claim that Hume's name was not unavailable during this time and that it is therefore not implausible to assume that he had an influence on the philosophical debate in Germany even before the 1750s.

3 See Kitcher (1990: 98) and Kühn (1987: 92–93, 92–93n). According to Kitcher, Kant and Tetens both read James Beattie, so that we can conclude that, when Kant wrote the *Critique*, he knew about Hume's theory of personal identity. Kitcher raises this point against Norman Kemp Smith (1962), who overlooked this connection and thereby concealed the target of "the Deduction's many references to the necessary unity of mental life" (Kitcher 1990: 98). Also see Wolff 1960 for an analysis of Kemp Smith's misrepresentation of Hume's influence on Kant.

4 See Kitcher (1990: 98).

5 See Zammito (2002) for an excellent study of the influences of British experimentalism on Herder and Kant. Also see Beiser (1987) on the German eighteenth-century debate on the status of reason. Garber

and Longuenesse's collection of essays (2008) examines Kant's thinking in relation to British and German early modern authors. Including the French eighteenth-century context, Jones (2005) offers a more general overview of Hume's influences on continental Europe.

6 The English translation of all passages from Kant is taken from *The Cambridge Edition of the Works of Immanuel Kant*, indicated by page numbers after the reference to the Akademieausgabe (volume and page number).

7 All passages quoted from Herder are taken from the edition *Werke in Zehn Bänden*, edited by Martin Bollacher, Frankfurt am Main: Deutscher Klassiker Verlag, and will be abbreviated FHA, volume number, page number. F will be used to indicate the use of the standard translation by Michel Forster.

8 In this respect, practitioners of the empirical method are like travelers who do not have a guiding principle and for this reason grope around; see Kant's 1788 essay "On the Use of Teleological Principles in Philosophy" (8: 161, 197)

9 See Allison for the related claim that "we can do the 'I' and be conscious of this doing, but cannot infer anything more than this" (Allison 1983: 290).

10 See Lifschitz (2012, 2f) for the claim that these signs are artificially instituted, even though the sounds used to refer to the sheep are part and parcel of one's natural environment.

11 For a particularly clear statement along these lines, see FHA 6, 375.

12 See Sloan (2002); Zammito (2003); and Waldow (2016) for a discussion of Kant's conception of reason as a pre-formed germ.

13 Herder himself states that life forces are principally invisible and can only ever be detected through their effects (see FHA 6, 100–101, 160–161, 165, 349).

14 See for instance De Pierris 2015 on Locke's conception of an *a priori* science and Kail (2011) for a comparison between Locke and Hume.

15 Müller-Brettel and Dixon (1990) stress the importance of Tetens for the history of developmental psychology.

16 See Thiel (2014: 89–90) and Schneidereit (2014: 181–183).

17 This argument is worked out in Schneidereit (2014).

18 See Tetens (2014) for this objection.

19 Thiel points out that Tetens tried to stay neutral with respect to the metaphysical question of whether the soul is material or immaterial, but he nevertheless thought of the soul as expressing its forces in our thinking and feeling; see Thiel (2014: 98).

References

Alanen, L. (2014) "Personal Identity, Passions, and 'The True Idea of the Human Mind,'" *Hume Studies* 40(1): 3–28.

Allison, H. (1983) *Kant's Transcendental Idealism*, New Haven: Yale University Press.

Beiser, F. (1987) *The Fate of Reason*, Cambridge, MA: Harvard University Press.

———. (2011) *The German Historicist Tradition*, Oxford: Oxford University Press.

De Pierris, G. (2015) *Ideas, Evidence, & Method*, Oxford: Oxford University Press.

DeSouza, N. (2012) "Language, Reason and Sociability: Herder's Critique of Rousseau," *Intellectual History Review* 22(2): 221–240.

Forster, M. (2002) *Herder: Philosophical Writings*, Cambridge: Cambridge University Press.

Garber, D. and B. Longuenesse (2008) *Kant and the Early Moderns*, Princeton: Princeton University Press.

Hampshire, S. (1991) "Nationalism," in E. Ulman-Margalit and A. Margalit (eds.), *Isaiah Berlin: A Celebration*, Chicago, IL: University of Chicago Press, pp. 127–135.

Herder, J. G. (1985) *Werke in Zehn Bänden*, edited by M. Bollacher, Frankfurt am Main: Deutscher Klassiker Verlag.

Jones, P. (2005) *The Reception of Hume in Europe*, London: Continuum.

Kant, I. (1995) *The Cambridge Edition of the Works of Immanuel Kant*, edited by P. Guyer and A. Wood, Cambridge: Cambridge University Press.

Kail, P. (2011) "Is Hume a Realist or an Anti-Realist?" in E. S. Radcliffe (ed.), *A Companion to Hume*, Oxford: Wiley-Blackwell.

———. (2016) "Hume and Nietzsche," in P. Russell (ed.), *The Oxford Handbook of Hume*, Oxford: Oxford University Press.

Kemp Smith, N. (1962), *A Commentary to Kant's 'Critique of Pure Reason'*, New York: Humanities Press.

Kitcher, P. (1990) *Kant's Transcendental Psychology*, Oxford: Oxford University Press.

Kühn, M. (1987) *Scottish Common Sense in Germany, 1768–1800: A Contribution to the History of Critical Philosophy*, Montreal: McGill-Queens University Press.

———. (1989) "Hume and Tetens," *Hume Studies* 15(2): 365–376.

———. (2005) "The Reception of Hume in Germany," in P. Jones (ed.), *The Reception of David Hume in Europe*, London: Continuum.

Lifschitz, A. (2012) *Language and Enlightenment: The Berlin Debates of the Eighteenth-Century*, Oxford: Oxford University Press.

Mossner, E. (1947) "The Continental Reception of Hume's Treatise, 1739–1741," *Mind* 56(221): 31–43.

Müller-Brettel, M. and R. Dixon (1990) "Johann Nicolaus Tetens: A Forgotten Father of Developmental Psychology," *International Journal of Behavioral Development* 13: 215–230.

Reimarus, Hermann Samuel. 1760. *Allgemeine Betrachtungen Über Die Triebe Der Thiere, Hauptsächlich Über Ihre Kunst-Triebe : Zum Erkenntniss Des Zusammenhanges Der Welt, Des Schöpfers Und Unser Selbst*. Hamburg: Bey Johann Carl Bohn.

Schneidereit, N. (2014) "Einheit der Vernunft und subjektive Notwendigkeit: Tetens Version einer Common Sense Philosophie," in G. Stiening and U. Thiel (eds.), *Johann Nikolaus Tetens (1736–1807)*, Berlin: De Gruyter.

Schliesser E. (2007) "Hume's Newtonianism and Anti-Newtonianism," in Edward N. Zalta (ed.), *The Stanford Encyclopedia of Philosophy* (Winter 2008 Edition), URL = <http://plato.stanford.edu/archives/win2008/entries/hume-newton/>.

Schnädelbach, H. (1984), *Philosophy in Germany: 1831–1933*, Cambridge: Cambridge University Press.

Sloan, P. (2002) "Performing the Categories: Eighteenth-Century Generation Theory and the Biological Roots of Kant's A Priori," *Journal of the History of Philosophy* 40(2): 229–253.

Sommers, A. (2014) "Geschichtsphilosophie und 'Perfektibilität' der Menschheit bei Johann Nikolaus Tetens," in G. Stiening and U. Thiel (eds.), *Johann Nikolaus Tetens (1736–1807)*, Berlin: De Gruyter.

Stiening, G. (2007/2008) "Physische Anthropologie als Antiskeptizismus bei Platner, Tetens und Wezel," *Wezel-Jahrbuch* 10/11: 115–146.

Tetens, H. (2014) "Johann Nikolaus Tetens und die Humesche Herausforderung," in G. Stiening and U. Thiel (eds.), *Johann Nikolaus Tetens (1736–1807)*, Berlin: De Gruyter.

Tetens, J. N. (1777) *Philosophische Versuche über die menschliche Natur und ihre Entwicklung*, 2 vols, Leipzig: Weidman.

Thiel, U. (2014) "Zwischen empirischer Psychologie und rationaler Seelenlehre: Tetens über das Selbstgefühl," in G. Stiening and U. Thiel (eds.), *Johann Nikolaus Tetens (1736–1807)*, Berlin: De Gruyter.

Waldow, A. (2016) "Natural History and the Formation of the Human Being: Kant on Active Forces," *Studies in the History and Philosophy of Science* 58: 67–76.

Wolff, R. P. (1960) "Kant's Debt to Hume via Beattie," *Journal of the History of Ideas* 21: 117–123.

Zammito, J. (2002) *Kant, Herder, and the Birth of Anthropology*, Chicago, IL: University of Chicago Press.

———. (2003) "'This Inscrutable Principle of an Original Organization': Epigenesis and 'Looseness of Fit' in Kant's Philosophy of Science," *Studies in History and Philosophy of Science* 34: 73–109.

30

HUME, THE PHILOSOPHY OF SCIENCE, AND THE SCIENTIFIC TRADITION

Matias Slavov

In his own time, Hume was known primarily as a historian and essayist. He was not known as a natural philosopher or, to use our terminology, a natural scientist.[1] Hume is usually not placed in the canonical listings of the history of early modern science, which include figures like Isaac Newton (1646–1727), Robert Boyle (1627–1691), Christiaan Huygens (1629–1695), and Carl von Linné (1707–1778).

Hume's contributions to "philosophy and general learning" revolve around his science of man and the study of the human mind. Even though he probably wanted to emulate the explanatory success of Newton's natural philosophy in his moral philosophy, the main concern of his philosophical work is in mapping the cognitive structures of the mind (Ott 2009: 191; Harris 2015: 85). Hume's objective is not to explain the "natural and physical causes" of our perceptions, as this task is for "the sciences of anatomy and natural philosophy" (T 2.1.1.2; SBN 275–276). Hume's ambition is to develop a human science which is different from natural science.

Although the main focus of Hume's career was in the humanities, his work also has an observable role in the historical development of natural sciences after his time. To show this, I shall center on the relation between Hume and two major figures in the history of the natural sciences: Charles Darwin (1809–1882) and Albert Einstein (1879–1955). Both of these scientists read Hume. They also found parts of Hume's work useful to their sciences. Inquiring into the relations between Hume and the two scientists shows that his philosophical positions had a partial but constructive role in the formation of modern biology and physics. This is accordingly a clear indication of Hume's impact on the scientific tradition.

Before proceeding to analyze Hume's contribution to the history of science, it is important to address his broader role in the history of philosophy of science. Hume's discussions concerning the topics of causation, induction, the distinction between mathematical and empirical propositions, and laws of nature have been important for the philosophy of science of the nineteenth and twentieth centuries.

Hume in the history of philosophy of science

Among scholars who contributed to the philosophy of science in the eighteenth century, the background of Hume (as well as the British empiricist tradition more broadly conceived) can be seen in the influential work *System of Logic* by John Stuart Mill (1806–1873). Mill was sympathetic to Hume's account of causation and induction. In some respects, he also developed it. He thought, as Hume had argued, that there are no objective necessary connections among species of objects or events. Inductive inference does not guarantee apodictic certainty. However, this is not to deny inductive inference. It is possible to address different levels of probability to propositions concerning matters of fact (Wilson 2016: section 3, Induction).

In the twentieth-century philosophy of science, Hume's impact can be seen most clearly in the doctrines of logical positivism. In Alexander Rosenberg's (1993: 64) estimation, the positivists and members of the Vienna Circle even preferred to call their program logical empiricism, to show their debt to Humean empiricism rather than to Auguste Comte's (1798–1857) positivism.

A particularly good example of Hume's influence on logical positivism can be found in A.J. Ayer's (1910–1989) 1936 book *Language, Truth and Logic*. In retrospect, as a popularization of "what may be called the classical position of the Vienna Circle," Ayer characterized "*Language, Truth and Logic* as being no more than Hume in modern dress" (Ayer 1959: 8, 1987: 24). Right from the beginning of his work, Ayer endorses, in no uncertain terms, Hume's distinction between the propositions concerning relations of ideas and matters of fact. Thus, he commences his work: "Like Hume, I divide all genuine propositions into two classes: those which, in his terminology, concern 'relations of ideas', and those which concern 'matters of fact.'" Within the former Ayer includes analytic "*a priori* propositions of logic and pure mathematics," and within the latter synthetic "propositions concerning empirical matters of fact." Ayer understood analytic propositions to be true in virtue of their meaning, and synthetic propositions to be "determined by the facts of experience." He took himself to be following Hume's footsteps, holding analytic statements to be necessary and certain, whereas empirical facts are "hypotheses, which can be probable but not certain" (Ayer 2001: 9, 72–73).

To produce textual evidence for his starting point, Ayer quotes the famous concluding paragraph of Hume's first *Enquiry*. In Ayer's (1959: 10) opinion, this paragraph is "an excellent statement of the positivist's position":

> When we run over libraries, persuaded of these principles, what havoc must we make? If we take in our hand any volume; of divinity or school metaphysics, for instance; let us ask, *Does it contain any abstract reasoning concerning quantity or number?* No. *Does it contain any experimental reasoning concerning matter of fact and existence?* No. Commit it then to the flames: For it can contain nothing but sophistry and illusion.
>
> (EHU 12.34; SBN 165)

In Ayer's view, Hume was the first hero of logical positivism. He thought that Hume championed the divide between the analytic and the synthetic. As the truths of mathematics and logic were to Ayer analytic and *a priori* necessary, he saw the movement of logical positivism to have vindicated "the empiricist claim that there can be no *a priori* knowledge of reality" (Ayer 2001: 83). If Ayer's Hume-interpretation were correct, he had a good reason in stating that "it is indeed remarkable how much of the doctrine that is now thought to be especially characteristic of logical positivism was already stated, or at least foreshadowed, by Hume" (Ayer 1959: 4).[2]

Although logical positivism was the most influential tradition in the philosophy of science between the two world wars, the movement eventually came to an end. In 1967, John Passmore (1967: 57) famously voiced that logical positivism "is dead, or as dead as a philosophical movement ever becomes." In its philosophy, there were a number of irresolvable problems. The principle of verifiability, according to which a cognitive statement is meaningful only if it is empirically testable, was self-refuting: the principle could not itself stand the test. Ludwig

Wittgenstein's (1889–1951) later philosophy indicated the problems of radical concept empiricism. In his *Philosophical Investigations*, Wittgenstein argued that the meaning of the word is its use in a language game. The Humean-positivist theory had maintained that words get their meaning by a reference to sensuous impressions; this was now seen as a commitment to an untenable doctrine of private language. W. V. Quine (1908–2000) set forth a detailed critique of the analytic synthetic divide in his groundbreaking article "The Two Dogmas of Empiricism" (1951). He argued that the truths of pure mathematics and logic are not in principle distinguishable from the propositions of empirical science. In Quine's holism, the totality of our knowledge and beliefs form a sphere "which impinges on experience only along the edges" (Quine 1951: 39). Although logical and mathematical truths are in the center of the sphere, and most unlikely to be revised, they are still not immune from the findings of the empirical sciences. In the 1970s, a rehabilitation of metaphysics was seen in the philosophies of Saul Kripke, Hilary Putnam (1926–2016), and David Lewis. Their works recreated traditional metaphysical questions of essences, natural kinds, and rigid designation (Ladyman and Ross 2007: 9).

Karl Popper's (1902–1994) philosophy of science was essentially a reaction to the positivist verification principle. He viewed Hume's account of induction both positively and negatively. He thought that Hume had shown that there cannot be legitimate truth-preserving inductive inference. However, Popper (1972, section 1) also argued that science does not and should not employ induction. In his view, the proper logic of science is falsificationism based on the *modus tollens* rule of inference. Popper has, however, been criticized for "smuggling" induction in his notion of corroboration of theories. William Edward Morris (2011: 460) argues that

> corroboration isn't really much different from confirmation, and seems to have an inductive inference embedded in it – the inference from the fact that a conjecture has thus far escaped falsification to the (admittedly fallible) conclusion that it will continue to do so.
>
> Since corroboration provides a way to accept conjectures [. . .], it is *ampliative*, and therefore should count as a non-demonstrative form of inference. To the extent that Popper's theory is inductive, it fails to evade Hume's argument.

The fact that Popper was not able to refute Hume on induction does not mean that philosophers of science after him would subscribe to induction as *the* logic of science. Contemporary philosophers of science, for example Peter Godfrey-Smith (2003: Chapter 3), have argued for pluralism of scientific inferences; there is no one valid mode of inference but several modes, including induction, deduction, and abduction.

Hume's regularity theory of causation (which is the traditional interpretation of his position)[3] has been reviewed critically by contemporary metaphysicians and philosophers of science. The basic problem of the regularity theory is that it does not properly distinguish between correlation and causation. To paraphrase Nancy Cartwright (1979), regularity is not sufficient for making a difference between effective and ineffective strategies. Buying a certain health insurance is statistically correlated with a longer lifetime, but the purchase of the insurance is not an effective strategy for prolonging one's life (as compared to physical exercise and proper diet). In addition to regularity, or probability of effects appearing after their causes, it has been suggested that causation needs also to be defined in counterfactual and interventionist terms. The counterfactual condition requires that if a cause did not happen, its effect would not ensue either (Menzies 2014). The interventionist position emphasizes the role of manipulability in causal relations: if the cause is intervened on, there will be a change in the effect (Woodward 2003).

In contemporary philosophy of physics, Hume's account of the metaphysics of laws of nature remains highly influential. It is commonplace to introduce two rival positions on the modal status of laws: the Humean and the non-Humean. According to the former position, laws are accurate records of universal generalizations. The non-Humean positions maintain that there is a specific modal character in laws of nature, namely physical necessity. Non-Humeanism in terms of laws maintains that the Humean view is not able to make a credible distinction between laws and accidentally true generalizations. To explain the non-Humean view, consider the following claims. There are no golden or uranium spheres larger than one mile in diameter. Although both of these claims are true, the first is true by accident: it would be physically possible to construct such a golden sphere. But it would not be physically possible to construct such an uranium sphere; this is restricted by the laws of nuclear physics (Carroll 2016). The non-Humeans maintain that, for example, massy particles *cannot* travel at the speed of light, whereas the Humeans hold the more cautious view that *so far* we have not been able to produce such accelerations.

Hume's science of human nature is also relevant for contemporary neuroscience and philosophy of mind. This is evident in Antonio Damasio's work *Descartes' Error* (1995). In his work, Damasio (1995: 108) explicitly draws on Hume's notion of mental images, which can be both "faint" and "lively." There are many important parallels in their positions: the centrality of representational images in our thought, the quintessential role that emotions play in cognition, and the denial of substantial self in which our mental states supposedly inhere. As Morris (2011: 471) puts it, Damasio brings "many of Hume's fundamental views into an exciting, plausible, and – ultimately – testable account of human cognition."

In the next section, I shall draw my attention to Hume's role in the history of science by concentrating on his relation to two major figures of the scientific tradition: Darwin and Einstein. I shall argue that Darwin's reading of Hume strengthened his naturalistic worldview, which maintains that the difference between human and animal reason and cognition is a matter of degree, not kind. This contributed to Darwin's theory of evolution and natural selection. Both Hume and Darwin thought that reason is not a special human faculty, but that it evolves gradually from animal instincts. In the subsequent section, I shall argue that Einstein inherited from Hume (and Mach) an empiricist theory of concepts, which he then went on to realize in his argument for the relativity of simultaneity. This fundamental result of the special theory of relativity debunked the Newtonian assumption that time is absolute. Hume, and the empiricist tradition more broadly, paved the way for a critical understanding of the ontology of time (and space) as not being absolute, self-sustaining structures.

Hume and Darwin: reason, cognition, and the human-animal distinction

To paint with a very broad brush, the dominant view in the history of Western philosophy regarding the relationship between humans and animals is anthropocentric. In ancient, medieval, and early modern philosophy, many prominent philosophers assumed that there is a categorical difference between human and animal reason.

Since Plato (427–347 BC) and Aristotle (384–322 BC), and especially since neo-Platonism in late Antiquity, a very popular view concerning the relationship between the beings of the world was expressed in the idea of the ladder of nature (*scala naturae*) (Bunnin and Yu 2004: 289; Lovejoy 1936: 58–59). According to this view – sometimes also referred to as the "Great Chain of Being" – there is a hierarchical structure in the world. This hierarchy includes the divine, living, and non-living parts of the universe. In the highest category there is God. In the next category come divine creatures like angels. After this there are humans, next animals, and then plants. Inanimate matter is placed at the lowest level.

In the scholastic period in Europe (roughly 1100–1500), theological considerations together with philosophical discussions based on the Aristotelian tradition emphasized the difference between human and animal reason. Thomas Aquinas shared the view of the ladder of nature. In his view, only humans and supreme beings like angels and God are intellectual. Human intellect is the lowest form of the intellect (Clark 2000: 66). Aquinas' conception is a direct continuation of the Aristotelian conception, which states that only humans have the rational part of the soul.

In the early modern period, Descartes' philosophy provides the clearest example of the view that there is a categorical difference between human and animal reason. In Descartes, only humans and angels are beings with minds. He thought that non-human animals are automata, sophisticated mechanical organs created by God. Descartes argues in his *Discourse of the Method* that reason is "the only thing that makes us men and distinguishes us from the beasts [lower non-human animals]." He did not think that "beasts have *less* reason than men," but that "they do not have reason *at all*" (Descartes 2000: 68, 148).

Hume's position regarding the distinction between human and animal reason is very different compared to the traditional view in the history of Western philosophy. This is evident both in his *Treatise* and his first *Enquiry*. On Hume's account, animal and human cognition works in fundamentally the same manner. This account concentrates on the notions of experience, causation, and uniformity of nature.

For Hume, we receive information of causal relations by experience (T 1.3.1.1; SBN 69). As reasoning concerning matters of fact is founded on experience, it is also the source of factual knowledge (EHU 4.14; SBN 32). The nature of experience is the following. We remember having observed two species of objects or events as being constantly conjoined in the past (T 1.3.6.2; SBN 87). For instance, I remember that when I placed my finger near to a candle flame, I felt heat. Experience enables me to infer the fact that flame causes heat. Hume contrasts experience to reason, since the latter does not "make us pass from one object to another." This requires the faculty of imagination:

> Reason can never shew us the connexion of one object with another, tho' aided by experience, and the observation of their constant conjunction in all past instances. When the mind, therefore, passes from the idea or impression of one object to the idea or belief of another, it is not determin'd by reason, but by certain principles, which associate together the ideas of these objects, and unite them in the imagination.
> (T 1.3.6.12; SBN 92; see also Garrett 1997: 76)

Both humans and non-human animals experience. They are both equipped with sensory systems and the faculty of memory. Humans and non-human animals are thus able to perceive objects and events, and infer some constant conjunctions and regularities between them. Both base their causal reasoning – the way in which they identify causality – on the uniformity of nature. "It seems evident," Hume writes, "that animals, as well as men learn many things from experience, and infer, that the same events will always follow from the same causes" (EHU 9.2; SBN 105). For example, an experienced horse knows, based on its previous experience, which fences it can jump, so it will not attempt to jump fences that it cannot handle. In chase, an experienced greyhound knows to leave the most fatiguing parts of the chase to the young, unexperienced hounds, instead waiting for the hare in a specific location where it is most likely to appear.

When animals infer from causes to effects, they do not base their inferences on any principle founded on reason. With an argument from analogy, Hume claims that the same is true with regard to humans:

Animals, therefore, are not guided in these inferences by reasoning: Neither are children: Neither are the generality of mankind, in their ordinary actions and conclusions:
Neither are philosophers themselves, who, in all the active parts of life, are, in the main,
the same with the vulgar [ordinary people], and are governed by the same maxims.

(EHU 9.5; SBN 106)

Hume's position on the relation between human and animal cognition is radical. He suggests
that reasoning is fundamentally an instinctive process. He maintains that

the experimental reasoning itself, which we possess in common with beasts, and on
which the whole conduct of life depends, is nothing but a species of instinct [. . .]
Though the instinct be different, yet still it is an instinct, which teaches a man to avoid
the fire; as much as that, which teaches a bird, with such exactness, the art of incuba-
tion, and the whole economy and order of its nursery.

(EHU 9.6; SBN 108)

Hume shrinks the gap between the human and animal reason into a difference of degree. Unlike
many of his predecessors, for which Descartes is an excellent example, he did not understand
reason as being a quasi-divine feature, a faculty by which humans can understand the God-
created world. Peter Millican (2007: xlviii–xlix) expounds on the controversiality of Hume's
position as compared to many of his predecessors:

Human reason was commonly [in the eighteenth century] thought to be quasi-divine
or angelic rather than beastlike, a faculty expressing the essence of our unique immaterial soul, capable of providing transparent insight into the nature of things and operating quite independently of brute animal instincts.

In the *Treatise*, Hume strongly criticizes the Cartesian conception by contending that "no truth
appears to me more evident, than that beasts are endow'd with thought and reason as well as
men" (T 1.3.16.1; SBN 176). He thinks that arguments for this case are "so obvious, that they
never escape the most stupid and ignorant" (T 1.3.16.1; SBN 176). In Hume's stance, human
reason is not opposite to animal instinct but emerges from it. Like animals, we humans acquire
knowledge of nature by sensory input and frequent experience.

Hume on the relation between human and animal reason and cognition made a deep impact
on Darwin. In August 1838, some 20 years before the publication of his *Origins of Species*, and
exactly at the time when Darwin was formulating his theory of natural selection, he was reading the first *Enquiry*. He wrote in his notebook (N101) that "Hume has section (IX) on Reason
of Animals . . . he seems to allow it is an instinct." As Hume had claimed, reasoning is a form
of natural instinct. By this he means that when humans or non-human animals infer "that like
events must follow like objects," they both rely on the assumption "that the course of nature will
always be regular in its operations" (EHU 9.5; SBN 106). This assumption of the uniformity of
nature is not founded on reasoning in any way. Rather, it is founded on non-voluntary, customary, habitual, and instinctive aspects of our natures.

Darwin wrote in his notebook (after reading Hume) that intellectual activity is a "modification of instinct – an unfolding & generalizing of the means by which an instinct is transmitted"
(*Darwin's Notebook* N48). As Robert J. Richards (2003: 95) expounds, to Darwin this meant that
"human intelligence was, then, not opposed to animal instinct but grew out of it in the course

of ages." Darwin's conception draws consciously on Hume, as he pointed out that in Hume's account the "origin of reason" is "gradually developed" (*Darwin's Notebook* N101).

Moreover, Hume's Copy Principle is also consistent with the position that animal and human mentality are in continuation. As our ideas and thoughts are copied from simple sensory impressions, there is no reason why animals, who possess similar sensory systems than humans, would not be capable of thought. Darwin explored this idea further, and went on to devise a sensationalist epistemology which he wrote down in one of his notebooks. Although Darwin does not explicitly mention Hume in this context, he argued, in a way that would have been very congenial to Hume, that the basis of complex thought is in the comparison of simple sensory images (*Darwin's Notebook* N21E; Richards 2003: 95).

Darwin's own scientific arguments for the difference of degree between human and animal cognition are made explicit in his main work *Of the Origin of Species by Means of Natural Selection* from the year 1859. Natural selection results from three combined principles: 1) tendency of offspring to resemble parents, 2) variation, and 3) superfecundity, that is, Malthusian production of more offspring than can possible survive. Thus, Darwin puts it as follows:

> As many more individuals of each species are born than can possibly survive; and as, consequently, there is a frequently recurring struggle for existence, it follows that any being, if it vary however slightly in any manner profitable to itself, under the complex and sometimes varying conditions of life, will have a better chance of surviving, and thus be *naturally selected*. From the strong principle of inheritance, any selected variety will tend to propagate its new and modified form.
>
> (Darwin 2006: 3)

Because of variation, it is not possible to draw a sharp dividing line between individual differences and slight varieties, between slight varieties and more distinct varieties, between more distinct varieties and sub-species, between sub-species and species, and finally, between species (Darwin 2006: 294). Darwin (2006: 34) stresses that he looks

> at the term species as one arbitrarily given for the sake of convenience to a set of individuals closely resembling each other, and that it does not essentially differ from the term variety, which is given to less distinct and more fluctuating forms. The term variety, again, in comparison with mere individual differences, is also applied arbitrarily, and for mere convenience sake.

The conclusion Darwin draws in the *Origin* is that all forms of life are part of one and the same tree of life. All species have probably evolved from a simple form or few forms of life (2006: 307).

In his *Descent of Man*, Darwin does, however, argue that humans have abilities that have developed further than in other animals. Such abilities include the development and application of an articulate language, manufacturing of weapons, tools, and traps, abstract thought, and self-consciousness. These capabilities have made human dominance in nature possible. Darwin also thinks that as self-reflecting beings humans are capable of making moral inferences. We can critically review our past actions and conclude that we could have acted differently (Darwin 2007: 83–84, 404). In this respect, he maintains that there are important differences between humans and other animals. Interestingly, Hume also thinks that non-human animals are not capable of making moral judgments, concerning neither their own actions nor what others should do (Boyle 2003: 21).

But these differences are nothing like what has been traditionally assumed in the history of Western philosophy. There is no ladder of life – "nature does not make jumps," as Darwin and many natural philosophers had claimed before him – but a tree of life. And humans are just one branch of this tree.

Hume did not say anything about the common tree of life, or about the way in which the branches of the family tree divide over and over again. It is not clear if Hume even had any position about the nature of species. Accordingly, Hume seems not to have theorized on sexual selection, which is one of the cornerstones of Darwin's work. In the *Dialogues*, there are some scattered remarks which suggest that Hume had some idea of evolution by means of natural selection. In the line of Philo, Hume writes the following:

> You ascribe, Cleanthes, (and I believe justly) a purpose and intention to Nature. But what, I beseech you, is the object of that curious artifice and machinery, which she has displayed in all animals? *The preservation alone of individuals and propagation of the species.*
>
> (DNR 10.26; KS 198, my emphasis)

Here Hume says that the purpose of living beings is to survive and produce offspring. This would be consistent with Darwinian evolution by means of natural selection.[4] Hume also did think, along the same lines with Darwin, that human mental faculties have gradually developed. They are not categorically different from those of the animals. In this respect, Hume's philosophy of animals instantiates a distinctly modern conception. It indicates that it is hopeless to draw a dichotomous and all-encompassing difference between humans and animals. In conclusion: the naturalistic worldview that is apparent in Hume's philosophy was clearly part of the intellectual background of Darwin's scientific work.

Hume and Einstein: empiricism and relativity of simultaneity

The commonsensical picture of time is that it flows like a river. We feel that time passes from past to future, no matter what. This picture is also apparent in Newton's major work *Principia: The Mathematical Principles of Natural Philosophy*, a work that laid the foundation for classical dynamic physics.[5] Thus Newton writes:

> Absolute, true, and mathematical time, in and of itself and of its own nature, without reference to anything external, flows uniformly, and by another name it is called duration.
>
> (Newton 1999: 408)

Newton's conception of time as flowing evenly and his understanding that duration is absolute has two consequences: all observers agree on the absolute simultaneity of events, since the duration between these events is zero and the durations between all non-simultaneous events are absolute (Earman 1989: 8). The absoluteness of time signifies that it exists entirely independent of observers, physical objects, or any kind of natural events, such as motion of objects. We can accelerate objects, but we cannot have any influence on the flow of time. In Newton's account, observers' relations to objects are insignificant for the structure and passage of time. Time is universal and independent of any specific location:

> The moment of duration is the same at Rome and at London, on the Earth and on the stars, and throughout all the heavens [. . .] each and every indivisible moment of duration is *everywhere*.
>
> (Newton 2004: 26; Newton 1999: 941)

From its inception, Newton's argument for absolute time (and space) has been taken with a grain of salt. To name some figures, important seventeenth- and eighteenth-century philosophers and natural philosophers such as Huygens, G.W.F. Leibniz (1646–1716), and George Berkeley (1685–1753) did not subscribe to Newton's absolutism. There are many reasons for their critical receptions, and there are many intricate issues in the philosophy and physics of time. In what follows, I shall zero in on Hume's influence on Einstein. I shall focus on the empiricist epistemology of concepts, and its relation to Einstein's argument for the relativity of simultaneity, which effectively gave Einstein the means to reject Newton's absolute conception of time.

In 1905, Einstein published his article "On the Electrodynamics of Moving Bodies" ("Zur Elektrodynamik bewegter Körper") in the physics journal *Annalen der Physik*. This is the original publication of the special theory of relativity, although Einstein was not the only scientist who took part in its creation.[6] The theory originated from a critical reflection of the nineteenth-century electrodynamic physics (see Norton 2014), but it is most well known for putting forth a novel theory of space and, perhaps more importantly, time. The processes that gave birth to the theory also have philosophical dimensions.

Einstein himself acknowledged the importance of his reading of Hume and Ernst Mach (1838–1916) several times. On December 1915, some ten years after the original publication of special relativity, and around at the time of a series of publications where he devised the general theory of relativity, Einstein was engaged in a correspondence with Schlick. In this correspondence, they discussed the philosophical issues related to special relativity. In one of his letters, Einstein (1998: 220) wrote that Schlick had been correct in recognizing that it was

> Mach, and, even more, Hume, whose *Treatise of Human Nature* I studied with passion and admiration shortly before discovering the [special] theory of relativity. Very possibly, I wouldn't have come to the solution without those philosophical studies.

Einstein had been reading the German translation of the *Treatise* in a reading group that he formed with his friends, philosophy student Maurice Solovine (1875–1958) and mathematician Conrad Habicht (1876–1958) around 1902–1903 in Bern (Howard 2005: 36; Janssen, Lehner 2014: 2). In his letter to Schlick, he noted that Hume's role was more important in the formulation of STR than Mach's. Later in 1948, he reiterated his opinion in his correspondence with his friend, engineer Michele Besso (1873–1955):

> How far (Mach's writings) influenced my own work is, to be honest, not clear to me. In so far as I can be aware, the immediate influence of D. Hume on me was great. I read him with Konrad Habicht and Solovine in Bern.
>
> (Speziali 1972: 153)

In the letters above, Einstein's debts to Hume are vague and unspecific. But there is one piece of textual evidence in his 1949 autobiographical notes where he is more specific. He points out that while forming the theory of special relativity, it was necessary to reject the false "axiom of absolute character of time, viz., simultaneity." This axiom, he writes,

> unrecognizedly was anchored in the unconscious. Clearly to recognize this axiom and its arbitrary character really implies already the solution of the problem. The type of critical reasoning required for the discovery of this central point [the denial of absolute time, that is, the denial of absolute simultaneity] was decisively furthered, in my case, especially by the reading of David Hume's and Ernst Mach's philosophical writings.
>
> (Einstein 1949: 53)

In general, historians and philosophers of physics have taken Hume's influence (or the influence coming from the empiricist and the positivist tradition more broadly) on Einstein to have focused on this central point (Norton 2010: 360, footnote 2). Understanding the relativity of simultaneity was a key to reconcile the two seemingly contradictory postulates of the theory: the light principle and the invariance principle. According to the first principle, the velocity of light in a vacuum, *c*, is constant. It is independent of the motion of the emitting source of the light. According to the latter, laws of physics are invariant in all inertial frames of reference. They apply in the same way for all uniformly moving or stationary observers (measuring devices).

As noted before, our commonsensical Newtonian picture of time tells us that time flows like a river. From the viewpoint of empiricist philosophy, the problem is that time in itself – if there were such a thing – is not something one can perceive. We do not acquire information of the putative flow of absolute time by our senses; time itself cannot be seen, touched, heard, tasted, or smelt.

If one is an empiricist about the idea or the concept of time, then its idea or concept has to be somehow related to a perception, observation, or experience. As John D. Norton (2010) shows, it was an empiricist account of concepts that Einstein learned from his reading of Hume (as well as Mach and possibly the empiricist and the positivist tradition of philosophy in general). Einstein's insight was to implement this empiricism into his argument for the relativity of simultaneity. In his popular book *Relativity. The Special and General Theory* from the year 1916, Einstein presents his argument with the following thought experiment.

Imagine two inertial frames of reference. These are two rigid bodies, a train and a railway embankment.[7]

There are two observers, M and M', and two places at the embankment, A and B. The observer M is at rest with respect to the embankment, while the observer M' is at rest with respect to the train. M sees the train passing her by with a constant velocity *v*. While M' passes M, they are both located at the mid-point of the line AB.

When the train passes M, two lightings strike to points A and B. The observers are both equipped with two mirrors that are inclined at 90 degrees. These mirrors enable them to see the receiving light coming from points A and B. The light travels with constant velocity *c* (all observers agree on the speed of light (in a vacuum), as established by the theory's light principle).

The observer M sees the lightning strikes to happen simultaneously. But how does the observer M' see the time ordering of the strikes? She is moving toward point B and away from point A. Therefore, she is also hastening toward the light beam coming from point B, and away from the light beam coming from point A. In her inertial frame of reference, the lightning striking point B occurs before the lighting strike at point A. Consequently, for her the strikes are non-simultaneous, that is, successive. "We thus arrive," Einstein (2001: 28–29) explains,

> at the important result: Events which are simultaneous with reference to the embankment are not simultaneous with respect to the train, and vice versa (relativity of simultaneity). Every reference-body (co-ordinate system) has its own particular time; unless we are told the reference body to which the statement of time refers, there is no meaning in a statement of the time of an event.

Crucial to Einstein's (2001: 25, 29) argumentation is the definition of the concept of simultaneity in empirical terms. Without the observation of lightning strikes in the experiment, one would not be "able to attach a meaning to the statement of simultaneity." The essential demand to this concept is "that in every real case it must supply us with an empirical decision as to whether or not the conception that has to be defined is fulfilled." Once simultaneity is so defined, the Newtonian absolutist assumption can be discarded, and the apparent tension between the two postulates of the theory of special relativity disappears. Einstein comments on the historical significance of the discovery of this central point:

> Now before the advent of the theory of relativity it had always tacitly been assumed in physics that the statement of time had an absolute significance, i.e. that it is independent of the state of motion of the body of reference.
>
> (Einstein 1920: 32)

With the aid of empiricist philosophy, Einstein rendered the concept of time an empirical one. It can be decided by experimental means that simultaneity and duration between two non-causally related physical events are relative to inertial frames of reference. Judgments about time are judgments about simultaneous events in which any freely chosen periodically recurring system, such as a clock, is compared to a reference-object, that is, to an inertial frame of reference. Time-interval between two ticks of a clock is shortest in the frame of reference where the clock is at rest (Knight 2008: 1158); there is no meaning in speaking of any "absolute" or "true" time to which any specific clock could be compared to. In special relativity (a theory which has now been extremely well confirmed), there is no absolute flow of time from earlier to later, from past to future.[8] Time is neither absolute nor universal the way Newton thought it would be.

Hume and the empiricist tradition shaped Einstein's views on the epistemology of concepts, but also, as I have argued (Slavov 2016), there are analogies between Hume's and Einstein's ontological positions concerning space and time. They are both relationists. An important aspect of both Hume's and Einstein's ontologies is this: they relate the idea or the concept of time to objects.

In Hume, the abstract idea of time is acquired by perceiving change. It "can never be convey'd to the mind by any thing stedfast and unchangeable," he writes (T 1.2.3.11; SBN 37). This change is perceivable through either succession or relative motion of objects. By hearing five successive flute chords, we can abstract the idea of time from the succession of the chords. Time is not something that is caused by an individual chord, a simple auditory impression. No single on-going chord could cause the idea of time to the mind, because there is nothing changing in this object. Rather, we need to perceive a sequence of chords and pauses to get time's idea. Another way for us to acquire the idea of time is to perceive relative change of motion of bodies. Motion gives us the idea of time as "every moment is distinguish'd by a different position" of the moving object (T 1.2.5.29; SBN 65; Baxter 2008: 30). Hume encapsulates his argument concerning the origin of the idea of time:

> Wherever we have no successive perceptions, we have no notion of time, even tho' there be a real succession in the objects. From these phaenomena, as well as from many others, we may conclude, that time cannot make its appearance to the mind, either alone, or attended with a steady unchangeable object, but is always discover'd by some *perceivable* succession of changeable objects.
>
> (T 1.2.3.7; SBN 35)

Time consists of indivisible moments that are parts of succession. For us to acquire the idea of time, it is requisite that these parts appear to be changing:

> Now as time is compos'd of parts, that are not co-existent; an unchangeable object, since it produces none but co-existent impressions, produces none that can give us the

idea of time; and consequently that idea must be deriv'd from a succession of changeable objects, and time in its first appearance can never be sever'd from such a succession.

(T 1.2.3.8; SBN 36)

To understand Hume's reasoning,[9] imagine a stationary observer in front of a huge gray wall. The wall is evenly painted, and it covers the observer's whole visual field. In this scenario, there is nothing changing in front of her. The wall is a steadfast object. It has no duration. Such an unchangeable object cannot be the source for the idea of time, alone.

Now, if something changing, like a blue object moving in front of the wall, appears, the observer will be able to acquire the idea of time through change of place of the object. Although the wall is a steadfast object, the "co-existing" moving item is not. It is changing its location as it is moving. Its moments, that is, different spatial locations with respect to the wall, are distinguishable. So there is apparent succession. However, this change, or the appearance of succession, is related to the observer's viewpoint. If the observer would be moving together with the object at the same relative velocity, there would not be any apparent change in her viewpoint.[10]

Hume's conception of time is clearly non-absolutist. There is no one universal time but different times. The way we perceive time depends on the observer's relations to objects. There is no absolute time (or we do not have its putative idea) independent of this relation. It is not "possible for time alone ever to make its appearance," as "time is nothing but the manner, in which some real objects exist," Hume says (T 1.2.3.7; SBN 35, 1.2.5.28; SBN 64; see also Isaacson 2008: 82).

Hume is conscious that his account of time is against the "common opinion of philosophers as well as of the vulgar," who assume that steadfast objects endure. Because of his strict empiricism, Hume cannot accept such a false notion. It is by means of "fiction," that is, without having ideas that "represent the objects or impressions, from which they are deriv'd" that "we apply the idea of time, even to what is unchangeable" (T 1.2.3.11; SBN 37). "There is no observable evidence that the structure of time is uniform across space," notes Baxter (2015: 214).

As in Hume, Einstein's ontology of time is also intrinsically related to his empiricism. Consider the following arguments of Einstein:

> in any ontological question, our concern can only be to seek out those characteristics in the complex of sense experiences to which the concepts refer.
>
> (1981: 271)

> [concepts] of space and time can only claim validity in so far as they stand in a clear relation to experiences.
>
> (Norton 2010: 369)

Although there are essential similarities between Hume and Einstein's philosophical analysis related to his special relativity, namely the intertwinement of empiricism of concepts and relationist ontology concerning space and time, there are also crucial differences. These differences pertain both to the epistemology of ideas and concepts as well as to the ontology of time (and space).

Hume's empiricism is much more radical than Einstein's. In Hume, simple ideas are caused by simple impressions; the origin of all of our simple ideas are in sensuous impressions. Einstein does not share this view. In his account, "physical concepts are free creations of the human mind" (Einstein, Infeld 1960: 31). He thought that the formation of concepts requires conventional stipulations. He did not subscribe to Hume's position concerning the origin of concepts (abstract ideas). On the other hand, both Hume and Einstein seem to have thought that the way ideas or concepts get their meaning and justification is by a reference to sensuous impressions.

Regarding the ontology of time, Hume is concerned with the way the mind acquires the idea of time. In Einstein's account, time is a physical quantity. This indicates that when the two are speaking about time, they are not referring to the exact same thing. Hume is more interested in the psychological and phenomenological dimensions of time, the way the human mind perceives time. Einstein is addressing physical time, that is, time as a natural phenomenon. To Einstein, "observer" is a technical term which denotes an inertial frame of reference with respect to with a measurement device is at rest. As Bradley Dowden comments, the observer "need not to have a mind" (Dowden 2017).

Moreover, according to Hume's view, the ideas of space and time are distinctly separable; there are successions of impressions (such as auditory impressions) which are not themselves physically located (T 1.4.5.10; SBN 235; Baxter 2008: 37). This means that in Hume there can be time without physical events taking place. To the contrary, Einstein's argument for the relativity of simultaneity connects temporal order to the order in which physical events take place (in a specific inertial frame). The order of events can be different from experimenters' direct observations of the timely order of events. To quote from a contemporary physics textbook (Knight 2008: 1153), the crux of the matter is this:

> Simultaneity is determined by when the events actually happen, not when they are seen or observed. In general, simultaneous events are *not* seen at the same time because of the difference in light travel times from the events to an experimenter.

In special relativity, it is a mistake to conflate "'simultaneously seen" and "simultaneously happening,'" as Einstein (1936: 358) himself asserts. It is not clear whether Hume's radical (and skeptical) empiricism could license us to infer that our perceptions are different from physical events *and* that our perceptions are caused by perception-independent natural events.

However, in both Hume and Einstein, their epistemology of ideas and concepts is related to their ontological commitments concerning time, so it is meaningful to compare their views. As there are salient confluences of their positions, and as there is evidence that Einstein was reading Hume before the formulation of his new theory, it can be concluded that Hume's philosophy did partly contribute to Einstein's work with his special relativity.

Notes

1 It is somewhat problematic to depict "natural philosophy" in the seventeenth and eighteenth centuries as "natural science." The disciplinary boundaries of our time are not the same as they were in the early modern world. Moreover, potential terminological confusions may arise when we use our contemporary language to interpret the past. The meaning of the word "philosophy" in the eighteenth-century context is quite close to the meaning of the word "science" in our contemporary use of the term. See the entry of "Philosophy" in Ephraim Chambers' dictionary from the year 1728 (Chambers 1728: 803).

2 Kevin Meeker (2011) has challenged Ayer's interpretation.

3 For different interpretations on Hume on causation, see Helen Beebee (2006: Chapters 5, 6 and 7).

4 For history of natural selection before Darwin, see Conway Zirkle (1941). On Hume's relation to Darwinism, see Simon Blackburn (2009).

5 To just say that our commonsensical picture of time is similar compared to Newton's conception of time is certainly an understatement. In short, the aim of Newton's argument for absolute space and time in the Scholium to the Definitions of the *Principia* is to make a difference between true and relative motion, that is, between acceleration exerted by a force and rest or motion with constant velocity.

However, in this chapter, it is not possible to properly analyze Newton's account. For a thorough analysis of Newton's argument for absolute space and time, see Robert DiSalle (2002).

6 Although Einstein is credited for the first publication of STR, many mathematicians and physicists took part in its creation, including Hendrik Lorentz (1853–1928), Henri Poincaré (1854–1912), and Hermann Minkowski (1864–1909) (Janssen, Lehner 2014: 11).

7 For reference, see "The relativity of simultaneity" in Einstein's (1920: 30) example.

8 However, there are other physical theories which indicate the direction of time, such as the second law of thermodynamics.

9 Donald L. M. Baxter (2008: 37) provides a "brick wall" diagram that is very helpful for understanding Hume's reasoning in this issue.

10 In this idealized example, observers' bodily motions are not taken into account. She could also have a succession of ideas in the mind, which would be a source for the idea of time.

References

Ayer, A. J. (1959) "Introduction," in A. J. Ayer (ed.), *Logical Positivism*, London: Free Press.

———. (1987) "Reflections on *Language, Truth, and Logic*," in B. Gower (ed.), *Logical Positivism in Perspective: Essays on Language, Truth and Logic*, London and Sydney: Croom Helm.

———. (2001) *Language, Truth and Logic*, London: Penguin Books.

Baxter, D. L. M. (2008) *Hume's Difficulty: Time and Identity in the Treatise*, London and New York: Routledge.

———. (2015) "Descartes and Hume on Duration," *Proceedings of the 42nd International Hume Society Conference Stockholm*: 203–216.

Beebee, H. (2006) *Hume on Causation*, New York: Routledge.

Blackburn, S. (2009) "Is Human Nature Natural?" in J. Hodge and G. Radick (eds.), *The Cambridge Companion to Darwin*, 2nd edn, New York: Cambridge University Press.

Boyle, D. (2003) "Hume on Animal Reason," *Hume Studies* 29(1): 3–28.

Bunnin, N. and J. Yu (2004) *The Blackwell Dictionary of Western Philosophy*, Malden, Oxford and Victoria: Blackwell Publishing.

Carroll, J. W. (2016) "Laws of Nature," in Edward N. Zalta (ed.), *The Stanford Encyclopedia of Philosophy* (Spring 2016 Edition), URL = <http://plato.stanford.edu/archives/spr2016/entries/laws-of-nature/>.

Cartwright, N. (1979) "Causal Laws and Effective Strategies," *Noûs* 13: 419–437.

Chambers, E. (1728) *Cyclopædia, or an Universal Dictionary of Arts and Sciences*, 2 vols, with the 1753 supplement. Digitized by the University of Wisconsin Digital Collections Center, URL = <http://digital. library.wisc.edu/1711.dl/HistSciTech.Cyclopaedia>.

Clark, M. T. (2000) *An Aquinas Reader*, New York: Fordham University Press.

Damasio, A. (1995) *Descartes' Error: Emotion, Reason, and the Human Brain*, New York: Avon Books.

Darwin, C. (2006) *On the Origins of Species by Means of Natural Selection*, Mineola and New York: Dover.

———. (2007) *The Descent of Man, and Selection in Relation to Sex*, New York: Penguin Books.

Descartes, R. (2000) *Discours de la méthode*, edited by D. Moreau, Paris: Librairie Générale Française.

DiSalle, R. (2002) "Newton's Philosophical Analysis of Space and time," in I. B. Cohen and E. Smith (eds.), *The Cambridge Companion to Newton*, New York: Cambridge University Press.

Dowden, B. (2017) "Time," *The Internet Encyclopedia of Philosophy*, ISSN 2161–0002, URL = <www.iep. utm.edu/time/>.

Earman, J. (1989) *World Enough and Space-Time: Absolute Versus Relational Theories of Space and Time*, Cambridge, MA and London: MIT Press.

Einstein, A. (1905) "Zur Elektrodynamik bewegter Körper," *Annalen der Physik* 332(10): 891–921.

———. (1936) *Physics and Reality*, trans. J. Piccard, *Journal of the Franklin Institute* 221(3): 349–382.

———. (1949) "Autobiographical Notes," in P. A. Schilpp (ed.), *Albert Einstein: Philosopher – Scientist*, vol VII in the Library of Living Philosophers, New York: MJF Books.

———. and L. Infeld (1960) *The Evolution of Physics, from Early Concepts to Relativity and Quanta*, New York: Simon Schuster.

———. (1981) "The Problem of Space, Ether, and the Field in Physics," in C. Seelig (ed.), *Ideas and Opinions*, trans. Sonja Bargmann, New York: Dell Publishing.

———. (1998) *The Collected Papers of Albert Einstein. Volume 8: The Berlin Years: Correspondence, 1914–1918*, edited by R. Schulmann, A. J. Kox, M. Janssen and József Illy, Princeton: Princeton University Press.

———. (1920) *Relativity. The Special and General Theory*, trans. R. W. Lawson, New York, NY: Henry Holt and Company.

Garrett, D. (1997) *Cognition and Commitment in Hume's Philosophy*, New York: Oxford University Press.

Godfrey-Smith, P. (2003) *Theory and Reality: An Introduction to the Philosophy of Science*, Chicago, IL and London: University of Chicago Press.

Harris, J. A. (2015) *Hume: An Intellectual Biography*, New York: Cambridge University Press.

Howard, D. (2005) "Albert Einstein as a Philosopher of Science," *Physics Today*, December, URL = <http://dx.doi.org/10.1063/1.2169442>.

Isaacson, W. (2008) *Einstein: His Life and Universe*, New York: Simon & Schuster Paperbacks.

Janssen, M. And C. Lehner (2014) "Introduction," in M. Janssen and C. Lehner (eds.), *The Cambridge Companion to Einstein*, New York: Cambridge University Press.

Knight, R. D. (2008) *Physics: For Scientists and Engineers*, 2nd edn, San Francisco: Pearson Addison-Wesley.

Ladyman, J. and D. Ross (2007) *Every Thing Must Go: Metaphysics Naturalized*, New York: Oxford University Press.

Lovejoy, A. O. (1936) *The Great Chain of Being: A Study of the History of an Idea*, Cambridge, MA: Harvard University Press.

Meeker, K. (2011) "Quine and Hume and the Analytic/Synthetic Distinction," *Philosophia* 39(2): 369–373.

Menzies, P. (2014) "Counterfactual Theories of Causation," in Edward N. Zalta (ed.), *The Stanford Encyclopedia of Philosophy* (Spring 2014 Edition), URL = <http://plato.stanford.edu/archives/spr2014/entries/causation-counterfactual/>.

Mill, J. S. (1963) "System of Logic, Ratiocinative and Inductive," in J. M. Robson (ed.), *Collected Works of John Stuart Mill*, vol 7 and 8, Toronto: University of Toronto Press.

Millican, P. (2007) "Introduction," in David Hume (ed.), *Enquiry Concerning Human Understanding*, New York: Oxford University Press.

Morris, W. E. (2011) "Hume's Epistemological Legacy," in E. S. Radcliffe (ed.), *A Companion to Hume*, Malden, Oxford and West Sussex: Wiley-Blackwell.

Newton, I. (1999) *The Principia: Mathematical Principles of Natural Philosophy*, trans. and edited by I. B. Cohen and A. Whitman, J. Budenz (assist.), Berkeley, Los Angeles and London: University of California Press.

———. (2004) "De Gravitatione," in A. Janiak (ed.), *Isaac Newton. Philosophical Writings*, New York: Cambridge University Press.

Norton, J. D. (2010) "How Hume and Mach Helped Einstein Discover Special Relativity," in M. Dickson and M. Domski (eds.), *Discourse on a New Method: Reinvigorating the Marriage of History and Philosophy of Science*, Chicago, IL and La Salle, IL: Open Court.

———. (2014) "Einstein's Special Theory of Relativity and the Problems in the Electrodynamics of Moving Bodies That Lead Him to It," in M. Janssen and C. Lehner (eds.), *The Cambridge Companion to Einstein*, New York: Cambridge University Press.

Ott, W. (2009) *Causation and Laws of Nature in Early Modern Philosophy*, New York: Oxford University Press.

Passmore, J. (1967) "Logical Positivism," in P. Edwards (ed.), *The Encyclopedia of Philosophy*, vol 5, New York: Palgrave Macmillan.

Popper, K. (1972) *Objective Knowledge: An Evolutionary Approach*, New York: Oxford University Press.

Quine, W. V. O. (1951) "Two Dogmas of Empiricism," *The Philosophical Review* 60(1): 20–43.

Richards, R. J. (2003) "Darwin on Mind, Morals and Emotions," in J. Hodge and G. Radick (eds.), *The Cambridge Companion to Darwin*, New York: Cambridge University Press.

Rosenberg, A. (1993) "Hume and the Philosophy of Science," in D. F. Norton (ed.), *The Cambridge Companion to Hume*, New York: Cambridge University Press.

Slavov, M. (2016) "Empiricism and Relationism Intertwined: Hume and Einstein's Special Theory of Relativity," *Theoria: An International Journal for Theory, History and Foundations of Science* 31(2): 247–263.

Speziali, P. (1972) *Albert Einstein, Michelle Besso. Correspondence 1903–1955*, Paris: Hermann.

Wilson, F. (2016) "John Stuart Mill," in Edward N. Zalta (ed.), *The Stanford Encyclopedia of Philosophy* (Spring 2016 Edition), URL = <http://plato.stanford.edu/archives/spr2016/entries/mill/>.

Wittgenstein, L. (2009) *Philosophical Investigations*, trans. and edited by G. E. M. Anscombe, P. M. S. Hacker and J. Schulte, 4th edn, Malden, Oxford and West Sussex: Wiley-Blackwell.

Woodward, J. (2003) *Making Things Happen: A Theory of Causal Explanation*, New York: Oxford University Press.

Zirkle, C. (1941) "Natural Selection Before the 'Origin of Species,'" *Proceedings of the American Philosophical Society* 84(1): 71–123.

31

HUME AND CONTINENTAL PHILOSOPHY

Jeffrey A. Bell

> The mind is a kind of theatre, where several perceptions successively make their appearance; pass, re-pass, glide away, and mingle in an infinite variety of postures and situations
> – David Hume, *A Treatise of Human Nature* (1.4.6.4; SBN 253)

Hume is one of the greatest philosophers in the English language, so it is no surprise that his work has had a profound influence upon the Anglo-American tradition in philosophy. When one surveys the work of continental philosophers, on the other hand, references to Hume are much less common, and those one does find are often quite critical of Hume. If one looks just under the surface, however, and especially if one looks to the post-Kantian tradition and its continuing response to problems Hume left in his wake, then one will quickly find that Hume's influence upon continental philosophy is far-reaching. A key aspect of the post-Kantian response to Hume, and one that begins with Kant himself, concerns what it means for the mind to be "a kind of theatre." What is the space that is the mind, and what is the relationship between the content that successively appears in the mind? Beginning with Kant's critique of Hume, and especially with his example of the incongruence of the right hand with its image in the mirror, we will set the stage for showing how a broad swath of work in continental philosophy can be seen as continuing the conversation Kant began with Hume. Moreover, it will be argued here that a common strategy among continental philosophers, beginning with Husserl, will be to return to Hume to assist in the development of their own philosophical projects. The following chapter will show how two key founding figures in continental philosophy – Henri Bergson and Edmund Husserl – and three important philosophers who were influenced by Husserl and Bergson – Jean-Paul Sartre, Maurice Merleau-Ponty, and Gilles Deleuze – were influenced by Hume. By showing how such critical figures in continental philosophy are continuing to develop the implications of a problem that Hume brought to our attention, it should become clear that a fuller understanding of continental philosophy will require returning to the work of Hume.

Kant and Hume

As is well known, Hume's philosophy led Kant to reconsider his philosophical presuppositions. As Kant put it, "David Hume was the very thing which many years ago first interrupted my dogmatic slumber and gave my investigations in the field of speculative philosophy a quite new direction" (Kant 1950: 8). In particular, Hume challenged Kant's long-held belief that there is a fundamental, necessary connection between a cause and its effect, and that this connection is rationally justified. Hume "demonstrated irrefutably," Kant admits, "that it was perfectly impossible for reason to think *a priori* and by means of concepts such a combination, for it implies necessity" (Kant 1950: 5). The problem concerns the origin of the concept of causal necessity, or the origin that accounts for the synthesis that connects causal elements, and a synthesis and connection that possesses, as Kant puts it, "an inner truth, independent of all experience. . . . This was Hume's problem" (ibid.: 7). As Kant will famously state this problem, the question is whether or not synthetic *a priori* judgments are possible.[1] For Hume, the answer is no, and for Kant, the answer is yes.

The key for Kant is to offer an account of a synthesis that is neither a conceptual or logical synthesis (such as when one says all unmarried men are bachelors) nor is it an empirical, *a posteriori* synthesis (such as when one asserts that the African elephant has larger ears than the Asian elephant). Many within the continental tradition will also attempt to demonstrate the possibility of a synthesis that is neither logical nor empirical, but is, rather, as Kant himself will describe it, genetic. To set the stage for this effort, let us turn to an important example Kant uses to justify his project that will recur in the work of Bergson and Deleuze – the example of the paradox of incongruent counterparts. As Kant formulates the paradox, it would seem that

> if two things are quite equal in all respects as much as can be ascertained by all means possible, quantitatively and qualitatively, it must follow that the one can in all cases and under all circumstances replace the other, and this substitution would not occasion the least perceptible difference.
>
> (Kant 1950: 33)

In other words, if we begin with the assumption that two entities share all the same extensive properties, and thus apparently exhaust "all means possible" whereby we can differentiate one entity from another, then it would seem that one entity could be substituted for another. This is not the case, however, and Kant offers his famous example to illustrate this point. If I take my right hand and take its image as reflected in a mirror, I cannot substitute the image in the mirror for my right hand, "for if this is a right hand," Kant claims, then "that in the glass is a left one," and a "left hand cannot be enclosed in the same bounds as the right one (they are not congruent)" (ibid.). What this example illustrates, for Kant, is that what we see of the hand is not the object as it really is. As Kant states it, what we have in this example are "not representations of things as they are in themselves . . . but sensuous intuitions, that is, appearances whose possibility rests upon the relation of certain things unknown in themselves to something else, namely, to our sensibility" (ibid.: 33–34). In short, for Kant it is space, as "the form of the external intuition of this sensibility," that accounts for this difference between the appearances of the right hand and this same hand's image in a mirror, and this difference "cannot be made intelligible by any concept, but only by the relation to the right and the left hands which immediately refers to intuition" (ibid.: 34). The spatial form of sensibility, therefore, is not itself an object represented through intuition, but the very form of sensibility itself, and this sensibility itself, as Kant noted, is in turn related to "certain things unknown in themselves" (ibid.: 34).

What the sensibility gives us, therefore, is mere appearances, and these, Kant argues, "are based upon a thing in itself, though we know not this thing as it is in itself but only know its appearances" (ibid.: 62). We cannot know the right hand as it is in itself, for this same hand in the mirror is incongruent with the actual hand even though all the extensive properties which exhaust the manner in which we ascertain and conceptually determine the hand are the same. The conclusion Kant draws is that knowledge itself presupposes a relationship between sensibility and "certain things unknown in themselves," and it is this relationship which provides for Kant a genetic account of "the origin of knowledge itself." Knowledge thus presupposes, for Kant, a synthetic process whereby appearances come to be combined in the form of judgments. The syntheses that make these judgments possible, however, are not derived from experience, as Kant argues against Hume, nor are they logical and conceptual. Instead, they presuppose the genetic relation of the sensibility to certain things unknown in themselves, which includes for Kant the "pure concepts of the understanding." With this move, Kant believes he has resolved the Humean problem that awoke him from his dogmatic slumber. What Kant recognized was "a completely reversed mode of connection" between the understanding and experience in that for Kant, unlike Hume, the pure concepts of the understanding "do not derive from experience, but experience derives from them."[2]

A central problem that will occupy much of the work that has been done in continental philosophy will be precisely that of demonstrating the role played by synthetic processes that are neither processes of logical and/or conceptual determination nor processes of empirical or psychological synthesis. The point of Kant's example of the right hand's image in the mirror was to show that determination in terms of extensive properties and qualities is insufficient in accounting for all differences, such as the difference between left hand and right hand. Kant turned to a non-conceptual sensibility and its *a priori* form of space to account for the difference between the two hands. The relationship between this sensibility and the pure concepts of the understanding makes possible the judgments regarding the appearances of experience. Within the continental tradition as well, a central concern is to account for the possibility of the extensive properties and qualities that constitute the content of our judgments. Two nearly exact contemporaries (both born in 1859) will set the stage for much of the work that will occur in twentieth-century continental philosophy – Henri Bergson and Edmund Husserl. What is of crucial concern to both of them is to provide an account of the syntheses that make knowledge possible. Both Bergson and Husserl argue that Kant ultimately failed to provide a sufficient account of the processes that allow for the possibility of judgments regarding experience, and in setting forth their criticisms of Kant return to Hume.

Bergson

Bergson's initial reaction to Hume appears to be largely critical, and it largely reprises Kant's critique. In short, Bergson argues that impressions are what need to be explained rather than presupposed. More to the point, he claims that "the truth is that this independent image [impression] is a late and artificial product of the mind" (Bergson 1988: 165). It was only because Hume assumed that the impression of a cause is distinct and independent of the impression of an effect that he was able to generate the problem of causality, the problem of showing how these two independent entities are necessarily connected. By turning instead to an account of the mind of which these impressions are "a late and artificial product," Bergson believes he is able, along with Kant, to resolve the problem of causality as Hume bequeathed it to posterity.

Before lumping Bergson into the post-Kantian camp, however, we must first note that Bergson is equally critical of Kant, and he turns to the right/left hand example to make his case. On the one hand, Bergson recognizes that Kant was right to note that the example of the right hand in the mirror demonstrates the inadequacy of conceptual determination – that is, the identification and differentiation of entities in terms of their extensive properties and qualities. For Bergson, "we cannot give a proper definition of right and left" if this entails a conceptual definition that involves a set of extensive properties and qualities. For Bergson, however, the very possibility of making a conceptual distinction presupposes "clean-cut distinctions and a kind of externality of the concepts or their symbols with regard to one another, . . . [and thus] the faculty of abstraction already implies the intuition of a homogeneous medium" (Bergson 2001: 97). Kant, Bergson argues, will also presuppose this conception of space as a "homogeneous medium," a "space separated from its contents," as Bergson puts it.

For Bergson, by contrast, space is not a homogeneous medium but what he will call a "pure heterogeneity" (Bergson 2001: 104). It is at this point where we find a similarity between Bergson and Hume.[3] In particular, Bergson also confronts the problem of accounting for how something new and different can arise out of the repetition of identical elements. As Hume states the problem, "'tis certain that this repetition of similar objects in similar situations produces nothing new either in these objects, or in any external body" (T 1.3.14.18). And yet when one perceives a necessary connection between two objects, one is perceiving something new, and thus the problem is to show how this is possible. Similarly for Bergson: he asks whether, "when the regular oscillations of the pendulum make us sleepy, is it the last sound heard, the last movement perceived, which produces the effect?" (ibid.: 105). If each of the oscillations, each of the ticks of the clock, is the same, then why is it the last one which produces the effect of sleepiness rather than the first? How did something new and different arise out of the repetition of the same?

Bergson also adopts a Humean solution to this problem. For Hume, it is indeed the case that "the several resembling instances, which give rise to the idea of power, have no influence on each other, and can never produce any new quality in the object," but it is nonetheless the case, Hume argues, that "the observation of this resemblance produces a new impression in the mind, which is its [the idea of necessary connexion's] real model" (T 1.2.14.20). The idea of a necessary connection is thus the result of a reflection on the impression of the easy transition the mind makes when, through habit, it comes to expect B upon being given A. It is therefore in the mind where we can account for the emergence of something new out of the repetition of identical instances. For Bergson, likewise, the emergence of something novel is to be accounted for by the mind, and thus while we cannot account for the effect of sleepiness by virtue of any determinate difference between the oscillations of the pendulum, "we must admit that the sounds combined with one another and acted, not by their quantity as quantity, but by the quality which their quantity exhibited, i.e. by the rhythmic organization of the whole" (ibid.: 105–106). In other words, what is perceived, Bergson argues, is not a quantitative effect that results from a composition of distinct, independent oscillations, but rather what Bergson calls an "intensive magnitude" or "pure duration" that "consciousness perceives" (ibid.: 106). The novel effect is a consequence of the mind, or it is, Bergson claims, "nothing else but the melting of states of consciousness into one another, and the gradual growth of the ego" (ibid.: 107).

It is at this point where Bergson's approach breaks with the one Hume takes, for although Bergson can be seen to adopt a Humean solution to the problem of novelty, Hume's solution does not go far enough. Bergson argues that it fails to account for the emergence of distinct, independent entities themselves, an emergence that arises for Bergson from the continuity of pure duration. The "capital error" of associationism, Bergson claims, "is that it substitutes for this continuity of becoming, which is the living reality, a discontinuous multiplicity of elements, inert and juxtaposed" (Bergson 1988: 134). What Hume in effect does is to think of the mind in terms of an abstract, homogeneous space, the empty stage upon which distinct impressions and ideas strut and fret their fitful hours. Bergson argues instead that the mind is not a homogenous space upon which the already determined and determinate appears but is "unceasing creation, the un-interrupted upsurge of novelty," and this continuity and upsurge of novelty is only "dissociated" (to use Bergson's term) into distinct, abstract elements "for the greater convenience of practical life" (ibid.: 164). In contrast to Hume's empiricism, therefore, Bergson offers what he takes to be the "true empiricism" which attempts "to get as near to the original itself as possible, to search deeply into its life, and so, by a kind of intellectual auscultation, to feel the throbbings of its soul; and this true empiricism is the true metaphysics" (Bergson 1999: 36–37). Rather than chart, measure, and quantify (using Bayesian analysis, for instance) the evidence of experience as given to us through our sense impressions, Bergson proposes developing an intuition of what he calls the absolute, or reality as continuous "upsurge of novelty," a freedom irreducible to any form of lawful determinism; it is thus the intuition of this absolute that is for Bergson simultaneously a true empiricism and a true metaphysics. As an illustration of this shift towards true empiricism he is calling for, Bergson claims that the

> absolute is synonymous with perfection. Were all the photographs of a town, taken from all possible points of view, to go on indefinitely completing one another, they would never be equivalent to the solid town in which we walk about.
>
> (Bergson 1999: 22)

The solid town is the absolute and the photographs taken of this town, no matter how exhaustive, will nonetheless never exhaust the reality that is the town, and it is this reality that is the condition for the possibility of understanding distinct, determinate existents (e.g. photographs) rather than the town itself being understood by way of distinct, determinate realities, as Bergson believes Hume does.

In the end, Bergson argues that Kant and Hume are two sides of the same coin. Despite their efforts to provide an explanation for the beliefs and judgments we arrive at, they both ultimately adopt a view of space as homogeneous medium, and a medium that is passive and neutral with respect to the distinct, successive entities that occur in this homogenous space. In doing this, both Hume and Kant fail to think the real as the free, creative upsurge of novelty, the pure heterogeneity that gives rise to the reality of distinct, successive entities.

Husserl

In contrast to Bergson, Bergson's contemporary Husserl draws much more fruitfully from Hume. Husserl's Humean influence, moreover, is arguably one of the key touchstones for subsequent generations of continental philosophers. Husserl is quite forthright in his praise for Hume, announcing in his *Formal and Transcendental Logic* that "Hume's greatness . . . [is] still unrecognized in this, its most important aspect, [which] lies in the fact that . . . he was the first to grasp the universal *concrete problem* of transcendental philosophy" (ibid.). This concrete problem, as Husserl understands it, consists of exploring "a transcendental subjectivizing, which is not merely compatible with genuine Objectivity but is the a priori other side of genuine Objectivity" (ibid.). In other words, the problem for Hume, and for Husserl as he takes up the *concrete problem* of transcendental philosophy, is to show how the very nature of the objective itself as objective is made possible by the constitutive conditions of the subject. The "Objective itself," as Husserl summarizes Hume's position, is "itself a product of that concreteness," by which Husserl means the "concreteness of purely egological internality" (ibid.). In short, Hume is the first to have outlined what Husserl calls "constitutional problems," in that Hume set out to understand the constitutive conditions for the very contents of our conscious experience. We can trace this influence more clearly and begin to see where Husserl breaks with Hume by turning to Husserl's reading of Hume's section on abstract ideas from the *Treatise*.

In the *Treatise*, Hume argues, *contra* Berkeley, that abstract ideas are more than simply individual ideas that are "annex'd to a certain term, which gives them a more extensive signification" (T 1.1.7.1). For Hume, an abstract idea arises through an association of ideas, most notably through resemblance, whereby the word that is "annex'd" to this idea revives a custom and habit. While it may perhaps be imperfect in its extension, this idea is nonetheless suitable for the "purposes of life" (T 1.1.7.7). For Husserl, however, Hume has not gone far enough in addressing the constitutional problem but simply leaves us with "particular individual ideas and their attendant habits" (Husserl 1969: 260). In short, Hume leaves us with a psychologistic account of abstract ideas whereby they are explained in terms of certain psychological and behavioral facts. We can thus trace to Hume the roots of the psychologism that Husserl sought to overcome through the development of his phenomenological method. It was this same psychologism that led Gottlob Frege to develop his highly influential distinction between *Sinn* and *Bedeutung* (*sense* and *reference*).[4] The prevalence of psychologism in Husserl's day led him to claim that "one can perhaps even say that Hume has never been more influential than he is now" (Husserl 1970: 419).

For Husserl, the fundamental mistake that kept Hume, and his psychologistic successors, from fully developing the implications of the constitutional problem with respect to abstract ideas is the failure to distinguish between an appearance and that which it is an appearance of – or, in Husserl's terminology, between the intentional content of consciousness and the intentional object this consciousness is a consciousness of. For Hume, Husserl argues, the "appearance and the apparent phenomenon coalesce" (Husserl 1970: 409). By turning to an analysis of the intentional syntheses of consciousness, an analysis Hume did not pursue, Husserl is able to distinguish between the manner in which a consciousness is determined in a particular way and the object that is the object of this consciousness.

This brings us to the core of Husserl's phenomenological approach. Unlike Hume, who assumes the already-constituted givenness of the data of experience, the impressions that conflate both "the appearance and the apparent phenomena," and unlike Kant, who presupposes the already constituted givenness of the formal categories of the understanding, Husserl, by contrast, argues for the necessary synthesis and constitution of these givens within and through the intentionality of consciousness itself. For Husserl, therefore, the phenomenological method consists of unpacking the givens of all aspects of experience, which entails an "unraveling of the intentionalities involved . . . [an] uncovering of the 'multiplicities' in which the 'unity' becomes constituted" (Husserl 1969: 262). Among the multiplicity of intentionalities that are synthesized into a unity are the various ways in which the consciousness is determined as well as the ways in which the object itself is presented. These intentional syntheses are in turn guided in their constitutive process toward unification by the fact, for Husserl, that there is an ego-pole which assures that the various consciousnesses are consciousnesses of one pure ego, and an object-pole which assures that the various presentations of the object are presentations of a unitary object. In other words, for Husserl there is a pure transcendental ego or ego-pole that assures that the multiplicity of consciousnesses will become unified as the unity of a particular ego, and the object-pole does the same for the unity of objects themselves. It was on this point where Jean-Paul Sartre famously broke with Husserl when, in *Transcendence of the Ego*, he in essence invoked the Humean challenge of accounting for the constitutive conditions of every identity by criticizing Husserl for presupposing the identity of the pure ego.

Sartre

Sartre's philosophical project can be seen as a continuing response to Hume's constitutional problem. In his first important philosophical work, *The Transcendence of the Ego*, Sartre takes up the Humean challenge and argues that Husserl's pure transcendental ego is unnecessary. As Sartre argues, "For our part, we readily acknowledge the existence of a constituting consciousness," but why, Sartre adds, "is not this psychic and psycho-physical *me* enough? Need one double it with a transcendental I, a structure of absolute consciousness?" (Sartre 1960: 36). In short, the question for Sartre is whether we must call upon the identity of a pure transcendental ego rather than simply drawing from what is given through psycho-physical processes. Sartre's answer to his own rhetorical questions is that no, we do not need this doubled I and can do perfectly well with a "transcendental field [that] becomes impersonal; or, if you like, 'pre-personal,' *without an I*" (ibid.) Like Bergson, we do not have a homogenous space upon which identities roam but rather have a dynamic field which is the condition for the identities that come to be conditioned by this field – hence the field is impersonal or 'pre-personal' in that it is the very constitutive condition for the identity of personhood. Sartre begins to draw the implications of this move to an impersonal field in *Being and Nothingness*.

At an important juncture in *Being and Nothingness*, Sartre calls upon Hume as he lays out his concept of the For-itself and In-itself and thus develops the implications of a constituting consciousness that presupposes an impersonal, transcendental field rather than, as Husserl does, an already constituted and individuated pure ego (the ego-pole) or an already constituted object (object-pole). Initially Sartre's use of Hume appears to be as a foil with which to contrast his own position. For example, Sartre argues that the association theory "is accompanied by a monistic conception to the effect that being everywhere is being-in-itself," and thus for Hume, "one can at will examine any impression, strong or weak [and yet] one will never find anything in it but itself so that any connection or a consequent . . . remains unintelligible" (Sartre 1956: 190). In other words, by dissolving the world into the atoms of impressions and ideas that are simply in themselves and without connection or relation to other impressions and ideas, Hume in effect removes the possibility of there being a relationship between impressions whereby one can be for another, or being-for-itself as Sartre understands it.[5] This criticism of Hume largely repeats Bergson's criticism, which faulted Hume for beginning with impressions which are, in fact, simply "a late and artificial product of the mind." Sartre, however, does not follow Bergson and endorse the notion that the mind is a continuous upsurge of novelty and that discrete, extensive differences are simply effects or abstractions derived from practical necessity. Sartre criticizes Bergson's approach and argues that Bergson unjustly ignores the fact that time is "a dissolving force" as much as a source of unity. It is the dissolving force of time that Hume recognized, Sartre claims, and with this comes a very Humean problem – namely, how to account for the unity of time if time is nothing but the passage of discrete instants. If A is prior to B, and if A and B are distinct, then how do we account for time such that B is before A (for instance)? If A and B are truly distinct beings, Sartre claims, then "it is impossible to establish between them the slightest connection of succession" (ibid.).

To address the Humean problem of accounting for how unity can arise out of a diversity of distinct elements, Sartre attempts, in a manner Deleuze will largely follow, to embrace both continuity *à la* Bergson and discrete elements *à la* Hume. This entails admitting, Sartre argues, that it is essential for there to be something that is both indistinguishable from two distinct elements – e.g. B is indistinguishable from A and C – while at the same time A and C remain distinct. Sartre admits that this would be the way one must go "but," he asks, "how can such a being exist?" (ibid.: 193). Sartre's answer is that it is the very nature of the For-itself to exist in this way, "to be what it is not and not to be what it is" (ibid.: 116). The nature of consciousness is to be what it is not – the objects it is consciousness of – and it is consciousness in the mode of not being these objects. The For-itself is thus indistinguishable from A and C for it is not an ego or I distinct from A and C but is simply the consciousness of A and C respectively. At the same time, A and C remain distinct for the For-itself is consciousness of A and C in the mode of not being A and C. There is thus a fundamental nihilation associated with the For-itself, and this in turn gives rise to what Sartre calls a "quasi-multiplicity" in that the "rising into being [of the For-itself] as the nihilation of the In-itself constitutes itself simultaneously in all the possible dimensions of nihilation." The For-itself, in other words, is not predisposed or predetermined by any identity for it is in the very nature of the For-itself "to be what it is not and not to be what it is." Thus the nihilations of the For-itself range a quasi-multiplicity. The For-itself, Sartre concludes, "is diasporatic," for it involves at once both "profound cohesion and dispersion" (ibid.: 195). It is this diasporatic nature of the For-itself that allows Sartre to resolve the Humean problem of accounting for unity out of a multiplicity of discrete elements while at the same time avoiding the dissolution of this unity into a diversity of discrete elements. Deleuze, as we will see, will also employ a concept of multiplicity that is neither reducible to being a collection of discrete elements nor is it a unity that reduces the multiplicity to being simply the unity of one nature or type. Deleuze's concept of multiplicity is also used, as it was for Sartre, to address the Humean problem as we have laid it out here. Before turning to discuss the influence of Hume on Deleuze, let us briefly examine the influence of Hume on Merleau-Ponty.

Merleau-Ponty

Merleau-Ponty's work extends Sartre's effort to push phenomenology beyond Husserl's reliance upon a pure transcendental ego and towards an impersonal transcendental field. For Merleau-Ponty, however, Sartre's understanding of our conscious lives was too abstract, and this left him unable to fully explicate the varied phenomena of conscious life. To remedy this situation, Merleau-Ponty begins with a phenomenological analysis of perception.

Merleau-Ponty shares with Sartre the Humean desire to lay bare the constitutive processes of conscious life in a way that does not presuppose something that in turn requires a constitutive explanation. Merleau-Ponty best typifies what is important about both Hume and Husserl for his own work when he argues that

> we may hold with Husserl that Hume went, in intention, further than anyone in radical reflection, since he genuinely tried to take us back to those phenomena of which we have experience, on the hither side of any formation of ideas, – even though he went on to dissect and emasculate this experience.
>
> (Merleau-Ponty 1962: 220)

Merleau-Ponty thus echoes both Kant's and Bergson's critique of Hume and rejects Hume's assumption that impressions, which serve as the "hither side of any formation of ideas," do not themselves require a constitutive explanation. Unlike Bergson, however, and more in line with Kant and Sartre, Merleau-Ponty argues for a constitutive difference in order to account for the content of conscious experience. For Kant, as we saw, this constitutive difference is the difference between the sensibility and that which remains unknown, a difference that Kant accounts for by way of the noumenal thing that remains unknown and the pure concepts of the understanding whereby the representations of this unknown come to be known. Under the influence of Husserl, however, both Sartre and Merleau-Ponty will criticize Kant's presupposed noumenal entities and pure concepts of the understanding, arguing, along Humean lines, that they themselves require a constitutive explanation. Merleau-Ponty likewise accepts Sartre's criticism of Husserl's pure transcendental ego and his call for a constitutive difference on an impersonal transcendental field; however, Merleau-Ponty rejects the constitutive difference Sartre claims is fundamental – namely, the difference between the For-itself and the In-itself. What Merleau-Ponty finds problematic in Sartre's approach is that the difference Sartre calls for is simply a binary opposition which repeats the problems that befell Descartes' mind–body dualism – in short, if mind and body are fundamentally different, then how do they relate? In the case of Sartre, as Merleau-Ponty puts it, "From the moment that I conceive of myself as negativity [For-itself] and the world as positivity [In-itself], there is no longer any interaction" (Merleau-Ponty 1968: 52).

For Merleau-Ponty, the constitutive difference that is on the "hither side of any formation of ideas" is the difference between figure and ground. This will remain a constant theme in Merleau-Ponty's work. Early in the *Phenomenology of Perception*, Merleau-Ponty argues that when

> when Gestalt theory informs us that a figure on a background is the simplest sense-given available to us, we reply that this is not a contingent characteristic of factual perception. . . . It is the very definition of the phenomenon of perception, that without which a phenomenon cannot be said to be perception at all.
>
> (Merleau-Ponty 1962: 4)

Nearly 20 years later, and in the notes to his unpublished manuscript, Merleau-Ponty wrote: "To be conscious = to have a figure on a ground – one cannot go back any further" (Merleau-Ponty 1968: 191). For Merleau-Ponty, what this entails is that perception involves a fundamental paradox of immanence and transcendence: "Immanence because the perceived object cannot be foreign to him who perceives; transcendence, because it always contains something more than what is actually given" (Merleau-Ponty 1964: 16). In a late essay, "Eye and Mind," this paradoxical nature of perception will be referred to as depth, "our participation in a Being without restriction" (ibid.: 173), and a participation whereby "there really is inspiration and expiration of Being, action and passion so slightly discernible that it becomes impossible to distinguish between what sees and what is seen" (ibid.: 167).

To clarify Merleau-Ponty's point, and set the stage for Deleuze's Humean critique of phenomenology, we can turn to Merleau-Ponty's discussion of hallucination. For one who is not suffering from hallucinations, Merleau-Ponty argues that

> the perceived world is not only my world, but the one in which I see the behavior of other people take shape for their behavior equally aims at this world, which is the correlative not only of my consciousness, but of any consciousness which I can possibly encounter.
>
> (Merleau-Ponty 1962: 338)

And in this world, moreover, Merleau-Ponty adds that "the experiences of other people or those which await me if I change my position merely develop what is suggested by the horizons of my present experience, *and add nothing to it*" (ibid., emphasis added). As I sit here and look around, I see the furniture and people before me from my particular perspective, though each person, in their experience, sees one another from yet another perspective, and one I could take up if I were to move to their location; and yet none of these perspectives adds anything to what is not already "suggested by the horizons of my present experience." My present experience, therefore, is full, or it implies more than that which is actually given. "I am," Merleau-Ponty adds, "in present communication with a consummate fullness [that] 'tolerates' nothing more than is written or foreshadowed in my perception" (ibid.: 338–339). It is this "consummate fullness" of our ordinary perceptual experience that is lacking, however, in cases of hallucination. For someone suffering a hallucination, the phenomena of their experience, Merleau-Ponty argues, "is not part of the world, that is to say, it is not accessible, there is no definite path [that] leads from [hallucinatory experience] to all the remaining experiences of the deluded subject" (ibid.: 339). In the shared world of normal experience, I can take up someone else's perception, for it is the "consummate fullness" of this world that is shared and my behavior as well as the behavior of others "aims at this world." In a hallucinatory experience, we discover that this is not an experience we can share. The person suffering from delusion, therefore, lives in an impoverished world rather than a world of consummate fullness. Within a delusional experience, the "hallucinatory thing," Merleau-Ponty claims, "is not, like the real thing, a form of being with depth" (ibid.). To suffer from hallucinations, therefore, is to be deprived of the fullness and depth of the proper world of perceptual experience.

Deleuze

We can now turn to Deleuze's Humean critique of phenomenology. Put simply, by calling upon a fundamental depth, a ground that is never figure but forever prefigures that which comes to be perceived, Deleuze argues that constitutive processes come in the end to be contained and pre-viewed by a fundamental *Urdoxa*, or what Deleuze, following Merleau-Ponty's own use of the term, calls a fundamental opinion that already contains and predetermines the possibilities that may arise. Rather than a true constitutive difference, we thus have a constitutive template, an organizing set of parameters that "'tolerates,'" as Merleau-Ponty argued, "nothing more than is written or foreshadowed in my perception" (Merleau-Ponty 1962: 338–339). The philosophical problem that motivates Deleuze is precisely to account for rather than presuppose an organizing, systemic template, an *Urdoxa*. Deleuze thus extends the Humean problematic that has been so influential among the central figures of continental philosophy. As Deleuze states in his early book on Hume, *Empiricism and Subjectivity*, the problem is to explain how a multiplicity of ideas can "become a system" (Deleuze 1991: 22). More precisely,

> the problem is as follows: how can a subject transcending the given be constituted in the given? . . . [or how can the] subject who invents and believes [be] constituted inside the given in such a way that it makes the given itself a synthesis and a system.
>
> (ibid.: 86–87)

The problem for Deleuze is precisely the problem we saw in Bergson and Hume as they sought to account for the emergence of something novel or new on the basis of the repetition of the same – or, the problem of accounting in terms of the given for that which transcends the given. Rather than presuppose, as Merleau-Ponty does, a systemic horizon or *Urdoxa* that serves as the ground that is never figure and yet prefigures all that comes to be, Deleuze adopts the Humean problem of attempting to understand the very emergence of systemic unity itself. The response to this problem will be the overarching task of much of Deleuze's philosophical writings, including what he wrote with Félix Guattari.

In his effort to account for the constitutive difference that provides the reasons for identity, systematic unity, etc., and in a way that does not presuppose either the identity that is constituted or a transcendent identity to which this difference is subordinate, Deleuze turns to Hume. In what is arguably Deleuze's most important philosophical work, *Difference and Repetition*, Deleuze brings Hume in at a critical point in his argument. Moreover, Deleuze brings in Hume in precisely the same way Bergson does – namely, in order to account for the emergence of something novel or new out of the repetition of that which stays the same. The first line of the second chapter from *Difference and Repetition* reads: "Repetition changes nothing in the object repeated, but does change something in the mind which contemplates it" (Deleuze 1994: 70). Thus, when A appears and we expect B, Deleuze notes that the expectation is "by no means a memory, nor indeed an operation of the understanding," but it is a synthesis which "contracts the successive independent instants into one another, thereby constituting the lived, or living, present" (ibid.). Deleuze will refer to this synthesis as "passive synthesis," arguing that while it is "constitutive it is not, for all that active. It is not carried out by the mind, but occurs in the mind which contemplates, prior to all memory and all reflection" (ibid.: 71).

What, then, is the place where the passive synthesis occurs? Is it a kind of theater, and a theater that serves as a homogeneous medium upon which successive states make their appearance? Deleuze does imply that this is precisely the type of theater Hume has in mind, the homogeneous space upon which "successive independent instants" appear and come to be contracted into habits by way of passive synthesis. For Deleuze, by contrast, this theater is what he will call a plane of immanence, by which he means an intensive field of pre-individual singularities and differences that are the sufficient reason for the determinate, distinct individuals that come to be identified. What is crucial here is that for Deleuze, like Bergson, the conditions that make possible the determinate, extensive properties and qualities are not themselves extensive and determinate but are rather intensive and indeterminate; or, as Deleuze argues, difference is inexplicable:

> It is not surprising that, strictly speaking, difference should be 'inexplicable.' Difference is explicated, but in systems in which it tends to be cancelled. . . . It [difference] is cancelled in so far as it is drawn outside itself, in extensity and in the quality which fills that extensity. However, difference creates both this extensity and this quality.
>
> (ibid.: 228)

In contrast to Bergson and more in keeping with Sartre's project, Deleuze argues for the importance of a fundamental, constitutive difference rather than call upon fundamental continuity or absolute as Bergson does. The key move in Deleuze's argument is the concept of multiplicity, understood by Deleuze to be a substance that is irreducible to extensive, determinate properties and qualities. By making this move, Deleuze is also able to avoid the Humean problem that beset Kant – the problem of accounting for the validity of synthetic *a priori* propositions. Rather than presupposing the reality of distinct, determinate existents that then give rise to the problem of how these distinct entities enter into necessary relations, Deleuze argues for the indeterminate substance or multiplicity as the sufficient reason for the emergence of determinate existence itself. In other words, by turning to the concept of multiplicity, Deleuze attempts to account for the constitutive conditions of determinate, individuated reality itself in a way that does not presuppose any predetermining identity or unity (such as Merleau-Ponty's *Urdoxa*).

So, how does Deleuze arrive at this concept? The first step is to set up an infinite series. For example, in *Difference and Repetition* Deleuze argues that "every phenomenon refers to an inequality by which it is conditioned" (ibid.: 228). That is, every determinate phenomenon in the end presupposes a multiplicity for it involves "a system [that] is constituted or bounded by at least two heterogeneous series . . . [of which] each is itself composed of heterogeneous terms, subtended by heterogeneous series which form so many sub-phenomena" (ibid.), and so on *ad infinitum*. Deleuze refers to the heterogeneous series that is presupposed by every determinate phenomena as intensity. "Intensity," Deleuze claims, "is the form of difference in so far as this is the reason of the sensible." Deleuze further clarifies this point:

> Every intensity is differential, by itself a difference. Every intensity is $E - E$,' where E itself refers to an $e - e$,' and e to $\varepsilon - \varepsilon$' etc.: each intensity is already a coupling (in

which each element of the couple refers in turn to couples of elements of another order), thereby revealing the properly qualitative content of quantity. We call this state of infinitely doubled difference which resonates to infinity disparity. Disparity – in other words, difference or intensity (difference of intensity) – is the sufficient reason of all phenomena, the condition of that which appears.

(ibid.)

We can clarify Deleuze's point in this passage by turning to Deleuze's book on Leibniz, a book he wrote nearly 25 years after *Difference and Repetition*. In this book, Deleuze finds an ally in Leibniz's philosophy as Deleuze continues to set out to reassert his claim that every determinate phenomenon presupposes an infinite series – or disparity. For example, with "the color green," Deleuze argues, "yellow and blue can surely be perceived, but if their perception vanishes by dint of progressive diminution, they enter into a differential relation (db/dy)" (Deleuze 1993: 88). The color green, in other words, presupposes the differential relation of blue and yellow, db/dy, and yet, as Deleuze continues, "nothing impedes either yellow or blue, each on its own account, from being already determined by the differential relation of the two colors that we cannot detect" (ibid.). And so on *in infinitum*. Deleuze will thus take up Bergson's critique of Kant and Hume and do so by bringing into play the notion of an infinitesimal, intensive difference that is not to be confused with any extensive property or quality. It is precisely the multiplicity of intensive, pre-individual singularities that is the sufficient reason for determinate extensive properties as the intensive difference is "cancelled." In contrast to Bergson, however, and drawing from Hume, Deleuze continues to assert that multiplicity is not a continuum, a continuous upsurge of novelty as Bergson put it, but is a multiplicity of pre-individual singularities or infinitesimal differences; or, drawing from Sartre, Deleuze will refer to this as an impersonal, transcendental field.

As he pursues his philosophical project, beginning with his 1953 book on Hume and ending with his essay "Immanence: a Life," Deleuze continues to work through the Humean problem of accounting for how a determinate, objective entity, along with its extensive properties and qualities, can be understood in a way that does not presuppose that which in turn requires an explanation. Since Kant's initial response to Hume, a key approach to this problem is to call upon a constitutive difference that is presupposed by the distinct, independent entities that are being accounted for. Subsequent philosophers within the continental tradition, as we have seen, have each attempted to remain true to the spirit of Hume's effort to offer an account of the constitutive conditions for the phenomena of the human mind while at the same time being cognizant of Kant's critical response to Hume. Bergson argues that both Hume's and Kant's conception of space as the homogeneous medium upon which independent entities manifest their extensive properties and qualities fails to address the problem of showing how such independent entities come to be in the first place. Husserl further develops what he sees as the constitutional problem that Hume was the first to recognize, and he argues that Kant did not reach the true transcendental conditions which are, for Husserl, the constitutive processes of a pure transcendental ego and its noematic correlates. Both Sartre and Merleau-Ponty extend the Humean concern with the constitutional problem by challenging Husserl's very notion of the pure transcendental ego. Deleuze, finally, draws explicitly and even more thoroughly upon the work of Hume and attempts to push the constitutional analysis to the point whereby a constitutive difference, or multiplicity for Deleuze, is the sufficient reason for all determinate phenomena. It would take us too far afield at this point to explicate the full details of Deleuze's project, but it should be clear at this point that Hume has cast a shadow that figures prominently across the continental tradition in philosophy.

Notes

1 Ibid., p. 23 (4: 275): "The real problem upon which all depends, when expressed with scholastic precision, is therefore: 'How are synthetic propositions *a priori* possible?'"
2 Ibid., 60 (4: 313)
3 Bergson does not explicitly draw from the work of Hume, though the similarities are quite clear and continental philosophers such as Gilles Deleuze will make the connections between Hume and Bergson explicit (as we will see below).
4 It is well known that Husserl and Frege corresponded about each other's work in the philosophy of mathematics, and for good reason given their shared interest in overcoming psychologism.
5 This was William James' criticism of Hume as well. In his arguments for radical empiricism, James faulted Hume for being unable to account for causal connections because relationships and connections were always subordinate to the reality of impressions, or to the In–itself, to use Sartre's terminology.

References

Bergson, H. (1988) *Matter and Memory*, New York: Zone Books.
———.Bergson, H. (1999) *An Introduction to Metaphysics*. Indianapolis: Hackett Pub.
———. (2001) *Time and Free Will: An Essay on the Immediate Data of Consciousness*, New York: Dover Publications.
Deleuze, Gilles. (1991) *Empiricism and Subjectivity*, New York: Columbia University Press.
———. (1993) *The Fold: Leibniz and the Baroque*, Minneapolis: University of Minnesota Press.
———. (1994) *Difference and Repetition*, New York: Columbia University Press.
Hume, D. and L. A. Selby-Bigge, ed. (1978) *A Treatise of Human Nature*, Oxford: Clarendon Press.
Husserl, E. (1969) *Formal and Transcendental Logic*, The Hague: Martinus Nijhoff.
———. (1970) *Logical Investigations*, 2 vols, Amherst, NY: Humanities Press.
Kant, I. (1950) *Prolegomena to Any Future Metaphysics*, New York: Bobbs-Merrill Company, Inc.
Merleau-Ponty, M. (1962) *Phenomenology of Perception*, New York: Routledge & Kegan Paul.
———. (1964) *The Primacy of Perception*, Evanston: Northwestern University Press.
———. (1968) *The Visible and the Invisible*, Evanston: Northwestern University Press.
Sartre, J. P. (1956) *Being and Nothingness*, New York: Washington Square Press.
———. (1960) *The Transcendence of the Ego*, New York: Farrar, Strauss and Giroux.

PART IV

Hume's legacy

PART IVA

Twentieth–twenty-first century

32

HUME'S MEANING EMPIRICISM

A reassessment

Tom Seppäläinen

Introduction

According to the standard twentieth-century interpretation, Hume is a semantic empiricist. The reason lies in his Copy Principle. According to it, "ideas," representations that are used in cognition, are copied from the senses, "impressions." Because of copying, ideas are images that resemble impressions. Hume's search for the true meaning of ideas in their copy-base, in impressions, indicates that resemblance extends also to semantic properties. This standard interpretation faces a number of obstacles that have left many recent scholars dismissive of Hume's ability to account for crucial semantic properties, intentionality, and complex structure. On the one hand, for Hume, simple impressions are non-intentional states and thus cannot serve to account for the "aboutness" of ideas. On the other hand, most complex mental representations are produced by associative principles of imagination and thus their structure cannot be said to resemble impressions.

In this chapter, I will offer a reassessment of Hume's semantic empiricism by, first, demonstrating that important recent discussions of Hume's semantic empiricism revolve around the problems of intentional content and complex structure and, second, by offering a solution to these two problems that complies with empiricism. Contrary to the standard interpretation, I will argue that Hume's semantic empiricism concerns the copying of a specific subclass of complex impressions, ones whose objects Hume describes as having the qualities of "constancy" and "coherence of change." These qualities constitute what I will call "change invariant" sense impressions and these, for Hume, underwrite the awareness of continuously existing objects. Continuous objects (of perception), in turn, are central for Hume's explanation of both the external situatedness of objects of perception and the experienced mind-independence of their properties. In other words, change invariant complex impressions explain the standard features of intentionality. As a consequence, senses are fundamental for semantics because they explain the intentionality of ideas.

The offered reassessment of Hume's meaning empiricism solves the problem of intentional content because the intentional objects of ideas are copied from impressions. It also solves the problem of complex structure. Although unique ideational processes result in kinds of complex structure not found in the senses, complex ideas must also agree in structure with impressions if they are to display intentional content. Because of this, intentional complex impressions also provide a tool for carrying out the type of meaning analysis *Humean* empiricists have always hoped for, one based in the "empirical cash-value" of ideas.

Problem-context for an empiricist interpretation
of Hume's semantics

According to the textbook image, Hume is a semantic empiricist on the grounds of the role that the Copy Principle bestows on the senses.[1] Copying results in ideas that resemble sensory impressions. Ideas are particular, "concrete" images or picture-like representations, and the meaning of cognitive representations is captured in such images. "Imagism" extends to the semantics of language because of Hume's commitment to a "Lockean," ideational theory of meaning. Linguistic representations refer to ideas. But because ideas are copies, linguistic meaning also rests on sensory impressions. In short, empiricism for the semantics of both linguistic and cognitive representations follows from Hume's Copy Principle.

The meaning empiricist interpretation rests not only on the theory of copying but also on Hume's use of it. Hume uses the Copy Principle "in-reverse" to explore the meaning of problematic ideas by attempting to trace them to impressions. In exploring the meaning of the idea of "substance," for example, Hume asks whether that idea be "deriv'd from the impression of sensation or reflexion?" (T 1.1.6.1; SBN 15–16). But Hume can only "find" impressions for particular qualities such as colors and sounds and their collections, so the requisite derivation is unattainable. By using copying in-reverse, Hume argues that we have no representation of substance distinct from the collection of ideas copied from sense impressions. The putative idea of a substance in which qualities "inhere" is thereby revealed to be a "fiction" (T 1.1.6.2; SBN 16). An established scholarly interpretation takes this and other similar illustrations of the use of copying to reveal the nature of Hume's semantics. Bennett, for example, argues that Hume ties the meaningfulness of words and expressions to their "empirical cash value" or "empirical cashability" (Bennett 1971: 231, 2002: 104). Similarly, for Price (1965: 7; italics original), Hume's empiricism is based in his contention that "our 'ideas' . . . have to be *cashed* by means of impressions."

Despite its standing, the empiricist interpretation of Hume's semantics faces several challenges. First, through its best known scholarly representatives, semantic empiricism is associated with a revisionist historiography. Both Price and Bennett, for example, offer an explicitly corrective interpretation of Hume. Second, the textbook Hume functions exclusively as a reminder of the abject failures of imagism. If the textbook interpretation is correct, Hume's very approach to semantics is a non-starter. Third, in focusing on copying, the empiricist interpretation overlooks the processes of imagination housed in the Humean mind. In this section, I will analyze these three challenges in order to formulate the precise problem-context for a reassessment of Hume's semantic empiricism.

According to many twentieth-century analyses, Hume's semantics is empiricist, although this interpretation requires a significant revision to the copy thesis and the approach to semantics it represents. According to Price, for example, copying – and the derivation of mental images from sensory impressions – is a "psychological doctrine" and, because of this, "not of the faintest philosophical interest" (1965: 5). Bennett (1971: 230), in turn, labels Hume's semantics a "genetic" theory because it attempts to answer questions of meaningfulness on the basis of past impressions. Past sensory exposure, Bennett (1971: 230) maintains, is "largely irrelevant" for semantics. According to both, to meet the criteria of a theory of semantics, Hume's psychological approach must be substituted by an analytic one. Bennett's version of what I will call the "analytic empiricist interpretation" is an illustrative example.

Bennett maintains that Humean copying can be 'translated' into analytic truths about the meaningfulness of expressions in relation to "empirical cashability" (1971: 231). "Empirical cashability" concerns our capacity to relate expressions "to bits of the objective world" or "the empirical world" (1971: 230), not just other expressions. The role of empirical cashability is fundamental for semantics because it is the basis of "our common understanding of a language" (ibid.). It is revealed, for Bennett, "in our ability to agree on statements of the form 'that is a . . .,' where 'that' refers to something accessible to all of us" (ibid.). Instead of ideas and their copying, for Bennett, Hume's meaning empiricism is revealed in tests of meaningfulness based in ostensive definitions for specific linguistic expressions. Such definitions are analytic truths. Bennett also maintains that his "translation" of Hume's semantics is not original but "underlies all the uses of Hume's work by twentieth century logical positivist and other 'meaning-empiricists' who acknowledge Hume as their leader" (2001: 213).[2]

The analytic empiricist interpretation is not intended as an accurate representation of Hume. It identifies Hume as a precursor of a later, twentieth-century empiricist tradition in semantics and represents his views in its analytic terms. The price of this explicitly revisionist historiography appears high. The interpretation discards copying, which for Hume was the "first principle in the science of human nature" (T 1.1.1.11; SBN 7). More specifically, Bennett characterizes Hume's semantic empiricism in terms of "linguistic abilities" (1971: 228). Our "capacities to use words correctly" replace Humean ideas and our specific capacity to connect expressions to publicly accessible entities – the "this" and "that" of ostensive definitions – replaces Humean copying (1971: 234).

Despite its departure from Hume's theory, the analytic empiricist interpretation does not as such refute Hume's psychology or psychosemantics. Both Price and Bennett judge copying irrelevant, not false. Furthermore, Bennett's linguistic "abilities" and "capacities" are dispositions. The analytic empiricist interpretation ignores or abstracts away from all matters of implementation, including those required for correctly pointing at "this and/or that" upon linguistic stimuli. As a result, ostensive definitions and other dispositional capacities cannot contradict the theoretical constructs of Hume's psychosemantics. The latter must be compatible with the former if the analytic account does not on additional interpretative grounds undermine Humean copying as a viable implementation of ostensive, linguistic capacities. I will use Bennett's account to illustrate how a further interpretative premise prevents Humean psychosemantics from realizing the public reference that ostensive definitions guarantee "analytically."

According to Bennett, Hume "sometimes equates 'impression' with 'perception of the outer world'" (2001: 214). Accordingly, for Bennett, Hume has a "preparedness" to treat meaning empiricism as concerned with the relationship between understanding and "*experience of the objective realm*" (1971: 224; italics original). However, Bennett maintains that, for theoretical reasons, Humean impressions cannot establish the relationship needed for such objective meaning or content. For him, equating the experiencing "of the objective realm" with impressions would be "simple to the point of idiocy" (1971: 225). This is shown by the fact that vivid dreams are indistinguishable from impressions, according to Hume's definition of impressions as vivid perceptions or "intense or violent sensory states" (ibid.). Non-veridical states such as dreams are obviously not experiences of the objective realm – despite their vivacity. More generally, Bennett believes that, for the purposes of objective content, Humean impressions ought to be defined in terms of "sensory intake" (2001: 214). But Hume's official definition is in terms of vividness. This shows, for Bennett, that Humean senses cannot connect our minds with an objective reality and, given the role that copying assigns to the senses, ideas and linguistic representations cannot be about anything objective, either. As a result, Bennett maintains that we "must understand the copy-thesis as saying something about how ideas relate to *sensory contact with the world of material objects*" (ibid.; italics original). Because Humean impressions cannot, according to Bennett, support such copying, ostensive definitions must replace it.

The above analysis shows that Bennett's revision of Hume's original semantic empiricism is premised on an interpretation of Hume's theory instead of Hume's "non-analytic" disciplinary orientation. It also indicates that the crux of Bennett's interpretation is not about copying but rather the nature of impressions. For him, impressions have a problem in connecting with "bits of the objective world." In other words, impressions are non-intentional states.[3] This purported problem coincides with the basis of the textbook dismissal of Hume's imagistic semantics. Lycan (2008: 68), for example, maintains that ideas and images are subjective – "held only in the minds of individual persons" – whereas meaning is "intersubjective, public and social."[4] Because of this difference, meaning cannot consist of imagistic ideas. But since, for Hume, linguistic expressions stand for ideas and ideas are copied from impressions, imagistic ideas are subjective only if impressions are subjective. The tacit premise behind Lycan's cursory dismissal of Humean imagism is that impressions cannot establish intersubjective reference. In other words, according to both the textbook and analytic empiricist interpretations, Humean semantics faces what I will call "the problem of intentional content" because of the non-intentional nature of impressions.

Humean semantic empiricism rests on the copy principle or Bennetian, modern "translations" of it. But the Humean mind contains many intra-ideational processes, those of imagination or, simply, "cognition." The second challenge to semantic empiricism arises from the role of cognitive processes for the meaning of ideas. For the remainder of this section, I will briefly review some of these processes and their role, and then analyze two critical interpretations of semantic empiricism based in processes unique to ideas. On these grounds, I will articulate the "problem of complex structure" for semantic empiricism.

According to Hume, ideas combine naturally on the basis of three principles of association – resemblance, spatio-temporal contiguity, and causation (T 1.1.4.1; SBN 10). These laws have a crucial role in the formation of complex ideas, structured cognitive representations. As a result, they are fundamental for semantics. Hume's explanation of "abstract ideas," concepts that refer to classes of entities, also invokes unique ideational processes. For Hume, ideas themselves are not abstract even though they have a general reference. Neither are abstract ideas reducible to any specific copied token idea. General reference is based in the mind's propensity to revive particular ideas on the basis of their resemblance to some token, exemplar idea that, in turn, is elicited by a word associated with it. Because of the phenomenon of "revival," Hume's explanation involves a process additional to resemblance-based association, a mental "habit" or "custom."[5] Hume's explanation of the identification of resembling (or otherwise related) ideas offers a final illustration of the importance of extra-sensory, cognitive processes for meaning. For Hume, identity requires an uninterrupted and invariable object, whereas impressions (and their exact copies) are never uninterrupted or without variation. As a result, the reference of ideas to persistent objects in which qualities "inhere" must also be in part explained by extra-sensory factors.[6]

The above shows that Hume employs many extra-sensory factors to account for what I will call "complex idea structure." Garrett's work illustrates how these lead to a non-empiricist interpretation of Hume's semantics. First, Garrett restricts the explanatory scope of the Copy Principle for semantics. It is not an "*a priori*" constraint on meaningful ideas; only "some" of the perceptions in its range concern the basis of thought (2015: 46).[7] Second, Garrett maintains that the meaning of ideas includes "relations" that by habit or custom have been "attributed to" them (2015: 57). These relations are based in the "mental transitions" that ideas partake in and, for Garrett, across psychological processes from reasoning through affect to volition. Garrett refers to the web of relations as ideas' "conceptual role" (ibid.) or, alternatively, their "causal–functional" role (2015: 72–73). For Garrett, the meaning of an idea is its conceptual or causal–functional role in the mental economy of an agent. As a result, Hume's semantics is an (intra-mental) use-based, holistic one.

Meaning holism diminishes the semantic function of the senses. Through causal-copying, ideas have a relation to impressions; through intra-ideational processes, ideas partake in many further relations. Since relations underwrite meaning, for holists, the presence of additional relations entails that ideas' meaning cannot be merely copied from impressions. By focusing on the effect of relations on ideas' complex structure, the challenge from Garrett's holistic interpretation can be expressed in precise Humean terms. Even though both ideas and impressions have (also) complex structure, the structure of the former is richer than that of the latter. Thus, the structure of complex ideas cannot be copied from the structure of impressions.

The holist's challenge to meaning empiricism runs deeper than the presence of additional structure among ideas. Holism undermines the special role that semantic empiricism confers on impressions. The analytic empiricist interpretation shows this role. It categorizes Hume's theory in a referential tradition of semantics. Some intentional relation to an extra-ideational (or extra-linguistic) reality is fundamental to meaning. Even though analytic empiricists think that copying fails to impart intentional content to ideas (and reference for language), impressions still have the role of contributing the extra-ideational, object-involving component to meaning. A holistic theory of semantics, in contrast, distances meaning from associations with an empirical world. When the meaning of an idea is its conceptual or causal–functional role, idea-relations are fundamental to meaning. Consequently, intentional empirical relations lose their special role for meaning. Garrett's holistic interpretation inherits these features.[8] Thus, for holists, not only do ideas have more structure than impressions, but their structure is also different in kind from that of impressions.[9]

Expressing the holist's challenge as a difference in the nature of the complex structure across ideas and impressions allows for the broadening of the interpretative basis of the challenge to compositional approaches to meaning. According to compositional semantics, the meaning of a complex representation (e.g. sentence) is derivable from features internal to the representation (e.g. words). Meaning is a function of the constituents of a representation together with the rules of composition that govern the constituents' arrangements. Fodor (2003) expresses the crux of the compositionalist critique of Humean empiricist semantics.

Fodor argues for a difference in the rules of composition for impressions and ideas on the basis of a difference in the decomposition of complex representations of the two domains. Fodor holds that only some parts of complex ideas have meaning, whereas all parts of impressions have meaning. More specifically, the decomposition of impressions is governed by the "picture principle." According to it, "every part of a complex impression has its corresponding content whichever way the complex is carved up" (2003: 35). This principle applies to impressions because, for Fodor (ibid.), they are representations of a "photographic kind" such as images or pictures.[10] Ideas, in turn, have a "canonical decomposition" into "canonical constituents" (ibid.). Canonical constituents are "guaranteed to be contentful," unlike parts of complex ideas that derive from "artificial" decompositions (ibid.). The principle of decomposition for ideas is thus opposite to the picture principle in that parts of complex ideas have content "under some *but not all* of the ways of carving it up" (2003: 37; italics original). Since, for Fodor, the rules of composition reflect rules of decomposition, he concludes that the complex structure of ideas and impressions is different in kind. As a result, complex ideas cannot be copied from complex impressions.

Fodor and Garrett offer opposing interpretations of the semantics of ideas. The former bases meaning in internal ideational relations and the latter in trans-ideational, external relations. Yet both challenge meaning empiricism on grounds of the difference in the nature of structured content across ideas and impressions. Meaning empiricists must explain what role copied structure can have for complex ideas' meaning to overcome this challenge. This "problem of complex structure" together with the problem of intentional content form the problem-context for a reassessment of Hume's empiricist semantics.

Hume's theory of intentional content

Hume develops his account of sensory intentionality in the context of an explanation of our belief in the "existence of body" (T 1.4.2; SBN 187). In this section, I will argue that the sensory component in Hume's explanation resembles one of the constituent ideas of the belief in the existence of body, the "continu'd existence" of bodies or objects. When the Humean belief in bodies' existence is seen to concern the intentional framework of ideas, this resemblance entails a central role for copying in the explanation of the intentionality of ideas. I will start the section by explaining how a belief concerning bodies' existence relates to intentional awareness. After that, I will explain how, for Hume, senses give rise to intentional awareness through complex impressions whose objects have the qualities of "constancy" and "coherence." Finally, I will clarify the role of copying for the intentionality of ideas through the role that intentional sense-impressions have in creating ideas' objects with continu'd existence.

For Hume, belief is a vivid idea (T 1.3.7; SBN 96). Human nature has not left the vivid idea concerning the existence of mind-independent bodies to our "choice" (T 1.4.2.1; SBN 187). We do not reason ourselves to believe it but instead are caused to do so through the senses and imagination. Hume's analysis of the belief in the existence of bodies gives the exact *explanandum* for the causal explanation concerning processes of both of these domains.

For Hume, the belief in the existence of bodies consists of two intimately connected ideas: that objects have "continu'd and distinct existence" (T 1.4.2.2; SBN 188). According to the former, "continu'd existence," perceptual objects continue to exist even while they are not being perceived. "Distinct existence," in turn, has two dimensions, the "situation" and "relation" of perceptual objects. From the perspective of their situation, distinctness refers to objects' "external position" (ibid.). Perceptual objects are situated not "in" the mind but external to it. From the perspective of their relation, "distinctness" refers to objects' independence in "existence and operation" (ibid.). Perceptual objects' existence defining properties and their change, movement, and causal interactions are not related to but are independent of us. Thus, "distinct existence" means that perceptual objects exist external to and independent of perception.

Hume's analysis of the idea of bodies' existence should be understood in experiential terms since belief–ideas are vivid mental contents. "Continu'd existence" refers to perceptual objects' presence in consciousness even when the objects are not strictly speaking present to the senses. Hume illustrates this experience in circumstances such as "turning about of our head" and "shutting of our eyes" (T 1.4.2.21; SBN 198). During these, objects are not strictly speaking perceived yet they have in experience what enactivist philosophers of perception (Noë 2004) call "presence in/as absence." Perceptual objects enjoy a robust phenomenological "presence" under many circumstances in which our body movements, including the movements and changes in our sensory systems, result in objects going in and out of our "view," in objects being "absent." Hume's "distinct existence," in turn, refers to the nature of perceptual consciousness when objects are strictly speaking perceived. Such "factual presence" involves perceptual objects' external location relative to our vantage point. It also concerns the experienced independence of perceptual objects' inherent and relational, causal properties from our contributions and activities. When objects are factually present, they appear both external to us and independent from us in their properties.

The structure of object-involving, intentional awareness needs to be characterized by both factual presence and presence in absence. This holds even if these two types are not understood dichotomously but as a matter of degree. Both are experientially real. If this is correct, Hume's twofold analysis of the belief in bodies' existence corresponds with the nature of intentional awareness. His generic vivid idea of bodies' existence refers simply to the intentional framework characteristic of (some) ideas.

Although Hume analyzes bodies' existence in terms of distinctness and continuity, he maintains that the two are "intimately connected" (T 1.4.2.2; SBN 188). This connection is causal: the "principle" of continu'd existence is "prior" to distinct existence and "produces the latter principle" (T 1.4.2.23; SBN 199). This supposition about causal priority founds Hume's explanatory strategy for intentionality. Hume explains objects' distinct existence through their continued existence. Before explaining the role of the senses in this explanatory scheme, Hume's general view of the intentionality of perceptions needs to be addressed.

Hume is well known for denying the inherent representational power of perceptions: "the reference of the idea to an object [is] an extraneous denomination, of which in itself it bears no mark or character" (T 1.1.7.6; SBN 20). In keeping with this, Hume argues against both the ability of the senses to "give rise" to continued existence (T 1.4.2.3; SBN 188) and to "offer their impressions" as independent and external to us (T 1.4.2.4; SBN 189). Correspondingly, he describes impressions at times as "internal and perishing existences" (T 1.4.2.15; SBN 194). Given all this, the causal explanation of the existence of intentional objects of ideas cannot be directly based in the copying of either continuously or distinctly existing objects of sense perception. Yet a denial of inherent intentionality does not preclude an explanation of intentionality. Just the opposite is the case.

Hume adds a caveat to his critical analysis of inherently intentional impressions. For him, it is a "single" perception that "can never give us the least intimation of any thing beyond" (T 1.4.2.4; SBN 194). More specifically, the content of a single perception cannot have an object that exists external to and independent of perception. It goes without saying that continued existence can never arise from a single impression, either. Continued existence requires minimally a sequence of objects. It is precisely to sequences that Hume turns in his explanation of the continued existence of objects of perception.

According to Hume, some complex impressions have the qualities of "coherence of change" and "constancy" (T 1.4.2.20; SBN 195). By the quality of "constancy," Hume means the qualitative uniformity in (some) objects of sense after interruptions such as those resulting from turning one's head. Mountains, houses, and trees, as well as his bed, table, and books, are for Hume examples of sensory objects that appear qualitatively "constant" across interruptions in sensing or sensory stimulation (T 1.4.2.18; SBN 194). Hume illustrates the coherence of change, in turn, through the recurring sequence characteristic of the fire burning in his chamber (T 1.4.2.19; SBN 195). After perceiving it after an hour's absence from his chamber, the fire does not resemble its previously noted condition yet exemplifies "a like alteration produc'd in a like time" (ibid.). "Coherence of change" refers then to resembling patterns of change.

Although Hume does not underscore it, both constancy and coherence of change in impressions concern change patterns. One is minimal and the other is not. The commonality between the two is not only order but robust change invariance. Both orders remain stable across a range of circumstances. In other words, Hume explains a certain kind of sensory order, the stability of sensory objects, on the basis of what I will call "change invariance" in (the qualities relevant for such) objects. This account of the origins of intentionality supports an empiricist explanation of ideas that Hume describes as follows:

> The notion of their [impressions] distinct and continu'd existence must arise from a concurrence of some of their qualities with the qualities of the imagination; and since this notion does not extend to all of them, it must arise from certain qualities peculiar to some impressions. 'Twill therefore be easy for us to discover these qualities by a

comparison of the impressions to which we attribute a distinct and continu'd existence with those which we regard as internal and perishing.

(T 1.4.2.15; SBN 194)

The passage shows that Hume's explanation of intentionality involves copying, but what is copied is not the intentional framework as such, objects of perception with distinct and continued existence. Instead, only the impressions that possess qualities that distinguish them from "internal and perishing" impressions constitute the copy-base. These are the change invariant ones, complex impressions with the qualities of constancy and coherence. The fact that Hume believes these qualities are copied is indicated by his use of the concept of "concurrence." It indicates both agreement and causal cooperation between the realms of impressions and ideas. As a result, for Hume, because change-invariant complex sense impressions have qualities resembling those that imbue complex ideas' objects with continued existence, a copy-based explanation applies to the latter. When we add to this scheme Hume's contention that continu'd existence causes distinct existence, we must conclude that the qualities of complex impressions comprising invariant ordered change explain ideas' intentional framework.[11]

Solutions to the problems of meaning empiricism

Hume's semantic empiricism aims to explain ideas' aboutness and linguistic representations reference through an account of sensory aboutness. Its central hypothesis is that intentional objects of certain complex sensory events are copied to the cognitive realm. In this section, I will use the account to solve the two problems facing Hume's semantic empiricism, the problem of intentional content and the problem of complex structure.

When Hume's semantic empiricism is seen to concern the copying of complex impressions with the qualities of constancy and coherence of change, copying becomes sufficient for relating understanding with what Bennett calls the "objective realm." Hume's semantic empiricism solves the problem of intentional content directly because the objects of some complex sense impressions are intentional. These present public and/or intersubjective criteria for the meaning of ideas and linguistic representations.

The reassessment of Hume's semantic empiricism helps identify the mistakes in both the analytic empiricist and textbook interpretation of Hume. Bennett (1971: 225, 2002: 99) describes Hume's actual meaning empiricism in terms of the universal version of the Copy Principle, according to which simple ideas are copied from simple impressions. This version fits Bennett's critique concerning the intentional content of ideas. For Hume, all simple perceptions are non-intentional states. Yet Bennett ignores the fact that, for Hume, copying also concerns complex perceptions, including ones with the qualities that underwrite "objective" or intentional ideas. This oversight led directly to a meaning empiricism that cannot connect "understanding" with an inter-subjectively accessible objective reality. In short, the universal version of copying leaves Humean semantic empiricism with the problem of intentional content. Not surprisingly, the subjectivity concerns that, for example, Lycan's textbook account associates with Hume's imagistic theory of meaning depend on the targets of copying. If words stand for ideas and ideas, in turn, are images copied from impressions, ideas are subjective only to the extent that the impressions targeted by copying are subjective. Alternatively, only if all copied impressions are without differences in objective, intentional content, subjectivity concerns follow for an imagistic theory of meaning. According to the proposed interpretation, Humean impressions differ in intentional content. Hence, they also differ in terms of subjectivity.

The proposed empiricist interpretation also entails a reassessment of the rationale behind the analytic meaning empiricist and related, twentieth-century logical positivist interpretation of Hume. These emphasize Hume's reverse use of copying. In doing so, they invariably take empirical constructs analogous to Hume's simple impressions as the foundation of meaning. When their Hume investigates the "empirical cash value" of words, he is seen to turn to simple impressions' analogues. The proposed interpretation turns to complex impressions and their structuring principles instead. That Hume, famously, can "find" no impression of "necessary connection," "substance," or "self" shows that complex impressions, for him, are not structured through these relations. When exploring the possible sensory causes of the belief in the existence of mind-independent objects or "bodies" – the intentional framework of perceptions – Hume argues explicitly that impressions are not structured by causation (T 1.4.2.4; SBN 189), a substance-like container framework (T 1.4.2.13; SBN 192–193), or non-ownership (T 1.4.2.5– 6; SBN 189–190). Hume's reverse use of copying, thus, mirrors if not "operationalizes" his empirical hypothesis about the sensory origins of intentionality based (only) in change invariant perceptions.

The holist challenge concerns the additional, including unique structure among complex ideas. The domain of ideas has unique associative and other processes so it has structure novel to that of impressions. But this does not constitute an insuperable problem for Hume's meaning empiricism. Its objective is not to account for all sources or "aspects" of meaning but, through complex impression copies that are change invariant, to indicate which ideas are about an extra-ideational reality.[12] To accomplish this, both perceptual domains must have entities with intentional content – even if both also include other types of content. Thus, the two domains (also) have complex representations that agree in structure.

The proposed reassessment of Hume's semantic empiricism allows for the identification of the mistake in the holistic interpretation. Hume explains the "standard" features of intentional objects – their independence from and external situation to us – on the basis of their continued existence. Continued existence is, though, not an explanatory primitive. Consciousness is regularly interrupted and perceptual objects are thus "perishing" or discontinuous. Yet, in some cases, their presence across "gaps" or "absences" is still a distinct phenomenological fact. Hume turns to change invariant patterns in the senses to explain this phenomenon. The same principle(s) also explain discontinuity.

The further from the senses processing occurs, the more opportunities for and occasions of perceptual objects' "absence" there exist. In realm(s) of "unconstrained," non-sensory mentation, the continu'd existence of perceptual objects becomes questionable because change invariance becomes vulnerable. According to Hume's meaning empiricism, this entails that the independent and external existence of perceptual objects also becomes doubtful. In other words, the more ideas' meaning revolves around non-sensory relations, the less likely it is that the ideas are intentional. Garrett's holistic interpretation is vulnerable to this consequence. According to Garrett, the meaning of ideas consists in their use in a "wide" intra-psychological context comprised of reasoning, affect, and volition. But such ideas threaten to become non-intentional states. As a result, the property of intentionality of mental states used in "wide" processing cannot be based in their wide functional roles but their relationship to the senses, in copying.

Despite its departure from standard meaning holism, Hume's semantic empiricism shares a feature with it. For Hume, aboutness or intentional meaning is a function of change, not just "constant" or uniform reference. Sensory objects must function in specific law-like ways for them to become intentional objects. But since Hume offers no constraints on what forms such change patterns may take, intentional objects can (only) be "defined" by the roles they play in functions concerning patterns of change. Thus, Hume's account of intentionality is a functional one. Furthermore, it is holistic. Ordered change profiles concern sequences of impressions and, for many kinds of objects, complex qualitative changes in them. As a result, Hume's semantics must be holistic. Yet his holism is of a narrow, sense-based kind.

The challenge against meaning empiricism concerning the unique structure of ideas also comes in a compositional version. According to Fodor's picture principle, any part of a meaningful complex impression is meaningful, whereas the opposite is true for ideas. Thus, for Fodor, complex impressions have no genuine structure because they have no constituent structure.

According to the proposed interpretation, Fodor's picture principle cannot be true for intentional complex impressions. Hume's account of the continu'd existence of objects of some impressions does not entail that all parts of such impression sequences are intentional. That, for Hume, no "singular" impression can be about anything already shows that. Singular impressions are parts of intentional complex impressions without themselves being intentional. Thus, Fodor's picture principle does not apply to impressions when meaning concerns representations' ability to be *of* this or that.

The above counter-argument, however, runs the risk of reducing to triviality. The worry is that none of the parts of Hume's intentional impressions are meaningful. In other words, Fodor's argument would be unsound, but only because Hume's semantic empiricism is not compositional at all. An adequate counter-argument to Fodor's must show that intentional complex impressions do have constituent structure that satisfies his necessary condition for idea-like representations, a canonical decomposition where some, but not all, parts are intentional.

Hume's approach to intentional impressions is compositional. Hume illustrates constancy in terms of the "sun or ocean returning" after an interruption in sensing "with like parts and order" (T 1.4.2.24; SBN 199). Yet, it is not clear from Hume's writings what the sensory constituents are on the basis of which change-invariance takes place. For example, "like parts and order" can characterize a similarity "metric" in any sensory modality or even sub-modalities. As a result, "likeness" or resemblance structures "naturally" not only the imagination (T 1.1.4.2; SBN 11) but also the senses, for Hume, yet he leaves open what the innate sensory similarity is in the case of complex, intentional perceptions. The same applies to the sense-perception of coherent change.

Although Hume's silence on the compositional basis of intentional sensory objects makes his account inadequate for theoretical purposes, the detail he offers is sufficient to refute Fodor's argument. Any version of compositionality that satisfies Hume's constraint concerning the non-intentionality of "singular" impressions suffices. For example, let us assume that colors are involved in learning through experience about the law-like change of Hume's fire. To satisfy Hume's constraint, as a constituent of the intentional experience of fire, color itself must involve a law-like change pattern. In other words, there must be invariant change in the color of fire (under changes in color-relevant circumstances). Furthermore, since lawful color change is a non-singular perception and, hence, a complex impression, it is consistent with Hume's account that such object-color is itself an intentional sense experience. Under this scenario, color is one of the constituents of the intentional object, fire, while the change invariant color sequence is itself an intentional experience. In this case, an intentional complex impression has intentional constituents. This explanation sketch applies *mutatis mutandis* to other qualitative dimensions of sensory variation that have a role in the causal origins of intentional objects.

The proposed reassessment of Hume's meaning empiricism allows us not only to solve Fodor's problem but also to explain Fodor's mistake. According to Fodor, the picture principle applies to impressions simply because Humean impressions are picture-like. But even if some Humean impressions are picture-like or more generally, imagistic, intentional complex

impressions are not. Moving pictures or moving images are better metaphors because the meaning of intentional impressions emerges from dynamic elements.[13]

There is more to Fodor's mistake. According to an alternative formulation of the picture
principle, Fodor maintains that photographs can be carved up spatially in any way possible and
"each of the resulting bits is a photograph too" (2003: 35). Were this true, the photographic
medium would be one example of Putnam's "magical theories of reference" (1981: Ch. 1). The
medium would reach out to its intended objects on its own. Furthermore, for Fodor, the magic
of this inherently intentional representational system would have to extend to all of its possible
parts. Apart from sheer magic, the only way to understand such a medium is by defining intentionality through resemblance. Not surprisingly, this is another feature of the textbook image
of Hume's semantics (e.g. Stainton 1996: 102). But Hume does not base intentionality in an
inherently intentional representational medium nor analyze it through resemblance. He bases it
in law-like change patterns and the resulting continuity of perceptual objects instead.

Concluding remarks

I have argued that the copy-based explanation of ideas' intentionality through specific complex impressions comprises the empiricism of Hume's semantics. This argument about "isms" is
underwritten by a robust characterization of empiricism as an "externalist" form of intelligibility
(Godfrey-Smith 1996). The system of the senses is external to that of the internal system of cognitions or ideas. Hume explains the semantic property of intentionality of the internal system
externally. This does not entail that other semantically relevant features of ideas are not based in
external sensory factors. Simple ideas, for example, are copied from impressions. But intentional
complex impressions are more significant for the semantics of ideas than simple impressions,
especially in light of Hume's empiricist epistemology. Because all ideas are composed of simple
ideas, simple ideas cannot be used to distinguish empirically warranted complex ideas from constructed, fictional ones. Intentional complex ideas copied from the senses, in turn, can. Thus, the
proposed reassessment of Hume's semantic empiricism leads to a more coherent understanding
of his philosophy, how his empiricist epistemology and semantics fit together.

The argument about "isms" is also based on coherence in the history of philosophy. Thinking
about Hume's semantics in the proposed manner creates historical continuity while pointing at
relevant differences. At least after Quine, meaning empiricism has been customarily associated
with holism. But Quine's views have inspired various forms of anti-empiricism. These include
network theories of meaning with theory-laden observations and referential or ontological
relativisms with coherentist epistemologies. Hume's meaning holism is different and fits his
empiricist epistemology.

Similar to current meaning holism, according to which reference is mediated by laws concerning the entities referenced, Hume denies a direct association between a representation and
its referent. Referenced intentional objects are constructed out of patterns of change so empirical objects are, for Hume too, based in law-like generalizations. Yet Hume's semantically relevant laws characterize a pan-human sense-perceptual mechanism for intentionality. Theoretical
laws and associated beliefs cannot influence Humean vivid beliefs concerning specifically external, mind-independent objects. These are copied from purely empirical objects. Given that these
objects are based in patterns of change, Hume's account still leaves room for variation across
individuals and cultures. Yet, such differences are a matter of experience and inherited habits,
respectively, not distinctions in the natural, sensory criteria of object-hood. Quinean ontological
relativity or insuperable referential ambiguities are not a consequence of "Humean" relativity.
Thus and despite their holistic nature, Hume's sensory criteria for intentional objects offer a

naturalistic analytic framework for meaning. Or at least they would, had Hume hypothesized about the compositional bases of intentional objects, the constituents in terms of which impression sequences exemplify constancy and coherent change. But even without such detail, Hume's semantics combines both holistic and compositional features within empiricism to explain our ability to connect through ideas with an external empirical reality.

Notes

1 The details of this image are based in three popular textbooks in philosophy of language: Alston (1964), Stainton (1996), and Lycan (2008).
2 Garrett (2015) also associates the (analytic) meaning empiricist interpretation to logical positivists and empiricists of the twentieth century. For Garrett, it is "natural" for proponents of these two movements to see the Copy Principle and the "accompanying directive to reject purported ideas" that cannot be traced to impressions as a "precursor to a method of logical analysis revealing relations to experience" (2015:329–330).
3 Most Hume scholars deny intentional content for Humean impressions. For example, Landy maintains that the "price of being a *strict* Humean" is "denying the sense in talk of an external world" because "impressions have no intentional content" (2006:137; italics original). Ott (2006: 242) argues that it is "anachronistic to import" reference to Hume's views on linguistic meaning and that Hume is "silent on the topic of reference." Ott's argument is premised on an indicator account of Humean "signification," the term Hume uses for the relationship between words and ideas, and his contention that the Copy Principle is "not concerned in the 1st instance with meaning" (248). These premises imply that impressions are non-intentional because, if they were intentional states, copying would automatically be concerned with what ideas are about and, indirectly, with terms' reference.
4 Alston (1964: 66, fn. 3) argues similarly that a "private language" is quite conceivable for Hume because meaning for him is a matter of intra-mental association. As a result, the conditions of words having meaning do not out of necessity coincide with meaning being publicly sharable.
5 See Garrett (2015: 52–57) for an account of the role(s) of custom in reviving individual tokens in the reference class of abstract ideas, what Hume describes also as individual tokens being "present in power" instead of present "in fact" to the mind (T 1.1.7.7); SBN 20. Price (1953) interprets "presence in power" as a robust conscious phenomenon that "as it were colours the image which is 'present in fact'" (1953: 274). For Price and Price's Hume, a person's capacity to revive token images in the reference class of a general idea imparts a "characteristic feel" to the image which is present "in fact" at any given occasion of verbal association so that the present image actually "feels somewhat different" on the basis of the additional images that a person has "the capacity to produce" (ibid.).
6 See Loeb (2002: 139–172) for Hume's explanation of the propensity to ascribe identity to related objects.
7 Although Garrett does not explain which specific perceptions in the range of the Copy Principle concern the basis of thought, on the grounds of Garrett's exclusive focus on simple impressions in the articulation of Hume's Copy Principle (1997: Ch. 2), simple impressions most likely comprise Garrett's "some" impressions that form the basis of thought for Hume.
8 Garrett interprets Hume's account of intentionality in holistic terms. According to him, for Hume, "perceptions represent at least partly in virtue of the kinds of causal or functional roles they come to play within the mind" (2015: 72). Garrett distinguishes this from a copy-based account according to which "intentionality of an idea consists in its representing something else simply in virtue of being a copy" (ibid.). Yet, Garrett also thinks that the two accounts coincide. This is because ideas "share all or nearly all features" with the impressions from which they are copied (ibid.). Although Garrett is not altogether clear on what all the two types of mental representations share, on the basis of his analysis of Hume's use of the term "representation" in other, non-mental contexts, Garrett concludes that a representing item "is taking on a significant part of a causal or functional role of what it is said to be represented" (2015:73). Schafer (2015) interprets Garrett (and especially Garrett 2006) to mean that Hume rests representation on functional similarities between ideas and the things they represent, such as impressions. If this were true, a copy-based and a functional role account of aboutness could coincide, but only if the domain of ideas and that of impressions share causal-functional features. But, since for Hume, complex ideas have additional structure to that of impressions, and because the functioning of

cognition is more complex than that of the senses, the two domains cannot be functionally similar. As a consequence, Garrett's interpretation of Hume's views on intentionality cannot overcome the difference in the role of intentionality in holistic and empiricist accounts of the semantics of ideas.

9   Garrett's views on the nature of ideas' relations demonstrate this. For him, "conceptual role" comprises inferential and causal-functional relations (2015: 57; 72–79). Yet Humean complex impressions are not structured by either inferential or causal relations, so the complex structure of impressions must be different in kind from that of ideas for Garrett.

10 Correspondingly, Fodor offers several alternative formulations of the principle such as "parts of a photograph of X are photographs of parts of X and this is true however you slice it" (2003: 35) and "parts of an image are images however the image is decomposed" (2003: 37).

11 If ideas' objects are taken as the (terminological) standard for aboutness or "object-directedness," Hume's explanation can be described as one where the "quasi-continuity" of objects of sense entails their "quasi-distinctness" which together through copying create similar objects for ideas (that are then processed further by additional laws and habits of imagination to reach intentional objects to which "identity" is applicable across occasions of perception). Cf. Loeb 2002: 162–172.

12 More specifically, the Humean mind tracks law-like change of ideas' objects to distinguish fact from fiction. Senses are put to use in this through an experiential indicator – the copied "feel" of vivacity – that tracks the stability of perceptual, idea-objects through their invariant change patterns. Stability of intentional objects emerges from such "vivacious" or stable change. See Seppalainen and Coventry (2012).

13 Similarly, Price points out (even if in a different and narrower context than this, one concerning the semantics of abstract ideas; see fn. 5 above) that Humean idea-images that are "present in power" include "changing or cinematographic" ones (1953: 273).

References

Alston, W. P. (1964) *Philosophy of Language*, Englewood Cliffs: Prentice Hall.

Bennett, J. (1971) *Locke, Berkeley, Hume: Central Themes*, London: Oxford University Press.

———. (2001) *Learning from Six Philosophers*, vol 2, New York: Oxford University Press.

———. (2002) "Empiricism about Meanings," in P. Millican (ed.), *Reading Hume on Human Understanding*, New York: Oxford University Press, pp. 97–106.

Fodor, J. (2003) *Hume Variations*, New York: Oxford University Press.

Garrett, D. (1997) *Cognition and Commitment in Hume's Philosophy*, New York: Oxford University Press.

———. (2006) "Hume's Naturalistic Theory of Representation," *Synthese* 152: 301–319.

———. (2015) *Hume*, London and New York: Routledge.

Godfrey-Smith, P. (1996) *Complexity and the Function of Mind in Nature*, Cambridge: Cambridge University Press.

Landy, D. (2006) "Hume's Impression/Idea Distinction," *Hume Studies* 32(1): 119–140.

Loeb, L. E. (2002) *Stability and Justification in Hume's Treatise*, New York: Oxford University Press.

Lycan, W. (2008) *Philosophy of Language: A Contemporary Introduction*, 2nd ed, New York: Routledge.

Noë, A. (2004) *Action in Perception*, Cambridge, MA: MIT Press.

Ott, W. (2006) "Hume on Meaning," *Hume Studies* 32(1): 233–252.

Price, H. H. (1953) *Thinking and Experience*, Cambridge, MA: Harvard University Press.

———. (1965) "The Permanent Significance of Hume's Philosophy," in N. Sesonske and A. Fleming (eds.), *Human Understanding: Studies in the Philosophy of David Hume*, Belmont, CA: Wadsworth Publishing, pp. 5–33.

Putnam, H. (1981) *Reason, Truth and History*, Cambridge: Cambridge University Press.

Schafer, K. (2015) "Hume's Unified Theory of Mental Representation," *European Journal of Philosophy* 23: 978–1005.

Seppalainen, T. and A. Coventry (2012) "Hume's Empiricist Inner Epistemology: A Reassessment of the Copy-Principle," in A. Bailey and D. O'Brien (eds.), *The Continuum Companion to Hume*, London: Continuum.

Stainton, R. J. (1996) *Philosophical Perspectives on Language*, Peterborough, ON and Canada: Broadview Press.

33

HUME'S LEGACY

A Cognitive Science Perspective

Mark Collier

Introduction

Hume's naturalistic approach to the study of human beings is a central part of his philosophical project (Stroud 1977; Garrett 1997). But the naturalist interpretation gives rise to an important challenge: how can we evaluate the status of Hume's positive account? Hume offers a series of empirical claims about why we think, feel, and act as we do. In order to determine the merits of these proposals, then, we must assess them in light of our best available theories and evidence from cognitive science.

How well does Hume's experimental philosophy fare when put to this test? Does it teach us anything of lasting importance? Some naturalist interpreters are pessimistic about its prospects. Consider the stance of Barry Stroud, for example, who refuses to endorse any of Hume's specific proposals:

> [If Hume's] contributions are to be judged as part of the empirical science of man ...
> then his 'results' will appear ludicrously inadequate, and there will be no reason to take
> him seriously.
>
> (Stroud 1977: 223)

This type of disparaging assessment is unfortunate. There is in fact a good deal of support for many of Hume's empirical claims about the workings of the mind. Several of his hypotheses have contemporary defenders in cognitive science; others can guide future research in the field.

The goal of this chapter is to examine the main proposals of Hume's experimental philosophy from a cognitive science perspective. It assesses the current status of Hume's proposals concerning the origin of ideas (particular and general), the development of our fundamental beliefs about the world (causes, objects, and gods/spirits), the operations of the emotions, the psychological prerequisites of cooperation, and the natural foundations of moral and aesthetic judgment.

Hume offers a wide-ranging account of the principles human nature, and as a result, this examination is broadly interdisciplinary and draws from every corner of cognitive science, including connectionist simulations of cognitive development, exemplar models of classification and memory, associative theories of contingency learning, appraisal theories of emotion, moral and cultural psychology, experimental game theory and neuroeconomics, the cognitive science of religion, and experimental aesthetics.

Concept empiricism

Hume attempts to explain how the mind is furnished with particular ideas. His central hypothesis is that complex ideas arise automatically from associative connections between sensory primitives. The laws of association function as "principles of union or cohesion among our simple ideas," as he puts it, and "supply the place of that inseparable connexion, by which they become united in the imagination" (T 1.1.4.6; SBN 12). Just as Newton discovered the gravitational attraction that governs the motions of celestial bodies, so Hume claims to have located the "gentle force" or mental dynamics that binds together the fluctuating contents of sensation (T 1.1.4.1; SBN 10; cf. T 1.1.4.7; SBN 13).

Connectionist models of concept acquisition allow us to develop Hume's proposal further by providing greater precision about the nature of associative learning.

> Connectionism can be regarded as the outcome of returning to the original vision of the associationists, adopting their powerful idea that contiguities breed connections, and applying that idea with an unprecedented degree of sophistication.
>
> (Bechtel and Abrahamsen 1991: 102)

Hume's classical version of associationism postulates that mental contents are naturally related in memory when they co-occur or resemble one another, but he does not attempt to explain the mechanisms that underwrite these connections. Neural networks fill this explanatory gap: connection strengths between processing units are adjusted over time in accordance with general-purpose learning rules.

Consider a simple connectionist model of associative learning: the Pattern Associator (Rumelhart, McClelland et al., 1986: 34). Its architecture consists of two layers of units connected to each other through weighted connections. Suppose the network's task is to associate the sight and smell of a rose. Each pattern of activation consists of a vector of four visual and olfactory sensory dimensions. Associative learning in pattern associators is governed by an unsupervised algorithm, known as Hebb's Rule, which gradually changes connection weights according to the inner product or similarity between input patterns. We can express this type of correlation learning in terms of a mathematical equation (Elman, Bates et al., 1996: 57).

When a pattern associator is presented with visual and auditory images of a rose, connections between units in the weight matrix are automatically adjusted to capture pair-wise regularities between sensory features. After training, each sensory pattern will automatically recall the other.

ΔWij = n • Ai • Aj

ΔWij = memory trace

n = learning rate
Ai = activation of visual feature i
Aj = activation of olfactory feature j

Figure 33.1   Hebbian Learning

This toy model illustrates how complex ideas can be learned from experience; the associative learning principles remain the same, moreover, when we scale up the model and include more sophisticated competitive algorithms such as backpropagation (Rumelhart, McClelland and the PDP Research Group 1986: 37). But is there any reason to think that human concept acquisition actually works this way? Jesse Prinz points to recent evidence from behavioral and neuroscientific studies in support of the Humean proposal that concepts are perceptually based. The behavioral tests prompt subjects to answer questions about the sensible qualities of objects (e.g. "Are lemons yellow?" "Are cranberries tart?"). Response times indicate a significant processing cost for switching between perceptual dimensions, which suggests that these objects are mentally represented in terms of sensory modalities. Neuroimaging studies provide further support for this account by revealing that sensory areas in the brain become active when we reflect on concepts (Prinz 2016: 779; cf. Prinz 2002: 127–132).

This research does not provide conclusive evidence, of course, that complex ideas are learned from experience rather than innately specified. More work is obviously required to settle the longstanding controversy over the origin of ideas. But these recent studies do show that the Humean approach to concept acquisition remains a "live theoretical option" embraced by a number of cognitive scientists (Prinz 2016; 781; cf. Prinz 2006: 111).

General ideas

Hume attempts to settle the early modern debate about whether categories, such as DOG, are mentally represented in terms of abstract ideas (Locke) or particular exemplars (Berkeley). The exemplar approach was traditionally criticized on the grounds that finite minds could not possibly represent, at one and the same time, a vast store of category members. But Hume demonstrates how the principles of association offer a rapid, parallel account of search and retrieval in memory. A category such as DOG is stored as a vast network of exemplars, according to Hume, connected by the perceptual similarity of their component features. We do not consciously entertain each of these items, since our attention span is quite limited; nevertheless, when we speak or think in general terms, these instances are activated at the level of habit, "as if they were actually present" in our awareness (EHU 12.20 n34; SBN 158n).

Contemporary exemplar theory provides a good deal of support for the plausibility of Hume's theory of general ideas. Concepts are represented in memory, according to exemplar theorists, as separately stored instances, and recall occurs in massively parallel fashion: instances automatically resonate with similar items in memory in much the same way that tuning forks vibrate (Collier 2005a: 204). There is evidence from behavioral experiments, moreover, that concepts are stored in memory as fully determinate particulars. When people are asked to describe dogs in the Arctic, for example, they typically refer to thick fur, even though this property is not mentioned in other contexts (Prinz 2016: 780).

Cognitive scientists have also run experiments, however, that support the Lockean alternative. In a classic study, Posner and Keele (1968) asked participants to categorize a variety of training instances. They subsequently presented them with the previously unseen prototype of each category and measured their response times. The results showed that subjects were able to recognize the prototypical member as quickly as the training instances, which suggests that they must have extracted and stored an abstract summary of the category during the learning phase (Posner and Keele 1968: 354).

But exemplar models can also explain these behavioral results. Subjects compute the summed similarity of category members, according to exemplar theorists, yet they do so on the fly during search and retrieval. Exemplar theory also predicts that unseen prototypes, therefore, will be recognized as quickly as training instances (Medin and Schaffer 1978: 214). It is extremely difficult to tease apart these rival explanations of prototype and exemplar theory, then, since they make very similar predictions about reaction times in categorization tasks (Collier 2005a: 204).

It appears that we are left, in the end, with two adequate accounts of general ideas. On one side are prototype theorists who, like Locke, believe that the mind stores abstract ideas of the shared features of category members; on the other side are exemplar theorists who, like Hume and Berkeley, maintain that the mind only stores fully determinate instances. Thus, cognitive science has not vindicated Hume's attempt to resolve the controversy over abstract ideas. But it does force us to rethink our assessment of Hume's positive account of how categories are represented in memory. Hume scholars have typically shied away from embracing his proposal; Passmore refers, for example, to the "notorious inadequacy" of Hume's theory of general ideas (Passmore 1952: 40). But this evaluation now appears unfair: contemporary versions of Hume's exemplar account lie at the cutting edge of research in cognitive psychology.

Probabilistic and causal induction

Hume offers a naturalistic account of how we make inductive inferences. He distinguishes between probabilistic and causal induction. The former type of inferences are prompted by *inconstant* conjunctions and characterized by varying degrees of uncertainty; the latter are triggered by *constant* conjunctions and constituted by feelings of necessity.

Hume maintains that our everyday probabilistic inferences can be fully explained in terms of the principles of association. When we observe either *small samples* of As' followed by Bs, *mixed frequencies* (As usually followed by Bs, but sometimes by Cs), or *partial resemblances* (As resemble each other in some respects, but not others), these event-types are weakly united in our imaginations, and novel A-tokens will lead us to expect Bs with "proportionably" low levels of inductive confidence (T 1.3.12.25; SBN 142).

There is empirical support from modern contingency learning theory for Hume's associationist explanation of probabilistic inference. Psychologists have developed an experimental paradigm to study how people learn about relations between events in the world. Subjects are presented with information about the relative frequencies with which event types co-occur, and they are asked to estimate their degree of statistical relationship. These studies converge on the fact that participants typically make implicit probability estimates that are proportional to the observed co-variation in the data (Collier 2005b: 30).

These experimental results can be explained, moreover, in terms of associative learning. A standard explanation of contingency learning in psychology is the Rescorla–Wagner model, a competitive learning rule that updates associative weights on a trial-by-trial basis. The results can also be mechanistically explained in terms of adaptive neural network models, whose learning algorithm, the delta rule, is formally equivalent to the Rescorla–Wagner rule. There is a good deal of evidence for Hume's proposal, then, that everyday probabilistic inferences can be psychologically explained at the level of associations.

What about Hume's naturalistic account of causal induction? Does it also receive support from cognitive science research? Hume maintains that when we observe constant conjunctions between events, there is a point where we no longer wait for additional confirmation: our inductive confidence jumps to a sense of certainty (T 1.3.14.20; SBN 165). This empirical proposal has not, however, been vindicated experimentally (David Shanks, personal communication). Confidence levels in causal learning tasks develop incrementally, and researchers have not observed any asymptotic jumps to maximal levels of assurance.

Hume acknowledges the limits of associationism, moreover, in explanations of causal cognition. His official position is that human beings are capable of sophisticated casual reasoning, even if many of our everyday inferences depend entirely on custom and habit. Indeed, there is a principled reason why he must hold this view: if causal inferences were based on nothing but associations, we could never discover that this was the case (Collier 2007: 179–180). Scientists of human nature would observe a *second-order* constant conjunction: their fellow men make causal attributions whenever they observe constant conjunctions, but they would not be able to figure out *why* they do so. In order to understand the psychological mechanisms responsible for these attributions, Hume recognizes, experimental philosophers must rely on explicit methodological rules for judging causes and effects.

Contemporary debates about the nature of causal reasoning often pit associative against rule-based proposals. But we can now see that framing the debate in this way gives rise to a false dilemma. Hume teaches us that both associations and rules are required in order to provide a complete account of causal inference.

Object permanence

Hume attempts to understand why we naturally believe in object permanence. Belief in the continued existence of objects is difficult to explain, however, in terms of perceptually based learning from experience. Our sensory encounter with objects, after all, is permeated by gaps. Whenever we blink or turn our heads, our acquaintance with objects become discontinuous. We can represent these broken sequences in the following way:

AAABBB___DDDEEE

The crucial question is how we learn to fill in the gaps, as it were, and infer that the occluded qualities (CCC) continue to exist unperceived.

Hume suggests at one point that belief in the persistence of objects can be explained in terms of the *coherence* of gappy series with complete sequences stored in memory. But he abandons this suggestive proposal because he failed to see how associative principles could impose a greater order than is perceived (T 1.4.2.21; SBN 197).

Research in cognitive science suggests that Hume might have been premature, however, in abandoning this coherence account of our natural belief in object permanence. Connectionist researchers have simulated the cognitive development of young children's belief in enduring objects, and these computational models provide a good deal of support for the proposal that the mind automatically fills in perceptual gaps by incorporating the sensory input into previously learned event categories (Munakata et al., 1997). The networks are trained on data consisting of sequences involving objects that pass behind occluders. In the early stages of training, the network's hidden units do not reveal any representations of temporal persistence. But as the network learns to predict the re-emergence of objects, the gaps in perception gradually cancel each other out, and the network comes to infer the continued existence of unperceived objects.

Connectionist models of cognitive development provide an existence proof for Hume's conjecture that our natural belief in a persisting world of objects can be learned through the association of partial sequences with complete standards in memory. Hume's theory of imagination was simply missing an important ingredient: a computational process, known as vector-completion, that enables the mind to recognize and fill in partially degraded input (Collier 1999: 162–164; cf. Churchland 1995: 280).

Emotions

Hume embraces a "feeling theory" of emotions, in which affections are individuated according to their distinctive phenomenological properties (Collier 2011a: 4–7; Prinz 2016: 783). This view has been subjected to severe criticism. It is often said that feeling theory cannot be reconciled with core aspects of emotions, such as their intentionality and susceptibility to rational assessment (Pitcher 1965: 327–329). But these standard objections are not as strong as they initially appear. It is true that emotions are *about* states of affairs; but they can derive this intentionality from the thoughts that cause them; similarly, emotions can be rationally assessed according to the reasonableness of their eliciting beliefs.

The armchair dismissal of feeling theory has prevented scholars from appreciating the insights of Hume's naturalistic approach to the emotions. Consider Hume's account, for example, of the causal antecedents of self-conscious emotions. Hume maintains that indirect passions such as pride and humility depend on two main variables: *valence* (pleasant or painful) and *agency* (relation to ourselves or others). This proposal receives a good deal of support from quantitative studies in social psychology in which subjects are asked to rate the causes of emotions along multiple dimensions. The experimental results confirm Hume's hypothesis that we feel pride when we perceive ourselves as responsible for pleasant outcomes, and we feel shame when we view ourselves as the source of unpleasant ones (Collier 2011a: 9–10).

There is also empirical support for Hume's conjectures about the psychological principles involved in emotional processing. Hume sketches an account where affective and cognitive pathways "assist and forward each other" (T 2.1.4.4; SBN 283). Suppose that you admire a beautiful house in your possession. This object produces a pleasant sensation and simultaneously turns attention toward yourself. It is this "double impulse" of ideas and impressions, according to Hume, that generates feelings of pride (T 2.1.5.5; SBN 287). There is ample evidence from contemporary psychology for the main outlines of Hume's proposal: affective and cognitive mechanisms are both involved in emotional processing (Zajonc 1984; Lazarus 1984).

Recent work in social psychology also corroborates Hume's speculations about the behavioral effects of emotions. Hume maintains that pride is a useful emotion that gives us "confidence and assurance" in our projects (T 3.3.2.8, T 3.3.2.14; SBN 597, 600). This claim has been vindicated by recent experiments: participants induced to feel pride demonstrate greater tenacity and perseverance in performing difficult tasks (Williams and DeSteno 2008: 1010).

Hume's feeling theory fares quite well, then, when examined from the perspective of contemporary research on the emotions. Cognitive scientists have not been directly influenced by Hume's writings, but their experimental findings "confirm and extend aspects of his account" (Prinz 2016: 785).

Moral sentimentalism

Hume attempts to understand the natural foundations of moral judgment. Why do we approve of some character traits and condemn others? Hume maintains that our evaluations are based primarily on affections and sympathy; reason is delegated a secondary role. But how well does this descriptive proposal fare when evaluated from the perspective of contemporary moral psychology?

It is helpful to distinguish two components of Hume's moral sentimentalism. The first involves *immediate* affective responses to the perception of character traits; the second involves moral judgments *mediated* by our sympathy with the welfare of others. An example of the first type of appraisal is our affective response to the perception of uncleanliness (EPM 8.13; SBN 266–267). We do not consider the downstream tendencies of such traits; rather, we automatically feel a type of moral disapproval constituted by feelings of repugnance. An example of the second type of judgment is our condemnation of almsgiving, which is based on thoughts about the harmful unintended consequences of this practice (EPM 2.18; SBN 180).

There is evidence from contemporary moral psychology that a significant portion of our everyday moral evaluations occur immediately. Consider Jonathan Haidt's influential research on implicit affective responses to vignettes such as harmless incest relations between siblings. We tend to judge the actions as morally wrong even though we cannot provide any explicit justification for these attitudes. It appears that our commitments are based on disgust reactions that take place before we have time to reason (Haidt 2012: 38). According to Haidt, the influence of the affects on our moral evaluations is corroborated by a wide range of studies in social psychology, and this experimental evidence serves to support "Hume's perverse thesis: that moral emotions and intuitions drive moral reasoning, just as surely as a dog wags its tail" (Haidt 2001: 830; cf. Haidt 2012: 49).

Another important line of evidence in favor of Hume's proposals concerning our immediate moral appraisals comes from research in experimental philosophy conducted by Shaun Nichols. Nichols asks participants to judge whether it is morally wrong for guest at a dinner party to spit in a cup and drink it. This type of transgressive behavior violates etiquette conventions, but it does not harm others or violate their rights; one would expect, then, that it would be judged to be morally neutral. But this is not what Nichols found: a statistically significant number of participants appraised the spitting behavior as morally wrong (Nichols 2004: 22). It appears that our moral judgments in such cases depend on automatic feelings of disgust. Nichols concludes his paper by writing that "cognitive science is poised to build an empirical case that would vindicate Hume's speculation" that moral judgments depend on our natural emotional repertoire (Nichols 2004: 29).

What about the second class of moral judgments described by Hume, where evaluations are mediated by sympathy with the psychological states of others? One crucial piece of support for this proposal comes from recent work on psychopaths, who lack the ability to care about the pains or pleasures of others. Psychopaths typically fail to distinguish between morality and convention; killing innocent persons is wrong, like chewing gum in class, merely because authorities forbid it. Research on psychopathy and moral reasoning is still in early stages, but these initial studies provide preliminary support for the claim that emotional concern for the welfare of others is a necessary condition for the capacity to make reflective moral judgments (Nichols 2004: 81–82; cf. Kennett 2006).

Jesse Prinz has challenged the Humean thesis that sympathy is a causal precondition of reflective moral judgments (2011). One of Prinz's principal arguments is that the Humean proposal cannot handle cases where we ourselves are victims of crimes; it is rather strange to suppose, after all, that our moral condemnation is based on sympathy with ourselves (Prinz 2011: 219). But Hume's account can accommodate such cases. When we adopt the general point of view, we rely on cognitive pretense to bracket our beliefs about our personal interests and simulate the attitudes we would have if were properly situated spectators (Collier 2010: 260). In this counterfactual scenario, we *would* feel disapproval toward the perpetrators, and thus when we judge a crime against us to be morally wrong, we are reporting this hypothetical disinterested feeling.

Hume's moral sentimentalism has clearly influenced the direction of contemporary moral psychology. Researchers have extended his proposal that moral evaluations are based on immediate as well as sympathy-based affective responses. Nichols is surely to correct when he remarks that "were Hume alive today, this research would be high on his reading list" (Nichols 2004: 4).

Moral diversity

In his essay, "A Dialogue," Hume argues that our core values are based on shared principles of human nature and, consequently, that moral disagreements between cultures can be rationally resolved. According to Hume, skeptics exaggerate the extent of moral diversity: there is in fact a great deal of overlapping consensus in the codes of different societies (EPM, D 27; SBN 334; cf. EPM 1.10; SBN 174). There are notable discrepancies as well. But these divergences can be explained away, he proposes, in terms of differences in factual belief or material circumstances: dueling was widely approved in France, for example, but only because they mistakenly thought that it promotes social utility (EPM, D 34; SBN 335).

The Humean approach to moral disagreement has recently been challenged on empirical grounds (Brandt 1954; Doris and Plakias 2008). Hume might have successfully explained away traditional cases of moral diversity, such as the disputes about the permissibility of infanticide. But critics claim to have isolated novel instances of moral disagreement that are *ultimate* in the sense that they remain even when we control for cognitive or socio-economic differences.

Richard Brandt was a pioneer in this approach. He conducted ethnographic studies on Hopi Reservations in the 1940s' that, he claims, reveal a fundamental moral disagreement between the Hopi and other citizens of the United States. Brandt observes in particular that the Hopi are more permissive about inflicting suffering on animals, and he could not find any factual disagreements that could explain away these attitudes (Brandt 1954: 214–215). There are reasons to doubt, however, that Brandt has discovered a genuine ultimate disagreement. It is not clear that the Hopi unanimously approve of animal cruelty, and even if they did, it is not obvious that the rest of the country exhibits greater concern for animal welfare (Collier 2013: 46).

Contemporary researchers in empirically informed moral psychology claim to improve on Brandt's approach and locate an indisputable case of ultimate moral disagreement (Doris and Stich 2005: 132; Doris and Plakias 2008: 316). These researchers do not point to ethnographic cases, such as the Nitsilik Inuits or Montenegrins; rather, they cite instances of moral disagreement much closer to home: divergent attitudes, among populations in different geographical regions of the United States, toward violent responses to personal affront. When presented with vignettes in which one person insults or cuckolds another, for example, Southerners are twice as likely as Northerners to assert that violent reprisals are "extremely justified" (Nisbett and Cohen 1996: 31–32). This disagreement appears, moreover, to be fundamental. It cannot be explained away in terms of cognitive differences, since everyone clearly understands the described facts; nor can one cite socio-economic factors, because these populations live in similar material conditions (Doris and Stich 2005: 135–136; Doris and Plakias 2008: 319–320).

The Humean approach to moral diversity can, however, accommodate this ethnographic data. First, subjects in the different regions do appear to have conflicting factual beliefs; Southerners who ascribe to codes of honor are more likely to believe, for example, that one's reputation is at stake in the vignettes. Second, these populations presumably have different conceptions of the utility of these codes; Southerners typically regard them, unlike Northerners, as serving a useful deterrence function. Finally, the available evidence indicates that honor codes are in fact dangerous when removed from their pastoral roots; the main conclusion of Nisbett and Cohen (1996)'s research, after all, is that the culture of honor is the primary factor responsible for higher rates of homicide in the South (Collier 2013: 48–49).

The Humean approach to moral diversity withstands challenges, then, from contemporary critics who draw on the emerging field of cultural psychology. Skeptics have yet to locate a single clear case of moral diversity that resists explanation in terms of the adaptation of universal values to particular contexts.

Justice

Hume offers a natural history of justice. His central thesis is that our ancestors gradually learned that they would each be better off if they mutually restrained from appropriating one another's possessions and reciprocated in economic exchanges of surplus goods and services. He recognizes that these justice conventions are difficult to explain in large-scale societies, however, where agents must trust that strangers will cooperate. These implicit agreements become even more puzzling when one assumes, as Hume does, common knowledge about the human tendency to discount the future. Why should we expect that strategically rational agents would act on their interests, given that human beings are shortsighted creatures prone toward impulsivity? (T 3.2.7.2–3; SBN 535)

One of Hume's central insights is that this dilemma, like collective action problems more generally, cannot be resolved by appeal to rational considerations alone; emotional dispositions are necessary to explain how we manage to cooperate with each other in large-scale societies. Consider Hume's solution to what we might call the Chastity Assurance Game. How can we trust our partners to remain faithful? Given the human propensity to discount the future, we would have little assurance that our partners will do so, even when they acknowledge that fidelity promotes their long-term interests. One can only cooperate with partners, therefore, who are emotionally disposed to feel "repugnance" at the very idea of infidelity (T 3.2.12.5; SBN 572). These emotional sanctions occur during deliberation and thus would reduce the immediate temptation to cheat, even in contexts where one can reasonably expect to get away with defections (Frank 1988: 82). This suggests a similar account of the psychological foundations of justice conventions: we can trust others to reciprocate in temporally extended games only if they are emotionally disposed to feel repugnance to the very idea of injustice.

What evidence is there for this conjecture? Hume reasonably worries that his proposals might be dismissed as "chimerical speculation" (T 3.2.12.6; SBN 572). Hume's natural history of justice refers, after all, to events that occurred before any written records. Does this mean that the psychological prerequisites of cooperation are beyond our empirical reach? Fortunately, researchers in game theory and neuroeconomics have developed experimental paradigms that allow us to put these speculative claims to the test. Neural activity of participants is measured during games involving social exchange and collective action. These studies indicate that areas of the brain dedicated to processing negative hedonic rewards become active when players make uncooperative moves in economic games; this reward circuitry enables participants to cooperate in these games, moreover, by inhibiting their impulsive desire for immediate gratification (Collier 2011b: 142).

Previous commentators have emphasized the game-theoretic notions in Hume's account of convention (Hardin 2007). But this is not what is distinctive about Hume's approach. Hume demonstrates that considerations of strategic rationality alone are insufficient to account for social cooperation. Our ancestors could not have established justice conventions unless they were also creatures with a heart.

Religion

In *Natural History of Religion*, Hume attempts to understand the psychological foundations of the widespread belief in gods and spirits. His explanation comes in the form of "motivated irrationality" (Kail 2007: 199). We naturally believe in the existence of supernatural agents because doing so reduces our fear and anxiety in the face of uncertainty. We acquire an illusion of control over our future welfare when we imagine that our fates are decided by anthropomorphic beings that can be propitiated by prayer and sacrifice.

Hume's account of the natural foundations of religious belief receives a good deal of support from recent work on our psychological responses to the perception of uncertainty. This research confirms that human beings are indeed vulnerable to biases such as wishful thinking and illusions of control in unpredictable situations; we also exhibit a strong tendency toward superstition and anthropomorphism in these circumstances. Hume's natural history is based on general psychological principles, then, which have been corroborated by experimental studies (Collier 2014a: 670; cf. De Cruz 2015: 658).

Contemporary researchers in the cognitive science of religion deny, however, that motivated reasoning accounts for the culturally recurrent belief in supernatural agents; they attempt to explain ontological commitment to gods and spirits, rather, in terms of purely cognitive principles, such as a "hyperactive agency detection device" (Barrett 2004: 32) or the cultural transmission of counterintuitive concepts (Boyer 1996: 95). These researchers agree with Hume that folk religious beliefs are based on universal principles of human nature rather than philosophical reasoning or argumentation, but they deny that that these commitments are motivated by passions and anxiety reduction.

The cognitive science of religion is a relatively new field, and it remains to be seen which of these alternative accounts will emerge as the best explanation of the natural foundations of religion. But it is clear that the Humean proposal, which assigns a central role to emotions, deserves a seat at the table.

Aesthetics

In his influential essay, "Of the Standard of Taste," Hume maintains that aesthetic values are based on principles of human nature. This empirical assumption buttresses his proposal that qualified (i.e. fully informed and unbiased) critics would arrive at a consensus on the merit of artwork. Skeptics would, of course, deny these claims; they maintain that aesthetic values are culturally conditioned, and as a result, that disagreements are rationally irresolvable disputes about taste (E 230). If Hume is going to refute the skeptic, then, he must discharge the assumption that aesthetic values are founded on universal aspects of the mind. But what empirical evidence could be marshaled for this controversial claim?

Recent work in experimental aesthetics provides some preliminary support for Hume's proposal. In these studies, subjects are presented with formal patterns and are asked to rank them in terms of their aesthetic appeal. These test figures consist of simple qualities and relations, so it is safe to assume that everyone is fully informed about their properties. Participants in these studies, then, would count as qualified critics. The crucial question is whether their aesthetic judgments would converge.

Consider the intriguing experiments run by Richard Latto and his colleagues. These researchers present subjects with two types of paintings: (a) early Mondrian paintings composed of horizontal and vertical spatial relations, and (b) "pseudo-Mondrian" paintings whose lines were rotated such that they became oblique. The experimental results show that participants systematically prefer the genuine over the pseudo-Mondrians (Latto et al., 2006: 983).

Why is this? The best explanation of these results, according to members of this research group, lies with the "oblique effect" in neuropsychology: orientation detection cells in the visual cortex have difficulty processing oblique contours (Latto et al., 2006: 986). There appears to be a neural basis, then, for these aesthetic preferences. The dynamic balance of the Mondrian paintings, it seems, is naturally attractive to our eyes.

Although the field of experimental aesthetics is still in its infancy, its initial results support Hume's proposal that aesthetic values are based on principles of human psychology (Collier

2014b). One might object that these studies are limited to simple formal qualities and relations; but these are the only types of stimuli that can be used in controlled experiments. As far as we can tell from experimental data, then, Hume appears to have been on the right track when he proposed that "some particular forms or qualities, from the original structure of the internal fabric, are calculated to please, and others to displease" (E 233).

Conclusion: Humean minds

When we examine Hume's science of human nature from the perspective of cognitive science, we can see that it has much more going for it than previously recognized. Let us conclude by mentioning one implication of this revisionary evaluation for a recent debate in the Philosophy of Mind.

Fodor and Lepore attempt to refute Paul Churchland's connectionist theory of mind on the grounds that it is Humean in character (Fodor and Lepore 1996: 160–161). Their argument runs along the following lines.

P1: Connectionism is Humean.
P2: Hume was "born pre-refuted."
C: Connectionism has been refuted.

Paul Churchland's official reply to this challenge is to deny the first premise (Churchland 1996: 278–283). There are independent reasons to doubt whether Churchland successfully distances connectionism from Hume (Prinz 2006: 107–110). But we can now see that the motivation for this reply has been undercut. Connectionists can reply to Fodor and Lepore by denying their second premise. Many of Hume's specific proposals about the workings of the mind have emerged as leading contenders in cognitive science. Neo-Humeans are in a position, moreover, to turn the tables on their opponents. One is left wondering whether Fodor's Neo-Cartesian approach would fare as well when put to the empirical test.

References

Barrett, J. L. (2004) *Why Would Anyone Believe in God?* Walnut Creek, CA: Altamira Press.

Bechtel, W. and A. Abrahamsen (1991) *Connectionism and the Mind: An Introduction to Parallel Processing in Networks*, Cambridge, MA: Wiley-Blackwell.

Brandt, R. (1954) *Hopi Ethics*, Chicago, IL: University of Chicago Press.

Boyer, P. (1996) "What Makes Anthropomorphism Natural: Intuitive Ontology and Cultural Representations," *Journal of the Royal Anthropological Institute* 2: 83–97.

Churchland, P. (1995) *The Engine of Reason, the Seat of the Soul: A Philosophical Journey into the Brain*, Cambridge, MA: MIT Press.

———. (1996) "Second Reply to Fodor and Lepore," in R. McCauley (ed.), *The Churchlands and Their Critics*, Oxford: Wiley-Blackwell, pp. 278–283.

Collier, M. (1999) "Filling the Gaps: Hume and Connectionism on the Continued Existence of Unperceived Objects," *Hume Studies* 25: 155–170.

———. (2005a) "Hume and Cognitive Science: The Current Status of the Controversy over Abstract Ideas," *Phenomenology and the Cognitive Sciences* 4: 197–207.

———. (2005b) "A New Look at Hume's Theory of Probabilistic Inference," *Hume Studies* 31: 21–36.

———. (2007) "Why History Matters: Associations and Causal Judgment in Hume and Cognitive Science," *Journal of Mind and Behavior* 28: 175–188.

———. (2010) "Hume's Theory of Moral Imagination," *History of Philosophy Quarterly* 27: 253–273.

———. (2011a) "Hume's Science of Emotions: Feeling Theory without Tears," *Hume Studies* 37: 3–18.

———. (2011b) "Hume's Natural History of Justice," in C. Taylor and S. Buckle (eds.), *Hume and the Enlightenment*, London: Pickering and Chatto, pp. 131–142.

———. (2013) "The Humean Approach to Moral Diversity," *Journal of Scottish Philosophy* 11: 41–52.

———. (2014a) "The Natural Foundations of Religion," *Philosophical Psychology* 27: 665–680.

———. (2014b) "Toward a Science of Criticism: Aesthetic Values, Human Nature, and the Standard of Taste," in M. Bruhn and D. Wehrs (eds.), *Cognition, Literature, and History*, New York: Routledge, pp. 229–242.

De Cruz, H. (2015) "The Relevance of Hume's Natural History of Religion for Cognitive Science of Religion," *Res Philosophica* 92: 653–674.

Doris, J. and A. Plakias (2008) "How to Argue About Disagreement: Evaluative Diversity and Moral Realism," in W. Sinnot-Armonstrong (ed.), *Moral Psychology*, vol 2, Cambridge, MA: MIT Press, pp. 303–332.

———. And S. Stich (2005) "As a Matter of Fact: Empirical Perspectives on Ethics," in F. Jackson and M. Smith (eds.), *The Oxford Handbook of Contemporary Philosophy*, New York: Oxford University Press, pp. 114–154.

Elman, J., E. Bates, M. Johnson, A. Karmiloff-Smith, D. Parisi and K. Plunkett (1996) *Rethinking Innateness: A Connectionist Perspective on Development*, Cambridge, MA: MIT Press.

Fodor, J. and E. Lepore (1996) "Reply to Churchland," in R. McCauley (ed.), *The Churchlands and Their Critics*, Oxford: Wiley-Blackwell, pp. 159–162.

Frank, R. (1988) *Passions Within Reason: The Strategic Role of the Emotions*, New York: W. W. Norton.

Garrett, Don. 1997. *Cognition and Commitment in Hume's Philosophy*. New York: Oxford University Press.

Haidt, J. (2001) "The Emotional Dog and its Rational Tail: A Social Intuitionist Approach to Moral Judgment," *Psychological Review* 108: 814–834.

———. (2012) *The Righteous Mind: Why Good People Are Divided by Politics and Religion*, New York: Pantheon.

Hardin, D. (2007) *David Hume: Moral and Political Theorist*, New York: Oxford University Press.

Kail, P. (2007) "Understanding Hume's Natural History of Religion," *Philosophical Quarterly* 57: 190–211.

Kennett, J. (2006) "Do Psychopaths Really Threaten Moral Rationalism?" *Philosophical Explorations* 9: 69–82.

Latto, R., D. Brain, and B. Kelly (2006) "An Oblique Effect in Aesthetics: Homage to Mondrian," *Perception* 29: 981–987.

Lazarus, R. (1984) "On the Primacy of Cognition," *American Psychologist* 39: 124–129.

Medin, D. and M. Schaffer (1978) "Context Theory of Classification Learning," *Journal of Experimental Psychology: Human Learning and Memory* 7: 241–253.

Munakata, Y., J. McClelland, M. Johnson and R. Siegler (1997) "Rethinking Infant Knowledge: Toward an Adaptive Process Account of Successes and Failures in Object Performance Tasks," *Psychological Review* 104: 686–713.

Nichols, S. (2004) *Sentimental Rules: On the Natural Foundations of Moral Judgment*, New York: Oxford University Press.

Nisbett, R. and D. Cohen (1996) *Culture of Honor*, Boulder: Westview Press.

Passmore, J. (1952) *Hume's Intentions*, Cambridge: Cambridge University Press.

Pitcher, G. (1965) "Emotion," *Mind* 74: 326–346.

Posner, M. and S. Keele (1968) "On the Genesis of Abstract Ideas," *Journal of Experimental Psychology* 77: 353–363.

Prinz, J. J. (2002) *Furnishing the Mind: Concepts and Their Perceptual Basis*, Cambridge, MA: MIT Press.

———. (2006) "Empiricism and State Space Semantics," in B. Keeley (ed.), *Paul Churchland*, New York: Cambridge University Press, pp. 88–112.

———. (2011) "Against Empathy," *Southern Journal of Philosophy* 49: 214–233.

———. (2016) "Hume and Cognitive Science," in P. Russell (ed.), *The Oxford Handbook of Hume*, New York: Oxford University Press, pp. 777–791.

Rumelhart, McClelland, and the PDP Research Group. (1986) *Parallel Distributed Processing: Explorations in the Microstructure of Cognition: Volume 1*, Cambridge, MA: MIT Press.

Stroud, B. (1977) *Hume*, London: Routledge & Kegan Paul.

Williams, L. and D. DeSteno (2008) "Pride and Perseverance: The Motivational Role of Pride," *Journal of Personality and Social Psychology* 94: 1007–1017.

Zajonc, R. (1984) "On the Primacy of Affect," *American Psychologist* 39: 117–123.

34

A HUMEAN SOCIAL ONTOLOGY

Angela M. Coventry, Alex Sager, and Tom Seppäläinen

Introduction

One of David Hume's major contributions to philosophy and the social sciences is an account of how people can coordinate their actions and resolve conflicts through stable, yet dynamic social institutions such as government, property, and money. Scholars have recognized the prescience of Hume's account and developed a sophisticated literature analyzing it, often employing the tools of game theory. Nonetheless, relatively little explicit attention has been given to Hume's social ontology – the metaphysical entities and relationships that ground Hume's social world. In particular, scholarship on Hume's account of conventions has proceeded separately from scholarship on Hume's associationist psychology. This neglect raises a fundamental question: do Humeans have the resources to construct a plausible social ontology?

There is reason for skepticism. Social ontology asks how it is possible for people to collectively create institutions that embody social facts such as norms, laws, money, and much else.[1] These social facts emerge from and depend on individuals' beliefs, desires, or intentions; nonetheless, they do not appear reducible, at least in a straightforward way, to these beliefs, desires, or intentions. People experience laws or money – to give just two examples – as independent of their psychological states, often impacting their lives in ways more analogous to physical barriers than to beliefs or desires.

The task for a Humean is to explain how we can ground the social world on individual associational processes. This places a burden on any Humean account of social ontology. Unlike prominent rival accounts of social ontology (e.g. Searle 1995, 2010), it cannot presuppose language and linguistically based logical structure to explain how people can come to recognize objective, yet mind-dependent facts. The advantage of presupposing language is that it builds a social component into the foundation of the account – theorists do not need to explain the social, but only explain how it can support real, but mind-dependent institutions. For this reason, Humean associational psychology may seem an unpromising starting point for explaining social institutions.

In response, we contend that Hume's philosophy in fact has resources for a compelling, empirical approach to social institutions. In fact, the Humean refusal to begin with the social and instead to construct it from experience allows for a broader, more powerful social ontology that can account for non-linguistic social entities, explain how people navigate the opacity of many of our social institutions, and show how individual motivations can conform to social norms.

Humean social ontology

Hume offers rich accounts of property, law, political authority, religion, and money. Much of this account – with the notable exception of his account of justice – occurs in the *Essays: Moral, Political, and Literary* and the multi-volume *History of England*, and proceeds independently of the psychological apparatus developed in Books I and II of the *Treatise*. Though Hume went on to devote Book III of the *Treatise* to morals, he never fulfilled his promise in the Advertisement to Books I and II to proceed to the examination of politics and criticism, at least within the structure of his philosophical system. Instead, his account of these topics (along with accounts of economics, religion, and family life) occurs in essays and throughout his *History*. These are usually read independently of his larger philosophical system.

This raises a number of possibilities. First, it might mean that Hume's contributions on these topics are in fact independent of his broader philosophy – an analysis of Hume's account of government or religion, for example, need not engage with the details of his associationist philosophy. This would not be problematic *per se*, but would undermine attempts to see Hume as a systematic philosopher who provides a foundational account of social reality. Second, and more problematically, it might be that his contributions to politics, economics, religion, and criticism – to list only some of the areas of Hume's most prominent interventions – cannot be reconciled with his account of the impressions, ideas, and passions. In particular, there is the worry that his associational psychology lacks the resources to explain his account of institutions. It is this possibility we wish to resist. Hume provides a potentially powerful social ontology built on individuals' psychology that includes internal mechanisms for the emergence of stable social structures.

Sympathy and the passions

Social entities involve our relations to others and others' relations to us. The relevant relations for social ontology (and for social science) must all be stable. Throughout his philosophical psychology, Hume's goal is to explain the genesis of structured experience. This explanatory goal is true for perceptual experience, Hume's "complex impressions and ideas of sensations" (perceptions of outer sense). It is also true for moral facts and experience, Hume's impressions and ideas. Both psychologies are empiricist and associationist. They rest on laws of individual psychology, associative processes, and individuals' conscious awareness of contents relevant for tracking stable relations.

For Hume, the "indirect passions" and moral emotions concern and inform us about stable social entities and thus provide the foundation of social science. These sorts of passions and emotions play a role in social science because they not only make us feel but also represent social objects. Passions or "impressions of reflection" based in pleasure such as pride or love and those based in pain such as humility or hate have representational or intentional content with specific intentional objects in addition to felt "qualia."

More specifically, their intentional content is structured by both self and others as objects. The self is always the object of pride and humility, whereas love and hate always take another person or "sensible being" as their object, such as family, friends, or rivals (T 2.2.1.2; SBN 329–330). Moral distinctions are based in the pleasurable and painful impressions of the indirect passions: virtue produces in the mind an impression of pleasure, whereas vice produces an impression of pain. The moral emotions also have representational content with intentional objects (T 3.1.2.11; SBN 475–476). The objects of moral evaluation are actions, sentiments, and characters, and these belong to either to oneself or another person. Virtues for Hume are classified as useful or agreeable to self or to others and vices are useless or disagreeable to self or to others (T 3.3.1.3; SBN 574–575). Both the indirect passions and moral emotions become specifically structured experiences through repeated experience of the diachronic structure of the represented objects that consist of particular relations between the self and others.

Hume speaks of the passions' "ideas and impressions," roughly, their represented and felt aspects, "concurring" in objects (T 2.1.5.10; SBN 289). This concurrence results from the mechanism of the double relation or impulse between associations of ideas and impressions. The imagination associates from one idea to another via the principles of resemblance, spatial–temporal distance, and causation (T 1.1.4.1; SBN 10–11; 1.3.6.13; SBN 92–93). Resemblance is the only principle which associates between impressions of reflection: a pleasant or painful impression will naturally lead us to experience other pleasant or painful impressions. For example, joy toward another person lends itself to feelings of love and generosity (T 2.1.4.3; SBN 283).

The first relation in the double relation between the subject and its object is an association of idea with another and the second association is the association of one impression with another impression, the feeling dimension. The double relation is when the two kinds of association of ideas and impressions unite together into a single action of the mind (T 2.1.4.4; SBN 283–284). The ideas and impressions tend to reinforce one another. Hume writes that when these "two attractions or associations of impressions and ideas concur on the same object, they mutually assist each other, and the transition of the affections and of the imagination is made with the greatest ease and facility" (T 2.1.5.10; SBN 289). The causes of these passions are numerous, ranging from mental qualities like virtue, wit, good sense, and good humor, to physical qualities such as beauty, strength, swiftness, and dexterity, to family, children, and relations, and material possessions like riches, property, and clothes, as well as nations, landscapes, and climate (T 2.1.2.5; SBN 279).

This "concurrence" in the emotional realm is what keeps society grounded in experience: the feeling dimension at the basis of moral emotions can be used by an individual to affectively track emotions' representational social relations. Emotions can be used to track associations across multiple kinds of we-intentional contents – mental states with both I- and other-involving contents – and in a manner principled enough to constitute a core inner epistemology for social, moral belief. As a result, moral emotions neither reduce social relations (and institutions) into individual subjects nor leave them independent holistic objects external to individuals.

The connection between individuals' emotions and others behooves further analysis to clarify both social ontology itself and the possibility of an affective epistemology for it. To accomplish this, we need to say a few words on the relationship between Hume's psychology and epistemology. We also need to contextualize the epistemology of moral belief through Hume's ideas for the epistemology of "factual" or non-moral beliefs – even if at the end both epistemologies are equally fact-based.

Given the explanatory goal of structured experience, Hume's psychology also harbors an epistemology. An individual's ability to distinguish between stable structured experience and its contrast is part of Hume's explanatory agenda. For him, we can track stability through conscious "feels" or "indicators." "Vivacity" is Hume's term of art for the conscious, feeling-based epistemology of belief. This epistemology for belief tracks the inner causal associative mechanisms behind structured experience and in both the perceptual or factual realm and the moral, affective one.[2] In the factual realm, vivacity works hand-in-hand with Hume's famous empiricist principle that keeps cognitions true to sense-perceptions, "copying." Ideas or intentional cognitive states that copy not only the contents of sense-perceptions but also the vivacity of sense-perceptions or "impressions" are genuine factual empirical beliefs.

The genesis and justification of social or moral beliefs is based in posits analogous to the ones responsible for non-social factual beliefs. Both are kinds of (causal) "copyings." In the case of emotional states, Hume adds to the process of regular copying another process of mimicry relevant for the intentional targets of emotions, "sympathy." Sympathy is a generic "mind-reading capacity." Hume states that our minds are "mirrors to one another" and "reflect each other's emotions" (T 2.2.5.21; SBN 365). This copying process affects vivacious or lively ideas about others. In fact, its effects are so "lively" that through it ideas of others' emotions can become actual experiences of the emotions of others (T 2.1.11.2–8; SBN 317–320). And since for Hume vivacity is what confers all perceptions their reality, their "belief-worthiness," sympathy is the major feature of structured moral experience and criterion for moral knowledge.

Sympathy ultimately accounts for our approval and disapproval of virtue and vices which mostly tend to the good or the detriment of society or of the person who possesses it (T 3.3.1.30; SBN 591). Moreover, since in some sense all of our experience is structured and since sympathy is part of human nature, Hume's consciousness is social. For Hume, the characteristic form of human awareness has a social causal origin through sympathy. Sympathy is for Hume functionally like copying. It has the same role in the epistemology of morality as "ordinary" copying functions for the epistemology of facts. Sympathetic copying-based emotional responses can function across many different levels and sizes of social hierarchy and be represented in emotions' contents.

Emotions for Hume contain the information rich representational structures that allow people to navigate shared social rules and expectations. They provide the cognitive content that explains the tendency to treat social objects as "real" though nonetheless mind-dependent. And as passions, conative states, they contain the motivational impetus that leads people to follow social conventions much of the time.

The above brief sketch of a Humean "passionate" social ontology can be further analyzed by contrasting it with two popular morality-based accounts of social order reflected in the meta-ethical "isms" of subjectivism and universalism, ones at times misleadingly associated with Hume. Morals are grounded in emotions and emotions have distinct feelings. Given the natural association of these with subjectivity,[3] many interpret Hume's morality as self-interest based.[4] This interpretation depicts Hume as one of the original individualists or even rational egoists who base morality and political stability on self-interested individuals. Moreover, since Hume describes feelings in terms of pleasure and pain, his subjectivism often acquires a hedonist bent.[5]

A subjectivist interpretation fails to take into account Hume's full theory of emotions by merely focusing on feelings. Emotions for Hume have representational structure – in addition to felt "qualia" – and include both the self and others as intentional objects. For example, Hume is explicit that morally relevant feelings such as pride and humility have the self as their "object," whereas feelings of love, hatred, or moral approval and disapproval take another person as their object. And Hume's "object" of emotions does not even constitute his full account of the representational content of emotions: it includes also "subjects" related to the "objects" (e.g. possessions to the self) and their quality (e.g. beauty of the possession). There is plenty more information in Hume's emotions than feelings.

Further, the sorts of feelings relevant for Hume's morality are of a "*peculiar* kind, which makes us praise or condemn" another person's character or action (T 3.1.2.4; SBN 472). It is what we feel *upon the general view or survey* that distinguishes virtue and vice from other feelings of pleasures and pains, and this distinguishes moral judgments from those based merely on individual subjective feelings or self-interest. We must rather "choose a point of view" that is common with others (EPM 9.6; SBN 272–273). Hume thinks that when a character or action "is consider'd in general, without reference to our particular interest, that it causes such a feeling or sentiment, as denominates it morally good or evil" (T 3.1.2.4; SBN 472). We learn to make these corrections of our expressions of praise or blame from experience. In some cases, we may be unable to correct our sentiments, where they are "more stubborn and inalterable," but we can at least correct our language. These sorts of corrections are needed for communication among members of society, otherwise "it would impossible we cou'd ever make use of language, or communicate our sentiments to one another, did we not correct the momentary appearances of things, and overlook our present situation" (T 3.3.1.16; SBN 581–582).

Another popular yet opposite, "universalist" misinterpretation derives from Hume's emphasis on sympathy.[6] Hume's use of sympathy as a principle of human nature "to receive by communication" the "inclinations and sentiments" of others resembling us easily leads to a theory of universal moral sense (T 2.1.11.2; SBN 316–317). This can take the form of universal benevolence towards humankind and from an abstract, universal point of view such as that of a universal, impartial spectator. But Hume's moral psychology does not demolish the separation among humans through innate means, without learned experience and the effects of imagination. And the importance of this learning history cannot be overstated. Just a brief sketch shows why.

Like all other causal mechanisms of Hume's empiricist epistemology, sympathy is "only" conscious data based in a structured form of consciousness. The "perspective" it affords on other humans is fully based on emotional structured content. Thereby, it can be more or less specific in its social, "other-involving" representational contents which depend on the individual's exposure, social experiences. For Hume, sympathy extends from others' feelings to their opinions; it becomes obvious that sympathy cannot be treated as a "moral sense" or other universal impartial perspective. Instead, it is dependent on specific intentional objects garnered through experience.

Sympathy follows further principles, and as always is the case for Hume, these concern imagination's associative principles. For Hume, perceptual information subject to modification by sympathetic enlivening varies in force depending on the resemblance, contiguity, and causation involved in the creation of the intentional social objects of emotions. Thus, a sympathetic response, an affective social response, is greater with those people who most resemble us in manners, including language. Sympathy also respects simple proximity relations so that the emotions about our close friends and neighbors are felt more strongly. In this way, the causal bases of sympathy for Hume are a way of "enlivening" our beliefs, ideas, concerning others' emotions to the point of feeling them ourselves and to varying degrees.

It is in this functional and variable sense in which Hume maintains that "we have no extensive concern for society but from sympathy" instead of some universal perspective (T 3.3.1.11; SBN 578–579). To put the Humean theory in most literal terms, human consciousness is social consciousness, and its social or moral "umph" varies as a function of principles pertaining to the social objects represented in consciousness.

Hume's account of sympathy is another exemplar of his empiricism, an experiential and developmental approach to morality and, thereby, social order. As a conscious indicator or tracking feature of a stable and coherent social environment, Hume's sympathy does not play intuitive or *a priori* favorites with respect to the foundations of social order. It is a mechanism directly subject to influence from new experiences and new habits. It also permits new social relations and, thereby, new affective relations. This is important since both subjectivist or egoist and universalist perspectives suffer in the face of such facts, social phenomena demonstrating the variability of moral experiences and social arrangements. Hume's naturalistic and empiricist moral theory surmounts these by showing how individual experience can ground intersubjective moral claims. Tracking stable social relations through emotions which, to boot, influence the very representation of the self is a conscious skill based in interaction and exposure.

Institutions

How do sympathy and the passions connect to social ontology? Put succinctly, Hume's social consciousness is a powerful explanatory tool, especially in light of empiricist epistemologies. Sympathetic emotional responses can function across many different levels and sizes of social hierarchy or order. Yet individuals themselves do not establish or justify all social orders they are exposed or subject to. Mostly individuals simply face political and social traditions and conventions, as members of a culture(s), and this culture is largely just communicated. Conventions, with systems of law, morality, and religion as three of the most important, have developed historically. They have a history. It is within this history that individuals encounter conventions that only at times and through different "media" of causal interactions trigger their literal vivacious sympathetic responses.

Hume's full political theory takes cognizance of this. For Hume, individual ontogeny need not recapitulate social or cultural phylogeny. In other words, the social order does not reduce to occurrent or "atemporal" social emotional "justifications." The brute facticity of some social orders is generally compatible and at times even supportive in phenomena of the sympathy-based psychology and epistemology. This can be best illustrated by contrasting a Humean account of the conventions of justice with a popular game-theoretic account of justice.

Game-theoretic approaches to convention focus on individuals' recognition of the mutual advantage of property rights. According to the contractarian interpretation of Hume,[7] the institution of property arises in which the circumstances of justice – limited benevolence and moderate scarcity – lead to conflict over external goods. To resolve this conflict, "rational moderately self-interested agents establish the rules of justice" because they all stand to benefit from them.[8] Each individual recognizes that they are better off with rules of property acquisition and transfer than they would be in their absence: "agents are willing to follow one of several possible social arrangements provided they have appropriate reciprocal expectations."[9] The rules of justice must be mutually advantageous, i.e. justifiable to each individual, as voluntary agreement only occurs when parties perceive that the arrangement is in their interest.[10] Here a convention is explained by identifying "useful" equilibria that people converge on in strategic interactions. Property is a useful institution that provides aggregate benefits by establishing rules for the acquisition and transfer of goods. The institution of property is a convention that resolves problems of partial conflict in which "some agents stand to gain only if other agents unilaterally make certain sacrifices."[11]

The starting point for the game-theoretical interpretation of property is individual self-interest. Institutions such as property emerge from the interaction of individuals coming to realize their enlightened self-interest in respecting other people's property rights insofar as others reciprocate. Game-theoretical interpretations fail to take seriously the main features that Hume underscores in his moral psychology and its relations to property.

First, at least in people's daily lives, enlightened self-interest is not what causes most people to respect property rights. Rather, mental principles such as custom or habit play a crucial role. There must be "some internal relation, that the property consists" or "some influence, which the external relations of the object have on the mind and actions" (T 3.2.6.3; SBN 527). Custom or habit bestows "a facility in the performance of any action or the conception of any object; and afterwards a tendency or inclination towards it" (T 2.3.5.1–5; SBN 422–424). This principle operates "on the tender minds of the children" and "makes them sensible of the advantages, which they may reap from society" and increases our esteem for justice (T 2.2.2.4; SBN 333; 2.2.2.26; SBN 345–345). We come to accept a complex convention of property through repeated exposures to structures, including diachronic transfers of property that contribute to stability and order. Social institutions are rarely the product of strategic calculation; rather they arise gradually and are maintained by copying already existing institutions. A game-theoretical approach to property depends on the appeal to self-interest – even when agents do not reflect on how the institution benefits them or are perhaps unaware of the benefits, the justification for the institution of property is self-interest. Hume agrees that property does benefit all. However, the justification for any particular set of property arrangements is that they are currently the ones adopted by the society, and this is explained partly by the force of habit (which is in turn explained by our psychology).

Second, game-theoretical interpretations insufficiently incorporate the passions and Hume's account of self. Conventions for Hume cannot be grounded on self-interested, rational agents strategizing in situations where utility (e.g. preference satisfaction) depends on the other agents' actions for the simple reason that Hume did not conceive of the self as a self-interested, rational agent. The self for Hume is composed of multiple, social relations that are associated in complex patterns highlighted by conscious indicators and by sympathy. Sympathy literally incorporates others into the associative web of the self.

The Humean self has two aspects (T 1.4.6.19; SBN 253). The first aspect is the self of thought and imagination in *Treatise*, Book 1 where Hume explains through the associative principles of resemblance and causality how we generate the fictional idea of the self. In Book 2, Hume posits an impression of the self as the object of the passions that "is always intimately present with us" (T 2.1.11.4; SBN 317). He says that nature has given an "emotion" to the idea of the self to make sure that it is produced all of the time (T 2.1.5.6; SBN 287). The self is posited as "an original and natural instinct" and this makes it "absolutely impossible, from the primary constitution of the mind, that these passions shou'd ever look beyond self, or that individual person, of whose actions and sentiments each of us is intimately conscious" (T 2.1.5.3; SBN 286). The presence of these associative relations enlivens the vivacity of this self at every moment of our lives – so that it approaches the vivacity of an impression (T 2.1.11.4; SBN 317). So our conscious experience always involves some degree of passionate feeling, and this feeling always involves some conception of self.

The consideration of other's sentiments is common when it comes to one's self. An extrinsic condition for the production of pride and humility is that the object that is pleasant or painful be very discernible and obvious, not only to ourselves, but to others also (T 2.1.6.3; SBN 291). This applies to joy as well, in that we think of ourselves as happier when others see us that way (T 2.1.6.3; SBN 291). When discussing the relation of the state of the body to the passions of pride and humility, Hume mentions the shame we feel for our maladies that may affect other people and are either "dangerous or disagreeable" to them (T 2.1.8.9; SBN 303).

When we judge ourselves, we always consider the sentiments of others. Hume states that "our reputation, our character, our name are considerations of vast weight and importance; and even the other causes of pride; virtue, beauty and riches; have little influence, when not seconded by the opinions and sentiments of others" (T 2.1.11.1; SBN 316). This is explained in terms of sympathy by which the feelings of others induce a similar feeling in ourselves. Sympathy is also at the basis of the mechanism of comparison. I may feel the pleasurable or painful passion of another person through sympathy and then comparatively I may feel my own pleasurable or painful passions all the more strongly. The key point is that our assessment of our own situation as more or less pleasing or painful to ourselves is done in comparison to our judgments of the situation of other people. Both sympathy and comparison together explain passions such as envy and malice.

The idea of our self is formed based on the ideas of others, through forming the impressions of another's self. Through sympathy we infer the pleasure and pains of others, and these are enlivened in our minds through their relation with the self. This allows that people can come to view themselves from a social perspective and one come to know themselves through others (Capaldi 1975: 92–93; Capaldi 1985: 279). Thus as Baier (1991: 130) writes for Hume, "the self is dependent on others for its coming to be, for its emotional life, for its self-consciousness, for its self-evaluations." The self as the object of the passions is the "socially constructed self" (Baille 2000: 35).

The social history of the self also establishes an irreducible socio-historical base and, thus, ontology for institutional facts. Selves "are" structured associations incorporating multiple agents who more or less share in emotions and other enlivened ideas, including information on history and tradition. These all influence action as emotions. Hume on justice and by extension property provides a good illustration of this ontology and its causal, explanatory potential.

Hume likens "the social virtue of justice" to "a vault, where each individual stone would, of itself, fall to the ground; nor is the whole fabric supported but by the mutual assistance and combination of its corresponding parts" (EPM App. 3.5; SBN 305). Justice involves "a kind of convention or agreement; that is, by a sense of interest, suppos'd to be common to all, and where every single act is perform'd in expectation that others are to perform the like" (T 3.2.1.22; SBN 498; EPM App.3.7; SBN 306). Once the convention concerning the "abstinence from the possessions of others is enter'd into," the ideas of justice and injustice emerge as well as that of property (T 3.2.2.11; SBN 490). The origin of justice thus "explains that of property" (T 3.2.2.11; SBN 491). Our own "property is nothing but those goods, whose constant possession is establish'd [. . .] by the laws of justice" (T 3.2.2.11; SBN 491).

Hume's account of justice and property incorporates multiple social relations mediated by emotions whose feeling dimension in its pleasure–pain dimension provides structure to the heterogeneity of intentional social objects. It has significant explanatory power, a cognitive value Hume himself emphasizes often. The laws of justice assigning stability of possessing and regulating the transfer of property emerge from individual interactions against a common problem background – the need for rules to prevent and resolve conflict over objects. These laws are sustained through the population's recognition and representation of these laws but at the same time shape the population's representations through continued feedback mechanisms.

For example, justice transforms avidity within society into various desires for the acknowledged symbols of status, privilege, and power. These desires emerge in a social context where a more extensive sympathetic mirroring increases awareness of how we stand in relation to one another, especially in terms of perceived social power, trustworthiness, and the markers of status or accomplishment. Because now "*Vanity* is rather to be esteem'd a social passion, and a bond of union among men," both the accumulation of wealth and the outlay of it on desirable goods draw the admiration of others (T 3.2.2.12; SBN 491–492). A high social status, secured by wealth, property, and position, produces not only pride in one's self and the esteem of others felt through ideas' sympathetic enlivening into real experiences, but these emotions in turn function to reinforce a sense of the desirability of high social status (T 2.1.11.1; SBN 316). In contrast, those lacking property or the wealth to secure it may find themselves subject to the power or authority of others. Both poverty and subjection to others are sources of shame or humility and tend to earn the contempt of others. Hume's naturalism leads him to present an account of the emotions that tracks the socio-economic status of persons, which directly affects how we treat each other.[12]

The above account illustrates how for Hume the self has a genuine social history in contrast to game-theoretical and other individualistic approaches. Moreover, this social history has explanatory value, not only for the precise shape our institutions take, but for the willingness of most people to abide by conventions. Our attachment to particular objects we own is only possible within a larger social web that clarifies and supports our ownership. This associative web referred to as the self is in a potentially perceptually changing "identity" through others – interrelations between other human beings mediated by historically caused social institutions. For Hume, society itself evolves and changes along with the psychological states of the agents whose actions sustain it. The two are in a coupled emergent interaction through and in time. Hume's historical ontology has thus ample room for emergence and contingency. There is no one single causal origin to society that could explain the nature of our conventions. As such, the game-theoretical interpretation lacks an adequate explanation for the nature of property relations and of people's motivations for upholding them.

Hume versus Searle

The Humean account of social ontology we have sketched provides an attractive alternative to non-empiricist, synchronic, linguistically based accounts of social ontology that privilege logical structure over causal mechanisms. To see this, it is helpful to contrast it with John Searle's account of social ontology. Searle's theory is based on three primitive notions: collective intentionality, the assignment of function, and constitutive rules.[13] Social facts exist when two or more people share intentional states or "we-intentions." We-intentionality is primitive: we-intentional statements cannot be reduced to sets of I-intentional statements. Collective intentionality occurs in cooperative activity and is necessary but not sufficient for social institutions. To move from social facts to institutional facts, Searle argues that we need to assign functions and impose constitutive rules, rules that bring social entities into existence. Human societies thus have a "*logical structure*, because human attitudes are constitutive of the social reality in question and those attitudes have propositional contents with logical relationships."[14]

When humans collectively accept that objects have a certain status, objects assume the status they intend. Searle gives the example of transforming pieces of paper into money and calls this a "status function." Status functions interlock with other institutional facts, creating a complex "series of obligations, rights, responsibilities, duties, entitlements, authorizations, permissions, requirements, and so on."[15] Status functions are "the vehicles of power in society."[16] Searle calls these entities "deontoic powers" which provide desire-independent reasons for action.

What is of particular significance for our purposes is the role of language in Searle's account. He claims that for "obligations, requirements, and duties to exist, they have to be represented in some linguistic or symbolic form."[17] Institutions are combinations of linguistic and non-linguistic facts, but the linguistic element is essential: "All other institutional facts require linguistic representation because some non-semantic fact is created by the representation."[18]

Searle mentions property as an institution many times in his written work, although he does not provide a detailed account of its nature. Nonetheless, we can construct a Searlean account of property. Property exists because we collectively accept that people have powers to do things with social and physical property. Property is defined by a set of deontic powers that determine rights to own, use, transfer, extract rents, etc., from resources. These deontoic powers have a linguistic basis and depend on "status indicators" that enable people to communicate and exchange property and to follow the rules governing the distribution of property.

As we have seen, Hume's account is very different. First, Searle's account and the Humean account differ at the level of motivation. For Searle, institutions provide desire-independent reasons for acting. Searle criticizes thinkers such as Hume who allegedly maintain that you can never have a motivation to for doing something unless you have a desire to do so (Searle 2010: 132). Humeans reject the possibility of people having reasons that they do not endorse. But this does not mean that people are not motivated to follow institutional rules, even if these rules are not directly connected to particular desires. Rather, motivation arises because institutional rules are embedded in the representational structure of the passions through custom and habit and intimately connected to the "feeling" aspect of emotion that provides motivational force. Hume explains, for example, how the force of the obligation to keep promises in a community is formed based on "principles and passions of human nature" (T 3.2.5.9; SBN 521). Similar to justice, Hume sees promise-keeping as a convention "founded on the necessities and interests of society" (T 3.2.5.6–7; SBN 519). Human self-interest provides the initial motivation for establishment of the convention of promises, but the obligation is brought about by the practice of the convention itself. Once we come to accept the social benefit of the fulfillment of our promises, the sentiment of moral approval of promise-keeping arises. Hume writes that "a sentiment of morals concurs with interest, and becomes a new obligation upon mankind" (T 3.2.5.12 SBN 523). This explains how people can insist on keeping promises even when in certain cases these promises clash in a significant way with their particular desires.

Second, the Humean account has an advantage in not appealing to Searle's controversial account of we-intentions as a primitive. As we have shown, Humeans can plausibly explain collective intentionality using the representative structure of the passions and the mechanism of sympathy – mechanisms that clearly connected to naturalistic forms of inquiry. Rather than having to negotiate the differences and interactions between non-reducible we-mode and I-mode frameworks (to adopt the influential terminology of Raimo Tuomela 2013), our Humean account suggests that this is a false dichotomy. This has the advantage of parsimony; it also, in our view, offers a more plausible reconstruction of the socially constructed self and of how it navigates the social world.

Third, unlike theorists of social ontology such as Searle who privilege language, Hume replaces identity and other similarly "transparency" evoking semantic notions with lesser or more opaque epistemological ones, copying, resemblance, and causal relations. And Hume never privileges linguistic interactions at the expense of lived, concrete shared experiences. Language is a useful convention for Hume that emerges from a causal process in which ideas are copied from impressions. In other words, his views about language are based in an empirical, psychological theory that unmasks some of the pretensions of language but also shows how appropriate language use is possible.

This is significant since it provides the Humean with a response to a damaging criticism against Searle's position by Jonathan Friedman and Steven Lukes: Searle seems unable to account for "non-intentional systemic realities" (Lukes 2006: 7). Lukes points out that social institutions "do not exhaust the realm of the social" and that they "are non-transparent to the extent that individuals who 'accept' them neither expect nor understand how they function and what their effects are." Another way to put the point is that social scientists are also interested in the "'brute' realities of social life" and Searle's account does not have clear resources to explain the causal impact of these brute realities.

The Humean response is that we should not expect institutions to be transparent. Lived, concrete shared experiences are constructed through causal relations, copying, and resemblance so that representations of institutions are non-transparent and limited. Representations are continually reformed through exposure to non-intentional objects and structures at multiple levels. These processes should not be confused with Searle's notion of the "background," which posits a mechanism that explains seemingly rule-governed behavior through unconscious adaptation to systems of rules.[19] On the Humean account, rules do not exhaust the explanation of institutions: brute reality is mediated through ideas and impressions in ways that we should expect will often surprise us. To explain how social institutions come about, the Humean must then take on work in different disciplines such as political science, economics, history, and evolutionary biology in addition to language and mind. We hope to have shown in this chapter at least the great potential of such an approach to social ontology.

Notes

1 See Epstein (2016) for an overview of the various approaches to the topics and problems in the field of social ontology.
2 The central concepts of epistemology, belief and belief-worthiness are for Hume simply an idea. Yet an idea is always a complex structured representational experience.
3 See James Rachels, *Elements of Moral Philosophy* (2003). In this best-selling text for introduction to ethics classes, Hume is given as the classic example of a "simple" or "basic" subjectivist in chapter 3.
4 Versions of this interpretation are held by Stroud (1977: Ch. I X); Mackie (1980: Ch. VI); Ardal (1966: Ch. VIII).
5 See for example Kail (2007: ch. 8).
6 See for example MacIntyre (1984); Livingston (1984), and Berry (2007).
7 This is put forward by authors such as David Gauthier (1979), Peter Vanderschraaf (1998, 2008), and Robert Sugden (2009, 2013),
8 Vanderschraaf (1998: 231).
9 Vanderschraaf (1998: 338), cf. Sugden (2013: 65).
10 Sugden (2009: 15–16).
11 Vanderschraaf (1998: 338).
12 See Taylor (1998, 2015) and Gross (2006: Chapter 4).
13 Searle (2006: 16).
14 Searle (2006: 15).
15 Searle (2006: 18).
16 Searle (2006: 18).
17 Searle (2006: 21).
18 Searle (2010: 113).
19 Searle (1995: 146).

References

Ardal, P. (1966) *Passion and Value in Hume's Treatise*, Edinburgh: Edinburgh University Press.
Baier, Annette (1991) *A Progress of Sentiments: Reflections on Hume's Treatise*, Cambridge, MA: Harvard University Press.
Baille, James (2000) *Hume on Morality*, London: Routledge.
Berry, C. (2007) "Hume's Universalism: The Science of Man and the Anthropological Point of View," *British Journal for the History of Philosophy* 15(3): 535–550.
Capaldi, Nicholas (1975) *David Hume: The Newtonian Philosopher*, Boston: Twayne Publishers.
———. (1985) "The Historical and Philosophical Significance of Hume's Theory of the Self," in A.J. Holland (eds.), *Philosophy, Its History and Historiography*. Royal Institute of Philosophy Conferences, vol 3, Dordrecht: Springer.
Epstein, B (2016) "A Framework for Social Ontology," *Philosophy of the Social Sciences* 46(2): 147–167.
Gauthier, David (1979) "David Hume, Contractarian," *The Philosophical Review* 88(1): 3–38.
Gross, D. (2006) *The Secret History of Emotion*, Chicago, IL: University of Chicago Press.
Kail, Peter (2007) *Projection and Realism in Hume's Philosophy*, Oxford: Oxford University Press.
Livingston, D. (1984) *Hume's Philosophy of Common Life*, Chicago, IL: University of Chicago Press.
Lukes, S. (2006) "Searle and His Critics," *Anthropological Theory* 6(1) (March 1): 5–11. doi:10.1177/1463499606061729.
MacIntyre, A. (1984) *After Virtue: A Study in Moral Theory*, Notre Dame, IN: University of Notre Dame Press.

Mackie, John (1980) *Hume's Moral Theory*, London: Routledge & Kegan Paul.

Rachels, James (2003) *The Elements of Moral Philosophy*. 4th edn, Boston: McGraw-Hill.

Sabl, Andrew (2012) *Hume's Politics: Coordination and Crisis in the History of England*, Princeton: Princeton University Press.

Searle, John R. (1995) *The Construction of Social Reality*, New York: Free Press.

———. (2006) "Social Ontology: Some Basic Principles," *Anthropological Theory* 6 (1) (March 1): 12–29. doi:10.1177/1463499606061731.

———. (2010) *Making the Social World: The Structure of Human Civilization*. Oxford and New York: Oxford University Press.

Stroud, Barry (1977) *Hume*, London: Routledge & Kegan Paul.

Sugden, Robert (2009) "Can a Humean Be a Contractarian?" *Rationality, Markets and Morals* 0(1): 11–23.

——— (2013) "Contractarianism as a Broad Church," *Rationality, Markets and Morals* 4: 61–66.

Taylor, Jacqueline (1998) "Justice and the Foundations of Social Morality in Hume's *Treatise*," *Hume Studies* 24(1).

———. (2015) *Reflecting Subjects: Passion, Sympathy, and Society in Hume's Philosophy*, Oxford: Oxford University Press.

Tuomela, Raimo (2013) *Social Ontology: Collective Intentionality and Group Agents*, New York: Oxford University Press.

Vanderschraaf, Peter (1998) "Knowledge, Equilibrium and Convention," *Erkenntnis* 49(3): 337–369.

——— (2008) "The Informal Game Theory in Hume's Account of Convention," *Economics and Philosophy* 14(02) (December 5): 215. doi:10.1017/S0266267100003849.

35

HUME'S MORAL PSYCHOLOGY AND CONTEMPORARY MORAL PSYCHOLOGY

Lorraine L. Besser

Over the past 20 years, contemporary moral psychology has taken a direction that fits nicely with Hume's overall agenda of introducing "the experimental method of reasoning into moral subjects" (T, title page). The central questions that Hume considered and the ways in which he advocated approaching these questions are very much alive and well in contemporary dialogue as the field tries more and more to integrate psychological research into philosophical analysis. For example, philosophers have appealed to empirical research into the causes of one's behavior to challenge the assumption, fundamental to virtue ethics, that one's character traits cause one's actions (Doris 2002; Harman 2000). They have used empirical research to challenge the role that many philosophers believe empathy can play in motivating us to act morally (Goldie 2011; Prinz 2011), and they have challenged the role that reason can play in governing our everyday lives (Doris 2015; Nichols 2002).

In this chapter, I will explore three areas within moral psychology that are central to both Hume and contemporary discourse: the nature of reason and passion; agency; and virtue and character. While, as we will see, Hume's influence on contemporary discussions of these issues is often taken to be relatively straightforward, my hope is to identify and develop insight into some more surprising connections between Hume's moral psychology and contemporary moral psychology.

Reason and passion

Hume's view of the nature and interaction of reason and passion has had a well-known and longstanding influence on contemporary discourse and specifically the sentimentalist tradition within ethics (Cohon 2008; Shaw 1993; Slote 2010). Most of the attention focuses on Hume's claims regarding the limited power of reason (T 3.1.1; SBN 455–419; and EPM App. 1; SBN 285–294). Reason, Hume argues, is limited to the discovery of truth and falsehood. Specifically, it looks to the agreement or disagreement that holds between relations of ideas or between matters of fact. Reason allows us to identify resemblances between our ideas of one thing and our ideas of another, or the lack thereof; it allows us to identify proportions in quantity and number and degrees of quality.

This, for Hume, constitutes the whole of what reason can do: it can make observations about the relations that hold between things and the kinds of relations that exist, as well as discover truth and falsity. Most important to Hume's discussion, however, is what reason cannot do, and what this consequently tells us about the nature of morality. While, as we have seen, reason allows us to identify relations of ideas or of matters of fact, Hume believes that we learn very quickly that morality does not consist in these kinds of relations. Consider, he suggests, the crime of ingratitude: this "has place wherever we observe good-will, expressed and known, together with good offices performed on the one side, and a return of ill-will or indifference, with ill-offices or neglect on the other" (EPM App 1.5; SBN 287). This is the defining relation of ingratitude and is the object of reason; however, as long as we consider the relation using reason alone, we will never find and reach any moral evaluations associated with this relation: "anatomize all these circumstances and examine, by your reason alone, in what consists the demerit or blame: You never will come to any issue or conclusion" (EPM App 1.5; SBN 287). Morality does not consist in the relation of ideas and must instead have its source in the passions which generate the feelings of approval and disapproval that arise when we consider the ingratitude that holds between the two parties:

> Consequently, we may infer, that the crime of ingratitude is not any particular individual *fact*; but arises from a complication of circumstances, which, being presented to the spectator, excites the *sentiment* of blame, by the particular structure and fabric of his mind.
>
> (EPM App 1.6; SBN 287)

The second component of Hume's view of the limitations of reason concerns reason's inability to motivate actions. Because reason is limited to identifying ideas and matters of fact and considering the various relations, it is a "wholly inactive" (T 3.1.1.10; SBN 458) principle and "can never be the source of so active a principle as conscience, or a sense of morals" (T 3.1.1.10; SBN 458). While reason can inform the passions and feed us important information about the objects of our passions, our passions are the only things that can motivate us. As, on Hume's account, morality is essentially motivating, this gives us further reason to assign the passions center-stage in our analysis of morality and to de-emphasize the role that reason can play within morality. Moral approbation "cannot be the work of the judgment, but of the heart; and is not a speculative proposition of affirmation, but an active feeling of sentiment" (T 3.1.1.10; SBN 458). We thus should recognize that "reason is, and ought to be, slave to the passions" (T 2.3.3.4; SBN 421) and turn to an examination of the passions in order to understand morality.

Hume's views of the limited role of reason, the primacy of the passions, and consequent understanding of morality as essentially grounded within one's passions are well-known; contemporary sentimentalists such as Shaun Nichols (2004) and Jesse Prinz (2007) acknowledge intellectual debts to Hume and very much see their defenses of sentimentalism as motivated by and advancing Hume's basic framework. Prinz (2007) opens his discussion with a preamble on Hume's understanding of moral judgments, noting that his view of morality as a construction of the passions is deeply influenced by Hume's own work. Nichols (2004) also opens his discussion of sentimentalism with a nod to Hume, claiming that, given Hume's extensive reliance on experiments derived from observations of human nature in practice, Hume would have "championed the use of controlled experiments in moral psychology," wherein individuals are placed in situations designed to minimize extraneous variables so as to better understand the variable in question (Nichols 2004: 4).

Within contemporary discourse, "sentimentalism" is used to describe an umbrella of moral positions rooted in the claim that moral judgments have their source in our emotional or affective responses. We have seen Hume's defense of this claim, which appeals to his understanding of the limited capacity of reason developed solely through reflection on the nature of the mind and to his extended discussion of the passions which do comprise morality. Many contemporary defenses take this reflection one step further by drawing on neuroscientific research regarding the sources of our moral judgments and the cognitive framework invoked in making moral decisions.

Nichols' initial defense of sentimentalism, for instance, begins with reflection on psychological research on psychopathy. Psychopaths are taken by Nichols to represent real life examples of amoralists insofar as they seem unable to make, or be motivated by, moral judgments.[1] Research by Blair suggests that psychopaths cannot distinguish moral norms from conventional norms; and that when they do make moral judgments, they do not seem to attribute to them the distinctive kind of weight that we take to reflect a proper understanding of those judgments. Blair's research indicates that most people take moral transgressions to be more serious and less permissible than conventional transgressions and less likely to be permissible than conventional transgressions. Moral transgressions are seen to be less contingent to rules and authority than are conventional transgression. Whereas transgressions, such as wearing pajamas to school, depend upon the existence of a rule and an authority figure to enforce the rule, moral transgressions, such as one student hitting another, are seen to be wrong even in the absence of explicit rules and authorities (Blair 1995: 6). This understanding of the distinctiveness of moral transgressions is evidenced in children as young as 39 months, but is lacking in psychopaths. Blair's research finds that psychopathic populations often cannot distinguish between conventional norms and moral norms, and that when they do make the distinction they are less likely to appeal to the welfare of others in their explanation of it than are non-psychopaths (Blair 1995: 25). That psychopaths experience this struggle with morality is seen to provide support for sentimentalism, insofar as psychopaths have a known defect to their affective processing systems and particularly their capacity to experience empathy, sympathy, remorse, and guilt (Blair 1995: 3–4).

The sentimentalist trend in contemporary moral psychology has been dominant and influential, particularly among those sensitive to the kinds of empirical research driving much of Nichols' and Prinz's elaborations of sentimentalism. As I argue elsewhere, sentimentalism has become the default position for empirically oriented moral philosophers; the task for those seeking to defend a more robust role for reason has been to show how this role is possible given empirical evidence that affirms Hume's basic position about dominance of the passions in the moral context (Besser-Jones 2012).

So what is the role of reason in the moral context? Thus far, we've focused on arguments defending sentimentalism insofar as there is evidence that affective processes drive our moral judgments and/or responses to them. Let us now turn to consider where and how reason contributes, and whether or not Hume's analysis of the limited power of reason holds up to contemporary examination.

Recent neuroscientific work on the role of cognition and affect introduces the idea of a dual process framework, whereby both affect and cognition work together in the production of moral judgments (e.g. Greene et al., 2001; Haidt 2001). Dual process frameworks thus study and target how both reason and affect are engaged in the course of moral deliberations and judgments; this focus on exploring the interactions between the two allows us to develop a more nuanced understanding of moral judgments. While at first we might think that this stands in tension with Hume's analysis, I would like to suggest that the two approaches are closer than we might first think, and that more research on the interaction between reason and affect would only advance Hume's aims of showing that morality is driven by passions, rather than reason.

Dual process frameworks hold that there are two systems involved in our moral decision-making: the first, system 1, is an intuitive process which is seen to be emotion-based and whose activation is both automatic and unconscious; the second, system 2, is a reasoning process which is seen to involve effort and to be a controlled process. Jonathan Haidt's "social intuitionist model," for instance, posits that our moral responses are the product both of (system 1) intuitions that come to us beyond our conscious control, and of a (system 2) reasoning process that justifies these intuitions post-hoc (Haidt 2001). His influential research presents vignettes detailing incidences of taboos, such as incest and cannibalism, that are framed so that they are harmless. The incest vignette, for example, details a consensual sexual encounter between a brother and sister, and excludes all potential harms associated with incest: multiple methods of birth control are used, the two have no remorse or hard feelings towards each other, and agree that while it was fun, they would not want to do it again (Haidt 2001: 814). When presenting the vignette to his subjects, Haidt found that subjects had an intuitive and immediate moral response to the scenario, but then struggled to come up with reasons that supported the moral judgment. This leads Haidt to postulate that there are two systems involved in moral judgments: the system 1 intuitive, affective responses, and the system 2 cognitive, deliberate rationalizations of those intuitive responses (Haidt 2001: 823–824).

Joshua Greene's MRI research also suggests a dual process framework, in which our emotional (system 1) responses are triggered by "up close and personal" encounters, while the reasoned (system 2) responses enter in later (2008). His research studies the brain activity of individuals considering the trolley problem and its various incarnations. He found that while individuals deliberating about whether or not to push a man onto the track to stop a train that would have otherwise killed several individuals engaged system 1 emotional responses, individuals deliberating about whether or not to pull a switch to move the trolley away from its intended path, which would kill one individual but save the lives of the several individuals who would be killed if the trolley stayed on track, employed system 2 reasoning process. Seemingly, the distance between the two scenarios determined which system was activated:

> the thought of pushing someone to his death in an 'up close and personal' manner . . . is more emotionally salient than the thought of bringing about similar consequences in a more impersonal way (e.g. by hitting a switch).
>
> (Greene 2008: 43)

Greene's own view is that the emotional (system 1) responses serve more as alarms than anything else, and that there is a valuable role for our reasoned (system 2) responses to play in allowing us to make reasoning judgments (Greene et al., 2001; Greene 2008).

Importantly, both of these models of our moral judgments share the same basic understanding of the interplay between emotion and reason: our initial responses to morally salient aspects of our experience are based in emotion, while explicit moral reasoning comes in later, to try to rationalize, justify, or even explain away those emotional reactions. In other words, while dual-process models affirm a fundamental role for emotions (albeit, in contrast to Hume, not necessarily an exclusive role for emotions) in the development of our moral judgments, they also affirm a fundamental role for reason in reflecting on and in regulating those emotional reactions. And it is in this respect that I think dual-process models may have the capacity to preserve and enhance Hume's basic understanding of our moral responses.

As we have seen, Hume's position holds that morality is entirely a matter of our affective responses. "Morality," he writes, "is more properly felt than judged" (T 3.1.2.1; SBN 470). But Hume, like Haidt and Greene, does not think that our initial affective responses ought to determine our moral judgments. Our initial affective responses are contingent to our place and circumstance: when, for example, we consider a ship facing a storm from afar while we are safely on shore, we "reap pleasure" from the consideration of the "miserable condition of those who are at sea in a storm" (T 3.3.2.5; SBN 594). But if the ship were close to shore, so that we "can perceive distinctly the horror, painted on the countenance of the seaman and passengers, hear their lamentable cries" (T 3.3.2.5; SBN 594), we could never have "so savage a heart as to reap any pleasure from such a spectacle" (T 3.3.2.5; SBN 594). Our initial affective responses are liable to morally irrelevant influences. Most generally, our sentimental reactions are partial and are more apt to favor ourselves and those close to us than they should. We thus should not embrace our initial affective responses as they need to be regulated to exclude the kind of contingencies that can alter their course.

Hume envisions that we regulate our affective responses through the development of a "general inalterable standard, by which we may approve or disapprove of characters and manners" (T 3.3.3.2; SBN 602). We reach this standard after experiencing the contingent nature of sympathy and the challenges that arise when trying to engage with others from the partial perspective that our partial sentiments generate:

> we every day meet with persons, who are in a different situation from ourselves, and who cou'd never converse with us on any reasonable terms, were we to remain constantly in that situation and point of view which is peculiar to us.
>
> (T 3.3.3.2; SBN 602)

Fixing on a general standard, and adopting a general point of view, allows us to engage with others and also allows us to develop a perspective from which to generate affective responses that are genuinely moral. True moral judgments thus consist in the feelings of approval and disapproval that we feel through contemplating the motives and actions of another from a general point of view, rather than from our own partial point of view.

In making this important qualification to his analysis of moral judgments, Hume recognizes that our immediate emotional reactions can be problematic. While they are indicative of something morally important, they are not the end all, be all when it comes to the formation of moral judgments. As Sayre-McCord argues, Hume's reliance of the general point of view "enables him to construct an account of moral judgment that sees those judgments as distinct from, but built upon, moral sentiment" (1994: 214). As we have seen, this is the same conclusion we get from defenders of the dual process model. Where there is disagreement, it is in what we do with our immediate emotional reactions. Hume hypothesized that we would be able to develop a mental state from which to experience emotional reactions that are regulated by a general standard. Contemporary research has not yet affirmed this. What it has affirmed is that there are cognitive processes through which we can build upon our emotional responses and to try to take some control over these otherwise unconscious, reactive, and intuitive processes.

Agency

Let us turn now towards consideration of the second theme essential to both Hume's and contemporary moral psychology. This is the area of agency, and specifically how we are to understand ourselves as agents: as people who deliberate about their actions and (seemingly, at least) act on the basis of those deliberations. Here, again, we find that Hume's observations about agency have had a significant influence on contemporary discourse, and that contemporary research affirms much of Hume's position. I will begin by exploring these connections and then turn towards consideration of whether some deeper, and relatively unrecognized, connections can be made between Hume's understanding of agency and our contemporary understanding of it.

Hume's initial approach to agency is dominated by his views of causality. Just as we cannot observe a causal connection between two billiard balls, we also cannot observe a causal connection between our will and our actions:

> in no single instance the ultimate connexion of any objects is discoverable, either by our sense or reason, and that we can never penetrate so far into the essence and construction of bodies as to perceive the principle, on which their mutual influence depends.
>
> (T 2.3.1.4; SBN 400)

We thus have "no adequate idea of power or efficacy in any object; since neither in body nor spirit, neither in superior nor inferior natures, are they able to discover one single instance of it" (T 1.2.14.10; SBN 400). While we cannot know for sure that our will causes our actions, we nonetheless experience a constant conjunction between our motives and our actions; this allows us to associate certain actions with certain motives, both in ourselves and in others. We observe that "the same motives always produce the same actions" (EHU 8.1.6; SBN 83) and in our moral evaluations of others we take one's actions as "signs" of one's motives (T 3.2.2.1; SBN 484).

Hume's theory of agency accepts a compatibilist framework of free will. Compatiblist views of free will hold that freedom (liberty) is compatible with a deterministic picture of the world. This framework emphasizes that what matters most when it comes to judging an action as free is not that we are free in some metaphysical sense, but that we are free insofar as our actions proceed from our motives. We act with liberty when our will precedes our actions (T 2.3.2; SBN 407–418). We experience ourselves as agents, thus, insofar as we experience the conjunction between our motives and our actions, an experience that generates an

> internal impression we feel and are conscious of, when we knowingly give rise to any new impression we feel and are conscious of, when we knowingly give rise to any new motion of our body, or new perception of our mind.
>
> (T 2.3.1.2; SBN 399)

Hume calls this internal impression the "will." This experience is all we need to go about acting; that philosophical introspection cannot secure a causal connection between our actions and motives does not prevent us from deliberating about how best to satisfy our passions and reflecting on the direction of those passions, from caring about what we do and praising and blaming others for their motives and preferences (or lack thereof).

Hume's formulation and defense of compatibilism has had a longstanding influence on contemporary discussions of free will, and compatibilist views of free will are alive and popular among many contemporary philosophers. Like Hume, compatibilists such as Frankfurt (1971) and Wolf (1993) take the basic task of an account of free will to consist in describing an agent's experience of it, as opposed to describing the metaphysical conditions that make actual free will possible (or not).

Before delving into philosophical debates on the experience of agency, let's take a moment to explore some psychological research on the connection between one's will and one's actions. This research has surged in recent years, as psychologists have moved away from the behaviorist views that dominated the field for many years. Behaviorism maintains that behavior is the product of the interaction between a person's actions and environmental stimuli; a person's mental states, on this position, have no influence on their behavior. Within psychology, a commitment to behaviorism entails that to understand human behavior, we look outside of the person, rather than within: an individual's mental experiences are tangential to her behavior.

While behaviorism certainly dominated the field for many years, psychology now has largely shifted its focus back to the individual's mental states as cognitive psychology has become more prominent. One of the psychological debates most salient to Hume's understanding of agency revolves around whether or not our experience of ourselves as agents is, in fact, an illusion. Hume's defense of this claim is straightforward: we experience ourselves as agents insofar as we take actions to be conjoined to motives, but introspective analysis of the causal connections between actions and motives reveals this experience to be illusory.

Psychologists Daniel Wegner and Thalia Wheatley offer a similar line of argument, acknowledging an explicit debt to Hume. Embracing Hume's definition of the will as an internal impression derived from the experience of willing new motions or thoughts (T 2.3.1.2; SBN 399), Wegner and Wheatley write in similar terms that the conscious will is simply "the perception of a causal link between one's own thought and action" (1999: 481),[2] that leads us to interpret our thoughts as the cause of our actions. Wegner and Wheatley argue that although we do in fact *experience* the conscious will, the perception that drives it is illusory, although not for that same reasons that Hume thought.

Wegner and Wheatley identify two main lines of psychological research they take to prove the conscious will is an illusion. The first involves evidence that we are habitually mistaken about the connection between our willings and our actions, such as when we think we have willed an action when we have not; in one experiment, a subject and a confederate played an I spy game on a computer, where they jointly moved the mouse (Wegner and Wheatley 1999: 487). The goal was to determine whether or not the subject believed she willfully moved the mouse when in fact the confederate had done so. Wegner and Wheatley found that this was a regular occurrence and that the experience of the will could itself be manipulated through thought and action even when it was not possible for the person's thoughts to have generated the action (Wegner and Wheatley 1999: 489). The second involves neuroscientific evidence (centered primarily on Libet's research (1985)) that suggests that our actions have their basis in brain activity that occurs before we form conscious intentions. Libet's research tracks individuals brain activity prior to performing simple acts, such as finger movements, as well as the timing of their awareness of any intention to move their finger. He found that movements were associated with cerebral activity, yet that the cerebral activity was initiated prior to an individual's awareness of any intention to act. This evidence is interesting in that it locates the source of actions within one's mental states, yet not within one's will.

What we see from this line of research is a more fine-grained analysis of the nature of agency than Hume was able to offer: for Hume, to understand the practical dimensions of the self and how it is that we engage as moral subjects, it was enough to identify the experience of agency. Exactly why the conscious will is an illusion did not really worry Hume. It is more important to Hume's agenda that we work with the experience of conscious will, and the feelings of agency that it delivers, than that we worry about whether or not the will (or any mental event, really) actually *causes* our actions.

This line of reasoning – moving discussion of agency away from arguments regarding the causes of our actions and towards discussion of the experience of ourselves as agents – fits squarely with both philosophical discussions of compatibilism (such as Frankfurt 1987 and Watson 1975) and social psychological perspectives on agency where questions of motivation take center stage (such as Deci and Ryan's influential self-determination theory (2000)). Within these discussions, much of the focus revolves around the process of identification. Identification involves some kind of reflection on one's desires or motives and endorsement of them. While identification does not presuppose that we freely choose any of our desires, it does provide us with a helpful way to distinguish between situations where we feel compelled by desires that feel foreign to us, and situations where we have desires that feel internal to us, that we embrace and want to act on. The latter delivers a sense of agency that is absent in the former.

Frankfurt's compatibilism holds that we experience our fullest sense of agency when we act on desires with which we can identify. Frankfurt argues that through the process of identification, an individual makes a choice to align herself with certain desires; the identified-with desire is thus "no longer in any way external to him" (Frankfurt 1987: 38). Moreover, he writes, "the person, in making a decision by which he identifies with a desire, *constitutes himself*" (Frankfurt 1987: 38).

The picture we see emerging from Frankfurt's focus on identification is one in which individuals can develop a robust sense of agency by making a choice to identify with certain of one's desires. Thus, even though we do not have control over the desires we have, we can still feel a sense of agency when we identify with certain desires, and in the process we develop our sense of self. The importance of identification, and the role it can play in the development of oneself, is something social psychological research affirms. Ryan and Connell's psychological research (1989), for example, suggests that when we identify with the principles guiding our actions, and come to see ourselves as the perceived locus of causality driving our actions, we satisfy an innate psychological need to experience autonomy; satisfaction of this need carries with it enhanced levels of psychological well-being.[3]

The term "identification" is not something that Hume invokes in his analysis of agency. Nevertheless, the process of identification is something Hume thought was an important component of how it is that we think of ourselves and others. The foundation of Hume's theory of virtues and vices depends upon us being able to attribute, to ourselves and others, durable and constant principles of the mind (T 3.1.1.13; SBN 460) – principles that, as I will discuss in the next section, contribute to our very understandings of character. The presupposition is that not all of one's motives ought to be salient to our moral evaluations, but only the ones that can be said to define a person.

While contemporary moral psychologists such as Frankfurt (1987) might say that the process through which we identify the durable and constant motives essential to a person is through a process of identification, Hume describes this process as a component of the production of pride. Part of what happens when we develop feelings of pride is that we come to think of our self in a certain way; we begin to think of ourselves as *agents*. Pride for Hume functions as a filtration process through which we narrow down the ideas we associate with the self, so that when we think of ourselves as an agent, we think only of the qualities in which we take pride and not necessarily all of the qualities that are somehow connected to the self.[4]

Pride leads us to focus on those qualities and characteristics that others approve of. These are the qualities and characteristics that inform our character and, consequently, our idea of ourselves as agents – the idea of the self "which [pride] never fails to produce" (T 2.1.5.6; SBN 287). One way of understanding what is happening here is that pride serves as a mechanism through which we come to identify with certain passions, motives, and commitments. In fact, we might even think that Hume's particular analysis of pride as framework through which we can make identifications is one which can help to inform current discussions of identification and help us make greater advancements in our understanding of identification, its connection to agency, and its connection to well-functioning.[5]

Virtue and character

The final topic I will address regards Hume's views on virtue and character. The notion of virtue plays a fundamental role in Hume's moral philosophy and many describe Hume's moral views as a species of virtue ethics (Hursthouse 1999; Slote 1995).[6] That Hume thinks virtues are the foci of moral philosophy seems clear from his assertion that we only care, morally speaking, about actions insofar as we presuppose that those actions proceed from certain motives: "If any *action* be either virtuous or vicious, 'tis only as signs of some quality or character. . . . Actions themselves, not proceeding from any constant principle, have no influence on love or hatred, pride or humility; and consequently are never consider'd in morality" (T 3.3.1.4; SBN 575).

This assertion places Hume straightforwardly within a virtue ethical tradition wherein the primary object of our moral evaluations are the virtues. Most virtue ethicists, following Aristotle, associate virtues with *dispositions*, whereas Hume associates virtues with *motives*. This is an important contrast and one that we will turn to later, particularly in our discussion of contemporary critiques of virtue ethics.

Hume's view of what constitutes the virtues is straightforward: the virtues are those qualities of the mind that we find useful or agreeable to ourselves or others, when we consider those qualities from a general point of view. Thus, he writes that: "every quality of mind, which is *useful* or *agreeable* to the *person himself* or to *others*, communicates a pleasure to the spectator, engages his esteem, and is admitted under the honorable denomination of virtue or merit" (EPM 9.1.12; SBN 276). Essential to Hume's theory is that we *feel* a sentiment of approval/disapproval when considering the qualities of others. This follows naturally from his overall understanding of morality as rooted in and driven by sentiments; it is another way of affirming his sentimentalist approach to morality and is one many contemporary sentimentalists, such as Michael Slote (2001), have embraced. Slote's agent-based virtue ethics is unique among contemporary virtue ethical accounts insofar as he follows Hume in framing the virtues as motives rather than dispositions. Slote even goes so far as to maintain that motives are worthy independently of their connection to the consequences they typically produce (Slote 2001: 38).

As we would expect from his definition of the virtues, Hume's catalogue of the virtues is broad; the virtues range from justice, modesty, and allegiance to one's government, to benevolence, prudence, and wit. Some of these virtues are natural, while some are artificial, insofar as they are convention-dependent: they "produce pleasure and approbation by means of an artifice or contrivance, which arises from the circumstances and necessities of mankind" (T 3.2.1.1; SBN 477).

Hume does believe that the virtues contribute to our character, but does not spend a lot of time discussing character as such. He notes that virtue depends "upon durable principles of the mind, which extend over the whole conduct, and enter into the personal character" (T 3.3.1.3; SBN 574). As we have already discussed, there are good grounds for thinking that pride plays an important role in determining which principles of the mind are durable and enter into one's character. But Hume's focus most of the time is on our evaluations of the particular virtues we attribute to another, rather than evaluations of one's character per se.

This is perhaps one of the reason Hume's virtue ethics has not been the target of the most recent and powerful contemporary critique of virtue ethics, which comes from situationist social psychology. The situationist critique, defended most notably by Doris (2002), calls into question the existence of character on the grounds that the attribution of dispositional states is unwarranted in light of psychological research regarding the causes of one's behavior.

Consider, for instance, the series of studies by Isen and Levin (1972), considering the effects of good moods on helping behavior. In these studies, researchers tested whether or not finding a dime in the change receptacle of a phone booth would lead to greater helping behavior. They planted dimes within a phone booth, and then arranged for subjects who found the dime to encounter a distressed stranger, who had dropped her papers on the sidewalk. The control group were subjects who used the phone but did not find a spare dime, and then had the same encounter with the distressed stranger. Those in the experimental condition, who were primed to feel good in virtue of finding a dime, ended up helping the distressed stranger at significantly higher rates than those in the control condition. The numbers are surprising, even to those familiar with this line of research: In one version of this study, 14 of 16 in the experimental condition helped, while only 1 of 24 in the control group helped. This experiment is just one of many that reveal the dramatic extent to which our actions are influenced by situations, suggesting that behavior is more the product of situational influences than one's internal dispositional states.

The situationist critique presents an important challenge to virtue ethics insofar as most virtue ethical theories are predicated on the assumption that the virtues are *dispositional* traits that lead a person to act in similar ways across a wide range of situations.[7] Aristotle, for example, defines virtue as the state which causes its possessor "to perform its characteristic activity well" (Aristotle 2014: sec. 1106a14–16). Contemporary Aristotelians, such as Julia Annas, fully embrace this idea that virtue is a dispositional state. Annas writes that virtues are active, such that "to have it is to be disposed to act in certain ways" (Annas 2011: 8).

Hume's theory, however, works slightly differently: what is crucial for Hume is not that we have dispositions to act, but that we have motives that others approve of. One way of framing this emphasis on motives is to see Hume as making the claim that what is most important is that we *care* about things in ways that others find useful/agreeable. We approve of those who *care* about justice, we approve of those who *value* honesty, and who *appreciate* wit. That (and if) our motives give rise to actions is secondary; we only care morally about actions insofar as they are signs of motives (T 3.3.1.4; SBN 604). Where actions are not indicative of motives, they fail to generate the sentimental reactions distinctive to our moral appraisal (T 3.3.1.4; SBN 593).

The proposal that there is an important difference between virtues conceived of as dispositions and virtues conceived of as motives warrants further reflection. Framing Hume's virtue ethics in this way, as essentially focusing on the development of motives, where those motives represent the principles of the mind that reflect what it is we (as informed by others) value and care about, allows us to begin thinking about character in a new way. Actions are not the end all, be all of morality: what is important is what we care about and what we feel motivated by. Whether or not we are actually moved by these motives is far less important than whether or not we experience these concerns.[8]

Conclusion

We have seen that the basic themes with which Hume's moral philosophy was most concerned are themes that are alive and well in contemporary debates. While contemporary discourse often invokes a standardized picture of what counts as "Humean," I have tried here draw attention to the possibility of developing some more novel and previously unnoticed connections. Hume would encourage the on-going enterprise of incorporating new insights regarding human nature to one's moral philosophy. He famously compares his methodology to one of a painter, who takes advice from the anatomist, and in doing so is able to develop a practical morality that is "more correct in its precepts, and more pervasive in its exhortations" (T 3.3.6.6; SBN 620). As the anatomist evolves, so too should the painter.

Notes

1 Exactly where psychopaths fail – in the making of moral judgments or in being motivated by moral judgments – is a subject of debate. See, for example, Blair (1995) and Cima et al. (2010).

2 Hume would resist labeling this as a perception of a "causal" link and would instead describe it as a perception of constant conjunction.

3 For further discussion of both the philosophical and psychological understanding of agency, see Besser-Jones (2014: chap. 4).

4 See Ainslie (1999); McIntyre (1989).

5 In Besser-Jones (2010), I develop some of these ideas with respect to pride taken in virtue.

6 Hume is often taken to be an early precursor to utilitarianism (Hayek 1966; cf Wand 1962). See also Gauthier (1979), who argues that Hume's view is contractarian.

7 For discussion and debate of this criticism, see Athanassoulis (2000), Besser-Jones (2008) Kamtekar (2004), Miller (2003), and Sreenivasan (2002).

8 In this way, we might find a connection between Alfano's suggestion that it is still functionally important to develop and attribute the virtues even though psychological research (on his account) shows them to be fictions (Alfano 2013).

References

Ainslie, D. C. (1999) "Scepticism About Persons in Book II of Hume's *Treatise," Journal of the History of Philosophy*. 37(3): 469–492.

Alfano, M. (2013) *Character as Moral Fiction*, New York: Cambridge University Press.

Annas, J. (2011) *Intelligent Virtue*, New York: Oxford University Press.

Aristotle and R. Crisp, ed. (2014) *Nicomachean Ethics*, rev. edn. Cambridge: Cambridge University Press.

Athanassoulis, N. (2000) "A Response to Harman: Virtue Ethics and Character Traits," *Proceedings of the Aristotelian Society* 100(1): 215–221.

Besser-Jones, L. (2008) "Social Psychology, Moral Character, and Moral Fallibility," *Philosophy and Phenomenology Research* 76(2): 310–332.

———. (2014) *Eudaimonic Ethics: The Philosophy and Psychology of Living Well*, New York: Routledge.

———. (2010) "Hume on Pride-in-Virtue: A Reliable Motive?" *Hume Studies* 36(2): 171–192.

———. (2012) "The Role of Practical Reason in an Empirically Informed Moral Theory," *Ethical Theory and Moral Practice* 15(2): 1–18.

Blair, R. J. R. (1995) "A Cognitive Developmental Approach to Morality: Investigating the Psychopath," *Cognition* 57(1): 1–29.

Cima, M., F. Tonnaer and M. D. Hauser (2010) "Psychopaths Know Right from Wrong but Don't Care," *Social Cognitive and Affective Neuroscience* 5(1): 59–67.

Cohon, R. (2008) *Hume's Morality: Feeling and Fabrication*, New York: Oxford University Press.

Deci, E. L. and R. M. Ryan (2000) "The 'What' and 'Why' of Goal Pursuits: Human Needs and the Self-Determination of Behavior," *Psychological Inquiry* 11(4): 227–268.

Doris, J. M. (2002) *Lack of Character: Personality and Moral Behavior*, New York: Cambridge University Press.

———. (2015) *Talking to Our Selves: Reflection, Ignorance, and Agency*, New York: Oxford University Press.

Frankfurt, H. (1971) "Freedom of the Will and the Concept of a Person," *Journal of Philosophy* 68(1): 5–20.

———. (1987) "Identification and Wholeheartedness," in F. Schoeman (ed.), *Responsibility, Character, and the Emotions: New Essays in Moral Psychology*, New York: Cambridge University Press.

Gauthier, D. (1979) "David Hume, Contractarian," *The Philosophical Review* 88(1): 3–38.

Goldie, P. (2011) "Anti-Empathy," in A. Coplan and P. Goldie (ed.), *Empathy: Philosophical and Psychological Perspectives*, New York: Oxford University Press.

Greene, J. D. (2008) "The Secret Joke of Kant's Soul," W. in Sinnott-Armstrong (ed.), *The Neuroscience of Morality: Emotion, Disease, and Development*, Cambridge, MA: MIT Press.

———., R. B. Sommerville, L. E. Nystrom, J. M. Darley and J. D. Cohen (2001) "An fMRI Study of Emotional Engagement in Moral Judgment," *Science* 293(5537): 2105–2108.

Haidt, J. (2001) "The Emotional Dog and Its Rational Tail," *Psychological Review* 108(4): 814–834.

Harman, G. (2000) "The Nonexistence of Character Traits," *Proceedings of Aristotelian Society (Hardback)* 100(1): 223–226.

Hayek, F. A. (1966) "The Legal and Political Philosophy of David Hume," in V. C. Chappell (ed.), *Hume*, New York: Springer.

Hursthouse, R. (1999) "Virtue Ethics and Human Nature," *Hume Studies* 25(1): 67–82.

Isen, A. M., & Levin, P. F. (1972). "Effect of Feeling Good on Helping: Cookies and Kindness," *Journal of Personality and Social Psychology* 21: 384–388.

Kamtekar, R. (2004) "Situationism and Virtue Ethics on the Content of Our Character," *Ethics* 114(3): 458–491.

Libet, B. (1985) "Unconscious Cerebral Initiative and the Role of Conscious Will in Voluntary Action," *Behavioral and Brain Science* 8(4): 529–566.

McIntyre, J. L. (1989) "Personal Identity and the Passions," *Journal of the History of Philosophy* 27(4): 545–557.

Miller, C. B. (2003) "Social Psychology and Virtue Ethics," *The Journal of Ethics* 7(4): 365–392.

Nichols, S. (2002) "How Psychopaths Threaten Moral Rationalism: Is It Irrational to Be Amoral?" *The Monist* 85(2): 285–303.

———. (2004) *Sentimental Rules: On the Natural Foundations of Moral Judgment*, New York: Oxford University Press.

Prinz, J. (2007) *The Emotional Construction of Morals*, New York: Oxford University Press.

———. (2011) "Is Empathy Necessary for Morality?" in A. Coplan and P. Goldie (ed.), *Empathy: Philosophical and Psychological Perspectives*, New York: Oxford University Press.

Ryan, R. M. and J. P. Connell (1989) "Perceived Locus of Causality and Internalization: Examining Reasons for Acting in Two Domains," *Journal of Personality and Social Psychology* 57(5): 749–761.

Sayre-McCord, G. (1994) "On Why Hume's 'General Point of View' Isn't Ideal – and Shouldn't Be," *Social Philosophy and Policy* 11(1): 202–228.

Shaw, D. (1993) "Hume's Moral Sentimentalism," *Hume Studies* 19(1): 31–54.

Slote, M. (1995) "Agent-Based Virtue Ethics," *Midwest Studies in Philosophy* 20(1): 83–101.

———. (2001) *Morals from Motives*, New York: Oxford University Press.

———. (2010) *Moral Sentimentalism*, New York: Oxford University Press.

Sreenivasan, G. (2002) "Errors About Errors: Virtue Theory and Trait Attribution," *Mind* 111(441): 47–68.

Wand, B. (1962) "Hume's Non-Utilitarianism," *Ethics* 72(3): 193–196.

Watson, G. (1975) "Free Agency," *Journal of Philosophy* 72 (April): 205–220.

Wegner, D. M. and T. Wheatley (1999) "Apparent Mental Causation: Sources of the Experience of Will," *The American Psychologist* 54(7): 480–492.

Wolf, S. (1993) *Freedom Within Reason*, New York: Oxford University Press.

36

HUME AND ANIMAL ETHICS

Deborah Boyle

The eighteenth century saw shifting attitudes towards non-human animals. By the time Hume wrote his *Treatise*, Descartes' arguments from the previous century that animals are mere machines,[1] and thus fundamentally different from humans, had already been subject to critiques by Pierre Bayle (1991: 213–235), David-Renaud Boullier (1728), David Hartley (1749: 413), and others. And during Hume's lifetime, there was a growing body of writing – poetry, sermons, pamphlets, speeches in Parliament, essays, novels, and children's literature – that depicted animals as worthy of compassionate treatment.[2] Hume's theory of sympathy has been invoked as an influence on this increased awareness of animal welfare.

However, Hume himself does not explicitly discuss animal welfare or whether animals have moral standing, and Hume's views on this issue have received relatively little scholarly attention. Instead, attention has focused on two other questions. First, does Hume think that animals can make moral judgments? Commentators who consider Hume's views on animals agree that Hume says animals cannot make moral judgments, but there is disagreement regarding whether Hume attributes this inability to a defect in animals' reasoning or to a defect of sentiment. A second question arises because even if an animal cannot make moral judgments itself, its character traits might nonetheless be subject to moral evaluation by *us*. Does Hume think that the character traits of animals are properly subject to moral approval or disapproval by humans? That is, does he think animals can be said to be virtuous or vicious? Again, the consensus in the secondary literature is that Hume said they cannot. This chapter will consider these two questions, ending with a discussion of the third question of what Hume's views imply about the moral standing of animals.

Hume's writings on animals

In the *Treatise*, Hume devotes three chapters to discussing the nature of animals: one chapter in Book 1, two in Book 2, but, interestingly, none in Book 3. This suggests that he thinks animals resemble humans in their mental faculties (the topic of Book 1) and their passions (the topic of Book 2), but not in their ethical capabilities (the topic of Book 3). In Book 1, "Of the Understanding," he observes that "no truth appears to me more evident, than that beasts are endow'd with thought and reason as well as men" (T 1.3.16.1; SBN 176).[3] In Book 2, "Of the Passions," Hume ends each of the three main parts with discussions of animals. In particular, at the end of

Part 1, "Of Pride and Humility," he argues that observations of animals provide "evident proofs, that pride and humility are not merely human passions, but extend themselves over the whole animal creation" (T 2.1.12.4; SBN 326). At the end of Part 2, "Of Love and Hatred," he similarly argues that we can tell from observation that animals experience love, hatred, and other passions such as grief and envy, and that such passions can be communicated among animals through the mechanism of sympathy (T 2.2.12.1–8; SBN 397–398).[4] Towards the end of Part 3, while he says that to avoid "prolixity" he will "wave the examination of the will and direct passions, as they appear in animals," he nonetheless says that "nothing is more evident, than that [the will and direct passions] are of the same nature, and excited by the same causes as in human creatures" (T 2.3.9.32; SBN 448). In other words, animals resemble humans in their reasoning abilities and their direct and indirect passions.

However, in Book 3, "Of Morals," Hume says nothing at all about animals possessing a moral sense; this absence is a clue that he thought they really do not possess it. Hume does mention animals in one example in Book 3 (what I will call the "incest example," at T 3.1.1.25; SBN 467), which commentators have generally taken as evidence that Hume thought animals cannot be subject to moral evaluations, although I shall argue later that the example should not be read that way.

In Hume's *Enquiry Concerning Human Understanding*, Section 9 addresses animals' reasoning abilities. As in the *Treatise*, Hume emphasizes the similarities between humans and other animals: "It seems evident, that animals as well as men learn many things from experience, and infer, that the same events will always follow from the same causes" (EHU 9.2; SBN 105). But he also observes that animals possess some knowledge that is derived "from the original hand of nature," "instincts" such as a bird's innate ability to build the appropriate sort of nest (EHU 9.6; SBN 108). In his essay "On the Dignity or Meanness of Human Nature," Hume also contrasts the human with other animals, writing that the former is "a creature, who traces causes and effects to a great length and intricacy; extracts general principles from particular appearances; improves upon his discoveries; corrects his mistakes; and makes his very errors profitable," while the latter is "the very reverse of this: limited in its observations and reasonings to a few sensible objects which surround it; without curiosity, without foresight; blindly conducted by instinct, and attaining, in a short time, its utmost perfection" (E 82).

First question: can animals make moral judgments?

For Hume, a moral judgment is a judgment about whether some character trait is a virtue or vice. Unfortunately, he did not explicitly address the question of whether animals can make such judgments; determining how he would answer the question requires identifying how Hume thought *humans* make moral judgments, and examining whether his remarks on animals imply that they have the same capacities. Hume scholars who have written on Hume's account of animals agree that Hume believes animals *cannot* make moral judgments, but they differ in their explanations of why Hume thought this.

For Hume, moral judgment requires a certain kind of both sentiment and reason. The sentiment, or "moral sense" (T 3.1.2; SBN 477–484), is a response to the character traits that Hume calls virtues and vices. Humean virtues are character traits that are pleasing or beneficial to the possessor or to those affected by the trait or action (T 3.1.2.11; SBN 475–476 and T 3.3.1.9; SBN 577); thus the moral sense is an ability to respond with approval or disapproval when we observe (in ourselves or others) such a trait. If the trait is not useful or agreeable directly to us, the observers, then our approval (or disapproval) derives from the sympathy we feel with those who *are* affected by the trait (T 3.3.3.2; SBN 602). However, the liveliness of the passions evoked

471

in us through sympathy can vary, because Hume thinks that sympathy exerts a greater influence when the person with whom we sympathize is closer to us:

> A statesman or patriot, who serves our own country, in our own time, has always a more passionate regard paid to him, than one whose beneficial influence operated on distant ages or remote nations; where the good, resulting from his generous humanity, being less connected with us, seems more obscure, and affects us with a less lively sympathy.
>
> (EPM 5.41; SBN 227)

Nonetheless, according to Hume, our moral judgments do not (and should not) vary correspondingly, because we are able to compensate for these disparities in our sympathetic responses; we "form some general inalterable standard, by which we may approve or disapprove of characters and manners" (T 3.3.3.2; SBN 603; see also EPM 5.42; SBN 229). We are able to do this, he says, because we do not have to "remain constantly in that position and point of view, which is peculiar to ourselves" (EPM 5.42; SBN 229). We can, in fact, give up our "peculiar point of view" and take up a *general* point of view (T 3.3.1.15; SBN 581–582). In the *Treatise*, Hume says that to take this point of view is to consider the effects of a character trait on all those who interact with the agent, regardless of the relationship we bear to those affected (T 3.3.1.17; SBN 582); it is to be impartial in our appraisal of the effects of the character trait on those affected, whether those affected are our family members, strangers, or sworn enemies. Hume refers to this process as "correcting our sentiments" (T 3.3.1.16; SBN 582).

Making a moral judgment requires the moral sentiment, but Hume also observes that

> in order to pave the way for such a sentiment, and give a proper discernment of its object, it is often necessary, we find, that much reasoning should precede, that nice distinctions be made, just conclusions drawn, distant comparisons formed, complicated relations examined, and general facts fixed and ascertained.
>
> (EPM 1.9; SBN 173)

Here Hume is noting that moral judgment in any given case requires being able to perceive or infer the pertinent matters of fact in the case. As Denis Arnold points out, making a moral judgment also requires discerning which actions derive from stable character traits and which ones were caused in some other way, such as from ignorance or haste (Arnold 1995: 306). And Hume's process of "correcting" our sentiments also involves reason, since considering the effects of a character trait on all those affected by the trait requires making inferences based on past experiences.

Thus, if Hume thought animals cannot make moral judgments, this must be because they lack one or more of the components required for such judgments. Perhaps other animals' reasoning abilities are lacking in some way, preventing them from identifying the pertinent matters of fact or preventing them from adopting the general point of view. Or perhaps they lack the moral sentiment that, in humans, causes an emotional response to virtues and vices. Or perhaps they lack sympathy, the propensity to come to share in the emotions of those affected for good or ill by someone's actions.

We can dispense first with the suggestion that Hume thought animals lack sympathy, for he explicitly states that animals *do* communicate passions through the mechanism of sympathy (T 2.2.12; SBN 398). Thus, if animals do not make moral judgments, it is not because they cannot come to share the passions of other animals around them.

What about reason? Various commentators have argued that the key moral difference between animals and humans lay, for Hume, in their differing abilities to reason. And if animals' inferior reasoning abilities prevent them from making moral judgments, it is presumably either because they lack the abilities adequately to ascertain relevant facts or because, even if they are able to discern the facts, they are unable to adopt a general, disinterested point of view.

Antony Pitson suggests that Hume thought animals lack *both* abilities. He writes that, for Hume, the moral sense requires "a kind of imaginative ability to detach ourselves from our personal relation to the agent whose mind or character is the subject of our appraisal"; this is the general point of view. But, Pitson goes on,

> in order that our moral judgements should achieve the objectivity associated with the general view distinctions need to be made, conclusions drawn, comparisons formed, relations examined, and facts ascertained (EPM 173). It is just this kind of exercise of understanding of which animals appear to be incapable; and it is also, therefore, this that would explain their lack of a moral sense.
>
> (Pitson 1993: 304)

According to Pitson, then, it is animals' failure to do the preliminary work of identifying facts and making inferences that leads them to the further failure, their inability to take a common point of view.

Knut Tranöy makes a similar point, focusing on Hume's claim that animals cannot imagine the effects of actions or traits on others, and so can "judge of objects only by the sensible good or evil, which they produce, and from that must regulate their affections towards them" (T 2.2.12.3; SBN 397). The failure here, as Tranöy sees it, is a failure to "reason from probabilities, to predict and foresee the consequences of alternative courses of action," for "it is only when, by this manner of reasoning, we see that a given 'character' or action will have certain good consequences for mankind, that we are able to feel the crucial and specific moral sentiment even though the character or action should go counter to our own private interests" (Tranöy 1959: 100).

On the other hand, some Hume scholars argue that Hume located the primary moral distinction between humans and animals in a difference in sentiment (Beauchamp 1999: 328; Seidler 1977: 368–369). Denis Arnold presents the most well-developed argument for this view, arguing that Hume's incest example provides evidence that the moral difference between humans and animals cannot be explained, for Hume, by differences in reasoning ability. The example occurs in a section of the *Treatise* (T 3.1.1; SBN 467–468) where Hume is objecting to the rationalist view that morality consists in certain relations and that moral judgment involves using reason to identify which relations obtain. Hume points out that his opponent's position would require ascribing the "same morality" to humans and animals. As he puts it,

> According to this system, then, every animal, that has sense, and appetite, and will; that is, every animal must be susceptible of all the same virtues and vices, for which we ascribe praise and blame to human creatures. . . . Animals are susceptible of the same relations with respect to each other, as the human species, and therefore wou'd also be susceptible of the same morality, if the essence of morality consisted in these relations. Their want of a sufficient degree of reason may hinder them from perceiving the duties and obligations of morality, but can never hinder these duties from existing.
>
> (T 3.1.1. 25; SBN 467–468)

Because Hume had already suggested that incest in animals has "not the smallest moral turpitude and deformity" (T 3.1.1.25; SBN 467–468), he is clearly providing a *reductio* of his opponent's view: if moral good and evil depend on certain relations between people or things obtaining, then, since animals engage in some of the same relations as humans (such as incestuous relations), such animals, like incestuous humans, should be judged to be immoral. But no one makes such a judgment about animals. Therefore, morality must consist in something other than relations, and it must be judged through some faculty other than reasoning.

As Arnold points out, Hume wants to show that if the wrongness of incest were discoverable by reason alone, then it wouldn't matter (for the purposes of moral assessments) that animals are unable to discern this; it would still be wrong for them to engage in incest. But, since it is clearly not wrong for them to engage in incest, the wrongness must not be discoverable by reason alone. As Arnold reads Hume's incest example, since reason does not make moral determinations, differences in reasoning ability are irrelevant to a creature's ability to make moral judgments; thus, if humans can make moral judgments and animals cannot, the difference is not in their reasoning abilities. Arnold concludes that the difference is in the sentiments that humans and animals feel. In Hume's account of human morality, the "sentiment of sympathy and humanity" (EPM 6.2; SBN 233) is a necessary condition for making moral judgments, but according to Arnold, animals lack "a species-wide sentiment akin to the sentiment of humanity" (Arnold 1995: 313). Animals thus cannot make moral judgments or act morally. Arnold does observe that if it were to turn out that some animals do have such a sentiment, then Hume could – and indeed would have to – say they are moral agents (Arnold 1995: 313–314).

According to Arnold, then, Hume's incest example shows that Hume thought animals lack the moral sentiment possessed by humans. But does the example really serve this function? According to Arnold, Hume proceeds by showing that his opponent's view "commits one to the view that nonhuman animal incest is morally wrong, and thus to the view that animals act morally," a conclusion that Hume takes to be "obviously absurd" (Arnold 1995: 308). But while Hume does say that it is absurd to think that non-human animal incest is morally wrong, he does not make the further point that Arnold attributes to him. That is, Hume does not say that it is "obviously absurd" to conclude that "animals act morally." Rather, he says that if his opponent's view is right, then animals "would also be susceptible of the *same* morality" and "susceptible of all the *same* virtues and vices, for which we ascribe praise and blame to human creatures" (T 3.1.1.25; SBN 467–468; emphasis added). The claim Hume denies is that animals and humans are subject to the *same* virtues, vices, and morality; but this is not equivalent to saying that animals do not act morally at all.

Even if Arnold were right that the incest example shows that animals lack a moral sentiment that humans possess, this lack would imply only that animals cannot *make moral judgments*. It would not automatically show, as Arnold claims it does, that "humans act morally and all other animals do not" (Arnold 1995: 308). This is because, as Beauchamp points out, whether a creature can make a moral judgment is a distinct question from whether humans can judge that creature to have moral qualities (Beauchamp 1999: 328; see also Driver 2011: 148). I turn to this distinct question in the next section.

So, what should we conclude about animals' abilities to make moral judgments? Pitson seems right about the limitations of animals' reasoning abilities. It also seems right to say that animals cannot take the general point of view. But does moral judgment *require* adopting the general point of view? Perhaps Hume thinks it is enough to feel, through sympathy with those affected by a character trait, a certain kind of sentiment. As Arnold points out, Hume says that moral sentiments can arise from observing certain "immediately agreeable" qualities of character (Arnold 1995: 312, citing SBN 589–590). If this is Hume's view, then even if animals cannot adopt the general point of view, an animal's response could be considered moral if the animal has enough reason to discern the facts of the situation and if it has a moral sense. As Arnold also points out, Hume does in fact suggest that animals have a species-wide concern for the well-being of other creatures: he says that animals are "susceptible of kindness, both to their own species and to ours" (EPM App 2.8; SBN 300; quoted in Arnold 1995: 313).

However, Hume does seem to think the "moral sentiment" is more than feeling love for another creature. He suggests that to feel a truly moral sentiment requires adopting the general point of view: "'Tis only when a character is considered in general, without reference to our particular interest, that it causes such a feeling or sentiment, as denominates it morally good or evil" (T SBN 472; cited in Arnold 1995: 312). As Annette Baier puts it, for Hume, "no sentiment can count as the moral sentiment unless it is 'steady and general,' unless it does arise from a reflective reasoned consideration of the good of all concerned" (Baier 1985: 154). If this is right, then an animal's inability to adopt a general point of view means that the animal cannot feel the moral sense, even if it can feel love for others whose character traits are pleasing or beneficial. Similarly, an animal cannot morally disapprove of a trait; as Baier puts it, while animals can "complain and protest," disapproval is a uniquely human, moral response to a character trait when considered from the general point of view (Baier 1985: 151).

In sum, animals seem to lack the abilities that Hume says are necessary for moral judgment; they lack the reasoning abilities to adequately identify the facts of a situation, and, even if they feel positive and negative sentiments towards others, they lack the specifically moral sentiment, which requires adoption of a more general perspective than animals can take. They may possess what Baier calls "the basic emotional prerequisites of a moral sense, including some, such as pride, that require a sort of self-consciousness" (Baier 1985: 147), but it seems that animals cannot be Humean moral judges.

Second question: can animals' actions be virtuous or vicious?

A creature that lacks the abilities to make moral judgments may nonetheless have the qualities of character that humans judge to be virtues or vices (Beauchamp 1999: 328; Driver 2011: 148). And, as Beauchamp observes, while Hume claims that animals "have little or no *sense* of virtue" (T 2.1.12.5; my emphasis), this does not mean that they do not have virtues or vices (Beauchamp 1999: 329). Some commentators have suggested that Hume's incest example shows that animals cannot be judged to be virtuous or vicious (Pitson 1993: 305 and Norton 2000: 179). However, as we saw in the previous section, Hume's incest example does not show that animals are "susceptible" of no virtues or vices; it establishes only that they are not subject to the same ones as us. Hume presents his argument as establishing "that morality consists not in any relations, that are the object of science" (T 3.1.1.26; SBN 468), and he draws that conclusion by identifying *one case* in which an action is subject to a moral evaluation when performed by humans, but not when performed by animals. But giving one case in which animals are exempt from moral evaluation does not show that Hume held that animals are *always* exempt from moral evaluation. The passage thus leaves open the possibility that animals' character traits might, in *other cases*, be virtuous or vicious. We need to investigate Hume's texts further, rather than relying only on the incest example, to settle whether animals fit Hume's criteria for counting as virtuous or vicious.

Humean virtues are those character traits that inspire moral approval, either through being directly pleasing or beneficial to someone, or through the sympathy an observer feels with those affected by the traits' usefulness or agreeableness. When a trait has beneficial effects (through being either useful or agreeable) on either the possessor of the trait or those around her, an observer can appreciate the beneficial effects; the observer's approval stems from sympathy with the feelings of those affected. As Hume puts it in the *Treatise*,

> When the natural tendency of [a man's] passions leads him to be serviceable and useful within his sphere, we approve of his character, and love his person, by a sympathy with the sentiments of those, who have a more particular connexion with him.
>
> (T 3.3.3.2; SBN 602)

Hume does say that animals have some natural abilities related to virtues, such as love, and some of the mental qualities that he calls virtues, such as friendliness, fidelity, industry, patience, and courage (Beauchamp 1999: 330–331; Driver 2011: 148). Thus, according to Beauchamp, Hume would probably be willing to say that animals can have virtues in a "primitive" sense (Beauchamp 1999: 330). But it is not clear that Hume thought that virtues and vices come in degrees. What would it mean for an animal to have virtue in a "primitive" sense? Perhaps it means that the animal demonstrates the pleasing or useful character trait in only a truncated way, to a lesser degree than humans exhibit it. But Hume does not suggest that we feel more or less approval or disapproval depending on the degree to which a character trait is expressed.

If we cannot make sense of the notion of a "primitive virtue" in Hume's ethics, then it seems we must either deny that Humean animals have virtues and vices altogether, or allow that they may have them in the same sense as humans. There are some reasons to think that Hume would deny altogether that animals can possess virtues or vices. First, Hume never himself describes any actual animals as virtuous or vicious. Second, in his discussion of ideas and impressions, Hume groups conceiving of a virtuous horse with conceiving of a golden mountain (EHU 2.5/SBN 19). Both, he says, are imagined by uniting two ideas of items "with which we were formerly acquainted" (EHU 2.5/SBN 19). His examples are supposed to show that we can combine ideas in new ways; but if horses could actually be virtuous, then the idea of a virtuous horse would not be an apt example. This suggests that Hume thought that virtues and vices do not, in fact, apply to animals.

On the other hand, it is hard to see how Hume can rule out the view that animals have virtues and vices, given his account of what it is to have a virtue or vice. For we can surely imagine both an animal possessing a character trait that positively affects other animals or humans, and a human observer coming to share, through sympathy, the sentiment felt by the affected person(s) or animal(s). For example, imagine a traumatized woman who benefits from the steady loyalty of her therapy dog. An observer, seeing that the dog's trait of loyalty is beneficial or pleasing to the woman, might come, through sympathy with the effects on the woman, to approve of the dog's loyalty. Hume says that "there are a numerous set of passions and sentiments, of which *thinking rational beings* are, by the original constitution of nature, the only proper objects" (EPM n17; SBN 213 n1; my emphasis). He contrasts these feelings with those produced by observing a useful or pleasing inanimate object, such as a useful kitchen knife. Hume does hold that animals are "thinking rational beings," so presumably the feeling of approval inspired by the loyalty of the dog is *not* like the feeling excited by the usefulness of an inanimate object.

What about cases where those benefited by an animal's character traits are other animals? In such cases, we must settle whether *animals* can feel the passions and sentiments that *humans* typically feel when they observe the utility or agreeableness of some character trait. If not, then there will be no feeling to be communicated by sympathy to a human observer, and so no judgment at all by the human observer concerning the virtue of the animal's character trait. But if there is, then we must ask whether Hume thinks a sentiment felt by an animal can be shared through sympathy with a *human* observer.

Hume does not explicitly address whether animals respond in the same way as humans to the utility of a thinking being. However, in "Of the love and hatred of animals," he writes: "As animals are but little susceptible either of the pleasures or pains of the imagination, they can judge of objects only by the sensible good or evil, which they produce, and from *that* must regulate their affections towards them" (T 2.2.12.3; SBN 397). This implies that animals *are* capable of judging that something is useful to them. Thus, Hume might say, when an animal is immediately benefited by a character trait displayed by another animal, it will feel love towards that animal. Of course, if the benefit is not immediately apparent, the animal will not feel any affection, because it lacks the imaginative capacity to follow out the train of ideas that would lead it to conclude that the action was beneficial. Similarly, if the cause of the action is not obvious, the animal would presumably not be able to infer who performed the action, and, again, the animal would not feel any affection for the creature that benefited it. But, if the animal is able to perceive the facts of the case, it could feel love for the animal whose character trait benefited it.

So let us assume that some animals, just like humans, can feel pleased when they are positively affected by some character trait exhibited by another animal. Can a human observer come to share that emotion through sympathy? The texts might suggest that Hume would say no, for in the second *Enquiry*, he emphasizes that we feel this sympathy with other *humans*: he calls it a "warm concern for the interests of our species," a feeling we extend to our "fellow-creatures" (EPM 5.39; SBN 225). Thus, Hume evidently thinks we cannot sympathize with another animal's pleasure.

However, we should note a certain qualification in Hume's account of sympathy. Hume thinks that we naturally sympathize when we contemplate the effects of a trait on those affected by the trait – so long as those affected either resemble us, are close to us in time or place, or are related to us by blood (T 2.1.11.5–6; SBN 318). Yet, as we have seen, Hume thinks that sympathy can be "corrected" so as to extend it to people in remote places or distant times, people for whom we do not naturally sympathize. And Hume has sought to establish that animals are much more like us than usually thought. So presumably we can, and perhaps should, extend sympathy to animals, too, just as we can extend it to people of more remote times and places (see Coventry and Hiller 2015: 173–174). If so, then when an animal's character trait positively affects other animals, we too can appreciate its utility, and morally approve of it. Character traits in animals, then, could count as virtues or vices, just as they do in humans.

Third question: do animals have moral standing?

I have argued that while Hume's account suggests that animals cannot make moral judgments, he can say that some animals possess some virtues and vices. But there is a third question related to animal ethics: what do Hume's views imply for how humans should treat animals? Do animals have moral standing, according to Hume?

There has been relatively little work on Hume's views about the moral standing of animals. Contemporary proponents of animal welfare have not made much use of Hume's writings on animals. Most contemporary writers on animal welfare argue on either utilitarian or deontological grounds, and, while some scholars see utilitarian strands in Hume's ethical thought, contemporary utilitarians such as Peter Singer do not draw inspiration from Hume; nor can we find in Hume any precedents for contemporary arguments that animals have rights. As Annette Baier has pointed out, "Hume would reject any attempt to give sense to the concept of rights of animals, since all rights arise from artifice" (Baier 1985: 147). In particular, Humean justice does not seem applicable to animals. Justice, as Hume explains it, concerns property and the "partition of goods" (EPM 3.2; SBN 183), and requires respecting the rules and conventions of property developed by a society. Baier suggests that humans can be said to have conventions with some animals, for a Humean convention "involves both a mutually expressed sense of common interest, and mutually referential intentions," and, she points out, "a horse and its rider, or a man and his dog, seem as good an example of this as Hume's boatload of rowers" (Baier 1985: 150; see also Kuflik 1998: 65 and Valls 2014: 124–126). But it would be a stretch to suggest that animals create conventions regarding the possession of goods, or that they have any such conventions with humans. Angela Coventry and Avram Hiller observe that Hume himself says that the "boundaries of justice" can expand, and that "the inclusion of moral duties towards animals might naturally be considered as part of the 'gradual enlargement' of the domain of justice" (Coventry and Hiller 2015: 171, citing EPM 3.1.21; SBN 192; see also Valls 2014: 126). But Hume's notion of justice is focused on the distribution of property; even if some animals could form conventions with humans regarding property (as Kuflik suggests perhaps porpoises and chimpanzees might [Kuflik 1998: 65]), the existence of such conventions would not provide much basis for arguing generally for improved animal welfare. To expand Humean justice in a way that secures rights for animals not to be used in (for example) experimentation or for food would require going far beyond Hume's own conception of justice.

While the utilitarian and deontological approaches to animal welfare often employed in the contemporary literature owe little to Hume, environmental ethicist J. Baird Callicott explicitly invokes Hume to support extending moral consideration to animals and even to plants, landscapes, and the ecosystem itself. On Callicott's reading, Hume is the "historical ancestor of Aldo Leopold's land ethic," for Leopold drew on Charles Darwin's "natural history" of ethics, and Darwin's views were shaped by Hume's (Callicott 1988: 166). Drawing on the work of Mary Midgley, Callicott points out that humans and domestic animals belong to a "mixed community," that we are "coevolved social beings participating in a single society" (Callicott 1988: 165).[5] Thus, "we and they share certain feelings that attend upon and enable sociability – sympathy, compassion, trust, love, and so on" (Callicott 1988: 165).

Hume would probably agree with Callicott so far, but Callicott makes two additional, suspect claims. First, having observed that humans are part of a "metahuman moral community" that is an interdependent biotic web of animals, plants, and the ecosystem, Callicott suggests that we can read Hume's references to "society" as including these other elements. Second, Callicott says that Hume's claim that humans have a "public affection" for society suggests a Humean basis for claiming that domestic animals have moral standing (Callicott 1988: 166 and 168).

Several commentators have criticized Callicott's attempt to read Hume as an early environmental holist. Alan Carter argues that Hume's reference to "public affection" and his claim that "the interests of society are not, even on their own account, entirely indifferent to us" (EPM 5.2.2; SBN 219) do not indicate that Hume was referring to interests "over and above [those] of the individuals who comprise that society" (Carter 2000: 8). As Carter correctly notes, in the pages immediately following the "public affection" passage, Hume's examples all concern how one person might share the sentiments of another individual person (Carter 2000: 8). Moreover, Carter argues that Humean sympathy cannot reasonably be read as extending to a biotic community. "Because another human resembles me," writes Carter, "because he or she can be injured like me, and because he or she reacts as I do when injured, I feel sympathy for that person" (Carter 2000: 9). Thus, it is quite implausible to suggest that Humean sympathy could be extended to water, the landscape, or other inanimate parts of the ecosystem (Carter 2000: 9; see also Coventry and Hiller 2015: 169; Varner 1991: 179; Valls 2014: 128; Welchman 2009: 205).

But while Carter is surely right both that Hume himself did not think sympathy extends to communities as such, above and beyond the individuals that comprise them, and that the mechanism of Humean sympathy does not make sense when applied to inanimate objects, Carter's critique of Callicott's interpretation does not show that we cannot give a Humean argument for extending moral standing to certain animals. We do not need to argue (as Callicott does) that Humean sympathy or moral sentiments extend to society as a whole or to inanimate objects in order to make a Humean case for extending moral concern to animals. Instead, we need only show that it is consistent with Hume's views to extend sympathy or other moral sentiments to animals. And, as we have seen, since Hume thinks that the similarities between us and people in remote places or distant times can lead us to extend sympathy to them, and since he thinks animals are much more like us than usually thought, it is indeed consistent with his claims to suggest that sympathy can extend to animals. Indeed, Hume says that even if our interactions with animals are not subject to the rules of justice, we are nonetheless "bound by the laws of humanity to give gentle usage" to animals (EPM 3.18; SBN 190). This principle can underwrite a Humean case for granting animals some degree of moral standing (Baier 1985: 154). As Baier writes, "because we can recognize what constitutes harm to them, because they, like us, are potential victims of human vices, we have both sympathetic and self-interested reasons to condemn humanly inflicted harm to them" (Baier 1985: 149–150; see also Coventry and Hiller 2015: 172–175; Driver 2011: 165; Gerrek 2004; Valls 2014: 125–126.).

But does the injunction to "give animals gentle usage" go far enough? One might worry that a principle dictating that we use animals "gently" is not enough to support a robust argument for animal welfare, or that it is too vague to provide guidance about which actions are permissible. This seems to be the reason that philosophers who argue for animal welfare from a virtue ethics perspective have not drawn on Hume's views for such an argument. To be sure, not many philosophers have taken a virtue ethics approach to animal welfare, but those who have, such as Rosalind Hursthouse, have taken Aristotle rather than Hume as inspiration, on the grounds that Aristotle's account of *phronesis*, or practical wisdom, provides more guidance for agents seeking to resolve difficult ethical cases (see Abbate 2014; Hursthouse 1999; Hursthouse 2011). Hursthouse suggests that Hume needs to offer an account of *phronesis*, and that perhaps a Humean could argue that adopting the common point of view and being a "good judge" are equivalent to *phronesis*, but she thinks the resources in Hume's writings for developing this view are thin (Hursthouse 1999: 77–80).[6]

Whether or not Hume has the resources to provide an adequate virtue ethics is beyond the scope of this chapter. However, if an adequate Humean virtue ethics can be developed for humans' interactions with other humans, then this could also be applied to humans' interactions with animals. "Gentleness" is a Humean virtue (T 3.3.3.9; SBN 606 and EPM 9.15; SBN 279), a character trait to which humans typically respond with moral approval (and to which animals may respond with love, even if, as I argued earlier, they cannot make moral judgments). And cruelty, he says, is "the most detested of all vices" (T 3.3.3.9; SBN 606). Hume thinks that most people care about possessing virtuous character traits (EPM 9.21–25; SBN 281–284). If gentleness is a virtue, and sympathy can extend to non-human animals, then virtuous human agents will be gentle not only towards other humans but also towards non-human animals. Thus, although animals have no special rights-based claim to just treatment on Hume's view, he does have the resources to argue against practices that are cruel to animals.

Notes

1 This chapter will use the term "animals" to mean "non-human animals."
2 For discussion of shifting attitudes towards animals in the writings of the late eighteenth century and early nineteenth century, see Perkins 2003; Spencer 2010, and Thomas 1983: 173–191.

3 For further discussion of Hume's account of animal reasoning and how he thought it compares to human reasoning, see Boyle 2003.
4 In T 2.2.12.6, Hume says we have "evident proof" that animals have a sense of the pain and pleasure of other animals, echoing his earlier claims that it is an "evident truth" that animals have reason and that we have "evident proof" that they feel pride and humility.
5 Callicott cites Midgley's 1983 book *Animals and Why They Matter* as inspiration for his holistic environmental ethic, arguing that Midgley and Leopold "share a common, fundamentally Humean understanding of ethics as grounded in altruistic *feelings*" (Callicott 1988: 166; emphasis in original).
6 For an opposing view, see Swanton 2007.

References

Abbate, C. (2014) "Virtues and Animals: A Minimally Decent Ethic for Practical Living in a Non-Ideal World," *Journal of Agricultural and Environmental Ethics* 27(6): 909–929.
Arnold, D. (1995) "Hume On the Moral Difference Between Humans and Other Animals," *History of Philosophy Quarterly* 12: 303–316.
Baier, A. (1985) "Knowing Our Place in the Animal World," in *Postures of the Mind: Essays on Mind and Morals*, Minneapolis: University of Minnesota Press, pp. 139–156.
Bayle, P. (1991) *Historical and Critical Dictionary: Selections*, trans. R. Popkin, Indianapolis, IN: Hackett Publishing.
Beauchamp, T. (1999) "Hume on the Nonhuman Animal," *Journal of Medicine and Philosophy* 24: 322–335.
Boullier, D. R. (1728) *Essai Philosophique sur L'Ame des Bêtes*, Amsterdam: Changuron.
Boyle, D. (2003) "Hume on Animal Reason," *Hume Studies* 26(1): 3–28.
Callicott, J. B. (1988) "Animal Liberation and Environmental Ethics: Back Together Again," *Between the Species* 4: 163–169.
Carter, A. (2000) "Humean Nature," *Environmental Values* 9(1): 3–37.
Coventry, A. and A. Hiller (2015) "Hume on Animals and the Rest of Nature," in E. Aaltola and J. Hadley (eds.), *Animal Ethics and Philosophy: Questioning the Orthodoxy*, London: Rowman & Littlefield, pp. 165–184.
Driver, J. (2011) "A Humean Account of the Status and Character of Animals," in T. L. Beauchamp and R. G. Frey (eds.), *The Oxford Handbook of Animal Ethics*, Oxford: Oxford University Press, pp. 144–171.
Gerrek, M. (2004) "Hume and Our Treatment of Animals," *Essays in Philosophy* 4(2): article 13.
Hartley, D. (1749) *Observations on Man*, London: S. Richardson.
Hursthouse, R. (1999) "Virtue Ethics and Human Nature," *Hume Studies* 25: 67–82.
———. (2011) "Virtue Ethics and the Treatment of Animals," in T. Beauchamp and R. G. Frey (eds.), *The Oxford Handbook of Animals Ethics*, Oxford: Oxford University Press, pp. 119–143.
Kuflik, Arthur. 1998. "Hume on Justice to Animals, Indians and Women." *Hume Studies* 24(1): 53–70. https://doi.org/10.1353/hms.2011.0124.
Midgley, Mary. 1983. *Animals and Why They Matter*. Paperback ed. Athens, GA: University of Georgia Press.
Norton, D. F. (2000) Introduction to *A Treatise of Human Nature*, edited by David Hume, Oxford: Oxford University Press.
Perkins, D. (2003) *Romanticism and Animal Rights*, Cambridge: Cambridge University Press.
Pitson, A. (1993) "The Nature of Humean Animals," *Hume Studies* 19: 301–316.
Seidler, M. (1977) "Hume and the Animals," *Southern Journal of Philosophy* 15: 361–372.
Spencer, J. (2010) "Creating Animal Experience in Late Eighteenth-Century Narrative," *The Journal for Eighteenth-Century Studies* 33(4): 469–486.
Swanton, Christine (2007) "Can Hume Be Read as a Virtue Ethicist?" *Hume Studies* 33(1): 91–113.
Thomas, K. (1983) *Man and the Natural World*. London: Lane.
Tranöy, K. (1959) "Hume on Morals, Animals, and Men," *The Journal of Philosophy* 56: 94–102.
Valls, A. (2014) "David Hume: Justice and the Environment," in P. F. Cannavò, J. H. Lane, Jr. and J. Barry (eds.), *Engaging Nature: Environmentalism and the Political Theory Canon*, Cambridge, MA: MIT Press, pp. 117–132.
Varner, G. (1991) "No Holism Without Pluralism," *Environmental Ethics* 13(2): 175–179.
Welchman, J. (2009) "Hume, Callicott, and the Land Ethic: Prospects and Problems," *The Journal of Value Inquiry* 43: 201–220.

37

HUME ON THE MINDS OF WOMEN

Katharina Paxman and Kristen Blair

Introduction

> Whether we consider mankind according to the difference of sexes, ages, govern-
> ments, conditions, or methods of education; the same uniformity and regular opera-
> tion of natural principles are discernible. Like causes still produce like effects; in the
> same manner as in the mutual action of the elements and powers of nature.
>
> There are different trees, which regularly produce fruit, whose relish is different
> from each other; and this regularity will be admitted as an instance of necessity and
> causes in external bodies. But are the products of Guienne and of Champagne more
> regularly different than the sentiments, actions, and passions of the two sexes, of
> which the one are distinguish'd by their force and maturity, the other by their deli-
> cacy and softness?
>
> (T 2.3.1.5–6; SBN 401)

In the passage above, Hume is seeking to emphasize that just as we find that there are natural principles that can account for events in the non-human world around us, so too we must admit to natural principles that account for regularities and uniformities in human behavior and social interaction.[1] Despite the great diversity of cultures, customs, environments, and circumstances, Hume takes it that there are certain universal principles of human nature that underlie our beliefs, passions, and actions. These principles of human nature play out in a great diversity of physical and social circumstances. This in turn results in rich variety in the details of individual human lives, as well as the norms of communities and cultures. But all are ultimately to be accounted for in terms of like causes producing like effects. An understanding of the universal principles of human nature, in conjunction with an understanding of the particular human and non-human contexts surrounding any given individual, allows us to recognize human phenom-ena in all its great variety as having the same kind of uniformity and regularity as is discovered in the natural world. Prominent among Hume's examples of regularity in human phenomena is the example of the differences between men and women.

Hume is here showing his methodological inclination towards social science:[2] observations we make about human beings should be understood in terms of causes, and ultimately these causes will lead us to principles of nature. Just as knowing that grapes grown in Guienne or Champagne will result in wines with distinctive qualities, knowing the sex of a person can allow us to predict things about their respective "force and maturity" or "delicacy and softness." At least on the surface, this is what Hume appears to be claiming in this passage.

It seems unlikely, however, that Hume, the great observer of human behavior, would really think that the differences between men and women are as easily understood and accounted for as the differences between various regional wines. Gender differences play out in complex social contexts. Despite Hume's assumption of "a uniformity in human motives and actions as well as in the operations of body" (EHU 8.9; SBN 84), he also acknowledges the "diversity of characters, prejudices, and opinions" (EHU 8.10; SBN 85) and the "great force of custom and education, which mould the human mind from its infancy" (EHU 8.11; SBN 86). We should expect, therefore, that a Humean account of gender difference would be sensitive to both the potential for 'natural' principles of difference, as well as those which are a result of various external and social circumstances.

This chapter intends to explore Hume's account of gender difference. There are of course obvious biological differences between the bodies of men and women, particularly as pertains to reproduction. Hume is not an anatomist, and these differences are not the focus of our interest here. It is rather Hume's understanding of the source of the differences in the behaviors, passions, cognitive capacities, and social norms that he observes between men and women that we seek to explore. Hume's incredibly rich account of mind includes reference to traits of mind that he took to be 'original' – that is, not themselves explained by the basic principles of his associationism, but rather a given part of human nature that we learn of via observation. Considering his time and cultural context, we may rightly ask whether he took there to be differences of this sort between the minds of men and women. In this chapter, we intend to address this question, with particular consideration of whether Hume's account of women and gender roles is indicative of a gender essentialism or a gender constructivism. We argue that Hume's account is mixed. While there are ample examples in his writing of a sophisticated awareness of the ways in which ideas about gender are culturally constructed, he is also inclined to occasional comments that betray certain beliefs about fundamental differences between the cognitive capacities and tendencies of men and women. This results in a lingering hint of gender essentialism in his otherwise constructivist characterizations of societal attitudes and norms surrounding women.

If the Humean account of the minds of women is dominated by constructivist explanations of gender difference, yet unable to fully disentangle itself from the essentialist assumptions of the time, we may ask an additional question: why? Hume offers a richly contextualized account of many human differences, and the social context he observes surrounding women appears sufficient to explain the apparent differences in passions, cognitive capacity, behavior, etc. Why appeal to original gender-based differences of mind to explain these? Is Hume in this respect merely a product of the thinking of his time? We wish to suggest that while the influence of received attitudes about women are certainly at play here, Hume's apparent endorsement of these norms is not that straightforward or unreflective. We will argue that Hume's gender essentialism can be usefully linked to his commitments to certain physiological theories of mind of his day, particularly the sort typified in the Cartesian physiology of Nicholas Malebranche. Were Hume's background assumptions about this false physical science of mind removed – assumptions to which we have good reason to think Hume was *not* strongly committed – we argue that what remains of Hume's considered position is a largely constructivist account of gender roles, and a picture of mind without sex-specific characteristics.

Section 1: Hume as a 'women's philosopher'

There has been some interest in Hume scholarship in the question of whether Hume is rightly identified as a 'women's philosopher' or even a proto-feminist. Some commentators have noted that his recasting of reason and his emphasis on emotion as the guide to moral judgment anticipate contemporary feminist reconstructions of rationality and moral reasoning. On the question of Hume's attitudes towards gender and reasoning abilities specifically, Don Garrett has suggested that Hume's account of reason does much to diffuse gender differences. He argues,

> Hume's naturalistic and highly specific conception of reason . . . creates a very strong burden of proof on anyone who wishes to suggest that men and women (or any two groups of human beings) differ in purely rational abilities, or to suggest that reason itself has any sex-specific (or race-specific, or class-specific) characteristics.
>
> (Garrett 2005: 188)

Other authors, such as Annette Baier, have argued that Hume's emphasis on the social nature of moral reasoning suggests that for Hume women can be expected to be strong, perhaps even superior, moral reasoners (Baier 1987). Yet others have pointed to Hume's accounts of sympathy, the passions, and virtue as all suggestive of a prioritizing of traditionally 'female' ways of engaging the world.[3] But scholars have also noted that there is clear textual evidence that Hume takes women to be inferior to men, not only physically but also intellectually. In considering the degree to which Hume's writing can be considered misogynistic, Anne Jaap Jacobson notes that "we should be pessimistic about the treatment of women in an eighteenth century text by a male writer, and the news about Hume is not terribly good" (Jacobson 2000: 14). And while championing Hume's conception of reason as feminism-friendly, Garrett concedes that his treatment of men and women more broadly is "a mixed performance" (Garrett 2005: 28).

One does indeed find a tension in Hume's treatment of gender. One way to explore this is to question the degree to which the female mind, on his account, is a product of socialization (or, in Hume's terms, 'education'), while on the other hand, questioning the degree to which Hume took the female mind to have sex-related 'original' propensities. In contemporary discourse, this issue might be framed as the question of whether or not Hume is a constructivist or an essentialist about gender. For the purposes of this discussion, we are using gender essentialism to refer to the conception of gender which assumes biological distinctions between the sexes to also determine certain mental and social characteristics. Gender constructivism, on the other hand, refers to the conception of gender which assumes mental and social characteristics attributed to particular genders to be products of socialization.[4]

We will answer the question of whether Hume is an essentialist or a constructivist about gender by first considering places in the text of the *Treatise*, as well as several of Hume's essays, where Hume accounts for expectations surrounding women and women's roles in terms of social constructs (in Hume's terms, such norms are 'artificially' determined). We will then turn to consideration of passages in which Hume appears to be endorsing a form of gender essentialism. Our discussion will culminate in an argument explaining Hume's apparent essentialism in terms of his implied commitments to a physiological account of mind of the sort presented by Nicholas Malebranche, a documented influence on Hume's philosophy, who himself offers an explicit account of the physiological differences between the brains of men and women.

Section 2: Hume's constructivist account of gender

There is much evidence throughout Hume's writings that he is inclined to explain the bulk of the difference in social roles and expectations attributed to men and women in terms of what we might now identify with socially constructed gender categories. While we will treat the evidence for Hume's gender essentialism in the next section, it will be useful to first say a little here about indications of essentialism we *do not* find in Hume, with an eye to setting up how his characterizations of women are open to a constructivist account. In particular, Hume offers no explicit treatment of anatomical differences between male and female brains. Indeed, when it comes to questions of anatomy, he claims a general distance, stating, for instance, that scientific explanations of brain and other bodily functions are not part of his project in the *Treatise*.[5] This is consistent with Hume's general purpose in the *Treatise*, where interest primarily lies in giving an account of mind from an examination of the experiential origins of our mental contents, including development as it is informed by social context, customs, and education. Such an account, while certainly open to the possibility of suggesting that some of our observations about human nature are examples of original properties of mind, not to be explained via experience (more on this below), will not incline towards explanations in terms of innate properties of mind. Rather, we find in Hume the impulse to explain mind in terms of human experience, which he understands to be richly social. Importantly for our project, his methodological approach means that his default position is to assume that all human minds in their original state are similarly constituted. Differences in belief and behavior from person to person are more likely to be accounted for in terms of experience and social context than essential, innate difference.

This impulse towards explanations of human nature through observation of lived context – without reference to foundational assumptions about differences in original mental capacities between particular groups – can be found throughout Hume's writing, and are importantly present in his discussions of women. Take for instance his essay "On Polygamy and Divorce," in which Hume states that "nature has established" a "nearness of rank, not to say equality" between the sexes (E 184). We might read this as a nod to some slight difference in original constitution of mind, but his point here is clearly to downplay any essential differences and emphasize the similarities in innate capacities. Hume offers his readers a starting point for thinking about men and women in a way that is not innately hierarchical. Instead, the "nearness of rank" suggests that differences we go on to observe between the attitudes and behaviors of men and women develop due to education and socialization. Indeed, Hume's point in this passage is to emphasize that societies in which marriage is allowed to consist in a tyranny of the male over the female do themselves a disservice, losing out on the benefits that would otherwise come from the sexual companionship and affection of an equal.

That the differences between the genders is not primarily a product of some original mental differences between men and women is perhaps best emphasized in Hume's *Treatise* discussion of the artificially determined social requirements of chastity and modesty. These he observes to be placed primarily on women. Hume notes that conditioning women to prize chastity is an important task of socialization in order to maintain the functions of society. Chastity and modesty are in fact presented as distinctly female virtues, and understood to "arise from education, from the voluntary conventions of men, and from the interests of society" (T 3.2.12.2; SBN 570). They are presented to women as essential duties of the female sex, but chastity, Hume notes, is not an easy requirement to make of any human. Sexual engagement is "a pleasure, to which nature has inspir'd so strong a propensity," that giving up the pleasure is quite backwards – especially since, Hume notes, it is a propensity that it is "absolutely necessary in the end to comply with, for the support of the species" (T 3.2.12.6; SBN 572). He must therefore explain how cultural norms of socialization ensures the adoption of these artificial virtues:

> In order, therefore, to impose a due restraint on the female sex, we must attach a peculiar degree of shame to their infidelity, above what arises merely from its injustice, and must bestow proportionable praises on their chastity.
>
> (T 3.2.12.4; SBN 571)

But though "this be a very strong motive to fidelity" (T 3.2.12.5; SBN 571), Hume expects it is not quite enough. Therefore it is necessary

> that, besides the infamy attending such licences, there shou'd be some preceding backwardness or dread, which may prevent their first approaches, and may give the female sex a repugnance to all expressions, and postures, and liberties, that have an immediate relation to that enjoyment.
>
> (T 3.2.12.5; SBN 571–572)

The aggressive socialization of women to not only feel shame at acting against their duties of chastity, but to feel 'repugnance' at anything potentially connected to infidelity will produce attitudes and beliefs in women about the desirability and propriety of such things that will appear to have universal acceptance within the cultural context (with individuals who deviate easily labeled as morally degenerate or in some way disturbed). Thus, some may come to think that women have a natural aversion to unchaste behavior, and a natural modesty that causes them to blush at things at all connected with infidelity. But Hume sees clearly that this is not the case. It is rather our active social efforts that result in the mere appearance of natural female virtues.

Hume's broader purpose in presenting this discussion is to support his contention that the artificial virtue of justice, and the related virtues deriving from it, can be understood to arise artificially, even should it be true that we can discover universal consent to any of these principles. That an explanation may be given with reference to observations of universal human circumstance is sufficient to explain the widespread acceptance of these constructed principles. The case of the artificial virtues of female chastity and modesty illustrates just such a phenomenon. In this case, the "trivial and anatomical observation" concerning the ease of determining maternity, and the challenge of determining paternity, results in "that vast difference betwixt the education and duties of the two sexes" (T 3.2.12.3; SBN 571). While something 'original' to each sex does play a role, it is the anatomical facts of human reproduction. The social tension that arises due to these anatomical differences Hume suggests is resolved via the creation of artificial virtues, which are in turn motivated via education and socialization.

With the exception of differences in reproductive anatomy, then, so far we see Hume as presenting women as different from men primarily in terms of education (or socialization) and related conventionally determined social roles, without any reference to innate differences of mind. Hume also accounts for the likelihood that individuals belonging to the same social categories will come to think in similar ways. In his essay on national character, Hume asserts that,

> The human mind is of a very imitative nature; nor is it possible for any set of men to converse often together, without acquiring a similitude of manners, and communicating to each other their vices as well as virtues. The propensity to company and society is strong in all rational creatures; and the same disposition, which gives us this propensity, makes us enter deeply into each other's sentiments, and causes like passions

and inclinations to run, as it were, by contagion, through the whole club or knot of companions.

(E 202)

Social reinforcement, or "imitation," as Hume states, dictates much of our behavior. Here Hume uses this sympathetic tendency of our social natures to explain consistency in attitudes and values within a culture, but the principle clearly can be applied to the way that gendered behaviors arise. It is to be expected that education (socialization) produces a similar effect on all those who are educated (socialized) in the same ways. Women who socialize with and are taught by other women "[acquire] a similitude of manners." Gendered behavior, much like culture, will be constructed for Hume through education.

It should be noted that Hume's apparent constructivism as thus displayed does not dismiss the reality of a gender hierarchy (or perhaps even condemn it with the strength we would hope for from a 'proto-feminist'), but rather presents gender hierarchy (with male dominance) as necessary for social function. For instance, Hume takes female chastity and modesty to be artificial virtues, but nevertheless unavoidable as an answer to the "trivial and anatomical observation" which will otherwise cause anxiety among presumed-fathers. The father's uncertainty is a threat to the stability of the family unit, which Hume takes to be the foundational social unit in establishing the artificial virtue of justice. As such, it would appear Hume takes us to be justified in using extreme social pressure to limit the freedoms of women, increasing the confidence of would-be fathers, thereby serving "the general interests of society" (T 3.2.12.1; SBN 570). What is significant for our purpose here is that Hume takes socially imposed female submission to be an 'artificially' constructed component of human experience, not a product of an innate gender inequality. Power dynamics largely define the interactions between the two genders and preserve clearly defined roles, which in turn preserve important social responsibilities and structures.[6] In "On Polygamy and Divorce," Hume discusses the positive and negative consequences of master/slave relationships. Regarding typical power dynamics between men and women, in which men are placed in superior positions, he suggests that

[The] sovereignty of the male is a real usurpation. We are, by nature, [women's] lovers, their friends, their patrons: Would we willingly exchange such endearing appellations, for the barbarous title of master and tyrant?

(E 184)

So why does Hume think men seek power over women, as opposed to developing more balanced relationships as lovers, friends, and patrons? Hume is of course aware of the physical advantage men typically have over women, and physical advantage he links directly to the positive (and desirable) passion of pride, which plays a key role in our pursuit and achievement of power. Hume notes that

'Tis not the beauty of the body alone that produces pride, but also its strength and force. Strength is a kind of power; and therefore the desire to excel in strength is to be consider'd as an inferior species of ambition.

(T 2.1.8.4; SBN 300)

Pride and ambition to power are here linked with physical strength, an important connection given the general observation of the relative size and physical capacities of men and women. The conclusion we can draw appears to be that humans with greater strength will naturally desire to assert that strength as a kind of power, which in turn acts as a source of pride. Hume characterizes pride as a pleasant feeling of self-love. Hume takes this pleasant passion to be central to explaining human nature (consider that he devotes a third of Book II of the *Treatise* to pride and humility). Therefore, one Humean explanation for any male desire to have power over females comes down to a difference in typical physical disposition, combined with a universal human impulse towards pride (or the objects of pride; in the case "the desire to excel in strength"). Again, the difference is *not* a natural difference in mental disposition between men and women.

Interestingly, in his essay, "Of Love and Marriage," Hume describes not men but women as having a "love of dominion" (E 558). The tone of the essay is playful, and at times verges on satirical, but Hume is clearly in earnest about the observations he is making concerning marital relationships. He goes so far as to suggest that some women marry fools to ensure ease in having power over their spouse. But what may appear at first to be a general observation about the female nature (in this case, a female drive to have control or power over a sexual partner) is ultimately explained by Hume in terms of the lived experience of women. Hume argues that "it is the fault of our sex [i.e. men], if the women be so fond of rule" for

> if we did not abuse our authority, they would never think it worthwhile to dispute it. Tyrants, we know, produce rebels; and all history informs us, that rebels, when they prevail, are apt to become tyrants in their turn.
>
> (E 560)

This essay begins by playfully chiding its female readers for being so easily offended by anything written that disparages marriage, and proceeds to explain to them the primary cause of complaints from men in marriage is the female love of dominion (Hume observes that "no passion seems to have more influence on female minds, than this for power" [E 558]). But there is a shift in tone and in the direction of the moral correction over the course of the essay. Having motivated the observations that may lead some to think that it is simply female 'nature' to seek dominion over their sexual partners, Hume turns the tables on his male readers by suggesting that the behavior of women in this regard is entirely predictable if we consider the typical abuse of authority by the man in a marital relationship. Women do not seek control over men by nature; rather, humans under tyrants seek to re-establish control over their lives, and when they achieve some degree of control are likely to seek dominion themselves in order to ensure it. This is not an explanation of typical marriage relations in terms of original differences between the dispositions of men and women. It is rather an explanation of gendered social behavior as arising due to social inequalities.

In these accounts, the only original attributes appealed to by Hume in explaining gender difference are differences of body pertaining to reproductive biology and physical strength. The former results in a social insecurity about paternity, requiring the stabilizing force of the female-specific artificial virtues of chastity and modesty. The latter physical difference accounts at least in part for the typical assertion of male authority, which establishes and maintains various gender discrepancies. In no case are Hume's observations about social norms surrounding gender explained with reference to some original difference between men and women in the functions or propensities of mind. That this is Hume's view is reinforced in the EPM, where he accounts for the tyranny of men over women with reference to physical strength alone, and notes that women often are able to compensate with other social skills in order to "share with the other sex in all the rights and privileges of society" (EPM 3.19). Short of these kinds of social compensations, the power dynamics which are established by physical authority work to preserve a master/slave relationship.[7] This dynamic is aided by education and cultural reinforcement; even in cases where a woman is equally or more physically capable, custom designates her role to be one of submission.[8]

It is true that ultimately Hume often appears committed to a description of gender roles in terms of essential social functions.[9] Thus, on a shallow reading, one might assume that Hume takes gender roles to be natural in the sense of 'original' to female nature. But closer readings of his treatments of various gendered social phenomena reveal an underlying constructivism concerning gender difference, and we find an 'original' equality of mind to be implied. Were this the entire picture, it might be easy to conclude that Hume has a constructivist account of gendered differences of mind. But there are moments of apparent essentialism about the female mind in his writings that stand in the way of such a straightforward diagnosis, and it is to an examination of these and a suggestion of their origin that we now turn.

Section 3: Hume's gender essentialism and Malebranchean physiology

Evidence of gender essentialism in Hume is mostly gleaned from comments made in passing, frequently in discussion of topics entirely distinct from the consideration of gender itself. It is telling that in Hume's focused discussions on social norms surrounding the sexes, his accounts tend to be more constructivist, but we are also left wondering how causally mentioned generalizations about the workings of women's minds are to be best understood. It is to a quick list of claims that give us a sense of Hume as an essentialist that we now turn.

In a *Treatise* discussion of sympathetic adoption of passions, Hume claims that women (and children) are most guided by imagination, making them more prone to pity, among other passions (see T 2.2.7.4; SBN 370 and T 2.2.9.18; SBN 388). Elsewhere this tendency of the female mind to be guided by imagination leads Hume to claim that women are more "apt to overlook remote motives in favour of any present temptation" (T 3.2.12.5; SBN 571). An easily influenced imagination is also used to explain why "education takes possession of the ductile minds of the fair sex in their infancy" (T 3.3.12.7).[10] On a Humean account, to be routinely guided by a 'ductile' imagination implies an inability to maintain vivacity of ideas that are not present to us. Given the role such maintenance of vivacity plays in reasoning, we can assume such a tendency would make women weaker reasoners. Such off-hand remarks implying an essential difference between the way that men and women think are also to be found in Hume's essays. Take for instance, Hume's essay, "Of the Study of History," in which he presents historical books as the type of reading "best suited both to [women's] sex and education," potentially implying a fit due not only to socialization, but also suited to the distinctly female mind, with its female strengths and weaknesses (E 563).

Two passages in particular stand out as most directly suggestive of a gender essentialism about mind in Hume. The first is found in Hume's EHU discussion of liberty and necessity (and in fact parallels the passage used at the beginning of this essay from the *Treatise*, as the EHU presents Hume's later treatment of the topic):

> Are the manners of men different in different ages and countries? We learn thence the great force of custom and education, which mould the human mind from its infancy, and form it into a fixed and established character. Is the behaviour and conduct of the one sex very unlike that of the other? It is thence we become acquainted with the different characters, which nature has impressed upon the sexes, and which she preserves with constancy and regularity.
>
> (EHU 8.11; SBN 86)

Here the naturalness of the differences in behavior between men and women are explicitly contrasted with the socialized differences between persons from different times and countries. Despite all we explored in the previous section that suggests the role of socialization in creating gender, here Hume is very quick to identify gender difference with nature's 'constancy and regularity.'

The second damning passage is in Hume's discussion of gallantry in "The Rise and Progress of the Arts and Sciences," where he says that, "nature has given *man* the superiority above *woman*, by endowing him with greater strength both of mind and body" (E 133). In the case of gallantry, Hume argues that in polite society we compensate for the weaker or more disagreeable positions of certain others by "throw[ing] the biass on the opposite side" and "yield[ing] superiority" to those in a marginalized position (E 132). This "generous attention," Hume argues, applies to the behavior of men towards women. Because a man is superior in mind and body, "it is his part to alleviate that superiority, as much as possible, by the generosity of his behavior, and by a studied deference and complaisance for all her inclinations and opinions" (E 133). While the type of social interaction described here that arises between men and women is characterized in a constructivist way, the basis for the behavior in this case is noted to be a real difference, not merely in physical strength, but also some sort of natural superiority of mind.

Hume goes on in this essay to emphasizes women's natural 'softness' and 'delicacy.' Interestingly, a woman's delicacy of mind is not always treated as a mental shortcoming. "Of Essay-Writing" offers a case for the particular value of women's judgements in certain areas due to their delicacy, which renders them, "much better Judges of all polite Writing than Men of the same Degree of Understanding" (E 536). Still, the tone of this discussion is highly essentialist in nature, and is echoed again in less flattering terms in "Of the Study of History," where Hume speaks of women's "tenderness of complexion," which prevents them from engaging "the severer studies" (E 565). It is noteworthy, though, that in the same passage Hume notes the "weakness of [women's] education" as a joint cause of their limitations in capacity for study.

What are we to make of this smattering of comments that suggest an essential difference between the workings of the male and female minds, particularly in light of the rich constructivist accounts given in Hume's more robust treatments of social norms surrounding gender? Our suggestion is that the degree to which Hume is an essentialist about gender and gender roles is a product of certain physiological theories he was aware of that appear to function as 'background' assumptions in some of his discussions of human nature. In particular, the physiology of brains traces and animal spirits, which he would have found in Descartes and seen developed in Malebranche and discussed by Mandeville, itself appears to leave traces over much of Hume's work. To make our case we suggest that the following are true: 1) Hume had encountered these theories as presented by thinkers known to have been important influences on his own work. 2) There is textual evidence that Hume sometimes applied this physiological theory as a kind of secondary evidence for his proposed systems of mind; 3) In light of 1 and 2, it is reasonable to think that Hume had accepted something like the Malebranchian version of the physiological theory of animal spirits as the best available science explaining the physical anatomy of mind (though his own theory of mind may stand independent of it). And 4) given the treatment of the nature of female brains in this theory, such a background commitment provides an explanation for Hume's scattered use of essentialist language when discussing the minds of women.

To make this case, we will begin by characterizing the account given of female brains in the physiology of animal spirits and brain traces. Malebranche is of particular interest here. Jacqueline Broad describes Malebranche as being "positively outspoken about the female sex" (Broad 2012: 374). As Broad points out, in his writings Malebranche does not shy away from including references to women and sex difference in discussions of human nature. The second book of

The Search After Truth[11] deals with the errors that arise in our reasoning due to the influence of imagination, and includes as entire section concerned with the imaginations of women. While not all of what he says about the female intellect is suggestive of inferiority, one of his main moves is to give an account of the physiological differences in the female brain that incline it towards errors in judgment.

Malebranche has in previous sections considered the "physical causes of disorder of men's imaginations," and found that "the delicacy of the brain fibers is one of the principal causes impeding our efforts to apply ourselves to discovering truths that are slightly hidden" (ST 130). With this general observation in hand, Malebranche moves to consider the case of women in particular.

> This delicacy of brain fibers is usually found in women, and this is what gives them great understanding of everything that strikes the senses. . . . Everything that depends upon taste is within their area of competence, but normally they are incapable of penetrating to truths that are slightly difficult to discover. . . . A trifle is enough to distract them, the slightest cry frightens them, the least motions fascinates them. . . . [B]ecause insignificant things produce great motions in the delicate fibers of their brains, these things necessarily excite great and vivid feelings in their soul, completely occupying it.
>
> (ST 130)

While all children start with "very soft and very delicate" brains, males typically grow out of it, and come to have "hardened and strengthened" brains, better suited to abstract reasoning and resisting the errors that are due to overpowering impressions of sensation on the imagination (ST 131). Women, on the other hand, typically retain the delicacy of brain fibers throughout their lives. So while Malebranche does acknowledge that this does not mean that all women will be poor reasoners (nor that all men will be relatively superior), he is also left with a physiological picture of mind that suggests that, all other things being equal, the physical state of the female brain will typically result in an inferiority in abstract reasoning skills to that of men. Thus, Malebranche appears to endorse a form of biological gender essentialism when it comes to the minds of women.

So now we must determine the answers to a series of related questions. Was Hume familiar with the Malebranchean physiological picture of mind? Did he accept it as a plausible physical theory? And did he adopt this take on the physiology of female brains in particular? There are good reasons, we argue, to believe that the answer to each question is yes.[12]

Hume's very use of the term 'impression' to mean our felt perceptions is suggestive of the physical model of perception that was contemporary to his theory of mind. While, as mentioned above, Hume is not interested in giving his own account of the physiological details of perception – and it is certainly true that he does not intend his system of mind to be dependent on some physical theory of brain states[13] – there is evidence that he takes his own understanding of mind to be compatible with this type of understanding of the physical reality of mental events. John Wright notes that Hume does acknowledge the likelihood that (at least some) mental events are caused by physical motions of the mind at the end of his discussion in "Of the immateriality of the soul."[14] Consider, also, Hume's explanation at T 1.2.5.20; SBN 60–61, which involves a description of the way in which animal spirits move through the physical brain, and influence our associations and reasoning:

> 'Twou'd have been easy to have made an imaginary dissection of the brain, and have shewn, why upon our conception of any idea, the animal spirits run into all the

contiguous traces, and rouze up the other ideas, that are related to it. But tho' I have neglected any advantage, which I might have drawn from this topic in explaining the relations of ideas, I am afraid I must here have recourse to it, in order to account for the mistakes that arise from these relations.

Hume's usage of the physiological explanation here is telling. He first notes that, despite a compatibility of the brain theory of animal spirits with his own non-physiological theory of mind, he has not to this point in the *Treatise* relied on this type of explanation to make his case. His tone here suggests that to rely on such a theory would have been to weaken his own case, which in general stands independent of anatomical theorizing. But in this instance, he feels it necessary to refer to this physical brain phenomenon to explain what he is observing about common mistakes made in reasoning. (Such an explanation of error has a very Malebranchean ring to it.) While this passage is unique in the degree to which reference to the physiology of brain plays a key role in supporting some aspect of Hume's theory of mind, it is not unique as a mention of animal spirit theory. Hume makes liberal use of the language of animal spirits in Books I and II of the *Treatise*.[15] It is clear that he was familiar with the theory and was inclined to adopt it insofar as he had reason to reference the workings of the brain and body.

And there is good reason to think that the version of this physiological theory of mind that Hume was particularly familiar with was that of Nicholas Malebranche. We know that Hume had read Malebranche, and in fact considered *The Search After Truth* to be a key text to read in order to understand his own work in Books I and II of the *Treatise*.[16] John Wright has argued persuasively for Hume's awareness and adoption of Malebranchean physiology of mind in particular, claiming that, "while Hume does not explicitly lay out all this physiology in the opening pages of the *Treatise*, he does assume that an account such as that given by Malebranche is true" (Wright 1983: 214). One need not agree with Wright about the importance of Malebranchean physiology in interpreting Hume's *Treatise* project overall[17] in order to acknowledge that Hume is clearly aware of it, and inclined towards it as a paradigm for understanding what is going on inside of sensing and thinking bodies.

Malebranche is not the only influence on Hume that is likely to have provided him with consideration of the Cartesian theory of animal spirits. Bernard Mandeville, himself a practicing doctor, wrote *A Treatise of the Hypochondriack and Hysterick Diseases*, in which he discusses contemporary theories of medicine and anatomy, including "the role of the animal spirits in the general economy of the body."[18] Mandeville's medical *Treatise* is written in dialogue form, and includes robust discussions between a physician and the hypochondriac he is treating, concerning a variety of medical explanations for his symptoms. James Harris has argued that Hume was significantly influenced by the work of Mandeville, particularly when Hume was himself struggling with his mental health as a young man.[19] Among the evidence of Mandeville's influence on the young Hume, Harris notes that Hume uses language in the letter to the anonymous physician that appears to be taken from Mandeville's *Treatise* discussion of the 'disease of the learned.'[20] (Harris 2015: 61) It is also worth noting that Mandeville's *Treatise* was a very well-received piece of eighteenth-century medical literature, having a particularly significant impact in Scotland, at the Edinburgh Medicine Faculty (Mauro Simonazzi 2016: 65–66.)

The likelihood of Mandeville's influence on Hume with regard to the adoption of the theory of animal spirits is particularly interesting given that the commitment of Mandeville himself to this theory is far from absolute. The tone of the dialogue is distinctly suspicious of medical practice that relies heavily on systems of thought about the body – speculative physicians "who ignore experience and let themselves be carried away by 'Flights of Invention in Physick'" (Simonazzi 2016: 70). Thus, Mandeville maintains a healthy skepticism about the theories he discusses, even while finding them practically useful insofar as they are found consistent with experience and observation. One could easily imagine that Hume would have adopted a similar attitude towards these contemporary theories of brain physiology.

Do we have reason to think he had such a low-stakes background commitment to this brain physiology of animal spirits as it applies to the minds of women in particular (taking Malebranche's account of the brains of women as our guide)? The instances of apparent essentialism about the minds of women listed above largely focus on the delicacy of the female imagination, which is exactly the difference of mind that Malebranche is interested in explaining in terms of physiology. Even the aligning of the 'softness' of the mind of women and children in Hume is consistent with the Malebranchean account of the similarity between the brains of women and the young. Malebranche's account of the fibers of the female brain explains that they are more easily physically disrupted and affected by the animal spirits, and thus we can expect women to be particularly subject to error in reasoning. Hume attributes to women limitations in their abstract reasoning and ability to form beliefs that remain consistent and motivating in the face of changes in sensation and impressions. In each case, impressionability and sensitivity to feeling is key. Hume offers no formal account of such an 'original' propensity of mind in women. But there is good evidence of an implied general adoption of Malebranchean physiology, and the details of this theory as they pertain to the minds of women can explain each instance of apparent essentialism concerning the female mind that we have documented here.

Where does this leave us with regard to the four points we set out prove in this section? First, we have shown that Hume had encountered detailed versions of these physiological theories in Malebranche and Mandeville, both thinkers who had considerable and early influence on his thought. We have also cited textual evidence that Hume on occasion applies this physiological theory as a kind of secondary evidence for his proposed systems of mind, and additionally uses the language of animal spirits casually across a wide range of topics in his discussions of mind. The influence of Malebranche and Mandeville, together with this textual evidence, makes it highly probable that Hume had adopted this type of physiological theory as a background assumption about the nature of the human brain. We do not suggest that it is central to his picture of mind – on the contrary, it seems plausible that he follows Mandeville in using the theory as long as it is practical, while remaining primarily committed to following his own empirical and naturalistic methodology. Finally, the nature of the characterization of the female brain included in such theories, typified in Malebranche, provides a unifying explanation for Hume's scattered use of essentialist language when discussing the minds of women, as these comments typically focus on tendencies of mind that can be explained in terms of brain impressionability and sensitivity.

Conclusion

We conclude that Hume is primarily a constructivist about gender, and in most instances is inclined to explain differences in the ways that men and women think in terms of culturally relative norms and artificially arising gender expectations. But a hint of essentialism about the ways in which the female brain works surfaces on occasion in his discussions, and we have argued that it is best accounted for with reference to his implicit commitments to a Malebranchean style physiology of brain. This leads us to conclude that were these commitments to a false physiological picture of mind removed, Hume's account of gender difference and associated inequalities could be presented as predominately constructivist in nature, with differences between how men and women think explained in terms of social situation and 'artificially' arising power dynamics, as opposed to original differences in the constitution of male and female minds.

What does this mean for Hume's status as a 'women's philosopher' or even a proto-feminist? Hume's sensitivity to the social influences that shape the norms that culturally govern women certainly anticipates contemporary understandings of gender. And it is worth remembering that much of what he says about mind is not sex-specific (including, arguably, his most important discussions about the nature of thought). The sex-specific comments about mental capacities are also not straightforwardly negative. Female delicacy and sensitivity of mind are not treated by Hume as a problem for women's cognitive potential in all cases, perhaps not even in most. As mentioned above, he takes women to be experts in certain areas, such as conversation and writing. In some areas, the assumption of this type of gender essentialism actually increases the female potential to engage in certain kinds of reasoning, particularly the generation of moral and aesthetic sentiments. The characterization of women's mind as different from men's in terms of their delicacy is also noteworthy, considering that Hume's essay, "Of the Delicacy of Taste and Passion," makes the case for a morally praiseworthy variety of delicacy. Therefore, we might think that the essential differences that Hume entertains between the minds of men and women are neither clearly nor consistently an indication of male superiority of thought. Perhaps there is even the potential for a Humean recognition of typically female cognitive virtues connected to delicacy of thought. Though this virtue will undoubtedly be balanced by the potential for a female tendency towards the morally problematic variety of delicacy as outlined in the essay mentioned above, not to mention the *Treatise* assumption that women are prone to errors in practical reasoning due to the female tendency towards active imagination concerning what is most immediately present to them. The point here is that the type of original cognitive difference that Hume may be (weakly) assuming exists between women and men is not straightforwardly an indication of greater mental ability for either sex.

This somewhat mixed attitude towards the mental powers of women may not be unique to Hume. Jacqueline Broad has argued that Malebranche, too. is not as much of an essentialist about female minds as his physiological account of female brains may initially make him appear. She argues that Malebranche can be read to understand the state of women's mental capacities to be primarily a product of education (as opposed to merely in-born abilities or limitations), and that there is room in his account for the possibility of the development of mental prowess in women.[21] Malebranche is clear that though "the delicacy of brain fibers is usually found in women it is not at all certain that it is to be found in all women," (ST 130), and (as Broad points out) his position overall is that all humans are susceptible to the errors of 'delicate brain fibers,' and the methods of improving on their cognitive abilities are not gender specific. The Humean perspective would be similar. Despite the existence of original tendencies of mind, including those linked to gender, Hume frequently prioritizes the role of socialization and circumstance, in understanding the characters and cognitive tendencies of individuals.[22] Male and female potential for cognitive ability appears to be roughly equal.

Still, there is reason to resist the urge to identify Hume's attitudes towards women as proto-feminist. Though there seems to have been some movement in Hume's literary essays and more mature writing towards gently correcting cultural norms that result in the oppression of women (think of Hume's suggestion in "Of Love and Marriage" that men should lean away from tyranny, and towards friendship), these calls for political change are mild, to say the least.[23] Despite Hume's self-report of having taken "particular pleasure in the company of modest women" and having "no reason to be displeased with the reception [he] met with from them" (*My Own Life*, 21), his affection for women does not appear to have motivated him towards real calls for cultural change, despite the potential for such ideas to come from the more constructivist aspects of his understanding of gender.

When considering "the difficult question of Hume's view of women's place in society" (Falkenstein 2015: 157), there is much that may still be said. But there are a few things we hope to have made clear here. First, that Hume's observations about norms and attitudes surrounding women were generally best understood as products of culture, not of nature. Gender-specific virtues, in particular, arise artificially, and do not reflect essential differences between the minds of men and women. Second, insofar as Hume does make comments that suggest an assumed original difference between the minds of men and women, these comments can be usefully linked to background assumptions about women's brains, based in influential physiological theories of mind that are decidedly non-central to Hume's considered views on human nature. Remove these commitments and you find Hume's general picture of mind unaffected, and what remains to be said of his understanding of what is distinct about the minds of women can be given a constructivist account, while what we can assume is original about their minds is found to be not particularly different from that of men.

Notes

1 Some may read this and worry about the difficulty of squaring this passage of Hume (and/or our reading of it) with Hume's well-known arguments against our ability to have knowledge of causal powers in Book I of the *Treatise*. I will not seek to engage this interpretive debate here. In general, Hume makes moves in Book II of the *Treatise* that rely on assumptions and forms of reasoning that he problematizes in Book I (consider, for instance, his assumption that we have an idea of the self in his treatment of sympathy at T 2.1.11, despite the argument against an idea of the self at T 1.4.6). In this chapter, we will follow Hume's lead and assume the use of causal language.

2 For an account of Hume as a social theorist engaging in an empirical and experimental methodology, see Jacqueline Taylor's *Reflecting Subjects* (2015).

3 See many of the essays in *Feminist Interpretations of David Hume* edited by Anne Jaap Jacobson (2000) for discussions of these and other feminism-related themes in Hume.

4 For further discussion of this distinction, see Charlotte Wit (2011) and Mari Mikkola (2017).

5 See T 1.1.2.1; SBN 7–8 and T 2.1.1.2; SBN 275–276.

6 Taylor (2015) offers a robust discussion of Hume's treatment of 'social power' in "Power and the Philosophy of Our Passions." This includes an account of Hume's take on power dynamics as it pertains to gender inequality.

7 See T 2.1.10.5; SBN 312: "When a person acquires such an authority over me, that not only there is no external obstacle to his actions; but also that he may punish or reward me as he pleases, without any dread of punishment in his turn, I then attribute a full power to him, and consider myself as his subject or vassal." Thus, physical dominance may reinforce specific roles and maintain the power dynamic.

8 For example, Hume presents the custom of passing on a name only through the male line as follows: "The case is the same with the transmission of the honours and fortune thro' a succession of males without their passing thro' any female. 'Tis a quality of human nature, which we shall consider afterwards, that the imagination naturally turns to whatever is important and considerable; and where two objects are presented to it, a small and a great one, usually leaves the former, and dwells entirely upon the latter. As in the society of marriage, the male sex has the advantage above the female, the husband first engages our attention; and whether we consider him directly, or reach him by passing thro' related objects, the thought both rests upon him with greater satisfaction, and arrives at him with greater facility than his consort ... And tho' the mother shou'd be possest of a superior spirit and genius to the father, as often happens, the *general rule* prevails, notwithstanding the exception" (T 2.1.9.13; SBN 308–309).

9 Whether his writing here is merely descriptive or also prescriptive is less clear, and we will take up this question again briefly in the conclusion.

10 Lorne Falkenstein (following Annette Baier) suggests that there may be another, more charitable reading of this passage. As opposed to suggesting that women in particular have ductile minds, Hume may intend only that it is the minds of infants that are ductile (see Falkenstein 2015: 165). Whether Hume intends this or not in this particular passage, I take it there is sufficient mention of women's impressionability of imagination in other passages to support the general claim that Hume is inclined to think there is some innate weakness of mind present in women, all other things being equal.

11 Nicholas Malebranche, *The Search after Truth*, trans. and edited by T. M. Lennon and P. J. Olscamp (Cambridge: Cambridge University Press, 1997). All citations from this text will be given as ST followed by the page number.

12 Baier has also noted a potential negative impact of Malebranche's views on women on Hume's own philosophy (Baier and Waldow 2008, 87n27).

13 Take for instance Hume's footnote at T 1.1.1.1n2, where he says, "By the term of *impression* I wou'd not be understood to express the manner, in which our lively impressions are produc'd in the soul, but merely the perceptions themselves."

14 See T 1.4.5.33; SNB 250, and also Wright (1983: 211).

15 See for instance: T 1.2.1.5; SBN 28, T 1.3.8.2; SBN 98; T 1.3.10.9–10; SBN 123, 630–631, T 1.3. 12.13; SBN 135, T 1.4.1.10; SBN 185, T 1.4.2.33, 45; SBN 203, 211, T 1.4.4.13; SBN 229, T 1.4.7.10; SBN 269, T 2.1.1.1; SBN 275, T 2.1.5.11; SBN 290, T 2.2.4.4, 7; SBN 352–353, 354, T 2.2.8.4; SBN 373, T 2.3.4.2, 5–6, 9; SBN 419–422, T 2.3.5.2–5; SBN 422–424, T 2.3.9.29; SBN 447. The theory of animal spirits is also referenced in the EHU discussion of necessary connections, as an explanation for the movement of limbs (EHU 7.14; SBN 66).

16 The case for the influence of Malebranche on Hume, particularly during the period in which he was writing the *Treatise*, is a strong one (see for instance Thomas Lennon's "Introduction," to *The Search After Truth* (ST xxii–xxiii). See also James Harris (2015: 80). That Hume was very aware of Malebranche and his work is also made evident when we take into account an 1847 letter to Michael Ramsey, in which Hume advises Ramsey that in preparation for reading Books I and II of the *Treatise*, he should read *The Search* (he also advises reading from Descartes, Berkeley, and Bayle).

17 Many commentators of course contest the importance of Malebranche's physiological picture of mind for Hume's theory of mind in the *Treatise*. James Harris, while acknowledging Wright's arguments in favor of a strong commitment of Hume to Malebranchean physiology, argues that Hume did not see physiology as playing a role in his account of mind (see Harris 2015: 84 and 491n29).

18 Bernard Mandeville, *A Treatise of the Hypochondriack and Hysterick Diseases (1730)*, Sylvie Kleiman-Lafon (ed.), Springer International Publishing, 2017: 10.

19 See "Pursuits of Philosophy and General Learning," in Harris (2015: 35–77).

20 John Wright argues that the phrase 'disease of the learned' is in fact unique to Mandeville (see Wright 1983: 236n10).

21 For her complete account of Malebranche's brand of proto-feminism (and the responses of some of his early female readers to his writing, which largely work to support her thesis), see her 2012 paper, "Impression in the Brain: Malebranche on Women, and Women on Malebranche."

22 For an excellent discussion of the relationship between Hume's universalism about aspects of human nature and his commitment to the prominent role of socialization in explaining the non-universality of human behaviors, beliefs, and values, see Christopher J. Berry (2007).

23 Falkenstein (2015) has suggested that though Hume's early views surrounding gender appear to be primarily non-normative descriptions of his observations of human society, the shift in his later work from a focus on "the female virtues of chastity and modesty to the male vices of gallantry and jealousy" represents a subtle theoretical shift in favor of shifting cultural attitudes concerning women.

References

Baier, A. (1987) "Hume, The Women's Moral Theorist," in E. Kittay and D. T. Meyers (eds.), *Women and Moral Theory*, Totowa, NJ: Rowman & Littlefield, pp. 37–55.

———. and A. Aldow (2008) "A Conversation between Annette Baier and Anik Waldow about Hume's Account of Sympathy," *Hume Studies* 34(1): 61–87.

Berry, C. J. (2007) "Hume's Universalism: The Science of Man and the Anthropological Point of View," *British Journal for the History of Philosophy* 15(3): 535–550.

Broad, J. (2012) "Impression in the Brain: Malebranche on Women, and Women on Malebranche," *Intellectual History Review* 22(3): 373–389.

Falkenstein, L. (2015) "Without Gallantry and Jealousy: Hume's Account of Sexual Virtues and Vices," *Hume Studies* 41(2): 137–170.

Garrett, D. (2005) "Hume as Man of Reason and Woman's Philosopher," *Feminist Reflections on the History of Philosophy* 25: 171–192.

Harris, J. (2015) *Hume: An Intellectual Biography*, Cambridge: Cambridge University Press.

Jacobson, A. J., ed. (2000) *Feminist Interpretations of David Hume*, University Park, PA: Pennsylvania State University Press.

Malebranche, N. (1997) *The Search After Truth*, trans. and edited by T. M. Lennon and P. J. Olscamp, Cambridge: Cambridge University Press.

———., T. M. Lennon and P. J. Olscamp (1997) *The Search After Truth: Elucidations of the Search After Truth*, trans. and edited by Thomas M. Lennon and Paul J. Olscamp, Cambridge: Cambridge University Press.

Mandeville, B. (2017) *A Treatise of the Hypochondriack and Hysterick Diseases (1730)*, edited by Sylvie Kleiman-Lafon, Cham, Switzerland: Springer.

Mikkola, M. (2017) "Feminist Perspectives on Sex and Gender," in E. N. Zalta (ed.), *The Stanford Encyclopedia of Philosophy*, URL = <https://plato.stanford.edu/archives/win2017/entries/feminism-gender/>.

Simonazzi, M. (2016) "Bernard Mandeville on Hypochondria and Self-Liking," *Erasmus Journal for Philosophy and Economics* 9(1): 65–66.

Taylor, J. (2015) *Reflecting Subjects: Passion, Sympathy, and Society in Hume's Philosophy*, Oxford: Oxford University Press.

Wit, C. (2011) "What Is Gender Essentialism?" in C. Witt (ed.), *Feminist Metaphysics* Dordrecht: Springer, pp. 11–25.

Wright, J. P. (1983) *The Sceptical Realism of David Hume*, Manchester: Manchester University Press.

38

HUME'S LEGACY REGARDING RACE

Andre C. Willis

Philosophers of race illuminate the extent to which Hume's racial reasoning relied on the observational methods of eighteenth-century natural science, which took races to be biological kinds hierarchically ordered by nature. Hume's adaptation of this approach to human difference led him to make racist assertions and to propagate the idea that whites were superior to non-whites.

Scholars of Hume focus their analysis on the extent to which Hume's claims about race comport with the methods and norms of his philosophical project, namely his aims to describe a universal science of human nature. For these thinkers, Hume's few comments about race are largely innocuous consequences of his naturalism, skepticism, and empiricism.

This chapter draws on features of both positions to evaluate Hume's legacy regarding race. It argues, via an assessment of a selection of Hume's writings on history, religion, and politics, that understanding Hume on race requires that we both candidly confront Hume's racism and thoughtfully assess his philosophical insights. Neither of these facts should be diminished, nor should they distract us from harnessing his important insights for generative intellectual work.

Introduction

Although David Hume never used the term race, his few yet significant comments on racial difference blatantly exposed the racial (il)logic of his day and candidly revealed the biases of Enlightenment natural sciences. From our contemporary perspective, his statement "I am apt to suspect the negroes to be naturally inferior to the whites" is abhorrent. It seems uncharacteristic for Hume, who was a fellow of moderate sentiment and a generous disposition. It has posed significant challenges to scholars of Hume and generated attention from critical race theorists. Much secondary literature has thoughtfully considered what to make of this line, the footnote that contains it, and the essay to which it was appended. While there is no consensus, it is generally accepted that the statement is racist in that it both situates the category 'negro' as a real, biological kind and reflects the belief that negro essence and character ranks beneath that of whites. The context for this remark and the extent to which racist sentiments permeate Hume's philosophical project are sources of robust scholarly debate, to which this chapter hopes to add (Popkin 1977, 1992; Immerwahr 1992; Garrett 2000, 2004; Garrett and Sebastiani 2017).

On one hand, critical race theorists interested in tracing the origins and development of anti-black and brown racism in the modern west often evaluate Hume's comments on race to ascertain the extent of his racism, the degree of his Eurocentrism, and the force of his anti-black sentiment. Beginning with the contemporary socio-political facts of racial inequality, persistent anti-black violence, and the history of non-white hatred, they search for the origins of white supremacy in the Western philosophical heritage and find them in Hume (Bracken 1973; Eze 2000, 2001; Morton 2002). On the other hand, scholars of Hume invested in defending the consistency of his philosophical thinking as well as his stated goal of revealing the 'universal springs and principles' of human nature regularly comb his writings to ascertain whether his comments about the fixed and natural inferiority of black people comport with his wider philosophical commitments – particularly his skepticism and naturalism – as well as his expressed moral aims. Venerating philosophical coherence and the desire to preserve the genius of *Le bon David*, they often minimize Hume's comments about non-whites and contend that racism requires more than just a stated belief (Palter 1995; Valls 2005).

If these bifurcating receptions of Hume on race are correct, then readers of Hume are left to choose between two extremes. This is unfortunate, as both positions reflect the problem of binary thinking about race, an adjunct to the larger crisis of racial interpretation in late modernity. Further, neither stance properly situates us to embrace the fundamental fact that we can more fully comprehend Hume's thoughts on race when we take into account his philosophical project *and* its wider socio-intellectual and political contexts, and that our sense of the wider socio-intellectual and political contexts as well as his philosophical project should be informed by how we understand his thoughts about race. Attentive consideration of Hume's thoughts about race can illuminate his naturalism (Eze 2001), demonstrate the boundaries of his sense of taste (Roelofs 2005), and display the limits of the psychological mechanism of sympathy (Levy and Peart 2004). It can also shed new light on his thoughts about religion, which I discuss below.

Beyond elucidating Hume's work, serious reflection on Hume and race is also instructive in that it allows us to highlight the various ways that the Western philosophical tradition has perceived human differences and convey some of the conceptual options Enlightenment thinkers devised to discuss variations between human beings. Early modern science, a discipline that developed ways to understand nature and classify differences between peoples, offered resources in this regard. It is important to keep in mind, however, that scientific approaches to race – like anything else – are always conditioned by history and shaped by culture. In a period when the socio-economic and political goals of Europe included colonial expansion, the Trans-Atlantic trade of Africans, the overthrow of indigenous peoples, and race-based plantation slavery, it behooves us to acknowledge that the political expediency of racist views and the economic benefit of racist practices supported the racial categories of the natural sciences as much as those categories bolstered racist views and practices.

Hume's engagement with race is an example of a fluid two-way exchange between practices and ideas. To put it another way, both non-discursive and discursive features of Hume's racial understanding are inseparable. We know that Hume was well aware of Scotland's extensive colonial slave-plantation systems; that he had knowledge of the viciousness of the Trans-Atlantic slave trade, as well as participated in (and may have personally profited from) the purchase and sale of a slave plantation (Harris 2015: 538). We also know that he worked in a context where *racial* differences (which included social, physical, cultural, *and* historical variances) were classified as *natural* differences (that is, fixed, essential types) and that – based on his distinctive form of naturalism – he thought of races largely as biological kinds. It follows that Hume could have considered blacks to be naturally inferior because he and his cultural group benefited from trading them, and it makes sense that he and his cultural group could have traded black bodies because they thought of them as naturally inferior.

My point here is that the bifurcated understanding that shapes contemporary reflections on Hume and race can result in deeper divisions between scholars and lead to logical dead ends: particularly, the idea that Hume was simply a racist whose views supported white supremacy reveals little and the notion that his work was consistent explains less. Hume's racism and his 'greatness of mind' (Hume 1739) are neither contradictory nor complementary features of his thought. Rather, they are each integral components of his flawed and insightful intellectual project, which both reflected and shaped the trends of his day. This chapter critically attends to Hume's racial understanding as a way of supplementing the various aspects and features of his thought discussed in this volume. In this way, it specifically acknowledges some problems of his work in a larger text that recognizes and celebrates it.

I begin from the premise that race is one of the worst ideas in Western thought. Beyond its conceptual problems, its impact on the history of humankind has been nothing short of horrendous. Given this, one wonders both how racial ideas in general, and black people ('negroes') in particular, came to be objects of interest for the Anglo imagination. Of course, it would be anachronistic to imagine that Hume could avoid participating in the quickly expanding discourse on race. Yet, why Hume took such a flat-footed position on race, and defended it, is less obvious. The following effort, which is divided into three sections, considers what to make of Hume's statements regarding race and discusses how we might understand the wider motivations behind his account. In section one, I present Hume's most well-discussed declaration about race, contained in a controversial footnote in the 1753 version of the essay "Of National Characters" (1748) (and its 1777 revision). I consult the wider socio-political and intellectual contexts regarding race that shaped the perspective in the footnote. In section two, I describe the essay itself, and gesture towards some of the ways that it might also reflect the racial understanding made explicit by the footnote. My hope is not only to illuminate the specific context for the footnote (that is, the essay "Of National Characters"), but also to demonstrate that the footnote obviates what remains implicit in the essay: Hume's Eurocentrism. In section three, I consider how Hume's belief that non-whites were unquestionably inferior to whites suffuses other comments in his corpus and silently saturates his work. Simply put, Hume's "tacit reference" when he wrote about 'people' was usually to whites (Mills 1998: 203). To spotlight Hume's racism in this way is not to diminish his value as a thinker; it is, simply, to locate more specifically where that value lies in light of his racial blind-spots and his profound affinity for and elevation of people of European descent.

The context of the footnote: Enlightenment thinking about race

It is widely agreed that Hume's position on race is expressed most extensively and explicitly in a controversial footnote added to his essay "Of National Characters" (1748) in 1753. It was edited for later publication (1777) to read:

> I am apt to suspect the negroes to be naturally inferior to the whites. There scarcely ever was a civilized nation of that complexion, nor even any individual eminent either in action or speculation. No ingenious manufactures amongst them, no arts, no sciences. On the other hand, the most rude and barbarous of the whites, such as the ancient GERMANS, the present TARTARS, have still something eminent about them, in their valour, form of government, or some other particular. Such a uniform and constant difference could not happen, in so many countries and ages, if nature had not made an original distinction between these breeds of men. Not to mention our colonies, there are NEGROE slaves dispersed all over EUROPE, of whom none

ever discovered any symptoms of ingenuity; though low people, without education, will start up amongst us, and distinguish themselves in every profession. In JAMAICA, indeed, they talk of one negroe as a man of parts and learning; but it is likely he is admired for slender accomplishments, like a parrot, who speaks a few words plainly.

(E 208, fn 10)

The racism articulated in this footnote by Hume is not exceptional. It correlated with a significant strand of the intellectual climate regarding racial differences that permeated the writings of Enlightenment *philosophes* Montesquieu, Voltaire, and Buffon (and later, Kant and Hegel) and conformed to the context of anti-black freedom that pervaded popular texts by Thomas Jefferson, Edward Long, and Samuel Cartwright. At the same time, another important strand of Enlightenment thought (e.g. Diderot, Herder, James Beattie, and Marquis de Condorcet) was animated by a "progressive universalism" (Harvey 2012: 108). These thinkers rejected hierarchical approaches to human difference and resisted racist rhetoric. Still others simply acknowledged human difference but gave little meaning to it.

Hume was neither a progressive universalist nor an agnostic when it came to the issue of race. Of course, one cannot deny that parts of Hume's work – with its claims about the "universal springs and principles" that guide human behavior, and his statement that "there is no universal difference discernible in the human species" (E 378) – accent the fundamental connection between humans. Yet, his stipulation of an 'original distinction' between blacks and whites supports the idea of poly-geneticism, the notion that blacks and whites emanate from distinct origins. That claim, along with his assertion that black people were "naturally inferior," seems to place them beyond the purview of the "universal springs and principles" or at least provisionally outside of the capacity for moral causes to properly shape their character. In other words, when Hume wrote about the fundamental connection between human beings, he did not have non-whites in mind (Mills 1998; West 1982).

It is tempting to imagine that Hume's claim that "nature, by an absolute and uncontroulable necessity has determin'd us to judge" (T 1.4.1.7; SBN 183), led him to embrace racial hierarchy and to justify white superiority. We must exercise caution, however, before assuming this to be the case. Hume never completely accepted the idea that nature was totally determinative or fully self-explanatory. In short, he rejected the positivist conception of nature, that assumed "reality [was] comprehensible and coextensive with nature" (Willis 2015: 106). Hume's distinctive form of naturalism, an awareness of the idea of the powers of nature and an acknowledgment of our lack of understanding the nature of these powers, is inflected by history and common life; thus, the way he thinks about race as a biological kind does not comport with his naturalism.

This does not mean that his thoughts about race were frivolous. Hume's addition of the racist footnote five years after the essay was published suggests that it was not an off-handed comment. Rather, it was a well-thought out statement and a reflectively considered conclusion: blacks were inferior. Legitimated by the standards of modern science and authorized by the methods of natural history (particularly its emphases on observation and codification), Hume's general position on blacks would not have been considered offensive by most readers. And, the fact that Hume placed these views in a footnote does not mean they were unimportant to him; rather, these comments were consistent with the racial sensibilities woven through his project. This is confirmed later in the same essay when he exclaimed, "You may obtain any thing of the NEGROES by offering them strong drink; and may easily prevail with them to sell, not only their children, but their wives and mistresses, for a cask of brandy" (E 214). I shall note some other examples of Hume's race-related statements and discuss the ways that he takes whiteness as normative below.

One of the ways to think about this infamous footnote, Hume's characterizations of non-whites throughout his corpus, and the tacit presumption of the norm of whiteness that pervades his thinking is in light of broader intellectual contexts and political conditions. Eighteenth-century modern science held that race was a naturally occurring and easily visible feature that distinguished human persons in ways that were non-trivial. Hume embraced this way of thinking about human difference, which had a long history that preceded French physician François Bernier's anonymously published essay *Nouvelle Division de la Terre* (1684), generally held to be the first modern use of the term race. Thoughts on race and species prior to Bernier included texts from Garcilaso de la Vega (*Royal Commentaries of the Incas*, 1607), as well as the Swiss naturalist Paracelsus (*Astronomia Magna*, 1571), Italian astronomer Giordano Bruno (*De Immenso et innumerabilibus*, 1591), and Italian Lucilio Vanini (*On the Marvellous Secrets of the Nature the Queen and Goddess of Mortals*, 1616). Paracelsus, Bruno. and Vanini subscribed to the theory of polygenesis.

Bernier's argument was innovative in that it gave "a physico-biological notion of race foundationalist status in the classification of the human species" (Stuurman 2000: 2). Casual in tone yet clever in content, Bernier reduced the variety of diverse physical combinations into four 'species' or 'races' (he used those terms interchangeably). His classificatory system worked as follows: (1) the 'first' race (constituted by Europeans, North Africans, Middle Easterners and Indians, Southeast Asians and Native Americans); (2) African negroes; (3) the east and Northeast Asian race, and (4) Lapps. Physical attributes, which Bernier noted during his travels, distinguished these peoples and were described by Bernier without the pretension of objectivity. For example, he reported that the hair of Africans was "not properly hair, but rather a species of wool, which comes near the hairs of some of our dogs"; the faces of East and Northeast Asians were "flat" with "a small squab nose, little pig's-eyes long and deep set, and three hairs of a beard"; and Lapps he logged as "little stunted creatures with thick legs, large shoulders, short neck, and a face elongated immensely; very ugly and partaking much of the bear . . . they are wretched animals" (Bernier 1684: 2–3).

Hume's articulations regarding race more closely reflected Carolus von Linné's taxonomy of races, which went beyond Bernier's physico-biological approach by correlating human differences with continental divisions and climate regions. Ideas of climate (humidity, altitude, seasons, soil, and topography) as well as culture and lineage had been discussed as important sources of human difference in classical antiquity (see Hippocrates 1868; Glacken 1967: 80–88). Partially following from this classical influence, the Swedish botanist von Linné, in his seminal *Systema naturae* (1735), relied on the same method he used for classifying plants and insects to contend that differences in physical attributes of humans observed in his travels – skin color, hair texture, nose shape, body type, etc. – were influenced by environmental factors. By its second edition in 1738 (a year before publication of Hume's *Treatise*), von Linné argued for fixed racial types and associated each with a general characteristic: black Africans were capricious; yellow Asians were opinionated; white Europeans were law-seekers; and red Americans were guided by customs. Overly normative, von Linné's natural order of human beings secured the foundations for anti-blackness (whites were the only group governed by law).

Among others, Justin E.H. Smith reminds us that the natural sciences developed within the context of expanding colonial interests of European nations. These political aims benefited from intellectual scaffolding and discursive support, just as the ideas were bolstered by certain political and social practices. Thus, it is not coincidental that many of the 'observations' of modern science buttress the imperial aims and colonial interests of European nations as well as their trading of Africans as slaves. Citing Edward Long, who relied on Hume's footnote for his argument in *History of Jamaica* (1774), Smith writes that Long's racial ideas (and by default, Hume's) "offered merely ad hoc theoretical support of an economic order he would have supported no matter what the evidence about human origins seemed to reveal" (Smith 2015: 5).

One of the fascinating yet underemphasized features of the modern discourse on race in which Hume participated was that the quality of 'observation' was linked to the quest of the natural sciences to present idealized objects for study and reflection. To be effective at the task of observation, the natural scientist was not simply to record the appearance of the object; he was to advance a creative rendering of how that object was intended to appear in nature. Additionally, the natural scientist was responsible for crafting categories of analysis and comparison to other objects by type and kind. These glorified observations and innovative classifications revealed the *truth-to-nature* of an object, not its *truth-to-experience*. Daston and Galison convincingly track the history of scientific observation to show that this eighteenth-century mode of scientific knowing – *truth-to-nature* – preceded the quest for objectivity that was to become the preferred method of scientific investigation in the nineteenth century. The *truth-to-nature* of an object was revealed by relying on the distinctive wisdom and particular genius of the observer to effectively synthesize, actively separate, and identify the genuine article from its varieties and distinguish its accidental features from its essential ones. Citing Goethe's 1798 quest for pure phenomena as indicative of this approach, they write: "To depict it [pure phenomena], the human mind must fix the empirically variable, *exclude* the accidental, *eliminate* the impure, *unravel* the tangle, *discover* the unknown" (Daston and Galison 2007: 59). Thus, we can think of Bernier and von Linné as notable not for their neutrality in observation, but for their creative interpretations and the comprehensibility of their systems of classification. The connections drawn by the interpretive biases of the observer were essential for distilling the essence of the object.

This originality in science may explain why von Linné was praised by French (Rousseau), German (Goethe), and Swedish (Strindberg) literati; his interpretive economy allowed him to present the object in its idealized and purest form. That is, von Linné's classic and celebrated system of fixed racial types that described Africans as "crafty, indolent, negligent" and Europeans as "gentle, acute, inventive" brilliantly reflected the *truth-to-nature* method of the eighteenth-century natural sciences (von Linné 1738: 9). Hume's thoughts about race both aligned with von Linné's categories and adopted his interpretive method.

In the eighteenth century, the terms 'race' and 'species' were used to designate a wide range of variations between humans. Sometimes these variances were based on climate alone (Montesquieu), other times they were linked to distinguishing lines of (degenerative) descent between groups (Buffon), and still others, they denoted groups that emanated from different sources (Kames; for more on this see Curran 2011; Harvey 2012; Sebastiani 2013; and Smith 2015). It is fair to say, however, that the central interest of eighteenth-century discourse on race was to effectively differentiate black, brown, and yellow bodies from white ones. African-derived peoples generated the most attention and gave rise to the most vitriolic commentary (Garrett 2006: 87–99).

The particular site of the footnote: Hume's essay "Of National Characters"

Hume's most well-known comments about race were made in the course of an argument in his 1748 essay "Of National Characters." In that essay, Hume aimed to disclose correlations between certain socio-political conditions and particular moral habits of different groups ('national character'). His objective, counter to the intentions of natural scientists Bernier and von Linné, was not simply to reveal how physico-biological traits might parallel the divisions of the continents or differences in air, temperature, or climate. He was concerned with the 'moral causes' of traits and manners as they interacted with the cultural heritage of a nation. He explained this as follows:

> By moral causes, I mean all circumstances, which are fitted to work on the mind as motives or reasons, and which render a peculiar set of manners habitual to us. Of this kind are, the nature of the government, the revolutions of public affairs, the plenty or penury in which the people live, the situation of the nation with regard to its neighbours and such like circumstances.
>
> (E 198)

Hume's premise was that each nation was constituted by communities with observable sets of manners that rendered them distinctive. He thought of these group characteristics as being produced in ever-changing socio-political contexts and believed that reflecting on the moral causes of a group's habits would provide a clearer understanding of both human society and group differences and give a more useful explanation of global trends. He wrote, "The same set of manners will follow a nation, and adhere to them over the whole globe, as well as the same laws and language. The SPANISH, ENGLISH, FRENCH, and DUTCH colonies are all distinguishable even between the tropics" (E 205). Thinking about the moral causes of 'national character,' then, given colonial interests, provided insights that superseded the effects of air and climate.

Hume's conversational tone in the essay displays the congenial style that marks his most thoughtful work. He associates style of political rule with effects on culture, arguing that stronger forms of government tend to create homogeneous character traits in its people:

> We may observe, that, where a very extensive government has been established for many centuries, it spreads a national character over the whole empire, and communicates to every part a similarity of manners. Thus the CHINESE have the greatest uniformity of character imaginable.
>
> (E 204)

He contends that close communication between groups that disperse beyond national boundaries helps them sustain characteristics that identify them as a group (Jews and Jesuits). And he engages the best arguments against his own position, including the idea that groups within the same national boundary will remain distinct if their language, religion, and culture keep them from mixing with others (Turks and Greeks) (E 205). Further, Hume agrees that physical causes are relevant for certain group characteristics, especially what he calls 'vulgar' differences (skin, hair, and eye color). He also notes the variety of traits derived from both non-moral and non-physical causes (like material prosperity and class status) and describes qualities that result from certain vocational commitments (priests tend to generally display similar character traits, as do soldiers and lawyers), as well as gender-based character differences (E 201, fn. 3).

Hume's interest in how types of government shape individual manners and thus form groups of people with distinctive habits aligns with his larger intellectual aims to understand the "universal springs and principles" that guide our behavior, which he exhibited in the *Treatise of Human Nature* (1739). There he wrote that:

> we ought to ascribe the great uniformity we may observe in the humours and turn of thinking of those of the same nation; and it is much more probable, that this resemblance arises from sympathy, than from any influence of the soil and climate, which,

though they continue invariably the same, are not able to preserve the character of a nation.

(T 2.1.11.2: SBN 316)

Investigating the 'moral causes' of national character enabled Hume to apply features of his previously articulated moral project. For example, in "Of National Characters," he demonstrates how proximity of persons – what he called 'contiguity' in the theory of association in the *Treatise* – and the psychological mechanism sympathy, fund our moral sentiments. National character is not merely a group disposition for approbation. On Hume's intervention in moral thought, moral approbation was not produced by an 'original quality' like benevolence; it required a secondary (though fully natural) principle, sympathy. The study of the moral or 'natural' causes of national character is, then, at the same time, a study in how sympathy is shaped by civil structures and social forces.

What seems to haunt Hume's quest for uncovering these moral causes, however, is the idea – propagated by von Linné and others (namely Montesquieu) – that climate is the incessant causal force behind human differences. Hume acknowledges that climate is a source of vulgar differences, yet he does not concede any predictable impact of climate on 'national character.' He writes:

> If the characters of men depended on the air and climate, the degrees of heat and cold should naturally be expected to have a mighty influence; since nothing has a greater effect on all plants and irrational animals. And indeed there is some reason to think, that all the nations, which live beyond the polar circles or between the tropics, are *inferior* to the rest of the species, and are incapable of all the higher attainments of the human mind.

(E 207)

Hume's suggestion that there "is some reason to think that all the nations" that live in the South and North Poles and between the Tropic of Cancer and the Tropic of Capricorn "are inferior to the rest of the species" demonstrates his awareness that his audience will recognize and resonate with the idea of a hierarchy of persons based on climate. One could argue that his hinting at the strong reliability of this racist logic, without critically undermining it, indirectly supports it. He claims, however, that the "general observations" regarding inhabitants of the South and North poles are "uncertain and fallacious"; and that national character within the "temperate climates" (that is, between the tropics) are "very promiscuous," ostensibly undermining the racial reasoning to which he had just appealed. Yet, Hume must have thought his position needed clarification; because five years later, he added a footnote that explained he was

> apt to suspect the negroes, and in general all the other species of men (for there are four or five different kinds) to be naturally inferior to the whites. There never was a civilized nation of any other complexion than white, nor even any individual eminent either in action or speculation.

(E 629, fn i; for more on Hume's use of 'species'
versus 'races,' see Zack 2002: 9–24)

He sharpened this point in the posthumously published version (1777) to read (the full citation is above): "I am apt to suspect the negroes to be naturally inferior to the whites" (E 208, fn. 10).

This footnote clarifies Hume's point: neither physical causes nor moral causes are sound explanations for the inferiority of peoples living between the tropics. They are naturally inferior;

those with a dark 'complexion' are not of human rank ('eminent') in either habits or reflections. Further, negroes are unique. They have "no ingenious manufactures amongst them, no arts, no sciences," while even "the most rude and barbarous of the whites, such as the ancient Germans, the present Tartars, have something eminent about them, in their valour, form of government, or some other particular" (E 208, fn. 10).

To what does Hume locate as the cause for "such a uniform and constant difference" between whites and negroes? His footnote answers: "an original distinction." This is a difference that is prior to history, culture, and politics. It is natural, primary, and fundamental. One observes it, he continues, both in the English-speaking colonies and all 'throughout Europe' where not one negroe slave "ever discovered any symptoms of ingenuity" while other "low people, without education, will start up amongst us, and distinguish themselves in every profession." He even notes, diminishing the reputation of the Jamaican poet Francis Williams (who wrote in Latin and allegedly trained in Cambridge), that "In JAMAICA, indeed, they talk of one negroe as a man of parts and learning; but it is likely he is admired for slender accomplishments, like a parrot, who speaks a few words plainly" (E 208n.10). Hume's egregious anti-black statements are counter to his empiricism and the stated aims of his philosophy.

Beyond the footnote: Hume on race

On the account provided above, Hume's racist footnote – the most explicit articulation of anti-black sentiment in his corpus – reflects the racial reasoning of early modern science, which supported racial hierarchy justified by observation. While the footnote is distinctively strident, it merely amplifies the basic position Hume staked out in the body of the essay "Of National Characters," which, in some ways, can be thought of as an excurses on the inferiority of tropical peoples. In this section, I want to demonstrate further that the position of the essay extends the racial understanding of Hume's corpus. In short, when Hume writes about human beings, he is thinking about whites: his philosophy of human nature might be best described as a philosophy of the nature of Anglo/Euro peoples.

The essay "Of National Characters" is not the only text where Hume articulates racist ideas. In his first *Enquiry* (1748), Hume wrote that "A Laplander or negro has no notion of the relish of wine" (EHU 2.7: SBN 20). On its surface, this statement appears to be an example of when an "object, proper for exciting any sensation, has never been applied to the organ" (EHU 2.7: SBN 20). Here he invoked the term "negro" in the second paragraph of a two-paragraph 'proof' that hoped to demonstrate "all our ideas or more feeble perceptions are copies of our impressions or more lively ones" (EHU 2.5: SBN 19). In the first paragraph, he asserted that the idea of God "arises from reflection on the operations of our own mind and augmenting, without limit, those qualities of goodness and wisdom" (EHU 2.6: SBN 19). That is, just as we cannot produce an impression of Deity with unlimited goodness, the Laplander or negro has no experience of wine and therefore cannot craft the idea of its taste.

On closer consideration, however, Hume's assertion regarding Laplanders and negroes is less banal. His formulation, which randomly pulls in race, should not be taken as the mere equivalent of the claim that certain groups without an impression of an object cannot have an idea of it. The next sentence supports this:

> And though there are few or no instances of a like deficiency in the mind, where a person has never felt or is wholly incapable of a sentiment or passion that belongs to his species; yet we find the same observation to take place in a less degree.
>
> (EHU 2.7: SBN 20)

It follows that Hume's use of the particular racial categories 'negro' and 'Laplander' – groups of low capacity in his hierarchical scheme – is intentional in problematic racial ways. For it is the unique deficiency of these groups that make them incapable of a sentiment that all others can access. These two groups are distinctively deficient: they do not possess the capacity to generate the sense of the characteristic taste (relish) of a civilized drink (wine). With other (that is, higher) races, "we find the same observation to take place in a less degree" (EHU 2.7: SBN 20). They "may possess many senses of which we can have no conception" (EHU 2.7: SBN 20), yet not the negro or the Laplander. Hume's racial hierarchy effectively situates Laplanders and negroes as primitive, perpetuates Eurocentrism, and extends white supremacist ways of thinking about difference.

On another example, Hume's 1752 essay "Of Commerce" relied on a racist distinction between people living 'between the tropics' and those in more temperate areas. Hume wrote,

> What is the reason, why *no people*, living between the tropics, *could ever yet attain to any art or civility*, or reach even any police in their government, and any military discipline; while few nations in the temperate climates have been altogether deprived of these advantages?
>
> (E 267, italics mine)

He describes that it is not simply the temperature, but what temperature causes (fewer clothes, houses, and possessions), which lead to fewer disputes between these peoples (and fewer outside enemies), and reduce the need for authority and protection. One may think that Hume's writing here is innocuous, that he is merely describing a pre-civilized people who have yet to evolve towards civilization. But his claim – an absolute one – that "no people living between the tropics" (that is, black and brown people) can "never yet attain to any art or civility" correlates with the racist logic of the footnote (as well as the claim I highlighted above from the first *Enquiry*). Of special note here is that Hume does not specifically use racial terminology. He relies on the racist logic of his day and appeals to a well-rehearsed notion: that black and brown people – who cannot progress to the standard of 'civilized' – live between the tropics. The inferiority of non-whites seeps into Hume's 'cosmopolitan' project as an unspoken premise after 1748. His moral, political, religious, and historical writings simply presuppose it.

A further example of this occurs in Book III, "Of Justice," in the *Enquiry Concerning the Principles of Morals* (1751). In his description of the unjust power relationship of men over animals, Hume reduces 'Indians' to near animal status and notes the "the *great superiority of civilized Europeans over barbarous Indians* tempted us to imagine ourselves on the same footing with regard to them" (that is, they related to Indians as they did to animals). This "made us throw off all restraints of justice, and even of humanity, in our treatment of them" (EPM 3.1.19; SBN 191, italics mine). When taken in the full context of Hume's racial reasoning, the 'superiority' Hume notes is not a descriptive statement about European military might; it is, rather, the normative idea that 'Indians' were less valuable human beings, a persistent temptation of the racist imaginary. Often excused as a critique of white mistreatment of Indians (Valls 2005: 143; Kuflik 1998: 62), the claim that Indians were "barbarous" is no mere "ethnocentrism" (Valls 2005: 142). Rather, the text – again, taken in light of the inferiority of non-whites in Hume's writings – actually exposes and legitimates the brutal rationale for the vicious treatment of native peoples at the hands of whites and offers no criticism for the lack of white restraint against them. He gives no "implication" or sense "that this was a mistake" (Valls 2005: 142). In fact, nowhere in the essay does Hume slightly challenge any act of white violence against 'Indians,' nor extend any minor criticism regarding white refusal to act justly to 'Indians.' Instead, he conjectures that white treatment of 'Indians' was linked to imagining them as a 'species of creatures,' the details of which he presents in the preceding paragraph (that might be considered as an apt description of the white genocide of those native to North America):

> Were there a species of creatures intermingled with men, which, though rational, were possessed of such inferior strength, both of body and mind, that they were incapable of all resistance, and could never, upon the highest provocation, make us feel the effects of their resentment; the necessary consequence, I think, is that we should be bound by the laws of humanity to give gentle usage to these creatures, but should not, properly speaking, lie under any restraint of justice with regard to them.
>
> (EPM 3.1.18; SBN 190)

Finally, the persistent inferiority of non-whites also factored into Hume's 1757 *Natural History of Religion*. Religion, for Hume, functioned as a way to examine the degree of civilization of a people. If a culture was civilized, 'religion' – a set of theistic beliefs and practices – might be present; if the culture was primitive or uncivilized, that culture was considered to be pagan, savage, or barbaric. To his credit, Hume thought that all races could be barbarous and pagan and he questioned the merits of 'civilization.' Yet, for him, negroes and Indians were *always* uncivilized; that is, they were *only* heathens and pagans. He wrote,

> In very barbarous and ignorant nations, such as the Africans and Indians, nay, even the Japonese, who can form no extensive ideas of power and knowledge, worship may be paid to a being whom they confess to be wicked and detestable.
>
> (NHR 8.4)

In this way, the supposedly neutral concept 'religion' was racialized: that is, shaped by and indebted to European forms of Protestant Christianity and based on a hierarchical logic of race.

Hume seemed to think that to be made clear, the category 'religion' required its contrary, 'pagan'; to make sense, the arc of history needed a palpable beginning – with savages; and that the category 'civilized' was comprehensible in the face of its opposite, 'barbarous.' The *Natural History of Religion* elected non-whites to serve as discursive points of contrast to whites, the only group that could access 'true religion.' In this way, non-whites functioned as negative binaries in the story of progress – always a 'flux and reflux' for Hume – in his concept of religion. Only non-whites were constrained to the roles of 'savages,' 'barbarians,' 'pagans,' and 'polytheists' in this text, and they were always only identified as practitioners of 'false' and 'vulgar' religion (Willis 2015).

The *Natural History of Religion* did refer to some whites as savages and barbarians (Laplanders, Ancient Athenians, etc.), as did the first three volumes of Hume's *History of England*. The important difference, to reiterate, is that non-whites were *only* referred to as savages, pagans, and barbarians; they were capable of superstition, not religion. 'Religion' described the beliefs and practices of more cultivated humans: "the savage tribes of America, Africa, and Asia are all idolaters. . . . Not a single exception to this rule" (NHR 1.4). In light of Hume's other claims about non-whites, I take this statement to mean that they could not control their un-moderated passions for deities. This led them to be, universally and absolutely (there is not a single exception) 'polytheists' and 'idolaters' (Hume uses the terms interchangeably). More specifically, Hume wrote that Egyptians were 'idolaters' and 'worshippers of dogs,' Chinese 'beat their idols,' and Laplanders worshiped "any large stone which they meet with of extraordinary shape" (NHR 4.3). He noted that monotheistic beliefs derived from calm passions and linked to "our ancestors in Europe," who, "before the revival of letters, believed, as we do at present, that there was one supreme God, the author of nature" (NHR 4.1).

One could argue that Hume's racist statements in the *Natural History of Religion* were attenuated by a moral equivalence between some ancient, uncivilized peoples and contemporary, civilized ones. For example, he wrote that it was "incontestable that about 1,700 years ago all mankind were polytheists" (1.2), yet claimed that 'the Gods of all polytheists are no better than the elves or fairies of our [European] ancestors' (NHR 4.2), thereby paralleling the European heritage with the broader inheritance of all humans. This impulse to universalize is supported by his declaration that "almost all idolaters, of whatever age or country, concur in these general principles and conceptions; and even the particular characters and provinces which they assign to their deities, are not extremely different" (NHR 5.10). Admittedly, these utterances appear to balance the proclivities of all polytheists and idolaters across time and maintain a sense of the unity of all. On closer investigation, however, the idolaters that Hume compares are mostly Greek, Roman, and Saxon peoples, and *never* Africans. Additionally, when Hume does seem to favorably compare the religious practices of non-whites to Ancient Jews, Greeks, and Romans, important differences remain. These groups – the Ancient Jews, Greeks, and Romans – developed traditions, narratives, and myths as well as temples, heroes, and nobility, and evolved into civilizations (they demonstrated some degree of character and culture). Hume states nothing about the (possible) development of non-whites, the evolution of their traditions, or the progress of their cultures.

Conclusion

The idea that non-whites were inferior to whites was a premise of Hume's writings (particularly after 1748). This notion manifests in uneven and unpredictable ways. Sometimes, as in the case of the notorious footnote, it is made explicit. At other times, as in his many references to 'human/s,' it remains implicit. Mostly, it bleeds out when he specifically mentions non-whites or alludes to the differences between human beings. To closely attend to how this racial thread runs through all of his work is not to diminish his contribution. Rather, it is to thoughtfully assess his broad corpus for both its insights and limitations.

The fact that Hume's writings on morals, the mind, politics, history, and religion constitute an Anglo-philosophy should not trouble the contemporary reader, for reflective consideration on white subjectivity, particularly the formation of Anglo moral character, white ways of being religious, the political history of Anglo peoples, etc., is vital for our Western intellectual inheritance. What is troubling, however, about Hume's approach to Anglo-thought, is his uncritical embrace of racism – the notion that phenotypical distinctions represented real biological and strict natural kinds that mapped onto racial categories, which were defined by their fixed location in a hierarchy (with blacks at the bottom).

Hume's uncritical embrace (for over 20 years) of the racist footnote, in addition to his ideas about white superiority that shaped his thought-project, means not only that Hume was shortsighted, but also that he propagated white supremacist discourse. When he mentioned black and brown people in his religious and historical texts, he confirmed their barbarity and savagery via description of their idolatrous practices. When he mentioned them in his political and moral works, they were examples of races that did not meet the standard for moral development. These racist ideas both supported and were shaped by the needs of an expanding European economy, whose colonial and imperial interests would be financed by hundreds of years of unpaid labor by those Hume called 'negroes.'

As scholarly interest in whiteness, anti-black racism, and colonialism continues to grow, Hume's racist remarks will continue to draw negative attention. If Hume scholars diminish the importance of his thoughts on race (and how they factor into other components of his thought), his corpus will generate less positive attention and his insights will be overlooked. If critical race theorists fail to attend to the significance of his deep insights in moral thought, religion, history, and philosophy, the breadth of his racism will not be understood. The challenge then, is twofold: we must be forthcoming about Hume's racism and honest about how it saturates his thought at the same time that we celebrate Hume's brilliant insights in philosophy, religion, morality, and politics.

References

Bernier, Francois. (2000 [1684]) "A New Dimension of the Earth," from *Journal des Scavans*, trans. T. Bendyshe, in Robert Bernasconi and Tommy Lott (eds.), *The Idea of Race*, Indianapolis, IN: Hackett Publishing.

Bracken, H. M. (1973) "Essence, Accident and Race," *Hermathena* 116: 81–96.

Curran, Andrew S. (2011) *Anatomy of Blackness: Science and Slavery in the Age of Enlightenment*, Baltimore: Johns Hopkins Press.

Daston, Lorraine and Peter Galison (2007) *Objectivity*, New York: Zone Books.

Eze, Emmanuel C. (2000) "Hume, Race, and Human Nature," *Journal of the History of Ideas* 61: 691–698.

———. (2001) "Hume, Race, and Reason," In *Achieving Our Humanity: The Idea of the Postracial Future*, New York and London: Routledge, pp. 51–76.

Garrett, Aaron (2000) "Hume's Revised Racism Revisited," *Hume Studies* 26: 171–177.

——— (2004) "Hume's 'Original Difference': Race, National Character and the Human Sciences," *Eighteenth-Century Thought* 2: 127–152.

——— (2006) "Human Nature," in Knud Haakanssen (ed.), *The Cambridge History of Eighteenth Century Philosophy*, Cambridge: Cambridge University Press.

——— and Silvia Sebastiani (2017) "David Hume on Race," in Naomi Zack (ed.), *The Oxford Handbook of Philosophy and Race*, Oxford: Oxford University Press, pp. 31–44.

Glacken, Clarence J. (1967) *Traces on the Rhodian Shore: Nature and Culture in Western Thought from Ancient Times to the End of the Eighteenth Century*, Berkeley: University of California Press.

Harris, James (2015) *Hume: An Intellectual Biography*, Oxford: Oxford University Press.

Harvey, David Allen (2012) *The French Enlightenment and its Others: The Mandarin, the Savage and the Invention of the Human Sciences*, New York: Palgrave Macmillan.

Hippocrates (1868) "On Airs, Waters, Places," in *Hippocrates Collected Works I*, trans. by W. H. S. Jones, Cambridge, MA: Harvard University Press.

Immerwahr, John (1992) "Hume's Revised Racism," *Journal of the History of Ideas* 53: 481–486.

Kuflik, Arthur (1998) "Hume on Justice to Animals, Indians and Women," *Hume Studies* 24: 53–78.

Levy, David M. and Sandra J. Peart (2004) "Sympathy and Approbation in Hume and Smith: A Solution to the Other Rational Species Problem," *Economics and Philosophy* 20: 331–349.

Mills, Charles (1998) *Blackness Visible*. Ithaca, NY: Cornell University Press.

Morton, Eric (2002) "Race and Racism in the Works of David Hume," *Journal on African Philosophy* 1–13.

Palter, Robert (1995) "Hume and Prejudice," *Hume Studies* 21: 3–24.

Popkin, Richard H. (1977–1978) "Hume's Racism," *Philosophical Forum* 9(2–3): 211–226.

———. (1992) "Hume's Racism Reconsidered," In *The Third Force in Seventeenth – Century Thought*, Leiden and New York: E. J. Brill, pp. 64–75.

Roelofs, Monique (2005) "Racialization as an Aesthetic Production: What Does the Aesthetic Do for Whiteness and Blackness and Vice Versa?" in George Yancy (ed.), *White on White/Black on Black*, Lanham, MD: Rowan & Littlefield, pp. 78–112.

Sebastiani, Silvia (2013) *The Scottish Enlightenment: Race, Gender and the Limits of Progress*, New York: Palgrave Macmillan.

Smith Justin E. H. (2015) *Nature, Human Nature and Human Difference: Race in Early Modern Philosophy*, Princeton: Princeton University Press.

Stuurman, Siep (2000) "François Bernier and the Invention of Racial Classification," *History Workshop Journal* 50.

Valls, Andrew (2005) "A Lousy Empirical Scientist': Reconsidering Hume's Racism," in Andrew Valls (ed.), *Race and Racism in Modern Philosophy*, Ithaca, NY: Cornell University Press, pp. 127–149.

von Linné, Charles (1800 [1738]) "A General System of Nature: Through the Three Grand Kingdoms of Animals, Vegetables and Minerals: Systematically Divided," in *Systema Naturae*, London: Lackington and Allen and Co.

West, Cornel (1982) "A Genealogy of Modern Racism," in *Prophesy Deliverance: An Afro American Revolutionary Christianity*, Philadelphia: The Westminster Press.

Willis, Andre C. (2015) *Toward a Humean True Religion: Genuine Theism, Moderate Hope, Practical Morality*, State College, PA: Pennsylvania State University Press.

Zack, Naomi (2002) *Philosophy of Science and Race*, New York: Routledge.

INDEX